Field Guide to the Native Plants of Sydney

Doryanthes excelsa Gymea *Lily* (page 226)

Field Guide to the
NATIVE PLANTS
OF SYDNEY

Les Robinson

'The first impression made on the stranger is certainly favourable. He sees gently swelling hills, connected by vales which possess every beauty that verdure of trees, and form, simply considered by itself, can produce...Every part of the country is a forest...'

– Watkin Tench, *A Complete Account of the Settlement of Port Jackson in New South Wales*, 1793.

Revised 2nd edition

Kangaroo Press

About the author

Les Robinson studied law at Sydney University and, logically, went on to become a cartoonist, helping found Streetwize Comics. His interest in botany grew from a love of bushwalking. His first plant specimens, stored in plastic, rotted, so he turned to drawing them instead. This became an obsession. After 700 drawings it occurred to him that he 'could make the book he wished someone had made for him'. He spent the next 3 years living on the south coast, working on the book and helping fight sand mining at Gerroa. He now works as a campaign consultant on environmental and social issues in Sydney.

About the second edition

The second edition contains a number of changes, including name changes to bring the *Field Guide* up to date with the final volumes of the *Flora of NSW*.

Changes include: – splitting *Helichrysum* into *Bracteantha*, *Chrysocephalum* and *Ozothamnus*; – splitting *Triglochin procera*; – new names: *Eucalyptus obstans, Dillwynia sieberi, Almaleea paludosa, Watsonia meriana*, Dampiera scottiana, Lepidosperma gunnii, Ptilothrix deusta, Glossogyne tannensis, Leptinella longipes, Eremophila debilis, Myoporum boninense, Rhytidosporum procumbens, Protasparagis aethiopicus**; – additional species: *Spaerolobium minus, Utricularia uniflora*; – and new illustrations: *Kunzea rupestris, Dipodium variegatum, Passiflora herbertiana, Utricularia* spp.

Acknowledgements

This book would not have been possible without the assistance of many experts, who willingly gave their time to read or offer advice on various parts of the book:

Dr Paul Adams (Aquatics, Seacoast and Estuarine Species)
Dr Elizabeth Brown (Goodeniaceae, Asteraceae)
Leo Cady (Orchids)
Dr Barry Conn (Dilleniaceae, Sterculiaceae)
Gwen Harden (Rainforest Species, Climbers)
Ken Hill (*Eucalyptus*)
Dr Surrey Jacobs (Grasses)
Van Klaphake (Sedges and Rushes, Grasses, *Eucalyptus*, Ferns)
Bob Mackinson (Pittosporaceae)
Dr Jocelyn Powell (Epacridaceae, Apiaceae)
Ron Tunstall (Orchids)
Dr Peter Weston (Proteaceae, Rutaceae, Fabaceae)
Karen Wilson (Casuarinaceae)

The following people deserve special thanks:

Ian Close, for good advice and reading many sections.
Barbara Wiecek, for constant and cheerful assistance in the National Herbarium.
Dr Barbara Briggs, for permission to use the collection of the National Herbarium, Royal Botanic Gardens, Sydney.
And Heather Carey, whose support made it all possible.

Cover painting by Heather Carey

Abbreviations

*	(after a species name) an exotic species, i.e. introduced into Australia since white settlement.
ex	(used in authors' names) out of, i.e. published by, e.g. Sieber ex Sprengel means Sieber's name, as published by Sprengel.
Gk.	Greek
Lat.	Latin
NG	New Guinea
NSW	New South Wales.
NT	Northern Territory
NZ	New Zealand
Qld	Queensland
SA	South Australia
sp. aff.	an unnamed species, with affinities to the species indicated.
sp.	species (plural: spp.)
ssp.	subspecies
Tas	Tasmania
var.	variety
Vic	Victoria
WA	Western Australia

Robinson, Les
Field Guide to the Native Plants of Sydney.

Bibliography.
Includes Index.
ISBN 0 86417 639 2
1. Botany – New South Wales – Sydney Region – Guidebooks. 1. Title.
581.99441

Reprinted in 1997
Second Edition published in 1994
First published in 1991 by Kangaroo Press Pty Ltd
3 Whitehall Road Kenthurst NSW 2156 Australia
P.O .Box 6125 Dural Delivery Centre NSW 2158
Printed by Australian Print Group, Maryborough, Victoria 3465

ISBN 0 86417 639 2

Contents

Foreword

Knowing about native plants has always been an important part of life in Australia.

For the Aboriginal people, an intimate knowledge of plants was vital to their way of life. The European explorers found our plants so impressive that Captain Cook named the area where he anchored Botany Bay. And just in case anyone wondered which particular botanists had been so impressed, he named the bay's two headlands Capes Banks and Solander.

Being familiar with wildlife still plays a vital role in society today. People consume documentaries on the natural world, and tourism focussing on wildlife has blossomed over the past decade.

Native plants are one of our few direct links with the natural world—a world that can balance the frantic pace of life today—and one that can give some perspective to our existence. It can inspire and fascinate: and, unlike animals, plants aren't very good at running away!

So the extraordinary sight of a giant fig strangling another tree is there for anyone with eyes to see it. The amazing trigger plant will perform its trick of whacking pollen onto the head of a visiting insect for anyone who cares to watch.

People who discover the natural world, can't help being impressed by it. And the more people who have this attitude, the greater is the chance of our embattled wildlife surviving.

What I really like about this book is the way Les has included conservation information about the species, and nice little bits of history and culture.

But where this book excels, is helping people come to grips with the often tedious process of identifying plants. When we humans are faced with something new, the first thing we want to know is what its called, and then, what does it do. I'm sure this book will be a great help to anyone trying to answer the former question, and a useful basis once a person starts wrestling with the latter.

I commend this book to all who would like to know our fascinating native plants better.

John Dengate
Radio and television naturalist

Using the Field Guide

Geographical coverage

The book covers the County of Cumberland, an area bounded by the Hawkesbury-Nepean system to the north and west, and the Cataract River to the south.

The book includes all native species found in this area, as recorded in the collection of the National Herbarium, Royal Botanic Gardens, Sydney, with the exception of the following:

- Many of the less common grasses, particularly those of the Cumberland Plain.
- A number of uncommon sedges and rushes.
- A handful of plants, mostly in Chenopodiaceae, which, although native, only occur as weeds in the area.

Included also are a number of exotic species which are either ecologically important or likely to be confused with native species.

Interpreting the illustrations

Dicotyledons

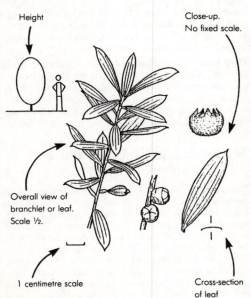

Height

Close-up.
No fixed scale.

Overall view of
branchlet or leaf.
Scale ½.

1 centimetre scale

Cross-section
of leaf

Monocotyledons

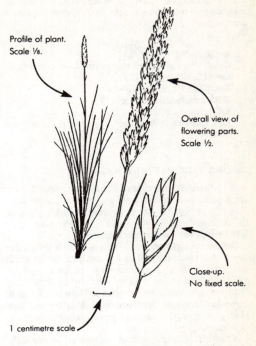

Profile of plant.
Scale ⅛.

Overall view of
flowering parts.
Scale ½.

Close-up.
No fixed scale.

1 centimetre scale

The illustrations attempt to show typical specimens, but the following points need to be borne in mind:

- The features of a plant can vary widely in different environments, particularly in different conditions of moisture and exposure.
- The juvenile and regeneration leaves of many species e.g. *Acacia, Eucalyptus*, are markedly different from adult leaves, usually being much larger and sometimes displaying ancestral features.
- Most species have several genetically distinct populations. Usually the differences are minor, but in some cases conspicuously different populations of a species occur in the area e.g. *Xanthosia pilosa, Grevillea diffusa, Grevillea linearifolia*.
- Salt-spray has a gross effect on many plants, producing small dense habits, crowded leaves and thicker protective layers of waxy cuticle or bloom.
- The height of woodland shrubs depends strongly on the fire history of a community. For instance, most shrubs which commonly appear 1-2m high will sometimes be seen 3-4m high in long-unburnt communities.
- The appearance of a plant can vary markedly through the yearly cycle of new growth-flowering-fruiting-dormancy.
- Hybrids between related species are not unknown, particularly amongst *Eucalypts*.

The habitat code

The habitat code is designed to assist identification by defining a number of broad habitat types with discrete vegetation associations.

These are:

Ss (sandstone woodlands)
Cumb (clay soils and alluviums of the Cumberland Plain)
Castl (Castlereagh woodlands)
Temp Rf (temperate rainforest)
STRf (subtropical rainforest)
Sal (saline environments)
Aqu (permanent freshwater, e.g. swamps, ponds and rivers)

■ **Ss** (sandstone woodlands)

'It is a singular fact that in Australia the most brilliant flowers are found on the most worthless country,' wrote A. G. Hamilton in 1930.[1] Sydney is fortunate in having plenty of this 'worthless country' dominated by shallow, poor, sandy soils derived from Hawkesbury Sandstone.

Despite their poverty these soils support a remarkable diversity of plants adapted to low nutrients, drying winds and frequent fires. The unsuitability of these soils for agriculture has resulted in the unintentional conservation of much of the sandstone vegetation. However suburban expansion and other developments such as freeways now place great pressure on areas not protected by national parks or reserves.

A number of distinct habitats are covered by this code.

Dry lateritic ridges: Laterites derived from the erosion of Wianamatta Shale cap most of the tops of the sandstone plateaus. Laterites are distinguished by large irregular ironstone nuggets and generally have a slightly higher nutrient level.

Poorly drained tops: These support marshy sedgeland and mallee communities.

Sloping country and valleys: These support extensive areas of heath and woodland (sometimes known as dry sclerophyll forest), grading into denser open forest in the valleys. The dominant trees are Sydney Red Gum (*Angophora floribunda*), Red Bloodwood (*Eucalyptus gummifera*), the Scribbly Gums (*E. racemosa* and *E. haemastoma*) and Sydney Peppermint (*E. piperita*). On the Woronora Plateau Silvertop Ash (*E. sieberi*) forms almost pure communities.

Gullies: These provide the humid and fire-free conditions for the development of temperate rainforest (see below).

Alluvial valleys: In a few places there are well developed alluvial soils supporting tall forests e.g. in parts of Port Hacking and the Lane Cove River Valley

Clay tops: An important feature of the sandstone plateaus is the capping of Wianamatta Shale which outcrops on high ridges. Usually this is reduced to a poor and deeply eroded laterite, but on the highest ridges of the coastal plateaus (Hornsby-Crows Nest, Epping-Castle Hill, Miranda-Kirrawee, the Garrawarrah Ridge in the Royal National Park) deeper

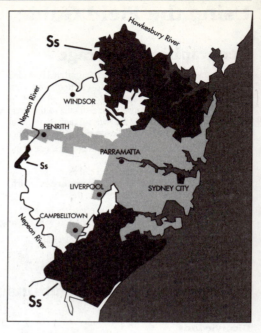

clay soils occur, giving rise to a tall forest dominated by Blackbutt (*E. pilularis*) and Sydney Blue Gum (*E. saligna*: mainly on the north shore), together with Grey Ironbark (*E. paniculata*) and a mixture of more typical sandstone species. In most areas only a few patches remain uncleared today, although isolated trees are quite common.

Deep sands: Consolidated coastal sand deposits with a rich heath vegetation occurred at several points along the coast, e.g. Narrabeen, the Eastern Suburbs, Kurnell and Jibbon Lagoon. The Jibbon Lagoon area at Bundeena is probably the best surviving example, but a small area at Jennifer Street, La Perouse has recently been reserved from development.

■ **Cumb** (clay soils and alluviums of the Cumberland Plain)

Western Sydney lies in an enormous basin composed of deeply weathered clay soils derived from Wianamatta Shale. Geologically it is a sag block which remained when the surrounding areas were raised to form plateaus. The rainfall is much lower than on the coast, although the clay soils retain moisture better than the surrounding sandy soils.

Most of the Cumberland Plain consists of undulating country of low hills and boggy depressions. A tall close-growing open forest once covered most of the plain but now only scattered patches remain. *Eucalyptus moluccana* and *E. tereticornis* are common on the better drained sites. Ironbarks abound in many places, especially on drier rises or lateritic soils. The original ground cover was mainly native grasses with scattered shrubs. Now introduced grasses and the opportunistic native shrub Blackthorn (*Bursaria spinosa*)

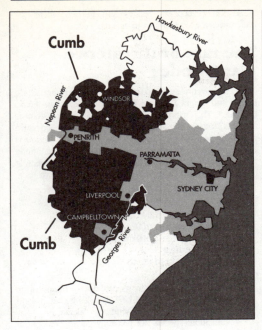

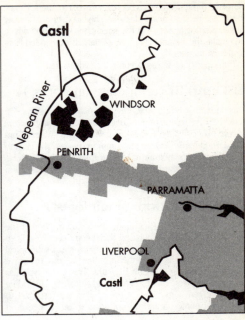

dominate. Marshy depressions are dominated by Cabbage Gum (*E. amplifolia*), *Melaleuca decora* and other paperbarks, with a marshy meadow of mainly native herbs. Swamp Sheoak (*Casuarina glauca*) follows the creek banks where saline groundwaters surface.

The rich alluvial flats along the Hawkesbury–Nepean River were dominated by a tall forest of *E. tereticornis* together with *Angophora subvelutina*, *E. deanei*, Blackbutt (*E. pilularis*), *Angophora floribunda*, with a semi-rainforest understorey. This was mostly cleared early in the last century. A number of freshwater lagoons remain, most notably Longneck Lagoon, Pitt Town.

◼ Castl (Castlereagh woodlands)

Between St Marys and Richmond is an interesting region of sclerophyll woodland which contrasts markedly with the surrounding clay forests. It consists of old sandy-clay alluviums which were laid down by the Hawkesbury River when it flowed to the east of its present course. They have since been eroded, so that what remains is a semi-consolidated laterite, low in nutrients. This supports an open woodland similar in appearance to that found on the coastal plateaus. The dominant species are *Angophora bakeri*, *E. sclerophylla* and *E. parramattensis*. The ground cover is a rich collection of heathy shrubs and grasses. Many would be well known to visitors to the sandstone country. However there are a number of rare or uncommon species which are relatively abundant there, e.g. *Micromyrtus minutiflora*, *Acacia bynoeana*, *Dodonaea falcata*, and *Macrozamia spiralis*.

Most of the area has been taken up by rural sub-divisions and the Hawkesbury Agricultural College, except for the Castlereagh State Forest, which conserves a good sample of the flora.

The Agnes Banks sands: An area of deep almost pure wind-deposited sand occurs at Agnes Banks, south of Richmond near the Nepean River. This supports an unusual flora dominated by *Banksia serrata*, *Banksia aemula*, and *Angophora bakeri*, with a complex understorey of heathy shrubs. For a time it appeared that sand mining would consume the whole of this site, but now part of the area is protected by the Agnes Banks Nature Reserve.

Rainforests

According to J.H. Maiden, a local rainforest or 'brush' corresponds to 'what in India would be called a jungle, and consists of well-watered sheltered rich soil areas in the coastal districts and valleys in the coast ranges, which not only support rich arboreal vegetation, but also creepers and climbers of various kinds, and shrubby undergrowth. The tree vegetation is of the most varied kind, but rarely includes eucalyps . . . a nearly smooth bark being of very common occurrence.'[2]

A rainforest is, simply, any forest with a closed canopy. The trees are usually closely spaced, broad-leaved, non-sclerophyll, with a distinctive sub-flora of epiphytes, vines, ferns and palms. The richest rainforests are based on soils with high nutrients, but rainforests can grow on sandy soils with very low nutrients. The Sydney area has more than adequate rainfall to maintain rainforests over all but exposed ridges. The real limiter of rainforest is fire. In the Sydney area, rainforests are restricted to small pockets in fire-free locations near creeks in deep gullies.

Australia is the only developed nation with rainforests.

However, three-quarters has been lost since settlement. Hence the remaining areas near Sydney have high conservation value. It is interesting to note that the sclerophyll vegetation which dominates the continent at present is largely descended from rainforest ancestors.

Two types of rainforest occur in the Sydney area.

■ Temp Rf (temperate rainforest)

This occurs along creeks in deep humid valleys on Hawkesbury sandstone. Coachwood (*Ceratopetalum apetalum*), Lillypilly (*Acmena smithii*) and Water Gum (*Tristaniopsis laurina*) are the common species. The ground layer is usually a mixture of ferns and broad-leaved shrubs. In deep gullies near the sea dense stands of Cabbage Palm (*Livistona australis*) occur.

■ STRf (subtropical rainforest)

In the Royal National Park, along the southern parts of the Hacking River and its tributaries, Narrabeen shales have been exposed. These support a dense complex subtropical rainforest, which is a northern outlier of the extensive subtropical rainforest of the Illawarra. This forest type has a dense and diverse canopy of trees and vines, often including large emergent Figs. Most of the species are restricted to subtropical rainforest and do not occur in other vegetation types.

A number of tiny remnants with subtropical rainforest species occur in other parts of the area: the 'Native Vineyard' near Cobbity is one, and a patch along Cattai Creek near Sackville is another. Gullies on Razorback Mountain west of Camden, just outside the area of this book, also have patches.

■ Sal (saline environments)

Salt-tolerant species are found within the ambit of sea-spray and in estuarine salt-marshes.

Sydney has 4 large estuarine river systems: The Hawkesbury River, Port Jackson, Georges River and Port Hacking, as well as the smaller Cooks River system draining into Botany Bay. Sand-dunes occur on long sandy beaches in Botany Bay and Cronulla and many at smaller breaks along coastline. Large saline coastal lagoons occur at Narrabeen and Dee Why.

The estuarine systems have extensive salt-marshes and mangroves although these have suffered much due to infilling. Seagrass beds also occur in all sheltered waters, especially in Botany Bay, although their fate has been even harsher (only about 20% of Botany Bay's seagrass beds remain).

For convenience salt-tolerant species are grouped in a separate chapter. The code Sal is used for plants in other parts of the book which have some salt tolerance, but normally grow in non-salty conditions.

■ Aqu (freshwater aquatic environments)

Plants growing in permanent water are grouped in a separate chapter. The code **Aqu** is used for plants in other parts of the book which are normally terrestrial but tolerate seasonal inundation (except in Sedges and Rushes where the preferences are too complex to be simply coded).

The rare or threatened plants code

Codes are given for all Sydney species which occur on the Briggs and Leigh *Rare or Threatened Australian Plants* database.[3] This national database and coding system is Australia's standard classification for rare and threatened native plants. As an example, the code for *Zieria involucrata* is 2VC-. The 2VC- code indicates that the species is confined to a geographical range of less than 100km, is vulnerable but reserved and the adequacy of reserve is not known.

The coding system is as follows:

Distribution category

1 = Known from type collection only
2 = Geographic range < 100km
3 = Geographic range > 100km
X = Presumed extinct
x = Presumed extinct in region

Conservation status

E = Endangered–species in serious risk of disappearing from the wild state within 1 or 2 decades if present land use and other causal factors continue to operate.
V = Vulnerable–species not presently endangered but at risk of disappearing from the wild over a longer period (20-50 years) through continued depletion, or which largely occur on sites likely to experience changes in land use that would threaten the survival of the species in the wild.
R = Rare (not threatened)–species which are rare in Australia but which overall are not currently considered endangered or vulnerable. Such species may be represented by a relatively large population in a very restricted area or by smaller populations spread over a wider range, or some intermediate combination of the distribution pattern.
K = Poorly known–species that are suspected, but not definitely known, to belong to any of the above categories.

Reservation adequacy code

C = Population reserved
a = Adequately reserved (> 1000 plants)
i = Inadequately reserved (< 1000 plants)
– = Adequacy of reservation unknown
t = Total population reserved
+ = Species with natural distributions outside Australia
? = Taxonomic status unknown

The arrangement of species

The order of species and genera is alphabetical except for a few occasions where obviously similar species are grouped together for easy comparison.

For ease of identification, certain species have been separated into groups, e.g. climbers and rainforest species. The family and genera descriptions for these species are usually found in earlier parts of the book.

Genera are placed in families according to the system of Cronquist (1981)[4] which is the system used in the *Flora of Australia*.[5]

Authors' names

The name(s) immediately after a species name is that of the botanist(s) who first scientifically described the plant. The discovery and early settlement of Australia occurred at a seminal time in the development of botanical science and many of the authors of Australian species were amongst the most distinguished names in botany: Linnaeus, Robert Brown, James Smith, De Candolle, Joseph Gaertner, W.J. and J.D. Hooker, Labillardière, George Bentham, Ferdinand Mueller, and Carl Willdenow, amongst others.

How to read author names

Example: *Phyllota grandiflora* (Sieber ex De Candolle) Bentham

The brackets indicate the authors who first published the species name but show that they placed it in a different genus. The abbreviation 'ex' indicates that the first author used the name in an unpublished manuscript and the second author first formally published the name. So the example tells us: Franz Sieber (a Bohemian commercial collector who worked in Australia from 1819–23) first used the specific name (*grandiflora*) in an unpublished manuscript (probably on a specimen sheet). The Swiss botanist De Candolle later published the name (in his immense *Prodromus Systematis Naturalis Regni Vegetabilis*) under a different genus. The British botanist George Bentham later placed the species in its present genus (in his *Flora Australiensis*).

Genus and subspecies names also have authors, e.g. *Phyllota* (De Candolle) Bentham. For genera the brackets indicate that the author originally coined the name at species rank. In this case, De Candolle originally used *phyllota* as a species name and Bentham raised it to genus rank.

The term 'emend' also occurs in a few cases, this shows that the definition of the genus was amended by the following author.

Sources of local Aboriginal plant names

There are 2 main sources for Aboriginal tree names in the Sydney area.

1. Specimens sent to Joseph Banks by his botanical collector George Caley between 1800 and 1810. Caley lived at Parramatta and most of his botanical work was on the Cumberland Plain and the foothills of the Blue Mountains. He lacked scientific names so he used the local Aboriginal names, probably provided by his Aboriginal assistant, Dan. He recorded the names on the specimen sheets which Joseph Banks widely distributed to British and European collections.

A large number of tree specimens retaining Caley's notes found their way to the Vienna Herbarium where they were discovered by J. H. Maiden at the beginning of this century.[6]

2. The catalogues for NSW products at the Paris World Exhibition of 1855 and the London World Exhibition of 1862, prepared by the prominent landowner William Macarthur. During his research he recorded the Aboriginal names for the colony's commercial timbers in languages from the Illawarra region, Brisbane Water and the Counties of Cumberland and Camden, often citing 3 different names.

Notes on the text

Use of plant dimensions

Scientific descriptions always state the total range of recorded dimensions, e.g. 'Shrub 1-3m high'. However, such a wide range can be unhelpful in the field. Hence the dimensions used in this book are median dimensions, i.e. those most commonly encountered. Hence 'Shrub 1.5-2m high' could be read as 'Shrub *usually* 1.5-2m high *but occasionally shorter or higher according to the environment and age of growth*'. In some cases a maximum growth figure is also provided e.g. 'Shrub 1-3m, occasionally to 6m'.

Flowering times

These have been collected from many sources and the author's observations. Because of lack of accurate local information they are often rather general. Hence 'spring' does not mean September–November but may refer to a shorter period. Usually a species will flower at a range of different times accoring to its shelter, aspect and other factors.

Some oft used terms

Sydney area: the area covered by this book (see above).

Sydney region: the area defined by Beadle, Evans and Carolin in *Flora of the Sydney Region*. It extends from the Hunter River in the north to the Shoalhaven River in the south and westward to include the Blue Mountains.

Woodland: on Hawkesbury Sandstone there is a fine transition between 'open heath' (i.e. heath recently burnt), 'closed shrubland' (i.e. heath unburnt for many years), 'woodland' (i.e. heath with a scattering of trees) and 'open forest' (where trees touch each other, usually on sheltered slopes and valleys). Here the term woodland is used to cover the last two of these types.

Open forest: this term is used mainly for moist open forests on clay soils on the Cumberland Plain.

Wetter sclerophyll forest: refers to Eucalypt forests which are transitional to rainforest. They occur in valleys near creeks, usually on alluvial soils, and have a shrub layer dominated by broad-leaved shrubs. The best developed examples around Sydney have tall canopies of Blue Gum and Blackbutt.

KEY

Ⓐ Is your plant in one of these groups?

If so, look in the separate sections at the back of the book.

1. Climbers and scramblers.

CLIMBERS 323

2. Parasitic shrubs, growing from the branches of trees.

MISTLETOES 345

3. Plants growing in closed-canopy forests in vallies, usually near streams. Non-sclerophyll, usually broad-leaved.

RAINFOREST SPECIES 348

4. Plants growing in salty environments beside the sea, in saltmarsh or in brackish estuaries.

COASTAL AND ESTUARINE SPECIES 386

5. Plants wholly or partly submerged in fresh water. Sometimes exposed on muddy banks.

AQUATICS 411

6. Plants submerged in bays and estuaries.

SEAGRASSES 410

7. Plants with spore-producing organs on the underside of leaves.

FERNS – see PRIMITIVE PLANTS 304

8. Small plants with spore capsules attached directly to stems or leaves.

PSILOPSIDA – see PRIMITIVE PLANTS 303

9. Small plants. Stems densely lined with short linear leaves.

LYCOPSIDA – see PRIMITIVE PLANTS 303

10. Plants with rigid palm-like leaves arising at ground level.

CYCADOPSIDA – see PRIMITIVE PLANTS 321

Ⓑ If not, use the following key.

Work your way through by making successive choices: either A or *A, then B or *B etc.. Where numbers occur (eg. 1,2,3 or H1, H2, H3) check each one.

A. Woody plants.

    B. Trees (woody plants over 8m tall, with a single trunk)...**Group 1**   13

    *B. Shrubs. ....**Group 2**   14

*A. Non-woody plants (herbs).

    C. Flower parts in 3s, leaves mostly with parallel veins (monocotyledons).........................**Group 3**   18

    *C. Flower parts in 4s or 5s, leaves mostly with branching veins (dicotyledons).

        D. Herbs with leaves mostly arising from the base...**Group 4**   19

        *D. Leaves arising mainly from aerial stems.

            E. Herbs creeping and rooting along the stems..**Group 5**   19

            *E. Remainder..**Group 6**   20

Group 1 Trees (woody plants over 8m tall, with a single trunk).

A. Leaves aromatic when crushed.
    B. Oil-dots visible in leaves (all **MYRTACEAE**).
        C. Bark papery.
            Melaleuca 55
      *C. Bark not papery.
        D. Leaves alternate.
           E. Leaves harsh and leathery, usually drooping.
                Eucalyptus 32

          *E. Leaves soft, spreading. Small tree with pale smooth bark.
              Tristaniopsis 61, 371
      *D. Leaves opposite or whorled.
        F. Fruits dry.
           G. Fruits united into an aggregate capsule.
              Syncarpia 60
          *G. Fruits consisting of independent capsules.
             H. Capsules smooth.
                Lophostemon 60

             *H. Capsules ribbed.
                Angophora 22

        *F. Fruits succulent.
             Acmena, Syzygium 370, 371

    *B. No visible oil-dots. Prominent yellow mid-vein present.

        LAURACEAE 321
        (located in RAINFOREST SPECIES
        except for *Cinnamomum camphora*)
*A. Leaves not aromatic when crushed.
    I. Leaves tiny and scale-like, or apparently absent.
        J. Scale-like leaves present, arranged in whorls on small green branchlets.
           K. Scale-like leaves in whorls of 3.
             CUPRESSACEAE 321

          *K. Scale-like leaves in whorls of 4 or more.
             CASUARINACEAE 149

      *J. Scale-like leaves absent, or if present, not whorled.
        SANTALACEAE 208

    *I. Leaves well developed.
        L. Leaves compound.
           M. Leaves 3-foliate.
        FABACEAE: *Erythrina* 79

      *M. Leaves bipinnate.
      MIMOSACEAE 64

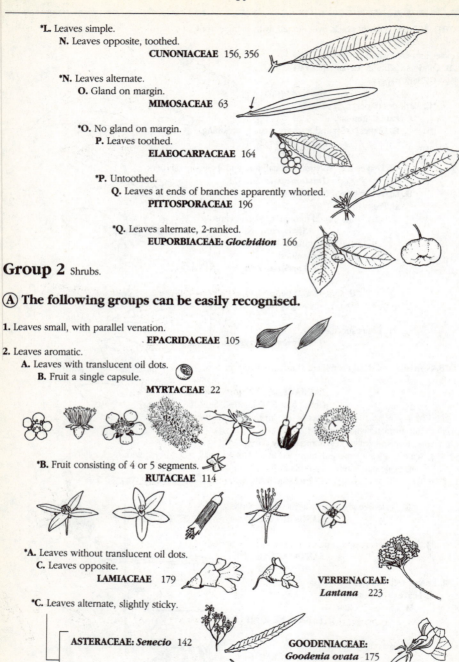

*L. Leaves simple.
    N. Leaves opposite, toothed.
        CUNONIACEAE 156, 356

    *N. Leaves alternate.
        O. Gland on margin.
            MIMOSACEAE 63

        *O. No gland on margin.
            P. Leaves toothed.
                ELAEOCARPACEAE 164

            *P. Untoothed.
                Q. Leaves at ends of branches apparently whorled.
                PITTOSPORACEAE 196

                *Q. Leaves alternate, 2-ranked.
                  EUPORBIACEAE: *Glochidion* 166

Group 2 Shrubs.

Ⓐ The following groups can be easily recognised.

1. Leaves small, with parallel venation.
        EPACRIDACEAE 105
2. Leaves aromatic.
    A. Leaves with translucent oil dots.
        B. Fruit a single capsule.
            MYRTACEAE 22

        *B. Fruit consisting of 4 or 5 segments.
            RUTACEAE 114

    *A. Leaves without translucent oil dots.
        C. Leaves opposite.
            LAMIACEAE 179   **VERBENACEAE:**
                                                  Lantana 223
    *C. Leaves alternate, slightly sticky.

          ASTERACEAE: *Senecio* 142   **GOODENIACEAE:**
                                      Goodenia ovata 175

          SAPINDACEAE: *Dodonaea* 210

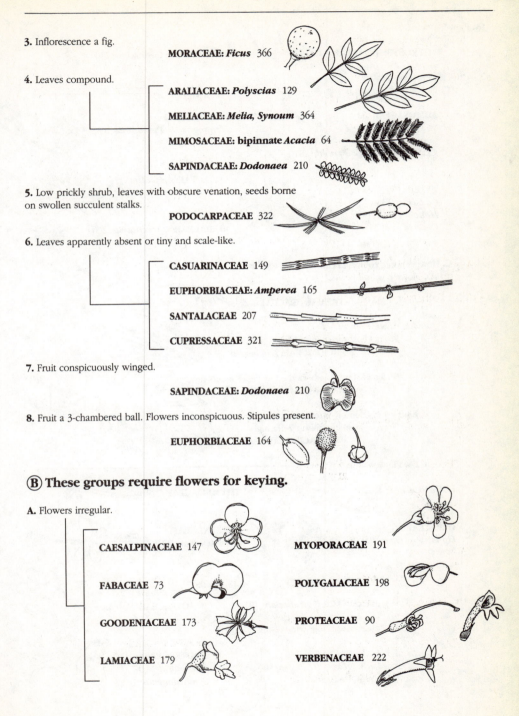

3. Inflorescence a fig.

      MORACEAE: *Ficus* 366

4. Leaves compound.

      ARALIACEAE: *Polyscias* 129

      MELIACEAE: *Melia, Synoum* 364

      MIMOSACEAE: bipinnate *Acacia* 64

      SAPINDACEAE: *Dodonaea* 210

5. Low prickly shrub, leaves with obscure venation, seeds borne on swollen succulent stalks.

      PODOCARPACEAE 322

6. Leaves apparently absent or tiny and scale-like.

      CASUARINACEAE 149

      EUPHORBIACEAE: *Amperea* 165

      SANTALACEAE 207

      CUPRESSACEAE 321

7. Fruit conspicuously winged.

      SAPINDACEAE: *Dodonaea* 210

8. Fruit a 3-chambered ball. Flowers inconspicuous. Stipules present.

      EUPHORBIACEAE 164

Ⓑ These groups require flowers for keying.

A. Flowers irregular.

      CAESALPINACEAE 147   **MYOPORACEAE** 191

      FABACEAE 73   **POLYGALACEAE** 198

      GOODENIACEAE 173   **PROTEACEAE** 90

      LAMIACEAE 179   **VERBENACEAE** 222

*A. Flowers regular.
   B. Flowers lacking petals.

      GYROSTEMONACEAE 176   **SAPINDACEAE: *Dodonaea*** 210

*B. Flowers with petals.
   C. Flowers in compact heads.

      MIMOSACEAE 62    **PROTEACEAE:**
                                    Isopogon 99 **_Petrophile_** 103

      CUNONIACEAE: *Callicoma* 157

                           APIACEAE: *Actinotus* 124

      ASTERACEAE:
      Cassinia 133
      Helichrysum 137
      Olearia 140    **RUBIACEAE: *Opercularia*** 206

*C. Flowers not in compact heads (flowers regular).
   D. Flowers with 4 petals.
      E1. Flowers pink.
         TREMANDRACEAE 221

      E2. Flowers red.
         F. Prickly shrub to 2m high.
            PROTEACEAE: *Lambertia* 99

        *F. Small shrubs with toothed leaves. Flowers tiny.
          HALORAGACEAE 177

      E3. Flowers densely covered in pale brown hairs.
         Flowers in spikes. Shrub 2-4m high.
          PROTEACEAE: *Xylomelon* 104

      E4. Flowers white.

LOGANIACEAE 187   **THYMELIACEAE** 219

OLEACEAE: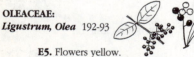
Ligustrum, Olea 192-93   **VERBENACEAE:**
                         Clerodendron 223

      E5. Flowers yellow.
         G. Flowers under 4mm wide.
           MYRSINACEAE: *Rapanea* 191 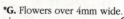   **OLEACEAE: *Notelaea*** 193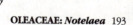

        *G. Flowers over 4mm wide.
           ONAGRACEAE:
           Ludwigia 420   **PROTEACEAE:**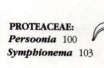
           (in AQUATICS)   **_Persoonia_** 100
                          Symphionema 103

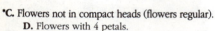
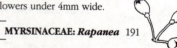

*D. Flowers with 5 petals.

> **H1.** Flowers nodding, often appearing shrivelled, covered in fine felty hairs.

STERCULIACEAE: *Lasiopetalum* 216

H2. Flowers white-cream.

APIACEAE:
Platysace, Xanthosia 126-27

PITTOSPORACEAE 195

CELASTRACEAE:
Maytenus 153

RHAMNACEAE:
Cryptandra, Pomaderris 201-02

OLACACEAE: *Olax* 192

STERCULIACEAE:
Commersonia, Rulingia 216-18

H3. Flowers yellow.

DILLENIACEAE 158

PITTOSPORACEAE 195

MALVACEAE:
Abultilon, Gynatrix 188

RHAMNACEAE:
Pomaderris 202

OCHNACEAE 191

H4. Flowers pink.

CUNONIACEAE: *Bauera* 156

MALVACEAE: *Pavonia* 190

H5. Flowers purple.

SOLANACEAE 212

H6. Flowers blue.

MALVACEAE: *Howittia* 189

H7. Flowers small, greenish.

SANTALACEAE: *Santalum* 209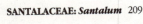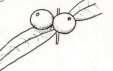

ULMACEAE 202

Group 3 Herbs with flower parts in 3s and leaves mostly with parallel veins (monocotyledons).

A. Flowering parts tiny, enclosed in scale-like bracts, forming spikelets.
    B. Stems hollow. Grasses.

POACEAE 265

    *B. Stems not hollow (or hollows restricted to distinct chambers or to discontinuities in the pith).

SEDGES and RUSHES 280

*A. Flowers conspicuous, or if small, then not enclosed within bracts.
    C. Flowers irregular.

ORCHIDACEAE 237
(Many flower shapes)

    *C. Flowers regular.

AGAVACEAE 226

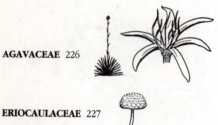

COMMELINACEAE 226

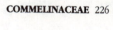

ERIOCAULACEAE 227

HAEMODORACEAE 227

IRIDACEAE 228

LILIACEAE 229

XANTHORRHOEACEAE 275

XYRIDACEAE 279

Group 4 Herbs with leaves arising mainly fom the base, dicotyledons.

A. Flowers regular.
    B. Flowers in erect spikes, brownish green.
                  PLANTAGINACEAE 197

   *B. Flowers in dense heads.
      C1. Flowers yellow.

                      ASTERACEAE:
                      Podolepis 141 ***Craspedia*** 135 ***Cymbonotus*** 135
      C2. Flowers white.

          D. Leaves highly divided.
                  APIACEAE: ***Trachymene*** 127

           *D. Leaves undivided.
                  ASTERACEAE: ***Lagenifera*** 140 ***Solenogyne*** 144

      C3. Flowers blue to mauve.
                  ASTERACEAE: ***Brachycome*** 131

*A. Flowers irregular.
    E1. Flowers yellow.
        GOODENIACEAE 173

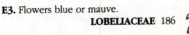

    E2. Flowers pink.
       STYLIDIACEAE 218

    E3. Flowers blue or mauve.
        LOBELIACEAE 186

Group 5 Herbs creeping and rooting along the stems, dicotyledons.

A. Leaves toothed.
    B. Flowers white or obsure.
        APIACEAE: ***Centella, Hydrocotyle*** 125

   *B. Flowers purple.

       VIOLACEAE 224

*A. Leaves not toothed.
    C. Leaves entire.

       CONVOLVULACEAE: ***Dichondra*** 155

    *C. Leaves 3-foliate.

       FABACEAE: ***Desmodium varians*** 333

Group 6 Remaining herbs.

Ⓐ The following groups are easily identifiable.

1. Leaves covered with sticky red hairs (plants carnivorous)
DROSERACEAE 162

2. Leaves with ochreous stipules.
POLYGONACEAE 420

3. Leaves succulent.

CACTACEAE 146   **CRASSULACEAE** 155

PORTULACEAE 199

4. Flowers in dense heads.

APIACEAE 124   **ASTERACEAE** 130

5. Leaves tiny, whorled.

RUBIACEAE:
Asperula, Galium 205

Ⓑ The remainder require flowers for keying.

A. Flowers regular.

B1. Flowers white or cream

AMARANTHACEAE 123   **PRIMULACEAE** 402, 422

CARYOPHYLLACEAE 355   **STACKHOUSIACEAE** 215

EUPHORBIACEAE: *Poranthera* 169

B2. Yellow or orange.

CLUSIACEAE 154   **RANUNCULACEAE** 200

OXALIDACEAE 195   **STACKHOUSIACEAE** 215

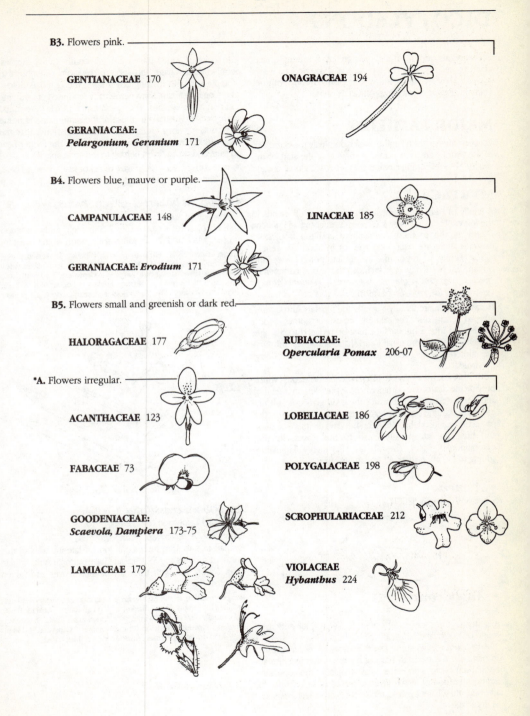

B3. Flowers pink.

GENTIANACEAE 170

ONAGRACEAE 194

GERANIACEAE:
Pelargonium, Geranium 171

B4. Flowers blue, mauve or purple.

CAMPANULACEAE 148

LINACEAE 185

GERANIACEAE: *Erodium* 171

B5. Flowers small and greenish or dark red.

HALORAGACEAE 177

RUBIACEAE:
Opercularia Pomax 206-07

*A. Flowers irregular.

ACANTHACEAE 123

LOBELIACEAE 186

FABACEAE 73

POLYGALACEAE 198

GOODENIACEAE:
Scaevola, Dampiera 173-75

SCROPHULARIACEAE 212

LAMIACEAE 179

VIOLACEAE
Hybanthus 224

DICOTYLEDONS

Dicotyledons are a major division of flowering plants, characterised by the embryo having 2 cotyledons (seed leaves). They are herbs and woody plants, mostly with net-veined leaves and flowering parts in 4s or 5s.

MAJOR FAMILIES

For convenience the 6 families which dominate the vegetation of the Sydney area are placed separately at the start of this section. The remaining families are then listed alphabetically.

MYRTACEAE

A family of trees and shrubs with translucent oil glands in the leaves. There are over 3000 species in about 155 genera, mainly in the southern hemisphere and the tropics. In Australia there are over 1500 species in about 75 genera.

The family is important for timber, pulp, honey and ornamental horticulture. It includes the exotic commercial species *Syzygium aromaticum* (cloves), *Psidium guavaja* (guava) and *Pimenta dioica* (allspice).

Botany: There are usually 5 sepals and 5 petals surrounding a broad nectary disc. The stamens are usually numerous and often fused into 5 bundles, or may be reduced to 5 single stamens. The fruits are usually cup-shaped capsules, although the rainforest genera retain more primitive succulent berry-like fruits.

All species have glands filled with volatile oils which provide the distinctive odours of eucalyptus, lemon, menthol and peppermint. The reason for these oil glands is still not understood. One current explanation is that they offer protection against dehydration: on hot days the oils evaporate and raise the air density close to the leaves, limiting evaporation of water. The oils are also highly flammable, adding to the intensity of Australian bushfires.

• *Acmena*
—See RAINFOREST SPECIES.

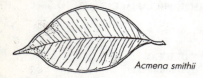

Acmena smithii

• *Angophora* Cavanilles
Apples

A genus of trees and shrubs with 11 species, all endemic, found on coasts and ranges of NSW, Qld and Vic.

Angophora retains some features ancestral to *Eucalyptus*. In particular the perianth has not been transformed into an operculum (cap) and the leaves retain the opposite arrangement found in the juvenile leaves of *Eucalyptus*. In addition, they have evolved modern Eucalypt features such as dry fruits.

In colonial times they were universally called 'Apples' because their foliage and show of blossom resemble that of apple trees. 'In looking down upon the rich flats below, adjoining the stream, I was perpetually reminded of a thriving and rich apple-orchard. The resemblance of what are called apple-trees in Australia to those of the same name at home is so striking at a distance in these situations, that the comparison could not be avoided, although the former bear no fruit, and do not even belong to the same species.'[1]

Name: *Angophora* = Gk. *angos*, vessel or vase, *phero*, to bear, i.e. goblet-carrying, referring to the fruit.

Angophora bakeri C. Hall **ssp.** *bakeri*
Narrow-leaved Apple **Ss, Cumb, Castl**

A shrub or small tree, usually 2-10m high, fairly common in open woodland in dry sandy soils, north of the harbour.

Range: coastal NSW. **Bark:** rough on all limbs. **Leaves:** opposite, mostly under 10mm wide. **Flowers:** CREAM, in terminal panicles. **Flowering time:** spring-early summer. **Capsules:** 7-10.5mm long, stalks mostly <10mm long. **Name:** *bakeri* = in honour of R. T. Baker (1855-1941), curator of the Technological Museum, Sydney, and pioneer in the development of the Eucalyptus oil industry.

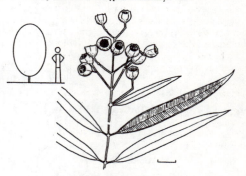

Angophora bakeri ssp. bakeri

Angophora crassifolia (not illustrated)
(G. Leach) L. Johnson & K. Hill

(previously *A. bakeri* ssp. *crassifolia*) **Ss**

A small tree to 15m high, common on lateritic tops in the northern suburbs and Ku-ring-gai Chase National Park. Similar to *A. bakeri*, but with thick tough rigid leaves and larger capsules.

Range: restricted to the Ku-ring-gai plateau between Sydney Harbour and the Hawkesbury River. **Bark:** rough on all limbs. **Leaves:** thick, rigid, usually olive-green, 7-15mm wide. **Flowers:** CREAM, in terminal panicles. **Flowering time:** spring-early summer. **Capsules:** 10-14mm long, stalks >10mm. **Name:** *crassifolium* = Lat. thick-leafed.

Angophora costata (Gaertner) Druce

(previously *A. lanceolata*)

Sydney Red Gum, Smooth-barked Apple, Kajimbourra **Ss**

'There too the angophora preaches on the hillsides With the gestures of Moses . . .'[2]

A medium-sized tree with smooth pinkish bark and convoluted limbs, 'festooning every hill and vale' on the poor sandstone soils of the Sydney region. It occupies a wide habitat between wet alluvial valleys and the poorest, most exposed tops, where only Scribbly Gum (*E. haemastoma*) is hardier. Usually it grows from crevices in rocks. The flesh-coloured limbs with their wrinkles and folds seem almost human.

Range: much of the NSW coast and a large part of southern Qld. **Bark:** smooth, mottled; orange after summer shedding, becoming purple and pink in winter. **Leaves:** opposite, *Eucalyptus*-like with very close lateral veins, paler on one side. **Flowers:** CREAM, in terminal panicles. **Flowering time:** October-January. **Capsule:** 13-15mm long, strongly ribbed. **Name:** *costata* = Lat. ribbed. *Kajimbourra* is an Aboriginal name from the Sydney area.

Angophora floribunda (Smith) Sweet

(previously *A. intermedia*)

Rough-barked Apple, Boonah **Ss**

A handsome small to medium tree with fibrous bark and sinuously contorted upper limbs. It prefers moist valleys with deep alluvial soils and almost certainly indicates habitats which would be rainforest if not regularly burnt. It is common in wet, sheltered forests in coast and mountain areas, with an understory of wetter sclerophyll or rainforest species. It has its best development in deep valleys of the mountains where its magnificently expressive limbs make it a memorable sight.

Range: from the NSW south coast, and northern NSW ranges, to southern Qld. **Bark:** brown, fibrous, on all limbs. **Leaves:** opposite, *Eucalyptus*-like with very close lateral veins, paler on one side. **Flowers:** WHITE. **Flowering time:** spring and summer. **Capsules:** 8-10mm long, thin walled, ribbed. **Name:** *floribunda* = abundant-flowered. *Boonah* is an Aboriginal name from the Sydney area.

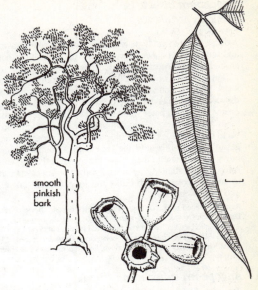

smooth pinkish bark

Angophora costata

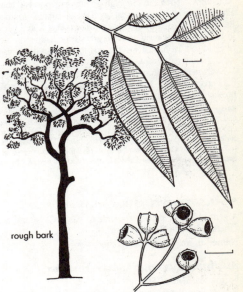

rough bark

Angophora floribunda

Angophora hispida (Smith) Blaxell

(previously *A. cordifolia*)

Dwarf Apple   **Ss**

A dense shrub to 4m high, with large stiff grey-green leaves, and red bristles on new leaves, stems and fruits. Common around Sydney, especially on ridge tops.

Dense masses of CREAM flowers in late spring produce a rich honey which attracts a fantastic collection of insects, especially jewel beetles. 'The brow of the hill would be a dreary place in summer without the dwarf apple . . . [in the morning] the slanting sun will shine upon the burnished backs of tiny beetles, whose blue and brown, green and red gleam like jewels against the creamy background. Honey-heavy bees drowse in their silky clusters; green-backed ants creep happily amongst them; while bright honey-eaters dart to and fro, poking sharp beaks and long, fringed tongues into the flowers' hearts.'[3]

Range: confined to coastal parts of the Sydney region. **Bark:** rough. **Leaves:** large, rounded, bluish, with small rigid hairs; the new branches and the inflorescence have dense bristly red hairs. **Flowers:** CREAM, dense. **Flowering time:** November-January. **Capsule:** ribbed, 15-19mm wide. **Name:** *hispida* = Lat. rough, from the stiff hairs that cover the plant.

Angophora hispida

Angophora subvelutina F. Mueller

Broad-leaved Apple   **Cumb**

A medium-sized tree to 25m high, common on poorly drained alluvial flats on the Hawkesbury-Nepean system, south of Richmond, often with *Melaleuca decora*. Alan Cunningham in 1827 noted that it was used by early settlers as an indication of good soil. Its habitat was the first to be cleared and used for crops and pastures.

Easily identified from a distance by its dense, non-droopy light-green foliage. Numerous juvenile leaves are usually present in the canopy (see illustration).

Range: NSW coast and ranges, except southern tabelands, and southern Qld. **Bark:** rough on all limbs, similar to *A. floribunda*. **Leaves:** opposite, mostly sessile (stalkless), stem-clasping, paler below, dull. Many adult leaves develop stalks and a drooping habit. **Flowering time:** spring-summer. **Capsules:** similar to *A. floribunda*, but covered in a fine felt and longer scattered reddish hairs (also on stems). **Name:** *subvelutina* = Lat. almost velvety.

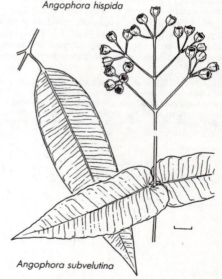

Angophora subvelutina

• *Austromyrtus* (Niedenzu) Burret

A genus with 12 species endemic to eastern Australia, and others in NG and New Caledonia.

Name: *austromyrtus* = Lat. southern Myrtle.

Austromyrtus tenuifolia (Smith) Burret

Narrow-leaf Myrtle   **Ss**

A sprawling, dense or more or less erect shrub 50-150cm tall. Scattered in sheltered places in woodland, mainly along creeks, north of the harbour. The leaves resemble *Ricinocarpos pinifolius*.

Range: restricted to sandstones in the Sydney region. **Leaves:** opposite, to 4cm long , about 2mm wide, with recurved margins and fine stiff points, hairless except for new shoots which are densely white silky below (and rosy above). **Flowers:** WHITE, in small axillary clusters, stamens numerous. **Fruit:** a dark purple berry. **Flowering time:** November-December. **Name:** *tenuifolia* = Lat. thin-leaved.

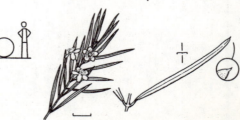

Austromyrtus tenuifolia

• *Baeckea* Linnaeus

Heath-myrtles
A genus of small shrubs with about 70 Australian species
and a few extending into Asia and New Caledonia.

Baeckea is distinguished by having 2 or 3 chambers in
a non-woody capsule and opposite leaves. There are 5-15
stamens, depending on the species. Most species are readily
identified by their miniscule leaves and tiny white flowers.

Name: *Baeckea* = Named by Linnaeus after his closest friend
Dr Abraham Baeck (1713-95), a medical doctor in Stockholm.

Baeckea brevifolia (Rudge) De Candolle

Ss

A shrub to 1m high, common in heathland.

Range: NSW coast and tablelands south from the Sydney region. **Leaves:**
about 2mm long, triangular in cross-section. **Flowers:** WHITE or
PINKISH. **Flowering time:** July-September. **Name:** *brevifolia* = Lat.
short-leaved.

Baeckea densifolia Smith

Ss

A shrub to 1.5m high, found in damp heath. Uncommon-
rare in the area, e.g. Georges River near Minto, Royal National
Park, Douglas Park. The densely 4-ranked leaves give the
branches a geometric beauty.

Range: coast and tablelands from the Sydney region to Qld. **Leaves:**
densely crowded, almost cylindrical, 4-6mm long, with a line of oil-dots
on each side (may need a hand lens to see these). **Flowers:** WHITE,
solitary in the upper axils. **Flowering time:** summer. **Name:**
densifolia = Lat. dense-leaved. **Similar species:** *Micromyrtus* spp.

Baeckea diosmifolia Rudge

Ss, Castl

A shrub to 1m high, found in low dry heaths.

Range: NSW coast and tablelands. **Leaves:** more or less flat, 2-3mm
long, 1mm wide, often with a microscopic margin of stiff hairs. **Flowers:**
WHITE. **Flowering time:** spring-summer. **Name:** *diosmifolia* =
Diosma-leafed. *Diosma* is a South African genus of small-leaved shrubs
in the family Rutaceae.

Baeckea imbricata (Gaertner) Druce

Ss

A shrub to 1m high. Found in damp heath, especially near
the sea.

Range: NSW coast and tablelands. **Leaves:** broad, more or less flat,
about 5mm long, 4-5mm wide. **Flowers:** WHITE to PINKISH.
Flowering time: spring-summer. **Name:** *imbricata* = Lat. with
overlapping edges.

Baeckea linifolia Rudge

Ss

'The prettiest of them all, is *B. linifolia*, a slender, linear-
shaped shrub, of a few feet, bearing a profusion of white
flowers, and gracefully bending over water-courses.'[4] Found
in sheltered rocky places along creeks in sandstone country,
especially around waterfalls.

Range: on coast and ranges from Vic to Qld. **Leaves:** soft, more or
less cylindrical. Branches often drooping. **Flowers:** WHITE.
Flowering time: spring-summer. **Name:** *linifolia* = Lat. linear-leaved.

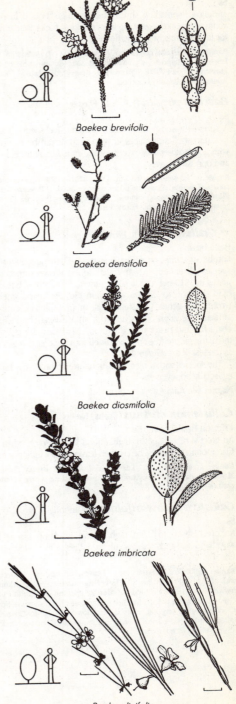

Baekea brevifolia

Baekea densifolia

Baekea diosmifolia

Baekea imbricata

Baekea linifolia

Baeckea ramosissima A. Cunningham
Ss

A delicate spreading shrub 10-20cm high. Found in open sunny heath, often growing from cracks in rocks. Remarkable for its delicate rose-purple flowers.

Range: on coast and ranges from Tas and SA to Coffs Harbour in NSW. **Leaves:** tiny, opposite, slightly flattened, soft, without visible oil-dots. **Flowers:** ROSE-PURPLE. **Flowering time:** June-February. **Name:** *ramosissima* = Lat. very branched.

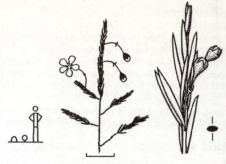
Baekea ramosissima

Baeckea virgata (J. R. & G. Forster) Andrews
Ss

A spreading shrub 2-4m high. An attractive species found in damp sheltered places in woodland. It can be confused with a *Leptospermum* except for the non-woody fruits in 3s, and opposite leaves.

Range: on coast and mountains from Vic to Qld and NT. **Leaves:** broad, fairly soft, with a Eucalyptus odour when crushed. **Flowers:** WHITE. **Flowering time:** spring-summer. **Name:** *virgata* = Lat. *virga*, a slender green twig, from the slender branchlets.

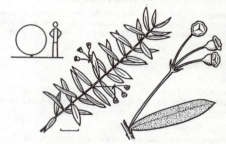
Baekea virgata

• *Callistemon* R. Brown
Bottlebrush

Shrubs in damp or swampy ground. There are about 30 species, all endemic to Australia. Robert Brown named this genus in 1810 but it took some time to be accepted because of its similarity to *Melaleuca*. Even in 1863 Ferdinand Mueller wrote 'The genus Callistemon is, in my opinion, entirely artificial, not safely distinguished from *Melaleuca* by a single character, and better united with it.'[5] Nowadays the fact that the filaments are free and not joined into bundles is regarded as the test of a *Callistemon*.

The species with long red filaments are pollinated by birds, especially honeyeaters.

Name: Gk. *Kallistos* = very beautiful.

Callistemon citrinus (Curtis) Skeels

Crimson Bottlebrush **Ss**

An erect shrub about 2m high. Found in swampy heathland. Common in the area. The crushed leaves have a lemon scent.

Range: from Vic to Qld. **Leaves:** hard, stiff, flat, sharply pointed. **Flowers:** with BRIGHT RED filaments. **Flowering time:** spring. **Name:** *citrinus* = lemony.

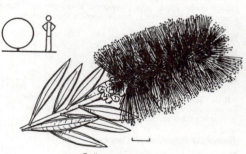
Callistemon citrinus

Callistemon linearifolius De Candolle
Ss

An erect shrub to 2.5m high, found in damp places in woodland on sandstone, usually in gullies (e.g. Audley), but uncommon.

Range: confined to the Sydney area. **Leaves:** stiff, hairless. **Flowers:** with bright RED filaments. **Flowering time:** spring. **Name:** *linearifolius* = Lat. straight-leafed. **Similar species:** distinguish from *C. pinifolius* by the lack of a swollen margin on leaves; distinguish from *C. saligna* by the very stiff leaves and red flowers; similar to *C. rigidus* except the leaves are usually larger and the marginal veins are much less prominent (see illustration).

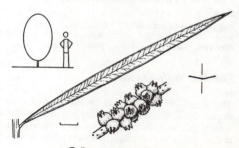
Callistemon linearifolius

Callistemon linearis De Candolle

Narrow-leaved Bottlebrush **Ss, Cumb**
An erect shrub 1.5-2m high, found in damp places in heath and woodland on sandstone and also on clay soils on the Cumberland Plain.

Range: restricted to NSW, from coast to western slopes. **Leaves:** narrow, stiff channelled above, rough due to raised oil dots, sharply pointed. **Flowers:** with bright RED filaments. **Flowering time:** October. **Name:** *linearis* = straight.

Callistemon pinifolius De Candolle

Ss, Castl
An erect shrub to 2.5m high. An uncommon species, found in the Castlereagh woodlands, and in wet coastal heath between Maroubra and Kurnell.

Range: Sydney area, also western slopes in central and northern NSW (e.g. Picton, Dubbo). **Leaves:** rough, with revolute margins (i.e. completely curled up) **Flowers:** with YELLOW-GREEN filaments. **Flowering time:** spring. **Name:** *pinifolius* = Pine-leaved.

Callistemon rigidus R. Brown

Stiff Bottlebrush **Ss, Cumb**
An erect shrub to 2m high, found in damp places in heath and woodland on sandstone and also on clay soils on the Cumberland Plain.

Range: restricted to the Sydney region. **Leaves:** stiff, often rough due to raised oil-dots, 3-6mm wide. **Flowers:** with RED filaments **Name:** *rigidus* = rigid.

Callistemon salignus (Smith) De Candolle

Willow Bottlebrush **Ss**
A tall shrub, usually 3-4m high, with corky bark. Found in freshwater marshes, rocky creek banks and moist forests in valleys, on a variety of soils.

Range: coastal areas from southern NSW to Qld. **Leaves:** stiff but flexible, hairless, alternate, with visible oil-dots. **Flowers:** with CREAM, YELLOWISH-WHITE, or LEMON filaments. **Name:** salignus = willowy.

Callistemon sieberi F. Mueller

(previously *C. paludosus*)
River Bottlebrush **Ss, Cumb**
An erect shrub 2-4m high, found in swamps and on stream banks along the Nepean River and on the Woronora Plateau.

Range: NSW coast, ranges and inland areas, Vic, Tas, SA and Qld. **Leaves:** 4-6cm long, 3-5mm wide, stiff, with a distinct point. **Flowers:** with WHITE filaments, spikes to 4cm long. **Flowering time:** January-May. **Name:** *sieberi* = after Franz Wilhelm Sieber of Prague, Bohemia, who collected extensively in Australia from 1819-23. **Similar species:** resembles *C. subulatus* except the flowers are WHITE and the capsules have only 3 chambers.

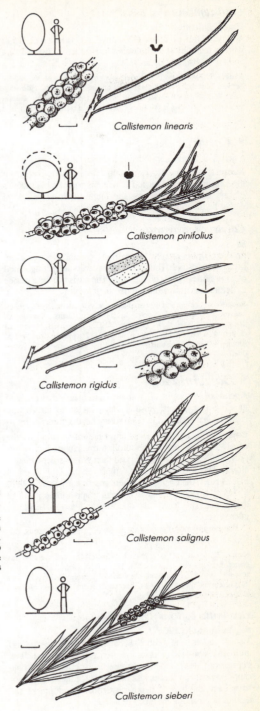

Callistemon linearis

Callistemon pinifolius

Callistemon rigidus

Callistemon salignus

Callistemon sieberi

Callistemon subulatus Cheel

Dwarf Bottlebrush **Ss**

A small shrub to 1.5m high. Found on rocky creek banks with its feet almost in the water, in Heathcote National Park and the Woronora Plateau.

Range: NSW coast and ranges south from the Sydney area, Vic and SA. **Leaves:** fairly stiff, with a sharp point and visible oil dots. **Flowers:** with RED filaments. **Flowering time:** October-January. **Name:** *subulatus* = Lat. *subula*, an awl, i.e. linear and tapering gradually to a fine point.

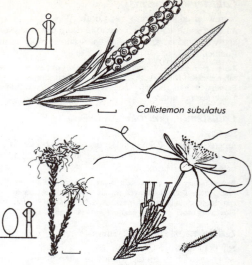

Callistemon subulatus

• *Calytrix* Labillardière

A genus of 45 species, endemic to Australia.

Name: *Calytrix* = Gk. *calyx*, cup, *thrix, trichos*, hair, from the long awns on the calyx. The name is one of Labillardière's elegant Latin combinations; the linguistically correct form would be the much more awkward *Calycothrix*.

Calytrix tetragona Labillardière

Ss

An erect shrub usually 1-1.5m high, common in open dry heath on sandstone. The small white flowers are distinguished by long sinuous awns on the calyx. The awns may be a device to detour ants away from the nectar.

Range: coast, ranges and western districts of NSW, also in all other states. **Leaves:** tiny, crowded, covered in short, erect hairs, blunt-tipped, triangular in cross-section. **Flowers:** WHITE or PINKISH, in terminal clusters, with 5 thread-like awns on the calyx. **Flowering time:** spring-summer. **Name:** *tetragona* = Gk. 4-sided, referring to the leaves (when dried).

Calytrix tetragona

• *Darwinia* Rudge

A genus of 45 species, all Australian and mainly concentrated in south-west Western Australia. Most are small shrubs with crowded leaves, found in open sunny heath country.

Botany: The tubular flowers are a radical variation on the usual Myrtaceae pattern. The corolla forms a tube which opens only briefly in its early stages and then remains permanently closed. This was a puzzle for early investigators; how could insects reach the enclosed anthers and so carry away pollen? In fact they don't; the style collects it and carries it out of the flower. The leaves are opposite and mostly triangular in cross-section.

The current populations are in small, restricted areas, but abundant where they occur.

Name: *Darwinia* (1815) = not after Charles Darwin, but after his grandfather Erasmus Darwin (1731-1802), a physician, inventor and amateur botanist. He translated the works of Linnaeus into English and then celebrated them in a long rather bawdy poem, *The Loves of Plants* (1789).

Darwinia biflora (Cheel) Briggs

Ss Vulnerable 2VCa

A small understorey shrub 20-80cm high, found in sedgeland and low scrubland with a preference for moist, shallow depressions. Restricted to ridge-tops in association with shale cappings over Hawkesbury sandstone. Since these ridge-tops have been the site of major residential development the current populations are much reduced.

Range: restricted to the northern suburbs of Sydney. Most stands are found in near-urban bushland near Asquith, Mt Colah and East Wahroonga, currently threatened by urban and Freeway development. There is a small population in Pennant Hills Park. It has also recently been discovered in Marramarra National Park. **Leaves:** triangular in cross-section, fairly soft. **Flowers:** in pairs, protected by two red bracteoles. The corolla is 6-8mm long. **Flowering time:** July-November. **Name:** *biflora* = Lat. two-flowered.

Darwinia diminuta Briggs

Ss Rare 3RCi

A spreading (sometimes sprawling) shrub to 1.5m high, with stout woody stems. Found in heath, scrub and woodland on poorly drained sandy soil or laterites.

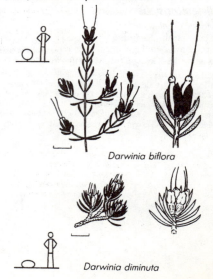

Darwinia biflora

Darwinia diminuta

Range: restricted to the Sydney area in two separate populations; on the plateau between Terry Hills and Manly, and on the Woronora Plateau between Sutherland and Helensburg. **Leaves:** 6-11mm long. **Flowers:** 2-4 per cluster, PINK-WHITE, floral tube 3-5mm long, style 4-9mm long. **Flowering time:** September-January. **Name:** *diminuta* = tiny.

Darwinia fascicularis Rudge
ssp. *fascicularis*
Ss

A spreading, much-branched shrub usually to 1.5-2.5m high. The most common *Darwinia* in the area, found in heathy scrubs. This is a beautiful species which resembles a bonsai conifer because of its clustered bunches of tiny pine-like leaves. The crushed leaves have a strong odour like 'a rather oily eau-de-cologne'.

Range: restricted to the sandstone coastal plateaus from north of Bulli to Gosford. (Around Katoomba in the Blue Mountains the species is represented by subspecies *oligantha*, which is basically the same plant with a decumbent habit and fewer flowers in each cluster.) **Leaves:** minute, densely crowded in clusters, more or less cylindrical. **Flowers:** WHITE becoming RED, in clusters of several (often 12). **Flowering time:** mainly June-September. **Name:** *fascicularis* = Lat. arranged in bundles, referring to the leaves.

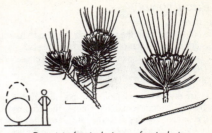

Darwinia fascicularis ssp. *fascicularis*

Darwinia grandiflora
(Bentham) Baker & Smith
Ss   Rare 2RC-

A robust prostrate shrub forming dense mats on open moist heath country. Found on higher parts of the Woronora Plateau where it is fairly common.

Range: restricted to the Sydney area. **Leaves:** 8-18mm long. **Flowers:** 4 (6) per cluster, white, becoming BRIGHT RED, floral tube 7-12mm long, style 12-20mm long. **Flowering time:** July-August. **Name:** *grandiflora* = Lat. large-flowered.

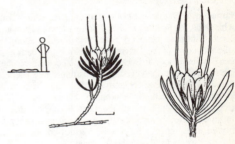

Darwinia grandifolia

Darwinia leptantha Briggs
Ss

A small heath shrub to 80cm high, preferring sandy soils, often on swampy ground.

Range: mainly in coastal heaths in three separate populations: Jervis Bay and Pidgeon House area, Sydney coast from Cronulla to North Head, and south of Forster. **Leaves:** triangular in cross-section, fairly soft. **Flowers:** 2 or 4 together, with yellow-green bracteoles 2-3.5mm long (falling off early). Floral-tube 4-6mm long. **Flowering time:** April-September. **Name:** *leptantha* = Gk. slender-flowered. **Note:** a closely related south coast and Woronora species is *D. camptostylis*, distinguished by its persistent bracteoles 3.5-6mm long.

Darwinia leptantha

Darwinia peduncularis Briggs
Ss   Rare 3RCi

A spreading shrub to 1.5m high, preferring shallow sandy soils in heath and woodland.

Range: restricted to the sandstone plateau between Hornsby and Hawkesbury River **Leaves:** 7-12mm long. **Flowers:** 1-2 together on a stalk 4-7mm long, floral-tube 9-12mm long, style 6-10mm long. The deep red bracteoles (4-8mm long) fall off early. **Flowering time:** July-August. **Name:** *peduncularis* = having prominent peduncles (floral stalks).

Darwinia peduncularis

Darwinia procera Briggs
Ss   Rare 2RCa

An erect shrub to 2m (3m) high. Found in sheltered places in woodland on sandstone slopes.

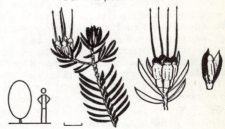

Darwinia procera

Range: Restricted to the Sydney area: mainly around Hawkesbury River, Cowan Creek and Berowra Creek, also Middle Harbour Creek and Narrabeen. **Leaves:** triangular in cross-section, fairly soft. **Flowers:** WHITE, becoming RED, floral tube about 10mm long, 4 (to 8) per cluster. Bracteoles deep red, falling off early. **Flowering time:** July-October. **Name:** *procera* = Lat. tall.

• *Eucalyptus* L'Héritier

Gum trees

'This noble genus, on the whole, may be said to have taken undisturbed possession of these Australian regions, clothing, as it does, with its stupendous mantle, the surface of both Van Diemen's Land and Australia.'
—Daniel Bunce, 1859[6]

There are over 500 species of Eucalypts, all endemic except for a handful extending into New Guinea, the Molucca Islands and the southern Philippines. They are always the tallest trees on the sites on which they occur and dominate the vegetation of much of the continent.

Name: In 1777 during Cook's epic third expedition, one of his ships, the *Resolution*, visited Bruny Island in Tasmania. Joseph Banks' collector on board was David Nelson. He collected a twig of the 'Dragon's Blood Tree' that Banks had seen 7 years before at Botany Bay. The specimen reached England and languished in Banks' herbarium at Kew Gardens until the visiting French botanist Charles-Louis L'Héritier de Brutelle examined it. He returned to France and in 1788 published its description with the name *Eucalyptus obliqua*. He created *Eucalyptus* from the greek *eu* well, *kalyptos*, covered, in reference to the cap covering the bud, and *obliqua* from the asymmetrical leaf of this species.

Botany: The bud cap or operculum is an adaptation of the petals which have joined and hardened into a thick protective lid. The numerous stamens have replaced the petals in the function of guiding insects to the flower. Pollination is by many species of nectar eating insects. The white or cream flowers suggest nocturnal pollinators.

Eucalypts are highly resistant to fire, and regenerate rapidly from epicormal buds hidden on the stems or from lignotubers hidden beneath the ground.

Identification: 'There is no family which is more perplexing to the botanist, as the species are so numerous and run so close to each other that it is exceedingly difficult to define them,' wrote William Woolls,[7] expressing the feelings of most people when faced with this genus.

Identification is rendered difficult by a number of factors: the close relationships of many species; the natural variability of characteristics used for identification; and the tendency of related eucalypts to interbreed forming hybrids with intermediate characteristics. In practice, generally more than one characteristic is needed for a firm identification as each type of bark, leaf or even fruit can appear to be shared by several species. The illustrations should enable immediate identification of all but stringybarks where several trees may have to be examined before a sure identification is reached.

The grouping here is an artificial arrangement based on bark types, since that is the most readily accessible characteristic.

Relationships within *Eucalyptus*: The relationships of the local species according to the system of Pryor and Johnson (1971) is given below. In this system *Angophora* is considered to have the same status as a *Eucalyptus* sub-genus

An attempt has recently been made to break *Eucalyptus* into 8 smaller genera, based upon recognised sub-genera. Together with *Angophora* this would make 9 genera in the

Eucalyptus alliance, one of which will still be called *Eucalyptus*. The argument is that if *Angophora* is allowed to be a separate genus, then equally distinct groups of Eucalypts should be raised to generic status in order truly to reflect variety within the alliance. This new arrangement has not been formally published yet and it remains to be seen whether it will be generally accepted.

For a short history of Eucalypt classification and an outline of the current system see—Brooker and Kleinig, *A Field Guide to Eucalyptus*,[8] available in most libraries.

A classification of the local species of *Eucalyptus* & *Angophora* according to Pryor and Johnson (1971)

Genus ANGOPHORA

- Series COSTATAE
  Hispidinae —
     A. hispida
  Floribundinae —
     A. subvelutina
     A. floribunda
     A. bakeri
  Costatinae —
     A. costata

Sub-genus CORYMBIA (Bloodwoods)

- Section RUFARIA
  - Series GUMMIFERAE
    E. gummifera
  - Series EXIMIAE
    E. eximia
  - Series MACULATAE
    E. maculata

Sub-genus MONOCALYPTUS
(single opercula)

- Section RENANTHERIA
  - Series ACMENOIDEAE (White Mahoganies)
    E. umbra
    E. acmenoides
  - Series CAPITELLATAE (Stringybarks)
    E. agglomerata
    E. eugenioides
    E. globoidea
    E. oblonga
    E. sparsifolia
    E. capitellata
    E. camfieldii
  - Series PILULARES (Blackbutts)
    E. pilularis
  - Series OBLIQUAE (Ashes)
    E. luehmanniana
    E. consideniana
    E. sieberi
    E. multicaulis
    E. obstans

- Series PIPERITAE (Peppermints and Scribbly Gums)
    - E. elata
    - E. piperita
    - E. haemastoma
    - E. sclerophylla
    - E. racemosa

Sub-genus SYMPHYOMYRTUS
(double opercula)

- Section EQUATORIA
    - Series TRANSVERSARIAE
        - E. deanei
        - E. saligna
        - E. botryoides
        - E. robusta
        - E. pellita
        - E. resinifera
        - E. punctata
        - E. longifolia
- Section BISECTARIA
    - Series SQUAMOSAE
        - E. squamosa
- Section EXSERTARIA
    - Series TERETICORNES (Red Gums)
        - E. parramattensis
        - E. amplifolia
        - E. tereticornis
- Section MAIDENARIA
    - Series VIMINALINAE
        - E. viminalis
        - E. benthamii
- Section ADNATARIA (Boxes)
    - Series MOLUCCANAE
        - E. moluccana
    - Series ODORATAE
        - E. bosistoana
    - Series PRUINOSAE (Ironbarks)
        - E. fibrosa
        - E. siderophloia
        - E. crebra
    - Series POLYANTHEMAE
        - E. bauerana
    - Series PANICULATAE (Ironbarks)
        - E. paniculata
        - E. beyeriana
    - Series MELLIODORAE (Ironbarks)
        - E. sideroxylon

Reading the *Eucalyptus* illustrations

Leaves: usually only adult leaves are shown; remember that Eucalypts have juvenile and intermediate leaves which can be quite different from adult leaves; the juvenile leaves are the most different, being usually large and broad and sometimes opposite. Intermediate leaves resemble adult leaves but are usually much larger.

Fruit: essential for good identification—some can almost always be found by scratching around in the leaf litter below mature trees.

Bark: the illustrations show the extent of bark on a supposed typical specimen; in practice, however, this varies widely.

Habit: this varies greatly according to soil and situation; the illustrations show well developed mature specimens but this is not necessarily an indication of the shape of trees likely to be encountered in the field.

Key to *Eucalyptus* groups

Smooth barks 32

Part barks 36

Full barks 40

Bark easily crumbles into small fragments or fibres.

'Crumbly' barks 40

Bark thick and pulls away in masses of long thin fibres.

Stringy barks 44

Bark dark, hard and deeply fissured, forming long stiff ridges.

Ironbarks 47

Mallees 49

SMOOTH BARKS

These are the trees that amazed early visitors by losing their bark in summer rather than their leaves in winter. In fact, since the bark (which is simply dead wood) is entirely shed each year, they could be called 'no barks'. Often the term 'gum' is applied to this bark type.

The most common smooth-barked gum in the area is the Sydney Red Gum, *Angophora costata* (see *Angophora*).

Eucalyptus amplifolia Naudin
ssp. *amplifolia*

Cabbage Gum   **Cumb**

A medium-sized tree found in swampy flats on shale-derived soils. Around Sydney it is common on low-lying parts of the Cumberland Plain. It is very similar to Forest Red Gum but can be easily distinguished at a distance by the very broad leaves.

Interestingly it was first described in 1891 when Charles Naudin, a sharp-eyed French botanist, realised that various trees, supposedly of Forest Red Gum (*E. tereticornis*), planted in Algeria, France, and Italy, differed from the normal characteristics of that species.

Range: coastal districts from Bega to Coffs Harbour.   **Bark:** smooth, with blotches in various shades from light to steel grey.   **Leaves:** very broad, same colour both sides.   **Flowering time:** summer.   **Capsules:** similar to *E. tereticornis* but more than 7 per umbel.   **Name:** *amplifolia* = Lat. large-leaf, referring especially to the juvenile leaves. The common name also refers to the juvenile leaves which, being enormous, round, tough and strongly veined, might resemble cabbage leaves.

Eucalyptus benthamii Maiden & Cambage

Nepean River Gum, Ribbon Gum, River White Gum, Kayer-ro   **Cumb   Vulnerable 2VCi**

A tall tree to 30m high. Restricted to a small population in Bents Basin and another at Kedumba Creek in the southern Blue Mountains, together with scattered individuals between Wallacia and Camden. It occurs with a wet sclerophyll understory on alluvial sandbanks.

Range: its original habitat was the flats of the Nepean River system, including the Coxs River but clearing and drowning by the waters of the Warragamba Dam have much reduced its area.   **Bark:** smooth and white on all parts, with numerous long loose ribbons, and a little persistent flaky bark at the base   **Leaves:** with irregular lateral veins, same colour both sides.   **Flowering time:** summer.   **Capsules:** small, usually bell-shaped, with a flat or slightly convex disc and exserted valves.   **Name:** *benthamii* = honours George Bentham (1800-1884), the English botanist who never visited Australia but wrote the immense and influential *Flora Australiensis*.[10]

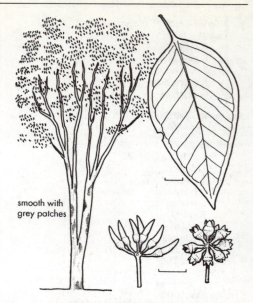

smooth with grey patches

Eucalyptus amplifolia ssp. *amplifolia*

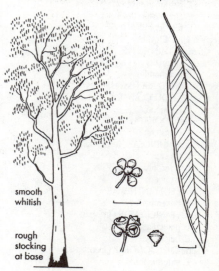

smooth whitish

rough stocking at base

Eucalyptus benthamii

Eucalyptus deanei Maiden

Mountain Blue Gum, Round-leaved Gum, Deane's Gum
A tall tree to 50m, closely resembling Sydney Blue Gum (*E. saligna*). Found scattered along alluvial flats on the lower Hawkesbury River (east of Wisemans Ferry), with Forest Red Gum, Blackbutt and *Angophora floribunda*. It also occurs in the Blue Mountains (e.g. the famous Blue Gum Forest) and along the Colo River system, where it may form dense forests on the alluvial flats.

Range: it has two occurrences; one in mountain valleys from Picton to near Singleton, and the other north from Armidale into southern Qld. **Bark:** similar to Sydney Blue Gum: smooth and white with bluish-grey patches, but with only a very short stocking of rough scaly bark at the base. **Juvenile leaves:** broad. **Adult leaves:** 8-12cm long, paler on one side. Intermediate leaves predominate on many trees, giving a very broad-leaved appearance. **Flowering time:** autumn. **Capsules:** about 5mm wide, with prominent stalks, valves sometimes slightly exserted. **Name:** *deanei* = after Henry Deane (1847-1924), railway surveyor, Engineer-in-Chief of the NSW railways and a keen amateur botanist.

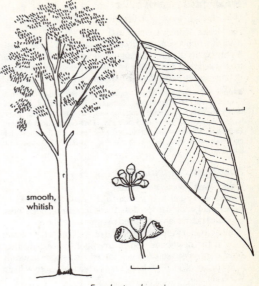

smooth, whitish

Eucalyptus deanei

Eucalyptus haemastoma Smith

Scribbly Gum, Tarinny, Wongnary **Ss**
A small gum tree to 15m high with bare, white and grey mottled bark showing distinctive 'scribbles' (the tunnels of moth larvae). It is the hardiest tree in the area. North of the harbour it occurs in pure stands, but south there are many hybrid stands of *E. haemastoma* x *racemosa*.

Range: restricted to sandstones in the Sydney region where it is very common on exposed skeletal-soiled ridges on the coastal plateaus. **Bark:** smooth on all limbs, white or yellowish, with grey mottling and 'scribbles'. **Adult leaves:** drooping, thick, dull, to 12cm long, 2-3cm wide. **Flowering time:** autumn-spring. **Capsules:** shaped like a pear. **Name:** *haemastoma* = Gk. *haema*, red, *stoma*, mouth. Smith does not explain why he choose this name, however the discs of the capsules are often red and this may be the reason. *Tarinny* and *Wongnary* are Aboriginal names from the Sydney area.

Eucalyptus racemosa Cavanilles

Snappy Gum, Scribbly Gum **Ss**
A small scribbly gum to 15m high with the same general appearance as *E. haemastoma* but distinguished by small fruit and narrow adult leaves. It prefers sandy soils near the coast (although at Mona Vale it is found on shales) and a moister and less exposed environment than *E. haemastoma*.

Range: restricted to coastal parts of the Sydney region. The pure stands occur mainly north of the harbour. A stand in the Domain was cut down in the 1920s. **Bark:** white with grey patches and occasional dark shreds of dead bark, especially at the base. Moth larvae 'scribbles' conspicuous. **Adult leaves:** long, drooping, narrow, to 14cm long, 10-15mm wide. **Flowering time:** August-November. **Capsules:** usually with reddish disc. **Name:** *racemosa* = having racemes. The name is a misnomer; it arose because the type specimens collected at Port Jackson in 1793 included parts of *E. crebra*, an ironbark which does have racemes.

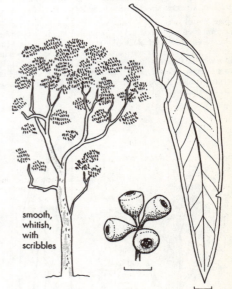

smooth, whitish, with scribbles

Eucalyptus haemastoma

Eucalyptus haemastoma x *racemosa*

These two species occur in pure populations north of the harbour, but south of the harbour (e.g. Royal National Park) they often form intermingled swarms, appearing as stands with intermixed features.

Eucalyptus racemosa

Eucalyptus sclerophylla

(Blakely) L. Johnson & D. Blaxell

Hard-leafed Scribbly Gum **Castl**

A small scribbly gum, usually to 15m tall in this area. Locally it only occurs in the Castlereagh woodlands. It is very similar to *E. racemosa*, fortunately its different distribution makes in unnecessary to distinguish them in the field.

Range: NSW coast and ranges, south from Howes Valley near Putty. Common in the Blue Mountains. **Bark:** typical scribbly bark. **Leaves:** hard and glossy with obscure venation; adult leaves mostly under 25mm wide, intermediate leaves to 5cm wide. **Flowering time:** summer. **Capsules:** 4-5mm wide, cup-shaped, disc exserted, flat or slightly enclosed, valves small, level with the disc. **Name:** *sclerophylla* = Lat. hard-leaved.

Eucalyptus maculata W.J. Hooker

Spotted Gum, Booangie **Cumb**

A medium or tall tree to 30m high, easily recognised by its beautiful smooth leopard-skin bark. It occurs in open forest on shales but has a very limited occurrence in the area.

Spotted Gum were once plentiful on the Cumberland Plain: ' . . . in the neighbourhood of Liverpool they extend over a surface of several square miles, sometimes rising majestically to the height of 80 to 100 feet without a branch', wrote William Woolls in 1867.[10]

The light, strong, durable timber was cut for many purposes, including wooden street paving in Sydney.

Range: coastal parts of NSW, extensively in south-eastern Qld and in one small stand near Orbost in Vic. **Bark:** smooth, pale yellow when fresh, greyish purple when old, shed in small patches, hence producing a spotted appearance. **Leaves:** same colour both sides. **Flowering time:** winter. **Capsules:** large, ovoid, with a broad descending disc and 3-4 deeply enclosed valves. The operculum (cap) is double: the inner one is thin and glossy. **Name:** *maculata* = Lat. spotted. *Booangie* is an Aboriginal name from Sydney area.

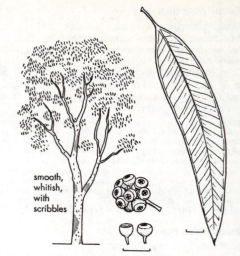

smooth, whitish, with scribbles

Eucalyptus sclerophylla

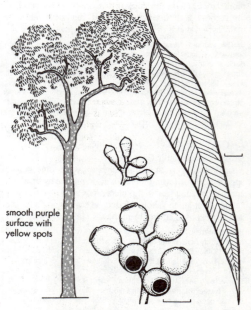

smooth purple surface with yellow spots

Eucalyptus maculata

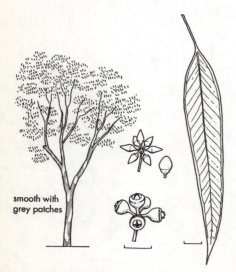

smooth with grey patches

Eucalyptus parramattensis ssp. *parramattensis*

Eucalyptus parramattensis C. Hall ssp. *parramattensis*

Drooping Red Gum, Parramatta Red Gum **Castl, Cumb**

A small tree 5-15m high, abundant in marshy parts of the Castlereagh woodlands. It looks like a Grey Gum or a dwarfed Forest Red Gum from a distance. The leaves are strongly aromatic.

Range: Cumberland Plain, Picton, Cessnock and Capertee Valley. **Bark:** pale grey, with mottled patches of yellow or cream. **Juvenile leaves:** slender (about 1.5cm wide, compared to 5-6cm wide for Forest Red Gum). **Adult Leaves:** mostly under 12cm long and under 2cm wide, dull, glaucous, same colour both sides. **Flowering time:** summer. **Capsules:** 4-6mm wide, similar in shape to Forest Red Gum. The buds vary from conical to almost spherical. **Name:** *parramattensis* = from Parramatta.

Eucalyptus punctata De Candolle

Grey Gum, Maandowie **Ss**

A tall open-crowned tree to 35m in tall open forests, reduced to 10m on poorer soils. It usually occurs on shallow sandy soils but seems to have a wide range of soil preferences and an unpredictable distribution. It is one of the most beautiful of gums in the area due to its matt steel-grey bark marked with patches of pink or cream.

The leaves of the Grey Gum, along with those of the Forest Red Gum (*E. tereticornis*), are the favourite food of koalas.

Range: NSW coast and mountains between Jervis Bay and Scone. **Bark:** smooth, falling in large irregular plates, cream, pink or orange, weathering to grey or brown with a grainy surface. The bark has a roughish or raspy appearance. . . It has smooth white patches in places, caused by the outer layer of bark falling off . . . Although rather difficult to properly describe, the bark of the Grey Gum is so characteristic that, when once pointed out it could not be confused with the bark of any other hardwood tree.'[11] **Leaves:** paler underneath, with a fine drawn-out point. **Flowering time:** December-April. **Capsules:** 12-14mm wide, with exserted valves. **Name:** *punctata* = Lat. dotted, referring to tiny black dots below the leaves. *Mandowe, Mundowey, Maandowie* are Aboriginal names from the Sydney area.

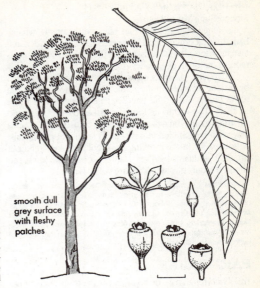

smooth dull grey surface with fleshy patches

Eucalyptus punctata

Eucalyptus tereticornis Smith

Forest Red Gum, Burringoa **Cumb**

A tall tree 30-40m high with a smooth pale trunk. The only red thing about Forest Red Gum is its timber; the bark is a mottled mixture of pale greys with dark grey shreds at the base. It prefers well-drained clay soils and alluviums and occurs on grassy wooded alluvial flats on the Cumberland Plain, with Grey Box (*E. moluccana*). It also occurs occasionally around the shores of the Parramatta and Georges Rivers on alluviums.

Closely allied to the important River Red Gum (*E. camaldulensis*) of the inland. It provides a strong hardwood timber, used for heavy construction, railway sleepers, poles and posts.

Range: from east Vic to northern Qld and NG. **Bark:** smooth, bluish-grey, whitish or ash-coloured with brown and grey patches, some rough dead bark remaining at base. **Leaves:** long and slender, 10-20cm. **Flowering time:** June-November. **Capsules:** always 7 per head, with valves strongly exserted. **Name:** *tereticornis* = Lat. *teretus* cylindrical or narrowly tapering, *cornus*, horn, refers to the long conical flower buds. *Burringoa* is an Aboriginal name from the Sydney area.

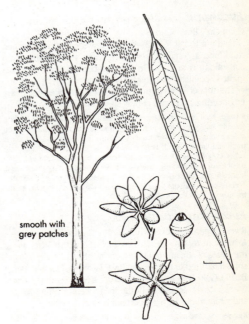

smooth with grey patches

Eucalyptus tereticornis

Eucalyptus viminalis Labillardière

Ribbon Gum, Manna Gum

A medium to tall tree, 20-40m high, with smooth, whitish bark. It has a limited local occurence between Camden and Menangle on alluvial soils beside the Nepean River but is more common in deep valleys in the Blue Mountains.

Gliders and possums often feed off the rich sugary sap by making incisions in the trunk. This sap gives rise to the name Manna Gum. The traveller Peter Cunningham wrote in 1827: 'The manna is found in flakes on the grass and adhering to the branches and trunks, and several pounds may often be gathered in a very short space of time. It must be looked for in the morning, as, should the sun shine out strong, it gradually dissolves. Manna is one of the safest and almost the only pleasant purgative we possess . . . '.[12]

Range: coast and ranges of NSW, Vic, and Tasmania, also SA. **Bark:** smooth, white or yellowish, with grey shreds collected around the base of trunk, shed in long ribbons which often remain caught in the forks. **Leaves:** long and slender, with irregular lateral veins, same colour both sides. **Flowering time:** most of the year. **Capsules:** 7-8mm wide, ovoid or hemispherical, with a domed disc and prominently exserted valves. **Name:** *viminalis* = Lat. twiggy.

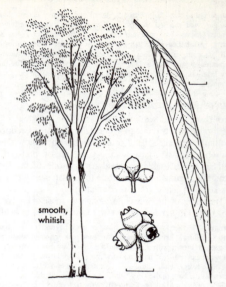

smooth, whitish

Eucalyptus viminalis

PART BARKS

Trees with rough bark on all or part of the trunk and smooth bare upper limbs. The species are otherwise unrelated.

Eucalyptus bosistoana F. Mueller

Coast Grey Box **Cumb**

A medium to tall tree, 25-40m high, with a tall unbranched trunk and a compact crown. It prefers good quality loam soils along river flats. On the Cumberland Plain it occurs in the Cabramatta–Bringelly–Prospect area.

The timber is very strong and durable, milled for heavy engineering, poles and railway sleepers.

Range: NSW coast and ranges south from Sydney, and Vic. **Bark:** a variable stocking of light grey, finely fibrous and rather flaky bark on at least some of the lower trunk; smooth pale grey or white on upper trunk and limbs. **Adult leaves:** slender, same colour both sides with rather irregular venation. **Juvenile leaves:** broad, heart-shaped, paler on one side. **Flowering time:** November-February. **Capsules:** small, hemispherical, disc descending, valves enclosed or at rim level. **Name:** *bosistoana* = honours Joseph Bosisto (1824-98), a pioneer in the manufacture of Eucalypt oils.

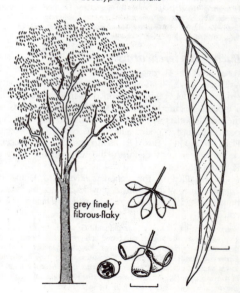

grey finely fibrous-flaky

Eucalyptus bosistoana

Eucalyptus elata Dehnhardt

River Peppermint, River White Gum **Cumb**

A medium to tall tree 20-45m high. Found in belts along the edges of streams in gullies, on moist and usually alluvial soils. Restricted to the Nepean River (Cobbity-Elderslie-Bents Basin), Colo-Putty and a few other areas (e.g. Kenthurst, Cattai Creek). Easily recognised by the sparse slender bluish foliage and white trunks with peppermint bark at the base.

Range: coast and ranges from eastern Vic to near Sydney (Putty). **Bark:** *upper trunk and limbs*—smooth, white, with small, sparse grey patches, falling in long loose ribbons; *lower trunk*—dark, rough, rather flaky, finely fibrous. **Juvenile leaves:** narrow, opposite, stalkless, paler on one side. **Adult leaves:** narrow, mostly 10-15mm wide, same colour both sides, thin textured, with steep vein angles. **Flowering time:** October-January. **Capsules:** numerous in each cluster (15-30), globular, 4-6mm wide, stalked; disc broad, level to steeply descending; valves enclosed. **Name:** *elata* = Lat. tall.

Eucalyptus longifolia Link

Woollybutt **Cumb**

A medium-sized tree to 25m high. It prefers heavy alluvial soils and clay flats which are moist but not swampy. On the Cumberland Plain it occurs as scattered individuals in open forest or in bands along small streams. In earlier times it was common around Ashfield, Homebush, Strathfield and Bankstown.

Range: coastal parts of NSW, usually within a few miles of the sea. **Bark:** rough and dirty grey, finely-fibrous and flaky, irregularly ridged and cracked, shed as flakes from smaller branches leaving them smooth, pale brown or greenish. **Leaves:** green or grey-green, same colour both sides, often very long. **Flowering time:** October-November. **Capsules:** large, bell-shaped, in pendant umbels of 3. **Name:** *longifolia* = Lat. long-leaved.

Eucalyptus moluccana Roxburgh

Grey Box **Cumb**

A medium-sized tree with a spreading crown. One of the most common species on the Cumberland Plain, usually with Cabbage Gum (*E. amplifolia*). It prefers wet but not soggy clay soils in undulating country. The timber which is very hard and durable, is used for heavy construction.

Range: drier parts of coastal areas from Jervis Bay to northern Qld. **Bark:** the word that instantly comes to mind when viewing the trunk is 'dirty'; finely tessellated, short-fibrous, grey. The upper trunk and branches are smooth, light grey, the bark falling in long ribbons. **Leaves:** same colour both sides. **Flowering time:** summer. **Capsules:** 7-8mm long, 4-5mm wide, elongated. **Name:** *moluccana* = from the area of the type specimen, on Ambon, in the Molucca Islands north of Australia. In fact it is not native outside Australia and the type specimen was probably planted.

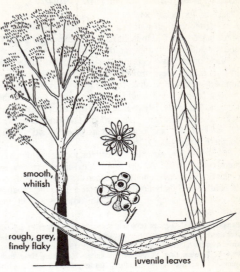

smooth, whitish

rough, grey, finely flaky

juvenile leaves

Eucalyptus elata

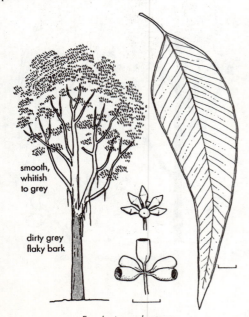

smooth, whitish to grey

dirty grey flaky bark

Eucalyptus moluccana

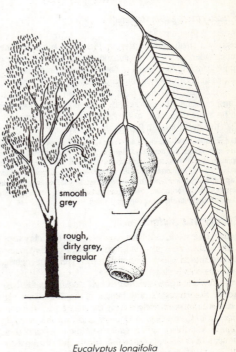

smooth grey

rough, dirty grey, irregular

Eucalyptus longifolia

Eucalyptus pilularis Smith ssp. *pilularis*

Blackbutt, Tarundea **Ss**

A tall stately tree 30-40m high, with a tall trunk and open spreading crown. Old individuals with immense stout trunks and spreading silver limbs can be a magnificent sight.

Blackbutt usually occurs in pure stands on poor sandy soils in high-rainfall areas near the coast. It was once found in impressive stands on shale tops in the Sydney area, where many individuals and small stands remain, e.g. between the City and Hurstville, between Crows Nest and Hornsby, and at Frenchs Forest, often in association with Sydney Blue Gum (*E. saligna*). The best local stands are on valley sides in the southern Royal National Park.

It is one of Australia's most important commercial hardwood timbers. 'To give some idea of the great utility of this timber, I may mention that a man in the neighbourhood of Baulkham Hills built himself a house from the produce of one tree—using I believe, no other wood in the construction.'[13]

Range: coastal districts of NSW and southern Qld. **Bark:** is smooth and whitish except for a distinctive 'sock' of fibrous bark around the lower trunk (which turns black after bushfires or rain, hence the common name). **Leaves:** long, narrow and drooping. **Flowering time:** early summer. **Capsules:** large, globular. **Name:** *pilularis* = Lat. little ball or knob, referring to the fruit. *Tarundea* is an Aboriginal name from the Sydney area.

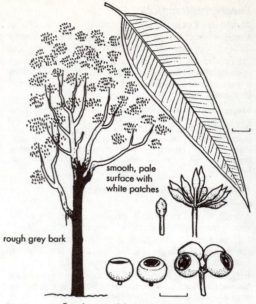

smooth, pale surface with white patches

rough grey bark

Eucalyptus pilularis ssp. pilularis

Eucalyptus piperita Smith

Sydney Peppermint **Ss**

Usually a small graceful tree to 15m high, but sometimes much taller, with grey rough-barked trunk and white upper limbs dangling long strips of bark. It occurs on moist valley slopes in poor rocky sandstone country. Sydney Peppermint was the first Australian plant to be used medicinally by Europeans. Its oil was found by a surgeon of the first fleet to be 'more efficacious in removing all cholicky complaints than that of the English Peppermint'.[14]

Range: from NSW extreme south coast to central north coast. **Bark:** fine grey fibrous on trunk and lower branches; smooth and pale on uppermost branches, falling in ribbons. **Leaves:** with irregular veins and a strong peppermint smell. **Flowering time:** early summer. **Capsules:** small and globular in dense clusters. **Name:** *piperita* = Lat. peppered, from the noun *piper* pepper, an allusion not to pepper but to *Mentha piperita*, the European peppermint.

Eucalyptus saligna Smith

Sydney Blue Gum, Calangara **Ss (on clay tops)**

A tall straight tree, 30—50m high, found in wet woodlands in deep alluvial valleys or on shale tops. It is easily recognised by the smooth bluish-

grey bark and relatively small rough stocking at the base. Sydney Blue Gum was a dominant of the 'Blue Gum high forest' which once stretched along the shale tops of the north shore from Crows Nest to Hornsby, and over the inner city suburbs, with Blackbutt (*E. pilularis*). Little remains of these forests today, although many individuals and small patches still exist on the north shore e.g. Dalrymple-Hay reserve (St Ives).

A Navy Board Purveyor's Report 15 in 1821 also noted that it was found in great plenty at Lane Cove where it supplied the government store in Sydney with ship's timbers and house

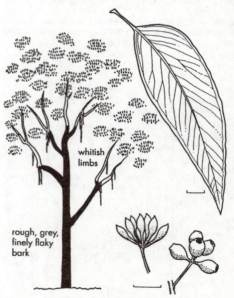

whitish limbs

rough, grey, finely flaky bark

Eucalyptus piperita

planks. Some small remnant stands still exist in the Lane Cove Valley.

Range: from the NSW mid-south coast into Qld. **Bark:** smooth, pale, usually bluish-grey, with a short fibrous stocking at the base. **Leaves:** paler underneath, similar to *E. botryoides*, but narrower. **Flowering time:** January-March. **Capsules:** 4-9mm wide. J. H. Maiden noted as a guide that there is a narrow space between the valves and the rim wide enough to insert a finger-nail or pen-knife.[15] **Name:** *saligna* = Lat. willowy (the reason is unclear). *Calangara* is an Aboriginal name from Parramatta.

Eucalyptus saligna x *botryoides* intergrades

South of Sydney Harbour pure *E. saligna* is replaced by populations intergrading with *E. botryoides*, a closely related species. The intergrades generally have leaves and fruits like *E. botryoides* but most of the upper branches are bare, with a smooth grey surface, as opposed to *E. botryoides* which has only the smallest branches bare.

The intergrades are very common in the Illawarra and south coast.

Range: Sydney to East Gippsland.

Eucalyptus sieberi L. Johnson

Silver-top Ash **Ss**

This varies from an untidily shaped small tree (as little as 6m high) on exposed rocky or damp heaths to a tall well-formed tree (to 45m) resembling Blackbutt, on moist valley slopes. It prefers sandy, well-drained sites with high rainfalls. Near to Sydney it is uncommon, tending to be restricted to the highest rainfall sites on sandstone ridges (e.g. Frenchs Forest, Royal National Park coastal heaths), however it is easily the most numerous tree on the Woronora Plateau south of Sydney.

It is one of the main species being logged for woodchipping in the Eden region. Its hard, fine-grained timber was popular in the past for tool handles and oars.

Range: from southern Vic to Gosford, and north-eastern Tas, in a wide variety of soils and forest types. **Bark:** on the trunk it is coarse, dark, dense, very rugged, resembling that of an Ironbark from a distance, rather flaky on the surface but densely fibrous inside. The upper branches are smooth and cream coloured. **Juvenile leaves:** bluish (glaucous). **Adult leaves:** green, curved, with distinctive, almost parallel venation. **Flowering time:** September-December. **Capsules:** pear-shaped, disc usually depressed, usually 3-valved. **Name:** *sieberi* = in honour of the Bohemian botanist Franz Wilhelm Sieber who collected in New South Wales in 1823. The common name Ash comes from the type of timber which is tough and fine-grained, like the European Ash. **Similar species:** *E. consideniana, E. multicaulis.* In its coppiced form following fire, *E. sieberi* is easily confused with *E. multicaulis.* However this mallee occurs on marshy ground, whereas *E. sieberi* prefers rocky sites.

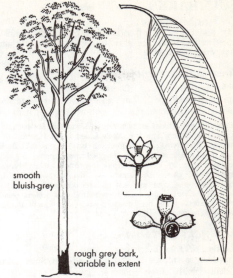

smooth bluish-grey

rough grey bark, variable in extent

Eucalyptus saligna

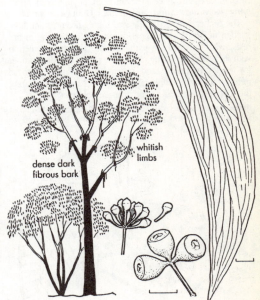

dense dark fibrous bark

whitish limbs

Eucalyptus sieberi

FULL BARKS

1. Crumbly barks

Short-fibred or scaly barked species whose bark crumbles easily in the hand. See also *Angophora floribunda* and *Angophora subvelutina*.

Eucalyptus acmenoides Schauer

White Mahogany, Barayly **Cumb**

A medium to tall tree 20-40m high, found on clay-influenced soils on the sandstone plateau north from Sydney harbour.

Range: NSW and Qld coast and ranges between Sydney and Rockhampton. Sydney is its southern limit. It is closely related to Broad-leaved White Mahogany (*E. umbra*), and the two species can easily be confused. **Bark:** rough on all limbs, tending to be stringy. **Leaves:** tapering to a long fine point, paler on one side. **Flowering time:** October-February. **Capsules:** wine-glass shaped, 6-9mm wide, disc narrow and level or steeply descending, valves enclosed. **Name:** *acmenoides* = *Acmena*-like; J. H. Maiden says that Schauer was reminded of *Acmena smithii* when viewing the leaves, but the similarity is far from obvious. *Barayly* is an Aboriginal name from the Sydney area.

Eucalyptus bauerana Schauer

Blue Box, Nettaring, Berryergro **Cumb**

A medium to tall tree 20-30m high with a rounded head of dense bluish foliage. Found uncommonly on clay soils and alluviums on the Cumberland Plain (e.g. near Camden). Near the Nepean River it occurs with Broad-leaved Apple (*Angophora subvelutina*) and Cabbage Gum (*E. amplifolia*).

The timber is very durable and highly fire resistant. J. H. Maiden noted that it is superior even to Turpentine in fire resistance. 'The durability in the ground, taken in conjunction with its resistance to fire, renders it almost an ideal timber for fencing purposes. Land-owners having clumps of these trees on their property should think twice before destroying them. Small and middle-sized trees are objects of beauty . . . '

Range: Sydney area and NSW coasts, and Vic. **Bark:** rough, short-fibred and grainy, pale to dark grey, on all limbs. **Leaves:** bluish, broad (to

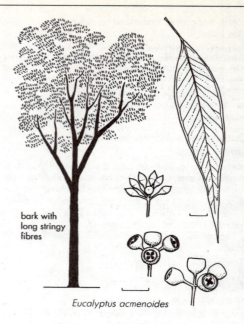

bark with long stringy fibres

Eucalyptus acmenoides

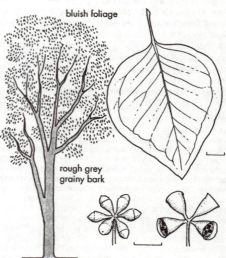

bluish foliage

rough grey grainy bark

Eucalyptus bauerana

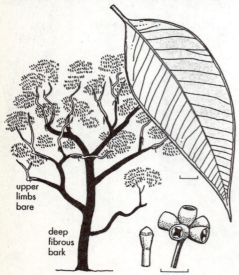

upper limbs bare

deep fibrous bark

Eucalyptus botryoides

5cm wide by 9cm long), same colour both sides. **Flowering time:** early summer. **Capsules:** conical, with enclosed valves. **Name:** *bauerana* = honouring Ferdinand Bauer, who with Robert Brown collected the type specimen on the Nepean River (1802-05). *Nettaring, Berryergro* are Aboriginal names from the Sydney area.

Eucalyptus botryoides Smith

Bangalay, Southern Mahogany **Ss**

A medium-sized tree 20-30m high, with rough reddish bark, short trunk and spreading crown. Restricted to sandy soils on the coast, usually just inland of the dune scrub, within the reach of coastal salt-mist. Tough salt-resistant leaves make it the first eucalypt to appear in the coastal succession. It is almost always associated with littoral rainforest and *Banksia integrifolia*. Immense old weathered trunks of Bangalay are a common sight in littoral rainforest pockets throughout the area.

There is a colonial record of the thick bark being removed in sheets by Aborigines to make canoe hulls.

Range: coastal districts from eastern Vic to just north of Newcastle. **Bark:** rough, fibrous, deeply fissured, reddish inside; except the small branches which are smooth and pale. **Leaves:** thick and broad, widest towards the base, paler on undersurface. **Flowering time:** January-March. **Capsules:** cup-shaped without individual stalks (sessile). **Name:** *botryoides* = Gk. clustered like a bunch of grapes, referring to the fruits. *Bangalay* or *Bengaly* is a local Aboriginal name. **Similar species:** *E. robusta*; distinguish by the fruits and smaller branches with bark.

rough, crumbly bark

Eucalyptus consideniana

Eucalyptus consideniana Maiden

Yertchuk **Ss**
A small straggly tree to 12m high (can be to 20m in mountain areas). Found in exposed heath country on shallow sandy or laterite soils, often with Scribbly Gums. A locally uncommon tree only found on exposed ridges in the Royal National Park. More common in the Blue Mountains and southern tablelands.

The buds, fruits and leaves resemble those of its close relative, Silver-top Ash (*E. sieberi*), however the bark is different, being finely fibrous and crumbly, not hard like *E. sieberi*. The rough bark covers most of the limbs, leaving only the smallest branches smooth and cream and with peeling ribbons of bark.

Range: NSW coast and ranges south from the Sydney region, also Vic. **Leaves:** green, curved, with distinctive, almost parallel venation. **Bark:** rough and crumbly (short-fibrous) on all but the smallest limbs which are smooth and cream or yellowish and marked by long peeling ribbons of bark. **Flowering time:** early spring. **Capsules:** conical, similar to *E. sieberi*, but usually smaller, 4-valved. **Name:** *consideniana* = after Denis Considen, an assistant surgeon on the First Fleet who took a keen interest in botany. He was probably the first to discover the medicinal effect of Sydney Peppermint (*E. piperita*) resin. On 18 November 1788 he wrote to Joseph Banks: 'We have a large peppermint tree which is equal, if not superior, to our English peppermint. I have sent you a specimen of it. If there is any merit in applying these and many other simples [herbal remedies] to the benefit of the poor wretches here, I certainly claim it, being the first who discovered and recommended them.'[16] *Yertchuk* is an Aboriginal name from Gippsland.

Eucalyptus eximia Schauer

Yellow Bloodwood **Ss, Castl**
A small tree usually to 16m tall, with scaly yellow bark, restricted to shallow sandy tops in the Sydney region usually with Red Bloodwood (*E. gummifera*), Narrow-leaved Angophora (*Angophora bakeri*) or Silver-top Ash (*E. sieberi*). It has limited occurrences at Elouera Reserve, Ku-ring-gai Chase National Park, along the Hawkesbury and at Bents Basin. Its massive bundles of white flowers in spring are a spectacular sight.

Range: confined to the Sydney region, mainly in the Colo area and Blue Mountains. **Bark:** soft, yellow, papery in young trees, scaly on mature trees, present on all limbs. **Leaves:** long, drooping, rather bluish, usually the same colour on both sides. **Flowering time:** spring. **Capsules:** stalkless. **Name:** *eximia* = Lat. *eximius*, excellent, referring to the showy flowers. George Caley collected it along the Grose River in 1804 and called it 'snuff-coloured bark Eucalyptus'.[17] **Similar species:** distinguish from *E. gummifera* by the yellow bark and stalkless fruits.

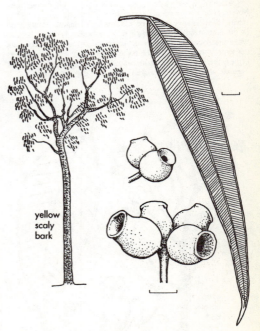

yellow scaly bark

Eucalyptus eximia

Eucalyptus gummifera

(Solander ex Gaertner) Hochreutiner

Red Bloodwood, Mannen **Ss, Castl**

This ranges from a mallee-like dwarf under 2m in coastal
heaths to a straight tree, 20-30m high, in sheltered forests.
It prefers poor shallow sandy soils and is common on dry
tops and slopes, with Sydney Red Gum (*Angophora costata*)
and Sydney Peppermint (*E. piperita*). Aborigines sucked the
flowers for nectar and around Sydney the resinous sap (kino)
was used by Aborigines to stop fibre fishing lines from fraying.
It well deserves its common name since it is rare to find
a specimen which has not shed great amounts of blood-
red resin from some wound.

Range: from the Vic border to southern Qld. **Bark:** rough on all limbs.
Leaves: covered in a thick rubbery cuticle, much paler below.
Flowering time: late summer to autumn. **Capsules:** large and urn
shaped, stalked. **Name:** *gummifera* = Lat. gum-bearing. *Mannen* is an
Aboriginal name from the Sydney area.

Eucalyptus resinifera Smith ssp. resinifera

Red Mahogany, Torumba, Booah **Ss**

A medium to tall tree 20-35m high, usually with a long straight
stem and stringy-flaky bark. It occurs in sheltered valleys and
clay-enriched sandy soils in high rainfall areas, especially near
water. Fairly common in the area. It produces a fine durable
timber which is milled for many construction purposes.

Range: from Jervis Bay to Taree. **Bark:** rough on all branches, stringy,
soft, fissured. **Leaves:** tapering to a long fine point. **Flowering time:**
November-January. **Capsules:** cup-shaped with strongly projecting
valves. **Similar species:** can be mistaken for a stringybark. Distinguish
by the fruits. **Name:** *resinifera* = Lat. resin-bearing (perhaps Surgeon
White mistook it for a species of *Angophora* as the local species are
not large kino producers). The common name comes from similarity
of the timber to the true Mahogany of South America, *Swietenia mabogani*.
Torumba and *Booah* are Aboriginal names from the Sydney area.

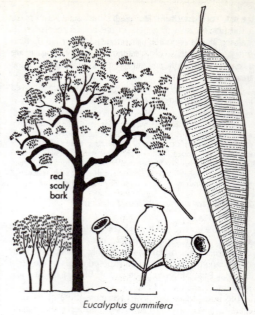

red
scaly
bark

Eucalyptus gummifera

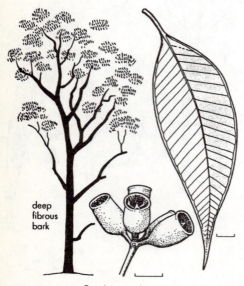

deep
fibrous
bark

Eucalyptus robusta

scaly to
fibrous bark

Eucalyptus resinifera ssp. *resinifera*

Eucalyptus robusta Smith

Swamp Mahogany, Bengaly **Ss**

A small to medium sized tree 20-30m high, closely resembling
E. botryoides. One of the few Eucalypts that prefers marshy
ground, it is common on swampy creek and estuary margins,
growing with Swamp She-oak (*Casuarina glauca*) and a
ground cover of marsh plants. The largest local stand is at

Dee Why lagoon. Often it is planted in parks and streets near the sea.

The timber is very durable and rot-resistant. It is milled for fencing and wharf construction. Swamp Mahogany has been planted extensively overseas for swamp draining (e.g. Hawaii, North Africa).

Range: from Jervis Bay in NSW to Rockhamptom in Qld. **Bark:** rough, fibrous-flaky, fissured, on ALL branches. **Leaves:** similar to *E. botryoides.* **Flowering time:** June-November. **Capsules:** elongated, much larger than *E. botryoides.* **Name:** named because its size and strength compared it with the European Oak *Quercus robur; robusta* = Lat. strong, firm, robust. The Common name comes from the similarity to the timber of the central American Mahogany *Swietenia mabogani.* The name was applied from the very beginning of the colony. *Bengaly* is an Aboriginal name recorded from the Sydney area.

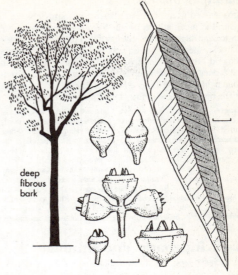

Eucalyptus scias ssp. scias

Eucalyptus scias L. Johnson & K. Hill
ssp. *scias*

(previously included in *E. pellita*)
Large-fruited Red Mahogany **Ss**
A medium-sized tree to 20m tall, although sometimes reduced to a mallee on exposed places near the sea. It prefers sandy soils in moist sheltered locations. When well developed it closely resembles *E. robusta,* with a tall trunk and heavily branched crown. Around Sydney it is occasionally found near the sea on shallow soiled ridges that are sheltered from strong winds, e.g. North Head, South Creek at Narrabeen, and formerly near Manly.

Range: sporadic, from North Head to inland of Newcastle. **Bark:** rough, reddish, thick, shortly fibrous, fissured, on all limbs (i.e. a typical Mahogany). **Leaves:** much paler underneath, similar to *E. robusta* and *E. botryoides,* but less broad (15-32mm wide). **Flowering time:** June-December. **Capsules:** shortly stalked, variable in size, 8-16mm long, 9-20mm wide. **Name:** *scias* = Gk. a shade, referring to the broad-leaved crown.

Eucalyptus squamosa Deane & Maiden

Scaly Bark **Ss**
A small or shrubby tree to 8m high. A rare species restricted to lateritic tops in the Sydney area. Its habitat preferences are similar to Red Bloodwoods. It was described by Henry Deane and J.H. Maiden as late as 1897, although Maiden later changed his mind and considered it a variety of Forest Red Gum (*E. tereticornis*).

Range: confined to the Sydney area. **Bark:** scaly, non-fibrous, on all limbs. **Leaves:** mostly 8-13cm long, thin-textured, with a hardened tip, marginal vein very close. **Flowering time:** winter to spring. **Capsules:** cup-shaped, 6-7mm wide, stalked, with a prominent disc and projecting valves. **Name:** *squamosa* = Lat. scaly

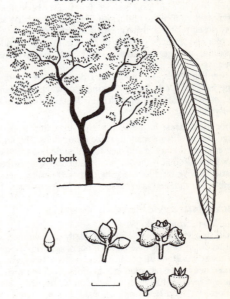

Eucalyptus squamosa

Eucalyptus umbra R. T. Baker

Broad-leaved White Mahogany, Bastard Mahogany **Ss**
A small to medium tree, usually 5-8m high in the area, but up to 20m high on the NSW north coast. It prefers sandy or rocky sites near the sea and the edges of breakaways (eroded breaks in sandstone tops) in plateau country. In the Sydney area it has a very scattered distribution in broken country in Ku-ring-gai Chase National Park.

The heavy, durable timber is used for construction work.

Range: in coastal areas from Sydney to Cooktown in Qld. **Bark:** fibrous, not as coarse as a typical stringybark. **Leaves:** thick and tough, usually curved (falcate), same colour both sides. **Flowering time:** early spring. **Capsules:** with conspicuous stalks, very similar to *E. acmenoides* in the early stage, but later with a broad disc which may be flat or slightly exserted. **Name:** *umbra* = Lat. shade, from the thick foliage. Common name from the resemblance of the timber to the South American Mahogany *Swietenia mahogani*. **Similar species:** *E. umbra* was long considered a 'coarse' form of *E. acmenoides* (White Mahogany), a shale species which is found in the Cumberland Plain. The two species are hard to distinguish reliably on any feature except the thickness of the leaves, those of *E. umbra* being thick, broad and coarse compared to those of *E. acmenoides*.

2. Stringybarks and similar species

Stringybarks are covered with a thick rough bark which can be rubbed off in long slender fibres. Everybody finds stringybarks difficult to distinguish. The true stringybarks are very closely related so that natural variations are often enough to blur species lines. Another problem is that stringybarks hybridise amongst themselves, and with certain other Eucalypts.

Note that some species from other groups can have a stringy-type bark: Red Mahogany (*E. resinifera*), White Mahogany (*E. acmenoides*), and Broad-leaved White Mahogany (*E. umbra*).

Aboriginal uses: In the Sydney area Aborigines stripped large sheets of stringybark to make canoe hulls. The ends were softened in a fire and then folded or tied up to make a waterproof hull. (Various species of Mahogany-barked Eucalypts were used for the same purpose.) Smaller pieces were rolled and used as torches for spear fishing at night.

Eucalyptus agglomerata Deane & Maiden

Blue-leaved Stringybark **Ss**
A tall stringybark tree 30-40m high, easily distinguished at a short distance by the blue-green colour of its foliage. Found on moist sandstone slopes in valleys, not on Hawkesbury sandstones, but on older sandstones which produce a higher nutrient level. It has been recorded in Ku-ring-gai Chase National Park and Heathcote National Park but is rare near the coast. It is very common west of Windsor and in the Blue Mountains and is one of the main stringybarks in its range. It is common north of Gosford and can be seen in big stands beside the Pacific Highway.

Range: from the Vic border to the Hunter River. **Bark:** typical stringybark. **Adult leaves:** with a distinctive hardened tip, same colour both sides, not especially blue close up. **Flowering time:** early winter. **Capsules:** stalkless, globular, compressed, with the disc forming part of the outside surface, usually collectively forming a tightly clustered globular mass. **Name:** *agglomerata* = Lat. collected in a head, referring to the fruits.

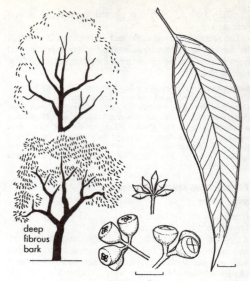

deep fibrous bark

Eucalyptus umbra

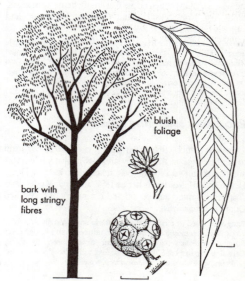

bluish foliage

bark with long stringy fibres

Eucalyptus agglomerata

Eucalyptus camfieldii Maiden

Heart-leaved Stringybark **Ss Vulnerable 2VCi**
A small tree to 8m high or a mallee to 2m in poorly drained sites. A rare species restricted to a few stands on shallow-soiled sandstone or lateritic tops amongst Dwarf Apple (*Angophora hispida*), Scribbly Gum (*E. haemastoma*) and Narrow-leaved Stringybark (*E. oblonga*). The thick, broad and oblong to almost circular leaves easily distinguish this from other stringybarks.

Range: restricted to Royal National Park, Middle Harbour and Ku-ring-gai Chase National Park. **Bark:** scaly-fibrous on all limbs. Coarsely fissured (more papery-fibrous than other stringybarks). **Juvenile leaves:** heart-shaped or circular. **Adult leaves:** broad, more or less oblong, thick, equally shiny on both surfaces. **Capsules:** compressed, stalkless (sessile). **Name:** in honour of Julius Henry Camfield (1852-1916), a gardener at the Royal Botanic Gardens, Sydney, for 34 years.

Eucalyptus capitellata Smith

Brown Stringybark, Bour-rougne **Ss**

A small to medium tree, usually to 10-20m high, often gnarled and shrubby in exposed places. Found in Ku-ring-gai Chase National Park and Royal National Park on lateritic or clay tops on shallow, often marshy soils, extending to more sloping sandstone country.

Its absence in bush reserves in Sydney is perhaps due to its excellent qualities as a timber. Being strong, durable and easily split it was extensively cut for fencing, building and shingles.

Range: restricted to the sandstones of the Sydney region. **Bark:** typical stringybark. **Juvenile leaves:** broad or round, rough, undulate. **Adult leaves:** leathery, shiny, with hardened tips, more or less same colour both sides. **Flowering time:** summer. **Capsules:** compressed, with barely exserted valves, stalkless. Buds angular. **Name:** *capitellata* = having heads, in reference to the clustered fruit. *Bour-rougne* is an Aborigianl name from the Camden district.

Eucalyptus eugenioides Sieber ex Sprengel

Thin-leaved Stringybark **Cumb**

A medium-sized stringybark 15-25m high. Mainly a clay species, fairly common on the Cumberland Plain, and also on sandstone in a few places such as Toongabbie Reserve, Lake Parramatta, near Silverwater and at Bents Basin. One of the most common stringybarks of NSW. Its best distinguishing feature is the presence of a distinct short stalk on the capsule.

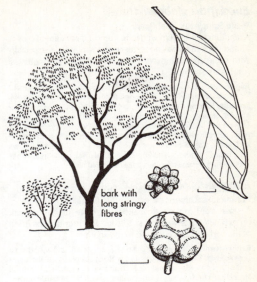

bark with long stringy fibres

Eucalyptus camfieldii

bark with long stringy fibres

Eucalyptus capitellata

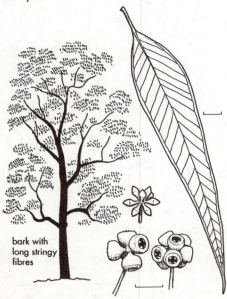

bark with long stringy fibres

Eucalyptus eugenioides

Range: from south coast of NSW to southern Qld, on coast and tablelands. **Bark:** typical stringybark. **Juvenile leaves:** broad, with star-hairs on margins, veins and stalks. **Adult leaves:** fairly large and finely pointed, not thick, same colour both sides, rather greyish-green from a distance, often sparse. **Flowering time:** spring to early summer. **Capsules:** usually 6-7mm wide, with a short stalk, cup-shaped to globular, disc exserted, level or slightly descending, valve tips sometimes slightly exserted. **Name:** *eugenioides* = like a *Eugenia*; a rather mystifying allusion.

Eucalyptus globoidea Blakely

White Stringybark   **Ss, Castl**

A medium tree 15-30m with long trunk and dark-green crown.
Found in open forests on better quality sandy soils, especially
with some clay influence. The spherical fruits distinguish it
from other species.

Range: coast and valleys in plateaus and lower mountains from Gippsland,
Vic to north coast of NSW.   **Bark:** typical stringybark, with deep furrows.
Juvenile leaves: alternate, paler below (discolorous), with crenate
margins, stems and leaf-edges and veins covered in star-hairs   **Adult
Leaves:** to 7-10cm (i.e. rather small), fairly thick, drawn to a long fine
point, generally slightly paler and duller underneath.   **Flowering time:**
April-June.   **Capsules:** stalkless (sessile), disc level, 7-10mm wide, not
compressed.   **Name:** *globoidea* = Lat. globe-shaped, of the fruits. White
in the common name refers to the light coloured timber.

Eucalyptus oblonga De Candolle

Common Sandstone Stringybark   **Ss, Castl**

A small tree, sometimes mallee-like, 3-6m high, abundant
on exposed shallow-soiled sandstone and lateritic tops north
of the harbour, less common to the south.

Range: restricted mainly to the Ku-ring-gai plateau, and inland from
Gosford, with small occurrences in the Royal National Park, the edges
of the Woronora Plateau, and the Kedumba Valley in the southern Blue
Mountains.   **Bark:** stringy, to the smallest branches.   **Juvenile leaves:**
broad (ovate), with wavy and uneven margins; stems and occasionally
margins with stellate hairs.   **Adult leaves:** variable in size according
to habitat (usually rather broad compared to *E. sparsifolia*), oblong, rather
thick and leathery, shiny, same colour both sides, usually with a hard,
abrupt point.   **Flowering time:** February-April.   **Capsules:** globular or
slightly depressed-globular with a flat or exserted disc and small valves,
sometimes slightly exserted.   **Name:** *oblonga* = Lat. oblong, referring
to the leaf shape.   **Similar species:** *E. sparsifolia, E. globoidea.*

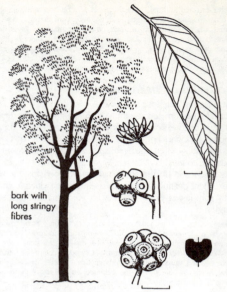

bark with
long stringy
fibres

Eucalyptus globoidea

bark with long
stringy fibres

Eucalyptus oblonga

juvenile leaf

bark with long
stringy fibres

juvenile leaf

Eucalyptus sparsifolia

Eucalyptus sparsifolia Blakely

Narrow-leaved Stringybark   **Ss**

A small to medium tree to 6-20m high, very slender,
sometimes with two or more stems from the same rootstock.
Common on poorly drained, slightly marshy heath on
sandstone tops north from Pennant Hills, also in the Blue
Mountains.

Range: central coast, central ranges and central western slopes. **Bark:** stringy on all but the smallest limbs which are smooth and dark greenish. **Juvenile leaves:** narrow (linear), with wavy and uneven margins; with stellate hairs on stems and occasionally on margins. **Adult leaves:** usually fairly small and narrow, rather thick and leathery, shiny, same colour both sides, usually with a hard, abrupt point. **Flowering time:** January-March **Capsules:** globular, with a raised disc broader than *E. oblonga*. The aperture is usually smaller than *E. oblonga* **Name:** *sparsifolia* = Lat. sparse-leaved. **Similar species:** *E. oblonga*.

Note: *E. oblonga* and *E. sparsifolia* have only recently been recognised as separate species, as first suggested by the early researcher Blakely. They can be difficult to distinguish, the fruits being more or less identical. The most useful distinguishing features are habitat (woodland versus marshy heath) and the leaves (more or less typical Eucalypt versus small, oblong). The real mark of distinction is in the shape of the juvenile leaves (broad versus slim). These may be found around the base of young or damaged trees or on seedlings growing nearby.

3. Ironbarks

An early commentator described these trees, 'Black and grimy and hard were they, as the metal from which they take their name. The deep cracks and fissures in the rugged bark were filled with a black glittering gum, that seemed as though molten iron had been run into them.'[18]

Ironbarks are easily recognised by this distinctive bark, which is dark, rigid, deeply fissured, impregnated with resinous kino and breaking off in stiff rectangular tessellations. The timber is famous for its great weight, density and durability. It was especially milled for railway sleepers and heavy construction.

The powerfully arching limbs and tall dark trunk of a typical ironbark make a fine sight. One early observer described them as 'fluted with the exquisite regularity of a Doric column . . . in truth the noblest ornaments of these mighty forests.'[19]

Eucalyptus beyeriana L. Johnson & K. Hill

Beyer's Ironbark, Mogargoo **Cumb**
A medium tree to 30m, widespread on sandy-clay soils on the Cumberland Plain. It has a similar distribution to *E. crebra*, which has almost identical fruits but longer, narrower leaves.

Range: Sydney area and also on the south coast. **Bark:** ironbark, on all limbs, dark and very coarse. **Leaves:** slender (5-15mm), not long (5-9cm), barely paler on one side. Although small they have 'normal' eucalypt proportions. **Flowering time:** spring. **Capsules:** small, 3-4(6)mm wide, pear-shaped, disc small, valves deeply enclosed. **Name:** *beyeriana* = after George Beyer (1865-1920), a clerk at the Sydney Technological Museum. He provided clerical assistance and indexing for Baker's Research on the Eucalypts (1920). The species was long known as *E. beyeri* R. Baker, but that name was found to be based upon a hybrid specimen. The new name was chosen to be sufficiently similar to minimise the effect of the change. *Mogargoo* is an Aboriginal name from the Sydney area.

Eucalyptus crebra F. Mueller

Narrow-leaved Ironbark **Cumb**
A medium tree to 30m tall with a long straight trunk, probably the most common ironbark in the area. It prefers drier sites on clay soils on the Cumberland Plain.

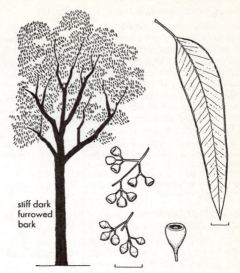

stiff dark
furrowed
bark

Eucalyptus beyeriana

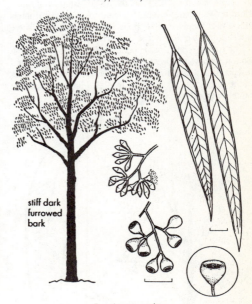

stiff dark
furrowed
bark

Eucalyptus crebra

Range: from Sydney to Cape York on coast, tablelands and inland slopes. Sydney is its southern limit. **Bark:** ironbark, hard, deeply furrowed, on all branches. **Leaves:** small, narrow, 7-16cm long, dull green, same colour both sides. **Flowering time:** May-January. **Capsules:** small, 5-6mm wide. **Name:** *crebra* = Lat. *creber* crowded, frequent, in reference to its abundance, especially on inland slopes of northern NSW and Qld.

Eucalyptus fibrosa F. Mueller ssp. *fibrosa*

Broad-leaved Ironbark **Cumb**

A medium to tall straight ironbark to 35m high, common on well-drained clay soils on the Cumberland Plain. It is easily recognised by large oval juvenile leaves. Its hard, strong, durable timber is milled for heavy engineering, poles and railway sleepers. J. H. Maiden describes it as having coarser fruits and bark than other species, 'Altogether a very sturdy tree, reminding one, in this respect of the British Oak . . . The fruits have exsert valves, which is usually quite sufficient to distinguish this from other ironbarks.'[20]

Range: NSW south coast, central ranges and slopes, and Qld. **Bark:** typical ironbark but rather flaky, deeply furrowed, on all limbs. **Leaves:** large, grey-green, dull, same colour both sides. **Flowering time:** November-January. **Capsules:** conical, with exserted valves, mainly in terminal panicles. **Name:** *fibrosa* = Lat. fibrous, referring to the bark, but hardly appropriate.

Eucalyptus paniculata Smith
ssp. *paniculata*

Grey Ironbark, Torrangora **Ss (clay tops)**

A medium sized tree 20-30m high with a long straight trunk. Grey Ironbark was formerly associated with Blue Gum and Blackbutt on the clay tops of the coastal plateau. Large remnant trees can still be found on the ridges running through Hornsby-Wahroonga-Pymble-Lindfield, also at Ryde, Hunters Hill, and at Kirrawee and Port Hacking (near Audley). There is also an old specimen in St John's church, Glebe.

The type specimen was collected at Port Jackson by David Burton who was Governor Phillip's 'public gardener' and Joseph Bank's short-lived botanical agent in the early years of the colony (he shot himself in 1792 while duck hunting on the Nepean).

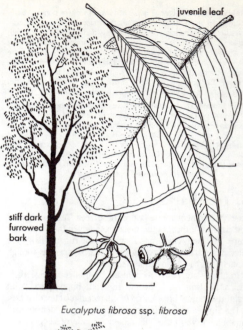

juvenile leaf

stiff dark furrowed bark

Eucalyptus fibrosa ssp. *fibrosa*

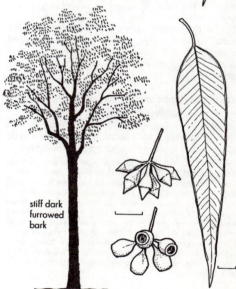

stiff dark furrowed bark

Eucalyptus paniculata ssp. *paniculata*

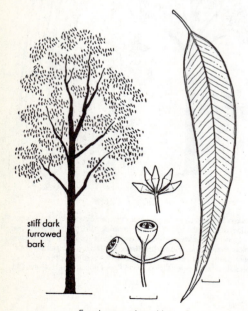

stiff dark furrowed bark

Eucalyptus siderophloia

Range: in coast and mountain country from Bega to north of the Manning River. **Bark:** ironbark, hard, deeply furrowed, usually grey (lighter than other ironbarks). **Leaves:** not thick, slightly paler on one side. Juvenile leaves not very different. **Flowering time:** autumn-spring. **Capsules:** with slightly depressed valves. **Name:** *paniculata* = Lat. the inflorescence type (usually a drooping panicle, extending from the ends of branchlets or from the final leaf joints). *Torrangora* is an Aboriginal name from the Sydney area.

Eucalyptus siderophloia Bentham

Northern Grey Ironbark, Terri-barri **Cumb**

A medium to tall tree 30-40m high. It prefers well-drained soils in undulating shale country. Uncommon to rare in the area, mainly found north of the Hawkesbury.

Range: from Sydney to Rockhampton in Qld, as far west as Dubbo. **Bark:** typical ironbark. **Leaves:** fairly long, with a fine point. **Flowering time:** July-January. **Capsules:** conical, 4-6mm wide, often with a single rib, disc narrow, enclosed by the rim, valves enclosed or sometimes exserted. **Name:** *sidero* = Gk. *sideros*, iron, *phloia* = Gk. *phloos*, bark. *Terri-barri* is an Aboriginal name from the Sydney area.

Eucalyptus sideroxylon

A. Cunningham ex Woolls **ssp.** *sideroxylon*

Red Ironbark, Mugga **Cumb, Castl**

A medium sized tree to 25m high, found on drier clay soils and laterites on the Cumberland Plain around Liverpool, St Marys and near Richmond, often with *E. fibrosa.* Easily recognised by its glaucous foliage.

Range: NSW western slopes, only crossing to the coastal side of the ranges on the Cumberland Plain. **Bark:** typical ironbark, but very dark (almost black) and deeply furrowed. The small branches are often smooth and light grey. **Leaves:** green, grey-green or bluish, same colour both sides, slender. The juvenile leaves are very narrow. **Capsules:** pendant, ovoid, with a fairly broad disc and deeply enclosed valves. **Name:** *sideroxylon* = Gk. iron-wood. *Mugga* is an Aboriginal name, probably from inland NSW.

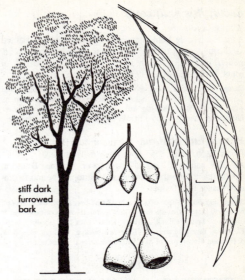

stiff dark
furrowed
bark

Eucalyptus sideroxylon ssp. *sideroxylon*

MALLEES

Small multi-stemmed trees usually less than 4m high. These are adapted to marshy, impoverished soils. Mallee is simply the name of the growth habit and doesn't imply any relationship between the species.

Eucalyptus luehmanniana F. Mueller

Yellow-top Ash **Ss Rare 2RCa**

A mallee, usually 4-6m high. An impressive and beautiful species remarkable for its large stiff leaves and stately somewhat drooping habit. It prefers sandstone tops where soil is marshy due to poor drainage. The identity of this species was disputed by botanists for many years (which is remarkable, given the distinctive leaves and fruit); it was confused with *E. haemastoma* and *E. stricta* (the Blue Mountains mallee). Its fruit appears beside Joseph Banks on the Australian $5 note.

Range: restricted to sandstone tops between Bulli and Gosford. **Bark:** smooth, bluish, even nearly white, sometimes with loose ribbons. Specimens from the north of Port Jackson have yellowish bark. **Leaves:** large, stiff, distinctly curved, bluish (specimens from the north of Port Jackson are green), rather drooping. **Flowering time:** spring. **Capsules:** large, somewhat wrinkled when dry. **Name:** by Ferdinand von Mueller in honour of Johann George Luehmann (1843-1904), his secretary for 28 years. He succeeded Mueller as Victorian Government botanist after Mueller's death. The common name presumably comes from the yellowish branchlets; *Ash* is from the tough fine-grained timber resembling a European Ash.

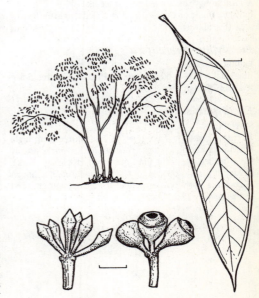

Eucalyptus luehmanniana

Eucalyptus multicaulis Blakely
Whip-stick Ash **Ss**
A mallee, usually 4-6m high. Found on rocky poorly-drained sandstone tops. It is closely related to the Silver-top Ash (*E. sieberi*) and varies mainly in the mallee habit and lack of rough bark. Locally present in the Royal National Park.

Range: an uncommon species recorded from the Blue Mountains and a few locations in the Sydney region. **Bark:** smooth. **Leaves:** drooping, with venation like Silver-top Ash. **Capsules:** similar to *E. sieberi.* **Flowering time:** June-July **Name:** *multicaulis* = Lat. multi-stemmed.

Eucalyptus obstans L. Johnson & K. Hill
Port Jackson Mallee **Ss** (previously *E. obtusiflora*)
A mallee usually 1.2-2m tall, rarely over 3 metres. Found in poorly drained heathland on sandstone tops. The most common mallee near Sydney.

Range: from Royal National Park to the Hawkesbury River. **Bark:** smooth, white with grey or greenish stripes, usually with fallen ribbons collected at the base. **Leaves:** thick, leathery, shiny, with hard abrupt points. **Flowering time:** late summer. **Capsules:** swollen, 10-11mm wide; buds with a short hemispherical cap. **Name:** *obstans* = Lat. persistent.

OTHER SPECIES OCCASIONALLY FOUND WITH MALLEE-LIKE HABITS

Eucalyptus camfieldii
Heart-leaved Stringybark
On poorly drained tops it often grows as a mallee-like tree down to about 2m high. (See above)

Eucalyptus oblonga
Common Sandstone Stringybark
A small stringybark, sometimes mallee-like, 3-6m high. Found on exposed shallow-soiled tops in the Sydney area. (See above)

Eucalyptus gummifera
Red Bloodwood
In coastal heaths it often grows as a mallee-like tree down to about 2m high. (See above)

Eucalyptus sieberi
Silver-top Ash
In coastal heaths it often grows as a small tree 3-6m high. When coppiced following regeneration after fire it usually has a mallee-like habit (and may even lack rough bark), making it hard to distinguish from *E. multicaulis*, although it does not grow on the poorly drained ground favoured by that species. (See above)

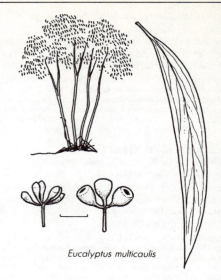

Eucalyptus multicaulis

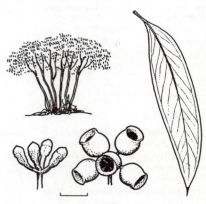

Eucalyptus obstans

• *Kunzea* Reichenbach

A genus of shrubs with about 27 Australian species. *Kunzea* resembles *Leptospermum* but may readily be distinguished by the long filaments on the flowers and the non-woody fruit (weak-walled, easily falling from the branch).

Name: *Kunzea* = in honour of Dr. Gustav Kunze (1793-1851), professor of botany in Leipzig. He published much of the Western Australian collections made by Ludwig Priess between 1844-48.

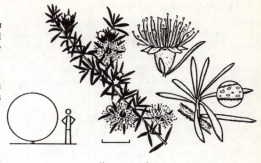

Kunzea ambigua

Kunzea ambigua (Smith) Druce

Tick Bush **Ss, Castl**

A tall spreading shrub usually 2-4m high with dense foliage. A fairly common shrub in heaths and scrubs, quickly colonising cleared ground and often forming dense thickets.

Range: from Tas to northern NSW on coast and tablelands. **Leaves:** tiny, crowded together on short lateral branchlets, narrow, concave above, covered in oil dots. **Flowers:** WHITE. **Flowering time:** early summer (October-November). **Name:** *ambigua* = Lat. doubtful, uncertain, perhaps because Smith had doubts about his decision to call it a *Leptospermum.* Tick Bush: origin not known.

Kunzea capitata Reichenbach **Ss, Castl**

A slender shrub to 1.5m high, found in damp places in sunny heath. It has button-like heads of bright violet-purple flowers at the tips of its ascending branches. A very common species in the area.

Range: from southern NSW to Qld. **Leaves:** more or less flat, alternate, with down-curved tips, with 3 veins visible. Young plants have very densely woolly leaves. **Flowers:** VIOLET-PURPLE, with long filaments, crowded in a head at the tip of each branch. **Flowering time:** spring and summer. **Name:** *capitata* = Lat. having heads.

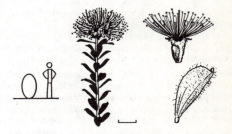

Kunzea capitata

Kunzea ericoides (A. Rich) J. Thompson

(previously *Leptospermum phylicoides*) **Ss**

An open shrub 1-2m (4m) high, Tea-tree-like, with numerous small slender leaves. Uncommon in the area (e.g. Excelsior Park, Baulkham Hills), mainly a Blue Mountains species. The leaves have a strong lemon-eucalypt scent.

Range: NSW coast (south from Sydney), ranges, and inland areas, Qld, Vic and SA. **Leaves:** narrow, dull, thin, numerous. **Flowers:** small (5-7mm wide), WHITE. **Capsules:** about 3mm diameter, only slightly woody, with valves enclosed in the rim, very finely hairy outside. **Flowering time:** summer. **Name:** *ericoides* = *Erica*-like, referring to the leaves.

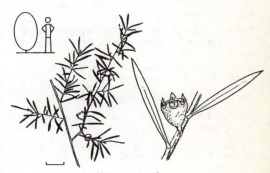

Kunzea ericoides

Kunzea rupestris Blakely

Ss Endangered 2ECi

A dense straggling shrub to 1.5m high. Found in woodland and heath on sandstone, usually on rock platforms. It is rare in the area, present only in a few locations in or near Marramarra National Park.

Range: restricted to the Sydney area. **Leaves:** crowded, mainly 6-10mm long, 2-3mm wide, woolly when young. **Flowers:** WHITE, in dense terminal heads. The calyx is top-shaped and densely covered in greyish woolly hairs, with woolly bracts at the base. **Flowering time:** October-November. **Name:** *rupestris* = Lat. rocky, referring to its favoured habitat. **Similar species:** Distinguished from white-flowering specimens of *K. capitata* by its lower habit and the densely hairy calyx.

Kunzea rupestris

• *Leptospermum* J. R. & G. Forster

Tea-trees

A genus with 79 species, all Australian except for 1 extending to NZ, 1 extending to NG, and 2 endemic to South-east Asia.

Tea-trees are tough shrubs with small aromatic leaves well adapted to drying winds and poor sandstone soils. They flower prolifically in spring and are a lovely sight 'waving high their wreathed spires of snowy flowers, like pure and hopeful spirits . . . '.[21]

Botany: The flowers have a cup-shaped calyx and 5 petals. Numerous stamens arise from the edge of a depressed disc which produces a rich honey nectar. This attracts many species of insects including flies, bees and beetles which force their way through the pallisade of stamens and perform the work of fertilisation. A single style arises from the centre of the disc. The fruit is a woody capsule with (usually) 5 chambers each containing numerous slender seeds.

Leptospermum is closely related to both *Kunzea* and *Baeckea*, but the large flowers and woody fruits make it easy to distinguish.

Common name: The name Tea-tree originated with Captain Cook. His crew drank tea made from the leaves of Manuka (*Leptospermum scoparium*) in New Zealand before their arrival in Australia, both as a tea substitute and to help prevent scurvy. There are many reports of *Leptospermum* and *Melaleuca* being used as tea substitutes in colonial times. However, these must have been in moments of ignorance or desperation as *Smilax* leaves and *Acacia* bark were well known and superior tea substitutes.

Name: *Leptospermum* = Gk. *lepto*, slender, *spermum*, seed. Pick a capsule, wait till it opens and you'll see why it deserves this name.

Note: Joy Thompson's 1989 revision of *Leptospermum* made significant changes to the genus in the Sydney area:
• The common and well-known *L. flavescens* was renamed *L. polygalifolium* (the name given by Salisbury in 1796, a year before Smith published *L. flavescens*).
• The common and well-known *L. attenuatum* was renamed *L. trinervium* (the name given by Smith to a specimen in 1790, 7 years before he gave the name *attenuatum* to a later specimen).
• *L. brevipes* was reduced to a species of rocky slopes in mountain areas. The new name *L. polyanthum* was given to those specimens found on river-banks.
• A new species, *L. deanei*, was recognised in the northern suburbs of Sydney.
• A large-leafed form of *L. polygalifolium* was raised to species status as *L. morrisonii*. It occurs on the southern Woronora Plateau.
• *L. scoparium* var. *rotundifolium* became *L. rotundifolium*.
• The NSW specimens previously referred to *L. scoparium* were recognised as a separate species, *L. continentale*.
• *L. lanigerum* was divided into two species: *L. grandifolium* and *L. lanigerum*.

Leptospermum arachnoides Gaertner

Spidery Tea-tree **Ss**

A low dense rigid shrub to 1m high, with a rather spidery habit and spiky leaves. A common species, forming colonies in open sandstone country, usually in moist places on rocky ground.

Leptospermum arachnoides

Range: NSW coast and ranges extending into Qld. **Leaves:** narrow, prickly, concave, about 1mm wide. **Flowers:** WHITE, 8-12mm wide. **Flowering time:** November-January. **Capsules:** 5-8mm wide, densely hairy (but hairless when old), tapering to the base. **Name:** *arachnoides* = Lat. spider-like (in general appearance).

Leptospermum continentale J. Thompson

Ss

A straggling slender shrub 1-2 (4)m tall with slender prickly leaves, found in moist woodland or sandy marshy heaths, on sandstone. It is present in the Royal National Park (e.g. near Audley, and near Warumbul) and on southern parts of the Woronora Plateau.

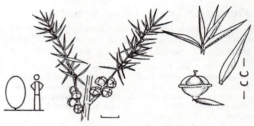

Leptospermum continentale

Range: NSW coast and ranges, Vic and SA. **Leaves:** about 10mm long, slender (1-3mm wide), thick, rigid, and spreading, folded along the mid-vein, tapering to a sharp point. **Flowers:** WHITE, about 10mm wide. **Flowering time:** November-January. **Capsules:** 6-7mm wide, hairless. **Name:** *continentale* = Lat. referring to its mainland distribution, in contrast to its close relative *L. scoparium*, which is largely restricted to Tas and NZ. **Similar species:** *L. squarrosum*; distinguish by the capsule size.

Leptospermum deanei J. Thompson

Ss Vulnerable 2V

A slender erect shrub to 1-2m (5m) tall, found in woodland. Only recently recognised, it is known from a small area on Sydney's north shore, on either side of the Pymble-Hornsby ridge, i.e. Pennant Hills Park, the southwest of Ku-ring-gai Chase National Park and Davidson State Recreation Area (also recently discovered in Marramarra Creek). It somewhat

Leptospermum deanei

resembles *L. polygalifolium* but the leaves are more slender and have a Eucalyptus scent.

Range: restricted to the Sydney area. **Bark:** peeling in long strips. **Leaves:** 10-15mm long, slender (1-2mm wide), not dense, hairless, with margins incurved above at least near the base, stalkless, distinctly pointed. **Flowers:** WHITE, 8-10mm wide. **Flowering time:** October-November. **Capsules:** about 3.5mm wide, hairless. **Name:** *deanei* = after Henry Deane, railway engineer, who collected the type specimen near Lane Cove in 1883 (it remained unidentified in the Royal Botanic Gardens Herbarium for over 100 years).

Leptospermum emarginatum

H. Wendland ex Sprengel **Ss**

A spreading shrub to 2.5m, shading the banks of rivers and permanent creeks. Basically a mountain species, but fairly common along the Nepean river as far north as Penrith.

Range: lower Blue Mountains and southern tablelands into Vic. **Leaves:** aromatic, 20-30mm long, similar to *L. polygalifolium* but with a tiny notch at the tip. **Flowers:** WHITE, about 7mm wide, in small clusters of 2-3 (5). **Flowering time:** November-January. **Capsules:** 3.5-5mm wide, small, hairless, with a satin sheen, falling easily. **Name:** *emarginatum* = Lat. notched at the tip.

Leptospermum grandifolium Smith

Woolly Tea-tree **Ss**

A tall shrub 1.5-3m, occasionally to 6m, high, with hard bark. Common beside creeks in sandstone country.

Range: NSW coast and ranges, Tas, Vic, and SA. The Sydney area is about its northern limit. **Leaves:** oblong, somewhat greyish green, with 3-5 strong parallel veins, length variable but usually 10-30mm long, upper surface glossy, lower surface felty (or both surfaces hairless on river forms), sharply-pointed, very silky when young. **Flowers:** WHITE, about 15mm wide. **Flowering time:** October-December. **Capsules:** 8-10mm wide, densely hairy (becoming hairless and rather flaky when old), broad at the base. **Name:** *grandifolium* = Lat. large-leaved.

Leptospermum juniperinum Smith

Prickly Tea-tree **Ss, Cumb**

A dense compact broom-like shrub usually to 1.5m high with many erect branches. It forms soft dense thickets near flowing water in marshy sandy heath country. Despite the prickly leaves the whole shrub has a soft willowy appearance which sets it apart from other species.

Range: south coast and tablelands extending along the coast to Qld. **Leaves:** 5-15mm long, sharp-pointed, crowded, flat or somewhat incurved towards the tip, at first erect then later becoming spreading. **Flowers:** WHITE, 6-10mm wide. **Flowering time:** November-December. **Capsules:** smooth, 5-7mm wide. **Name:** *juniperinum* = like a Juniper, a small prickly European conifer.

Leptospermum laevigatum

—See COASTAL AND ESTUARINE SPECIES.

Leptospermum lanigerum

(Solander ex Aiton) Smith

Woolly Tea-tree **Ss**

A tall shrub to 3m with dense greyish foliage, found on the Woronora Plateau on marshy ground and sunny creek banks.

Range: NSW coast and ranges south from Sydney into Vic, SA and Tas. **Leaves:** oblong, greyish with fine dense hairs, very silky when young, 8-15mm long. **Flowers:** WHITE, about 15mm wide. **Flowering time:** spring. **Capsules:** 5-10mm wide, densely hairy at flowering time, becoming bare and flaky when old. **Name:** *lanigerum* = woolly.

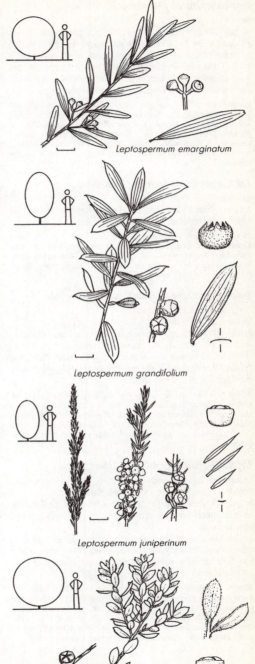

Leptospermum emarginatum

Leptospermum grandifolium

Leptospermum juniperinum

Leptospermum lanigerum

Leptospermum morrisonii J. Thompson

Ss

A tall shrub, usually 3-4m high. Very similar to *L. polygalifolium*, but with larger leaves and flowers. It occurs in moist places in heath or woodland or on rocky creek banks, on sandstone or basalt. Locally restricted to the Georges River (Kentlyn), southern Nepean River, southern Woronora Plateau (e.g. Cataract River) and Illawarra escarpment.

Range: southern Blue Mountains, Woronora Plateau, Illawarra, south coast and southern tablelands. **Leaves:** mostly 20-30mm long, flat, strongly aromatic (but not strongly lemon-scented like *L. polygalifolium*). **Flowers:** WHITE, 12-15mm wide. **Flowering time:** December-January. **Capsules:** 6-10mm wide, hairless. **Name:** *morrisonii* = after David Morrison, a botanist whose work assisted its recognition as a separate species.

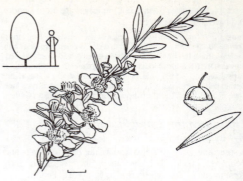

Leptospermum morrisonii

Leptospermum parvifolium Smith

Ss, Castl

An erect shrub to 2m high, found in dry heath and woodland north of the harbour, usually in stony places.

Range: NSW coast and ranges, from the north-west slopes to Nowra. **Leaves:** 3-6mm long, flat, erect, thick, blunt, with visible oil dots. **Flowers:** PINK or white, about 10mm wide. **Flowering time:** September-November. **Capsules:** about 4mm wide, hairy. **Name:** *parvifolium* = Lat. small-leaved.

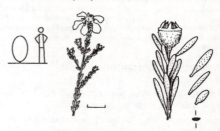

Leptospermum parvifolium

Leptospermum polyanthum J. Thompson

(previously *L. brevipes*, in part)

Slender Tea-tree **Ss**

A tall willowy shrub 2-5m, weeping over the banks of creeks and rivers. Basically a mountain species, but occurs uncommonly along the Nepean (e.g. Douglas Park) and Hawkesbury systems. It appears similar to *L. polygalifolium*, but the capsules are very small.

Range: NSW coast and ranges from Armidale south to Wombeyan Caves. **Leaves:** 10-20mm long, slender, soft, with a single vein. They have a Eucalyptus-menthol scent when crushed. **Flowers:** WHITE, 5-6 (10)mm wide. **Flowering time:** October-January. **Capsules:** about 3mm wide, usually hairless and shiny, falling easily. **Name:** *polyanthum* = Gk. many-flowered.

Leptospermum polyanthum

Leptospermum polygalifolium Salisbury

(previously *L. flavescens*)

Lemon-scented Tea-tree **Ss, Cumb, Castl**

A graceful shrub usually to about 2.5m high. One of the most common Tea-trees of the region, found in moist places in woodland.

The lemon-scented leaves were sometimes used as a tea substitute in the early days of settlement. The Cribbs report that their strongly aromatic flavour is acceptable but with no resemblance to normal tea.[22]

Range: a widespread species ranging from southern NSW to Cape York. **Bark:** hard, not flaky or papery. **Leaves:** mostly 10-15mm long, soft and narrow with one rather obscure vein, visible oil-dots and a strong lemon odour when crushed. **Flowers:** WHITE, about 10-14mm wide. **Flowering time:** October-December. **Capsules:** 5-8mm wide, smooth, with a distinct stalk. **Name:** *polygalifolium* = Lat. *Polygala*-leaved.

Leptospermum polygalifolium

Leptospermum rotundifolium

(Maiden & Betche) F. Rodway ex Cheel **Ss**

An erect or spreading shrub 1-2m high, found in heath on coastal plateaus. Occurs locally in the Royal National Park which is its northern limit. It has the largest flowers of any local species, a spectacular sight in spring

Range: NSW coast and ranges, south from Sydney. **Leaves:** 4-7mm long, rounded, glossy, stiff, thick, sharply pointed, crowded. **Flowers:** WHITE or purplish, to 30mm wide. **Flowering time:** October-December. **Capsules:** large, hairless. **Name:** *rotundifolium* = Lat. round-leaved.

Leptospermum squarrosum Solander ex Gaertner

Ss

A small dense erect shrub to 2.5m high, common in dry heath scrublands on coastal plateaus, especially on laterites. Its masses of pink flowers and dark prickly foliage make it an attractive species for horticulturists and several cultivars with 'double' flowers are available.

Range: Sydney area and Blue Mountains, NSW south coast and southern ranges. **Leaves:** glossy, 5-10mm long, sharply pointed, thick, rigid, folded along the mid-vein, crowded, often purplish. **Flowers:** PINK to WHITE, 10-20mm wide. **Flowering time:** March-April. **Capsules:** smooth, 8-12mm wide. **Name:** *squarrosum* = Lat. crowded and rigid, referring to the leaves.

Leptospermum trinervium (Smith) J. Thompson

(previously *L. attenuatum*)
Paperbark Tea-tree **Ss, Cumb, Castl**
A tall shrub usually to 3m, with a stout trunk and papery-flaky bark. One of the most common Tea-trees in the region, found in damp shrubby understories in woodlands on sandstone. The leaves have a strong eucalyptus odour when crushed.

Range: Vic to Qld, on coast and ranges. **Bark:** flaky-papery, grey. **Leaves:** flat, oblong, 10-20mm long, with three rather obscure veins (look at mature leaves). **Flowers:** WHITE, to 15mm wide. **Flowering time:** spring. **Capsules:** 3-6mm wide, densely woolly with a very short stalk, falling soon after flowering. **Name:** *trinervium* = Lat. 3-veined.

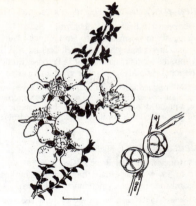

Leptospermum rotundifolium

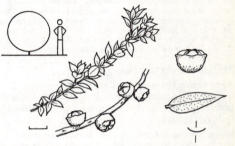

Leptospermum squarrosum

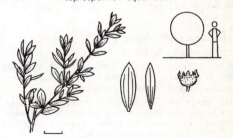

Leptospermum trinervium

• *Melaleuca* Linnaeus

Paperbarks
A genus of swamp and marsh-loving shrubs including many species with thick cream papery bark. *Melaleuca* has about 140 Australian species with a few extending to Malaysia and New Caledonia.

Flowers: in dense 'bottle-brush' spikes which are terminal but soon left behind by the continued growth of the branches. The petals are inconspicuous. The staminal filaments are numerous and fused into 5 bundles (called claws) arising from the margins of a cup-like nectary disc.

Uses: Melaleucas are amongst those shrubs whose flowers were soaked in water by Aborigines to produce a sweet beverage. The bark was used for shelters, to make fire, as an all-purpose 'bush gladwrap', and as an oven bag for cooking food in the earth.

Melaleucas have been exploited by Europeans since colonial times for Tea-tree oil; *M. lineariifolia, M. ericifolia*, and *M. decora* being three of the local species so used. The north coast species *M. alternifolia* is the main source of Tea-tree oil today.

Identification: *Melaleuca* and *Callistemon* are easily recognised by the distinctive flower spikes with long projecting filaments. With only a little experience the two genera can be easily distinguished in the field, although botanically the only distinction is the stamens which in *Melaleuca* are fused into 5 bundles or claws, while in *Callistemon* they are free.

Name: Gk. *melas* = black, *leucos* = white; from the black wood and white branches on the first specimens collected. In country areas they are often called 'Tea-trees'.

Melaleuca armillaris (Solander ex Gaertner) Smith

Giant Honeymyrtle, Bracelet Honeymyrtle **Ss**

A tall dense shrub or small tree to 5m high with hard corky bark, found in coastal scrubs on well-drained soil. In the Sydney suburbs it occurs naturally at La Perouse, Kurnell and Royal National Park. Also a popular street and garden shrub.

Range: NSW coast and ranges, also Qld, Vic, Tas. **Leaves:** crowded, alternate, 12-25mm long, less than 1mm wide and with a recurved tip. **Flowers:** with CREAM filaments. **Capsules:** 5mm diameter. **Name:** *armillaris* = encircled with a bracelet or collar, perhaps referring to the leaves.

Melaleuca armillaris

Melaleuca deanei F. Mueller

Deane's Honeymyrtle **Ss Rare 3RC-**

A shrub to 3m with paperbark, found in marshy heath on coastal sandstone plateaus. Uncommon in the area.

Range: restricted to the sandstones of Sydney region and south coast. In the Sydney suburbs it is only recorded from Pennant Hills Park, Elouera Reserve and Davidson State Recreation Area. **Leaves:** 1-2cm long, flat, twisted so the edges turn towards the stem. **Flowers:** with CREAM filaments. **Capsules:** 7-10mm diameter. **Name:** named by Ferdinand von Mueller in honour of Henry Deane (1847-1924), noted botanist, especially of Eucalypts, and Engineer-in-Chief of the NSW Government Railways (he took the zig-zags out of the Blue Mountains line).

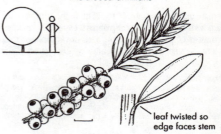

leaf twisted so edge faces stem

Melaleuca deanii

Melaleuca decora (Salisbury) Britten

White Feather Honeymyrtle **Cumb, Castl**

A shrub or large tree, 6-20m high, with dense foliage and paper bark. Common in marshy ground on clay soils on the Cumberland Plain.

Range: NSW coastal districts, and Qld. **Leaves:** just over 1mm wide, 10-15mm long, twisted at the base so one edge faces the stem, with one inconspicuous vein. **Flowers:** with WHITE filaments. **Flowering time:** summer. **Capsules:** about 2.5mm diameter. **Name:** *decora* = Lat. ornamental.

Melaleuca ericifolia Smith

Swamp Paperbark **Ss, Sal**

A small rounded tree usually to 6m high, with corky bark. Found in semi-saline swampy ground near coastal estuaries, streams and lagoons. Common in the area.

Range: along the east coast from Melbourne to Qld. **Leaves:** tiny, narrow, recurved, fairly soft. **Flowers:** in spikes with WHITE filaments. **Flowering time:** spring and early summer. **Name:** *ericifolia* = *Erica*-leafed; *Erica* is the European Heath or Heather.

Melaleuca decora

Melaleuca ericifolia

Melaleuca erubescens (Bentham) Otto

Pink Honeymyrtle **Castl, Cumb**

A straggling shrub, often with several ascending stems, 50cm to 3m high, with corky bark. Found in the Castlereagh woodlands and on clay-laterites on the Cumberland Plain. Recorded in earlier times from the Lidcombe-Hurstville area.

Range: NSW northern and central western slopes, only crossing the ranges on the Cumberland Plain. **Leaves:** slender (1mm wide), cylindrical, crowded, dull green, with conspicuous oil dots. The tips are not always as hooked as those in the illustration. **Flowers:** with BRIGHT PINK filaments. **Flowering time:** December-January. **Name:** *erubescens* = Lat. reddening, referring to the pink flowers. **Similar species:** *M. ericifolia*, distinguish by cylindrical leaves.

Melaleuca erubescens

Melaleuca hypericifolia Smith **Ss**

A shrub usually 2-3m high (6m in some places) with corky bark, found in sunny seepages in sandstone woodland. It also pops up opportunistically in almost any damp soils.

The large spikes of rich rusty-red filaments make it an attractive species. In 1796 the botanist James Smith described it as 'the most beautiful of the genus. It grows in swampy ground . . . and was generally taken for a *Hypericum*, till it lately produced, in several collections in London, its elegant flowers.'[23]

The oily aromatic leaves were used as a bush remedy for headaches and colds.

It is the only local *Melaleuca* with long reddish filaments adapted for bird pollination.

Range: mostly restricted to the sandstones of the Sydney area and Blue Mountains. **Leaves:** opposite, aromatic. **Flowers:** with large RUSTY-RED spikes. **Flowering time:** spring-summer. **Name:** *hypericifolia* = *Hypericum*-leafed.

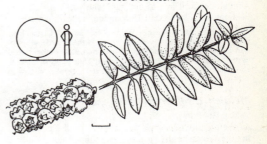

Melaleuca hypericifolia

Melaleuca lineariifolia Smith

Snow-in-summer **Ss, Cumb, Castl**

A small tree to 8m high with paperbark. Abundant in marshy places in forests and gullies, especially beside swamps on the Cumberland Plain where it forms dense fringing thickets.

Ranges: along the NSW coast and ranges. **Leaves:** narrow, opposite, crowded, fairly soft and thin. **Flowers:** in dense spikes with CREAM stamens. Flowering time: summer. **Capsules:** in small globular clusters. **Name:** *lineariifolia* = straight-leaved. The common name Snow-in-summer is from the extraordinary show of flowers about Christmas time.

Melaleuca lineariifolia

Melaleuca nodosa (Solander ex Gaertner) Smith

Ball Honeymyrtle **Ss, Cumb, Castl**

A shrub or small tree usually to 6m high with paperbark. Fairly common in forests near marshy ground, on sandstone or shale.

Range: south coast of NSW to Qld and SA. **Leaves:** linear, stiff, sharply pointed, fairly crowded. **Flowers:** in globular clusters with CREAMY YELLOW filaments. **Flowering time:** October. **Capsules:** in small dense spherical clusters. **Name:** *nodosa* = knotted or knobbly, referring to the clustered fruit capsules.

sharp point

Melaleuca nodosa

Melaleuca quinquenervia (Cavanilles) S. T. Blake

Broad-leafed Paperbark **Ss**

A handsome tree 8-12m high, the largest of our paperbarks. Found in marshes and nearby forests. The Cribbs report that the leaves, boiled with ordinary tea, make a pleasant, refreshing brew.[24]

Range: from Botany Bay to Cape York, also New Guinea and New Caledonia. A very common park and street tree around Sydney. **Leaves:** broad, tough, with 5 main veins. **Flowers:** in dense spikes with CREAM filaments. **Name:** *quinquenervia* = Lat. five-veined, of the leaves.

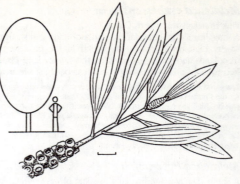

Melaleuca quinquenervia

Melaleuca sieberi Schauer

Sieber's Paperbark **Cumb**

A shrub or small tree to 5m high with paper bark, found in swamps on clay ground. Uncommon in the Sydney area.

Range: Sydney area, NSW north coast and Qld. **Leaves:** 4-12mm long, twisted so the edges turn towards the stem. **Flowers:** in dense spikes with CREAM filaments. **Capsules:** 2-4mm diameter. **Name:** named by the German botanist J. H. Schauer in honour of his principal collector, Franz Wilhelm Sieber (d. 1844) who collected specimens in NSW in 1823.

leaf twisted so edge faces stem

Melaleuca sieberi

Melaleuca squamea Labillardière

Swamp Honeymyrtle **Ss**

An erect shrub 1-2m high with pretty pink flowers. Found in damp coastal heath (e.g. La Perouse, Kurnell, Royal National Park).

Range: NSW coast, Vic, SA, Tas. The Sydney area is its northern limit. **Leaves:** crowded, erect, flat, rigid. **Flowers:** with ROSE PINK filaments, in short heads at the tips of branches. **Name:** *squamea* = Lat. scaly, perhaps in reference to the stiff crowded leaves.

Melaleuca squamea

Melaleuca styphelioides Smith

Prickly-leaved Paperbark **Ss, Cumb, Castl**

A small to medium tree 6-15m high with paper bark, found in swampy places near creeks and estuaries, on sandstone and shale. Common in the area, especially on the Cumberland Plain, where it is occurs in less swampy conditions than *M. lineariifolia.*

William Woolls wrote 'I believe that no wood in the colony is more tenacious of life, or better adapted for buildings which stand in damp soils.'[25]

Range: NSW coast north from the Shoalhaven River, Blue Mountains and Qld. Also planted in streets and gardens. **Leaves:** stiff, twisted, sharply pointed, crowded along the stems. **Flowers:** in spikes with white filaments. Flowering time: mid-summer. **Name:** *styphelioides* = *Styphelia*-like: 'It has altogether the habit of a *Styphelia.* The leaves are thick-set, twisted, harsh, pungent and striated, exactly as in several of that genus, and very slightly aromatic, so that it could hardly be taken for one of the Myrti, except for the fructification.'[26]

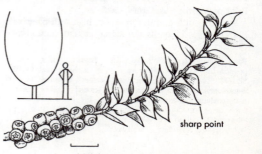

sharp point

Melaleuca styphelioides

Melaleuca squarrosa Donn ex Smith

Scented Paperbark Ss

An erect shrub to 6m high, densely foliaged, with corky bark. Found in dense thickets lining steams in heath and woodland. Locally restricted to the Royal National Park and Woronora Plateau.

Range: Woronora Plateau, south coast, southern Blue Mountains, Vic, Tas and SA. **Leaves:** opposite, 4-ranked, short, stiff, and sharp. **Flowers:** scented, with YELLOWISH-CREAM filaments. **Flowering time:** October-February. **Name:** *squarrosum* = Lat. crowded and rigid, referring to the leaves.

Melaleuca thymifolia Smith

Ss, Cumb, Castl

A small shrub to about 1m high with slender wiry stems, corky bark, and delicate feathery violet-purple flowers. The leaves are very fragrant. Found scattered in damp places in heath, open forests and swamp margins on both sandstones and clays.

Ranges: from southern NSW to Qld. **Leaves:** opposite, small, crowded on slender, wiry stems, with visible oil-dots. **Flowers:** with VIOLET-PURPLE staminal claws. **Flowering time:** mainly October. **Capsules:** with distinctive permanent horns; in small clusters. **Name:** *thymifolia* = Thyme-leaved.

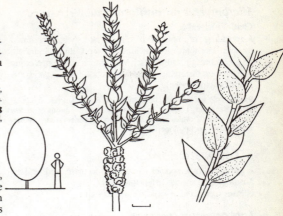

Melaleuca squarrosa

• *Micromyrtus* Bentham & W. J. Hooker

An endemic genus of 20 species, distributed in all states.

It resembles *Baeckea* but is mainly distinguished by having a single chamber in the fruit. The flowers are only a few mm wide, solitary and axillary, appearing as clusters at the tips of branches. There are 5 sepals, 5 petals and 5 stamens. **Name:** *micromyrtus* = Lat. tiny-Myrtle.

Micromyrtus blakelyi (J. W. Green)

Ss Vulnerable 2VC-

A compact spreading shrub to 30cm high, often cushion-like. Found in crevices or depressions on sandstone platforms. Occurs only in a few localities near the Hawkesbury River (e.g. Cowan, Muogamarra Nature Reserve).

Range: restricted to the Hawkesbury area. **Leaves:** similar to *M. ciliata*, except that the leaves are ciliate on the lower keel as well as the margins (view with a hand lens). **Flowers:** WHITE to red, 4 ovules per ovary, the deciduous sepals are densely fringed (need a hand lens; the other species have unfringed sepals). **Flowering time:** August-October. **Name:** *blakelyi* = after W.F. Blakely who collected many specimens between 1918 and 1929.

Melaleuca thymifolia

Micromyrtus blakelyi

Micromyrtus ciliata (Smith) Druce

Ss

A spreading shrub to 50cm high, found on low damp heath on sandstone, usually near the coast.

Range: coast and ranges in central and south-eastern NSW, and separately in western Vic and south-eastern SA. **Leaves:** opposite, four-ranked, with a row of oil-dots on each side, margins fringed with minute hairs. **Flowers:** WHITE to red, 4 ovules per ovary. **Flowering time:** September (July-November). **Name:** *ciliata* = fringed with hairs.

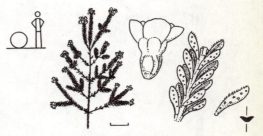

Micromyrtus ciliata

Micromyrtus minutiflora (F. Mueller) Bentham

Castl Vulnerable 2V

A spreading shrub 50-150cm high. A rare species, confined to open forest on old alluviums on the Cumberland Plain (e.g. Castlereagh State Forest). Very similar to the preceding species, best distinguished by the location (*M. ciliata* is only found on sandstones).

Range: only known from the Cumberland Plain. **Leaves:** similar to the above, linear, 1-3mm long. **Flowers:** WHITE, tube more narrow than *M. ciliata*, 2 ovules per ovary. **Flowering time:** spring. **Name:** *minutiflora* = Lat. tiny-flowered.

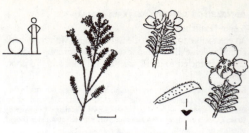

Micromyrtus minutiflora

• *Lophostemon* Schott

A genus with 4 species, found in northern and eastern Australia. One species extends to New Guinea.

Name: *Lophostemon* = Gk. crested-stamen.

Lophostemon confertus•

(R. Brown) P. G. Wilson & J. T. Waterhouse

(previously *Tristania conferta*)

Brush Box

A tall shady tree, usually 30-40m high in northern NSW rainforests, but kept trimmed to around 6-10m by dedicated council workers in Sydney suburbs. It was adopted as a street tree by the Municipality of Strathfield early this century and is a now a common sight in Sydney streets. Naturalised in Royal National Park and many urban bushlands.

Range: from just north of Newcastle to northern Qld. **Bark:** smooth pinkish orange, with a very variable stocking of rough grey bark, falling in small ribbons. **Leaves:** glossy, thin, apparently whorled (i.e. arising in a circlet from the same point on the stem) at the tips of branchlets.

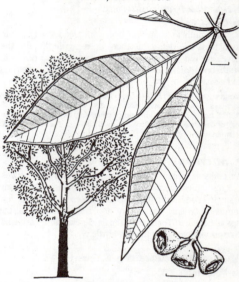

Lophostemon confertus

Flowers: with WHITE stamens joined into prominent claws. **Fruit:** a Eucalyptus-like capsule. **Name:** *confertus* = Lat. crowded closely together, referring to the leaves clustered at the ends of the branchlets. The common name: 'Brush' is a colonial term for rainforests, while 'Box' refers to the wood which resembles the European Box (*Buxus sempervirens*), being close-grained, hard, heavy and durable.

• *Syncarpia* Tenore

An endemic genus with 2 species, distributed in eastern NSW and Qld.

Name: *Syncarpia* = Gk. joined fruit.

Syncarpia glomulifera (Smith) Niedenzu

Turpentine **Ss**

A tall handsome tree, often over 40m high, with a straight trunk, deep fibrous bark and dull grey-green foliage. Found in all types of forest in this area. It prefers moist, well-drained soils and reaches its best development in places transitional between tall Eucalypt forest and rainforest. Common in the area. Its olive, non-droopy foliage makes it easy to distinguish from surrounding Eucalypts.

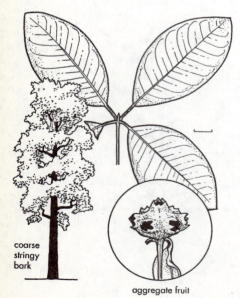

coarse stringy bark

aggregate fruit

Syncarpia glomulifera

Contrary to popular belief no part of the tree smells of turpentine. 'Turpentine timber has scarcely any odour, but I have known of perfectly well-authenticated instances in which men, insisting that turpentine timber is so-called because of the odour of turpentine, were obliged by accommodating timber-getters who sprinkled their logs with turpentine prior to inspection.'[27]

The timber is very resistant to fire and very durable in salt water. It is highly regarded and milled extensively for structural purposes such as telegraph poles, beams and wharf piles (the London docks are made of Australian Turpentine).

Range: coast and ranges from Batemans Bay, NSW, to the Atherton Tableland in northern Qld. **Bark:** very coarse, thick, stringy, deeply fissured. **Leaves:** opposite or whorled, glossy grey-green above, thin, stiff, tough, grey underneath. **Flowers:** with prominent CREAMY-WHITE filaments; clustered in united heads. **Flowering time:** September-November (mainly October around Sydney). **Fruit:** a fused woody cluster. **Name:** *glomulifera* = ball-carrying, from the compact flower clusters. 'Turpentine' because it exudes a clear liquid quite different from the dense red resin of a Eucalypt.

• *Tristania* R. Brown

An endemic genus of one species. It once had 12 Australian species and many others in south-east Asia and the Pacific. However all but one have been shifted into *Tristaniopsis, Lophostemon* and other genera.

Name: *Tristania* = honours Jules de Tristan (1771-1861), a French botanist.

Tristania neriifolia (Sims) R. Brown
Ss

A small shrub, usually to 1.5m high, gracing rocky creek banks, often under the shelter of its cousin *Tristaniopsis laurina*.

Range: restricted to the sandstones of the Sydney region. **Leaves:** opposite, usually 4-6cm long, fairly tough. **Flowers:** GOLDEN YELLOW, in axillary cymes. **Name:** *neriifolia* = leaves like a *Nerium* (Oleander).

• *Tristaniopsis* Brongniart & Gris

An Indo-Australian genus with about 36 species, including 3 in Australia.

Name: *Tristaniopsis* = *Tristania*-like.

Tristaniopsis collina
P.G.Wilson and J.T.Waterhouse   **Ss, Temp Rf**

An attractive tall shrub or small tree with pale sheeny bark. Found on sheltered valley slopes away from creeks. Uncommon in the area. Similar to *T. laurina* but distinguished by its smaller leaves with tapering (accuminate) tips and hillside habitat.

Range: coastal NSW and southern Qld. **Leaves:** satin, dark green above, very pale below, hairless, with drawn out (accuminate) tips and obscure venation. The juvenile leaves can be very large. **Flowers:** GOLDEN YELLOW, same as *T. laurina* **Flowering time:** December-January. **Name:** *collina* = Lat. pertaining to hills, referring to its prefered habitat.

Tristaniopsis laurina
—See RAINFOREST SPECIES.

Tristania neriifolia

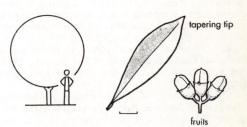

tapering tip

fruits

Tristaniopsis collina

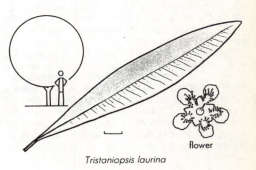

flower

Tristaniopsis laurina

MIMOSACEAE

A large family distributed mainly in warm or tropical regions of the world. There are about 3000 species in about 60 genera. Australia has about 960 species in 17 genera, the largest by far being *Acacia*. Mimosaceae is closely allied to the other legume producing families, Fabaceae and Caesalpinaceae.

• *Acacia* Miller

Wattles

A genus of Gondwanaland origin with about 900 species in Australia. It is also widely distributed in Africa, South America and India although Australia has the majority of species. *Acacia* is one of the two genera which dominate the Australian landscape. They are tough, quick growing and opportunistic shrubs or trees, quickly colonising cleared or disturbed ground. The showy masses of flowers in winter and spring have often been celebrated in art and literature. The wattle is Australia's national flower, officially represented by Golden Wattle, *A. pycnantha* (an inland species). Wattle Day is 1 September.

Uses: The seeds of some local species were collected by Aborigines and roasted as food. The gum of some species was also used as food, as Daniel Bunce recorded in the Dandenongs in 1859. 'The native women sometimes went out by themselves, and returned with a quantity of the liquid amber gum which exudes from the *Acaciæ decurrens*, or black wattle tree. This gum they call korong. They prepare it as a relish for their food in the following manner: having formed, of a sheet of wattle bark, a trough to hold water (willum), the women soak the gum until it assimilates with the water, and forms a thin glutinous liquid; a little sugar, or manna, is then added to make it palatable.'[1]

William Woolls wrote that it 'yields a gum similar to gum arabic, but more astringent in nature. It is often mixed with sugar and lemon and called by our colonial youth "gum jelly" '.[2]

Acacia leaves and bark were important to Aborigines as 'fish poisons'. They were thrown into pools to stupify fish. Several local species were used in this way. It is thought tannins are responsible for the effect.

With the arrival of Europeans different uses emerged. The long flexible branches of some species were exploited as a source of 'wattle'. This is an old Anglo-Saxon word for interwoven saplings used in plaster or mud walls, hence the 'wattle and daub' huts which were the first home of most pioneer settlers in the last century.

The bark of pinnate-leafed trees such as *A. mearnsii* and *A. decurrens* contains 20-30% tannic acid. Early colonists discovered that this bark was an excellent tea substitute. A small amount of old black bark boiled in water makes a refreshing cup of tea. It has the tannin flavour of normal tea as well as a fine fragrance all its own. The tea has medicinal properties, 'A decoction of the bark has become a remedy amongst the diggers for diarrhoea and dysentery, and its efficacy in some cases has proved successful when all other remedies have failed.'[3]

The bark became a major colonial industry as a source of tannin for the leather industry. There are records of as much as 150kg of bark being removed from a single tree. Extract of Mimosa Bark became an important export. By 1892 A. G. Hamilton complained of the 'indiscriminate ravages of bark-strippers'[4] which had almost destroyed the species in many districts.

Because of their showy flowers Acacias quickly became popular with British aristocrats as greenhouse plants, although one writer warned ' . . . it has been remarked in England that the roots of all the Australian species of acacia smell of garlic. For this reason when acacias are kept in a greenhouse, adjoining the living rooms of a house, care should be taken to give the house abundance of ventilation.'[5]

Botany: *Acacia* divides into two groups; those with feathery bipinnate leaves and those with stiff, leathery phyllodes.

Bipinnate-leaved species show the ancestral leaf form which our Acacias share with those of Africa. Most bipinnate leaves have hundreds of tiny soft leaflets (called pinnules) attached to subsidiary stalks (called pinnae) which are in turn attached to a central stem or rhachis. The rhachis is lined with glands for transpiration. Such a leaf is vulnerable to heat and dryness. Consequently as the Australian continent dried over the last 14 million years feathery-leafed wattles were only able to survive in the damp sheltered habitat beside creeks or rivers, where they still abound today.

Meanwhile in the dry remainder of the continent phyllode-bearing species evolved. They are now the most abundant. Phyllodes are not true leaves but only the central stem (rhachis) of a bipinnate leaf which has lost its leaflets and grown wings. Phyllodes are tough skinned to resist evaporation, aligned vertically to limit exposure to the sun and usually have only a single marginal gland near the base of the leaf. All phyllode-bearing *Acacia* have bipinnate leaves in the juvenile stage and the process by which phyllodes evolved can be seen as plants grow. Bipinnate leaves may also reappear were the plant is damaged or infested by insects or disease. Phyllodes have a wide range of distinctive forms which make identification easy.

The flowers are tiny, yellow, with a 5-lobed calyx, 5 petals and numerous stamens. They are gathered together in distinctive inflorescences which are either balls or cylinders.

All species produce pods or legumes containing a single row of seeds. The seeds have a tough outer coat which must be split, usually by fire, for germination to occur. The seeds are commonly harvested by ants which are attracted by an oil-rich organ (called an elaiosome or aril) on the seed. Because the seeds are stored underground by ants, high intensity fires are required for effective germination.

Name: *Acacia* is the Greek name for *Acacia arabica*, a tropical African and West Asian species known from antiquity. The name is derived from *akis*, a sharp point, because of its thorns. It was used by the German botanist Willdenow in his reformation of the old genus *Mimosa* early in the last century.

KEY TO *ACACIA*

1. BIPINNATE SPECIES
A. Leaflets over 3mm wide.
    B. Leaflets same colour both sides.
        = *A. schinoides*
    *B. Leaflets paler below.
        = *A. elata*
*A. Leaflets under 2mm wide.
    C. Mostly 3-4 glands per division.
        D. Rhachis (i.e. central axis of leaf) with fine hairs, leaflets 3-5mm long, pinnae 14-30 in number.
            = *A. parvipinnula*
        *D. Rhachis felty, leaflets 4-9mm long, pinnae 5-14 in number.
            = *A. filicifolia**
    *C. Usually two glands per division, leaflets glossy, 2-3mm long.
        = *A. mearnsii*
    **C. Usually one gland per division.
        E. Leaflets 3-5mm long, inconspicuous ridges on stem, flowers pale yellow.
            = *A. parramattensis*
        *E. Leaflets 5-12mm long, wing-like ridges on stems, flowers bright yellow.
            = *A. decurrens*
        **E. Glands absent from most divisions.
            F. Leaflets tough, about 2mm wide, single gland at base of leaf.
                = *A. terminalis*
            *F. Stems and branchlets with rough ridges, gland only at tip or base of rhachis.
                = *A. irrorata*
            **F. Shrub with conspicuously hairy brachlets.
                = *A. pubescens*

* *A. filicifolia* is not described here, it is a small tree with bluish branches, and bright yellow flowers, found along creeks to the north of the Sydney area.

2. PRICKLY SPECIES

A. Leaves flat, 2-3mm wide.
    = *A. oxycedrus*
*A. Leaves about 1mm wide.
    B. Flowers CREAM, phyllode swollen at gland.
        = *A. ulicifolia*
    *B. Flowers BRIGHT YELLOW, phyllode not swollen at gland.
        C. Phyllodes cylindrical, 5-9mm long.
            = *A. echinula*
        *C. Phyllodes compressed, 13-25mm long.
            = *A. brownei*

3. ALL OTHER SPECIES
A. One main vein.
    B. Cylindrical flower heads.

            A. floribunda

            A. longissima

    *B. Globular flower heads, solitary or in pairs.

    A. hispidula   *A. stricta*

    **B. Globular flower heads, in racemes.

    A. buxifolia   *A. prominens*

    A. falcata   *A. myrtifolia*

    A. falciformis   *A. rubida*

    A. fimbriata   *A. suaveolens*

    A. linifolia

*A. 2 or more main veins.
    C. Cylindrical flower heads.

    A. binervia   *A. maidenii*

    A. longifolia ssp. *longifolia*   *A. obtusifolia*

     A. longifolia ssp. *sophorae*

    *C. Globular flower heads, solitary or in pairs.

    A. bynoeana   *A. elongata*

    **C. Globular flower heads, in racemes.

    A. binervata   *A. implexa*

1. Bipinnate species

Many of these species were long confused under the name of *A. decurrens*, a situation that remained in some cases until the 1960s when several new species were described.

Identification of bipinnate wattles can be difficult. *A. decurrens*, for instance, is often said to be distinguished by wing-like ridges on the branches, but all species have stem ridges in various degrees. Generally a keen eye or hand lens is necessary to examine the glands and the hairiness of the leaves.

Acacia decurrens (Wendland) Willdenow

Sydney Green Wattle, Book-kerriking
Cumb, Castl

A handsome tree 10-16m high, common in forests on the Cumberland Plain, rarely on sandstones. Distinguish from similar species by the angular branchlets, hairless leaves with long, well spaced leaflets, and bright yellow flowers.

Aborigines used the gum as a 'relish' (see *Acacia*: Uses, above). It was heavily exploited in colonial times as a source of tannin for tanning hides. Where tea was too expensive or unavailable the bark was used as a tea substitute.

Range: Sydney area, Blue Mountains, southern tablelands, naturalised in all other states except NT. **Bark:** smooth, and green or grey when young, dark and crumbly when old, stained black with tannin. **Leaves:** rhachis hairless, one gland at each division, leaflets 5-12mm long, well spaced compared to other species. There are conspicuous wing-like ridges extending down the stems from each leaf joint. **Flower heads:** BRIGHT YELLOW, globular. **Flowering time:** July-September. **Name:** *decurrens* = referring to decurrent leaf stalks that run down the stem, producing angular branches. Common name 'green' from smooth green limbs. *Book-kerriking* is an Aboriginal name from the Sydney area.

Acacia elata A. Cunningham ex Bentham

Mountain Cedar Wattle **Rf, Ss**

A medium-sized tree to 20m high with dense spreading foliage. Native to rainforest valleys and volcanic tops in the Blue Mountains, occasionally naturalised in coastal areas. A very handsome tree now common in parks and gardens.

Range: NSW coast and ranges south from the Sydney area. **Leaves:** bipinnate, large, to 25cm long. The leaflets are fairly tough and glossy, paler below. **Flower heads:** PALE YELLOW, in dense masses. **Flowering time:** December-March. **Name:** *elata* = Lat. tall.

Acacia irrorata Sieber ex Sprengel **ssp. *irrorata***

Ss

A small handsome tree to 15m high, common along watercourses in sandstone gullies. Easily recognised by the stiffly hairy leaf rhachis, lack of glands and the golden tinge on new leaves.

Range: NSW coast and ranges from Bega to southern Qld, moister western slopes, and Tas. **Leaves:** rhachis covered in a dense felt of tiny stiff hairs, one gland only present at the tip of the rhachis or occasionally another near the base, leaflets 2-4mm long. Harsh stiff ridges extend down the stems. **Flower heads:** PALE YELLOW. **Flowering time:** November-January. **Name:** *irrorata* = Lat. covered in minute grains or dew, referring to the hairy covering of the leaf rhachis.

Acacia mearnsii De Wildeman

Black Wattle **Ss**

A small tree to 15m high, found in damp places in woodland

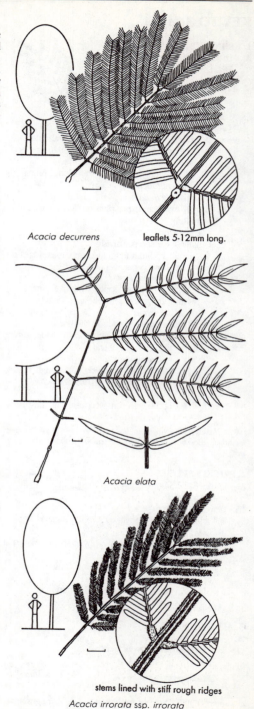

Acacia decurrens   leaflets 5-12mm long.

Acacia elata

stems lined with stiff rough ridges

Acacia irrorata ssp. *irrorata*

on sandstone or clay soils. Its northern limit seems to be about Bargo, just south of Sydney, but specimens can occasionally be found as 'blow ins' in the area. The common name Black comes from the trunk and limbs being stained dark with resin. The species was widely cultivated overseas for fuel and tannin, and is now a weed in many countries.

Range: NSW coast and ranges south from Sydney, Vic, Tas and SA. Very common on the NSW south coast, especially in the Illawarra where it is the only feathery-leafed wattle. **Leaves:** rhachis minutely felty, usually two glands in each division, leaflets 2-3mm long, glossy above with a layer of fine hairs underneath. **Flower heads:** PALE YELLOW. **Flowering time:** October-December. **Name:** The Black Wattle obtained its botanical name in an unusual way. In 1809, the German botanist, Carl Willdenow, in his great revision of the old genus *Mimosa*, described some specimens of *Acacia pubescens*, giving them the name *Acacia mollissima* (= Lat. very soft). Unfortunately Sweet's *Flora Australiensis* in 1827 incorrectly combined this name with an illustration of the Black Wattle. Bentham in 1842 compounded this error by actually publishing a description of Black Wattle under the same name. The mistake continued until 1967 when two Kew researchers realised what had happened. At the same time they discovered that Black Wattle had been independently described and named in 1925 by the Belgian botanist De Wildeman based on a specimen from Thika in Kenya. He had named it *Acacia mearnsii* after the collector, Mearns, and believed it was endemic to a small area near Nairobi. It was, of course, a wandering Australian Black Wattle. This was the first time true Black Wattle had been formally named, so it superseded the incorrect name *A. mollissima.*

Acacia parramattensis Tindale

Parramatta Green Wattle **Ss, Castl, Cumb**

A shrub or small tree usually to 8m high. Found in woodland on dry shallow sandy or clay soils. The first sighting of this species by Europeans was probably made on 14 May 1788 when Surgeon Worgan, Captain Hunter and Lieutenant Bradley 'Went by boat about 12 miles up the harbour' (i.e. to Parramatta). Worgan wrote 'We now and then, in our walk, met with clusters of a very delicate looking tree, the trunks of some of them were 12, 14, 20 inches round, covered with a green bark, the leaves of a peculiarly beautiful Verdure, and growing like the fern, but more delicate.'[6]

Because of the similarity between many feathery-leafed wattles, its separate identity was not established until 1962.

Range: coastal and mountain areas from Sydney to south of Nowra. **Leaves:** bipinnate, dark-green, with very fine blunt leaflets, glands at the base of each division (very rarely with smaller ones in between), apparently hairless (but finely hairy when young). **Flower heads:** PALE YELLOW. **Flowering time:** late November-early February. **Name:** *parramattensis* = inhabiting Parramatta, where the type specimen was collected.

Acacia parvipinnula Tindale

Ss, Castl

A shrub or small tree 2.5-4, occasionally to 10m, high, found in woodland on sandy soils, especially along creeks. It occurs in northern parts of the area (e.g. tributaries of the Hawkesbury) and is easily recognised by its bluish branches and numerous leaf glands.

Range: coast north from Sydney and Blue Mountains. Common north of the Hawkesbury. **Leaves:** rhachis minutely hairy, with 2-4 glands between each division, leaflets 3-5mm long, usually hairless. **Pods:** blue-brown or blue-black. **Flower heads:** PALE YELLOW. **Flowering time:** September-early December. **Name:** *parvipinnula* = Lat. with small leaflets.

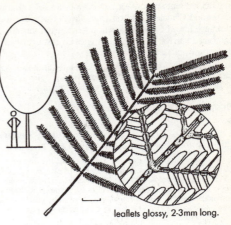

leaflets glossy, 2-3mm long.

Acacia mearnsii

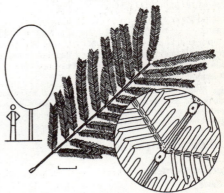

Acacia parramattensis   leaflets ±hairless, 3-5mm long.

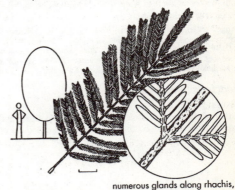

Acacia parvipinnula   numerous glands along rhachis, leaflets 3-5mm long.

Acacia pubescens (Ventenat) R. Brown

Cumb Vulnerable 2VCa

A bushy or weeping shrub 1-3m high. A rare species, found in open forest on clay soils. Restricted to a few locations in inner western Sydney (e.g. Lansdowne Park at Bankstown, Rookwood Cemetery, and on Duck River, Granville). Land clearance for urban development poses a major threat to its continued survival in the wild. It is easily distinguished by the conspicuously hairy branchlets.

Range: restricted to the Sydney area. **Leaves:** rhachis densely hairy, often no glands present, leaflets 2-4mm long, hairless. **Flower heads:** BRIGHT YELLOW **Pod:** bluish. **Name:** *pubescens* = Lat. finely hairy.

Acacia schinoides Bentham
Ss

A tall shrub to 16m high, found in deep shady sandstone gullies in the upper parts of the Lane Cove River system.

Range: restricted to the Lane Cove River, Gosford area and north to the Hunter Valley. **Leaves:** only 4-5 pairs of pinnae present, leaflets 3-5mm wide, same colour both sides. The branches and trunk are silvery grey. **Flower heads:** PALE YELLOW, globular. **Flowering time:** late November-February. **Name:** *schinoides* = *Schinus*-like, referring to the leaves. *Schinus ariera* is the Pepper Tree that graces many farm houses in country areas.

Acacia terminalis (Salisbury) Macbride
Sunshine Wattle **Ss**

An attractive open shrub usually about 1.5m high. Abundant on moist ground in heath and woodlands. One of the most spectacular flowering wattles in the area. Aborigines collected witchetty grubs from the branches. It was once known as Port Jackson Wattle.

Range: NSW coast and ranges, Vic and Tas. **Leaves:** with leaflets thick, tough, pointed, hairless. **Flower heads:** BRIGHT YELLOW, globular, in spectacular masses. **Flowering time:** late summer and winter. **Name:** *terminalis* = refers to the terminal inflorescences.

2. Prickly species

Acacia brownei (Poiret) Steudel
Ss, Castl

A low spiky shrub to 1m high, found in woodland on sandy soils. Less common than *A. ulicifolia*, but easily distinguished by the bright yellow flowers.

Range: NSW coast, ranges and western slopes, Qld and Vic. **Phyllodes:** compressed, very sharply pointed, gland not swollen. **Flowers:** BRIGHT YELLOW, globular, solitary, axillary. **Flowering time:** August-November. **Name:** *brownei* = after Robert Brown (1773-1858), botanist on Matthew Flinders' 1801-05 circumnavigation of Australia.

Acacia echinula De Candolle
Hooked Wattle **Ss**

A much-branched shrub to 2m high. Found in heath and woodland. Much less common than either *A. ulicifolia* or

Acacia echinula

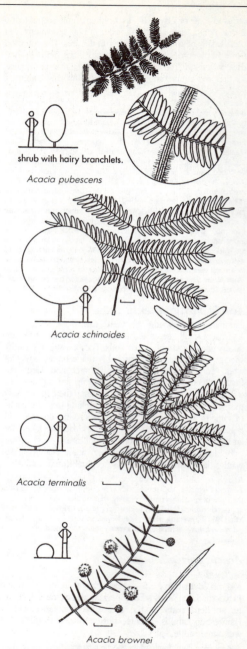

shrub with hairy branchlets.

Acacia pubescens

Acacia schinoides

Acacia terminalis

Acacia brownei

A. brownei. Recognised by the yellow flowers and very short phyllodes.

Range: NSW coast and Blue Mountains. **Phyllodes:** cylindrical, short (5-9mm long), very sharply pointed, gland not swollen. **Flower heads:** BRIGHT YELLOW (but not as richly coloured as *A. brownei*), globular, solitary, axillary. **Flowering time:** spring (from June). **Name:** *echinula* = Gk. spiny, originally from Echinus, the Sea Urchin.

Acacia oxycedrus Sieber ex De Candolle

Spike Wattle **Ss**

A spreading shrub to 3m high, densely armed with stiff spiky phyllodes. Found in heath and scrubland, especially on disturbed ground, north of the harbour.

The British botanist Robert Sweet was strangely taken by this alarmingly prickly shrub: 'This fine plant is of late introduction to this country, and we believe was first raised at His majesty's Botanic Garden at Kew. It is a very desirable plant for the Greenhouse or Conservatory, both for the elegance and delightful fragrance of its flowers.' (1828)

Range: Hornsby Plateau, and separately in coastal Vic and SA. **Phyllodes:** stout, stiff, very sharply pointed. **Flower heads:** BRIGHT YELLOW, cylindrical. **Flowering time:** August-September **Name:** *oxycedrus* = Gk. sharp-*Cedrus*, or Cedar (a genus in the Pine family).

Acacia ulicifolia (Salisbury) Court

Prickly Moses **Ss, Cumb, Castl**

A wiry, prickly shrub to about 1.5m high, abundant in drier woodlands.

Range: NSW coast, ranges and western slopes, Qld, Vic and Tas. **Phyllodes:** short, stiff, thin, very sharp pointed, swollen at the gland. **Flower heads:** CREAM, solitary. **Flowering time:** autumn and winter. **Name:** *ulicifolia* = leaves like an *Ulex*, the prickly European Gorse or Furze. The common name is a corruption of 'Prickly Mimosa'.

3. All other species

Acacia baueri Bentham

Ss

A small shrub with spreading stems to 20cm long, found in heathland. Very rare or extinct near Sydney. Two subspecies have been collected in the area:

• **ssp. *baueri*** (leaves smooth): this occurred in coastal heaths between Rose Bay and La Perouse, but was last collected in 1911, so it is probably locally extinct. It has a limited range, only occuring in a few other places on the north coast and in Qld.

• **ssp. *aspera*** (leaves rough): its principal population is in heathland at Wentworth Falls in the Blue Mountains, but it has been recorded at Wilton near Picton, above Bulli, and on the road to Warrumbul in the Royal National Park.

Leaves: cylindrical, hooked, in whorls of 5-8. **Flower heads:** BRIGHT YELLOW, solitary, axillary. **Flowering time:** May-June. **Name:** *baueri* = after Ferdinand Bauer (1760-1826), the fine scientific artist who accompanied Robert Brown on Matthew Flinders' 1801-03 circumnavigation of Australia.

Acacia binervata De Candolle

Two-veined Hickory **Rf, Ss**

A dense dark tree to 16m high, covered in masses of large cream flowers in spring. Found in moist coastal forests and rainforest margins, mainly in near-coastal districts. Very restricted in the Sydney area (mainly in moist valleys in the southern Royal National Park) but very common north and south of the area.

Range: from NSW south coast to Qld, on coast and ranges. **Phyllodes:** drooping, curved, fairly tough, with two main veins and prominent net veins. **Flower heads:** CREAM, globular, numerous in large axillary racemes. **Flowering time:** October. **Name:** *binervata* = Lat. 2-veined.

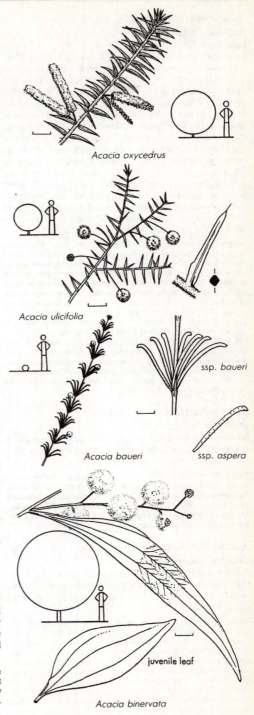

Acacia oxycedrus

Acacia ulicifolia

ssp. *baueri*

Acacia baueri

ssp. *aspera*

juvenile leaf

Acacia binervata

Acacia binervia (Wendland) Macbride

(previously *A. glaucescens*)
Coast Myall, Kaarreewan **Ss**

An elegant shrub or small tree with beautiful silvery blue-grey foliage and dark flaky bark. Found in rocky places near rivers and creeks and now planted widely in parks and gardens. Coast Myall has everything going for it: beautiful silver-grey foliage, flowers that cover the tree in early spring and a fine fragrant timber. 'It almost seems beyond the power of art to depict the exquisite fluffiness of the spikes of flowers of the Coastal Myall'.[7] The 'wood exhales a delicious perfume like violets . . . I have a small cup of Myall-wood, which has been in my possession for the last 14 years, and retains its fragrance as powerfully as ever'.[8] Because of its hardness and perfume it was a favourite timber for smoking pipes. 'Smokers who pride themselves on their pipes greatly affect the myall, and thousands of wooden pipes are sold in London perfumed and coloured so as to imitate it'.[9] The timber is extremely hard and was used by Aborigines for boomerangs.

Range: NSW coast and ranges. **Bark:** very dark, flaky. **Phyllodes:** silver-grey, sickle-shaped, finely furry to feel, with three main veins. **Flower heads:** cylindrical, bright YELLOW. **Flowering time:** spring. **Name:** *binervia* = Lat. two-veined. This inappropriate name deserves some explanation: In 1806 the German botanist Willdenow described Coast Myall and named it, appropriately, *A. glaucescens*. It was known by this name throughout the last century. However, in 1798 another German botanist, Wendland, had given the name *Mimosa binervia* to material which consisted of the leaves of the two-veined species *A. binervata* mixed up with some cylindrical flower heads. Although his description was nonsense Wendland many years later claimed he had intended it to apply to Coast Myall. In 1919 the American botanist Macbride considered that this was sufficient reason to give Wendland's earlier name precedence under the International Rules of Botanical Nomenclature, so *A. glaucescens* was overturned, and the current name applied. *Kaarreewan* is an Aboriginal name from the Sydney area.

Acacia buxifolia A. Cunningham

Box-leaf Wattle **Castl, Ss**

An erect shrub to 3m high with pale slate-green foliage, found in open forest in the Castlereagh woodlands, and occasionally in the far north of the area.

Range: inland slopes from Vic to Qld, only appearing east of the ranges in the Sydney region (common on tops in Yengo National Park). **Phyllodes:** dull, thick, with one inconspicuous vein, hairless (branchlets also hairless). **Flower heads:** deep BRIGHT YELLOW, in axillary racemes. **Flowering time:** August-October. **Name:** *buxifolia* = Box-leaved. *Buxus* is the European Box Tree.

Acacia bynoeana Bentham

Castl, Ss Vulnerable 3VC-

A low spreading shrub with stems under 40cm long, finely hairy all over. Found in heath and woodland on sandy soils. Very uncommon, probably extinct over much of its range due to settlement.

Range: scattered populations have been recorded from the Sydney area: Port Hacking, Kogarah (extinct), Middle Harbour, Frenchs Forest, Kenthurst, the Castlereagh woodlands (relatively common there), near Gosford, in the Blue Mountains (Mount Tomah, Lawson), and at Morriset in the Hunter Valley. The author has collected a specimen from beside Heathcote Road at Lucas Heights, so there may be a population south of the harbour. **Phyllodes:** straight or curved, flat, spreading, 1-2mm wide, rigid, with 3-4 raised parallel veins, covered in fine stiff hairs. **Flower heads:** BRIGHT YELLOW, globular, solitary, axillary. **Flowering time:** summer. **Pod:** 2-3cm, finely hairy, striate. **Name:** *bynoeana* =

Acacia binervia

leaf variants

Acacia buxifolia

leaf variants

Acacia bynoeana

Acacia elongata

after Benjamin Bynoe, a surgeon on the Beagle's 1837-43 expedition (with Charles Darwin). He collected plants at various stops on the voyage, including around Sydney where he spent a few months in 1838, collecting the type specimen of this species.

Acacia elongata Sieber ex De Candolle

Ss, Castl

An open shrub to 3m high with stiff, spreading or erect foliage. Found in heath and woodland. A fairly common species, usually in colonies on damp ground.

Range: coast and ranges of NSW. **Phyllodes:** 6-12cm long, fairly rigid, dull, with 3 main veins. **Flower heads:** rich LEMON YELLOW, globular, axillary, in pairs. **Flowering time:** August-September. **Name:** *elongata* = Lat. stretched or lengthened, referring to the leaves.

Acacia falcata Willdenow

Cumb, Castl

A tall open shrub to 5m high with droopy Eucalyptus-like leaves. Found in woodland on clay soils, and occasionally on sandstone. Common on the Cumberland Plain. Aborigines used an 'embrocation from bark' for skin diseases.

Range: NSW coast and ranges and Qld. **Phyllodes:** light grey-green, thick, leathery, arising at 90° from the stems. **Flower heads:** CREAM, globular, in axillary racemes. **Flowering time:** mid-winter. **Name:** *falcata* = Lat. curved like a scythe.

Acacia falciformis De Candolle

Broad-leaved Hickory **Ss**

An erect shrub or slender tree, 3-12m tall, with large drooping blue leaves, found in woodland on sandstone and rocky soils. Basically a Blue Mountains species, but it occurs at Bents Basin. It takes a close inspection to realise it is not a *Eucalyptus.*

The bark on old trees in dark and corrugated, rich in tannin.

Range: ranges and western slopes throughout the eastern mainland. **Phyllodes:** curved, blue-green, rather fleshy, same colour both sides, to 20cm long. **Flower heads:** cylindrical, CREAM to PALE YELLOW, on stalks covered in golden felt (also on young branches). **Flowering time:** October-January. **Name:** *falciformis* = Lat. sickle-shaped. **Similar species:** distinguish from A. *falcata* by the marginal gland being joined to the mid-vein.

Acacia fimbriata A. Cunningham ex G. Don

Fringed Wattle **Cumb**

A shrub or small tree, found in open forest on clay soils on the Cumberland Plain.

Range: mainly NSW inland slopes, only crossing the ranges in the Sydney region. **Phyllodes:** thin, with a fringe of tiny hairs on the margin (a hand lens may be necessary); the hairs may be almost absent on some specimens. **Flower heads:** LEMON YELLOW, globular, in axillary racemes. **Flowering time:** July-September. **Name:** *fimbriata* = Lat. fringed.

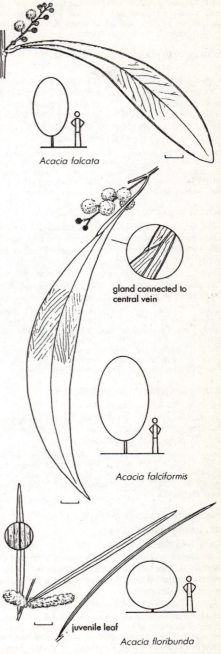

Acacia falcata

gland connected to central vein

Acacia falciformis

microscopic hairs

Acacia fimbriata

juvenile leaf

Acacia floribunda

Acacia floribunda (Ventenat) Willdenow

White Sallow Wattle, Sally, Marrai-uo **Ss, Cumb**

A dense rounded shrub usually to 2-4m high, but can be 10-15m. Common along river and creek banks throughout the area; also planted in gardens and streets. Closely related to A. *longifolia*. It was one of the main species used for 'wattling' in colonial times.

Range: NSW coast and ranges, also southern Qld and Vic. **Phyllodes:** thin, narrow, crowded, with numerous branching veins visible and one slightly stronger central vein. Mature phyllodes are usually 3-5mm wide, but young shrubs often have very slender phyllodes about 2mm wide. **Flowers-heads:** PALE-YELLOW, cylindrical. **Flowering time:** late winter. **Name:** *floribunda* = Lat. abundant-flowering. The common name Sallow is an English name for Willow, white possibly refers to the colour of the timber and Sally is a corruption of Sallow. *Marrai-uo* is an Aboriginal name from the Illawarra.

Acacia hispidula (Smith) Willdenow

Ss

A low sandpaper-leafed shrub to 1m high with a wiry, much-branched stem. Uncommon, in woodland, often occurring as an isolated specimen. The English botanist James Smith first described it in 1793: 'We know of no other species that has so much asperity about it; certainly every other simple-leaved one yet discovered is perfectly smooth.'[10]

Range: NSW coast and ranges, extending to the western slopes in the north of the state; also Qld. **Phyllodes:** small and stiff, covered in hard short hairs and teeth, rough to touch. **Flower heads:** PALE YELLOW, solitary, globular, in leaf axils. **Flowering time:** much of year. **Name:** *hispidula* = Lat. rough with minute hairs or spines.

Acacia implexa Bentham

Hickory, Lightwood, Wee-tjellan **Ss, Cumb**
A slender graceful shrub or small tree 4-10m high, with light willowy foliage. Found in moist sandstone gullies in the Sydney area, and also occasionally on clay soils on the Cumberland Plain. Aborigines used the leaves as a fish poison. They also used the bark as a medicine by soaking it in water to produce a treatment for skin diseases.

Range: NSW coast, ranges, western slopes and plains, Qld and Vic. **Phyllodes:** very variable in width from 8-25mm wide, with 3 main veins and many smaller parallel veins; usually drooping. **Flower heads:** PALE YELLOW, globular, in axillary racemes. **Name:** *implexa* = Lat. infolded, refering to the twisted pod. Wee-tjellan is an Aboriginal name from the Sydney area. **Similar species:** *A. longifolia, A. maidenii*; distinguish by the phyllode venation and cylindrical flower heads.

Acacia linifolia (Ventenat) Willdenow

Flax-leafed Wattle **Ss, Cumb**
A graceful shrub to 2m high, common in heath and woodland. Easily recognised by its soft, crowded foliage on tall swaying stems. Often abundant on disturbed ground.

Range: restricted to the Sydney region. **Phyllodes:** small and narrow (1-3mm wide), fairly soft and thin, very numerous. **Flower heads:** CREAM, globular, in axillary racemes, often forming dense pyramidal masses at the ends of branches. **Flowering time:** December to April. **Name:** *linifolia* = Lat. straight-leaved.

Acacia longifolia (Andrews) Willdenow
var. *longifolia*

Sydney Golden Wattle, Marrai-uo **Ss**
An attractive tall or rounded shrub usually 3-4m high. Very common in moist forest understories and in successions on cleared or disturbed ground. Its hardiness and showy flowers make it a popular street tree.

The phyllodes were used as a fish poison by Aborigines.

Range: coast and ranges of NSW, and Vic; naturalised in SA. **Phyllodes:** thin and flexible, fairly stiff, erect or spreading, with two main veins (one more prominent than the other) and many smaller parallel veins. **Flower heads:** GOLDEN YELLOW, cylindrical. **Flowering time:** July-November. **Name:** *longifolia* = Lat. long-leaved. *Marrai-uo* is an Aboriginal name from the Illawarra.

Acacia longifolia var. *sophorae*

—See SEACOAST AND ESTUARINE SPECIES.

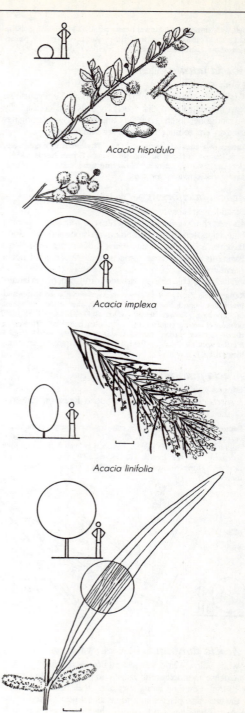

Acacia hispidula

Acacia implexa

Acacia linifolia

Acacia longifolia var. *longifolia*

Acacia longissima Wendland

Ss

An erect shrub to 2-4m high usually with willowy, drooping foliage. Found in sheltered places in woodland. Uncommon locally, mainly north of the harbour.

Range: coastal NSW into Qld. **Phyllodes:** long and slender, with one main vein. **Flower heads:** PALE YELLOW, cylindrical. **Flowering time:** much of the year. **Name:** *longissima* = Lat. very long.

Acacia maidenii

—See RAINFOREST SPECIES.

Acacia myrtifolia (Smith) Willldenow

Myrtle Wattle **Ss**

A small erect heath shrub usually 50-100cm high, with attractive red-tinged foliage. Common in woodland on sandstone.

It was introduced into English hot houses in 1789 where its red colouring made it popular. Early settlers used the leaves as a hop substitute for making beer. A strange feature is that the pods point rigidly upwards instead of loosely dangling as in most other wattles.

Range: NSW coast and ranges, also all other states except NT. **Phyllodes:** tough, hairless, with thickened, usually red margins and red stems. Marginal gland prominent. **Flower heads:** PALE YELLOW, globular, in axillary racemes. **Flowering time:** late winter. **Name:** *myrtifolia* = leaves like the European Myrtle.

Acacia obtusifolia A. Cunningham

Ss

An erect shrub to 3m high, common in woodlands. Care needs to be taken to distinguish this species from the closely related *A. longifolia*. It has thick, erect leaves which always have an irregular, rather ragged margin, caused by withering in the bud stage.

Range: coast and ranges from Vic to Qld. **Phyllodes:** erect, thick, leathery, blunt, with a ragged, often reddish margin, very variable in size and shape. **Flower heads:** PALE YELLOW, cylindrical. **Flowering time:** December-February. **Name:** *obtusifolia* = Lat. blunt-leaved.

Acacia prominens A. Cunningham ex G. Don

Gosford Wattle **Ss Rare 2RCa**

An erect shrub 3-6m high, found in woodland. Now rare. Maiden described it as 'the glory of the southern suburbs of Sydney'.[11] The English botanist Sir William Hooker wrote 'although it may, in its native regions, be truly said to be, like Goldsmith's village thorn, "unprofitably gray," no one

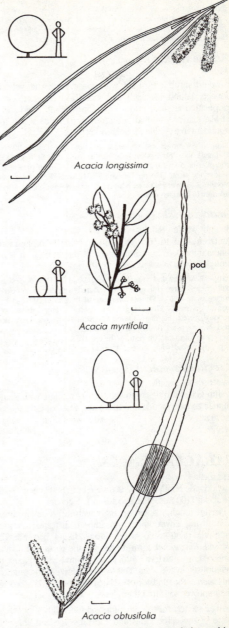

Acacia longissima

pod

Acacia myrtifolia

Acacia obtusifolia

Acacia prominens

caring to receive it into his garden, it nevertheless seldom fails, even there, in the month of September, when decked with blossoms, to commend itself to the notice and admiration of the passing, way-worn colonist, not less by the extreme richness and profusion of its flowers, than by the delicious fragrance they diffuse around.'[12]

Range: Hurstville area and Gosford, also scattered in the Blue Mountains and south to the Snowy River. **Phyllodes:** slightly grey-green, with one main vein and a prominent gland. **Flower heads:** LEMON YELLOW, globular, in axillary racemes. **Flowering time:** July-September. **Name:** *prominens* = Lat. prominent, referring to the gland.

Acacia rubida A Cunningham

Ss

An erect shrub 2-2.5m tall, with dense, somewhat yellowish foliage. Found in heath and woodland on sandstone. A population around Loddon Falls (above Bulli), and another at Maroota, are the main occurrences in the area. It is more abundant in the Blue Mountains.

Range: NSW ranges and western slopes, but uncommon on the coast, Qld and Vic. **Phyllodes:** erect, often pale or yellowish, with a conspicuous marginal gland. Bipinnate foliage is usually present at the base of the plant. **Flower heads:** BRIGHT YELLOW, in dense axillary racemes. **Flowering time:** July-September. **Name:** *rubida* = Lat. red, referring to the often reddish stems.

Acacia stricta (Andrews) Willdenow

Straight Wattle **Ss**

An open shrub to 3m high, found in colonies in open forest. Uncommon locally, mainly north of the harbour. It is very similar to *A. suaveolens.*

Range: NSW coast and ranges, Qld, Vic, Tas and SA. **Phyllodes:** erect, dull, hairless, often pale green, thin-textured, with one main vein and numerous net veins. **Flower heads:** small, BRIGHT YELLOW, globular, axillary, in pairs. **Flowering time:** spring. **Name:** *stricta* = Lat. bundled or erect, referring to the leaves. **Similar species:** the phyllodes of *A. suaveolens* are fleshy blue-green, while those of *A. stricta* are dull grey-green with a thin, dry texture. The veins of *A. suaveolens* are invisible or poorly marked, while those of *A. stricta* are clearly visible.

Acacia suaveolens (Smith) Willdenow

Sweet-scented wattle **Ss**

A slim graceful blue-green shrub to 1.5m high, with sharply angular stems. Abundant in heath and woodland throughout the area.

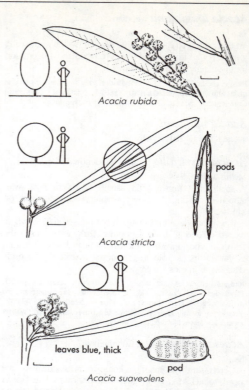

Acacia rubida

pods

Acacia stricta

leaves blue, thick

pod

Acacia suaveolens

Range: coast and ranges of NSW, Qld, Vic, Tas and SA. **Phyllodes:** blue-green, arising at 90° on angular stems, stiff and spirally arranged. **Flower heads:** CREAM, globular, in short racemes. **Flowering time:** winter. **Name:** *suavolens* = Lat. sweet smelling.

FABACEAE Papilionaceae

Peas, Beans

A worldwide family with 12 000 species in 500 genera. There are about 1100 Australian species in 136 genera.

Peas are tough, adaptable plants which are present in almost every living environment. An important feature is their symbiotic relationship with nitrogen-fixing bacteria. The bacteria, *Rhizobium*, form nodules in the roots and convert atmospheric nitrogen into ammonium which can be metabolised by the plant. This lets peas thrive in low-nutrient soils such as the sandstones of the Sydney region. The process also improves soils for other plants.

Flower structure: the calyx forms a tube with 5 lobes, the shape of the calyx lobes and the presence and shape of bracteoles are important diagnostic features. The corolla consists of 5 free petals: a broad erect *standard* usually with markings to guide insects, two narrow *wings*, and a *keel* of two tightly clasped petals enclosing the sexual parts. The staminal filaments are clasped in a tube around the ovary and style.

Fruit: the fruit is called a *legume*. It consists of a shell (*pericarp*) enclosing a row of seeds. The legume usually splits along both sides when opening. Due to the bacterial symbiosis in the roots, the seeds are very rich in protein and form an important food source for insects, animals and humans.

Pea flowers produce little or no scent 'but as Don Quixote pointed out to Sancho Panca, beauty is of two kinds, so scent is of two kinds, and therefore, if the Papilionaceae do not possess the positive quality of wafting any grateful odour to the breeze, it is consolatory to know that they have the negative virtue of emitting no unpleasant one'.[1]

• *Almaleea* Crisp & P. Weston

An endemic genus with 5 species in eastern Australia. They were formerly included in *Pultenaea* and *Dillwynia*.

Name: *Almaleea* = in honour of Alma Lee (1912-90), a botanist at the Royal Botanic Gardens, Sydney, who specialised in this family.

Almaleea paludosa (J. Thompson) Crisp & P. Weston

Ss (previously *Pultenaea paludosa*)

A slender erect or sprawling shrub usually to 40cm high, found in damp open heath. An uncommon species in the area (eg. Royal National Park).

Range: NSW coast and Victoria. **Leaves:** tiny, crowded, erect, flat, 6-8mm long, with uneven margins and small hard points. **Flowers:** tiny, YELLOW with RED markings, in small dense terminal heads, calyx densely hairy. **Flowering time:** spring. **Name:** *paludosa* = Lat. pertaining to swamps.

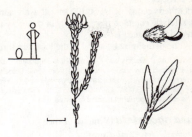

Almaleea paludosa

• *Aotus* Smith

An endemic genus of 8 species distributed in all states except NT.

Name: *Aotus* = Gk. earless, referring to the lack of bracteoles on the calyx.

Aotus ericoides (Ventenat) G. Don

Aotus **Ss**

A small variable heath shrub 0.5-2m high, locally very common in heath, and woodland on sandstone. There are two distinct forms: a compact, dense, erect-leaved form found in open heath, and a taller more open form, with spreading leaves, found in more sheltered locations. In the heath form the flowers are so dense that the stems often appear as solid cylinders of yellow.

Range: NSW coast and ranges, Qld, Vic, Tas and SA. **Leaves:** vary considerably in proportions but are always recognisable by the raised keel below. **Flowers:** YELLOW with RED markings, axillary, usually very dense on the branches. **Flowering time:** spring. **Name:** *ericoides* = *Erica*-like, referring to the small leaves. Erica is the European Heath or Heather.

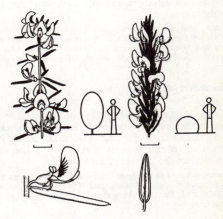

Aotus ericoides

• *Bossiaea* Ventenat (Boss-ee-EE-a)

An endemic genus of 42 species distributed in all states except Qld (19 in NSW).

Name: *Bossiaea* = after Boissieu de la Martinière. He was medical officer and botanist on the *Astrolabe,* one of La Pérouse's ships in his southern expedition of 1785-88. He perished with the rest of the expedition when the ships were wrecked on a reef in the Santa Cruz group, Melanesia, shortly after their meeting with the first fleet at Sydney in 1788.

Bossiaea ensata Sieber ex De Candolle

Small Leafless Bossiaea **Ss**

A weakly erect or sprawling shrublet, usually leafless, to 50cm high, with broad winged stems. Found in heath and woodland on sandstone. Less common than *B. scolopendria.*

Range: NSW coast and ranges, into Qld. **Leaves:** none, or reduced to tiny scales, although a few small leaves can be found on seedlings

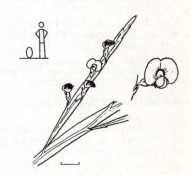

Bossiaea ensata

or on regrowth after fire. The stems are green, stiff, with broad flattened wings. **Flowers:** YELLOW with RED markings and GREEN keel, smaller than *B. scolopendria*, and with longer, more slender stalks. **Flowering time:** spring. **Name:** *ensata* = Lat. *ensis,* sword, referring to the broad stems.

Bossiaea heterophylla Ventenat

Variable Bossiaea **Ss**

A slender herbaceous plant 50-100cm tall with attractive flowers. A locally common plant, usually in dry rocky places in heath and woodland.

This is one of the most beautiful of the local pea shrubs.

Range: NSW coastal districts into Qld; also Blue Mountains. **Leaves:** very variable in size and shape (and absent from some branches), 2-ranked on erect stems which may be flattened into wide wings. **Flowers:** attractively patterned YELLOW, ORANGE and RED. **Flowering time:** spring. **Name:** *heterophylla* = Lat. variable-leaved.

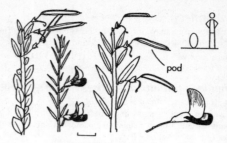

Bossiaea heterophylla

Bossiaea obcordata (Ventenat) Druce

Spiny Bossiaea **Ss, Castl, Cumb**

A stiff shrub to 1.5m high, found in woodland on sandstone and shales. A fairly common species in the Sydney area, north of the harbour.

Range: NSW coast and ranges, into Vic. **Leaves:** small, heart-shaped, notched at the tip. **Flowers:** YELLOW with red markings, RED wings and keel. **Flowering time:** spring. **Name:** *obcordata* = Lat. *ob-*, opposite of, *cordate*, heart-shaped, referring to the reversed heart-shaped leaves.

Bossiaea obcordata

Bossiaea prostrata R. Brown

Cumb

A small prostate shrub with thick woody stock and slender branches to 20cm long. A rare species locally, found in widely scattered locations, mainly on clays on the Cumberland Plain (e.g. Liverpool area, Prospect, St Marys, Clyde, Scheyville), but also recorded from sea cliffs at Mona Vale.

Range: NSW coast, tablelands and south-western slopes. **Leaves:** small, elliptic, with tiny hairs. **Flowers:** small, REDDISH PURPLE except for YELLOW inside of standard. **Flowering time:** spring. **Name:** *prostrata* = Lat. prostrate.

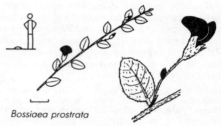

Bossiaea prostrata

Bossiaea rhombifolia Sieber ex De Candolle

Ss, Castl

An erect, dense, much-branched shrub 1-2m high, found in sheltered woodland. A spectacular sight in early spring when flowers cover the branches.

Range: coast and ranges north from the Sydney area into Qld. **Leaves:** erect, flat. **Flowers:** YELLOW with DARK RED keel. **Flowering time:** early spring. **Name:** *rhombifolia* = diamond-shaped leaf.

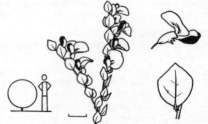

Bossiaea rhombifolia

Bossiaea scolopendria (Andrews) Smith

Ss

A slender weakly erect or sprawling shrub usually leafless, 0.5-1m high, with broad winged stems. A common species in heath and woodland on sandstone.

Range: limited to the sandstones of the Sydney region. **Leaves:** none, or only minute scales, except on seedlings or regrowth after fire. **Flowers:** YELLOW with RED markings, with a DARK RED keel. **Flowering time:** spring. **Name:** *scolopendria* = Gk. scolopendra, millipede, from the general appearance of the plant. **Similar species:** compared to *B. ensata*, the stems are broader and the flowers are larger, with short rather stout stalks, and large bracts and bracteoles. The different coloured keels are the easiest way to distinguish the two species.

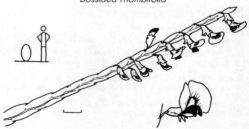

Bossiaea scolopendria

Bossiaea stephensonii F. Mueller

Ss

A small weakly erect shrub with winged stems, to 1m high. Found amongst taller shrubs in heath and woodland on sandstone.

Range: from Royal National Park to Morrisset and Port Macquarie, on the coastal strip only. **Leaves:** soft, softly hairy, with large conspicuous leaf-like stipules. **Flowers:** solitary in the axils, YELLOW with RED markings and keel. **Flowering time:** spring. **Name:** *stephensonii* = in honour of Lawrence Stephenson, the Sydney botanist who collected the type specimen from near Loftus in the Royal National Park.

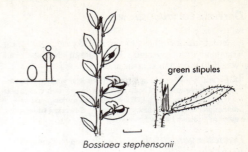

green stipules

Bossiaea stephensonii

• *Canavalia*

—See COASTAL AND ESTUARINE SPECIES.

• *Chorizema* Labillardière

An endemic genus of 20 species distributed in WA, NT, Qld and NSW.

Name: *Chorizema* = *chorizo*, I separate, *nema*, filament, an example of Labillardière's elegant joining of Latin.

Chorizema parviflorum Bentham

Castl, Ss

A shrub 20-50cm high with several erect or sprawling stems arising from a woody base. Found in heath country, in the Castlereagh woodlands, and a scattering of other locations on sandstone.

Range: coastal NSW into Qld. **Leaves:** slender, with recurved margins, 10-25mm long, with a short usually downcurved point, microscopically hairy below, on angular stems. **Flowers:** in racemes at the end of branches, small, YELLOW with RED centre. **Name:** *parviflorum* = Lat. small-leaved.

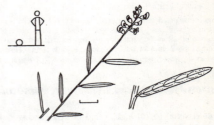

Chorizema parviflorum

• *Daviesia* Smith

An endemic genus of 110 species distributed in all states.

Name: *Daviesia* = after a Welsh botanist, the Reverend Hugh Davies (1739-1821), in honour of his work on Welsh plants.

Daviesia acicularis Smith

Castl, Ss

A small spiky shrub to 50cm high, found in heath and woodland. Locally restricted to the Castlereagh woodlands and upper Georges River.

Range: NSW coast, ranges, southern tablelands and slopes, and Qld. **Leaves:** stiff, pungent pointed, concave above. **Flowers:** YELLOW with DARK RED markings, solitary, axillary. **Flowering time:** spring. **Name:** *acicularis* = Lat. needle-like.

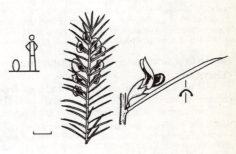

Daviesia acicularis

Daviesia alata Smith

Ss, Castl

A small leafless sprawling plant with winged green stems to 40cm long. Found in open heath, and woodland on sandstone.

Range: NSW coastal districts and Blue Mountains. **Leaves:** reduced to minute scales on broad winged stems. **Flowers:** YELLOW or ORANGE with RED or BROWNISH markings, RED wing petals and hidden pink keel, in small clusters subtended by ragged green bracts. **Flowering time:** spring-early summer. **Name:** *alata* = Lat. winged.

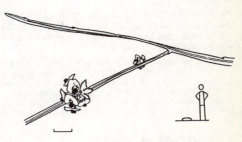

Daviesia alata

Daviesia corymbosa Smith

Ss

An erect shrub 1-2m high, found on rocky creek banks, e.g. Woronora River, Georges River, Royal National Park (Waterfall). Uncommon in the area.

Range: mainly restricted to sandstones of the Sydney region. **Leaves:** leathery, variable in width (linear to narrow ovate), with conspicuous net veins. **Flowers:** bright YELLOW with RED markings and keel, in dense axillary clusters (corymbose racemes). **Flowering time:** spring. **Name:** *corymbosa* = Lat. having a corymb.

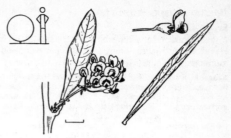

Daviesia corymbosa

Daviesia genistifolia A. Cunningham ex Bentham

Cumb

An erect shrub 1-2m tall, now restricted to remnant woodland at Prospect Reservoir. Once more common on the Cumberland Plain.

Range: widespread in inland eastern Australia, only occurring on the coast in a few places. **Leaves:** rigid, pungent pointed, more or less cylindrical, 10-25mm long, spreading. **Flowers:** in clusters or very short racemes; calyx 2-3mm long, lobes reduced to short teeth. **Flowering time:** spring. **Name:** *genistifolia* = Lat. *Genista*-leaved. *Genista* is another pea genus.

old pods

Daviesia genistifolia

Daviesia mimosoides R. Brown **var. *mimosoides***

Ss

An erect shrub to 2m high, found in heath and woodland on sandstone.

Range: coast, ranges and western slopes of NSW, into Qld and Vic. In the Sydney area it occurs at Kurnell and Menangle Park (more common in the southern tablelands and Blue Mountains). **Range:** widespread in coast, ranges and western slopes in eastern mainland Australia. **Leaves:** flat, veins not conspicuous. **Flowers:** YELLOW with RED-BROWN markings, in axillary racemes. **Flowering time:** spring to early summer. **Name:** *mimosoides* = *Mimosa*-like, referring to the similarity of the leaves to *Acacia* phyllodes (*Mimosa* is the old name for *Acacia*).

Daviesia mimosoides var. mimosoides

Daviesia squarrosa Smith **var. *squarrosa***

Cumb, Castl

A weak spreading shrub usually to 40cm high. Locally uncommon, found in woodland on the Cumberland Plain. The leaves have an uncanny resemblance to *Epacris* species.

Range: NSW coast and ranges. **Leaves:** sessile, heart-shaped, tapering to a fine pungent point, 6-10mm long, on stems covered in tiny stiff hairs. **Flowers:** small, YELLOW with RED markings and red keel, solitary, axillary, on slender peduncles, with a hairless calyx. **Name:** *squarrosa* = Lat. thickly crowded and rigid, referring to the leaves.

Daviesia squarrosa var. squarrosa

Daviesia ulicifolia Andrews

Ss, Castl

An erect spiky shrub to 1.5m high covered in sparse stiff prickly leaves. Found in most types of drier woodland, but rare near the coast. Usually on bare stony ground. The stems end in sharp spines.

Range: coastal districts, mountains and western districts of NSW, and all other states except NT, (including the Great Victoria Desert, WA). **Leaves:** rigid, pungent, often slightly concave underneath. **Flowers:** small, YELLOW with RED-BROWN markings. **Name:** *ulicifolia* = *Ulex*-leaved. *Ulex* is the spiky European Gorze or Furze. (*Ulex europaeus* is naturalised in many places in eastern Australia).

old pods

Daviesia ulicifolia

• *Desmodium*

—See CLIMBERS.

• *Dillwynia* Smith

Parrot Peas

An endemic genus of 15 species of small shrubs distributed in all states except NT.

Name: *Dillwynia* = in honour of Lewis Weston Dillwyn (1778-1855), a British botanist, who specialised in Confervae (a now discredited grouping of primitive plants).

Dillwynia acicularis Sieber ex De Candolle

Cumb, Castl

An erect bushy shrub to 1-2m high, found in woodland on sandstone, e.g. Marramarra National Park and Cowan. Rare in the area. Similar to *D. floribunda* and *D. retorta*, except the leaves are very dense and pressed against the stem.

Range: Sydney area, Blue Mountains and southern tablelands. There is a concentration around Bargo, just south of Sydney. **Leaves:** cylindrical, with a channel above, with a firm but not sharp point, mostly 10-15mm long. **Flowers:** YELLOW (sometimes orange) with RED markings, calyx with fine grey hairs, clustered at the ends of branches. **Flowering time:** spring. **Name:** *acicularis* = Lat. needle-like (in fact the leaves are not sharp).

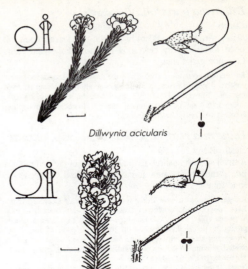

Dillwynia acicularis

Dillwynia floribunda Smith **var.** *floribunda*

Ss

A bushy shrub 1-2m high, generally restricted to wet places in heath and woodland on sandstone. Common in the area.

Range: NSW coastal districts, into Qld. **Leaves:** 5-15mm long, crowded, flattened, rough to touch due to raised hair-bases. **Flowers:** YELLOW with RED markings, in pairs, dense towards the ends of branches. **Flowering time:** early spring. **Names:** *floribunda* = Lat. abundant-flowered.

Dillwynia floribunda var. floribunda

Dillwynia floribunda **var.** *teretifolia*

(De Candolle) Blakely

Ss

A bushy shrub 1-3m high. Found in heath and woodland on sandstone. Similar to var. *floribunda* except the leaves are smooth and the habit generally taller and more robust. Not confined to wet soil.

Range: restricted to the Sydney region. **Leaves:** crowded, cylindrical, smooth, channelled above. **Flowers:** YELLOW with RED markings, in pairs, dense towards the ends of branches. **Name:** *teretifolia* = Lat. cylindrical-leaved.

Dillwynia floribunda var. teretifolia

Dillwynia glaberrima Smith

Ss, Castl

A small soft spreading shrub 30-100cm high, found in heath and open forests, especially on deep coastal sands.

Range: coastal districts of NSW, Qld, Vic, Tas and SA. **Leaves:** flat or cylindrical, soft. **Flowers:** YELLOW with RED centres, in terminal clusters (corymbs). **Flowering time:** spring. **Name:** *glaberrima* = Lat *glabellus*, bald. **Similar species:** distinguish from *D. tenuifolia* by the numerous flowers in a terminal inflorescence.

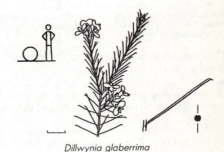

Dillwynia glaberrima

Dillwynia sieberi Steudel

Cumb, Castl (previously part of *D. juniperina*)

A rigid prickly shrub 1-2m high. Found in dry heath, woodland or forests on shale or alluvium. In the Sydney area restricted to the Cumberland Plain (and Bents Basin).

Range: coastal districts from the Sydney region into Vic, also NSW ranges and western slopes into Qld. **Leaves:** stiff, pungent pointed. **Flowers:** YELLOW with RED markings. **Flowering time:** April-November. **Name:** *sieberi* = after Franz Wilhelm Sieber (see under *Eucalyptus sieberi* p39).

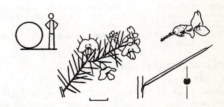

Dillwynia sieberi

Dillwynia parvifolia R. Brown
Cumb

A low wiry shrub to 80cm high, with tiny leaves. Found in open forest on dry clay soils on the Cumberland Plain. Common in the area.

Range: NSW coast, also recorded from the southern tablelands and central western slopes. **Leaves:** 2-3mm long, smooth, twisted, with recurved margins. **Flowers:** YELLOW with RED markings, stalkless or on stalks under 3mm long; in short terminal spikes. **Flowering time:** spring. **Name:** *parviflora* = Lat. small-leaved.

Dillwynia parvifolia

Dillwynia retorta (Wendland) Druce **ssp. *retorta***
Heathy Parrot Pea **Ss**

A small spreading shrub to 1m high. One of the commonest pea shrubs in the area, found in heath and woodland on sandstone.

Range: all states except WA, on coast and mountains. **Leaves:** 6-12mm long, crowded, smooth, twisted, almost cylindrical, with a channel beneath. **Flowers:** YELLOW with RED markings, in pairs in each leaf-axil, usually producing dense floral masses on the upper parts of the stems. **Flowering time:** July-September. **Name:** *retorta* = Lat. turned or twisted, referring to the leaves. **Similar species:** distinguish from *D. floribunda* by the twisted leaves.
Note: *D. retorta* is a complex which has not been properly studied. One problem is that ssp. *trichopoda* and ssp. *retorta* are distinct and non-interbreeding in the Sydney area but are blurred together elsewhere in the state; a 'nasty situation' in the words of one botanist.

Dillwynia retorta ssp. *retorta*

Dillwynia retorta ssp. *peduncularis*
(Bentham) Tindale

Ss

A small spreading heathy shrub to 1m high, found in heath and woodland on sandstone. Fairly common in the area, mainly north of the harbour.

Range: NSW coast north from Sydney, Blue Mountains and Qld. **Leaves:** similar to ssp. *retorta*. **Flowers:** YELLOW with RED markings, obviously stalked, in short terminal racemes. **Flowering time:** August-November. **Name:** *peduncularis* = Lat. stalked. **Similar species:** distinguish from *D. floribunda* by the twisted leaves.

Dillwynia retorta ssp. *peduncularis*

Dillwynia retorta R. Brown **ssp. *trichopoda***
(Blakely) Tindale

Ss

An erect-spreading shrub 1-2m tall. Locally recorded from clay woodland in the Liverpool-Casula-Fairfield area and on sandstone at Bents Basin. Common in the lower Blue Mountains south from Glenbrook, and north and south of the area. Similar to *D. parvifolia*, except the flowers occur on long peduncles.

Range: Sydney area, southern tablelands and central western slopes. **Leaves:** 2-3mm long, smooth, twisted with recurved margins. **Flowers:** YELLOW with RED markings, in umbels, on slender peduncles over 6mm long. **Flowering time:** spring. **Name:** *trichopoda* = Gk. hair-pod, as the pod is finely hairy.

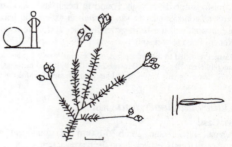
Dillwynia retorta ssp. *trichopoda*

Dillwynia rudis Sieber ex De Candolle
Ss, Castl

A small shrub to 1m high, found in dry sandy heath. It temporarily lost its name when it was thought to be a subspecies of the Blue Mountains species *D. sericea*, but the old identity has been re-established.

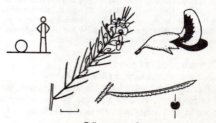
Dillwynia rudis

Range: NSW coast and ranges south from the Sydney region into Vic, also on the western slopes. **Leaves:** crowded, rough to touch, channelled above. **Flowers:** YELLOW with RED markings and RED keel, in pairs, dense towards the ends of branches, calyx hairless. **Flowering time:** spring. **Name:** *rudis* = Lat. reddish. **Similar species:** *D. floribunda;* distinguish by the colour of the floral keels and twisting of leaves.

Dillwynia tenuifolia Sieber ex De Candolle

Castl, Cumb   Vulnerable 2VCi

A small spreading shrub 40-100cm high, uncommon in the area. Found in the Castlereagh woodlands and shales on the Cumberland Plain.

Range: Sydney area and NSW north coast. **Leaves:** very slender, hairless, soft, erect, downcurving at the tip. **Flowers:** ORANGE with RED-BROWN markings, solitary, terminal. **Flowering time:** spring. **Name:** *tenuifolia* = Lat. thin-leaved. **Similar species:** distinguish from *D. glaberrima* by the flowers being orange and solitary.

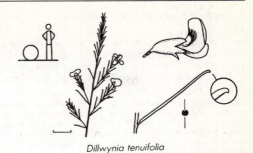

Dillwynia tenuifolia

• *Dipogon*
—See CLIMBERS.

• *Erythrina* Linnaeus

A pantropical genus with 4 representatives native or naturalised in Australia. Includes *E. vesperilio*, the Batswing Beantree of Qld, NT and WA whose hard reddish beans are used by Central Australian Aborigines for ritual and decorative necklaces.

Name: *Erythrina* = Gk. *erythros*, red.

Erythrina x *sykesii** Barneby & Krukoff

Coral Tree   Ss, Cumb

A stout deciduous tree with numerous 'hands' of large red flowers. Common, both planted and wild, throughout the east coast. It is deciduous in autumn and winter, when it displays a brilliant show of flowers. The tree is an exotic hybrid of uncertain parentage.

Range: widely naturalised in NSW, Qld, and NZ. **Bark:** smooth, armed with thorns. Wood very soft. **Leaflets:** 3, large, thin, soft. **Flowers:** RED. **Flowering time:** autumn and winter. **Name:** *sykesii* = from the NZ botanist W. R. Sykes, who drew attention to the hybrid nature of the tree.

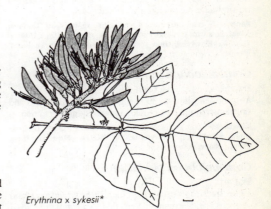

Erythrina x sykesii*

• *Gompholobium* Smith

Golden Glory Peas

An endemic genus of 25 species distributed in all states except NT, and New Guinea. These are among the most beautiful and spectacular flowering plants in the area. The flowers are lemon yellow, and the calyces and leaves are an unusual dark dull olive-green, unique to this genus.

Name: *Gompholobium* = Gk. *gomphos*, a wedge-shaped nail, *lobos*, a pod.

Gompholobium glabratum
Sieber ex De Candolle

Ss, Castl

A small, weakly ascending shrub, with stems 20-30cm long, 'quite a humble plant' according to J.H. Maiden.[2] Fairly common in heath and woodland on sandstone.

Range: coastal districts north from Vic to Newcastle, and in the Blue Mountains. **Leaflets:** usually 5, in tiny 'hands', soft, olive-green. **Flowers:** LEMON YELLOW. **Flowering time:** spring. **Name:** *glabratum* = Lat. hairless, referring to the calyx.

Gompholobium glabratum

Gompholobium grandiflorum Smith

Ss

An erect shrub 1-2m high, found in heath and woodland on sandstone. A common species in the Sydney area. As a piece of historical trivia it was introduced to British gardens in 1803 and was called 'Air-pod' on account of the inflated fruits.

Range: mainly restricted to the Sydney region, south from Gosford. **Leaflets:** 3, slender, very concave below, firm, usually with a hard point. **Flowers:** large, LEMON YELLOW. **Flowering time:** early spring. **Name:** *grandiflorum* = Lat. large-flowered, but only compared to the specimens available to Smith at the time. In fact many species (e.g. *G. latifolium*) have larger flowers.

Gompholobium latifolium Smith

Broad-leaf Wedge-pea **Ss**

An erect shrub 1-2m high, found in heath and woodland on sandstone. A common species in the area.

Range: NSW coast and ranges, extending into Vic and Qld. **Leaflets:** 3, fairly broad, flat or slightly concave below. **Flowers:** large, LEMON-YELLOW. **Flowering time:** spring. **Name:** *latifolium* = Lat. broad-leaved.

Gompholobium minus Smith

Dwarf Wedge-pea **Ss, Castl, Cumb**

A small weak shrub to 30cm high, found in many soils and situations, but not on exposed sandy tops. Fairly common.

Range: NSW coast and ranges north to the Sydney region. **Leaflets:** 3, tiny, pointed, soft. **Flowers:** LEMON YELLOW. **Flowering time:** spring. **Name:** *minus* = Lat. lesser.

Gompholobium pinnatum Smith

Ss, Castl

A weak shrub to 30cm high high, found in heath and woodland on sandstone. Uncommon. Recorded locally from the Royal National Park and Castlereagh woodlands.

Range: coastal NSW from Jervis Bay into Qld. **Leaflets:** 20-30. **Flowers:** LEMON YELLOW. **Flowering time:** spring-early summer. **Name:** *pinnatum* = Lat. pinnate, referring to the pinnate arrangement of the leaves.

• Glycine

—See CLIMBERS.

• Goodia Salisbury

An endemic genus with 2 species.

Name: *Goodia* = after Peter Good, the Kew gardener who accompanied Robert Brown and Ferdinand Bauer in their 1802-03 circumnavigation of Australia. Unfortunately he died of dysentery in Sydney in 1803.

Goodia lotifolia Salisbury

Clover-tree **Ss**

An erect open shrub 2-3m tall. Uncommon or rare in the area. Recorded from the Nepean River at Douglas Park. More common in drier parts of the Blue Mountains.

Range: NSW coast, ranges and some inland areas, Qld, Vic and Tas. **Leaves:** with 3 leaflets, soft, 12-18mm long. **Flowers:** YELLOW with RED markings, about 1cm long; in loose terminal or leaf-opposed racemes.

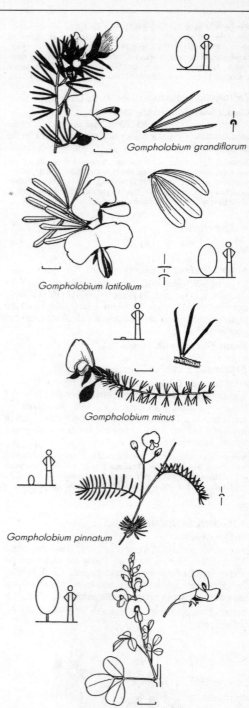

Gompholobium grandiflorum

Gompholobium latifolium

Gompholobium minus

Gompholobium pinnatum

Goodia lotifolia

Flowering time: spring.   **Name:** *lotifolia* = *Lotus*-leaved. *Lotus* is another pea genus.

• *Hardenbergia*
—See CLIMBERS.

• *Hovea* R. Brown
An endemic genus of 20 species, distributed in all states. Both the local species are uncommon in this area.

Name: *Hovea* = in honour of Anton Pantaleon Hove, died 1798, a Polish botanist from Warsaw. He collected for Joseph Banks in West Africa, India, Persia and the Crimea, in the late 1700s.

Hovea linearis (Smith) R. Brown
Ss, Castl
A small shrub, erect or sprawling, usually to 50cm high. Found sheltering beneath other shrubs in dense scrubland or forest on sandstone.

Range: NSW coast and ranges, Qld, Vic, Tas and SA.   **Leaves:** stiff, to 7cm long, concave below, upper surfaces rough due to raised net-veins, finely hairy below.   **Flowers:** PURPLE with pale yellow centres, 1-3 in the axils. Calyx covered in fine hairs.   **Flowering time:** early spring.   **Name:** *linearis* = Lat. straight, with parallel sides, referring to the leaves.

Hovea longifolia R. Brown ex Aiton
Ss
An erect shrub to 1.5-2m high, found in woodland on sandstone. Less common than *H. linearis*.

Range: Confined to the Sydney region, mainly in coastal districts.   **Leaves:** slender, to 8cm long, with revolute (curled beneath) margins, and a dense layer of rusty felt below.   **Flowers:** PURPLE, with pale yellow centres, larger in all respects than *H. linearis*. Calyx covered in dense rusty felt.   **Flowering time:** spring.   **Name:** *longifolia* = Lat. long-leaved.   **Similar species:** the leaves are easily confused with *Astrotricha ledifolia*.

Hovea purpurea Sweet
(previously *Hovea pannosa*)   **Ss**
An erect shrub 1.5-2.5m tall, found in woodland on sandstone (e.g. Kentlyn on the Georges River). Uncommon in the area.

Range: NSW coast and ranges, Vic and Qld.   **Leaves:** 4-7cm long, stiff, blunt, hairless above, densely rusty-felty below, with strongly recurved margins. Fine but strong reticulation is visible above.   **Flowers:** PURPLE with dark purple markings and pale yellow centres, in axillary clusters of 1-3.   **Flowering time:** spring.   **Name:** *purpurea* = Lat. purple.   **Similar species:** the leaves are easily confused with *Astrotricha ledifolia*.

• *Indigofera* Linnaeus
A genus of tropical and sub-tropical plants with about 700 species worldwide. There are 30 Australian species, all endemic. It includes *Indigofera tinctoria* of Asia and Africa, the source of the indigo dye. The local species also produces some dye.

Name: *Indigofera* = Lat. indigo-bearing.

Indigofera australis Willdenow
Cumb, Ss (clay tops)
A small lightly foliaged shrub usually about 1-1.5m high, found in forests on clay soils.

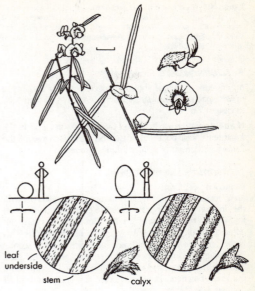

leaf underside   stem   calyx

Hovea linearis   *Hovea longifolia*

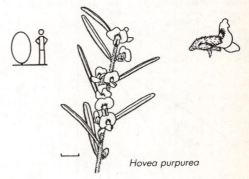

Hovea purpurea

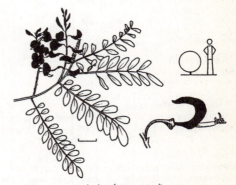

Indigofera australis

Range: NSW coast, ranges and western districts, also in all states except NT. **Leaves:** pinnate, soft, dull, dark, rather greyish. **Flowers:** PINK, in erect axillary racemes. The petals are easily deciduous, all except the standard falling upon opening. **Flowering time:** spring. **Name:** *australis* = Lat. southern.

• *Jacksonia* R. Brown

An endemic genus of about 50 species, mainly distributed in WA, extending through northern WA, NT, Qld, and NSW to eastern Vic.

Name: *Jacksonia* = in honour of George Jackson (1780-1811), a gardener and botanical artist who was in charge of the famous herbarium of Aylmer Bourke Lambert.

Jacksonia scoparia R. Brown

Dogwood **Ss, Castl**

An erect greyish green leafless shrub, to 3m tall. Found in the dry stony forests, but not near the coast. It is uncommon in Sydney, mainly found on the Cumberland Plain, but occasionally on sandstone. According to William Woolls 'This is the only one of the Papilionaceae which has any scent'.[3] The common name comes from a resemblance of the hard wood to the European Dogwood. It was used for the same purpose—butchers' skewers, hooks, fine pegs and small pointed wooded instruments.

Range: NSW and Qld, mainly in mountain areas. **Leaves:** none except for minute scales, often greyish-green. **Flowers:** YELLOW with RED markings. **Flowering time:** early summer. **Name:** *scoparia* = Lat. broom-like.

Jacksonia scoparia

• *Kennedia*

—See CLIMBERS.

• *Lotus* Linnaeus

A cosmopolitan genus of herbs with about 100 species worldwide. There are 2-3 native species and 3 species introduced in Australia. The local introduced European species all have yellow flowers.

Name: *Lotus* = the ancient Greek name for certain legumes. The lotus-eaters of Homer's Odyssey, whose lives were rendered a permanently forgetful dreaminess, were probably addicted to the Jujube Tree (*Zizyphus lotus*, in the family Rhamnaceae).

Lotus australis Andrews

Cumb

An erect perennial herb to 60cm tall, found in grasslands and open forest on the Cumberland Plain. Fairly common.

Range: widespread throughout the state, and in all other states. **Leaves:** with 5 leaflets, soft, hairless or finely hairy; two of the leaflets are borne at the very base of the leaf-stalk. **Flowers:** WHITE, in terminal heads. **Flowering time:** spring. **Name:** *australis* = Lat. southern

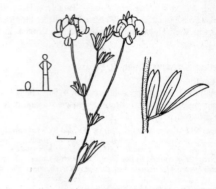

Lotus australis

• *Mirbelia* Smith

An endemic genus of 27 species distributed in all states except SA and Tas.

Name: *Mirbelia* = in honour of C. F. B. de Mirbel (1776-1854), a French botanist who did pioneering work on plant structure and physiology.

Mirbelia rubiifolia (Andrews) G. Don

Ss, Castl

A tiny sprawling or erect shrub with stems usually 20-30cm long. Easily recognised by the strong net-veins in the leaves. Fairly common, but inconspicuous, in heaths on sandstone.

Range: NSW coast and ranges, into Qld. **Leaves:** in whorls of 3, stiff, pungent pointed, concave below, with strong venation. **Flowers:** PURPLE with a hidden yellow centre, axillary. **Flowering time:** spring–early summer. **Name:** *rubiifolia* = *Rubus*-leaved, referring to the spiky leaves which perhaps resemble some species in the Blackberry genus.

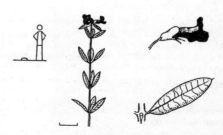

Mirbelia rubiifolia

Mirbelia speciosa Sieber ex De Candolle

Purple Mirbelia **Ss**

A slender erect shrub to 1m high, found in heath and woodland. An uncommon species recorded locally only from the Royal National Park and Woronora Plateau.

Range: Sydney region (also Blue Mountains and north of the Hawkesbury), north coast and Qld. **Leaves:** linear, in whorls of 3, varying from blunt to pungent, very revolute (curled below). **Flowers:** large, RICH ROSE-PURPLE with pale purple markings, but quickly fading to mauve-purple, axillary. **Flowering time:** spring. **Name:** *speciosa* = Lat. showy, referring to the flowers.

Mirbelia speciosa

• *Oxylobium* Andrews

An endemic genus of about 40 species distributed in all states except NT and SA.

Name: *Oxylobium* = Gk. sharp-pod, referring to the pointed pod.

Oxylobium cordifolium Andrews

Heart-leaved Shaggy Pea **Ss**

A low sprawling shrub with branches to 40cm long, sometimes forming wiry cushions. Found in coastal heath and scrubland on sandstone, south of the harbour.

Range: NSW coast and ranges south from Sydney. **Leaves:** tiny, heart-shaped, stiff, mostly in whorls of three. **Flowers:** ORANGE with RED markings and keel. Usually in 3s at the ends of branches. **Flowering time:** spring and early summer. **Name:** *cordifolium* = Lat. heart-shaped leaf.

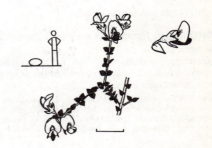

Oxylobium cordifolium

Oxylobium ilicifolium (Andrews) Domin

Native Holly **Ss**

An erect spiky shrub usually 1.5m high, found in dry stony woodland. Not common near the coast.

Range: NSW coast and ranges into Qld. **Leaves:** opposite, stiff, with pungent-tipped lobes. **Flowers:** YELLOW with RED markings, in axillary racemes. **Flowering time:** spring. **Name:** *ilicifolium* = *Ilex*-leaved; *Ilex* is the European Holly.

Oxylobium scandens
—See CLIMBERS.

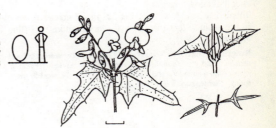

Oxylobium ilicifolium

• *Phyllota* (Sieber ex De Candolle) Bentham

An endemic genus of 10 species distributed in all states except NT.

Name: *Phyllota* = Gk. leaf-ear, referring to the large leafy bracteoles. It resembles *Pultenaea* except for the large leafy bracteoles which are longer than the calyx.

Phyllota grandiflora
(Sieber ex De Candolle) Bentham

Ss

An erect shrub usually to 1m high, found in heath and woodland on sandstone. Fairly common north of the harbour.

Range: restricted to the Hornsby plateau in the Sydney region. **Leaves:** slender, revolute (curled below). **Flowers:** YELLOW with RED markings, about 15mm long (including calyx). Bracteoles slender, linear. **Flowering time:** spring, early summer. **Name:** *grandiflora* = Lat. large-flowered.

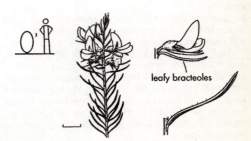

leafy bracteoles

Phyllota grandiflora

Phyllota phylicoides

(Sieber ex De Candolle) Bentham

Ss

An erect shrub usually to 1m high, found in heath and woodland on sandstone. This species is more common than *P. grandiflora.*

Range: NSW coast and ranges into Qld. **Leaves:** slender, revolute (curled below). **Flowers:** YELLOW with RED markings, about 10mm long (including calyx). Bracteoles broad. **Flowering time:** spring—early summer. **Name:** *phylicoides* = Gk. leaf-like, referring to the leafy bracteole (or perhaps *Phylica*-like).

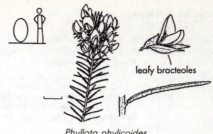

leafy bracteoles

Phyllota phylicoides

• *Platylobium* Smith

An endemic genus of 4 species distributed in all states except WA and NT.

Name: *Platylobium* = Lat. broad pod.

Platylobium formosum Smith ssp. *formosum*

Handsome Flat-Pea **Ss**

A scrambling pea-shrub to 1m high, found in colonies in sheltered woodland. Easily recognised by the broad round rusty-coloured calyx lobes.

Range: NSW coastal districts, Qld, Vic and Tas. **Leaves:** opposite, heart-shaped, with prominent reticulation (network veins) and recurved points. **Flowers:** YELLOW with RED markings, calyx 8-10mm long, standard about 18mm long. **Flowering time:** spring. **Name:** *formosum* = Lat. beautiful.

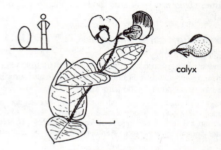

calyx

Platylobium formosum

Platylobium formosum ssp. *parviflorum*

(Smith) Lee

(not illustrated) **Ss**

This is like ssp. *formosum*, but has much smaller flowers. It occurs in a few places on the north shore and Blue Mountains.

Range: NSW coast, Blue Mountains, Qld and Tas. **Leaves:** longer and narrower than ssp. *formosum*. **Flowers:** similar to ssp. *formosum*, except calyx 4-5mm long and standard 5-8mm long. **Flowering time:** spring. **Name:** *parviflorum* = Lat. small-flowered.

• *Pultenaea* Smith (pult-en-EE-a)

Bush Peas

An endemic genus of 120 species distributed in all states except NT. It has a centre of diversity in south-eastern Australia, with many species present.

The flowers are typical 'bacon and egg' type, but differ from other genera by the scaly brown stipule-bracts at the base of the leaves and flower stalks (sometimes these are developed into large scales enveloping the base of flower heads), and by the scaly brown bracteoles on the sides of the calyx. The shapes of the bracts and bracteoles are important diagnostic features. A hand-lens can be useful to distinguish species.

Name: *Pultenaea* = in honour of Dr William Pulteney MD, an English botanist who wrote a biography of Linnaeus.

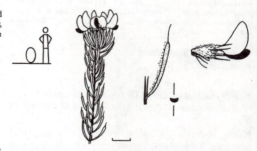

Pultenaea aristata

Pultenaea aristata Sieber ex De Candolle

Ss Vulnerable 2VC-

An erect shrub to 1m tall, found in heath and woodland on sandstone. Uncommon. Restricted to the Woronora Plateau from Helensburgh to Mt Kiera.

Range: confined to the Sydney area. **Leaves:** crowded, 5-20mm long, upcurved, channeled above, with hairy margins and a long bristle at the tip. **Flowers:** YELLOW with RED markings and keel, in a terminal head. The calyx is very hairy, with long dark slender lobes and bracteoles. **Flowering time:** spring. **Name:** *aristata* = Lat. tipped with a bristle.

Pultenaea blakelyi J. Thompson

Blakely's Bush-Pea **Ss**

A graceful open shrub 1-4m high, found in humid sheltered understories in woodland, usually near streams. Moderately common in deep gullies. The branches are angular. When flowering it forms impressive carpets of gold in the Blackbutt forests in southern coastal parts of the area (e.g. Royal National Park, Stanwell Park).

Range: mainly coastal parts of NSW. **Leaves:** narrow, 2-3cm long, opposite, appearing flat but with barely upturned margins. **Flowers:** YELLOW, in short terminal racemes. **Flowering time:** October. **Name:** *blakelyi* = in honour of the Sydney botanist W.F. Blakely (1875-1941). He was a gardener and later botanical assistant at the Royal Botanic Garden, Sydney. He made extensive collections north of the harbour and co-authored, with J. H. Maiden, a monumental critical revision of the Eucalypts.

Pultenaea daphnoides Wendland

Ss

A slender attractive shrub to 2-3m high, common in denser moist understories in woodlands on sandstone.

Range: NSW coast, Blue Mountains and southern ranges, extending to Vic, Tas and SA. **Leaves:** flat, flexible. **Flowers:** YELLOW with RED markings and a red keel, clustered in dense heads at the tips of branches. **Flowering time:** spring and early summer. **Name:** *daphnoides* = Daphne-like, referring to the leaves.

Pultenaea dentata Labillardière

Ss

A slender shrub 20-100cm high, found in marshy heath next to the sea (La Perouse to Jibbon Lagoon, Royal National Park). Rare in the area.

Range: in the Sydney region: coastal plateaus south of Botany Bay, also scattered locations in the NSW ranges, Vic, Tas and SA. **Leaves:** 5-12mm long, margins strongly incurved above. **Flowers:** small (about 5mm long), ORANGE with red-brown markings and dark keel, in a dense head, surrounded at the base by dense overlapping bracts. The calyx is densely silky-hairy. **Flowering time:** spring. **Name:** *dentata* = Lat. toothed, allusion not clear.

Pultenaea elliptica Smith

Ss, Castl

An erect shrub up to 1m high, found in heath and woodland on sandstone and laterites. One of the more common local species.

Range: NSW coastal districts and Blue Mountains. **Leaves:** less then 3mm wide, concave above, crowded, with distinct stalks, raspy to touch, with long loose hairs when young. **Flowers:** rich YELLOW with dark RED markings and red keel, in a dense terminal head, each flower with a broad leaf-like bract below (the bracts are not much larger than the leaves), covered in loose hairs. **Flowering time:** September-October. **Name:** *elliptica* = Lat. elliptical, referring to the leaf shape.

Pultenaea ferruginea Rudge **var. *deanei***
(R.T. Baker) Williamson

Ss

A bushy shrub usually about 1.5m high, found in woodland on sandstone, mainly north of the Hawkesbury River, but with a few recordings from the extreme northern suburbs.

Range: NSW coast north from Sydney. **Leaves:** soft, hairy, blunt. **Flowers:** YELLOW, axillary, the calyx has bracteoles divided to the base into three segments. **Flowering time:** spring. **Name:** *ferruginea* =

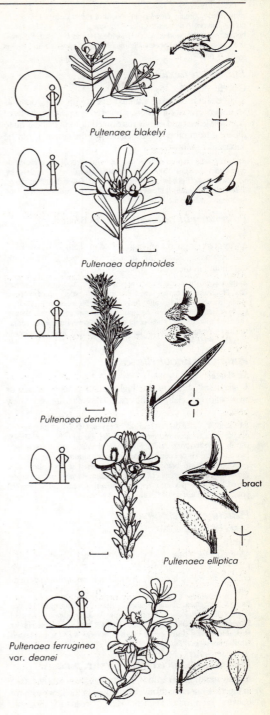

Pultenaea blakelyi

Pultenaea daphnoides

Pultenaea dentata

Pultenaea elliptica

bract

Pultenaea ferruginea
var. deanei

rusty, reason obscure. *Deanei* = in honour of Henry Deane (1847-1924), railway surveyor, Engineer-in-Chief of railways, a knowledgeable amateur botanist who often worked with J. H. Maiden. He was the first to recognise this variety. **Similar species:** distinguish from *P. elliptica* by the flowers being all yellow.

Pultenaea flexilis Smith

Graceful Bush-Pea **Ss**

A large shrub or small rounded tree to 4m high, found as an understorey shrub in dry, sheltered open forest. Its large size, soft leaves and evenly distributed flowers make it quite different from other local members of the genus. It can be spectacular in flower.

Range: coastal districts of NSW into Qld also parts of the great divide north from the Blue Mountains. **Leaves:** 2 small, more or less flat, hairless, soft and flexible. **Flowers:** small, YELLOW with RED markings, in short leafy racemes. **Flowering time:** spring. **Name:** *flexilis* = Lat. flexible, referring to the leaves.

Pultenaea hispidula R. Brown ex Bentham

Ss

A wiry erect shrub to 1.5m high, found in heath and woodland, mainly on sandstone. An uncommon species, but widely distributed in the area.

Range: south from the Sydney region into Vic, also in the southern Blue Mountains. **Leaves:** tiny, 6-8mm long, crowded, concave above, mildly rough to touch, stiffly hairy below. **Flowers:** pale YELLOW (without red), keels green, bracteoles red-brown and broad; axillary, clustered towards the ends of branches. **Flowering time:** spring-summer. **Name:** *hispidula* = Lat. rough to touch. **Similar species:** *P. villosa, P. microphylla*.

Pultenaea linophylla Schrader

Ss, Castl

A spreading shrub to 1m high, found in open heath or woodland, especially on the coast. The stems are very finely hairy.

Range: NSW coastal districts into Vic. **Leaves:** with a distinctive narrow-oblong shape, a small recurved point under the tip (often very small), usually a notched apex and finely hairy undersurface. **Flowers:** in tight heads at the ends of branches. The heads are surrounded by persistent overlapping brown bracts. The calyx is covered in long grey hairs. **Flowering time:** September-October. **Name:** *linophylla* = Lat. straight-leaved. **Similar species:** *P. retusa*; it has hairless stems, no tiny recurved point under the leaf-tip and easily deciduous bracts.

Pultenaea microphylla

Sieber ex De Candolle

Cumb

An erect much-branched shrub to 2m high, found in open forest on clay soils on the Cumberland Plain. A moderately common species. It closely resembles *P. hispidula* in general habit.

Range: Cumberland Plain and high parts of the Blue Mountains. **Leaves:** small, stiff, 4-8mm long, with a stiff sharply downcurved point, crowded. **Flowers:** axillary, ORANGE with RED-BROWN markings and red-brown keel **Flowering time:** spring. **Name:** *microphylla* = Lat. tiny-leaved. **Similar species:** *P. hispidula*.

Pultenaea palacea Willdenow **var. palacea**

A small weakly erect shrub 50-120cm high. Now almost extinct in the area, but once relatively common in the inner suburbs (Clyde, Parramatta, Pennant Hills, Greenacre, Kogarah,

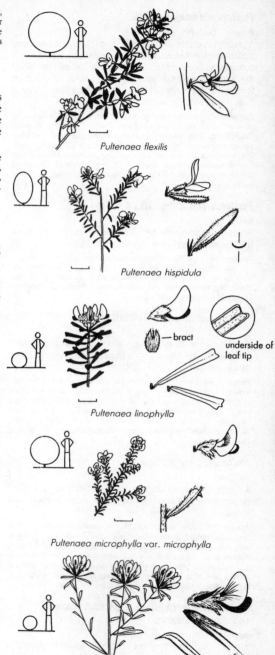

Pultenaea flexilis

Pultenaea hispidula

— bract

underside of leaf tip

Pultenaea linophylla

Pultenaea microphylla var. microphylla

Pultenaea palacea var. palacea

Carlton). Found in damp places in heath or woodland, on or near clay.

Range: Sydney area, part of the north coast, and in the southern tablelands.
Leaves: 10-16mm long, with fine appressed silky hairs beneath, and a fine recurved point. **Flowers:** ORANGE-YELLOW with RED markings and dark keel, in small dense terminal heads surrounded by long dark bracts. The calyx is densely silky-hairy. The bracteoles are broad and as long as the calyx. **Name:** *palacea* = Lat. spade-shaped, reference obscure.

Pultenaea parviflora Sieber ex De Candolle
Cumb, Castl   Vulnerable 2V

A small much-branched shrub to 1m high, found in open forest on heavy shale soils (also in the Castlereagh woodlands).

Range: restricted to the Cumberland Plain. **Leaves:** 3-5mm long, hairless when mature, hooked downward at the tip. **Flowers:** YELLOW with RED markings, solitary, axillary. The calyx is hairless, with long slender lobes and bracteoles. **Flowering time:** spring. **Name:** *parviflora* = Lat. small-leaved. **Similar species:** *P. microphylla*. Distinguish by the hairless, slender-lobed calyx.

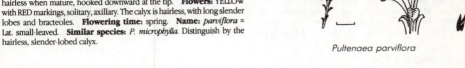

Pultenaea parviflora

Pultenaea pedunculata W. J. Hooker
Cumb

A prostrate, mat-forming shrub with branches to 50cm long. Found in open places on clay soils. A rare species, reported locally from Casula, Cabramatta, Canley Vale and Yennora.

Range: from the above sites in NSW; also Vic, Tas and SA. **Leaves:** rigid, with recurved margins and appressed hairs below. **Flowers:** small, axillary, on slender peduncles. Calyx, fruit pod and peduncle are covered with tiny fine hairs. **Name:** *pedunculata* = Lat. having peduncles (floral-stalks).

Pultenaea pedunculata

Pultenaea polifolia A. Cunningham
Ss

A weak ascending or spreading shrub to 1m high, found in heath and woodland on sandstone.

Range: coastal NSW into Qld and Vic; also Blue Mountains (Blackheath). Not recorded south of the harbour in the Sydney area. **Leaves:** linear, with recurved or revolute margins, often gently upcurving, with a long slender point, sparsely hairy underneath. **Flowers:** YELLOW with RED markings and keel, in terminal heads surrounded by bracts, calyces densely hairy. **Flowering time:** spring. **Name:** *polifolia* = Gk. grey-leaf.

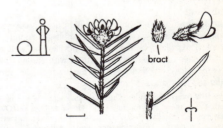

bract

Pultenaea polifolia

Pultenaea retusa Smith
Ss

A small erect shrub 0.5-2m high, found in heath and woodland on sandstone. Uncommon in the area. Recorded from the Royal National Park, Menai and Kurnell.

Range: NSW coast and ranges, Qld and Vic. **Leaves:** narrow oblong to wedge-shaped, notched at the tip and without a point. **Flowers:** small, YELLOW with RED-BROWN markings in a head less than 2cm diameter, with deciduous bracts. **Flowering time:** spring-early summer. **Name:** *retusa* = very obtuse, with an indentation at the tip. **Similar species:** *P. linophylla*.

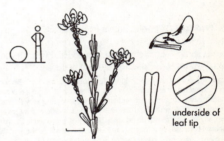

underside of leaf tip

Pultenaea retusa

Pultenaea rosmarinifolia Lindley

Ss

A slender erect shrub to 2m high, found in heath and woodland on sandstone. The whole plant has appressed silvery or white hairs.

Range: Hornsby Plateau, south coast and southern tablelands. **Leaves:** long, spreading, with strongly recurved margins and a fine recurved point. **Flowers:** YELLOW with RED markings and keel, in a dense terminal head. **Flowering time:** spring. **Name:** *rosmarinifolia* = having leaves like *Rosmarinis officinalis*, the Rosemary of the Mediterranean and Turkey.

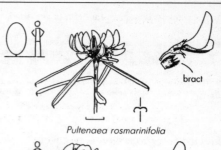

bract

Pultenaea rosmarinifolia

Pultenaea scabra R. Brown ex Aiton **var. *scabra***

Ss

An erect shrub usually 1-1.5m high, found in dry understories of woodland on sandstone.

Range: NSW coast, Blue Mountains and southern ranges into Vic and SA. **Leaves:** covered in short stiff hairs and rough to touch, with recurved margins and a long down-facing point. **Flowers:** YELLOW with RED markings, axillary. **Flowering time:** spring. **Name:** *scabra* = Lat. rough. **Note:** var. *biloba* (R. Brown) Bentham: a similar plant except the leaves are distinctly bi-lobed at the ends. Found in clay soils (e.g. at Frenchs Forest).

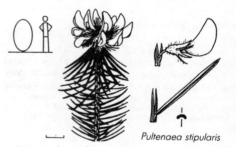

Pultenaea scabra var. scabra

Pultenaea stipularis Smith

Ss

An erect shrub to 2m high, found in heath and woodland on sandstone. A fairly common species in the area.

Range: confined to the coastal plateaus of the Sydney area. **Leaves:** very crowded, long and slender, upcurving from the base, with thickened margins. **Flowers:** YELLOW except for faint red markings on the standard. **Flowering time:** September. **Name:** *stipularis* = having stipules. In this case the stipules are exceptionally long (up to 1cm), scaly, and rusty-brown.

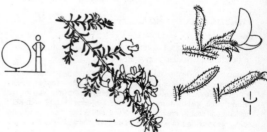

Pultenaea stipularis

Pultenaea villosa Willdenow

Cumb, Castl

A softly spreading or erect shrub 0.5-2m high, densely covered in soft white hairs, especially the new foliage. Found in sclerophyll woodland on the Cumberland Plain, as well as other dry sites on clays. Easy to confuse with *P. hispidula* except the foliage is soft textured and the bracteoles are very slender and hairy, about 3mm long.

Range: NSW coastal districts into Qld. **Leaves:** concave above, hairy beneath, the hairs are on small tubercles. **Flowers:** RICH YELLOW, axillary, crowded towards the ends of branches; note the narrow green bracteoles 2-3mm long. **Flowering time:** spring. **Name:** *villosa* = Lat. villous, with long loose hairs. **Similar species:** *P. hispidula, P. microphylla.*

Pultenaea villosa

Pultenaea viscosa R. Brown ex Bentham

Ss

An erect shrub 1-2m high, found in woodland (e.g. Devlin's Creek, Pennant Hills Park). Uncommon in the area.

Range: NSW coast south from Sydney, Blue Mountains, and Vic. **Leaves:** deeply channeled or revolute above, upcurving, drawn out to a recurved point, not sharp, undersurface and stems with spreading greyish hairs. **Flowers:** YELLOW with RED keel, calyx ribbed, sparsely hairy, glossy brown, slightly sticky, with broad shiny bracteoles, protected at the base by shiny brown sticky 2-lobed bracts; in loose heads at the ends of branchlets. **Flowering time:** spring. **Name:** *viscosa* = Lat. sticky.

Pultenea viscosa

• *Sphaerolobium* Smith

An endemic genus of 14 species distributed in all states except NT.

Name: *Spaerolobium* = Lat. spherical pod.

Sphaerolobium minus Labillardière

Ss, Castl

A small heath shrub with erect, usually leafless stems under 50cm high. An inconspicuous inhabitant of sandy or peaty open heath country. Common in the area.

Although first described 180 year ago, botanists almost immediately confused it with *S. vimineum* and it was not separately recognised again until 1993. The two species may be found growing together.

Range: widespread on coast and ranges in eastern Australia. **Leaves:** tiny, falling early and usually absent. **Flowers:** PURE LEMON YELLOW, in pairs; calyx uniformly lead grey; the style is sharply flexed down and then up again. **Flowering time:** spring. **Name:** *minus* = Lat. lesser.

Sphaerolobium vimineum Smith

Ss, Castl

A small heath plant with erect, usually leafless stems to 1m high. Found in sandy or peaty open heath country. Probably also common locally, but its exact distribution is unclear.

Range: occurs in scattered populations in south-east Qld, NSW and eastern Vic. **Leaves:** tiny, falling early and usually absent. **Flowers:** ORANGE-YELLOW with conspicuous RED markings, in pairs; the calyx is covered in tiny dark spots on a light green background; the style curves evenly upwards forming almost a complete circle. **Flowering time:** spring. **Name:** *vimineum* = Lat. *vimen*, a swirch of twig, referring to the leafless stems.

• *Viminaria* Smith

An endemic genus with only one species.

Name: *Viminaria* = Lat. *vimen*, a switch or twig, referring to the leafless stems.

Viminaria juncea (Schrader) Hoffmannsegg

Golden Spray **Ss**

An erect leafless shrub usually 2-3m high, common in wet ground and beside watercourses in heathland. Numerous whip-like green stems arise from stout orange-brown branches; in spring the stems are lined with sprays of small yellow pea flowers, making a lovely sight.

Range: coastal districts of all states except NT. **Leaves:** in botanical terms each stem is a reduced pinnate leaf of which only the central stalk (rhachis) remains. Rarely a few leaflets can be found on young stems. **Flowers:** all YELLOW. **Flowering time:** spring. **Name:** *juncea* = Lat. Juncus-like, referring to the green stalks.

• *Zornia* Gmelin

A pantropical genus of about 75 species with 13 Australian representatives, distributed in WA, NT, Qld and NSW.

Name: *Zornia* = in honour of Johann Zorn (1739-99), a Bavarian apothecary, botanist and senator, author of *Icones Plantarum Medicinalium*, a work on medicinal plants.

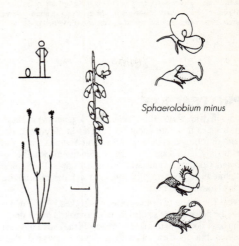

Sphaerolobium minus

Sphaerolobium vimineum

Viminaria juncea

pod

Zornia dyctiocarpa ssp. dyctiocarpa

Zornia dyctiocarpa De Candolle

Cumb

A small weak perennial herb, often prostrate, found in grasslands on clay soils on the Cumberland plain. Faily common.

Range: NT, Qld, inland NSW, and the Cumberland Plain. **Leaflets:** 2, variable in shape, 4-25mm long, on long stalks, with a pair of leafy stipules at the base. **Flowers:** YELLOW with RED markings, almost hidden in a pair of leafy bracts. **Flowering time:** spring-summer. **Name:** *dyctiocarpa* = Gk. net-fruits, referring to the strongly veined pods.

PROTEACEAE

A family with about 1500 species in 75 genera worldwide. In Australia there are about 900 species in 45 genera. The main distribution is in South Africa and Australia but it also occurs in China, southern India and South America. It is an ancient Gondwana family with no close relatives. The tropical rainforests of northern Qld contain a number of primitive relict Proteaceae genera.

Uses: The nectar of many species was sucked by Aborigines and the flowers were soaked in water to make a sweet drink. The large flowers of this family impressed the early European visitors but its lack of economic value lowered their estimation. 'The order must be regarded as one of the most useless to man'.[1] 'Perhaps as a whole this order is one of the most useless which we have and the removal of which in the process of cultivation will be the least regretted.'[2]

The timber of two rainforest species, *Grevillea robusta* (Silky Oak) and *Cardwellia sublimis*, is used for furniture. Two species of *Macadamia* produce the Macadamia nut. Many species are now common as garden plants, especially since their abundant nectar attracts native birds.

Botany: The flowers have 4 perianth segments and no calyx. There are 4 stamens, each attached to a perianth segment. There is a single style, with a sticky disc around the stigma at its tip. The flowers are usually in pairs.

The flowers are pollinated mainly by bees or honey-eaters. The method is unusual: before the flower opens the anthers deposit their pollen on the sticky style. Bees are attracted by nectar which exudes from cup-shaped nectaries just below the ovary. While collecting the nectar the bees naturally cling to the style and the pollen is brushed onto their leg hairs. The stigma is not ready to receive the pollen for some time, during which visitors gradually remove all the pollen, but some may remain to cause self-pollination.

• *Banksia* Carl von Linné
Honeysuckle
A genus of 72 species, all endemic except for one that extends to NG.

Botany: *Banksia* is distinguished from other Proteaceae by the dense flower spikes and distinctive woody follicles.

The flowers are attached to a woody axis that expands and clasps the woody fruits (called follicles) at maturity. Each follicle has two valves which protect two small winged seeds. These are stored on the tree for a year or more. If the tree dies or the follicles are stimulated by fire they open and release the seeds. All except *B. serrata* and *B. aemula* (which regenerate from stem-buds and lignotubers) are killed by

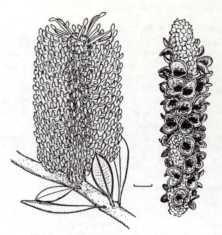

Banksia spike and cone *(B. integrifolia)*

severe burning and depend on seeds for regeneration. Hence fires in close succession can destroy Banksias in an area.

Banksias are abundant nectar producers. One spellbound nineteenth century English commentator wrote: 'It is so abundant in *B. ericifolia* and *B. collina* that when in flower the ground underneath large cultivated plants is in a complete state of puddle; bees and wasps become intoxicated, and many lose their lives in it.'[3]

Banksias and mammal pollinators: Although honey-eaters visit all Banksias several local species are also visited by small nectar-feeding mammals. Recent studies have shown these mammals are more efficient pollinators than the birds. The species are: *B. ericifolia, B. spinulosa, B. paludosa, B. robur* and *B. oblongifolia*. The mammals are Brown Antichinus (*Antichinus stuartii*), the Eastern Pigmy Possum (*Cercartetus nanus*) and the Sugar Glider (*Petaurus breviceps*).

Uses: Aborigines were reported to suck the nectar from Banksia flowers (e.g. *B. ericifolia* at Jervis Bay) or soak them in water to produce a sweet beverage. Europeans were attracted by the fine grain and rich red colour of the timber. Large species have been cut for furniture, decorative work, boats (*B. serrata*) and biplane construction (*B. integrifolia*).

There is even a colonial record that 'The smaller and barren cones being porous, were used with fat by the bushmen in the early days of the colony, as night lights'.

Banksias and popular culture: *Banksia* spikes have been frequently depicted in art and decoration, notably in the paintings and woodblocks of Margaret Preston. The withered spikes have been immortalised as the evil 'Banksia-men' in May Gibbs' *Snugglepot and Cuddlepie* stories.

Name: Named by Carl von Linné (the son of Linnaeus) in honour of Joseph Banks, who provided him with specimens from Botany Bay.

Banksia aemula R. Brown

(previously *B. serratifolia*) **Ss, Castl**
A hardy coastal shrub to 4m high but often dwarfed to 1m
in exposed coastal heaths (e.g. Malabar). It also crops up
as a tall shrub (to 7m high) in the sand dune country at
Agnes Banks near Richmond. Its main interest is its local
rarity and its similarity to *B. serrata* (the stigmas are the only
reliable distinguishing feature—see illustration).

Range: from NSW to southern Qld, very common on the northern NSW
coast. **Leaves:** generally a little smaller and slimmer than *B. serrata*.
Spikes: YELLOWISH GREEN, about 10cm high. **Flowering time:** April-
May. **Name:** *aemula* = Lat. vying with, in allusion to its close affinity
to *B. serrata*.

Banksia ericifolia Carl von Linné

Heath-leaved Banksia, Lantern Banksia **Ss**
A rounded shrub 2-5m high, usually abundant in heaths and
woodlands. 'There is, I think, no more decorative plant in
the bush than this particular banksia, when the bottle brushes
are newly-opened and the little hooked styles are deep red
with yellow tips. A bunch of them arranged with their own
green in a big bronze jar is a sight to gladden a whole
household . . . '.[4]

    This is one of the most important species for nectar feeding
birds such as honeyeaters because it carries a heavy load
of blossom in the otherwise lean winter months. Small birds
may disappear from areas where *B. ericifolia* has been killed
by fire.

Range: coastal NSW, southern tablelands and Blue Mountains **Leaves:**
tiny, crowded. **Spikes:** ORANGE, to 20cm high with hooked red to
black styles. **Flowering time:** winter (April-August). **Name:** *ericifolia*
= *Erica*-leaved (*Erica* is the European Heath or Heather).

Banksia integrifolia

—See COASTAL AND ESTUARINE SPECIES.

Banksia marginata Cavanilles

Silver Banksia **Ss**
A rounded shrub or small tree to 6m high which has a rather
scattered distribution in heaths and woodland in the Sydney
area. Its fine beefy-red timber has been used for cabinet-
making.

Range: A widespread species, ranging from SA, through Vic to northern
NSW. **Leaves:** small, white below, and oblong with very variable
numbers of teeth. Most leaves on large specimens are untoothed. The
juvenile leaves are deeply and evenly toothed. **Spikes:** YELLOW, usually
about 8cm high, with straight styles. **Flowering time:** February-June.
Name: *marginata* = the Spanish botanist Cavanilles used the name to
draw attention to the down-curled leaf margins, though this is not a
very notable or distinctive feature.

Banksia oblongifolia Cavanilles

(previously *B. asplenifolia*) **Ss, Castl**
A spreading shrub to 0.5m (in heath) or 2m (in woodland).
Fairly common in the area.

Range: from the Sydney area along the coast to Qld.
Leaves: stiff, leathery, variably toothed, covered when young in a thick
rusty felt which is retained on the main underside vein of mature leaves.
Spikes: PALE YELLOW to 10cm high, with a yellowish style. **Flowering
time:** March-July. **Name:** *oblongifolia* = oblong-leaved.

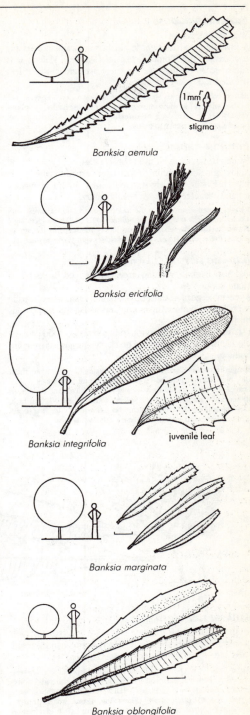

Banksia aemula

1mm
stigma

Banksia ericifolia

Banksia integrifolia

juvenile leaf

Banksia marginata

Banksia oblongifolia

Banksia paludosa R. Brown

Swamp Banksia **Ss**

A low shrub to 1m high, found in wet heathland. Locally restricted to the Woronora Plateau (Maddens Plains). It is similar to *B. oblongifolia*, but the leaves are more or less whorled and lack visible hairs.

Range: coast and ranges south from the Sydney region. **Leaves:** stiff, toothed, white below with a microscopic felt, otherwise hairless. **Spikes:** YELLOWISH, to 10cm long. **Flowering time:** April-August. **Name:** *paludosa* = Lat. pertaining to swamps.

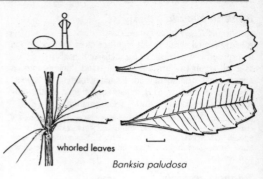

whorled leaves

Banksia paludosa

Banksia robur Cavanilles

Swamp Banksia, Large-leaved Banskia **Ss**

A low spreading shrub to 1m high, extraordinary for its immense, stiff, coarsely serrated leaves. Found in marshy ground near creeks in open heath country.

Range: coastal districts from the Sydney area to Qld. **Leaves:** with a dense rusty felty undersurface. **Spikes:** GREY-GREEN, to 15cm high. **Flowering time:** late summer (January-July). **Name:** *robur* = Lat. strong, refering to the tough leaves. **Note:** hybridises with *B. oblongifolia*.

Banksia serrata Carl von Linné

Old Man Banksia, Wattung-urree, Saw-toothed Banksia, Red Honeysuckle **Ss**

A venerable, gnarled, thick-trunked shrub or small tree, usually 4-8m high. Common in heaths and forests on sandy soils in coastal areas.

It carries large underground lignotubers, food storage mechanisms which also allow quick regeneration after severe burning.

Range: in coastal districts from Wilsons Promontory, Vic, to southern Qld, only extending inland on the sandstones of the Sydney region. **Leaves:** are large, stiff, leathery, evenly serrated, glossy and dark green above; dull, pale green below. **Spikes:** GREY-GREEN, 10-15cm high. **Flowering time:** December-March. **Name:** *serrata* = Lat. saw-edged. *Wattung-urree* is an Aboriginal name from the Sydney area.

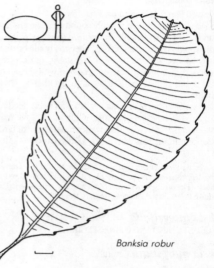

Banksia robur

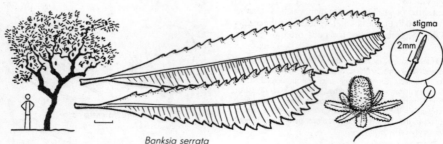

Banksia serrata

stigma

2mm

Banksia spinulosa Smith

Hair-pin Banksia **Ss, Castl**

An erect rounded shrub to 2m high, very common in sheltered woodland. It is an indicator of moist conditions.

Range: from Vic to Qld in mountains and coastal woodlands. **Leaves:** very narrow, fairly stiff and tough, toothed on the upper half and concave beneath. **Spikes:** to 15cm high, GOLDEN YELLOW to ORANGE with hooked red to black styles. **Flowering time:** winter (March-September). **Name:** *spinulosa* = Lat. spinula, a small spine, in reference

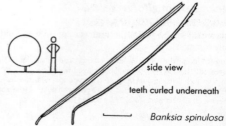

side view

teeth curled underneath

Banksia spinulosa

to the spiny appearance of the plant. Common name from the stiff black hooked styles. *Wattangre* is an Aboriginal name from Port Jackson: the name seems the same as for *B. serrata*, so perhaps it was a general name for Banksias.

• *Conospermum* Smith

Cone-seed, Smoke Bush

A genus with 38 endemic species, distributed in all states except NT. Most species are in WA where it is known as Smoke Bush.

Conospermum flower

fruit

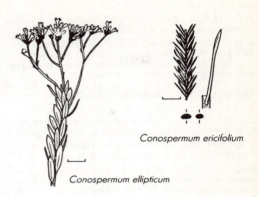

Conospermum ellipticum

Conospermum ericifolium

This is an highly modified genus with no obvious similarity to any other members of the family. The flower forms a tube with 2 lips. There are only 3 anthers, and 2 of these have only 1 cell (instead of 2). The fruit is a tiny upside-down cone with a fringe of silky hairs, containing a single seed. A. G. Hamilton explained the unusual method of pollination. 'Conospermum is remarkable for having sensitive anthers. The style lies behind them, and is held up by them. At a certain stage, if a bee inserts its proboscis, the anthers burst open and throw the pollen downwards on the insect. At the same time, the elasticity of the style brings it down, so that any future visitor will have to push under it to reach the nectary.'[5]

Name: *Conospermum* = Lat. cone-seed.

Conospermum ellipticum Smith

Ss

A slender erect shrub 50-100cm tall, common in the area in heath and woodland on sandstone.

Leaves: flat, more or less oblong, erect. **Flowers:** WHITE. **Flowering time:** early spring (from June). **Name:** *ellipticum* = elliptical, of the leaves.

Conospermum ericifolium Smith

Ss

A slender erect shrub 50-100cm tall, common in the area in heath and woodland on sandstone.

Leaves: tiny, slender, erect, 5-15mm long. **Flowers:** WHITE. **Flowering time:** early spring (from June). **Name:** *ericifolium* = *Erica*-leaved. *Erica* is the European Heath or Heather.

Conospermum longifolium
Smith **ssp.** *longifolium*

Ss

A slender erect shrub to 1-1.5m tall. Common in the area in heath and woodland on sandstone.

Range: restricted to coastal districts in the Sydney area mostly north of Port Jackson, and the Blue Mountains. **Leaves:** erect, broad, tapering gradually to the base, 10-20cm long. **Flowers:** WHITE. **Flowering time:** July-November. **Name:** *longifolia* = Lat. long-leaved.

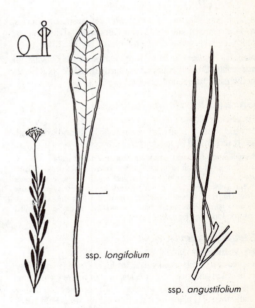

ssp. *longifolium*

ssp. *angustifolium*

Conospermum longifolium

Conospermum longifolium
ssp. *angustifolium*

(Meisner) Johnson & McGillivray

Ss

A slender erect shrub to 50-100cm tall. Common in heath and woodland on sandstone.

Range: coastal districts in the Sydney Region, mostly south of Port Jackson. **Leaves:** erect, slender, sinuous, 10-20cm long. **Flowers:** WHITE. **Name:** *angustifolium* = Lat. narrow-leaved.

Conospermum taxifolium Smith
Ss

A slender erect shrub 50-100cm tall, common in the area in heath and woodland on sandstone.

Range (of the *C. taxifolium* complex): NSW coast and ranges, Vic, Tas and Qld. **Leaves:** slender, erect, 10-30mm long. **Flowers:** WHITE. Flowering time: July-October. **Name:** *taxifolium* = *Taxus*-leaved. *Taxus* is the genus of Northern Hemisphere Yew trees.

Conospermum tenuifolium R. Brown
Grass-leaved Conospermum **Ss**

A shrub with prostrate main stems and ascending branches, to 1m long. It forms tangled grass-like masses in damp, low-lying situations in heath and woodland on sandstone. The least common of the local species.

Range: mainly coastal parts of the Sydney area and Blue Mountains. **Leaves:** erect, slender, sinuous, often about 20cm long, arising from a prostrate stem. **Flowers:** SKY BLUE. **Flowering time:** September-January. **Name:** *tenuifolium* = Lat. thin-leaved.

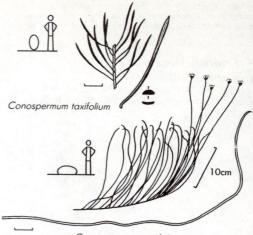
Conospermum taxifolium

Conospermum tenuifolium

• *Grevillea* R. Brown ex Salisbury

A large genus mainly of shrubs with 250 Australian species, and others extending to NG, New Caledonia and the Celebes. Much loved by gardeners for their floral beauty.

Name: *Grevillea* = in honour of Charles Francis Greville, an aristocratic English collector and propagator of NSW plants in the early nineteenth century.

Grevillea buxifolia (Smith) R. Brown
Grey Spider Flower **Ss**

An erect shrub to 1.5m high, common in heath and woodland. Easily recognised by its grey hairy flowers.

Range: mostly restricted to sandstones on the Sydney region. **Leaves:** rounded or oblong, hard and stiff with a flattened layer of silvery hairs underneath. **Flowers:** in dense terminal heads, all covered in dense RUSTY hairs, the inside of the flowers being densely grey hairy. **Flowering time:** August-November. **Name:** *buxifolia* = Lat. Box-leaved. *Buxus sempervirens* is the European Common Box. Its timber was called Box-wood and used for making boxes.

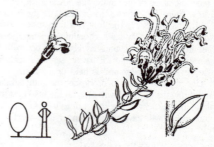
Grevillea buxifolia

Grevillea caleyi R. Brown
Ss Vulnerable 2VCi

A spreading shrub usually to 2.5m high, covered with rusty hairs. A tall and beautiful species, one of the few truly rare and endangered plants in the area. The species has a very small range and plans for the expansion of Mona Vale Road, if carried out, would destroy about 70% of the known plants. The restricted range is due to its preference for an equally restricted soil type, a deeply eroded Narrabeen shale.

The flowers often produce so much nectar that it may readily be sucked out.

Range: restricted to two hilltops in the Terry Hills area (it can be seen around the Baha'i temple) and in a few other small relic groups nearby. **Leaves:** deeply lobed, covered with dense soft rusty hairs. **Flowers:** in combs, grey, finely furry, styles DARK RED. **Flowering time:** October-December. **Name:** by Robert Brown, after George Caley, Banks' botanical agent in NSW. Brown and Caley collected together during Brown's 1803 visit.

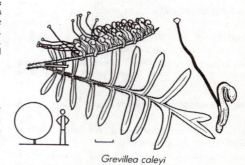
Grevillea caleyi

Grevillea diffusa Sieber ex Sprengel **ssp. *diffusa***
(previously *G. capitellata*) **Ss**

A low spreading shrub to 1.5m high. Moderately common in heath and scrubland. This is a variable species with a two different forms in the area.

1 • Menai-Holdsworthy, and south to Appin, is a form with hairy leaves giving it a silky-grey appearance, to 50cm high.

2 • Above Wollongong is the 'Bulli' form, to 50cm tall, with longer leaves and longer hairs and a rather shaggy appearance.

Range: from the Royal National Park to the Appin and Illawarra areas.
Leaves: slender, under 7cm long, with a flattened layer of silvery hairs
below and often sharply recurved margins. **Flowers:** RED, all covered
in fine hairs. The inside of the flower has fine dense hairs. **Flowering
time:** July-November. **Name:** *diffusa* = loosely spreading, referring to
the habit.

Grevillea juniperina R. Brown

Ss, Cumb, Castl

A prickly much-branched shrub 1-2m high. A locally
uncommon species, found in open forest on clay soils on
the Cumberland Plain. A popular garden shrub with many
cultivated varieties.

Range: NSW coast and ranges, mainly in mountain districts. **Leaves:**
crowded, stiff, pungent-pointed, with revolute margins (curled
underneath). **Flowers:** in short clusters (umbels) at the ends of
branches, YELLOWISH GREEN to RED. **Flowering time:** September-
November. **Name:** *juniperina* = Lat. Juniper-like. Juniper is a prickly
small-leaved European Conifer.

Grevillea linearifolia (Cavanilles) Druce

(now includes *G. parviflora*)
White spider flower **Ss**

A graceful slender spreading shrub usually to 2m high (in
the Sydney sandstone form). Found in heath and woodland.
The species represents a complex of forms stretching from
Vic to Qld, of which 3 occur in the Sydney area.
1 • Sydney sandstone form (illustrated) with white flowers,
only found north of the harbour.
2 • Royal National Park to southern tablelands; flowers mainly
pink-red and, just to confuse things, a longer style, about
the same length as *G. sericea.*
3 • a clay species usually under 1m high, found in the upper
Georges River, Maroota and Arcadia areas with much shorter
leaves with strongly curled margins and pink to purple flowers.

Leaves: 1 and **2:** long, slender, with a layer of silver-silky hairs below.
3: short with strongly curled margins. **Flowers: 1:** WHITE, style usually
about 7mm long. **2:** RED (sometimes pink, purple or white), style over
10mm long. **3:** PINK-PURPLE, style under 10mm long. **Flowering time:**
July-October. **Name:** *linearifolia* = Lat. straight-leaved.

Grevillea longifolia R. Brown

Ss   Rare 2RC-

A medium-sized shrub 2-4m high, found on sheltered valley
sides on sandstone, usually close to creeks, but occasionally
on scrubby tops. It is common along the Woronora River,
also along the Georges River (Kentlyn) and scattered along
the southern rim of the Cumberland Plain. The leaves are
large, mostly deeply serrated, and silver below.

Range: restricted to the Sydney area. **Leaves:** long, broad, ranging from
deeply serrated to entire, with a silvery layer of appressed silky rusty
hairs below. **Flowers:** (similar to *G. caleyi*) in combs, grey, finely furry,
styles DARK RED. **Flowering time:** October-December. **Name:**
longifolia = Lat. long-leaved. **Similar species:** There is a closely related
species, *G. asplenifolia*, in the southern Blue Mountains. It has dull felty
rather than sheeny silky hairs on branchlets and leaf undersides, and
round rather than angular branchlets.

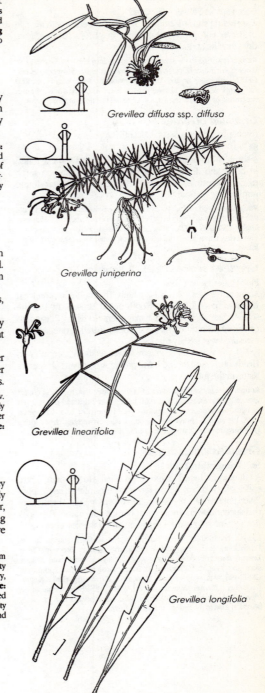

Grevillea diffusa ssp. *diffusa*

Grevillea juniperina

Grevillea linearifolia

Grevillea longifolia

Grevillea mucronulata R. Brown

Green Spider Flower **Ss, Castl**

A spreading shrub 1-2m high. A variable species with a range of flower colours and leaf forms, in various habitats, from dry sandy heath to rocky river banks.

Range: restricted to the sandstones of the Sydney region. **Leaves:** soft, covered in loose hairs, strongly hollow beneath. **Flowers:** usually GREEN with more or less red-brown markings, hairy, with bright RED to purplish style. **Flowering time:** April-October. **Name:** *mucronulata* = Lat. having a small hardened leaf tip (mucro).

Grevillea oleoides

(Sieber ex Schultes & son) McGillivray

Ss

A shrub to 2m or more high with brilliant red flowers, found in heath and dry woodland on sandstone. Common south of the harbour. It is closely related to *G. speciosa*, found north of the harbour.

Range: restricted to the Sydney region. **Leaves:** more than 5cm long, stiff, with a layer of silvery hairs below and recurved margins. **Flowers:** bright CRIMSON RED, in a short stalked axillary inflorescence. **Flowering time:** July-October. **Names:** *oleoides* = like an olive, of the leaves.

Grevillea sericea (Smith) R. Brown

Pink Spider Flower **Ss**

An attractive heath shrub 1-2m high. The most common local *Grevillea* species. William Woolls noted 'Brown says that the style is half an inch, and I may mention as an illustration of the uniformity of nature's works, that the one which I measured was exactly that length.'[6]

A form with stiff pungent leaves is fairly common in Heathcote National Park. It will probably be given sub-species status in the future.

Range: throughout the sandstones of the Sydney area, mainly in coastal districts. **Leaves:** tough, stiff, with hard pointed tips and downcurved margins, silver underneath with a layer of fine silky hairs. **Flowers:** PINK, the style is always over 12 mm long. **Flowering time:** spring (July-November). **Name:** *sericea* = Lat. silky

Grevillea shiressii Blakely

Ss Vulnerable 2VCit

A tall graceful broad-leaved shrub usually to 3m high. A rare species known only from a few tributaries of the Hawkesbury River. Found near creeks in gullies on sandy soils. The delicate translucent flowers are unusual because the anther-cup does not split into the usual 4 segments when the flower opens.

Range: confined to a few valleys on the northern shores on the Hawkesbury River, e.g. Mullet Creek and Mooney Mooney Creek. **Leaves:** distinguished by prominent intra-marginal veins some distance from the margins. **Flowers:** delicate, translucent, pale purple or GREENISH with purple-brown markings. **Flowering time:** August-December. **Name:** *shiressii* = named by W.F. Blakely in honour of his friend David Shiress, an accountant, who accompanied him on many botanical trips in the Sydney area in the 1920s.

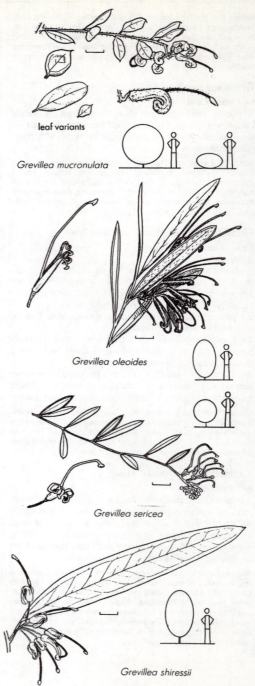

leaf variants

Grevillea mucronulata

Grevillea oleoides

Grevillea sericea

Grevillea shiressii

Grevillea speciosa (Knight) McGillivray

(previously *G. punicea*)
Red Spider Flower **Ss**
A shrub to 1.5m high with brilliant red flowers, found in heath and woodland on sandstone. Common north of the harbour.

Range: restricted to the Sydney region. **Leaves:** less than 5cm long, stiff, with a layer of silvery hairs below and recurved margins. **Flowers:** bright CRIMSON RED, in a conspicuously stalked terminal inflorescence. **Flowering time:** June-September. **Names:** *speciosa* = Lat. showy, of the flowers.

Grevillea speciosa

Grevillea sphacelata R. Brown

Grey Spider Flower **Ss**
An erect shrub to 1.5m high, common in dry heath and dry woodland. Like *G. buxifolia* but smaller in every part.

Range: mostly restricted to sandstones in the Sydney region. **Leaves:** more or less linear, small, hard and stiff with a flattened layer of silvery hairs underneath. **Flowers:** in dense terminal heads, all covered in dense GREYISH hairs, the inside of the flowers being densely rusty hairy. **Flowering time:** August-November. **Name:** *sphacelata* = Lat. withered.

Grevillea sphacelata

• *Hakea* Schrader

A genus with about 125 species, all Australian (about 23 in NSW). 'This genus appears to me to be one of the most useless of the Proteaceae,' wrote William Woolls.[7]

The fruit is a dense woody follicle, often rough and knobbly, with a swollen projection (called a beak) which is often armed with 2 sharp projections or 'horns' (these are the swollen woody remains of nectar glands). The fruit splits open after fire or death of the plant, to release 2 seeds each with a fibrous wing. There are 2 semi-circular nectar glands in the base of each flower. Some species are bird pollinated (e.g. *H. bakerana*), but most local species have tiny pale flowers and are pollinated by insects.

Hakeas are killed by severe fire, but readily regenerate from seed stored on the branches.

Name: *Hakea* = named by the German botanist Heinrich Schrader (1767-1836) in honour of his patron, Baron Hake of Hanover. The early writer Louisa Anne Meredith called it 'Porcupine-Tree'.

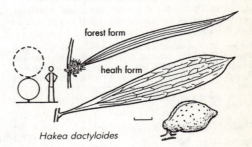

Hakea bakerana

Hakea bakerana F. Mueller & Maiden

Ss
A prickly shrub usually about 2m high, found in heath and woodland north of the harbour.

Range: northern Sydney to NSW north coast. **Leaves:** more or less hairless, swollen compared to those of *H. sericea*, mostly 5-7cm long, just over 1mm diameter. **Flowers:** REDDISH-PINK, 8-15mm long, style 40-50mm long. **Fruit:** large, very rugged, with 2 horns. **Flowering time:** May-July. **Name:** *bakerana* = named by Ferdinand von Mueller and J. H. Maiden after their colleague and friend, the economic botanist R. T. Baker (1854-1941) who succeeded Maiden as curator of the Sydney Technological Museum in 1888. Baker's research and encouragement did much to establish the Eucalyptus oil industry.

forest form

heath form

Hakea dactyloides

Hakea dactyloides (Gaertner) Cavanilles

Finger Hakea, Broad-leaved Hakea
Ss, Cumb, Castl
A shrub to 1.5m (heath) or 4m (forest). A common species, widely distributed in heaths and dry forests on sandy soils. The leaves vary according to the habit: the heath form has wider, tougher leaves and more prominent net-veins than the forest form.

Range: from the extreme north of Vic (rare) to southern Qld; extending inland to the western slopes of NSW. **Leaves:** stiff, tough, with 3 main veins and prominent net-veins. **Flowers:** tiny, WHITE, numerous in clusters in the leaf-joints. **Fruit:** smooth except for tiny tubercles, with a short point. **Flowering time:** September-October. **Name:** *dactyloides* = finger-like, referring to the leaves.

Hakea gibbosa (Smith) Cavanilles

Ss

A grotesque prickly shrub to 2m high, found mainly in heathy country near the coast. The new stem and leaves are densely covered with loose white hairs, giving the plant a frosty look. The incredibly dense foliage consists of a solid mass of intermingled spines and generally looks less like a plant than an alien in a B-grade movie.

Range: restricted to the Sydney region. **Leaves:** covered in fine hairs, at least when young, 4-8cm long, a little over 1mm diameter. **Flowers:** CREAM, 5-6mm long before opening. **Fruit:** rugged, with 2 horns. **Flowering time:** June-September. **Name:** *gibbosa* = having a short blunt spur, or beak, referring to the fruit.

Hakea propinqua A. Cunningham

Ss

A prickly shrub to 2m high with very large warty fruits. Found in heath and woodland, mainly north of the harbour.

Range: Sydney region and Blue Mountains. **Leaves:** swollen, 1.5-2mm diameter, 2-4cm long, covered by minute raised white vesicles. **Flowers:** PALE YELLOW, similar to *H. sericea.* **Flowering time:** June-October. **Fruit:** rugged, with a short blunt point but no horns. **Name:** *propinqua* = Lat. allied; Cunningham thought it was nearly allied to *H. nodosa.*

Hakea salicifolia (Ventenat) B. L. Burtt.

Willow-leaved Hakea **Ss**

A broadleaved tall willowy shrub or small tree, found in moist sheltered gullies on sandstone. The tallest member of the genus.

Range: in coast and mountains from southern NSW to Qld. Also planted in gardens. **Leaves:** drooping, hairless, but shoots silky, to 12cm, mid-vein only prominent. **Flowers:** tiny, WHITE, 12mm long, in dense clusters. **Fruit:** silvery grey with black warts, and 2 small horns. **Flowering time:** September-November. **Name:** *salicifolia* = Lat. willow-leaved.

Hakea sericea Schrader

Bushy Needlebush **Ss, Cumb, Castl**

A prickly shrub usually 2-3m high. The most abundant local species, widely distributed in heathy scrubs and woodland, especially south of the harbour. Also found on clay soils on the Cumberland Plain.

Range: coast and mountains from Tas to the north coast of NSW. **Leaves:** slender and needle-like, cylindrical, stiff, pungent-pointed, just under 1mm diameter, finely hairy when new, otherwise hairless, 3-5cm long. **Flowers:** tiny, pale YELLOW, in clusters at the leaf-joints. **Flowering time:** June-September. **Fruit:** a dense woody follicle, rough and knobbly, with two sharp horns. **Name:** *sericea* = Lat. silky, referring to the hairs on new leaves.

Hakea teretifolia (Salisbury) J. Britten

Dagger Hakea **Ss**

A stiff prickly shrub, usually to 1m high, very abundant in low moist heaths on the NSW coast and tablelands. The common name comes from shape of fruit—though people would be forgiven for thinking it comes from the leaves.

Range: from Tas to the NSW north coast. **Leaves:** stiff and needle-sharp, 1.5-2mm diameter. **Flowers:** small, WHITE, 4-6mm long before opening, silky-hairy. **Flowering time:** January-April. **Fruit:** narrow, with a rather devilish appearance. **Name:** *teretifolia* = Lat. cylindrical-leaved.

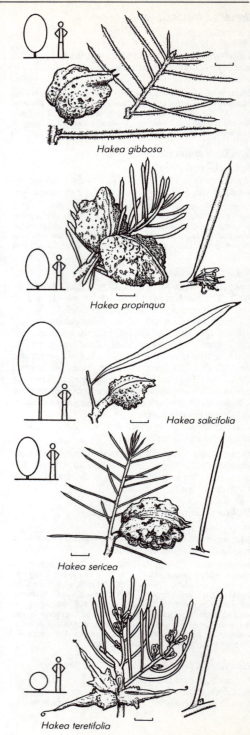

Hakea gibbosa

Hakea propinqua

Hakea salicifolia

Hakea sericea

Hakea teretifolia

• *Isopogon* R. Brown ex Knight

Drumsticks

A genus of 35 species, all endemic, distributed in all states except NT. Both local species are common in the area and frequently occur together.

After flowering the inflorescence develops into a spherical woody cone which gives the plant its common name. The cone is made up of scales clothed in pale fur. These scales are really the fruits. If the plant dies or is burnt, the cone disintegrates and the individual fruits fly away with some force.

Name: *Isopogon* = equal-bearded, referring to the hairy fruits.

Isopogon anemonifolius (Salisbury) Knight

Ss, Castl

A shrub usually 1-1.5m high, mainly restricted to heath shrublands.

Range: coast and mountains from southern NSW to Qld. **Leaves:** subdivided into narrow flat segments, fairly hard and tough. **Flowers:** YELLOW, arising from a dense globular mass of furry protective bracts. **Flowering time:** September-November. **Name:** *anemonifolius* = *Anemone*-leaved (*Anemone* is a genus of daisies).

Isopogon anethifolius (Salisbury) Knight

Ss, Castl

Similar to *I. anemonifolius*, except for the leaves. It has a wider habitat range, often occuring in sheltered forest situations, where it is taller (to 3m) and has finer and more spreading leaf segments.

Range: more restricted than *I. anemonifolius*, being limited to the Sydney sandstones and to the southern NSW coast and ranges. **Leaves:** with slender cylindrical segments. **Flowers:** YELLOW, arising from a dense globular mass of furry protective bracts. **Flowering time:** September-November. **Name:** *anethifolius* = *Anethum*-leaved; *Anethum graveolens* is Dill.

• *Lambertia* Smith

An endemic genus of 9 species, 8 in south-western WA and 1 in the Sydney region.

Name: *Lambertia* = named by James Smith, president of the Linnean Society, in honour of his friend Aylmer Bourke Lambert (1761-1842), English botanist and vice-president of the Linnean Society. J.H. Maiden describes Lambert as 'a wealthy and cultured patron of botany, who busied himself in collecting Australian herbarium specimens and raising Australian plants. His herbarium was second only in importance to that of Sir J. Banks, but it was broken up on his death'.[8]

Lambertia formosa Smith

Mountain Devils   **Ss**

A spreading prickly shrub to 1.5m high. Common in the Sydney region, abounding in heath scrubs and dry forest understories. Second only to Dagger Hakea in sheer spikyness. The long red flowers are designed for bird pollination. It was originally named *Protea nectarina*, from the amount of honey it contains. The woody fruits can sometimes be seen in tourist shops in the Blue Mountains dressed up as little devils.

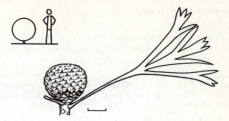

Isopogon anemonifolius

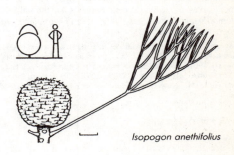

Isopogon anethifolius

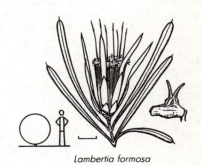

Lambertia formosa

Range: mainly restricted to the sandstones of the Sydney region. **Leaves:** olive-green, hard, stiff, in whorls of 3, hollow below, tapering gradually to the base and with a very sharp point. **Flowers:** 7 in a spectacular, dense terminal cluster, brilliant red, surrounded by numerous orange-green bracts. **Fruit:** woody, with two long projections, resembling a little devil with horns. **Flowering time:** much of the year, but especially September-May. **Name:** *formosa* = Lat. beautiful.

• *Lomatia* R. Br.

A highly varied endemic genus of 8 species. The flowers and fruits of both the local species are similar although their leaves and habits could hardly be more different.

Name: *Lomatia* = Gk. *loma*, a fringe or border, referring to the seed-wing.

Lomatia myricoides (Gaertner f.) Domin

River Lomatia **Ss**

A tall shrub to 4m high with dense, somewhat drooping foliage. Common along creek banks in gullies, shadowing the waters but not actually getting its feet wet.

Range: Coast and ranges north from Vic to the Sydney area. **Leaves:** to 20cm long, hard and smooth, ranging from entire to deeply toothed. **Flowers:** WHITE, similar to *L. silaifolia*. **Flowering time:** December-January. **Name:** *myricoides* = resembling *Myrica*, Wax Myrtles.

Lomatia silaifolia (Smith) R. Brown

Crinkle Bush **Ss**

A low shrub with rigid, highly divided leaves, forming a tuft at ground level. A common understorey plant in dry forests. At flowering time a tall straight inflorescence rises to about a metre above the leaves. In earlier times it had the unlikely common name of 'wild parsely' because of the segmented leaves.

Range: on coast, mountains and slopes from the Sydney region to Qld. **Leaves:** stiff, tough, divided 2 or 3 times into toothed segments. **Flowers:** WHITE, *Grevillea*-like, in an erect inflorescence much taller than the leaves. **Fruit:** a woody follicle which splits to reveal 2 rows of winged seeds. **Flowering time:** November-February. **Name:** *silai* = Lat. finely cut leaf.

• *Persoonia* Smith

Geebungs

An endemic genus with 42 species, distributed in all states except NT. Persoonias are shrubs with small yellow flowers and diverse leaf shapes, important in the understorey and shrub layer of woodlands. Their fruit is edible and formed part of the diet of local Aborigines. It was also said to be

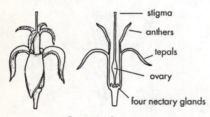

Persoonia flower

a popular bush fruit with European children. The fruit is astringent until it turns purple, at which time the skin can be broken and the flesh is sweet. The best fruit is found lying on the ground. Unfortunately, however, the ripe fruits are almost always consumed by birds or ants.

Name: *Persoonia* = in honour of the Dutch botanist Christiaan Henrick Persoon (1755-1837), for his work on Fungi.

It's not clear whether the common name *Geebung* is an Aboriginal name or a name used by European children. It was certainly in use from an early time; Peter Cunningham in 1827 wrote 'The Jibbong is another tasteless fruit, as well as the five corners, much relished by children.'[9] George Bennet in 1833 refered to 'the yellow flowers of the native *Jibbong*'.[10]

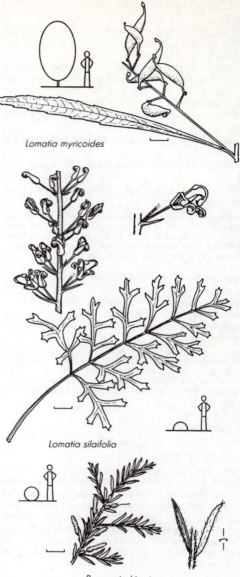

Lomatia myricoides

Lomatia silaifolia

Persoonia hirsuta

Persoonia hirsuta Persoon

A Geebung **Ss Poorly known 3KCi**

A spreading shrub to 1m high, covered in rusty hairs. Found in heath and woodland on sandstone. Rare.

Range: from the Georges River to Gosford. **Leaves:** small, crowded, covered in rusty hairs, with revolute margins. **Flowers:** GOLDEN YELLOW, very hairy. **Flowering time:** November-January. **Name:** *hirsuta* = Lat. stiffly hairy.

Persoonia isophylla L. Johnson & P. Weston

Ss

A spreading shrub to 2m with similar leaves to *P. pinifolia*. Common north of the Hawkesbury, extending as far south as Frenchs Forest.

Range: Restricted to northern coastal plateaus in the Sydney area. **Leaves:** 15-25mm long. **Flowers:** similar to *P. pinifolia* except the inflorescence leaves are not reduced in size and the inflorescence continues into a leafy shoot. **Flowering time:** spring. **Name:** *isophylla* = Gk. equal-leaved, referring to the inflorescence leaves being as long as the stem leaves.

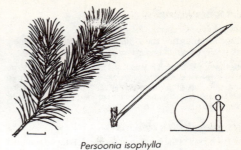

Persoonia isophylla

Persoonia lanceolata Andrews **ssp. *lanceolata***

A Geebung **Ss**

A bushy erect shrub to 2m high, common in heath. The leaves are often yellowish.

Range: restricted to the Sydney area and Blue Mountains, extending north on the coast. **Leaves:** flat, stiff, bright green or yellowish. **Flowers:** GOLDEN YELLOW. **Flowering time:** summer (much of the year). **Name:** *lanceolata* = Lat. lance-shaped, of the leaves.

Persoonia lanceolata

Persoonia laurina Persoon **ssp. *laurina***

Golden Geebung **Ss, Castl**

A low spreading shrub to 1m high, widespread in woodlands. Found on both sandstone and shale. Relatively common but easily missed as it shelters amongst taller shrubs. Memorable from the rich golden felt that covers the flowers.

Range: mainly restricted to the Sydney region. **Leaves:** opposite, thick and leathery, not rigid, veins just visible, with a hard tip. **Flowers:** very attractive, in short clusters in the leaf joints, covered in a rich dense cloak of GOLDEN-RUSTY hairs. **Flowering time:** October-December. **Name:** *laurina* = resembling a Laurel, of the leaves. **Note:** *P. laurina* **ssp. *intermedia***, a similar shrub, has been recorded from the upper Georges River (east of Leumeah). It is distinguished by scabrous (rough) leaves.

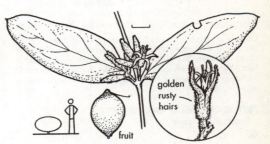

golden rusty hairs

fruit

Persoonia laurina ssp. *laurina*

Persoonia laxa L. Johnson & P. Weston

Ss Extinct 2X (not illustrated)

A low, much-branched shrub related to *P. nutans*, was collected early this century at Manly and Newport. As these were the only known locations it is now certainly extinct.

Persoonia levis (Cavanilles) Domin

Smooth Geebung **Ss**

A tall shrub usually about 4m high, common in heath and woodland. When it grows in open heath it is a small shrub usually under 1m high, with almost round leaves. The forest form is tall, with large long leaves. It has black flaky-papery bark which is brilliant red underneath. The large rich green leaves often look bizarre and out of place amongst the dull sclerophyll vegetation.

Range: coast and mountain districts from Vic to northern NSW. **Leaves:** somewhat thick and fleshy, rich green in colour, hairless, droopy, to 20cm long in the forest form (the heath form has shorter, broad, rounded leaves). **Flowers:** GOLDEN YELLOW. **Flowering time:** mainly September-November. **Name:** *levis* = Lat. smooth, referring to the leaves.

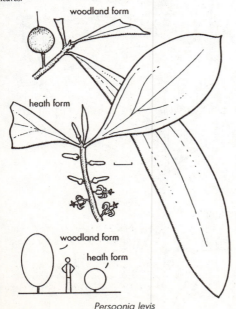

woodland form

heath form

woodland form

heath form

Persoonia levis

Persoonia linearis Andrews

Narrow-leaved Geebung Ss, Cumb, Castl

A large shrub usually about 3m high with dark flaky-papery bark. A very common understory shrub in many habitats.

Range: widely distributed in coastal and mountain forests from Vic to Qld. **Leaves:** variable, narrow, stiff, fairly crowded, not stiff, finely furry when young, dull, dark green. **Flowers:** GOLDEN YELLOW. **Flowering time:** December-July. **Name:** *linearis* = Lat. linear, i.e. thin and straight, of the leaves.

Persoonia levis x *linearis*

This is a hybrid of the 2 common species, it is found scattered in areas where both *P. levis* and *P. linearis* grow. All its characteristics are intermediate between those of the parent species. It's easily recognised as a tall willowy shrub (to 5m) with dense drooping foliage. It has the typical dark papery bark of the larger persoonias. Robert Brown collected a specimen, probably in Lane Cove Valley in 1803, and called it *P. lucida.*

Persoonia mollis ssp. *maxima*

S. Krauss & L. Johnson

Ss   Endangered 2EC

A tall shrub 2-5m high, found in sheltered woodland on sandy soils. Restricted to the Hornsby-Asquith-Cowan/Bobbin Creeks area. Only a few small populations are known. It is geographically isolated from other subspecies, but closely related to ssp. *mollis*, which is common in the Blue Mountains.

Range: restricted to the above area. **Leaves:** drawn out to a fine point, 6-12cm long, 10-17mm wide, soft, softly hairy on the undersurface when young. **Flowers:** YELLOW, densely covered in erect copper-coloured hairs. **Flowering time:** Late December-April. **Name:** *mollis* = Lat. soft, refering to leaves. *maxima* = Lat. greatest, since it is larger in all its parts than the other subspecies.

Persoonia mollis ssp. *nectens*

S. Krauss & L. Johnson

Ss

A shrub 1.2-3m high, found in moist sheltered sites in woodland on sandstone. Uncommon locally, recorded from the Royal National Park, O'Hares Creek and Loddon Falls.

Range: Woronora Plateau, from Loddon Falls and Sublime Point south to Hill Top. **Leaves:** 4-10cm long, 8-15mm wide, opposite or in 3s (whorled), pliable but not soft, finely silky-hairy on the undersurface. **Flowers:** YELLOW, sparsely covered in fine silky hairs. **Flowering time:** late December-April. **Name:** *nectens* = Lat. connecting, referring to its geographical and botanical relation to other subspecies.
Note: *Persoonia mollis* is a complex species which has recently been divided into 9 subspecies.[11] It ranges from narrow leaved forms in the Budawang Ranges and Jervis Bay to broad-leaved hairy forms in the Blue Mountains and Sydney.

Persoonia nutans R. Brown ssp. *nutans*

Cumb, Castl   Endangered 2E

An erect much-branched shrub to 1m high, found in open forest on clay soils and old alluviums on the Cumberland Plain. Closely related to the widespread *P. oxycoccoides.*

Range: restricted to the Cumberland Plain. **Leaves:** slender, with recurved margins, apparently hairless but with microscopic fine hairs on both sides. Stems finely hairy. **Flowers:** nodding, YELLOW, hairless, on fine stalks which are 5-12mm long and often sharply bent. **Flowering time:** December-March. **Name:** *nutans* = Lat. nodding, referring to the flowers.

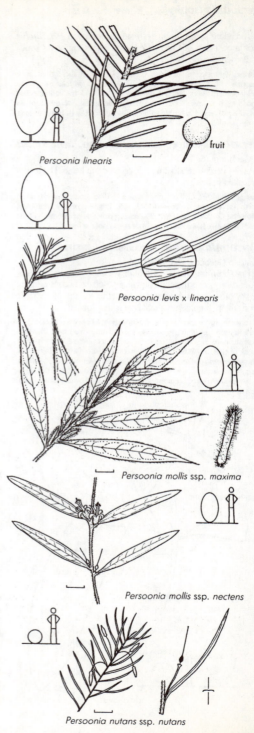

Persoonia linearis

fruit

Persoonia levis x linearis

Persoonia mollis ssp. maxima

Persoonia mollis ssp. nectens

Persoonia nutans ssp. nutans

Persoonia oblongata R. Brown

Ss

An erect shrub 1-2m high, found in dry woodland on sandstone. It occurs mainly north of the Hawkesbury, but extends south into the north-west of the area (e.g. Windsor, Sackville).

Range: northern parts of the Sydney region.   **Leaves:** 2-5cm long, bright green, flat, smooth, shiny, hairless, flexible, not thick, and with a short point.   **Flowers:** YELLOW, axillary, on long drooping slender stalks which are mostly 15-20mm long.   **Flowering time:** March-July.   **Name:** *oblongata* = Lat. oblong, of the leaf shape.

Persoonia pinifolia R. Brown

Pine-leaf Geebung   **Ss**

A spreading shrub 2-4m high, with crowded pine-like leaves. Very common in sheltered open forests on sandstone.

Range: restricted to the Sydney region.   **Leaves:** 30-50mm long, slender with a groove beneath. Note the floral leaves are much reduced in size. **Flowers:** GOLDEN YELLOW, crowded towards the ends of branches.   **Flowering time:** March-May.   **Name:** *pinifolia* = Lat. Pine-leaved.

• *Petrophile* R. Brown ex Knight

Cone-sticks

A genus of 42 species, all endemic, found in NSW, Qld, SA, and WA.

   Petrophile is closely related to *Isopogon* except that the floral tube splits to the base when the flower opens and the cones are egg-shaped with smooth scales.

Name: *Petrophile* = Lat. rock-loving, in allusion to the habitat of the first specimens described.

Petrophile pulchella (Schrader) R. Brown

(previously *P. fucifolia*)   **Ss, Castl**

A shrub to 2m high, found in dry heath and woodland on sandstone. Very common in the area. The leaves are almost identical to *Isopogon anethifolius* but the egg-shaped cones easily distinguish it.

Range: coast and mountains of NSW.   **Leaves:** with flexible segments all ascending in about the same direction. **Flowers:** YELLOW. **Flowering time:** mainly December-March.   **Name:** *pulchella* = Lat. *pulcher*, beautiful.

Petrophile sessilis

Sieber ex J. A. Schultes & son

Ss

A shrub to 2m high, found in dry heath and woodland on sandstone. Less common than *P. pulchella*. Easily distinguished by the rigid leaves and generally harsher appearance.

Range: coast and mountains south from the Sydney region.   **Leaves:** with stiff, sharply pointed segments spreading in all directions. **Flowers:** YELLOW.   **Flowering time:** mainly December-January.   **Name:** *sessilis* = stalk-less, of the fruit.

• *Stenocarpus*

—See Rainforest species.

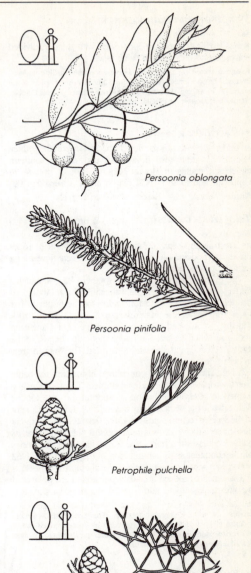

Persoonia oblongata

Persoonia pinifolia

Petrophile pulchella

Petrophile sessilis

• *Symphionema* R. Brown

An endemic genus of 2 species. The other species is *S. montanum*, with broad flat leaf segments, found in NSW mountain heaths.

Name: *Symphionema* = Gk. *symphyo*, to unite, *nema*, a thread, because the staminal filaments cling together at the top.

Symphionema paludosum R. Brown
Ss

A small delicate shrub to 30cm high with slender, divided leaves. Found only in open damp heath.

Range: restricted to coastal NSW. **Leaves:** opposite, usually cylindrical, divided 1, 2 or 3 times. **Flowers:** tiny, CREAM, in short spikes at the ends of ascending branches. **Flowering time:** August-October. **Name:** *paludosum* = Lat. pertaining to swamps.

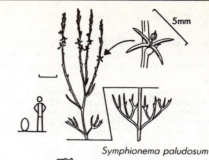

Symphionema paludosum

• *Telopea* R. Brown

An endemic genus of 4 species; *T. speciosissima* in the Sydney region, *T. mongaensis* in a small part of the southern tablelands, mainly in Morton National Park, *T. oreades* in Gippsland and southern NSW ranges, and *T. truncata* in Tas.

Name: *Telopea* = Gk. *Telopos*, perceived from afar.

Telopea speciosissima (Smith) R. Brown

Waratah **Ss**

An erect shrub usually 2-3m high. Usually found in rocky places in woodland on sandstone. A magnificent flower long valued for its exceptional beauty.

The Burragorang people in the southern Blue Mountains told a story of the origin of the Waratah: Krubi, an Aboriginal maiden, waited on a sandstone ridge for the return of her lover from battle. She was dressed in the red skin of a rock wallaby, ornamented with the red crests of a Gang-gang cockatoo. When he failed to return she willed herself to die and passed away into the sandstone ridge. The Waratah grew in her place.[12]

A little-known aspect of our cultural history was the battle over the choice of Australia's floral emblem. The Wattle League formed in 1911 in Melbourne to support the case for the Wattle, while the Waratah party was led by R. T. Baker, Curator of the Sydney Technological Museum. Despite some eloquent newspaper articles he was unsuccessful (he wrote that its name 'expresses the hope of all Australians that the glories of the continent shall light the rest of the world'). In 1962 however, it was chosen as the state floral emblem of NSW.

The flowers produce abundant nectar and are pollinated by birds. A lignotuber allows quick regeneration after fire.

Range: from Braidwood to the Hunter River, coast and mountains. **Leaves:** stiff, leathery, irregularly toothed. **Flowers:** CRIMSON RED in a dense globular inflorescence surrounded by prominent red bracts. **Flowering time:** September-October. **Name:** *speciosissima* = Lat. most beautiful. Waratah is an Aboriginal name.

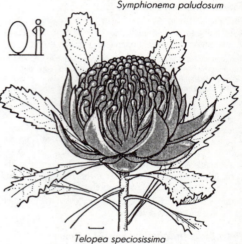

Telopea speciosissima

• *Xylomelum* Smith

An endemic genus of 5 species, distributed in south-western WA, eastern NSW and Qld.

Name: *Xylon* = Gk. woody-apple.

Xylomelum pyriforme Smith

Woody Pear, Meridja-courroo **Ss**

A tall shrub 2-4m high with soft flaky bark and attractive foliage. Widely distributed but not common around Sydney. Found on sandstone soils in sheltered forests. The far-famed "Wooden Pear" of Australia' was held up in colonial times as a typical example of the bizarre flora of the southern land.

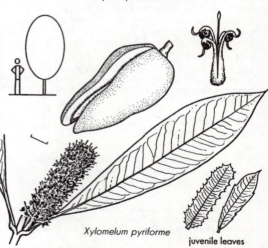

Xylomelum pyriforme

juvenile leaves

Range: coast and ranges from Picton to southern Qld. **Leaves:** opposite, fairly stiff and tough, hairless, glossy above, dull below, drawn out to a fine accuminate point, red when young, net veins prominent. Juvenile leaves are deeply toothed, adult leaves entire. **Flowers:** in dense rusty-furry spikes in the leaf joints. **Flowering time:** October-November. **Fruit:** a massive dense woody pear-shaped follicle. **Name:** *pyriforme* = Lat. pear-shaped. *Meridja-courro* is an Aboriginal name from the Sydney area.

EPACRIDACEAE

Southern Heaths

A southern or Gondwana family, distributed in Australia, South-east Asia and Argentina. Worldwide there are about 426 species in 31 genera. In Australia there are about 335 species in 28 genera.

The family is closely related to Ericaceae, the northern Heaths of Europe.

Botany: Epacrids are mostly small-leaved shrubs, tolerant of poor acidic soils and exposed places.

The leaves have parallel veins and are usually small and sharp pointed. The flowers are small, often hairy, protected by rows of scale-like bracts, with 5 scale-like sepals, a perianth tube ending in 5 lobes and 5 stamens attached to the inside of the perianth tube near the lip. A single style surmounts a superior ovary. The fruit is usually an edible drupe.

Some local species have been recorded with 'double flowers', i.e. where the stamens appear as deformed extra petals, a very unusual feature in native plants.

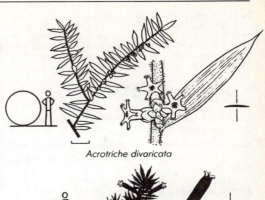

Acrotriche divaricata

• *Acrotriche* R. Brown (ac-ro-TRICK-ee)

An endemic genus of 14 species, distributed in all states.

Name: *Acrotriche* = *acro*, extremity, *triche*, hair, referring to the tufts of hair on the tips of the perianth segments.

Acrotriche divaricata R. Brown **Ss**

A prickly spreading shrub to 2m high, found scattered in sheltered places in woodland on sandstone. An uncommon species in this area.

Range: coast and ranges from Vic to Qld. **Leaves:** flat, pungent, usually dark green. **Flowers:** GREEN, about 1mm long, with tufts of hairs in the throat and at the tips of the segments. **Flowering time:** July-September. **Name:** *divaricata* = Lat. straggling and much branched.

Astroloma humifusum

• *Astroloma* R. Brown

An endemic genus of 18 species, distributed in all states except Qld.

Name: *Astroloma* = Gk. *astron*, a star, *loma*, a fringe, referring to the tufts of hair inside the floral tube.

Astroloma humifusum (Cavanilles) R. Brown

Cranberry Heath **Ss, Cumb, Castl**

A small shrub to 15cm high forming dense prickly cushions in exposed rocky places. Maiden wrote that the fruits were 'much appreciated by schoolboys and aboriginals . . . They have a viscid, sweetish pulp, and a relatively large stone.'[1]

Range: NSW coast and ranges, Tas, Vic, SA and WA. The Sydney region is its northern limit. **Leaves:** small, narrow, very dense, pungent and finely toothed. **Flowers:** bright RED 'cigars' about 14mm long. **Flowering time:** summer. **Name:** *humifusum* = Lat. ground-spreading, referring to its habit.

Astroloma pinifolium

Astroloma pinifolium (R. Brown) Bentham

Ss

A low sprawling or prostrate shrub with stems to 1m long. Found occasionally in sheltered sandy places in woodland, e.g. near creek banks in the Royal National Park. Uncommon in the area.

Brachyloma daphnoides

Range: coastal districts from Tas to northern NSW. **Leaves:** less than 0.5mm wide, fairly rigid, rough (due to stiff microscopic hairs), with a hard but not sharp tip. **Flowers:** RED, becoming YELLOW and GREEN at the tip, falling off easily at maturity. **Flowering time:** winter-spring. **Name:** *pinifolium* = Pine-leaved.

• *Brachyloma* Sonder (brack-ee-LO-ma)

An endemic genus of 7 species, distributed in all states.

Name: *Brachyloma* = Gk. *brachys*, short, *loma*, edge or fringe, referring to the hairs or scales at the throat of the floral tube.

Brachyloma daphnoides (Smith) Bentham

Daphne Heath **Ss, Castl**

A lovely shrub usually to 50cm tall with small prickly leaves, distinctive cream flowers and a small, low, rather scraggly appearance with many wiry branches. A common species in heathlands.

Range: NSW coast, ranges and inland slopes, Vic, Tas and SA. **Leaves:** small, oval, with a pungent point, often reddish. **Flowers:** CREAM, with a rich honey fragrance, about 5mm long, with a constricted floral tube, hairy inside, and with recurved perianth segments. **Flowering time:** August-October on the coast, to December in the Blue Mountains. **Name:** *daphnoides* = Daphne-like; of the fragrance.

• *Dracophyllum* Labillardière
(drac-o-FILL-um)

A genus of 4 endemic species, distributed in Tas, NSW, Qld, Lord Howe Island, New Caledonia and NZ.

Name: *Dracophyllum* = Lat. dragon-leaf, because the stiff, narrow leaves suggest a small *Dracaena draco* (Dragon's Blood tree).

Dracophyllum secundum R. Brown
Ss

A graceful shrub with arched stems to 50cm long, drooping from crevices in damp sandstone cliffs. Very common in the Blue Mountains but less so on the coast. '. . . its long, bright foliage falling from a single stem, and the crowning spike of blossoms, often bent fantastically, gleaming out like the rose tint of a pearl shell, every little tube drooping from the same side of the stem in a continuous wreath.'[2]

Range: NSW coastal districts and Blue Mountains. **Leaves:** stiff, stem clasping. **Flowers:** PINK, in a long curving one-sided terminal raceme. **Flowering time:** August-October. **Name:** *secundum* = arranged on one side only.

Dracophyllum secundum

• *Epacris* Cavanilles
An endemic genus of 35 species, found in all the eastern states and SA.

Name: *Epacris* = Lat. *epi*, upon, *akros*, the top, supposedly referring to a habitat on hill tops (hardly a precise name).

Epacris coriacea A. Cunningham ex De Candolle
Illawarra Coral Heath **Ss 3RC-**

A shrub, sprawling or erect, 50cm to 3m high, restricted to the tops of sandstone cliffs on the edge of the Illawarra escarpment south of Sydney. The habitat includes poor sandy soil, very exposed windy conditions and very high rainfall.

The type specimen was probably collected by Allan Cunningham during his Illawarra expeditions in 1818 or 1824.

Range: confined to the Illawarra escarpment, including southern parts of the Royal National Park. **Leaves:** with short stems, ovate, concave and glossy above. **Flowers:** WHITE, similar to *E. microphylla*. **Flowering time:** spring. **Name:** *coriacea* = leathery, referring to the leaves.

Epacris crassifolia R. Brown
Ss

A low spreading shrub less than 30cm high, confined to crevices and ledges in sandstone cliffs. Uncommon in the area.

Range: restricted to the Sydney area and Blue Mountains. **Leaves:** thick, stiff, shiny, dark green, with a distinctive rounded tip. **Flowers:** WHITE, 6-9mm long, swollen in the middle of the tube. **Flowering time:** late winter-early spring (from June). **Name:** *crassifolia* = Lat. thick leaf.

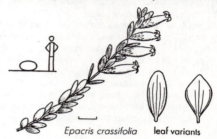

Epacris crassifolia   **leaf variants**

Epacris longiflora Cavanilles
Native Fuschia **Ss**

A slender graceful heath shrub to 1.5m high, with drooping rows of red and white flowers 'so well known to the ramblers round the shores of Port Jackson, where many a "desert wild" is adorned by its exquisite beauty'.[3] A very common species, preferring rocky ground in sheltered woodland understories.

Range: eastern Vic and NSW on coast and ranges. **Leaves:** small, 5-12mm long, heart shaped, tough and sharply pointed. **Flowers:** tubular, RED and WHITE, axillary, in pendant rows along stiff wiry stems. **Flowering time:** winter and spring. **Name:** *longiflora* = Lat. long-flowered. **Note:** It has the distinction of being the subject of the first poem ever published in Australia:

'When I first landed on Australia's shore,
. . . A flower gladden'd me above the rest, shap'd
   trumpet-like, which from a leafy stalk
Hangs clust'ring, hyacinthine, crimson red
Melting into white . . .

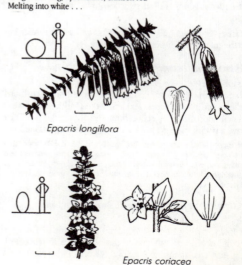

Epacris longiflora

Epacris coriacea

But, having lived the circle of the year,
I found . . . this the sole plant that never ceas'd to
   bloom . . . '4
—Barron Field, 1820s.

Epacris microphylla R. Brown

Coral Heath **Ss**

A slender, erect, wiry, few-branched shrub to 1m high. A very common species in all damp rocky heaths in the Sydney Region, often growing fairly densely and creating a snowy appearance in spring. Early this century the Sydney botanist Agnes Brewster noted that bees and black wasps were the main pollinators.

Range: SA, Vic, NSW and Qld, on coast and ranges. **Leaves:** tiny , heart-shaped, 2-4mm long, held erect against the wiry stem. **Flowers:** WHITE, small but often dense on the stem, concealing the leaves in a snowy mass. **Flowering time:** late winter-early spring (from July). **Name:** *microphylla* = Lat. tiny-leaved.

Epacris obtusifolia Smith

Ss

A slender erect shrub to 1.5m high 'met with in damp and yet sunny vales, its slender stems wreathed with minute leaves and blossoms.'5 Found in marshy heath and wet sandstone ledges.

Range: Tas to Qld on coast and ranges. **Leaves:** erect, rather thick, pressed against the stems, diamond shaped with a distinctive thickened blunt tip. **Flowers:** WHITE, swollen, all reaching outwards to one side of the stems. **Flowering time:** August-October. **Name:** *obtusifolia* = Lat. blunt-leaved.

Epacris paludosa R. Brown

Swamp Epacris **Ss**

A stiff slender few-branched shrub usually 1-1.5m tall, very attractive when flowering. Found in sedge swamps, e.g. Maddens Plains. Uncommon in the area. More common in the Blue Mountains.

Range: Woronora Plateau, NSW south coast and ranges, Vic and Tas. **Leaves:** thin-textured, stiff, sharply pointed. **Flowers:** WHITE, axillary, forming head-like masses at the tips of branches. **Flowering time:** August-November. **Name:** *paludosa* = Lat. pertaining to swamps.

Epacris pulchella Cavanilles

NSW Coral Heath **Ss**

An erect few-branched shrub to 1.5m high, common on rocky heaths and understories in woodland. When fully flowering the branches form beautiful swaying ivory limbs.

Range: NSW coast and ranges, extending into Qld. **Leaves:** very similar *E. longifolia*, pungent pointed. **Flowers:** WHITE, larger than *E. microphylla* **Flowering time:** mid to late summer. **Name:** *pulchella* = Lat. pulcher, beautiful. **Similar species:** distinguish from *E. microphylla* by the larger size of all its parts and by its summer flowering time.

Epacris purpurascens R. Brown
var. purpurascens Ss

A stiff prickly shrub 1-1.5m high, very beautiful when in flower. It occurs in damp places in woodland on sandstone. Uncommon.

Range: confined to coastal plateaus in the Sydney region. **Leaves:** like *E. longiflora*, but much longer, 8-15mm long, pungent pointed. **Flowers:** PINK-WHITE, swollen, each in the fold of a single leaf.

Epacris microphylla

thickened blunt tip

Epacris obtusifolia

Epacris paludosa

Epacris pulchella

Epacris purpurascens var. purpurascens

Flowering time: spring. **Name:** *purpurascens*, Lat. becoming purple, referring to the flowers.

• *Leucopogon* R. Brown (loo-co-PO-gon)

Beard-heath

A genus with 143 species in Australia, and others occurring from Malaysia to NZ. The fruits of all *Leucopogon* are sweet, succulent and edible. *Leucopogon* species are easily distinguished from other genera by the dense 'beard' of hairs on the inside of tiny white flowers.

Name: *Leucopogon* = Gk. *leuco*, white, *pogon*, beard, referring to the bearded flowers.

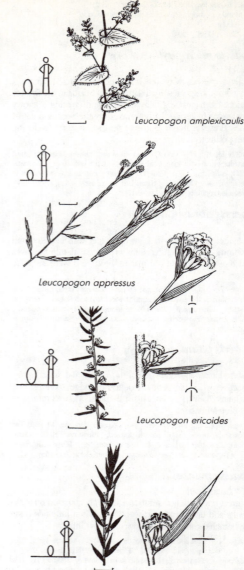

Leucopogon amplexicaulis

Leucopogon amplexicaulis (Rudge) R. Brown

Ss

A small weak shrub to 1m tall with distinctive leaves, found amongst the tangle of undergrowth in woodlands which have not been burnt for many years.

Range: restricted to coastal districts in the Sydney Region, e.g. Royal National Park near Engadine. **Leaves:** thin, flexible, heart-shaped, stem-clasping, with fringed margins. **Flowers:** WHITE in narrow spikes longer than the leaves. **Flowering time:** spring and winter. **Name:** *amplexicaulis* = Lat. stem-clasping, referring to the leaves.

Leucopogon appressus R. Brown

Ss

A slender straggling wiry shrub under 1m high with wiry branches, found in heath and woodland on sandstone.

Range: restricted to northern Sydney suburbs (Gordon to Hawkesbury River), and Blue Mountains. **Leaves:** erect, closely appressed to the stem, pungent, margins smooth. **Flowers:** with blunt sepals, solitary, axillary, partly hidden by the leaves. **Flowering time:** summer-autumn. **Name:** *appressus* = pressed down, referring to the leaves pressed against the stem. **Similar species:** *L. virgatus*, distinguish by the leaf margins.

Leucopogon appressus

Leucopogon ericoides (Smith) R. Brown

Bearded Heath   **Ss, Castl**

A slender erect prickly shrub, usually 0.5-1.5m high, common in scrub and woodland on sandstone.

Range: NSW coast and ranges, also Vic, Qld, Tas and SA. **Leaves:** small, stiff, pungent pointed. **Flowers:** WHITE, perianth segments fully opening and recurving upon maturity. **Flowering time:** late winter-early spring (from July). **Name:** *ericoides* = *Erica*-like, *Erica* is the European heath or heather. **Similar species:** *L. juniperinus.*

Leucopogon ericoides

Leucopogon esquamatus R. Brown

Ss

A slender erect spiky shrub to about 50cm high. Found in open heath country on sandstone.

Range: coastal areas from Tas to Qld; also in the Blue Mountains. **Leaves:** erect, flat, pungent pointed. **Flowers:** WHITE, hidden by the leaves; the sepals are as long as the floral tube. **Flowering time:** August-October. **Name:** *esquamata* = Lat. without scales, possibly to distinguish it from the scale-like leaves of other species.

Leucopogon esquamatus

Leucopogon exolasius F. Mueller

Ss   Vulnerable 2VC-

A small shrub, found in heath on sandstone. A rare and threatened species known only from a few locations.

Range: confined to upper Georges River, Woronora Plateau and the Grose River (Blue Mountains).   **Leaves:** slender, pungent, stiff, with revolute margins.   **Flowers:** WHITE, hairy outside, usually solitary in the leaf axils.   **Name:** *exolasius* = Gk. *exo*, outside, *lasios*, hairy, woolly, refering to the hairy outside of the floral tube.

Leucopogon fletcheri Maiden & Betche

Pendant Beard-heath   **Ss   Rare 3RC-**

A wiry spreading shrub 1-1.5m high, found in open dry heath on sandstone. It is easily recognised by the neat rows of drooping white flowers with long floral tubes and projecting styles.

Range: a rare species confined to Springwood and the northern Sydney area: Kenthurst, Kurrajong, Terrey Hills, Frenchs Forest, Elouera Reserve.   **Leaves:** short, slender, usually revolute (i.e. curled below), pungent tipped.   **Flowers:** WHITE, drooping, solitary in the leaf axils, on stalks under 1mm long.   **Flowering time:** spring (starting in August).   **Name:** after J.J. Fletcher who collected the type specimen near Springwood in 1887.

Leucopogon juniperinus R. Brown

Bearded Heath   **Ss, Cumb**

A small dense prickly shrub to 1m high. A fairly common understorey species in forest, especially on clays and enriched soils. The small white fruits are sweet and succulent but with a thin flesh (in December-January). Distinguish from *L. ericoides* by the longer flowers and tightly crowded leaves.

Range: Vic to Qld on coast and ranges.   **Leaves:** are small, crowded, narrow, hard, concave below and with pungent points.   **Flowers:** slender, WHITE, tubular, arising singly or in pairs in the leaf axils, perianth segments not recurved upon maturity.   **Flowering time:** spring (from August).   **Name:** *juniperinus* = like a Juniper, the prickly European conifer.   **Similar species:** *L. ericoides.*

Leucopogon lanceolatus (Smith) R. Brown

Lance Beard-heath   **Ss**

An erect shrub to 1.5m high. A common species, preferring sunny but sheltered understoreys in woodland on sandstone. The red fruits are sweet and edible (in November).

Range: NSW coast and ranges, Vic, Qld, Tas and SA.   **Leaves:** flexible, 1-4cm long, soft pointed, flat.   **Flowers:** tiny, WHITE, arising in spikes much longer than the leaves.   **Flowering time:** spring and early summer.   **Name:** *lanceolatus* = lance-like, referring to the shape of the leaves.

Leucopogon microphyllus (Cavanilles) R. Brown

Ss

A slender erect shrub to 1m high, found in wet heath, but sometimes weak and straggling in dense scrubs. A very common species in the area. According to one author the flowers have a subtle odour; 'A breath of nutty fragrance told of the presence of the little whitebeard.'[6]

Range: NSW coast and ranges into Qld.   **Leaves:** tiny, mostly about 3mm long but sometimes up to 6mm, scale-like.   **Flowers:** WHITE.   **Flowering time:** June-January.   **Name:** *microphyllus* = Lat. tiny-leaved.   **Similar species:** *Cryptandra amara* (Rhamnaceae).

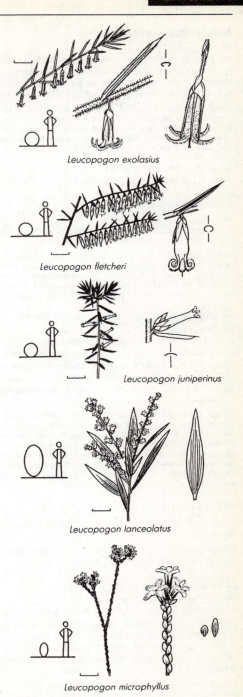

Leucopogon exolasius

Leucopogon fletcheri

Leucopogon juniperinus

Leucopogon lanceolatus

Leucopogon microphyllus

Leucopogon muticus R. Brown

Ss

An erect lightly foliaged shrub to 1.5m high, found in woodland on sandstone. It is locally rare, only reported from Bents Basin and Nortons Basin on the Nepean River and from Dural (but more common north of the Hawkesbury).

Range: NSW coast, ranges and western slopes, and Qld. **Leaves:** crowded, rather diamond-shaped, thin, concave below, erect, tapering gradually towards the base, with obscure venation. **Flowers:** WHITE, in small axillary racemes. **Flowering time:** spring. **Name:** *muticus* = Lat. unarmed, as the leaves have no sharp point.

Leucopogon parviflorus

—See COASTAL AND ESTUARINE SPECIES.

Leucopogon setiger R. Brown

Ss

A wiry spreading shrub to 1m high, found in open dry heath country on sandstone. An uncommon species.

Range: confined to the Sydney area and Blue Mountains. **Leaves:** short, slender, flat with recurved margins, pungent tipped. **Flowers:** WHITE, in drooping racemes of 1-4 in the leaf axils, on long stalks; the sepals are longer than the floral tube. **Flowering time:** spring (starting in August). **Name:** *setiger* = Lat. bristly, referring to the short spiky leaves.

Leucopogon virgatus (Labillardière) R. Brown

Ss, Castl, Cumb

A small ascending or trailing shrub to 50cm high with many slender stems arising from a woody rootstock. In the Sydney region it occurs mainly in coastal heaths between La Perouse and North Head, in the southern Blue Mountains, and on clays in the Appin area. It may be hard to distinguish from *L. appressus*.

Range: coast, ranges and western slopes of all eastern states and SA. **Leaves:** slender, erect, pungent, often appressed on the stem, margins lined with fine teeth; may be tightly crowded in coastal specimens. **Flowers:** with blunt sepals, solitary or more often in short dense head-like racemes, always at the ends of branches. **Flowering time:** spring and summer. **Name:** *virgatus* = Lat. twiggy or much-branched. **Similar species:** *L. appressus.* Distinguish from that species by the finely toothed leaf margins.

• *Lissanthe* R. Brown

An endemic genus of two species distributed through the eastern states.

Name: *Lissanthe* = Gk. smooth-flowered, to distinguish it from the bearded flowers of *Leucopogon*.

Lissanthe strigosa (Smith) R. Brown

Native Cranberry **Cumb, Ss, Castl**

A stiff prickly shrub to 50cm high. Mainly a shale species. In the Sydney area found on the Cumberland Plain and also in the Castlereagh woodlands.

The white fruits (with persistent style) are edible. The Cribbs say they are 'juicy and, although small, well worth seeking out for their excellent honey flavour'.[7]

Range: coast, ranges and inland slopes of all eastern states and SA. **Leaves:** 4-10mm, rigid, pungent. **Flowers:** urn-shaped, PINK to WHITE, numerous, in short dense racemes, with sparse hairs inside (on the lobes). **Flowering time:** July-September. **Name:** *strigosa* = Lat. with stiff bristles, referring to the general habit.

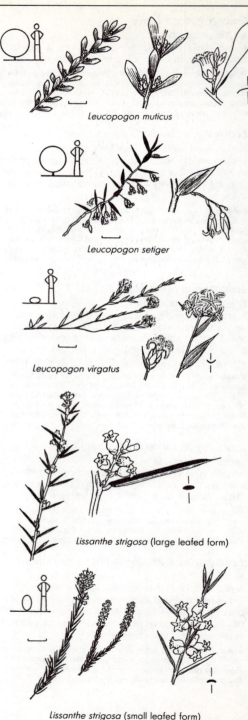

Leucopogon muticus

Leucopogon setiger

Leucopogon virgatus

Lissanthe strigosa (large leafed form)

Lissanthe strigosa (small leafed form)

• *Melichrus* R. Brown (mel-ICK-rus)

An endemic genus of 4 species distributed in the eastern mainland states.

Name: *Melichrus* = Gk. honeyed.

Melichrus procumbens (Cavanilles) Druce

Jam Tarts **Ss, Castl**

A low shrub with densely crowded prickly leaves on sprawling stems. Found in heath on sandstone.

This species is famous for its rich nectar. The Cribbs note that the flowers 'are largely hidden from sight on the undersides of the branches, but they contain so much nectar they are worth searching for'.[8] The fact that the flowers are face downwards close to the ground suggests pollination by ground-crawling insects such as ants.

Range: coast and ranges north from the Sydney Region into Qld. **Leaves:** numerous, densely crowded, with hairy margins, finely pointed but not pungent, 12-25mm long. **Flowers:** CREAMY WHITE, widely opening, 10-12mm wide, drooping and partly hidden by the branches. **Flowering time:** winter and spring. **Name:** *procumbens* = Lat. procumbent, referring to the habit.

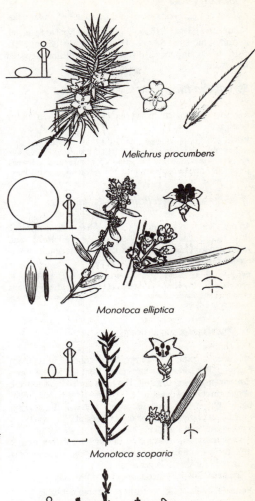

Melichrus procumbens

Monotoca elliptica

• *Monotoca* R. Brown

A small endemic genus of 11 species, found in all states.

Name: *Monotoca* = Gk. single-offspring, referring to the single seed in each fruit.

Monotoca elliptica (Smith) R. Brown

Tree Broom-Heath, Pidgeon Berry **Ss**

A large rounded prickly shrub usually to 3m, occasionally to 6m, high. Plentiful near the coast, in shrublands, forest understories and regrowth. The succulent fruit (in summer) is edible and was consumed by Aborigines. In colonial times the hard fine-grained wood was sometimes used for tool handles.

Range: Tas to Qld on coast and ranges. **Leaves:** oval or oblong, concave below, pungent pointed. **Flowers:** in dense short racemes in the leaf axils, WHITE with swollen red anthers. **Flowering time:** late winter-early spring (from July). **Name:** *elliptica* = elliptic, referring to the leaves.

Monotoca scoparia (Smith) R. Brown

Ss, Castl

A small erect heath shrub usually 30-50cm high. A common species, found in dry stony and lateritic heaths. The flowers are pollinated by ants. ' . . . tiny white, cup-like flowers are half-filled with nectar and look very like small cups. We noted on these plants dozens of ants—the mound or gravel ant (*Iridiomyrmex detectus*). They went from flower to flower and drank the nectar, their heads just fitting into the top of the cup. Italian Hive bees visited too.'[9]

Range: coast and ranges of all eastern states and SA. **Leaves:** stiff, pungent pointed. **Flowers:** WHITE, tiny, 1-3 in the leaf axils. **Flowering time:** April to July. **Name:** *scoparia* = Lat. broomy.

Monotoca scoparia

Monotoca ledifolia

A. Cunningham ex De Candolle

Ss Rare 3RC-

A small erect shrub to 1m high, found in dry open heath on shallow soils, restricted to Heathcote National Park and

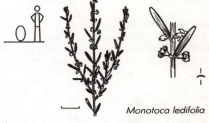

Monotoca ledifolia

rarely in Heathcote-Waterfall area in Royal National Park. It is similar to *M. scoparia* but has blunt leaves.

Range: above areas and also scattered locations in the southern Blue Mountains. **Leaves:** small, erect, thick, blunt. **Flower:** WHITE, similar to *M. scoparia*, solitary or in pairs. **Name:** *ledifolia* = Lat. *Ledum*-leaved. *Ledum* is a small genus of northern hemisphere shrubs in the family Ericaceae.

• *Sprengelia* Smith

A genus of 4 endemic species distributed in eastern Australia.

Name: *Sprengelia* = in honour of Christian Konrad Sprengel, Rector of the High School of Spandau, near Berlin, 1750-1816. He was the principal discoverer of the relations between insects and flowers.

Sprengelia incarnata Smith
Ss

A slender stiff shrub to 1m high, growing abundantly in marshy heathlands.

Range: NSW coast and ranges, Vic, Tas and SA. **Leaves:** stiff, stem clasping, pungent pointed. **Flowers:** WHITE with slender lobes; with rigid pink sepals, as long as the petals. **Flowering time:** late winter (from July). **Name:** *incarnata* = Lat. to cover, referring to the leaves which conceal the stem.

Sprengelia sprengelioides (R.Brown) Druce
Ss

An erect shrub to 1m high (more bushy than *S. incarnata*). Rare, recorded from swampy heath near West Head Road in Ku-ring-gai Chase National Park. In the last century it was recorded at Bondi, Waterloo and Narrabeen.

Range: in coastal districts from Sydney north into Qld. **Leaves:** stiff, stem-clasping. **Flowers:** with broad lobes and broad green sepals resembling the leaves. **Name:** *sprengelioides* = *Sprengelia*-like (it was originally in a different genus).

• *Styphelia* Smith (sty-FEEL-ee-a)
Five-corners

An endemic genus with 12 species, distributed in southern Australia. The common name comes from the 5 calyx lobes that remain around the fruit. The fruits are edible and were popular in colonial times. In 1833 George Bennet found them being sold in fruit shops in Sydney but Rolf Boldrewood in *Robbery Under Arms* used the expression 'You won't turn a five corner into a quince'.

Most species are adapted to dry sandy soils but cannot bear the exposure of an isolated position, thriving only beneath the shelter of larger shrubs.

Styphelias are pollinated mainly by honeyeaters.

Name: *Styphelia* = Gk. dense, from the compact habit.

Styphelia angustifolia De Candolle
Five-corners **Ss** (previously *S. laeta var. angustifolia*)

An erect shrub to 1.5m high, found in heath and woodland. Recorded only from Loftus in the Sydney area. Very similar

Styphelia angustifolia

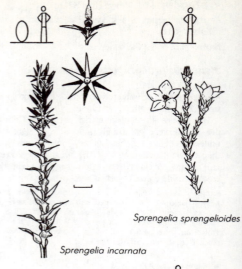

Sprengelia sprengelioides

Sprengelia incarnata

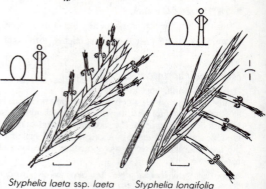

Styphelia laeta ssp. *laeta*   *Styphelia longifolia*

to *S. longifolia* but distinguished by the presence of tiny teeth on the leaf margins and the smaller flowers.

Range: Loftus and the Blue Mountains south to Pigeon House Mountain, also in the Warialda district. **Leaves:** 10-29mm long, narrow, finely toothed. **Flowers:** PALE GREEN, tube 15-19mm long. **Flowering time:** March-August. **Name:** *angustifolia* = Lat. narrow-leafed.

Styphelia laeta R. Brown *var. laeta*
Five-corners **Ss, Castl**

An erect shrub 1-2m high, found in heath and woodland.

Range: restricted to a few locations in the Sydney area and Blue Mountains. **Leaves:** 15-35mm long, ovate to broad-oblong. **Flowers:** PALE YELLOW-GREEN or RED, tube 14-26mm long. **Flowering time:** March-August. **Name:** *laeta* = Gk. *laios*, left, as the flowers tend to fall to one side of the stem.

Styphelia longifolia R. Brown
Five-corners **Ss**

An erect shrub 1-2m high, found in woodland.

Range: Waterfall to Broken Bay. **Leaves:** 25-50mm long, with smooth margins. **Flowers:** PALE GREEN or YELLOW, tube 20-25mm long. **Flowering time:** March-August. **Name:** *longifolia* = Lat. long-leafed.

Styphelia triflora Andrews

Ss

An erect or bushy shrub to 2m high, found in sheltered understories in woodland.

Range: NSW coast, ranges and western slopes, to Qld. **Leaves:** broad, flat, pungent-pointed. **Flowers:** light PINK. **Flowering time:** spring. **Name:** *triflora* = three-flowered.

Styphelia tubiflora Smith

Ss

A small wiry straggling shrub with attractive red flowers, common in heath and woodland on sandstone.

Range: mainly restricted to the Sydney area and Blue Mountains. **Leaves:** narrow and sharply pointed. **Flowers:** tubular, RED, drooping in rows on the stems. **Flowering time:** spring. **Name:** *tubiflora* = tubular-flowered. **Note:** In 1793 English botanist James Smith wrote: 'It has lately been a complaint among cultivators of plants, that the vegetable productions of New Holland, however novel and singular, are deficient in beauty . . . and if it were so, the shrub here delineated might atone for a multitude of unattractive ones, by its own transcendent elegance, as well as by its resemblance to the favourite *Erica tubiflora*. We hope it will one day be introduced into our gardens, and remain a perpetual asserter of the botanical honour of its country.'[10]

Styphelia viridus R. Brown *ssp. viridus*

Ss

A stiff shrub 1-2m high, found in sheltered places in heath and woodland on sandstone, especially near the sea.

Range: in coastal districts from Botany Bay into Qld. **Leaves:** more or less flat, with a long sharp point. **Flowers:** GREEN, tube 16-18mm long. **Flowering time:** April-August. **Name:** *viridus* = Lat. green, referring to the flowers.

• *Trochocarpa*
—See RAINFOREST SPECIES.

Trochocarpa laurina

• *Woollsia* F. Mueller

An endemic genus with a single species.

Name: Ferdinand Mueller took this species out of the genus *Lysinema* and named it after his friend, the Reverend William Woolls.

Woollsia pungens (Cavanilles) F. Mueller

Snow Wreath **Ss**

An erect shrub 0.5-2m high with dense spiky leaves, found in sheltered damp places in heath and woodland on sandstone. A common species. The flowers exude one of the richest and most beautiful fragrances in the Sydney bush.

Range: NSW coastal areas, Blue Mountains and Qld. **Leaves:** pungent-pointed, very dense on the stem. **Flowers:** WHITE (sometimes purplish), fragrant, dense, covering the upper parts of the plants. The perianth lobes have fine corrugations. **Flowering time:** spring. **Name:** *pungens* = pungent, referring to the leaves.

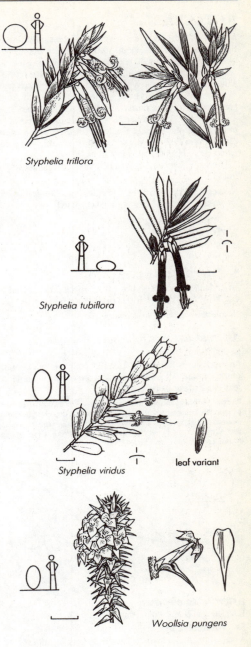

Styphelia triflora

Styphelia tubiflora

Styphelia viridus   leaf variant

Woollsia pungens

RUTACEAE

A family of trees and shrubs with translucent oil glands in
the leaves. There are about 1800 species in 150 genera
worldwide, and about 320 species in 41 genera in Australia.

Rutaceae is probably a family of Gondwanan origin
although it is now widely distributed through warmer parts
of the world. The leaves of all species are dotted with glands
containing strongly aromatic volatile oils. The flowers have
4 or 5 petals. The number of stamens is usually equal to,
or twice that of the petals. The fruits consist of 4 or 5 joined
carpels. Most fruits are dry and open explosively, but some
rainforest genera have succulent fruits.

The family is economically important since it includes citrus
fruits.

Name: Rutaceae = from the European Rue, *Ruta graveolens*,
grown since ancient times as a medicinal herb.

• *Acronychia*
—See RAINFOREST SPECIES.

• *Asterolasia* F. Mueller

An endemic genus of shrubs with 5 species, distributed in
Qld, NSW and Vic. Closely related to *Phebalium*.

Name: *Asterolasia* = Gk. star-wool.

Asterolasia correifolia Bentham
Ss

An erect shrub 1-2m high, found in gully rainforests north
of the harbour. All parts of the plant are covered in a dense
felty cloak of star hairs.

Range: Sydney area and NSW north coast, also recorded from the southern
tablelands.   **Leaves:** flat, blunt-tipped, thin and soft, densely stellate hairy
below, barely hairy above.   **Flowers:** CREAMY-WHITE, in clusters, axillary
and terminal, densely felty on outside.   **Flowering time:** spring.
Name: *correifolia* = *Correa*-leaved.

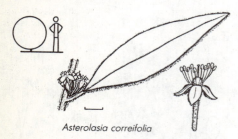

Asterolasia correifolia

Asterolasia elegans
L. McDougall & M.F. Porteners

Ss   Vulnerable 2V

A leafy shrub to 3m high. A very rare species, first discovered
in the 1970s north of Maroota, in a moist gully which is
still its only known location. About 200 plants exist there.
It is similar to *A. correifolia*, but much larger in all its parts.

Range: restricted to the Sydney area.   **Leaves:** to 16cm long, soft, densely
covered in star hairs on both surfaces.   **Flowers:** WHITE, about 25mm
wide; in small clusters surrounded by rusty-hairy bracts, mainly terminal.

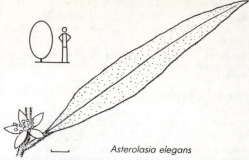

Asterolasia elegans

Flowering time: August-October.   **Name:** *elegans* = Lat. elegant, from
its appearance when flowering.

• *Bauerella = Sarcomelicope*
—See RAINFOREST SPECIES.

• *Boronia* Smith

A genus with 95 endemic species, found in all states. Boronias
are small aromatic heathy shrubs with opposite, usually
pinnate leaves. The local species have rich purple, pink or
white star-shaped flowers. Each flower has 4 petals and 8
anthers which closely imprison the style and ovary. The ovary
has 4 chambers, each with 1 seed. The fruit opens explosively.

Name: *Boronia* = 'in memory of Francis Borone, an Italian,
the faithful personal attendant of Dr. Sidthorp, the author
of the colossal and exceedingly beautiful *Flora Græca*. A
certain plant was observed near Athens, in a situation difficult
of access, and, in spite of the doctor's warnings, Borone
endeavoured to secure the prize for him, but, alas!
overbalanced himself and was killed.'[1]

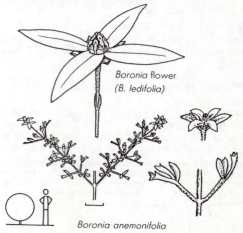

Boronia flower
(B. ledifolia)

Boronia anemonifolia

Boronia anemonifolia A. Cunningham

Sticky Boronia **Ss**

An erect shrub usually 1-1.5m tall, with a strong oily fragrance,
found in rocky places in woodland. Uncommon. Only

recorded locally along the banks of the upper Nepean (e.g. Menangle). Also found north of the Hawkesbury River.

Range: NSW coast and ranges, Vic and Tas. **Leaves:** with 3 leaflets, each with 3 lobes at the tip, covered in short stiff hairs, sometimes slightly sticky. **Flowers:** WHITE to slightly pink, axillary, solitary or in pairs. **Flowering time:** September-November. **Name:** *anemonifolia* = *Anemone*-leaved. *Anemone* is a genus in the Ranunculaceae family.

Boronia anethifolia A. Cunningham ex Endlicher

Narrow-leaved Boronia **Ss**
A small shrub to 50cm high, with a rich peppermint fragrance. Found in sheltered woodland on sandstone. Uncommon locally. Recorded from Bargo, on the Nepean River and also north of the Hawkesbury River.

Range: scattered locations in the Blue Mountains and foothills. **Leaves:** pinnate, some leaflets further divided into secondary leaflets, sometimes sticky. **Flowers:** PALE PINK to WHITE, in axillary cymes. **Flowering time:** August-September. **Name:** *anethifolia* = *Anethum*-leaved. *Anethum graveolens* is Dill, a species in the Apiaceae family.

Boronia anethifolia

Boronia barkeriana F. Mueller

Barker's Boronia **Ss**
A slender erect shrub 50-100cm high, found in marshy heath. Similar in appearance and habitat to *B. parviflora* except larger in all its parts. Recorded locally only from the Royal National Park.

Range: NSW coast and ranges, and Qld. **Leaves:** with finely toothed margins (serrulate). **Flowers:** RICH ROSE PINK, anthers orange, petals 6-8mm long; several in a terminal cyme. **Flowering time:** spring. **Name:** *barkeriana* = after C.A. Barker, who supplied the type specimen to Ferdinand von Mueller.

Boronia floribunda Sieber ex Sprengel

Pale Pink Boronia **Ss**
An erect shrub usually about 1.5m high, found in sheltered moist places in woodland. Rather uncommon in the area.

stigma

Boronia floribunda

Boronia barkeriana

B. pinnata and *B. floribunda* are very similar and can only be practically distinguished by the stigmas (see illustrations).

Range: Sydney area and Blue Mountains. **Leaves:** pinnate, the leaflets finely pointed. **Flowers:** usually a PALE PINK, in dense axillary cymes, stigmas large and swollen. **Flowering time:** spring. **Name:** *floribunda* = Lat. abundant-flowered.

Boronia fraseri W.J. Hooker

Fraser's Boronia **Ss Rare 2RCa**
An erect shrub usually 1-1.5m high, found in the moist woodland in sandstone gullies. Closely related to *B. mollis*, which is distinguished mainly by its conspicuous hairiness.

Range: confined to the northern bushlands of Sydney as far north as Woy Woy and also on the lower eastern slopes of the Blue Mountains. **Leaves:** almost hairless. The whole plant is apparently hairless but on close examination the branches are covered in minute tufts of stiff stellate hairs. **Flowers:** large (18-24mm wide) in small axillary cymes. **Flowering time:** spring. **Name:** *fraseri* = in honour of Charles Fraser, died 1831. The first official superintendent of the Royal Botanical Gardens, Sydney, originally a private soldier in the 46th regiment.

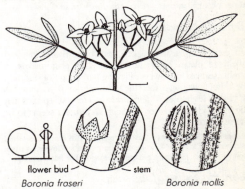

flower bud — — stem

Boronia fraseri

Boronia mollis

Boronia mollis A. Cunningham ex Lindley

Soft Boronia **Ss**
An erect shrub usually 1-1.5m high, found in moist sandstone gullies. Uncommon in the area; mainly on the far north shore. The leaves have a most unpleasant lemon-bitumen odour.

Range: Sydney area and NSW north coast. **Leaves:** similar to *B. fraseri*. The branches and leaf stalks are densely covered in soft stellate hairs (often much thicker than illustrated). **Flowers:** RICH PINK in axillary cymes. Note the slender sepals compared to *B. fraseri* and the hairs on the outside of the petals. **Flowering time:** spring. **Name:** *mollis* = Lat. soft, refers to leaves and soft hairs on stems.

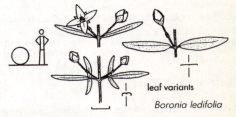

leaf variants

Boronia ledifolia

Boronia ledifolia (Ventenat) J. Gay

Sydney Boronia, Ledum Boronia **Ss**
An erect shrub 30-100cm high, abundant in heath and

woodland. The hardiest and also the earliest flowering of the local species.

Range: Sydney area, Blue Mountains, south coast, central western slopes and Vic. **Leaves:** slender, entire, 3-foliate or rarely pinnate, with recurved margins, dark green, dotted above with star-hairs, whitish below due to a microscopic felt. The stems are cloaked in a rusty layer consisting of tiny glands covered in rough microscopic rusty star hairs. **Flowers:** rich ROSE-PINK, solitary or in small axillary cymes. **Flowering time:** late winter-early spring, from July. **Name:** *ledifolia* = with leaves resembling *Ledum*, a small genus of northern hemisphere shrubs in the family Ericaceae.

Boronia parviflora Smith

Swamp Boronia **Ss**

A slender erect shrub, 30-100cm high, usually found in marshy heath country, amongst sedges and taller shrubs. Smaller in all its parts than *B. barkeriana*.

Range: south from the Sydney area into Vic, also Qld, Tas and SA. **Leaves:** erect, with entire or very finely toothed margins. **Flowers:** terminal and usually solitary, RICH PINK, petals 3-4mm long. **Flowering time:** spring and summer. **Name:** *parviflora* = Lat. small-leaved.

Boronia pinnata Smith

Ss

An erect shrub usually about 1.5m high. Found in moist sheltered places in dry woodland. This plant makes an immense mass of flowers in spring and is one of our most beautiful flowering plants (the same goes for *B. floribunda*). It closely resembles *B. floribunda* and the two species may be found close together, although *B. pinnata* seems to be more common.

Range: NSW coastal areas. **Leaves:** pinnate, with slender segments. **Flowers:** rich ROSE PINK, in dense axillary cymes. **Flowering time:** spring. **Name:** *pinnata* = pinnate, referring to the leaf arrangement.

Boronia polygalifolia Smith

Milkwort Boronia **Cumb, Castl**

A small shrub to 20cm high, primarily a shale species, found on the Cumberland Plain. Also recorded from Lake Parramatta reserve.

Range: NSW coast and ranges. **Leaves:** small, undivided, hairless, oil dots only visible below. **Flowers:** axillary, solitary, REDDISH to PALE PINK. **Flowering time:** spring. **Name:** *polygalifolia* = leaves like a *Polygalia* (Milkwort) species.

Boronia rigens Cheel

Stiff Boronia **Ss**

A low wiry spreading shrub usually under 40cm high. An uncommon and inconspicuous species in heath and woodland. Locally common in low coastal heath at La Perouse.

Range: Sydney area, Blue Mountains, southern tablelands and Qld. **Leaves:** small, thick, stiff, 3-foliate, grooved above. **Flowers:** WHITE or pinkish, tiny, usually solitary in the axils. **Flowering time:** spring. **Name:** *rigens* = Lat. stiff, referring to the leaves.

Boronia ruppii Cheel

Ss

A small erect shrub to 1m high, closely related to *B. fraseri*. Only recorded locally in woodland at Annangrove Rd in the Kenthurst area.

Range: patchily distributed in the Sydney area and Blue Mountains, mainly around the Colo River and Newnes-Glen Alice area, also on the north

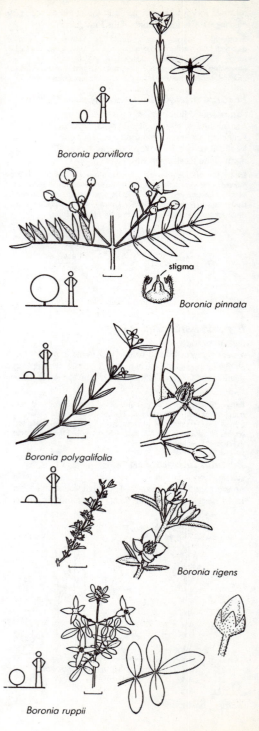

Boronia parviflora

stigma

Boronia pinnata

Boronia polygalifolia

Boronia rigens

Boronia ruppii

and central western slopes of NSW. **Leaves:** pinnate, mostly with 5 leaflets, blunt, covered below with fine stellate hairs. (Specimens from other parts of the range have larger leaves than illustrated.) **Flowers:** PINK, the calyx and outside of the petals covered in fine stellate hairs. **Flowering time:** spring. **Name:** *ruppii* = after the Reverend H.H.R. Rupp (the author of *The Orchids* of NSW) who collected the type specimen in the Blue Mountains in 1912.

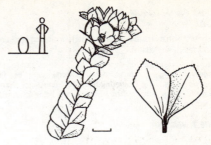

Boronia serrulata

Boronia serrulata Smith

Native Rose **Ss**
A small slender erect heath plant usually under 1m high. Common in damp sandy open heath near the coast. The tight clusters of pink flowers do resemble roses.

Range: restricted to the Sydney area. **Leaves:** erect, diamond shaped, finely toothed, flat, concealing the stem. **Flowers:** in a dense terminal cyme, ROSE-PINK. **Flowering time:** spring (September-October). **Name:** *serrulata* = Lat. finely toothed, referring to the leaves.

Boronia thujona Penfold & Welch

Ss
An erect shrub to 2m high, found in damp shady places in heath and woodland, usually at higher altitudes. Only occurs in a few places in the Sydney area, e.g. Royal National Park, Davidson State Recreation Area and Katandra Reserve. The whole plant is surrounded with a powerful and disturbing odour somewhat like mentholated dried meat.

Range: NSW coastal plateaus south from Sydney and Blue Mountains. **Leaves:** pinnate, with slender segments, apparently toothed due to oil glands on the margins. **Flowers:** usually LIGHT PINK, in dense axillary cymes. **Flowering time:** spring. **Name:** *thujona* = from Thujone, the essential extract of oil of *Thuja*, an aromatic genus of Northern Hemisphere plants of the Pine family: *Thuja plicata* is the western Red Cedar of the United States.

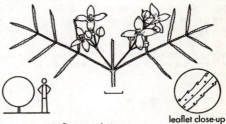

Boronia thujona leaflet close-up

• *Correa* Andrews

An endemic genus of 11 shrubs, distributed in all states. Correas have broad, opposite leaves. The flowers are tubular for at least part of their length, with 4 lobes at the tip. There are 8 stamens and the ovary is 4-chambered, each chamber producing 2 seeds.

Name: *Correa* = in honour of Joseph Correa de Serra, a celebrated Portugese botanist.

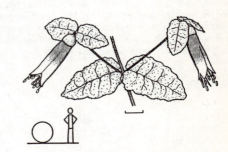

Correa reflexa var. reflexa

Correa alba
—See SEACOAST AND ESTUARINE SPECIES.

Correa reflexa (Labillardière) Ventenat **var. *reflexa***

Ss, Cumb, Castl
A spreading shrub under 1.5m high, always found in sheltered moist sites in woodland, on both sandstone and clay soils. The geometric shape of this plant is often exceedingly beautiful. 'The arrangement of its leaves and flowers is exact almost to formality; even the demure little acorn-like buds seem trained to the extreme of primness, as they look modestly down, beneath their light little skull-cap calyces.'[2]

Range: NSW coast, ranges and western slopes, Qld, Vic, Tas and SA. **Leaves:** opposite, covered in star hairs, heart-shaped, papery, often with undulating margins, dark green above, pale below with rusty star hairs on the veins (and stems). **Flowers:** terminal (1-3 together), drooping, tubular, RED passing into white and GREEN towards the tips, or rarely entirely WHITE. **Flowering time:** spring (from June). **Name:** *reflexa* = Lat. bent backwards.

• *Crowea* Smith

An endemic genus of small shrubs with 3 species, distributed in NSW, Qld, Vic and WA.

Crowea flower
(C. exalata)

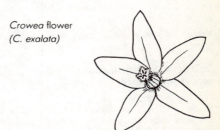

Name: *Crowea* = in honour of James Crow, a British botanist who studied mosses and fungi, and collected willows in his Norfolk garden.

Crowea exalata F. Mueller

Ss

A small erect shrub, usually 30-50cm high, found in sheltered rocky places in woodland.

Range: NSW coasts, ranges and slopes, and Vic. **Leaves:** slender, with slightly recurved margins; on angular stems. **Flowers:** RICH ROSE-PINK, petals usually 9-12mm long. **Flowering time:** December-June. **Name:** *exalata* = Gk. lacking wings, referring to the stems being less angular than *C. saligna.*

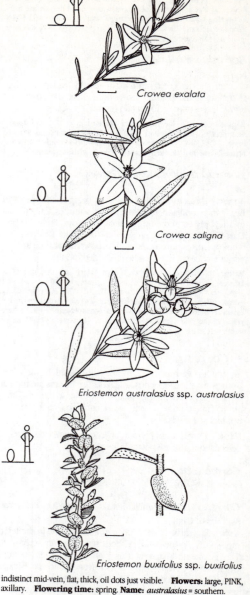

Crowea exalata

Crowea saligna Andrews

Ss

A small erect shrub usually less than 1m high, found in dry sandy forest under the shade of taller shrubs. Moderately common around Sydney. Because of its large, long-lived flowers it was a popular greenhouse plant in Britain after its introduction in 1790.

Range: confined to the Sydney area. **Leaves:** shiny, on very angular branches. **Flowers:** RICH ROSE-PINK, axillary, solitary, petals 12-15mm long. **Flowering time:** January to June. **Name:** *saligna* = Lat. of a willow, referring to the shape of the leaves.

Crowea saligna

• *Eriostemon* Smith

Wax Flowers

An endemic genus of 32 species found in all states. Most are small hardy heath shrubs with conspicuous oil glands. Some are highly valued horticultural plants. Their hardiness in poor soils points to mycorrhizal associations which supply the plant with additional nutrients. The stems and leaves are usually covered with conspicuous warty glands filled with volatile oils.

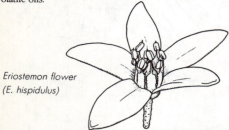

Eriostemon flower
(E. hispidulus)

Eriostemon australasius ssp. *australasius*

The flowers have 5 petals and 10 stamens. The stamens have flat translucent filaments with hairy margins which interlace to form a tube around the ovary. This ensures that insects can only reach the nectar after brushing against the anthers and stigma.

Name: *Eriostemon* = Gk. *erion*, wool, *stemon*, stamen, referring to the hairy stamens.

Eriostemon australasius Persoon
ssp. *australasius*

Pink Wax Flower **Ss**

An erect heath shrub usually to 1.5m high. Common in heath and woodlands throughout the sandstone plateaus. Easily recognised by its large pink flowers and thick grey-green foliage. This is one of our most beautiful heath plants, producing a spectacular mass of flowers in spring.

Range: NSW coast, Blue Mountains and Qld. **Leaves:** grey-green with

Eriostemon buxifolius ssp. *buxifolius*

indistinct mid-vein, flat, thick, oil dots just visible. **Flowers:** large, PINK, axillary. **Flowering time:** spring. **Name:** *australasius* = southern.

Eriostemon buxifolius Smith

Ss

A small erect shrub usually 50-100cm high, found in heath on sandstone. There are two subspecies in the area.

• **ssp. *buxifolius*:** leaves with even margins, heart-shaped. Found south of the harbour.

• **ssp.** *obovatus:* leaves with warty margins, more or less square at the base. Found north of the harbour.

There are hybrid populations of *E. buxifolius* x *scaber* in the Royal National Park (see illustration).

Range: Sydney area and south coast (both subspecies). **Leaves:** short and broad, sometimes heart-shaped, stiff, with prominent oil glands, with a sharp or hard point. **Flower:** axillary, PINK. **Flowering time:** spring. **Name:** *buxifolius* = Box-leaved, i.e. leaves like the European Box (*Buxus*).

Eriostemon hispidulus Sieber ex Sprengel
Rough Wax Plant **Ss**
An erect shrub, usually about 50cm high, found in heath and woodland on sandstone. Restricted to northern parts of the area (north of Hornsby).

Range: Blue Mountains and Hornsby Plateau. **Leaves:** stiff, covered in prominent oil glands, often with downcurved point, covered in short stiff hairs above and softer hairs below. **Flowers:** WHITE above with pink tinges, usually pink below. **Flowering time:** September-October. **Name:** *hispidulus* = Lat. rough.

Eriostemon myoporoides De Candolle
ssp. *myoporoides*
Long-leaved Wax Flower, Native Daphne
Cumb
An erect or spreading shrub 1-2m high, found on the banks of the Nepean and Cataract Rivers, also recorded from South Creek at St Marys. Because of its hardiness and masses of white wax flowers it is a popular garden plant.

Range: NSW coasts and ranges south from Sydney, Qld and Vic. **Leaves:** broad, dull greyish green, more or less fleshy, erect, with oil dots clearly visible. **Flowers:** WHITE in axillary clusters of 2-4. **Flowering time:** spring. **Name:** *myoporoides* = resembling a *Myoporum*.

Eriostemon scaber Paxton ssp. *scaber*
Ss
A low spreading shrub, to 1m high, found scattered in heath and woodland in coastal districts south of Botany Bay. Be careful not to confuse it with *Philotheca salsolifolia.*

Range: NSW coast south of Botany Bay. **Leaves:** narrow, rough to touch due to tiny stiff hairs, covered in small tubercles (oil glands). **Flowers:** WHITE, 1 per leaf joint. **Flowering time:** September. **Name:** *scaber* = Lat. rough, referring to the tubercles covering the plant.

• *Euodia = Melicope*
—See RAINFOREST SPECIES.

• *Phebalium* Ventenat
A genus of aromatic shrubs with 44 endemic species, distributed in all states except NT, and 1 species in NZ. The flowers are white or yellow, with 5 petals and 10 anthers on long slender filaments. The ovary has 5 chambers which form separate hard-pointed segments, each containing a single seed.

Some *Phebalium* species have 'scurfy' scales. These are tiny scales with a silver or bronze metallic sheen which form a dense cloak on stems and leaf undersides. They sometimes give the whole plant a most beautiful metallic lustre.

Name: *phebalium* = Gk. *phibalee*, a kind of Myrtle.

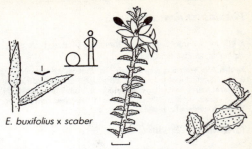

E. buxifolius x scaber

Eriostemon buxifolius ssp. *obovatus*

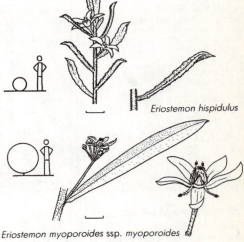

Eriostemon hispidulus

Eriostemon myoporoides ssp. *myoporoides*

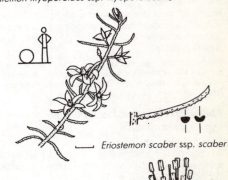

Eriostemon scaber ssp. *scaber*

Phebalium flower, showing scurfy scales
(*P. squamulosum*)

Phebalium dentatum Smith

Ss

A tall erect shrub 2-3m high, found in sheltered places in gullies on sandstone. Uncommon.

Range: NSW coast and ranges north from Sydney. **Leaves:** slender, flexible, fairly thin, the teeth are small and hidden by the recurved margins. **Flowers:** WHITE with pale yellow anthers, in axillary umbels forming dense masses at the ends of branches. **Flowering time:** spring. **Name:** *dentatum* = Lat. toothed.

Phebalium diosmeum A. Jussieu

Ss

A small erect shrub with crowded leaves, 50-150cm high. Uncommon in the area, in heath (e.g. Royal National Park).

Range: NSW coast and ranges south from Sydney. **Leaves:** dense, crowded about hairy stems, narrow and stiff with very downcurled margins (i.e. hollow beneath). **Flowers:** bright YELLOW, crowded in dense terminal heads. **Flowering time:** spring. **Name:** *diosmifolium* = leaves like a *Diosma*.

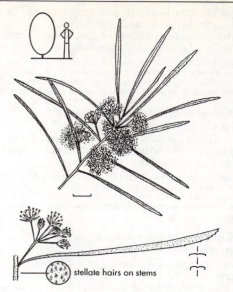

Phebalium dentatum

stellate hairs on stems

Phebalium diosmeum

leaf variant

Phebalium squameum (Labillardière) Engler

Satinwood **Ss**

A tall graceful shrub 2-4m high with an extraordinary metallic sheen due to bronze and silver scurfy scales on branches and leaf undersides. Found in sheltered gullies on sandstone. Uncommon in the area, in the Royal National Park and Woronora Plateau.

Range: NSW coast, Blue Mountains, Qld, Vic and Tas. **Leaves:** broad, flat, satiny silver on the undersides (stems are bronze). **Flowers:** WHITE, on short, thick, scaly stems, in axillary clusters. **Flowering time:** spring. **Name:** *squameum* = Lat. scaly.

Phebalium squamulosum Ventenat
ssp. *squamulosum*

Scaly Phebalium **Ss**

An open slender lightly foliaged shrub 0.5-1.5m high, with scurfy scales. Found in heath and woodland on sandstone. Fairly common in the area.

Range: NSW coast and ranges, Qld and Vic. **Leaves:** very variable in shape, undersurface with brownish scales and silvery hairs, shiny on upper surface. **Flowers:** petals pale YELLOW inside. **Flowering time:** spring (from August). **Name:** *squamulosum* = Lat. *squamosa*, scaly.

Phebalium squamulosum
ssp. *argenteum*

—See COASTAL AND ESTUARINE SPECIES.

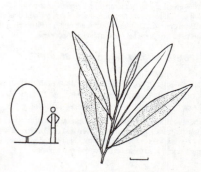

Phebalium squameum

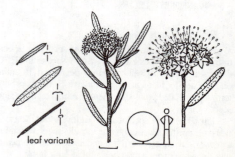

leaf variants

Phebalium squamulosum ssp. *squamulosum*

• *Philotheca* Rudge

An endemic genus of 3 species, 1 in WA and the other 2 in NSW and Qld. The anther filaments are fused into a transparent cylinder, imprisoning the stigma and ovary in a similar manner to *Eriostemon*, and for the same purpose, i.e. to prevent insects reaching the nectar without first brushing against the anthers and stigma.

Name: *Philotheca* = Gk. *philos*, loving, *theke*, box, referring to the fused anther filaments.

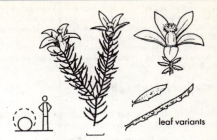

leaf variants

Philotheca salsolifolia (Smith) Druce

Ss, Castl

A small erect shrub usually under 50cm high (but over 1m high in taller heaths). Abundant in sunny, sandy, coastal heaths.

Range: NSW coasts, Blue Mountains, southern ranges and central and northern slopes. **Leaves:** crowded, slender, with prominent lumpy oil glands on lower surface. **Flowers:** PINK or MAUVE, solitary, terminal. **Name:** *salsolifolia* = *Salsola*-leaved. *Salsola* is a genus of salt-resistant, small-leaved, often prickly plants in Chenopodiaceae.

Philotheca salsolifolia

• *Sarcomelicope*
—See RAINFOREST SPECIES.

Zieria compacta

• *Zieria* Smith

A genus of aromatic shrubs with 25 endemic species. Found in all eastern states and New Caledonia.

Zierias have opposite, tri-foliate leaves. The flowers have

Zieria flower with two petals removed

(*Z. laevigata*)

4 petals and 4 stamens. The ovary has 4 chambers, each producing a single seed.

Name: *Zieria* = by James Smith in honour of his friend, the botanist Jan Zier, who had just passed away.

Zieria cytisoides

Zieria compacta C. T. White

Ss

An erect shrub to 1.5m tall, found in woodland on sandstone. Mainly a mountain species, but occurs in the Sydney area at Bent's Basin. It is very similar to *Z. cytisoides*, but easily distinguished by the hairless upper surface of its leaves.

Range: coast and ranges, mainly north from the Sydney area, into Qld. **Leaves:** smooth, satin, hairless above, pale below with a fine felt, margins recurved. **Flowers:** PINK to WHITE, in small dense axillary cymes at the end of a short stalk. **Flowering time:** spring. **Name:** *compacta* = Lat. compact. **Similar species:** distinguish from *Z. cytisoides* by the hairless upper surface of the leaves and by the hairless fruits.

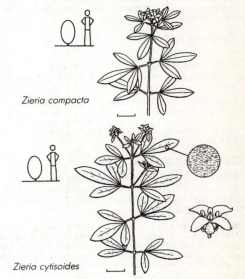

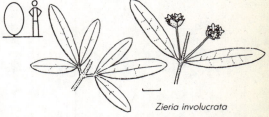

Zieria involucrata

Range: ranges and western slopes throughout the eastern mainland. **Leaves:** densely furry above, densely white-hairy below, with recurved margins. **Flowers:** PINK to WHITE, in small dense axillary cymes at the end of a stalk 10-25mm long. **Flowering time:** spring. **Name:** *cytisoides* = Gk. like *Cytisus*, a genus in the Pea family with similar leaves; *C. scoparius* is English Broom. **Similar species:** distinguish from *Z. compacta* by the leaves furry on both sides and the hairy fruits.

Zieria cytisoides Smith

Downy Zieria **Ss**

An erect shrub to 1.5m tall, found in woodland on sandstone, especially in rocky places. Mainly a mountain species, but occurs in the Sydney area at Bent's Basin. Easily recognised by its softly furry, sometimes greyish, leaves.

Zieria involucrata R. Brown ex Bentham

Ss Vulnerable 2VC-

A robust shrub to 2m high. A rare species, found in a few moist gullies near Maroota and in Marramarra National Park (also near Colo Heights and in the Blue Mountains, e.g. Springwood, Valley Heights and Kurrajong).

Range: restricted to the Sydney area. **Leaves:** opposite, simple or with 3 leaflets, oblong, to 6cm long, both sides covered in dense soft whitish hairs, dull olive green above, whitish green below. **Flowers:** petals WHITE with pink tinges, sessile, numerous in a compact head, surrounded by persistent overlapping bracts. The calyx is reddish and densely hairy. **Flowering time:** spring. **Name:** *involucrata* = Lat. enwrapped, referring to the floral bracts.

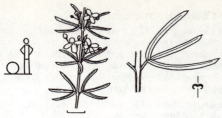

Zieria laevigata ssp. *laevigata*

Zieria laevigata Bonplaud

Ss

A small open shrub usually under 1m high, found in sunny places in heath on sandstone. Not common.

Range: NSW coasts, Blue Mountains and northern ranges. **Leaflets:** 3, slender, with recurved margins. **Flowers:** WHITE or PINKISH, in axillary inflorescences. **Flowering time:** spring (June—October). **Name:** *laevigata* = smooth and polished.

Zieria pilosa Rudge

Ss

A low sprawling shrub with stems to 1m long, common in woodland, usually in rocky places. It has a lemon fragrance when crushed.

Range: NSW coast and Blue Mountains. **Leaves:** small, opposite, 3-foliolate, fairly tough, with recurved margins, and translucent oil-dots. **Flowers:** tiny, PINK, 1 per leaf joint. **Flowering time:** September-November. **Name:** *pilosa* = Lat. softly hairy, from the hairs that cover the stems.

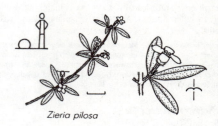

Zieria pilosa

Zieria smithii Andrews

Sandfly Zieria **Ss, Cumb, Temp Rf margins**

An erect shrub to 1.5m with strongly fragrant foliage, abundant in sheltered places in all types of forests. The *Pyrethrin*-like oil in the leaves is a good insect repellent.

Range: NSW coast, Blue Mountains, northern ranges, Qld and Vic. **Leaves:** opposite, 3-foliate, hairless, rough with raised translucent oil-glands, fairly thin and soft, usually glossy. **Flowers:** WHITE in small cymes in the leaf joints. The whole plant flowers at once and can be very spectacular. **Name:** *smithii* = in Honour of the celebrated English botanist James Smith (1759-1828).

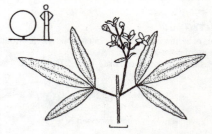

Zieria smithii

LESSER FAMILIES

ACANTHACEAE

A family of herbs and small shrubs with about 2500 species in about 250 genera, mainly tropical. There are about 40 species in 21 genera in Australia. The family is closely related to Scrophulariaceae.

• *Brunoniella* Bremekamp

A mainly endemic genus of small perennial herbs with 6 species, distributed in eastern mainland Australia, Darwin and the Kimberleys. One species extends to NG.

These little plants have swollen succulent roots. Since a related Qld species has edible roots, those of the local species may also be edible.

The seeds are covered in specialised hairs which, although matted and inconspicuous when dry, produce a mass of sticky mucus when wet, aiding dispersal by birds and small animals.

Name: *Brunoniella* = little-*Brunonia*, presumably from some resemblance to *Brunonia*, which is however quite a different plant in a different family (Brunoniaceae).

Brunoniella australis (R. Brown) Bremekamp

Blue Trumpet, Blue Yam   **Cumb, Castl**

A small erect herb, to 15cm, occasionally to 30cm, tall. Common in marshy clay understories in open forest on the Cumberland Plain.

Range: an inland species, only found east of the Great Dividing Ranges on the Cumberland Plain. **Leaves:** opposite, mostly 10-30mm long, roughly furry both sides. **Flowers:** BLUE-MAUVE, about 15mm wide, sepals slender 0.5-1mm wide, scabrous-hairy. **Flowering time:** October-January. **Name:** *australis* = Lat. southern.

Brunoniella pumilio (R. Brown) Bremekamp

Dwarf Trumpet   **Cumb, Castl**

Similar to *B. australis*, except smaller (to 10cm tall), with smaller flowers which have wider hairless sepals.

Range: NSW coastal areas.   **Leaves:** similar to *B. australis*, except almost hairless, often purple below.   **Flowers:** BLUE-MAUVE, about 10mm wide, sepals relatively broad and apparently hairless.   **Flowering time:** October-January.   **Name:** *pumilio* = Lat. low, small.

• *Pseuderanthemum* Radlkofer

(seu-der-ANTH-e-mum)

A genus of small herbs with about 120 species. There are 3-4 species in Australia. The narrow tube and pale flowers suggest pollination by night-flying moths. There are only 2 stamens. In the capsules the seeds are attached by hook-like woody stalks called jaculators. They position the seed for forcible ejection as the capsule bursts open.

Name: *Pseuderanthemum* = Gk. false *Eranthemum*, a similar related genus.

Pseuderanthemum variabile

(R. Brown) Radlkofer

Pastel Flower   **Ss, Cumb, Temp Rf, STRf**

A small erect herb with stems 10-30cm tall, arising from creeping roots. Moderately common in the area (especially on the north shore), in moist shady situations in gullies or in forests on the Cumberland Plain. Also in rainforests.

Range: NSW coast, Qld and NT. **Leaves:** opposite, 2-7cm long (mostly 2-3cm in the Sydney area), glossy, dark green above, sometimes with pale markings following the veins. **Flowers:** PALE MAUVE, PALE BLUE, PALE PINK or WHITE, 15-22mm wide, with a narrow tube and 5 broad unequal lobes, sometimes with purple markings on the upper lobe, in a short terminal spike (although only 1-2 flowers mature at a time). **Flowering time:** December-January. **Name:** *variabile* = Lat. variable.

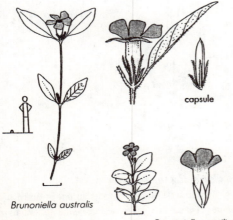

capsule

Brunoniella australis

Brunoniella pumilio

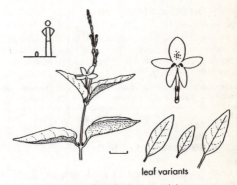

leaf variants

Pseuderanthemum variabile

AMARANTHACEAE

A family with about 900 species in 65 genera, including 131 species in 14 genera in Australia. It is notable for having small papery flowers, usually surrounded by conspicuous papery bracts. The family is closely related to Chenopodiaceae.

• *Alternanthera* Forsskal

A genus with about 200 species worldwide, including 5 native and 3 introduced species in Australia.

Name: *Alternanthera* = Lat. alternating anther, since the stamens often alternate with staminodes.

Alternanthera denticulata R. Brown

Lesser Joyweed **Cumb, Ss, Aqu, Sal**

A weak sprawling herb with stems 20-50cm long, found in marshes, especially on the Cumberland Plain.

Range: widespread on mainland Australia. **Leaves:** opposite, 1-6 cm long, with very tiny teeth, on more or less square stems. **Flowers:** stalkless, about 2mm long, with 5 white papery perianth segments; in small dense axillary clusters. **Flowering time:** spring-summer; but the papery perianths remain all year. **Name:** *denticulata* = Lat. having tiny teeth.

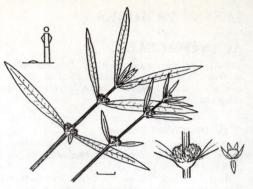

Alternanthera denticulata

• *Deeringia*

—See CLIMBERS.

APIACEAE Umbelliferae

A family mainly of herbs, with about 3000 species in about 300 genera. Australia has 167 species in 36 genera, distributed in all states, including many introduced species. The family includes the culinary plants carrot, dill, coriander, celery, parsley, fennel and others.

The flattened, 2-chambered fruits are distinctive.

• *Actinotus* Labillardière

An endemic genus with 15 species, found in all states except SA (one species extends to NZ). The flower-heads are surrounded by large furry bracts.

Name: *Actinotus* = Gk. having rays, referring to the ray-like bracts.

Actinotus helianthi Labillardière

Flannel Flower **Ss**

A strange and beautiful herbaceous plant, to 1m high, common in dry sunny rocky places. The whole plant is covered in a dense layer of whitish woolly hairs, and its flower heads mimic those of a daisy.

Range: NSW coast, ranges and western slopes, into Qld. **Leaves:** much divided into blunt slender segments. **Flowers:** tiny, densely hairy, clustered into a dense central knob surrounded by large furry ray-like bracts, the whole 4-7cm wide. **Flowering time:** spring. **Name:** *helianthi* = Gk. a sunflower.

Actinotus minor (Smith) De Candolle

Ss

A small sprawling or ascending shrub with wiry stems to 40cm long, abundant in open heathland.

Range: Sydney area, Blue Mountains, south coast and southern tablelands. **Leaves:** few, small, divided, with pointed segments. **Flowers:** similar to *A. helianthi*, but usually only about 12mm diameter. **Flowering time:** much of the year. **Name:** *minor* = Lat. lesser.

• *Apium*

—See COASTAL AND ESTUARINE SPECIES.

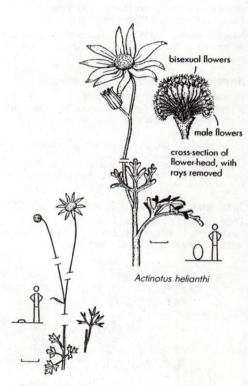

bisexual flowers

male flowers

cross-section of flower-head, with rays removed

Actinotus helianthi

Actinotus minor

• *Centella* Linnaeus

A genus with about 40 species, including one in Australia.

Name: *Centella* = Gk. little prickle, referring to features on the type species.

Centella asiatica (Linnaeus) Urban
Ss, Cumb, Castl, Aqu

A creeping herb, rooting along the stems, common in marshy places on clays or sandy soils. In India the juice is used as a medicine for sores, skin irritation, prickly heat and leprosy.

Range: Sydney area and NSW north coast; also recorded from the south-western plains, Lord Howe Island, all states except NT, and widespread in Asia. **Leaves:** serrated, 2-5cm wide. **Flowers:** tiny, in small clusters of 3-4, protected by small broad bracts, on peduncles much shorter than the leaves. **Flowering time:** summer. **Name:** *asiatica* = Asian.

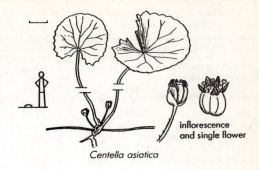

inflorescence and single flower

Centella asiatica

• *Daucus* Linnaeus
A genus of small herbs with about 60 species, including 1 native and 1 introduced species in Australia.

Name: *Daucus* = from the Greek name *daukon*, used by Theophrastus for another plant in this family.

Daucus glochidiatus (Labillardière)
Fischer, C. A. Meyer & Avé-Lallemant
Ss, Cumb

A sprawling or ascending herb with stems 30-50cm long. Rare in the area, only recorded north of the harbour. The fruits are small and globular, armed with numerous barbed projections.

Range: found in all parts of NSW, all other states and NZ. **Leaves:** pinnate, the segments much divided, soft, usually slightly hairy. **Flowers:** WHITE. **Name:** *glochidiatus* = Gk. bearing barbs.

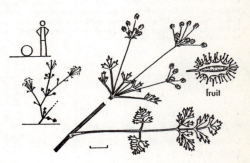

fruit

Daucus glochidiatus

• *Hydrocotyle* Linnaeus (hy-dro-COT-il-ee)
Pennyworts

A genus of small marsh herbs with about 100 species in temperate and tropical regions of the world. There are 32 species native to Australia with 1 species introduced (*H. bonariensis*) 'all insignificant weeds' wrote William Woolls.[1] Found in all states.

Name: *Hydrocotyle* = Gk. water-cup, from the leaf shape of the European type species.

*Hydrocotyle bonariensis**
—See SEACOAST AND ESTUARINE SPECIES.

Hydrocotyle geraniifolia F. Mueller
Forest Pennywort **Ss**

A weak scrambling herb with stems to about 50cm long, found in sheltered gullies, in wet shrubbery beside streams. Very uncommon in the area (e.g. Lady Carrington Drive, Royal National Park), but common on creek flats and volcanic tops in the Blue Mountains.

Range: NSW coastal areas and Blue Mountains. **Leaves:** soft, thin, deeply divided into toothed or lobed segments. **Flowers:** SNOWY WHITE, in small fragile umbels. **Flowering time:** spring and summer. **Name:** *geraniifolia* = *Geranium*-leaved.

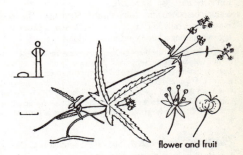

flower and fruit

Hydrocotyle geraniifolia

Hydrocotyle peduncularis R. Brown ex A. Richard
Ss

A creeping herb with small toothed leaves, common in sheltered marshy spots. Forms with large leaves are sometimes known as *H. acutiloba*, but that species only occurs in Qld.

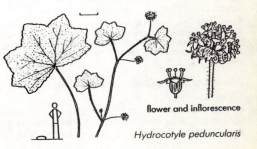

flower and inflorescence

Hydrocotyle peduncularis

The species is under revision and a number of subspecies may be recognised in future.

Range: coast and ranges of NSW. **Leaves:** slightly or densely hairy, with shallow lobes, not hard or stiff, mostly 5-25mm wide (rarely to 70mm). **Flowers:** tiny, in dense clusters on long flower stems. **Flowering time:** summer. **Name:** *peduncularis* = Lat. pedunculate, referring to the long flower stalks.

Hydrocotyle tripartita R. Brown ex A. Richard
Ss

A small creeping herb, rooting from the stems. Found in sheltered places and beside streams, and occasionally as a weed in lawns. Rare in the area, but more common north of the Hawkesbury and in the Illawarra.

Range: confined to the Sydney region. **Leaves:** deeply divided into 3 toothed or lobed segments less than 6mm long (rarely to 12mm long). **Flowers:** about 1mm wide, pale green, in globular clusters on peduncles much shorter than the leaves. The flowers are rarely seen, either because of their small size and obscured position, or because the plant, spreading well by vegetative means, rarely produces them. **Name:** *tripartita* = Lat. 3-sectioned, referring to the leaves.

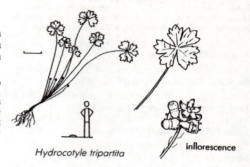

Hydrocotyle tripartita inflorescence

• *Lilaeopsis*
—See AQUATICS.

• *Platysace* Bunge (plat-ee-SACE-ee)

An endemic genus with about 20 species, distributed in all mainland states.

Name: *Platysace* = Gk. flat-shield, describing the fruit.

Platysace clelandii (Maiden & Betche) L.A.S. Johnson
Fan Platysace **Ss Rare 2RCa**

A much-branched scrambling shrub to 50cm high. The species is very rare, only known locally from Berowra Creek where it grows amongst large sandstone boulders.

Range: restricted to the Berowra Creek area, Sydney, and to several spots in the Colo-Wiseman's Ferry-Glen Davis area north-west of Sydney. **Leaves:** numerous, fan-shaped with 5-9 teeth on the outer margin, hairless above and sparsely bristly underneath. Young branches are densely covered in short, rigid, spreading bristles. **Flowers:** WHITE, in terminal compound umbels. **Flowering time:** late summer. **Name:** *clelandii* = after Dr Cleland who collected the type specimen at Berowra Creek in 1911.

Platysace clelandii

Platysace ericoides (Sieber ex Sprengel) C. Norman
Heathy Platysace **Ss, Castl**

A low sprawling shrub with stems to 10-50cm long. Fairly common in heath and sclerophyll forest.

Range: NSW coast, ranges and western slopes, from the Sydney area into Qld. **Leaves:** slender, erect, fairly stiff. **Flowers:** WHITE, in very small, compact umbels at the ends of branches. **Flowering time:** spring-summer. **Name:** *ericoides* = *Erica*-like. *Erica* is the heath or heather of Europe.

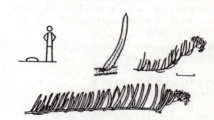

Platysace ericoides

Platysace lanceolata (Labillardière) Druce
Native Parsnip **Ss**

An erect leafy shrub 1-1.5m high. Abundant in woodland, often forming dense masses in gullies. There are two distinct forms which have yet to be named. One has spear-shaped

narrow-leafed form broad-leafed form

Platysace lanceolata

leaves, thin and flexible. The other has heart-shaped leaves which are fairly stiff.

Range: NSW coast, ranges and western slopes, also Queensland and Victoria. **Leaves:** alternate, dull, hairless, sessile, with distinctive almost parallel venation. **Flowers:** WHITE, in dense compound umbels. **Flowering time:** summer. **Name:** *lanceolata* = Lat. spear-shaped.

Platysace linearifolia (Cavanilles) C. Norman

Carrot Tops **Ss**
A slender open shrub to 1.5m high with soft thread-like foliage. Common in woodland, usually in dense colonies.

Range: confined to the Sydney region and Blue Mountains. **Leaves:** erect, soft, almost cylindrical. **Flowers:** WHITE, in dense clusters on long peduncles near the tips of branches. **Flowering time:** February-March. **Name:** *linearifolia* = Lat. straight-leaved.

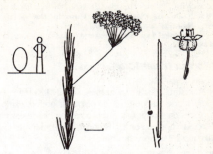

Platysace linearifolia

Platysace stephensonii (Turczaninow) C. Norman

Stephenson's Platysace **Ss Rare 3RC-**
An erect or spreading shrub to 30cm high. Very uncommon, scattered in coastal heaths.

Range: Sydney area and also on Point Perpendicular (Jervis Bay). **Leaves:** divided into 3 segments, rigid, sharp-pointed. **Flowers:** small, WHITE, in small dense terminal umbels. **Flowering time:** summer. **Name:** *stephensonii* = in honour of Lawrence Stephenson, the Sydney botanist who collected the type specimen. It would be interesting to know how it reached Turczaninow, a Russia botanist with a passion for Australian plants.

Platysace stephensonii

• *Trachymene* Rudge (track-ee-MEE-nee)

A genus of herbs with about 40 species, including about 20 in Australia, distributed in all states.

Name: *Trachymene* = Gk. rough-skin, referring to the fruits.

Trachymene incisa Rudge **ssp. *incisa***

Ss
An erect herb to 50cm high, found in sheltered woodland, especially in gullies. Uncommon in the area. The thickened taproot is edible cooked or raw, tasting rather like a parsnip.

Range: NSW coasts, also northern tablelands, north-western slopes and Qld. **Leaves:** 2-4cm wide, highly dissected; mainly located at the base of the stem. **Flowers:** tiny, fragile, WHITE, in a dense terminal umbel. **Flowering time:** summer. **Name:** *incisa* = Lat. deeply cut.

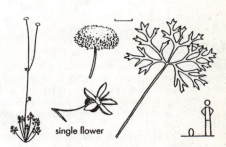

single flower

Trachymene incisa ssp. *incisa*

• *Xanthosia* Rudge (zanth-O-zhee-a)

An endemic genus with 20 species, found in all states except NT.

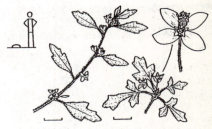

Xanthosia pilosa

Xanthosia flower
(*X. pilosa*)

Name: *Xanthosia* = Gk. *xanthos*, yellow, from the yellow flowers of the type species (though most have white flowers).

Xanthosia pilosa Rudge

Woolly Xanthosia **Ss**
A small straggling shrub with stems under 50cm long, common in sheltered woodland on dry sandy soil. This is a very complex species with a number of widely differing forms*: those with compound umbels previously went under the name *X. vestita*.

Range: NSW coast and ranges, Qld, Vic and Tas. **Leaves:** lobed and hairy, densely hairy below. **Flowers:** GREENISH WHITE, in few-flowered umbels with small pale wing-like bracts. **Flowering time:** spring and summer. **Name:** *pilosa* = Lat. softly hairy.
* a very large-leaved form occurs beside the Lane Cove River, at the end of Mars Road.

Xanthosia tridentata De Candolle
Rock Xanthosia **Ss**
A shy little shrub that's easy to miss, usually less than 30cm high and hidden amongst taller plants. It prefers damp or rocky places on sandy soils and is common near creeks and in sheltered woodland on sandstone. It also sometimes forms mat-like masses in open heathland.

Range: Sydney area, Blue Mountains and NSW south coast into Vic. **Leaves:** 3-toothed at tip, finely hairy, erect. **Flowers:** inconspicuous, hidden by leafy bracts. **Name:** *Lat. tridentata* = 3-toothed.

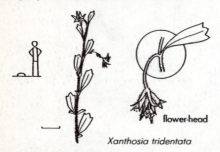

flower-head

Xanthosia tridentata

ARALIACEAE

A family of trees, shrubs and climbers with about 700 species in 55 genera. There are about 28 species in 10 genera in Australia. The family includes the English ivy (*Hedera helix* cultivars), ginseng (*Panax quinquefolia*), and the umbrella plant, *Schefflera actinophylla*, an indoor inhabitant of many an Australian home.

The family is closely related to Apiaceae, and has similar flowers and fruits.

• *Astrotricha* De Candolle (ass-tro-TRICK-a)
Star-hairs
An endemic genus with about 10 species, distributed in NSW, Qld and WA.

Astrotricha flower
(*A. longifolia*)

Name: *Astrotricha* = Gk. *astron*, star, *trichos*, hair, from the dense covering of star-hairs.

Astrotricha crassifolia Blakely
Thick-leaf Star-hair **Ss**
An erect shrub 2-3m tall. A rare species. Recorded from Port Hacking (south of Audley), Woronora Plateau (e.g. Heathcote Creek), and also near Gosford.

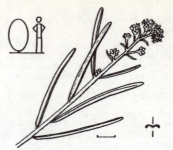

Astrotricha crassifolia

Range: restricted to the Sydney area; also in Vic. **Leaves:** stiff, blunt, with recurved margins, hairless above, covered in a dense brownish wool below. **Flowers:** WHITE, with mauve anthers, in a terminal panicle of umbels. **Flowering time:** September. **Name:** *crassifolia* = Lat. thick-leaved. **Note:** the leaves may be mistaken for those of *Hovea* species (see MAJOR FAMILIES: Fabaceae).

Astrotricha floccosa De Candolle
Flannel leaf **Ss**
An erect leafy shrub 2-3m tall, found in sheltered gullies near streams. Common on sandstone. Easily recognised by the very dense woolly hairs on the underside of leaves and on stems.

Range: restricted to the Sydney area. **Leaves:** flat, densely woolly below, stalks under 25mm long. **Flowers:** WHITISH. **Flowering time:** October-November. **Name:** *floccosa* =Lat. woolly.

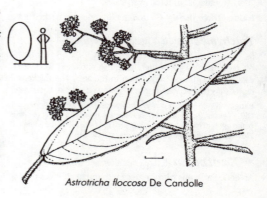

Astrotricha floccosa De Candolle

Astrotricha latifolia Bentham

Ss

An erect leafy shrub 2-3m tall, found in sheltered gullies near streams. Rare in the area, restricted to the Georges River (Woolwash, Kentlyn) and Norton's Basin.

Range: NSW coast and ranges, and Qld. **Leaves:** glossy, thin textured, dark green above, covered with a fine felt below, stalks at least 30mm long. **Flowers:** WHITISH. The inflorescence is larger and more open than *A. floccosa.* **Flowering time:** October-November. **Name:** *latifolia* = Lat. broad-leaved.

Astrotricha longifolia Bentham

Ss

An erect shrub 1-2m tall, found in sheltered woodland on sandstone. Uncommon, occurring only north of the harbour.

Range: NSW coast and ranges, north from Sydney harbour into Qld. **Leaves:** dull green above, finely rusty-felty below. **Flowers:** WHITE. **Flowering time:** October-December. **Name:** *longifolia* = Lat. long-leaved.

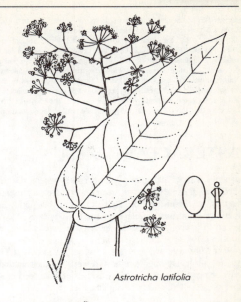

Astrotricha latifolia

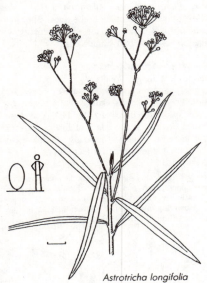

Astrotricha longifolia

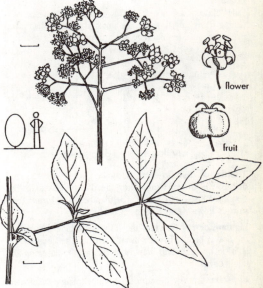

flower

fruit

Polyscias sambucifolia

• *Polyscias* J. R. & G. Forster

A genus with about 80 species, including 7 species in Australia, all in the eastern states.
Name: *Polyscias* = Gk. many-canopied, referring to the numerous umbels.

Polyscias elegans
—see RAINFOREST SPECIES.

Polyscias murrayi
—see RAINFOREST SPECIES.

Polyscias sambucifolia
(Sieber ex De Candolle) Harms

Elderberry Panax **Ss**

An erect shrub usually about 2m high, found in sheltered woodland on sandstone, usually on gully sides. Common in the area. The wood is very tough and was much used for axe handles and other tools by early timber cutters.

Range: NSW coast and ranges north from the Sydney area into Qld.
Leaves: pinnate, usually with 5-7 leaflets and also a pair of small stipule-like leaflets at the base of the stalk; the leaflets are hairless, medium-textured, toothed. **Flowers:** GREENISH with yellow anthers, about 5mm wide, in a terminal panicle of umbels. **Fruits:** bluish-green, becoming purple and succulent when ripe. **Flowering time:** December-January. **Name:** *sambucifolia* = *Sambucus*-leaved. *Sambucus* is a genus in the family Caprifoliaceae. **Note:** There are a number of surprising variants of this species whose status has yet to be determined. The leaves may be bipinnate, and the leaflets may be very slender and variously lobed or toothed.

ASTERACEAE Compositae

Daisies

A family with 25 000 species in about 1100 genera, distributed in all continents except Antarctica and well represented in all environments from alpine to desert (but poorly in rainforests). In Australia there are about 970 species in 205 genera. The family is important in deserts where ephemeral species cover large areas after rain.

Most Asteraceae are, let's face it, weeds. Even our native species are highly opportunistic and weedy in their natural environments. The reason for this is their massive seed production and short, often annual, life cycles.

Botany

Daisy 'flowers' are not single flowers but dense heads containing many tiny flowers. The unusual anatomy has given rise to a special terminology –

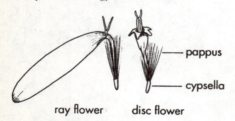

ray flower   disc flower

Tubular or disc flowers: the flowers forming the central disc of the flower head. They are usually bisexual. The petals are fused into a tube. The 5 anthers also form a tube surrounding a 2-armed style.

Ligulate or ray flowers: the flowers forming the rays of the flower head. They are usually female. The floral tube is split on one side and drawn out into a long flat wing-like ligule or ray.

Cypsella: the tiny cylindrical or winged single-chambered ovary at the base of each flower

Pappus: the cluster of long silky hairs, scales or barbs encircling the top of the cypsella. The pappus allows distribution by wind (when hairy) or by animals (when barbed).

Receptacle: the broad disc-like structure on which the cypsellas sit.

Involucre: the rows of involucral bracts which surround the flower head. They may be green or coloured, fleshy or papery.

The method of pollination is as follows. The anthers release their pollen inwards onto the sticky style which then grows upward, carrying the pollen out of the anther tube to where it may brush against visiting insects. Shortly afterwards the style arms open and the stigmas become receptive. Daisies are popular with bees and other insects but self-pollination is also common.

The combination of prodigious seed production and efficient distribution makes Daisies amongst the most abundant, successful and wide ranging plants on the planet.

• *Actites*

– See COASTAL AND ESTUARINE SPECIES.

• *Ageratina* Spach

An almost cosmopolitan genus of opportunistic shrubs, with about 230 species, especially in America. There are 3 naturalised species, in NSW, Qld and SA.
Name: *Ageratina* = from *Ageratum*, a Greek name for some blue-flowered members of the genus. The older name *Eupatorium* is from Eupator, the King of Pontus, who was reputed to have first used it in medicine.

*Ageratina adenophora**

(Sprengel) R.M. King & Robinson
(previously *Eupatorium adenophorum**)
Crofton Weed   **Ss, Cumb**
An erect leafy shrub usually to 2.5m high. Very common in disturbed ground on the edges of forests and roadsides, always in dense colonies. The stems and inflorescence are sticky with glandular hairs. Introduced from Central America.

Range: NSW coast and ranges north from the Sydney region into Qld.
Leaves: opposite, soft, thin, toothed. **Flower heads:** disc flowers WHITE, with long white style arms, ray flowers absent, pappus of fine hairs. **Flowering time:** summer. **Name:** *adenophora* = Gk. *aden*, gland, *phoros*, carrier, referring to the glands on the stem and floral bracts.

Ageratina adenophora*

*Ageratina riparia** (Regel) R.M. King & Robinson
(previously *Eupatorium riparium**)
Mist Flower   **Ss, Cumb, Temp Rf, STRf**
A low sprawling shrub, found in damp places on better soils, especially beside creeks in gullies and on the edges of rainforests where it forms such dense masses that the white flowers resemble a mist, hence the common name.

Introduced from North America. The flowers have a strong honey fragrance.

Range: NSW coast and ranges. **Leaves:** opposite, soft, thin, toothed. **Flowers:** as for *A. adenophora*. **Flowering time:** spring. **Name:** *riparia* = Lat. pertaining to creek banks.

• *Brachycome* Cassini
(bra-KICK-o-me, or brack-ee-CO-me)
A genus with 60 species in Australia and 5 species in NG and NZ. Most are small herbs with typical daisy flower heads. The rays are mostly mauve, blue or white and the disc flowers are yellow. There is a pappus of fine hairs.
Name: *Brachycome* = Gk. *brachy,* short, *kome,* hair, referring to the pappus. Sometimes incorrectly called *Brachyscome* (this was Cassini's own mispelling).

Brachycome aculeata (Labillardière) Lessing
Ss, Cumb
An erect perennial herb 20-60cm high. An uncommon species, recorded in the past from scattered locations in the area. Probably a 'blow-in' from other districts

Range: NSW coast and ranges, except for north coast; also Qld, Vic, Tas and SA. **Leaves:** soft, thin, toothed, hairless. **Flower heads:** solitary on long rough scapes, ray flowers WHITE, LILAC or BLUE, disc flowers YELLOW. **Flowering time:** mainly summer. **Name:** *aculeata* = Lat. covered in spines, reference obscure.

Brachycome angustifolia
A. Cunningham ex Bentham *var. angustifolia*
Cumb, Castl, Ss
A tiny ascending or sprawling herb with stems to 20cm long. Common in moist forests on the Cumberland Plain, sometimes in wastelands and on roadsides. Rare on the coast.

Range: NSW coast and ranges, except the north coast, Vic, Tas and SA. **Leaves:** ascending, soft, slender, toothless, variable in shape and width. **Flower heads:** to 2cm wide, solitary on slender stalks, with GOLDEN YELLOW disc flowers and MAUVE or BLUISH ray flowers, pappus of fine hairs. **Flowering time:** summer. **Name:** *angustifolia* = Lat. thin-leaved.

• *Bracteantha* Anderberg & Haegi
An endemic genus with 5 species, found in all states.
Name: *Bracteantha* = Lat. bract-flower.

Bracteantha bracteatum
(Ventenat) Anderberg & Haegi   Golden Everlasting
Ss (previously *Helichrysum bracteatum*)
A slender erect herb usually 40-80cm tall, with bright golden flower heads. Found in sunny places in forests on high-nutrient soils. Uncommon in the area, only occurring in the southern parts of the Royal National Park, especially beside roads. The bright show of golden bracts makes this a beautiful species which is popular in gardens & dried flower arrangements.

Range: widespread throughout NSW, also all other mainland states. **Leaves:** soft, to 10cm long, more or less stem-clasping, hairless or slightly hairy **Flower heads:** GOLDEN YELLOW, solitary, terminal, to 25-

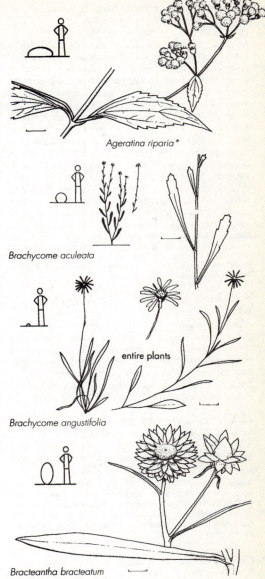

Ageratina riparia *

Brachycome aculeata

entire plants

Brachycome angustifolia

Bracteantha bracteatum

35mm wide (when bracts open), surrounded by several rows of stiff golden yellow bracts. **Flowering time:** spring-summer, but the dry golden bracts remain for much of the year. **Name:** *bracteatum* = Lat. having bracts.

• *Calomeria* Ventenat (cal-o-MEER-ee-a)
An endemic genus with a single species.
Name: *Calomeria* = Gk. beautiful-part, referring to the flowers.

Calomeria amaranthoides Ventenat
(previously known as *Humea elegans*)
Plume Bush **Cumb**

An extraordinary looking plant to 3m or more high, with a tuft of very large leaves at the base, reaching up to a magnificent terminal panicle with thousands of cascading glossy, reddish flower heads. Found uncommonly along the Nepean, and in gullies in the Blue Mountains. It has a 'powerful resinous odour...which is by no means pleasant' wrote William Woolls.[2] Another early commentator, George Bennet, wrote 'I observed about the Rocky Hills a very large herbaceous plant, growing in great luxuriance upon the scarped ridges, and bearing flowers of a reddish hue, in large drooping panicles; it was the Elegant Humea (*Humea elegans*). The whole plant, on being bruised, emits a delightful scent, so overpowering as sometimes to produce headache. I am of the opinion that a very valuable perfume might be obtained from it'.[3] Each plant lives for 2 years.

Range: NSW coast, Blue Mountains and Vic. **Leaves:** mostly about 30cm long, fairly soft, stem-clasping, crowded, spirally arranged, with rough glandular hairs above and white wool below; on white woolly stems. **Flower heads:** 3mm long, surrounded by SILVERY-REDDISH bracts, drooping in an immense open panicle. **Flowering time:** spring. **Name:** *amaranthoides* = *Amaranthus*-like.

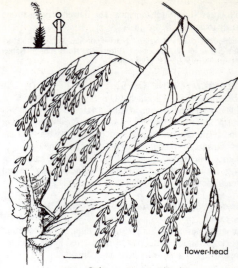

Calomeria amaranthoides

flower-head

• *Calotis* R. Brown
Burr Daisies

A genus of small weedy herbs with 24 species in Australia and 2 in Asia. *Calotis* are innocent looking Daisies until they fruit and the heads develop into fiendish masses of rigid needle-sharp barbs. They are mostly opportunistic inhabitants of grasslands, easily spread by stock.

Name: *Calotis* = Gk. beautiful-ear, alluding to the ear-shaped pappus scales of *C. cuneifolia*, the type species.

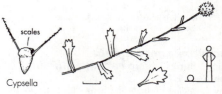

scales

Cypsella

Calotis cuneifolia

Calotis cuneifolia R. Brown
Bindi-eye, Blue Burr-daisy **Cumb, Castl**

A perennial herb to 60cm high. A weedy species from inland NSW, probably spread by stock. Found in grasslands and open forests on the Cumberland Plain.

Range: all parts of NSW; also Qld, Vic, NT and SA. **Leaves:** spathulate (spoon-shaped), usually with 5 short lobes near the tip, covered in short stiff hairs; the leaf bases are stem-clasping. **Flower heads:** 7-10mm dia, ray flowers WHITE or MAUVE, disc flowers YELLOW, pappus of 2 barbs and 2 scales. **Flowering time:** much of the year. **Name:** *cuneifolia* = Lat. wedge-leaved.

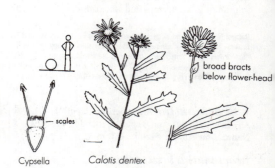

broad bracts below flower-head

scales

Cypsella *Calotis dentex*

Calotis dentex R. Brown
White Daisy Burr **Cumb**

A leafy perennial herb with stems to 80cm high and white daisy flowers. Found in grassland and open forest on clay soils, and clay enriched sandy soils. Common and widespread on the Cumberland Plain and adjacent sandstone areas, probably the most common of the local species.

Range: NSW coast and ranges north from Sydney, also Qld. **Leaves:** usually deeply toothed, soft, green, all parts covered in fine soft hairs. **Flower heads:** ray flowers WHITE (drying mauve), rays about 10mm long, bracts broad, pappus of 2 barbs and 2 scales with fringed margins. **Flowering time:** most of the year. **Name:** *dentex* = toothed.

Calotis hispidula R. Brown
Boganflea (and worse names) **Cumb**

A small annual herb, prostrate or ascending, to 25cm high. Found in dry places in grasslands and open forests. Uncommon on the Cumberland Plain. Probably an inland species spread by stock. It often forms extensive colonies after rains and is one of the most annoying of the inland burrs.

Range: western NSW, Qld, Vic, NT, SA, WA, including Central Australia. **Leaves:** tiny, with 3 teeth at the apex, covered in stiff hairs, lower leaves sometimes with 5 teeth. **Flower heads:** ray flowers about 1mm long, very slender, YELLOW, pappus of 5-6 barbs, several finely dissected scales and a mass of woolly hairs **Flowering time:** mainly winter. **Name:** *hispidula* = covered in dense stiff hairs.

Calotis lappulacea Bentham
Woolly-headed Burr-daisy   **Cumb**
A small stiff perennial herb with many ascending branches, 10-30cm high. Found in grasslands and open forest on the Cumberland Plain.

Range: NSW coast, ranges and inland areas, Qld, Vic, SA and WA. **Leaves:** tiny, entire (sometimes a few basal leaves lobed), covered in short hairs. **Flowers:** ray flowers YELLOW, about 3mm long, pappus of 2 large and usually 4 small barbs with some woolly hairs. **Flowering time:** most of the year. **Name:** *lappulacea* = like a *Lappula*, a genus of stiffly hairy plants (Stickseeds) in the Boraginaceae family, found in temperate regions, from Lat. *lappa*, a burr.

• *Cassinia* R. Brown
A genus of shrubs with 18 endemic species in Australia (all states except NT), and 3 in NZ. **Name:** *Cassinia* = after Count Henri Cassini (1781-1832), a French botanist who specialised in this family.

Cassinia flower head (*C. denticulata*)

Cassinia aculeata
(Labillardière) R. Brown
Common Cassinia, Dogwood, Mountain Itch   **Ss**
An erect shrub 1-2m high, found in sheltered places in forests. Probably locally restricted to a few places in the Royal National Park. The leaves are reputed to cause skin irritation. It can be difficult to distinguish from *C. uncata*, but the leaves are usually much longer.

Range: NSW coast and ranges spreading into Vic, Tas and SA. **Leaves:** linear, slightly rough and sticky, margins rolled underneath almost concealing the white woolly undersurface (or rarely almost flat), crowded. **Flower heads:** 1-3mm diameter, bracts pink or white, and of 2 types; the outer ones round and papery and the inner ones hard and slender (though this can be hard to see on living specimens). **Flowering time:** mainly summer. **Name:** *aculeata* = Lat. spiny, reference obscure.

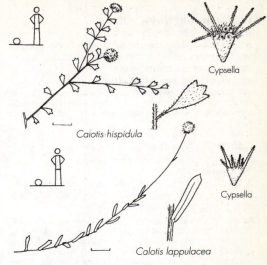

Calotis hispidula

Cypsella

Cypsella

Calotis lappulacea

green below. Stems green. **Flower heads:** similar to *C. longifolia*, except the bracts are LEMON YELLOW (fading to brown). **Flowering time:** spring-summer. **Name:** *aureonitens* = Lat. shining gold.

Cassinia compacta F. Mueller
Long-leaved Cassinia, Shiny Cassinia   **Ss**
An erect shrub to 2m high, closely related to *C. longifolia* except the floral bracts are brownish ('straw') coloured. Found in moist forests and gullies. An uncommon species, recorded locally from Bobbin Head and Cowan Creek.

Range: NSW coast and ranges north from Sydney, into Qld. **Leaves:** 2-7cm long, 1-3mm wide, sticky, dark, and shiny or rough with glandular hairs above, ±white below. **Flower heads:** similar to *C. longifolia* except the bracts are brownish. **Flowering time:** spring-summer. **Name:** *compacta* = Lat. compact.

Cassinia aculeata

Cassinia aureonitens N. A. Wakefield
Golden Cassinia   **Ss** (illustration: see *C. longifolia p134*)
An erect shrub to 2m high, very closely related to *C. longifolia* except the floral bracts are bright lemon yellow. A beautiful shrub that is fairly common in sheltered places in woodland, especially in the Royal National Park.

Range: NSW coast and ranges. **Leaves:** similar to *C. longifolia* except

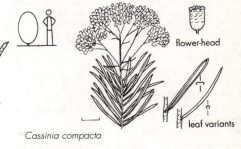

flower-head

leaf variants

Cassinia compacta

Cassinia denticulata R. Brown
Stiff Cassinia   **Ss**
An erect shrub usually about 1.5m high. An abundant local species, found in heath and woodland on sandstone.

Range: restricted to the Sydney area and Blue Mountains. **Leaves:** glossy, fairly stiff, finely toothed, with a layer of white felt underneath. **Flower heads:** with SILVERY-WHITE bracts (the flowers are yellow when they protrude). **Flowering time:** spring. **Name:** *denticulata* = Lat. finely toothed.

Cassinia longifolia R. Brown

Long-leaved Cassinia, Shiny Cassinia **Ss**

An erect shrub 2-3m high, found in moist forests and gullies. Only recorded locally from the Royal National Park but more common in southern ranges.

Range: NSW coast and ranges south from the Sydney area into Vic and Tas. **Leaves:** more or less flat, dull, usually white below with a layer of fine felt (also on stems), 4-8cm long, 3-10mm wide. **Flower heads:** enclosed in WHITE bracts. **Flowering time:** spring. **Name:** *longifolia* = Lat. long-leaved.

Cassinia trinerva N. A. Wakefield

Long-leaved Cassinia, Three-veined Cassinia

Ss, Temp Rf

A tall shrub or small tree 3-8m high, with pale brittle branches. Found in wetter woodlands in the Royal National Park. Not common locally.

Range: NSW coast and ranges, Vic and Tas. **Leaves:** soft and thin-textured, flat, variable in size (the largest size is illustrated), usually with strong parallel veins near the margins, apparently hairless, green underneath. **Flower heads:** SILVERY WHITE, very slender (<1mm wide), surrounded by silvery bracts, forming very dense terminal corymbs. **Name:** *trinerva* = Lat. 3-veined.

Cassinia uncata A. Cunningham ex De Candolle

Bent Cassinia **Ss**

An erect shrub to 2m high, found in rocky forest understories on sandstone or shale. Not common in the area. This shrub is very easily mistaken for *Ozothamnus diosmifolium**.

Range: in scattered populations in inland NSW, Vic and SA; also in mountains and coast of eastern Vic. **Leaves:** leaf tip with a slightly hooked point, 15-20mm long, rough, cylindrical with margins varying from inrolled (concealing the white underside) to merely recurved. **Flower heads:** usually WHITE (can be brownish or yellowish). **Flowering time:** much of the year. **Name:** *uncata* = Lat. hooked. **Similar species:** *Ozothamnus diosmifolium*. Close inspection of the leaf to find *C. uncata*'s slightly hooked tip is the most convenient method to distinguish the 2 species, though the hook may be rather obscure on some specimens. *O. diosmifolium* also has dark green leaves compared to the mid-green leaves of *C. uncata*.

• Centipeda

– See Acquatics

• Chrysanthemoides Medikus

A genus of with 2 species in southern Africa. One species is naturalised in Australia.

Name: *Chrysanthemoides* = like a *Chrysanthemum*, a large genus of old world daisies, literally gold-flower-like (Gk.).

Chrysanthemoides monilifera*

(Linnaeus) T. Norlindh **ssp. monilifera**

Bitou Bush, Bone Seed **Ss, Cumb**

An erect shrub usually to 1.5m high. This is a sub-species of Bitou Bush, the common weed on coastal sand-dunes. It is an erect shrub with coarsely toothed leaves, occurring on the Cumberland Plain and in coastal valleys.

Range: NSW coast south from Sydney, Vic, Tas, SA and WA.

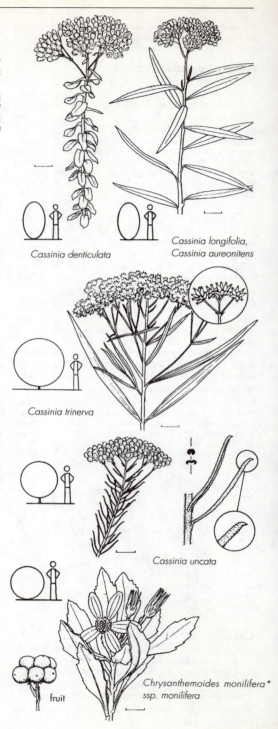

Cassinia denticulata

Cassinia longifolia,
Cassinia aureonitens

Cassinia trinerva

Cassinia uncata

fruit

Chrysanthemoides monilifera*
ssp. monilifera

Leaves: coarsely toothed, rather fleshy, covered in cotton wool when young (less so than *ssp. rotundata*). **Flower heads:** a few in a terminal panicle, ray flowers 12, GOLDEN YELLOW, disc flowers GOLDEN YEL-LOW, pappus absent. The seeds are about as broad as long, and smooth. **Flowering time:** mainly spring. **Name:** *monilifera* = Lat. necklace-bearing, referring to the seeds.

*Chrysanthemoides monilifera** ssp. rotundata*
– See COASTAL AND ESTUARINE SPECIES.

• *Chrysocephalum* Walpers
A genus with 8 species endemic in Australia, found in all states. Previously included in *Helichrysum*.
Name: *Chrysocephalum* = Gk. golden-head.

Chrysocephalum apiculatum

floral bract

Chrysocephalum apiculatum
(Labillardière) Steetz   Yellow Buttons   **Ss, Cumb**
(previously *Helichrysum apiculatum*)
A perennial herb to 50cm high, often with a woody base, found in grasslands and forests on the Cumberland Plain.

Range: NSW coast, ranges and inland; also all other states including Central Australia. **Leaves:** decurrent, covered in silvery felt. **Flower heads:** roughly spherical, flowers and papery bracts GOLDEN YELLOW. The bracts are erect, spreading after maturity. **Flowering time:** spring-summer. **Name:** *apiculatum* = Lat. having a small abrupt point, referring to the leaves.

• *Coreopsis* Linnaeus
A genus with 120 species in America and tropical Africa. One species is naturalised in Australia.
Name: *Coreopsis* = Gk *koris,* a bug, an allusion to the cypsella.

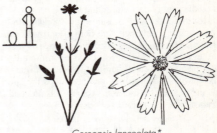

*Coreopsis lanceolata**

*Coreopsis lanceolata** Linnaeus
Ss, Cumb
A small erect herb to 50cm high. An exotic species that turns roadsides into fields of gold in spring. Very common locally. Introduced from North America.

Range: NSW coast and ranges. **Leaves:** slender, hairless, soft, with 2 lobes. **Flower heads:** solitary on leafless stalks, ray flowers GOLDEN YELLOW, the rays lobed, disc flowers GOLDEN YELLOW. **Flowering time:** spring-summer. **Name:** *lanceolata* = shaped like a lance head, referring to the leaves.

• *Cotula*
– See COASTAL AND ESTUARINE SPECIES.

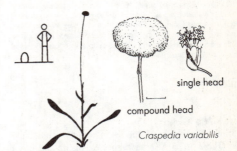

single head

compound head

Craspedia variabilis

• *Craspedia* G. Forster
Billy Buttons
A genus of herbs with 12 species, mainly Australian but with some in NZ.
Distinguished by having a compound head with numerous flower heads joined into a single globular mass.
Name: *Craspedia* = Gk. fringed, referring to the feathery pappus.

Craspedia variabilis Everett & Doust
(previously *C. glauca, and included in C. sp. C)*
Billy Buttons, Emu Flowers   **Cumb**
A tufted herb with an erect more or less leafless scape to 50cm tall bearing a globular compound head of yellow flowers. Found in grasslands and forests on the Cumberland Plain. 'The Emu flowers were now abundant, and in full blossom; the colonial appellation has been given from the emus feeding upon them, that is, when emus were to be seen...for they have been driven by the encroaching settlements far into the interior of the colony, and before long an emu will be as great, if not a greater rarity, at Sydney than in England...', wrote George Bennet in 1832.[4]

Range: NSW coast, ranges and western slopes, Vic and Qld. **Leaves:** thick, rather succulent, hoary green (glaucous), ±hairless above, pale and hairy below. **Flower heads:** many combined into a dense tight compound globular head, disc flowers YELLOW, ray flowers absent, pappus of fine hairs. **Flowering time:** spring-autumn. **Name:** *variabilis* = Lat. variable.

• *Cymbonotus* Cassini (sim-bo-NO-tus)
Bear's Ears

A small endemic genus with 3 species, mainly restricted to NSW.

Name: *Cymbonotus* = Gk. *kymbos,* a boat or cup, *notos,* the back, referring to the concave depression on one side of cypsella.

Cymbonotus lawsonianus Gaudichaud-Beaupré
Austral Bear's Ear, Native Thistle   **Cumb**

A small perennial herb with a tuft of broad woolly leaves arising from a rootstock. Found in *Eucalyptus moluccana* forests on the west of the Cumberland Plain.

The thick rootstocks were consumed by Aborigines in the NSW Alps and Vic (they are very fibrous and need some preparation). J.H. Maiden recorded how European settlers in southern NSW used the leaves as an ointment for wounds: 'Alternate layers of lard and leaves are made, the mass is allowed to cool slowly, and afterwards the lard is run out and is ready for use. Some country folk are loud in their praises of its quick healing effects.' [5]

Range: NSW coast, ranges and inland districts.   **Leaves:** entire to deeply toothed, furry above, densely white cotton woolly below.   **Flower heads:** on flowering stems shorter than the leaves, disc and ray flowers both YELLOW.   **Flowering time:** August-November.   **Name:** *lawsonianus* = after William Lawson, an ensign in the NSW Corps, who guided the French botanist Gaudichaud on his visit to the Blue Mountains and Bathurst in 1819, where the type specimen was collected. The common name 'Bear's Ear' comes from its resemblance to a European species of that name, *Primulus auricula.*

• *Eclipta*
– See AQUATICS

• *Epaltes* Cassini
A genus of herbs with 17 species in warmer parts of the world. There are 5 Australian species, distributed in all states except Tas.

Name: *Epaltes* = Gk. healing, because the root of an Indian species is used as a tonic.

Epaltes australis Lessing
Ss, Castl, Cumb, Aqu

A small perennial herb with weak, often prostrate branches, 10-25cm long. Common in marshy places, both on sandy and clay soils. Also on permanently wet rocks near the coast.

Range: all states except Tas, including Central Australia.   **Leaves:** usually toothed, spoon-shaped.   **Flowers:** YELLOW or RED, disc flowers only present, the inner disc flowers are bisexual, the smaller outer flowers are female. Pappus absent.   **Flower heads:** button-like, 4-6mm diameter, sessile (stalkless) in the leaf axils, surrounded by obtuse green bracts.   **Flowering time:** summer.   **Name:** *australis* = Lat. southern.

• *Erigeron* Linnaeus
A worldwide genus with over 200 species, mainly in North America. There are 8 species in Australia: 5 endemic and 3 naturalised.

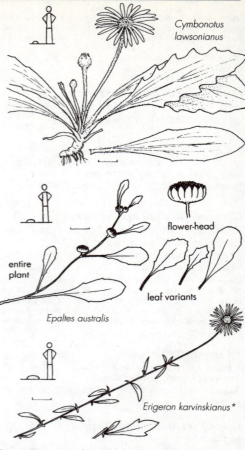

Cymbonotus lawsonianus

flower-head

entire plant

leaf variants

Epaltes australis

*Erigeron karvinskianus**

Name: *Erigeron* = the name used by Theophrastus for *Senecio vulgaris,* meaning spring–old man, since some species have downy covering in spring.

*Erigeron karvinskianus** De Candolle
Fleabane   **Ss**

A scrambling herb with stems usually about 40cm long, common in moist sheltered situations in gullies. Introduced from Central America. The flowers and habit resemble those of a native *Calotis* or *Brachycome.*

Range: NSW coast and ranges.   **Leaves:** thin, hairless, soft, large basal leaves often toothed.   **Flower heads:** disc flowers YELLOW, rays purplish pink when young, becoming WHITE. A very short pappus is present. Involucral bracts are green, numerous and slender.   **Flowering time:** October-February.   **Name:** *karvinskianus* = in honour of a certain Karvinski, who collected the type specimen in Mexico.

• *Glossogyne* Cassini
A genus of small herbs with 8 species in South-east Asia and Australia. There are 2 native species in Australia, found in all states except Tas. The genus is closely related to *Bidens,* well know from the common weed *Bidens pilosa* or

Cobbler's Pegs, whose distinctive cypsellas everyone has caught in their socks at some time.

Name: *Glossogyne* = Gk. tongue-female, referring to the tongue-like style lobes.

Glossogyne tannensis (Sprengel) Garnock-Jones
Cumb   (previously *G. tenuifolia*)   Cobblers Tack

A small erect herb with a slender flower stalk arising from a small tuft of much-divided leaves. A locally uncommon species found in grasslands and open forests usually on clay soils, e.g. Doonside, Ingleburn, Glenfield.

Range: coast and northern ranges and inland parts of NSW, all mainland states, the Pacific, Asia and India **Leaves:** fairly soft, apparently hairless, often grey-green, much divided. **Flower heads:** few, on a long slender stalk, disc and ray flowers both GOLDEN YELLOW. Cypsellas with 2 stiff barbed awns. **Flowering time:** summer. **Name:** *tannensis* = from Tanna, an island in Vanuatu where Forster collected the type specimen on Cook's 1774 visit.

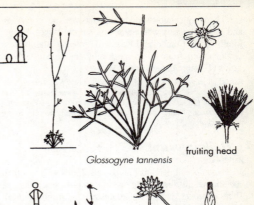

Glossogyne tannensis

fruiting head

• *Gnaphalium* Linnaeus (naf-AIL-ee-um)
Cudweeds

A genus of small herbs with about 200 species worldwide. In Australia there are about 30 species including 5 naturalised. Weedy exotic Gnaphaliums (e.g. *G. americanum*) are very common in Sydney streets and lawns. The native species have strictly globular clusters of flower heads whereas the introduced species have flower heads in elongated clusters that straggle up the stem.

The flower heads are stalkless. There are no ray flowers. The disc flowers are held in a tight involucre of shining yellowish or brownish-green bracts. There is a pappus of fine hairs. The flower heads are arranged in clusters, each subtended by 1 or more leaves.

All 3 local species were previously known under the name *G. japonicum*.

Name: *Gnaphalium* = Gk. soft down, referring to the woolly leaves. The name is very old and was used by Dioscorides.

Gnaphalium gymnocephalum De Candolle
Cudweed   **Ss**

An erect or ascending herb to 30cm high, found in moist forests, grasslands and riverbanks. Locally restricted to the Royal National Park.

Range: NSW coast, ranges and inland districts, Vic, Tas and WA. **Leaves:** silvery-white below, with a basal rosette of long leaves. **Flower heads:** about 2mm diameter, in globular clusters subtended by a single leaf (sometimes 2). **Flowering time:** much of the year. **Name:** *gymnocephalum* = Gk. naked-head, referring to the paucity of subtending leaves, compared to other *Gnaphalium* species.

Gnaphalium involucratum J. R. Forster
Cudweed   **Cumb, Ss**

A small erect herb to 30cm high. Similar to *G. gymnocephalum* except the flower heads have 3-5 subtending leaves and the basal rosette dies away at flowering time. An uncommon species locally.

Range: NSW coast and ranges south from Sydney into Vic, Tas and SA. **Leaves:** similar to *G. gymnocephalum*. **Flower heads:** about 2mm

single head

Gnaphalium gymnocephalum

Gnaphalium involucratum

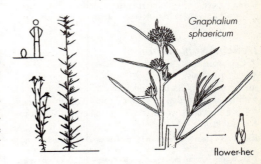

Gnaphalium sphaericum

flower-head

diameter, in globular clusters subtended by 3-5 leaves. **Flowering time:** summer. **Name:** *involucratum* = having an involucre, presumably referring to the subtending leaves.

Gnaphalium sphaericum Willdenow
Cudweed   **Cumb**

An erect herb 20-60cm high, found in grasslands, wasteground and moist forests. There seem to be 2 forms; one a small herb with almost spoon-shaped leaves, the other taller and more vigorous with numerous narrow leaves. Found locally on the Cumberland Plain and probably other places. Distinguished from other species by the slender flower heads (1-1.5mm diameter).

Range: all parts of NSW and all other states except NT. **Leaves:** slender, silvery-white below, basal rosette absent. **Flower heads:** 1-1.5mm diameter, in globular clusters subtended by several leaves. **Flowering time:** summer. **Name:** *sphaericum* = Gk. spherical, referring to the globular clusters of flower heads.

• *Helichrysum* Miller (heel-ee-CRIS-um)
Paper-daisies, Everlastings

A genus of small perennial herbs and shrubs with less than 300 species distributed worldwide except in the Americas. There are over 32 species in Australia, distributed in all states except NT.

Name: *Helichrysum* = Gk. *helios*, sun, *chrysos*, golden, an ancient name for a species of Mediterranean everlasting daisy.

Note: The old *Helichrysum* genus was considered to be too diverse and the Australian species have now been split off into *Chrysocephalum*, *Bracteantha*, and *Ozothamnus*. The remaining Australian *Helichrysum* are also considered to be distinct and will soon be placed in two as yet unnamed genera!

Helichrysum collinum De Candolle
Ss

An erect herb to 50cm high with golden yellow flower heads. Easily recognised by numerous slender brownish transparent bracts surrounding the flower heads. Found in woodland on sandstone. Locally restricted to the Georges River (Panania to Como).

Range: NSW coast, ranges and inland slopes, and Qld. **Leaves:** soft, pale below with matted hairs (also on stems). **Flower heads:** solitary on a tall stem, flowers GOLDEN YELLOW, surrounded by membranous brown pointed bracts. **Flowering time:** spring-summer. **Name:** *collinum* = pertaining to hills, presumably the habitat of the type specimen.

Helichrysum elatum
A. Cunningham ex De Candolle
White Paper Daisy   Ss

An erect herb to 2m high (often woody towards the base) with large white papery flower heads. A fairly common species in wetter woodlands (e.g. valleys in the Royal National Park).

Range: NSW coast and ranges and Qld. **Leaves:** dull, covered in cotton wool. **Flower heads:** surrounded by erect WHITE papery bracts, several in an open terminal inflorescence, disc flowers YELLOW. **Flowering time:** spring (from July). **Name:** *elatum* = Lat. tall.

Helichrysum rutidolepis De Candolle
Ss

An erect or decumbent perennial herb, to 40cm high. Found in a range of environments from sheltered woodland to moist open heath and on various soils. Fairly common in the area, but not on the Cumberland Plain.

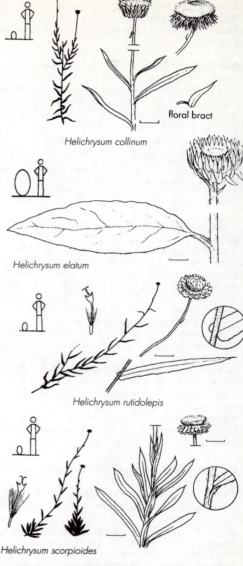

floral bract

Helichrysum collinum

Helichrysum elatum

Helichrysum rutidolepis

Helichrysum scorpioides

Range: NSW coast and ranges, also Vic, SA. **Leaves:** rough above, white-furry below, wide at the base, not decurrent (i.e. it has a distinct joint at the stem). **Flower heads:** 8-15mm diameter, solitary, terminal, all flowers tubular, GOLDEN YELLOW, surrounded by blunt YELLOW bracts. **Flowering time:** most of the year. **Name:** *rutidolepis* = Gk. wrinkled-scale, referring to the bracts.

Helichrysum scorpioides Labillardière
Ss, Castl

An erect or ascending herb usually about 30cm high. Similar to *H. rutidolepis* except for its more strongly tufted habit, decurrent leaves (i.e. arising directly out of the stem with no obvious joint) and larger flower heads. Found mainly on clay soils on the Cumberland Plain and on shale remnants in the suburbs, also sometimes on enriched sandy soils. Less common than *H. rutidolepis*.

Range: NSW coast, ranges and western slopes, Vic, Tas and SA. **Leaves:** rough (scabrous) above, white-furry below, decurrent, often with wavy margins. **Flower heads:** GOLDEN YELLOW, similar to *H. rutidolepis* except the head is wider (1-2cm) and the pappus is longer (5-7mm). **Flowering time:** May-June. **Name:** *scorpioides* = curved like a scorpion's tail, referring to the general habit.

• *Lagenifera* Cassini (pronounced with a soft 'g')

A genus of small tufted herbs with 18 species, distributed in the western Pacific from NZ to Japan, and in Central and South America. There are 4 native species in Australia. Closely related to *Solenogyne* (see below).
Name: *Lagenifera* = Lat. flagon-bearing, because the mature cypsellas are that shape.

Lagenifera stipitata (Labillardière) Druce
Ss, Castl, Cumb

A small tufted perennial herb, often with purple leaves, found in moist forests. Common throughout the area, mainly on sandstone.

Range: NSW coast and ranges, Qld, Vic, Tas, SA and NZ. **Leaves:** usually 5-10cm long, lax, toothed. **Flowers-heads:** solitary on slender scapes, ray flowers strongly developed, MAUVE, disc flowers WHITE, cypsellas not beaked (pointed), not glandular. **Flowering time:** spring-summer. **Name:** *stipitata* = Lat. stalked.

• *Melanthera*

– See COASTAL AND ESTUARINE SPECIES.

• *Olearia* Moench
Daisy Bushes

A genus of shrubs with 180 species in Australia, NZ and NG. There are 130 endemic species in Australia.

Both disc and ray flowers are present. The ray flowers are female, the disc flowers are bisexual. The flower colour is usually white. A pappus of fine hairs is present.
Name: *Olearia* = after Adam Olearius (1603-71), author of a flora of Halle, Germany.

Olearia elliptica De Candolle
Sticky Daisy Bush **Ss**

A shrub usually 50-100cm high, found in rocky places near the coast, often on sea cliffs (e.g. Royal National Park).

Range: NSW coast and ranges north from the Sydney area; also Qld and Lord Howe Island. **Leaves:** oblong or elliptical, 5-9cm long including distinct stalks, glossy above, dull below, sticky when rubbed (glands may be visible), hairless. **Flower heads:** several in an open terminal corymb, ray flowers WHITE, disc flowers YELLOW. **Flowering time:** spring-summer. **Name:** *elliptica* = the leaf shape.

Olearia microphylla (Ventenat) Maiden & Betche
Bridal Daisy Bush **Ss, Castl**

A shrub to 1.5m high with dense shows of fragrant flower heads on long gracefully curving branches. Moderately

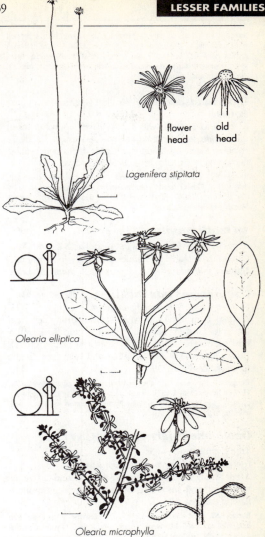

flower head   old head

Lagenifera stipitata

Olearia elliptica

Olearia microphylla

common in woodland. William Woolls called it 'the harbinger of spring'. [7] Amy E. Mack wrote that 'its million stars make a milky way beneath the trees'. [8]

Range: NSW coast, ranges and western slopes, and Qld. **Leaves:** tiny, crowded along the branches, with recurved margins and a layer of white cotton wool underneath. **Flower heads:** solitary on the ends of short lateral branchlets, rays WHITE. **Flowering time:** September. **Name:** *microphylla* = Lat. tiny-leaved.

Olearia tomentosa Bentham
Ss, Sal

A shrub 50cm (near sea) to 2m (inland) high, with densely hairy leaves and stems. Found in sheltered forests in coastal gullies (e.g. north shore) and also on exposed cliffs near the sea (e.g. Royal National Park).

Range: NSW coast and ranges. **Leaves:** rough above, with impressed veins, pale and woolly underneath. **Flower heads:** solitary, terminal, ray flowers WHITE or MAUVE, disc flowers YELLOW. **Flowering time:** spring-summer. **Name:** *tomentosa* = Lat. felty, referring to the hairs on the branches and leaf undersides.

Olearia viscidula (F. Mueller) Bentham
Ss, Cumb

A shrub to 2m high with sticky leaves, found in forest understories on sheltered valley sides, usually in dense colonies. Rarely on sandstone. It often forms impenetrable thickets on valley sides in the Blue Mountains.

Range: NSW coast, ranges and western slopes. **Leaves:** opposite, soft, dull, sticky. **Flower heads:** solitary or a few in short axillary corymbs, disc flowers YELLOW, ray flowers WHITE. **Flowering time:** spring. **Name:** *viscidula* = Lat. sticky.

• *Ozothamnus* R. Brown

A genus with 53 species in Australia, NZ, and New Caledonia, including 44 endemic species in Australia.
Name: *Ozothamnus* = Gk. *ozo*, to smell, *thamnos*, shrub.

Ozothamnus adnatus De Candolle
Ss (previously *Helichrysum adnatum*)

A shrub 1-2m high, with white stems and tiny decurrent leaves (i.e. leaf margins joined directly onto the stem). A rare species recorded in the past from Oatley (1894), Hurstville (1900), Waterfall (1906), and Palm Creek in the Royal National Park (1975).

Range: mainly found on higher parts of the NSW ranges and in Vic. **Flower heads:** with WHITE bracts, in a *Cassinia*-like dense terminal corymb. **Flowering time:** spring. **Name:** *adnatum* = Lat. attached, referring to the decurrent leaves.

Ozothamnus ferrugineus (Labill.) Sweet
Tree Everlasting **Ss**
(previously *Helichrysum dendroideum*)

A tall shrub or small tree 2-4m high, found in wetter woodland near the coast, often near swampy ground. Rare in the area.

Range: NSW coast and ranges, Vic and Tas. **Leaves:** mostly under 4cm long, with recurved, often wavy, margins, and a cloak of pale or brownish felt below. **Flower heads:** numerous in dense terminal corymbs, with WHITE flowers surrounded by straw coloured bracts. **Flowering time:** summer. **Name:** *ferrugineus* = Gk.rusty, refering to the leaf undersides.

Ozothamnus diosmifolium
(Ventenat) De Candolle   Everlasting, Paper Daisy
Ss, Cumb, Castl   (previously *Helichrysum diosmifolium*)
A shrub usually about 2m high, common in woodlands.

Range: NSW coast, ranges and inland districts and Qld. **Leaves:** tiny and narrow, dark green above and white below, rough to the touch due to tiny hard hairs, margins recurved. **Flowers:** white, in numerous small heads surrounded by papery white bracts, arranged in a dense *Cassinia*-like terminal corymb. **Flowering time:** spring and summer. **Name:** *diosmifolium* = leaves like a *Diosma* species. *Diosma* is a small South African genus of fragrant small-leaved shrubs in the Rutaceae family.

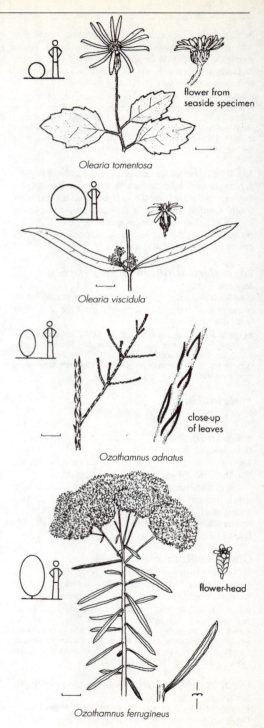

flower from seaside specimen

Olearia tomentosa

Olearia viscidula

close-up of leaves

Ozothamnus adnatus

flower-head

Ozothamnus ferrugineus

• *Podolepis* Labillardière (pod-o-LEEP-is)

An endemic genus with 20 species, distributed in all states except Tas and NT.

Name: *Podolepis* = Gk. foot-scale, referring to the stalked involucral bracts.

Podolepis jaceoides (Sims) Voss
Cumb

A perennial dandelion-like herb usually about 50cm high with spectacular yellow flower heads. Found in grasslands and open forests. Uncommon locally (Campbelltown-Bargo-Appin). The root is reported to be edible.

Range: NSW coast, ranges and inland districts to the far west, Qld, Vic, Tas and SA. **Leaves:** soft, finely hairy, decurrent, with recurved margins. **Flower heads:** solitary, surrounded by brown membranous bracts, disc and ray flowers both BRIGHT YELLOW, the rays deeply 3-lobed. **Flowering time:** mainly spring. **Name:** *jaceoides* = *Jacea*-like. *Jacea* is an old name for *Centaurea*, in the same family.

• *Pseudognaphalium* Kirpichnikov
(seu-do-naf-AIL-ee-um)

A genus of woolly annual herbs with about 50-60 species worldwide and one species native in Australia.

Name: *Pseudognaphalium* = Gk. false *Gnaphalium*.

Pseudognaphalium luteo-album
(Linnaeus) O. M. Hilliard & B. L. Burtt
(previously *Gnaphalium luteo-album*)
Jersey Cudweed　　**Cumb, Ss, Castl**

An ascending herb 20-50cm high, found in grasslands and as a weed in fields. Not common locally.

Range: all parts of NSW and all other states, including Central Australia. Also in Java, NG, South-east Asia, India, Madagascar, Mauritius, Africa and Europe. The type specimen is from Nepal. **Leaves:** pale green, woolly, same colour both sides. **Flower heads:** about 4mm diameter, in small clusters with inconspicuous subtending leaves. The involucral bracts are translucent, with blunt tips. There is a pappus of fine hairs. The flowers are pale yellow. **Flowering time:** all year. **Name:** *luteo-album* = Lat. yellowish-white, referring to the flower heads.

• *Rhodanthe* Lindley

An endemic genus with 46 species.

Name: *Rhodanthe* = Gk. rose-flower.

Rhodanthe anthemoides
(Sieber ex Sprengel) De Candolle　　Chamomile
Cumb? (previously *Helipterum anthemoides*)

A perennial herb to 30cm high with heads of yellow flowers surrounded by white papery bracts. Found in grasslands and open forests. Probably extinct locally but once common on the Cumberland Plain. 'I have seen this plant growing even in the town of Parramatta, but the last place in which I noticed it in any quantity was near the residence of an old friend of mine, Mrs Lowe, of Bringelly, who informs me that the country people call it Chamomile, and use a decoction of it as a tonic.' wrote William Woolls in 1857. [6]

Range: NSW coast, ranges and western slopes, Qld, Vic and Tas. **Leaves:** linear, crowded, about 1cm long, hairless. **Flower heads:** solitary, 2-3cm diameter, tubular flowers YELLOW, surrounded by radiating WHITE bracts; the outer bracts are broad, membranous and brown-tinged; the inner bracts are petal-like and white. **Flowering time:** spring-summer. **Name:** *anthemoides* = *Anthemis*-like; *Anthemis nobilis* is the European Chamomile.

• *Senecio* Linnaeus (sen-EE-see-o)

A cosmopolitan genus of herbs and shrubs with about 2000 species; reputed to be the largest genus of flowering plants. There are about 50 native species and about 7 introduced.

Senecios are weedy opportunists in wet sheltered places like gullies or rainforest margins.

Name: *Senecio* = Lat. *senex,* an old man, referring to the white pappus. The name was first used by Pliny.

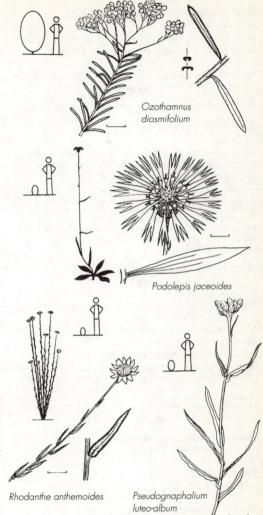

Ozothamnus diosmifolium

Podolepis jaceoides

Rhodanthe anthemoides

Pseudognaphalium luteo-album

Senecio bipinnatisectus Belcher

Ss, Temp Rf

An erect herb to 1.5m high with rough and highly divided leaves. Found in gullies and rainforest margins. Not common locally.

Range: NSW coast and ranges, also Qld. **Leaves:** highly divided, smooth or rough. **Flower heads:** small, often very numerous, disc flowers YELLOW, ray flowers absent. **Flowering time:** spring-summer. **Name:** *bipinnatisectus* = twice pinnatisect, referring to the leaf shape.

Senecio diaschides Drury

Ss, Cumb

An erect herb to 1m high, found in moist places in gullies and on disturbed ground, mainly near the coast, but also on the Cumberland Plain (uncommon).

Range: NSW coast, ranges and western slopes, and Qld. **Leaves:** soft, toothed (except sometimes the young leaves), hairless, flat or with recurved margins, usually with 2 short pointed lobes on either side of the stem at the base of the leaf. **Flower heads:** in a moderately dense terminal corymb, disc flowers YELLOW, ray flowers absent. **Flowering time:** summer. **Name:** *diaschides* = Gk. split, or cloven, referring to the base of the leaves.

Senecio hispidulus A. Richard

Rough Groundsel **Ss, Cumb**

An erect annual herb to 1m high with rough leaves. Opportunistic in many moist sunny environments. There are 2 varieties in the area:

• **var. *hispidulus*:** leaves undivided but coarsely toothed. This seems to be the most common form.

• **var. *dissectus*:** leaves deeply divided.

Range: var. *hispidulus*: NSW coast and ranges, Vic, Tas, SA and WA; var. *dissectus*: NSW coast, ranges and inland districts, also Vic and SA. **Leaves:** narrow, hastate (i.e. with a base that extends backwards in short projections on either side of the stem), toothed, feeling rough to touch due to small hard hairs. **Flowers:** disc flowers only, BRIGHT YELLOW. **Flowering time:** much of the year. **Name:** *hispidulus* = Lat. rough.

Senecio lautus ssp. maritimus

—See COASTAL AND ESTUARIES.

Senecio linearifolius

—See RAINFOREST SPECIES.

Senecio madagascariensis* Poiret

(previously incorrectly known a *S. lautus* ssp. *lautus*)
Variable Grounsel **Ss, Cumb**
A small hardy soft-leaved shrub to 50cm high, hairless. An

Senecio madagascariensis*

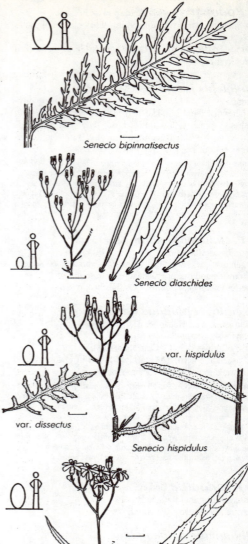

Senecio bipinnatisectus

Senecio diaschides

var. *hispidulus*

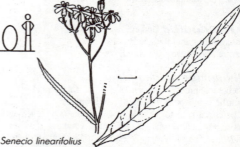

var. *dissectus*

Senecio hispidulus

Senecio linearifolius

opportunistic little plant found in almost any sunny place and a declared pest in pastures.

Range: common and widespread in south-eastern Australia. **Leaves:** narrow, soft, toothed and decurrent (i.e. growing directly out of the stem without a narrowed stalk), with distinct 'ears' at the base, and with recurved margins. **Flower heads:** disc and ray flowers both BRIGHT YELLOW. **Flowering time:** most of the year. **Name:** *madagascarensis* = Lat. from Madagascar.

Senecio mikanioides *
—See CLIMBERS.

Senecio minimus Poiret **var. *minimus***

Saw Groundsel **Ss**

An erect shrub to 1.5m high, found in moist sheltered places in gullies. Not a common species in this area.

Range: NSW coast and ranges, Vic and Tas. **Leaves:** dark green, toothed, both surfaces covered in fine rough hairs, with distinct 'ears' at the base. Stems often dark red. **Flower heads:** slender, numerous in an open terminal panicle, disc flowers YELLOW, ray flowers absent. **Flowering time:** spring-summer. **Name:** *minimus* = Lat. small, referring to the flower heads.

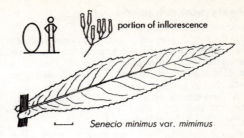

portion of inflorescence

Senecio minimus var. *mimimus*

Senecio quadridentatus Labillardière

Ss, Cumb

A perennial herb 40-100cm high with matted white cottonwool on the leaf undersides and stems, giving it a silvery appearance. Found in forests and wastelands. Moderately common on the Cumberland Plain. Also found along creeks in the Hornsby area.

Range: NSW coast, ranges and inland, Qld, Vic, SA, Tas, SA and WA, including Central Australia. **Leaves:** slender (to 2mm wide) and toothless with white cotton wool beneath, margins recurved, (some older basal leaves may be toothed and up to 6mm wide, tapering to both ends). **Flower heads:** slender, in a spreading panicle, disc flowers YELLOW, ray flowers absent. **Flowering time:** much of the year. **Name:** *quadridentatus* = Lat. 4-toothed, since the flowers have 4 perianth lobes (instead of the usual 5).

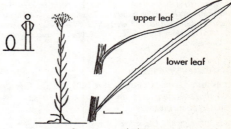

upper leaf

lower leaf

Senecio quadridentatus

Senecio sp. E (aff. *apargiifolius*)

Ss

An erect herb 30-50cm high, found in moist sheltered places. A rare species recorded locally only from Bobbin Head and Georges River at Kentlyn. It has yet to be properly studied or described, hence the provisional designation sp. E.

Range: widely scattered records from NSW coast, ranges and western slopes, Vic, Tas and NT (though some of these may eventually be attributed to other species). **Leaves:** erect, toothed, rough above, pale and finely woolly beneath, rather variable in shape. The specimens from Kentlyn are purple underneath. **Flower heads:** few to many in a open terminal corymb on a relatively long leafless flowering stem; disc flowers YELLOW, ray flowers absent. **Flowering time:** summer.

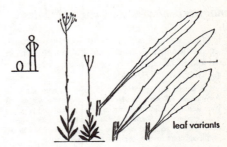

leaf variants

Senecio sp. E (aff. *apargiifolius*)

Senecio vagus F. Mueller **ssp. *eglandulosus*** Ali

Ss

An erect perennial herb to 1.5m high, found in gullies in wetter woodlands (e.g. Royal National Park).

Range: NSW coast and ranges north from the Sydney area. **Leaves:** glossy, thin, soft, deeply lobed, hairless. **Flower heads:** several in an open panicle, large, lower part of involucre swollen, ray flowers 8, YELLOW, disc flowers numerous, yellow. **Flowering time:** most of the year. **Name:** *vagus* = Lat. wandering, perhaps in reference to its distribution, *eglandulosus* = lacking glands, since ssp. *vagus* has conspicuous red glands on its involucral bracts.

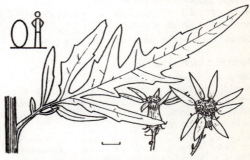

Senecio vagus ssp. *eglandulosus*

• *Sigesbeckia* Linnaeus

Indian-weeds

A genus with 5 species widely distributed in warmer parts of the world, with 1 representative in Australia.

Name: *Sigesbeckia* = after Johann Georg Sigesbeck (1686-1755), director of the Apothecary's Physic Garden in St Petersburg. He was a bitter opponent of the Linnaean sexual system, saying: 'Never would God allow such detestable vice within the vegetable kingdom, that several men should own a communal wife, and in certain composite flowers, a husband should have a mistress so near to his wife.'[9]

Sigesbeckia orientalis Linnaeus
Indian-weed **Rf, Ss, Cumb**
A bushy herb to 1.5m high, found in rainforests and moist sheltered gullies on good soils. Remarkable for the unusual flower heads which are surrounded by bracts covered in sticky gland-bearing hairs (red or green). The outer 5 bracts spread outwards.

An opportunistic weed found in many tropical and temperate parts of the world. It probably reached Australia without the aid of Europeans.

Range: all states except Tas, also Asia and Africa. **Leaves:** opposite, thin, soft, covered in short stiff hairs, often deeply toothed, on red stems. **Flower heads:** in a leafy inflorescence, small, surrounded with red bracts bearing sticky glandular hairs, ray flowers 5, YELLOW, 3-lobed, disc flowers several, YELLOW. **Flowering time:** spring-autumn. **Name:** *orientalis* = Lat. belonging to 'The East'.

Sigesbeckia orientalis

• *Solenogyne* Cassini
A genus with 1 species, distributed in NSW and Tas. Closely related to *Lagenifera* (see above). Its separate status is disputed by some botanists.

Name: *Solenogyne* = Gk. *solen*, tube, *gyne*, female, referring to tubular ray flowers.

Solenogyne bellioides Cassini **var. *bellioides***
Cumb
A small tufted perennial herb, found in forest understories. A rare species locally (recorded from St Marys, Homebush, Glenfield and Richmond). 'It is a very small flower with a very long name,' wrote J.H. Maiden.[10]

Range: coast, ranges and western plains of NSW. **Leaves:** similar to *Lagenifera stipitata*. **Flower heads:** solitary on slender scapes, ray flowers have absent or rudimentary rays, cypsellas are covered in glands and beaked (i.e. pointed). **Name:** *bellioides* = *Bellis*-like (*Bellis* is a genus of European daisies). **Similar species:** distinguish from *Lagenifera stipitata* by the apparent absence of rays in the flower head.

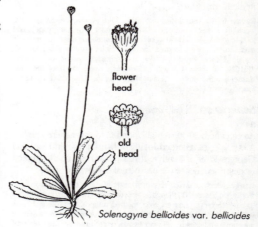

flower head

old head

Solenogyne bellioides var. *bellioides*

• *Sonchus* Linnaeus (SONG-cus)
A genus with about 50 species worldwide. There are 2 native species and 4 introduced to Australia.

Name: *Sonchus* = the name used by Pliny for these plants.

Sonchus oleraceus * Linnaeus
Common Sowthistle **Ss, Cumb, Sal**
A weak annual herb to 1m high, widespread in the area. Introduced from Europe, although some authorities believe it is native to Australia. The leaves are edible, raw or cooked, and were eaten by Aborigines.

Range: most parts of Australia, also Europe. **Leaves:** soft, toothed and deeply lobed, in a basal rosette and borne on the stem. **Flower heads:** YELLOW, all flowers are ray flowers, pappus present; in an irregular terminal corymb. **Flowering time:** most of the year. **Name:** *oleraceus* = Lat. pertaining to gardens.

• *Triptilodiscus* Turczaninow
An endemic genus with a single species. It was placed in *Helipterum* until 1988.

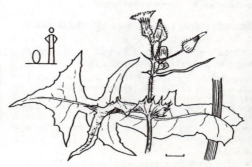

Sonchus oleraceus

Name: *Triptilodiscus* = Gk. 3-feathered disc, referring to the pappus of usually 3 feathery bristles on the top of the cypsella.

Triptilodiscus pygmaeus Turczaninow

(previously *Helipterum australe*) **Cumb**
A tiny erect herb found in seasonally swampy grasslands and
forests on the Cumberland Plain.

Range: coast and inland NSW, also in all other states except NT and
Tas. **Leaves:** decurrent, soft, sparsely hairy. **Flower heads:**
surrounded by silver papery bracts with hairy margins; the inner bracts
are darker and covered in fine hairs; the flowers are all tubular and
YELLOW. **Flowering time:** spring-summer. **Name:** *pygmaeus* = Lat.
pygmy.

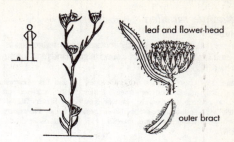

leaf and flower-head

outer bract

Triptilodiscus pygmaeus

• *Vernonia* Schreber

A very large genus of herbs mainly found in America, Africa
and Asia. There is a single Australian species.

Name: after William Vernon (1688-1711), an early plant
collector in North America, and an expert on mosses and
liverworts.

Vernonia cinerea (Linnaeus) Lessing **var. *cinerea***
Cumb, Ss

A small erect perennial herb to 50cm high, either hairless
or with matted woolly hairs. Found in forest understories
on the Cumberland Plain and occasionally in wetter forests
near the coast. A common weed in India where it is used
medicinally.

Range: NSW coast and ranges, Qld, Central Australia, Africa and Asia.
Leaves: small, toothed, not numerous. **Flower heads:** few on slender
stems, disc flowers PURPLE, ray flowers absent, pappus of soft hairs.
Flowering time: summer-autumn. **Name:** *cinerea* = Lat. ash-grey,
referring to those specimens with matted hairs.

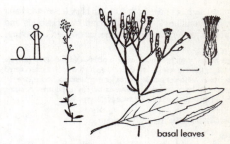

basal leaves

Vernonia cinerea var. cinerea

• *Vittadinia* A. Richard

Fuzzweed, New Holland Daisy
A genus of 27 species in Australia, 1 in New Caledonia, and
1 in NZ. All are small weedy herbs, ascending or erect,
sometimes woody near the base. The local species are mostly
found in forests and grasslands on clay soils.

Name: *Vittadinia* = in honour of Carlo Vittadini (1800-65),
a doctor of medicine who lived in Milan and wrote many
works on fungi.

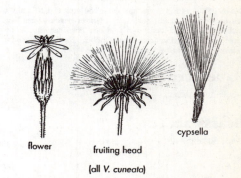

flower　　　fruiting head　　　cypsella

(all *V. cuneata*)

Vittadinia cuneata De Candolle **var. *cuneata***

Fuzzweed **Cumb**
An erect woody herb to 40cm high covered in short sharp
stiff hairs. There are 2 local forms of this variety; form *cuneata*
and form *minor*. Form *minor* is a little smaller in all its parts
but the real distinction is the hairiness of the cypsella (see
illustration). Both are found in grasslands and forests on the
Cumberland Plain.

Range: form *cuneata*: inland NSW, Sydney area, Vic, Tas and SA; form
minor: NSW coast and ranges. **Leaves:** folded along the mid-vein, mixed
entire and lobed, hairy. **Flower heads:** ray flowers PALE BLUE to
MAUVE. Cypsella ribbed, covered in short silky hairs; form *cuneata*: the
hairs are dense, short and appressed on the lower portion; form *minor*:
the lower portion is hairless or sparsely hairy. **Name:** *cuneata* = Lat.
wedge-shaped, referring to the leaves, *minor* = Lat. smaller.

cypsella:
form *cuneata*

cypsella:
form *minor*

Vittadinia cuneata var. cuneata

Vittadinia muelleri N. Burbidge

Cumb

A perennial herb with woody rootstock and tufted stems, covered in scattered stiff hairs. Found in grasslands and forests on the Cumberland Plain.

Range: NSW coast, ranges and inland slopes, Vic and Tas. **Leaves:** folded along midrib, most with spreading slender lobes, scattered stiff hairs on midribs and margins. **Flower heads:** ray flowers BLUISH PURPLE, cypsellas not strongly ribbed, with spreading hairs. **Flowering time:** spring-summer. **Name:** *muelleri* = in honour of Ferdinand Mueller.

Vittadinia pustulata N. Burbidge

Cumb

An annual herb or undershrub 10-30cm high, leaves and habit closely resembling *V. cuneata.* Found on grasslands and disturbed sites. A fairly common species on the Cumberland Plain.

Range: Sydney area, NSW north-western plains, Qld and WA. **Leaves:** folded along the mid-vein, mostly entire or with a few small teeth, covered in rough hairs. **Flower heads:** 5-6mm long, cypsella not ribbed, covered in sparse short hairs. **Name:** *pustulata* = Lat. having pustules, referring to the 1 or more pimples near the base of the cypsella.

Vittadinia sulcata N. Burbidge

Cumb

An erect annual herb 10-30cm high with soft hairs. Rare in forests and near rivers on the Cumberland Plain.

Range: NSW coast and ranges, northern inland areas, Qld, NT and WA. **Leaves:** most or all lobed, softly hairy. **Flower heads:** 7-9mm long, ray flowers PURPLE, cypsellas with prominent ribs, finely hairy on the upper part. **Flowering time:** August-October. **Name:** *sulcata* = Lat. furrowed, referring to the cypsella.

Baueraceae

—See Cunoniaceae.

Brassicaceae

—See Aquatics.

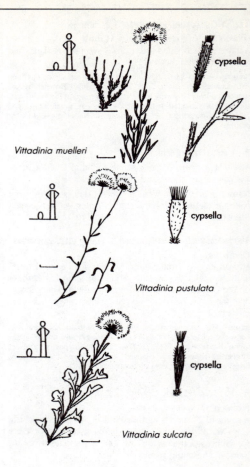

Vittadinia muelleri

cypsella

cypsella

Vittadinia pustulata

cypsella

Vittadinia sulcata

CACTACEAE

A family with about 2000 species in 75-220 genera, native to North and South America, mainly in desert areas. There are about 32 species in 8 genera naturalised in Australia.

• *Opuntia* Miller

A genus with about 90 species, native to the Americas, with 15-20 species naturalised in Australia.

Some species have become widespread pests and most are declared noxious weeds in NSW. *O. stricta* once threatened the national economy (see below).

The succulent fruit of some species, especially *O. stricta,* is edible raw and makes a good jam.

Name: *Opuntia* = Lat. an inhabitant of Opus, a town in Greece where the type specimen of the genus was collected (it had been introduced from the Americas).

Opuntia elatior Miller

(not illustrated)

A densely branched cactus to 4m high, found on wasteland and disturbed ground. Uncommon in the area. Naturalised in isolated areas. A native of South America.

Range: mostly in coastal NSW, Qld and SA. **Segments:** flattened, oval, 10-20cm long. **Areoles:** with at least 3 (up to 8) spines. **Flower:** YELLOW, anthers pink. **Name:** *elatior* = Lat. tall.

Opuntia vulgaris• Miller
Drooping Pear, Smooth Tree Pear
Often a tall tree-like cactus, drooping at the tips, found on
wasteland and the edges of bushland. Common in the area.
A native of South America.

Range: NSW coast, Qld, Vic and SA. It was once the most widely naturalised
prickly pear in Australia but is now eradicated from inland NSW.
Segments: *light green, glossy,* 12-15cm long, ±oblong, flattened.
Areoles: filled with short woolly hairs and *usually 2 large spines.*
Flower: YELLOW, outer perianth segments often with red stripes.
Name: *vulgaris* = Lat. common.

Opuntia stricta• (Haworth) Haworth
. Prickly Pear (not illustrated)
A bushy cactus, forming clumps to 1.5m high, lacking distinct
trunks. Found on wasteland and the edges of bushland.
Common in the area. A native of South America.

This species was first introduced as a hedge plant and
as food for the cochineal insect which furnished the red dye
for soldiers' coats, but by the 1920s it had become the worst
plant pest in Australia's history, devastating large areas of
pastoral country, mainly in southern Qld and inland NSW.
Prickly Pear eradication gangs became a common sight in
many areas. By 1925, despite the use of 3 million kilograms
of arsenic poison, it covered some 25 million hectares and
was estimated to be advancing at 100 hectares per hour. Only
the introduction of its natural predator, the *Cactoblastis* moth,
in 1926, brought it under control. By 1933 about 90% of
the plants were destroyed.

Range: widespread in all mainland states. **Segments:** mostly a *dull
bluish green, not glossy,* mostly under 20cm long, oval, flattened.
Areoles: filled with brown woolly hairs, and mostly lacking spines,
although 1-2 spines often present. **Flower:** YELLOW. **Name:** *stricta*
= Lat. bundled.

CAESALPINIACEAE

This is the third of the leguminous families, occupying a
position between Fabaceae (Peas) and Mimosaceae (Wattles).
It has 2500-3000 species in about 150 genera, mainly in
tropical and subtropical parts of the world. There are about
85 species in 19 genera in Australia, especially in arid areas.

• *Senna* Miller
A genus with about 240 species, including about 50 species
in Australia. They were previously placed in *Cassia*, but that
genus has now been broken into a number of smaller genera.
Several introduced and one native species occur in the area.

Name: *Senna* = from the Arabic name for the plant, *Sana*.

Senna barclayana (Sweet) Randell
var. *barclayana* Ss
An erect shrub to 1m tall. Rare in the area. Recorded from
railway nature strips at Ingleburn, Doonside and Menangle
Park. Mainly a western slopes species, probably introduced
into the area.

Range: NSW north and central western slopes, infrequently in other
districts. **Leaves:** mainly 10-14cm long, hairless, with a prominent gland
at the base of the rhachis. **Flowers:** GOLDEN YELLOW. There are 4
short stamens, 2 long stamens and 4 staminodes (this is the only native

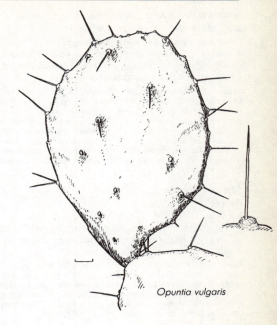

Opuntia vulgaris

Senna barclayana var. barclayana

Senna with staminodes). **Flowering time:** spring. **Name:** *barclayana* = after the gentleman who first raised the species in Britain. The
botanist Robert Sweet wrote 'Our drawing was made from fine specimens
sent to us in September last, from the collection of Robert Barclay, Esq.
of Bury-Hill; and we are informed by Mr D. Cameron that it was raised
from New Holland seeds in 1824 . . .'[11]

*Senna coluteoides** (Willdenow) Irwin & Barneby
var. *glabrata* (J. Vogel) Irwin & Barneby
(previously *Cassia coluteoides*) **Ss, Cumb**
A shrub to 1.5-3m tall, very common in bush gullies and
disturbed ground throughout the area. A garden escapee,
introduced from South America.

Range: Sydney region, including Blue Mountains, Qld and South America.
Leaves: pinnate, 7-10mm long; the leaflets 2-4cm long, dull, soft, hairless
except for microscopic hairs on the stems and base of the leaflets. A
stout conical gland about 1mm long is visible on the upper side of
the rhachis between the lowest pair of leaflets. **Flowers:** GOLDEN
YELLOW, about 35mm wide, with 3 long stamens, 4 short stamens and
3 staminodes. **Flowering time:** late summer-autumn. **Name:**
coluteoides = like *Colutea*, a genus in the family Fabaceae, of similar
appearance.

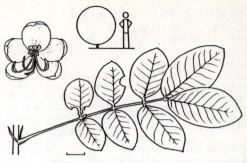

Senna coluteoides var. glabrata

Senna odorata (Morris) Randel
(previously *Cassia odorata*)
Southern Cassia **Ss**
An open erect shrub to 1m, occasionally to 2m, tall. Found
in woodland in the Liverpool-Ingleburn area, also on the
Nepean River south of Menangle.

Range: NSW coast and ranges, excepting the south coast, and Qld.
Leaves: pinnate; the leaflets thin-textured, 1-3cm long, with
microscopically hairy veins and margins. A bristle-like gland is visible
below each pair of leaflets. **Flowers:** GOLDEN YELLOW, about 15mm
wide, with 10 stamens; in long-stalked axillary racemes. **Flowering
time:** spring-early summer. **Name:** *odorata* = Lat. fragrant.

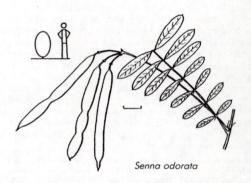

Senna odorata

CAMPANULACEAE

Wahlenbergia, Native Bluebells
A family of small herbs with about 600 species in 35 genera
worldwide. There are 27 species in 2 genera in Australia.
It includes *Campanula*, the Harebells of Britain* (English
Bluebells are in fact lilies).

Campanulaceae is related to Lobeliaceae, Stylidiaceae and
Goodeniaceae; all have anthers joined in a tube surrounding
the style.

* 'Here and there amidst the scanty and withered herbage . . . gleamed
a bright blue starry flower, looking fearlessly to the fervid sky from its
slight and hair-like stem; but its bolder aspect did not prevent my claiming
it as a relative from my own dear land, the harebell . . . that so merrily
waves over British heaths and hills.'[12]

• *Wahlenbergia* Schrader
Native Bluebells
A genus of slender graceful herbs with sky blue flowers. There
are about 200 species worldwide, and 26 in Australia
(including 1 naturalised), distributed in all states.

The method of fertilisation is unusual. The style is tipped
by large glands which secrete a sticky fluid. The anthers are
caught in this at an early stage, literally torn off their filaments
and projected out of the flower where the pollen is available
to be brushed off on insects. This is why anthers are never
seen inside the flower. The flowers were eaten by Aborigines
and are good in salads.

Name: *Wahlenbergia* = after Göran Wahlenberg (1780-1851),
a Swedish botanist who specialised in mosses and lichens.

Wahlenbergia communis Carolin

(previously *W. bicolor*)
Tufted Bluebell **Cumb, Castl**
A slender erect herb, often with many stems, to 40cm tall.
Found in sunny places in open forest, but not on sandstone.
Uncommon in the area.

Range: throughout the eastern mainland, including arid areas. **Leaves:** opposite or alternate, slender, to 30cm long, usually with scattered teeth. **Flowers:** SKY BLUE, 10-25mm wide. The style has 3 swollen lobes at the tip. **Flowering time:** spring-summer. **Name:** *communis* = Lat. common.

Wahlenbergia gracilis (G. & J. R. Forster) Schrader

Native Bluebell **Ss, Cumb, Castl**
A slender erect herb with many fine stems to 35cm high.
Abundant in sunny situations.

Range: NSW coast, scattered in ranges and slopes, also Lord Howe Island, Qld, Tas and Vic. **Leaves:** narrow, with scattered teeth, 10-40mm long, 1-3mm wide. **Flowers:** SKY BLUE, 5-6mm wide. **Flowering time:** spring-summer. **Name:** *gracilis* = Lat. slender.

Wahlenbergia littoricola P.J. Smith

Ss, Cumb
A slender erect herb 10-80cm tall, with narrow leaves. Rare
in the area. Recorded from The Valley at Hornsby (1914)
and St Marys (1966).

Range: NSW coast south from Sydney, ranges and far south-western plains, also Vic, Tas, SA, WA and NZ. **Leaves:** all slender, 1(-4)mm wide, to 60mm long, hairless. **Flowers:** SKY BLUE, tube 2-3mm long, lobes 5-9mm long, the style has 3 lobes. **Flowering time:** spring-summer. **Name:** *littoricola* = Lat. seashore-dwelling.

Wahlenbergia stricta Sweet **ssp. *stricta***

Tall Bluebell, Austral Bluebell **Ss**
A slender erect herb with a few stems to 40cm tall, found
in sunny places in open forest. Widely scattered but
uncommon in the area (common in the Blue Mountains).
Easily recognised by its large flowers.

Range: NSW coast, ranges and western slopes, and all states except NT. **Leaves:** mostly opposite, mostly 10-15mm long, 3-5mm wide. The lower stems are covered with stiff hairs. **Flowers:** SKY BLUE (rarely mauve), 25-30mm wide. The style is not swollen at the tip. The calyx is often scabrous. **Flowering time:** spring-summer. **Name:** *stricta* = Lat. bundled, perhaps referring to the stems.

CASUARINACEAE

She-oaks
A family with 90 species in 4 genera distributed in South-
east Asia, NG, the Pacific and all Australian states. In Australia
there are 66 Australian species in 3 genera. It is an ancient
and highly evolved family with no close relatives.

She-oaks are well adapted to hot, dry conditions. Their
leaves are reduced to rings of tiny teeth on specialised
branchlets. Along the length of the branchlets are grooves
sheltering the stomata. In hot dry conditions the branchlets
fall, relieving the plant from the strain of high evaporation.
An interesting feature of she-oaks is the beautifully haunting
song of wind in the foliage. The effect is caused by the wing
playing over the joints and grooves of the branchlets. It can
be either a mournful or refreshing sound, depending on one's
mood. It has frequently been commented on in literature
and sometimes compared to harps of Aeolus, the God of
the Winds. 'Perhaps none of all the novel trees of the colony
have so completely strange and un-English an aspect as these;
and in a moderate breeze the notes uttered amongst their
thousands of waving, whispering strings, are far from
unmusical, and reminded me of the lower, wailing notes
of an Aeolina harp . . . It is said that the name has been
borrowed from sheac, or cheoak, of America, in consequence
of some resemblance of the wood.'[13]

The wood is strongly cross-grained and makes an excellent
shingle and furniture timber. She-oaks were cut for shingles
from the very beginning of white settlement.

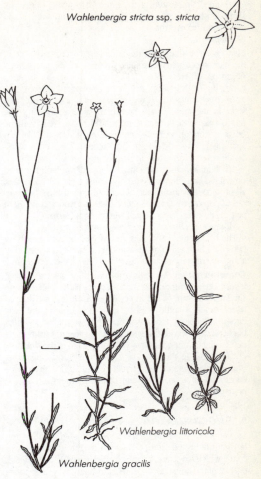

Wahlenbergia stricta ssp. *stricta*

Wahlenbergia littoricola

Wahlenbergia gracilis

Wahlenbergia communis

An interesting feature is the insect galls which mimic the shape of the fruiting cones. They occur on all species and are produced by the larvae of several species of bugs (*Hemiptera*).

Flowers: The floral structures are highly unusual. Most of the local species are dioecious, i.e. male and female flowers occur on different plants. The male flowers are simple, consisting of little more than a single stamen, protected by a structure similar to a leaf-tooth and set in a dense whorled spike at the end of each branchlet. At flowering time the reddish stamens project from behind these teeth and the effect is enough to make the male plant turn rusty-brown and appear quite dead from a distance. The pollen is wind-borne, a very rare feature in large Angiosperms.

The female flowers are clustered in a dense globular head on a stalk. Each flower has an ovary, a style and 2 bracteoles, all protected by a stiff bract. After fertilisation the bracteoles develop into woody valves embedded in a woody cone. Each pair of valves encloses a small winged fruit (samara).

Most species flower in late winter and early spring.

The root hairs of She-oaks are infected by nitrogen-fixing bacteria which explains their ability to thrive on poor sites and their early appearance in successions on cleared ground.

Common name: The origin of the name She-oak is a mystery. It may be a corruption of an Aboriginal name, although no similar names are found in vocabularies. It may be derived from Sheack, a name used by English officers in the early days of the colony for an American tree producing a similar beef-coloured wood, though there is no record of the name being used in America. It may have originated in the similarity of the timber to the true Oak of the northern hemisphere, 'she' being reference to female trees. It could even be a corruption of a word for the sound of the wind in the branchlets.

Allocasuarina diminuta ssp. *mimica*

Allocasuarina distyla

Allocasuarina glareicola

• *Allocasuarina* L.A.S. Johnson

An endemic genus of 59 species, distributed in all states. It is distinguished from *Casuarina* by the anatomy of its cones, which have, by comparison, thickly woody valves which only slightly protrude and are surmounted by a separate angular woody crest. The winged fruits are also a point of distinction: in *Casuarina* they are pale and dull, while in *Allocasuarina* they are dark brown and shiny.

Name: *Allo* = Gk. *allos*, other i.e., different from *Casuarina*.

Allocasuarina diminuta L.A.S. Johnson
ssp. *mimica* L.A.S. Johnson
Ss

An erect shrub to 1.5m high, often many stemmed at the base, recognised by its glaucous erect branchlets. Found in heath, woodland and the margins of sedge-swamps. Uncommon or rare in the area; restricted to a few small populations, one along Heathcote Road at Lucas Heights, one in woodland on the Appin–Bulli Road, and another in the eastern suburbs (Long Bay–Little Bay).

Range: the Sydney area and also in the Blue Mountains from Blackheath to Taralga and Bundanoon. **Branchlets:** glaucous, rigidly erect, (0.5-)1mm wide, with 6-7 (-10) leaf-teeth. **Cones:** almost globular-cylindrical, 10-12mm wide, to 17mm long, on a 3-6mm stalk. **Note:**

Unlike most local species, this one is monoecious (male and female flowers occur on the same plant). **Flowering time:** January-February. **Name:** *diminuta* = Lat. small, *mimica* = Lat. mimicking, since it looks like a dwarf *Allocasuarina distyla*.

Allocasuarina distyla (Ventenat) L.A.S. Johnson
Ss, Castl

A dense elegantly brushy shrub to 4m tall, common in the area, in dry heathy scrubland, often on poor rocky ground. The male plants are very densely foliaged and turn a brilliant rusty-red when in flower.

Range: NSW coast south of Port Stephens, and Blue Mountains. **Branchlets:** 1-1.5mm diameter, erect, with 6-8 leaf-teeth, often rather greyish from a distance. **Cones:** 15-18mm diameter, cylindrical, with a pointed apex. **Name:** *distyla* = double-styled (a feature in common with all other She-oaks).

Allocasuarina glareicola L.A.S. Johnson
Castl Vulnerable 2V

An open erect shrub 1-2m high, restricted to a few small populations in the Castlereagh woodlands.

Range: restricted to the Castlereagh woodlands. **Branchlets:** very thin, 0.5-0.7mm diameter, to 20cm long, with 5-7 leaf-teeth. **Cones:** 10-13mm long, 7-8mm wide, on stalks 4-7mm long. **Name:** *glareicola* = Lat. gravel-dwelling.

Allocasuarina littoralis (Salisbury) L.A.S. Johnson

Black She-Oak, Dahl-wah **Ss, Cumb, Castl**

A shrub or small tree usually 3-6m tall. Common in dry scrubs and woodland, often on rocky ground. It often forms pure stands where the combination of deep shade and the dense carpet of fallen branchlets inhibits the development of ground-cover.

Range: NSW coast, ranges and western slopes, Tas, Vic and Qld. **Bark:** deeply fissured with ridges of hard cork. **Branchlets:** thin, 0.7-1mm diameter, with 6-8 leaf-teeth. **Cones:** 15-20mm diameter, cylindrical, with a flattened apex. **Name:** *littoralis* = pertaining to the sea-shore (not a very appropriate name). *Dahl-wah* is an Aboriginal name from the Camden area.

Allocasuarina nana (Sieber ex Sprengel) L.A.S. Johnson

Dwarf She-oak **Ss**

A low dense heathy shrub, usually multi-stemmed, 0.5-1.5m high. Found in dense colonies in high, exposed, often stony, heath country. Uncommon in the area, mainly in heath scrubs, e.g. Berowra, Long Bay, Royal National Park. Easily recognised by its short branchlets (under 6cm long).

Range: coast and ranges of NSW and north-eastern Vic. Generally a higher altitude mountain species. **Branchlets:** slender (about 0.6-0.8mm diameter), under 6cm long, erect, crowded, usually with 5 leaf-teeth. **Cones:** 10-15mm diameter, 18-24mm long, with a rounded or pointed tip. **Name:** *nana* = Lat. dwarf.

Allocasuarina paludosa

(Sieber ex Sprengel) L. Johnson **Ss**

A spreading shrub 0.4-2m high with ascending or curvaceous green branchlets. Found in damp heath scrubs and the margins of sedge-swamps. Uncommon to rare in the Sydney area, restricted to the Narrabeen-Avalon area (where it grows with *Allocasuarina distyla*, although it may now be rare or extinct there) and to Maddens Plains on the Woronora Plateau. Mainly a south coast and southern tablelands species.

Range: coast and ranges south from the Hawkesbury River into Vic, Tas and SA. **Branchlets:** with 6-8 leaf-teeth, usually densely micro-hairy in the furrows. Sometimes the whole branchlet may be conspicuously

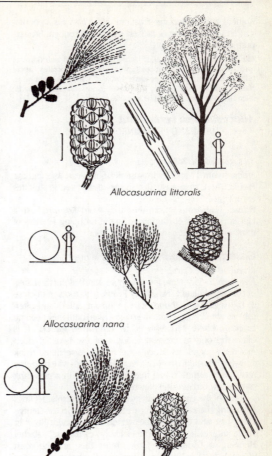

Allocasuarina littoralis

Allocasuarina nana

Allocasuarina paludosa

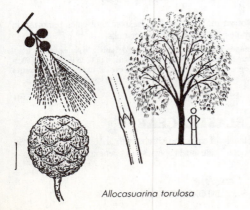

Allocasuarina torulosa

hairy. **Cones:** more or less stalkless, mostly about 15mm long, fairly flat on top. **Note:** unlike most other local species, it is monoecious (male and female flowers on the same plant). **Flowering time:** January-February. **Name:** *paludosa* = Lat. pertaining to swamps.

Allocasuarina portuensis L.A.S. Johnson

(not illustrated) **Ss Endangered 2ECit**

A shrub 2-3m tall, related to *A. diminuta*. It was first discovered in 1986. The entire known population consists of 8 specimens in Sydney Harbour National Park. The National Parks and Wildlife Service is carrying out a planting program to increase the population.

Name: *portuensis* = Lat. inhabiting a port.

Allocasuarina torulosa (Aiton) L.A.S. Johnson

Forest Oak **Ss**

A small rounded tree with drooping, greyish foliage, usually to 8m high in the Sydney area but up to 20m on the north coast. Occurs as an understorey tree in woodland and forest, often forming dense groves. Generally grows in higher-nutrient soils and moister situations that *A. littoralis*. A popular garden plant because of its neat shape and frequent bronze-purplish hue.

Range: Nowra to northern Qld. **Bark:** deeply fissured with ridges of hard cork. **Branchlets:** drooping, with 4 leaf-teeth, pendent, about 0.2mm diameter. **Cones:** pendent, ball-like, warty, 15-25mm wide. **Name:** *torulosa* = Lat. *torulus*, little protuberance, *-osus* abounding in, referring to the warts on the cone segments.

Allocasuarina verticillata
—See COASTAL AND ESTUARINE SPECIES.

• *Casuarina* Linnaeus

A genus with 17 species in Australia, South-east Asia and the Pacific. There are 6 Australian species distributed in all states except Tas.

Name: *Casuarina* = from the Malay word *Kasuari*, from a fancied similarity of the foliage to the drooping feathers of the Cassowary bird.

Casuarina cunninghamiana Miquel

River She-oak **Cumb**

A tall tree 20-35m high, found in pure stands along the banks of the Nepean and Hawkesbury Rivers, with roots in or close to the water. It is abundant in mountain valleys and often follows watercourses onto the coastal plain until they become brackish, where it is replaced by *Casuarina glauca*.* It is often the only permanent resident of the beds of deep mountain gorges; its strong roots and massive fluted trunk allowing it to survive regular catastrophic floods which destroy most other plants. Young trees usually grow in a neat rank on the downstream side of parent trees.

Some of the early colonists were struck by dismal feelings on seeing these magnificent trees. Bank's collector George Caley first saw them on the western Hawkesbury River in 1801 and called them 'melancholy casuarinae'. Rachel Henning at Bathurst in 1856 wrote 'They are the most melancholy of vegetable productions. Cypresses are gay to them. They are quite black at a little distance, and only grow in muddy, slimy places.'[14] George Bennet in 1860 thought 'The dark, mournful appearance of this tree caused it to be planted in cemeteries'.[15]

Range: NSW, Qld and NT. **Branchlets:** thin, about 0.5mm diameter, with 8-10 leaf-teeth. **Cones:** pea-size, globular, about 1cm diameter. **Name:** *cunninghamiana* = in honour of Allan Cunningham (1791-1839), pioneering botanist of inland NSW.
* On the western side of the Great Dividing Range it is gradually replaced by *Eucalyptus camaldulensis*, the River Red Gum.

Casuarina glauca Sieber ex Sprengel

Swamp She-Oak, Grey She-Oak **Ss, Cumb**

A tree to 20m high, prefering brackish marshes and estuaries, but also lining muddy creeks on the Cumberland Plain, and appearing as a dwarf on exposed coastal headlands. Neat and pyramidal when young, but maturing into a tall but scraggly tree with contorted, misshapen branches, often decorated with lichens. It usually grows in dense stands, often in belts just inland from mangroves, following the boundary between brackish and fresh waters.

It was probably the bark of this species which Surgeon

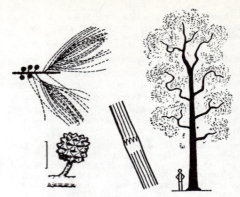

Casuarina cunninghamiana

Casuarina glauca

Worgan in 1788 saw Port Jackson Aborigines removing in whole cylinders to make canoe hulls.

Range: from Eden to southern Qld (also a common street tree). **Branchlets:** thick, about 1-2mm diameter, with 12-16 leaf-teeth, 30-50cm long. **Cones:** a stumpy cylinder, about 14-20mm diameter, with a hollowed apex. **Name:** *glauca* = blue-grey, from the grey foliage.

CELASTRACEAE

A family of trees and shrubs with about 800 species in 50 genera. There are 34 species in 14 genera in Australia.

• *Cassine*
—See RAINFOREST SPECIES.

• *Maytenus* Molina

A genus with about 200 species widely distributed in the tropics and subtropics. There are about 9 species in Australia.

Name: *Maytenus* = from *maytén*, the Spanish name for the South American type species.

Maytenus silvestris (F. Mueller) Lander & L. Johnson

(previously *M. cunninghamii*)

Ss, Cumb

A low spreading or erect shrub 30-150cm, occasionally to 3m, high. Found in the moist understorey of wetter sclerophyll forests on a variety of soils. Relatively common north of the harbour, but rare or absent from the south.

Range: from Sydney to Darling Downs in Qld, but recorded as far south as the Shoalhaven River. **Leaves:** 2-8cm long, fairly tough, entire or with a few teeth towards the upper end, with conspicuous net-veins. **Flowers:** WHITE or PALE GREEN, 4-5.5mm wide, with a fleshy nectary disc, axillary, solitary or in small clusters or racemes. **Fruit:** a leathery capsule splitting in 2, globular, yellow when fresh, brown when dry, smooth, seeds 1-4. **Flowering time:** summer (October-January). **Name:** *silvestris* = Lat. pertaining to forests.

CHENOPODIACEAE

Salt-bushes

A family with about 1500 species worldwide in about 100 genera. There are about 300 species in 31 genera in Australia. The fleshy leaves are often covered in a waxy bloom or 'meal'. This is the remains of sap-filled hairs which collapsed when the leaf was young.

    The family includes silverbeet and beetroot (both cultivars of *Beta vulgaris*), but few other cultivated plants. It is related to Amaranthaceae and Caryophyllaceae.

• *Atriplex*

—See COASTAL AND ESTUARINE SPECIES.

Atriplex semibaccata R. Brown

Half-berried Salt-bush   **Cumb, Sal**

A prostate or clump-forming perennial shrub with stems 20-80cm long. Found on dry creek-banks and vacant allotments on the Cumberland Plain and occasionally in estuarine salt-marshes. It indicates saline soils. Moderately common. A valuable fodder plant in inland NSW.

Range: all parts of NSW, all other states, especially on salt-plains. **Leaves:** variable, ranging from toothed to entire and silvery-mealy to green., 1-3cm long. **Flowers:** tiny, axillary, in small clusters. **Fruits:** the diamond-shaped bracteoles of the female flowers usually become BRIGHT RED and succulent at fruiting time. **Flowering time:** much of the year. **Name:** *semibaccata* = Lat. berry-like, referring to the bracteoles.

• *Einadia* C.S. Rafinesque-Schmaltz

A genus of small herbs and shrubs with 6 species; 4 endemic to Australia, and 2 in NZ.

    There are similarities to *Chenopodium* except the fruit becomes red, swollen and succulent (3-4mm wide). It is also closely related to *Rhagodia* except there is only 1(-3) stamen.

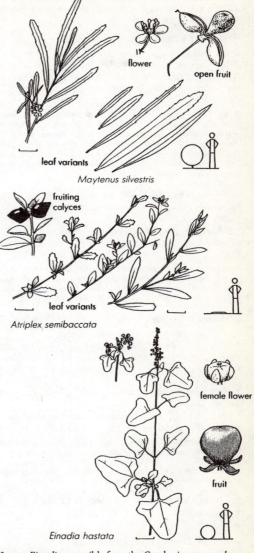

Maytenus silvestris

Atriplex semibaccata

female flower

fruit

Einadia hastata

Name: *Einadia* = possibly from the Greek *ein*, one, *andros*, man, referring to the single stamen of the type species (*E. polygonoides*).

Einadia hastata (R. Brown) A. J. Schott

(previously *Rhagodia hastata*)

Cumb, Temp Rf, STRf

A small erect or ascending herb to 50cm tall, common in open forest on the Cumberland Plain and occasionally in rainforests or gullies on good soils.

Range: coast, ranges and inland areas of eastern Australia. **Leaves:** opposite, soft, green, thin-textured, blunt-tipped and bluntly lobed at the base. **Flowers:** unisexual, tiny, GREEN; in terminal and near-terminal axillary spikes. **Flowering time:** summer. **Name:** *bastata* = triangular with spreading lobes at the base.

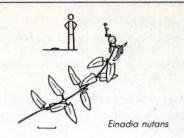

Einadia nutans (R. Brown) A. J. Schott

(previously *Rhagodia nutans*)
Native Seaberry, Saloop-bush **Cumb, Sal**
A small weak prostate herb with stems to 1m long. Rare on the Cumberland Plain, but more common on sea-coasts in the Illawarra.

Range: NSW coast and ranges, Qld and Vic. **Leaves:** opposite, small, more or less succulent, pointed, shaped like arrow-heads. **Flowers:** similar to *E. bastata*. **Flowering time:** summer. **Name:** *nutans* = Lat. nodding, referring to the fruiting spikes. The name saloop refers to a non-alcoholic herbal beverage which was widely drunk in colonial times. True saloop is made from an Indian orchid root. Presumably our plant supplied a local substitute.

Einadia nutans

Einadia polygonoides (Murray) P. G. Wilson

(previously *Chenopodium polygonoides*)
Cumb
An inconspicuous prostrate herb with slender stems usually to 40cm long. Common in open forest on the Cumberland Plain.

Range: NSW coasts north from Sydney, northern tablelands and inland slopes. **Leaves:** slender, green, sometimes slightly lobed at the base, with slightly recurved margins, mealy below. **Flowers:** tiny, in small axillary clusters. **Name:** *polygonoides* = *Polygonum*-like.

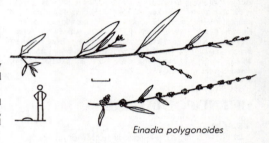

Einadia polygonoides

Einadia trigonos (Roemer & Schultes) P. G. Wilson

(previously *Chenopodium trigonon*) **Cumb**
A small trailing herb with slender stems usually to 40cm long. Fairly common in open forest on the Cumberland Plain. There are 2 sub-species in the area, distinguishable only with a strong lens.
• **ssp. *trigonos:*** perianth segments rounded (ovate-obovate), fruit smooth.
• **ssp. *stellulata:*** perianth segments narrow (spathulate-linear), fruit covered in tiny warts, often black.

Range: NSW coast and ranges and Vic. **Leaves:** triangular, 10-35mm long, hairless, green, not shiny, not fleshy, slightly mealy below. **Flowers:** tiny, GREEN, stalkless; numerous, in small clusters arranged in terminal spikes and axillary spikes or clusters. **Flowering time:** summer. **Name:** *trigonos* = Gk. 3-sided.

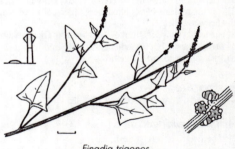

Einadia trigonos

• ***Enchylaena***
• ***Rbagodia***
• ***Salsola***
• ***Sarcocornia***
• ***Suaeda***

—See COASTAL AND ESTUARINE SPECIES.

CLUSIACEAE Hypericaceae

A family of trees, shrubs, climbers and herbs, with about 1200 species in 50 genera, found especially in moist tropical regions of the world. There are 15-19 species in about 6 genera in Australia.

The family includes the Mangosteen (*Garcinia mangostona*) and the Mammy-apple (*Mammea americana*), a fruit widely cultivated in tropical America.

The family is related to Theaceae, Dilleniaceae, and possibly to Myrtaceae.

• *Hypericum* Linnaeus

St John's Wort (pronounced wert)
A genus with about 350 species, including 2 species native and 3 naturalised in Australia. Some authors place it in the families Guttiferae or Hypericaceae.

Name: *Hypericum* = Gk. *hypereikon*, from *byper*, above, *eikon*, picture, as the flowers of some species were placed above images to ward off evil at the ancient midsummer festival which later became St John's feast (June 24), hence the common name (wort simply means plant).

Hypericum gramineum G. Forster

Ss, Cumb, Castl

A slender erect perennial herb, to 30cm tall, with golden flowers. Common in the area in moist sheltered forests.

Range: NSW coast, ranges and inland areas, and all other states. **Leaves:** opposite, soft, hairless, thin-textured, stalkless. **Flowers:** GOLDEN-YELLOW, solitary, terminal, with 3 styles and numerous stamens. **Flowering time:** summer. **Name:** *gramineum* = Lat. grassy.

Hypericum japonicum Thunberg

Ss

A weak prostrate perennial herb with stems to 30cm long. Uncommon or rare in the area, in wet shady situations.

Range: NSW coast and ranges, Vic, Tas and widespread in Asia. **Leaves:** opposite, soft, blunt, with short stalks, hairless, 6-20mm long. **Flowers:** similar to *H. gramineum.* **Name:** *japonicum* = Japanese, because the type specimen was collected there.

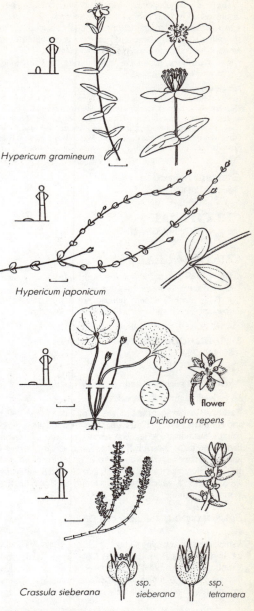

Hypericum gramineum

Hypericum japonicum

Dichondra repens

flower

Crassula sieberana

ssp. sieberana

ssp. tetramera

CONVOLVULACEAE

—See CLIMBERS for family treatment.

• *Dichondra* J. R. & G. Forster

A genus of creeping herbs with about 5 species, including 2 native species in Australia.

Name: *Dichondra* = Gk. 2-grained, from the 2 free carpels (a feature not found in related genera).

Dichondra repens J. R. & G. Forster

Kidney Weed **Ss, Cumb, Temp Rf, STRf**

A low creeping herb with ascending kidney-shaped leaves on stalks to about 10cm long. Common in moist shady situations. It often forms dense carpets.

Range: coast and ranges through eastern Australia and Tas; also NZ. **Leaves:** finely hairy on both sides, soft, on long weak stalks. **Flowers:** WHITE, about 5mm wide, solitary, on long stalks. **Flowering time:** spring-early summer. **Name:** *repens* = Lat. creeping. **Note:** it often grows with *Viola hederacea* and can be easily confused with it. Remember that *Dichondra* always has non-toothed, hairy, dull leaves, while those of *Viola hederacea* are toothed, hairless and slightly glossy.

CRASSULACEAE

A family of succulent herbs and shrubs, with about 1500 species in 35 genera, especially in South Africa and Central America.

• *Crassula* Linnaeus

A genus of small succulent herbs with about 300 species worldwide, about half in South Africa, and 8 species in Australia.

The species are adapted to dry conditions by Crassulacean Acid Metabolism, a water-efficient pathway for respiration, which also occurs in Aizoaceae and Cactaceae.

The family is closely related to Saxifragaceae.

Name: *crassula* = Lat. *crassus,* thick or fat.

Crassula sieberana (Schultes) Druce

Austral Stonecrop **Ss, Sal**

A minute succulent herb 3-20cm long, common in moss on sandstone rocks. It may be single-stemmed and erect or a branched prostrate tuft to 20cm wide. The flowering spikes are erect and leafy, to a few cm high. The stems turn red with age or in dry conditions.

There are 2 subspecies, both found in the area, best distinguished by their habits.

• **ssp. *sieberana***: an annual or perennial with weak, often sprawling stems to 20cm long, forming roots along their length. This is the most common sub-species.

• **ssp. *tetramera***: an annual, rigidly erect, to 15cm long, not rooting from the branches.

Range: widespread throughout NSW, except north coast, and Lord Howe Island. **Leaves:** opposite, succulent, 3-8mm long, 1-3mm wide. **Flowers:** about 1mm wide, with 4 petals; in the axils of leaf-like bracts, arranged in an erect leafy spike. The flower stalks elongate at fruiting time. **Flowering time:** spring and summer. **Name:** *sieberana* = after Franz Wilhelm Sieber of Prague, Bohemia, who collected extensively in Australia from 1819-23, spending 7 months in NSW; *tetramera* = Gk. 4-parts.

Crassula helmsii
—See AQUATICS.

CRUCIFERAE
See AQUATICS: BRASSICACEAE

CUNONIACEAE
A family with about 250 species worldwide in 26 genera. There are about 19 species in Australia in 14 genera.

It is a mainly southern hemisphere family, related to Pittosporaceae. Often included in the family Saxifragaceae.

• *Aphanopetalum*
—See CLIMBERS.

• *Bauera* Banks ex Andrews (BOW-er-a)
An endemic genus with 3 species.

Name: *Bauera* = after the brothers Franz Bauer (1758-1840) and Ferdinand Bauer (1760-1826), fine botanical artists who painted Australian species. Franz was employed by Joseph Banks. Ferdinand, possibly the finest botanical artist ever to have lived, travelled with Robert Brown on Matthew Flinders' 1801-03 circumnavigation of Australia. He collected many species himself, which eventually found their way to the Vienna Herbarium.

Bauera capitata Séringe ex De Candolle
Ss

A small erect or straggling shrub to 25cm tall. It is only known locally from coastal heath at La Perouse where Banks and Solander collected it in 1770. However, it was last recorded there in 1913. It is similar to *B. rubioides* except the flowers are stalkless, forming small leafy heads, and the leaves are lobed.

Range: NSW coastal areas from La Perouse north into Qld. **Leaves:** 5-6mm long, blunt, mostly 3-lobed, opposite, in 3s. **Flowers:** PINK, petals 7-8mm long; crowded at the ends of branches. **Flowering time:** September-October. **Name:** *capitata* = Lat. having heads.

Bauera microphylla Sieber ex De Candolle
Ss

A small low-growing shrub, found in wet heath country.

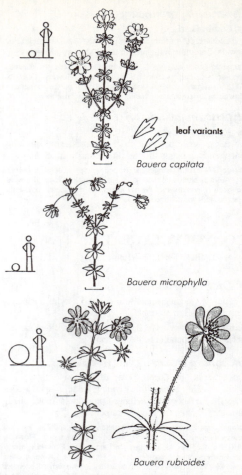

leaf variants

Bauera capitata

Bauera microphylla

Bauera rubioides

Uncommon in the area. Similar to *B. rubioides*, but smaller in all its parts.

Range: NSW coast and ranges north from the Sydney area. **Leaves:** 3-4mm long. **Flowers:** WHITE (rarely pink), about 5mm wide. **Flowering time:** spring-summer. **Name:** *microphylla* = Lat. small-leaved

Bauera rubioides Andrews

River Rose **Ss**

A straggling shrub 0.5-1.5m high, forming dense tangled masses in moist sheltered places, especially creek banks, on sandstone. Common in the area.

Range: coast and ranges south from the Sydney region into Vic, Tas and SA. **Leaves:** 3-foliate, stalkless, opposite (appearing 6-whorled), sparsely hairy, barely toothed, 6-15mm long. **Flowers:** BRIGHT PINK, 12-18mm wide, with usually 8 petals and numerous yellow stamens, on long slender stalks. **Flowering time:** spring-summer. **Name:** *rubioides* = Lat. ruby-like.

• *Callicoma* Andrews

A genus with a single species.

Name: *Callicoma* = Gk. beautiful-hair, referring to the fluffy flowers.

Callicoma serratifolia Andrews

Callicoma, Black Wattle, Tdgerruing
Ss, Temp Rf, STRf

A large spreading shrub (usually about 4-5m but can be 10-15m high) with wattle-like flowers. A common shrub in gullies and damp sheltered cliff ledges, on sandstone, and in rainforests. This is a really beautiful shrub. It was probably the first plant used for wattling by the early settlers (see *Acacia*). The new soft leaf shoots are furry with dense bronze hairs (a popular food for possums).

Range: from the Clyde River to southern Qld. **Leaves:** opposite, shiny, tough, coarsely serrated, whitish below with a fine felt. **Flowers:** CREAMY YELLOW, in dense ball-shaped heads, on long hairy peduncles. **Flowering time:** October-November. **Name:** *serratifolia* = Lat. saw-leaved. *Tdgerruing* is an Aboriginal name from Camden.

• *Ceratopetalum* Smith

An endemic genus of 5 species, mostly rainforest trees. A peculiar feature is that after pollination the sepals swell and turn bright red, giving the distinctive red 'flowering' in December. The colour attracts birds to distribute the capsules held within the sepals.

Name: *Ceratopetalum* = lat. antler-petalled, referring to the lobed petals.

Ceratopetalum apetalum

—See RAINFOREST SPECIES.

Ceratopetalum gummiferum Smith

New South Wales Christmas Bush **Ss**

A light erect shrub usually 2-4m high (although in rainforest

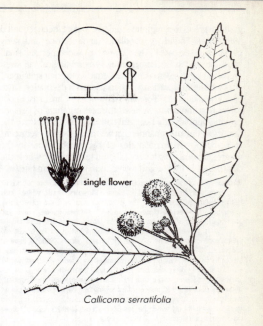

single flower

Callicoma serratifolia

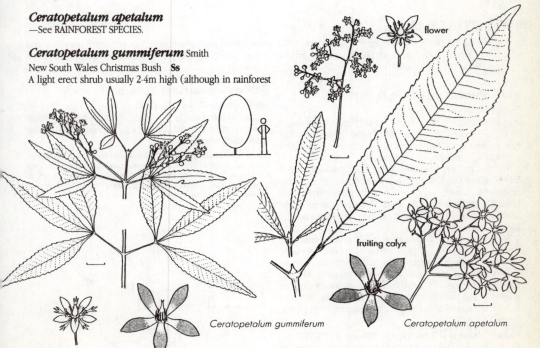

flower

fruiting calyx

flower

fruiting calyx

Ceratopetalum gummiferum

Ceratopetalum apetalum

gullies it grows to a medium-sized tree and has been recorded 30m high). Found in woodland on sandstone and fairly common in the area. The flowers in November are small and white, but in December-January the fruiting calyces swell and turn bright red, making it an attractive garden specimen.

The beautiful sprays have been used as a decoration since early colonial times. 'For some days before Christmas, in our drives near the town, we used to meet numbers of persons carrying bundles of a beautiful native shrub, to decorate the houses, in the same manner that we use holly and evergreens at home . . . Great quantities of the shrubs grow in the neighbourhood of Sydney or I should fear that such wholesale destruction as I witnessed would soon render them rare.'[16]

Range: NSW coasts and Blue Mountains. **Leaves:** 3-foliate, opposite, thin, fairly soft, finely toothed, hairless. **Flowers:** small, white, fairly numerous in axillary cymes. The petals are tiny and slit into narrow segments. **Flowering time:** November. **Name:** *gummifera* = Lat. gum-bearing, since Surgeon White told James Smith that it produced a red gum. It was once known as 'Officer Plant' from its bright red appearance. **Note:** This species prompted James Smith's famous statement: 'When a botanist first enters on the investigation of so remote a country as New Holland, he finds himself as it were in a new world. He can scarsely meet with any fixed points from whence to draw his analogies; and even those that appear most promising, are frequently in danger of misleading, instead of informing him. Whole tribes of plants, which at first sight seem familiar to his acquaintance, as occupying links in nature's chain, on which he has been accustomed to depend, prove on a nearer examination, total strangers . . . '[18]

Schizomeria ovata

• *Schizomeria*
—See RAINFOREST SPECIES.

DILLENIACEAE

A mainly tropical family with about 400 species in 10-12 genera. In Australia there are about 110 species in 5 genera, the largest of which is *Hibbertia*.

• *Hibbertia* Andrews (hib-ER-sha)

Guinea Flowers

A genus of small shrubs or climbers with bright yellow flowers. There are about 115 species, distributed in Australia, NG, New Caledonia and Madagascar. About 110 species are native to Australia, distributed in all states.

The flowers are short-lived, solitary and terminal with 5 fragile yellow petals that are easily deciduous. The stamens are usually numerous and there are 2 or more independent ovaries, each with a single style. The arrangement of the stamens around the ovaries is an important aid to identification.

Hibbertia is a difficult genus because there are several local species with virtually identical leaves: *H.* sp. aff. *riparia*, *H. cistiflora*, *H. pedunculata*, *H.* sp. aff. *serpyllifolia* and *H. empetrifolia*, as well as forms with no clear identity. Identification requires close attention to leaves, stamen numbers, and stamen arrangement. The genus is under revision at present and a clearer delineation will emerge in future.

Name: *Hibbertia* = after George Hibbert (1757-1837), a London merchant who had a private botanic garden at Chelsea

in London. He was interested in propagating exotics and introduced many NSW plants to the hothouses of the British aristocracy.

Hibbertia acicularis (Labillardière) F. Mueller

Prickly Guinea Flower **Ss, Castl**

A small shrub, erect or prostrate, 30-150cm high. Found in moist heath near the coast (e.g. Kurnell) and in the Castlereagh woodlands.

Range: coast, ranges and western slopes in eastern Australia. **Leaves:** linear, stiff, pungent pointed, with recurved margins, mostly 6-20mm long, 0.5-2mm wide. **Flowers:** axillary, with 6-8 stamens all on one side of 2 densely hairy carpels. **Flowering time:** September-December. **Name:** *acicularis* = needle-like.

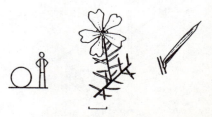

Hibbertia acicularis

Hibbertia aspera De Candolle

Rough Guinea Flower **Ss, Cumb**

A weakly erect shrub usually to 50cm high, common in shrubby understories in woodland on both sandstone and clay soils.

Range: coastal areas throughout eastern Australia. **Leaves:** small, fairly stiff, ovate, rough to touch (due to stiff star-hairs with swollen bases), felty below, with recurved margins, 4-20mm long, 2-7mm wide. **Flowers:** terminal, 6 stamens all on one side of 2 hairy carpels **Flowering time:** spring (October-November). **Name:** *aspera* = Lat. rough.

Hibbertia aspera

Hibbertia bracteata

(R. Brown ex De Candolle) Bentham

Blue Mountains Guinea Flower **Ss**

A shrub usually to 1m high, found in heath and woodland. Each flower arises from a ring of brown bracts.

Range: restricted to the Sydney area and Blue Mountains. **Leaves:** broad, with a short point, 10-30mm long, 4-7mm wide, with flat or slightly recurved margins. **Flowers:** terminal or axillary, with about 16 stamens all placed on one side of 2 silky carpels. **Flowering time:** spring. **Name:** *bracteata* = Lat. with bracts.

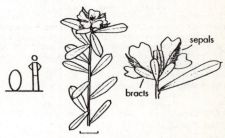

sepals

bracts

Hibbertia bracteata

Hibbertia circumdans Conn

(previously *H.* sp. aff. *monogyna*) **Ss**

An erect shrub to 60cm high. A recently recognised species, locally found in woodland on the Cataract River near Appin, and at Wilton. It is closely related to *H. monogyna.*

Range: scattered populations occur from Nadgee on the far south coast to the Pilliga Scrub on the north-western slopes of NSW. **Leaves:** similar to *H. monogyna,* but folded along the length, with prominently recurved point and prominent teeth at the apex. **Flowers:** terminal, with 15-30 stamens completley surrounding usually 3 hairless carpels. **Flowering time:** spring-autumn. **Name:** *circumdans* = Lat. encircling, referring to the stamens surrounding the carpels.

Hibbertia circumdans

Hibbertia cistiflora

(Sieber ex Sprengel) N. A. Wakefield
Ss

A wiry shrub 40-100cm high with stout stems. Found in heath and woodland on sandstone. Uncommon in the area.

Range: Sydney area, Blue Mountains and southern tablelands, into Vic. **Leaves:** rough due to small warty projections, with revolute margins, a short blunt yellowish point, a thickened keel underneath, 5-10mm long, about 1mm wide. **Flowers:** terminal, with about 6 stamens all on one side of 2 hairless carpels. **Flowering time:** spring. **Name:** *cistiflora* = *Cistus* flowered. *Cistus* is a genus of mainly Mediterranean shrubs known as Rockroses. **Similar species:** distinguish from *H.* sp. aff. *riparia* by the hairless ovaries (need a hand lens) and the short yellowish leaf point.

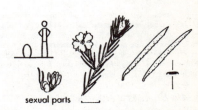

sexual parts

Hibbertia cistiflora

Hibbertia dentata
—See CLIMBERS.

Hibbertia diffusa R. Brown ex De Candolle
Cumb

A small prostrate or sprawling shrub with stems rarely over 50cm long, often forming mats. Fairly common in dry clay soils on the Cumberland Plain.

Range: coast and ranges in eastern mainland Australia. **Leaves:** blunt, sometimes toothed, tapering gradually to the base, and usually with a small notch at the tip, lacking a distinct recurved point, hairless except

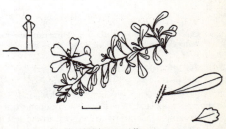

Hibbertia diffusa

for the margins, 4-30mm long, 3-9mm wide. **Flowers:** mostly terminal, with 20-25 stamens completely surrounding 2-3 hairless carpels, sepals usually 8mm long. **Flowering time:** spring-autumn. **Name:** *diffusa* = Lat. spreading and much branched. **Similar species:** *H. obtusifolia*, *H. monogyna*.

Hibbertia empetrifolia (De Candolle) Hoogl.

Trailing Guinea Flower **Ss**

A sprawling multi-stemmed shrub with branches to about 40cm long. Found in open heath usually on sandstone.

Range: Sydney area, south coast, western slopes, Vic and Tas. **Leaves:** rough to touch, fairly stiff, with a short point (the point often recurved), 5-7mm long, 1-3mm wide. **Flowers:** terminal, on prominent stalks 6-12mm long, with 6-12 stamens all placed on one side of 2 hairy carpels. **Flowering time:** spring-early summer. **Name:** *empetrifolia* = *Empetrum*-leaved. *Empetrum* is a genus of low alpine shrubs found in the northern hemisphere. **Similar species:** distinguish from *H.* sp. aff. *riparia* by the prominent recurved point and generally broader leaves and sprawling habit.

Hibbertia fasciculata R. Brown ex De Candolle

Ss

A low spreading shrub to 50cm high, usually found in open heath on sandy soils.

Range: NSW coast, Blue Mountains and northern ranges. **Leaves:** slender, 4-6mm long, crowded, convex underneath, margins not recurved. **Flowers:** variable; axillary, with 8-12 stamens usually completely surrounding 3 hairy or hairless carpels. **Flowering time:** spring (August-October). **Name:** *fasciculata* = Lat. clustered. **Similar species:** distinguish from *H.* sp. aff. *riparia* and other similar species by the leaves lacking recurved margins.

Hibbertia hermanniifolia De Candolle

Ss Rare 3RCa

An erect shrub to about 150cm tall, found in woodland on sandstone. A rare species, only locally known from a small area at Bents Basin. The nearest population is 300km to the south, in Wadbilliga National Park.

Range: Sydney area, also separate populations in the southern tablelands and Vic. **Leaves:** furry above, densely pale-hairy below (star-hairs), with recurved margins and rounded notched tips, 5-30mm long, 3-10mm wide. Branches covered in white or rusty felt. **Flowers:** axillary, with 15-20 stamens completely surrounding 2 hairy carpels. **Flowering time:** April-May. **Name:** *hermanniifolia* = *Hermania*-leaved. *Hermannia* is a genus in Sterculiaceae.

Hibbertia linearis R. Brown ex De Candolle

Showy Guinea Flower **Ss**

An erect shrub to 1.5m high, found in heath and woodland on sandstone and sands. A hairless species, except for young shoots.

Range: NSW coast, into Qld. **Leaves:** fairly soft, with recurved margins, 8-30mm long, 1-5mm wide. **Flowers:** terminal or axillary; with 15-25 stamens completely surrounding 3 hairy carpels. **Flowering time:** June-October. **Name:** *linearis* = Lat. straight, referring to the leaves.

Hibbertia monogyna R. Brown ex De Candolle

Leafy Guinea Flower **Ss**

A shrub usually 40-60cm high, found in shallow sandy soils in heath and woodland. Very difficult to distinguish from *H. diffusa*; close attention has to be given to the leaf tip (see illustration) which has a tiny recurved point. Not common but widely distributed in the area.

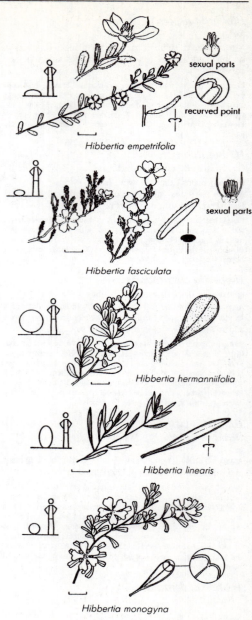

Hibbertia empetrifolia

sexual parts

recurved point

Hibbertia fasciculata

sexual parts

Hibbertia hermanniifolia

Hibbertia linearis

Hibbertia monogyna

Range: NSW coast, Blue Mountains, central and north western slopes and Qld. **Leaves:** hairless, with a distinct recurved point and recurved margins, fairly dense in clusters on short lateral branchlets, 5-12mm long, 2.5-5mm wide, often with some prominent teeth at the apex. **Flowers:** terminal on short shoots, with 10-12 stamens completely surrounding often only 1 hairless carpel, sepals usually 4-6mm long. **Flowering time:** spring-autumn. **Name:** *monogyna* = Lat. having a single set of female parts. **Similar species:** distinguish from *H. diffusa* by the presence of a distinct recurved tip on the leaf.

Hibbertia nitida (R. Brown ex De Candolle) Bentham

Shiny Guinea Flower   **Ss**

A spreading shrub to 1m high, found in heath and woodland on sandstone. An uncommon species recorded mainly from various spots on the Georges River but also from Middle Harbour, West Head and Upper Lane Cove River.

Range: restricted to the Sydney area.   **Leaves:** shiny, 10-20mm long, 3-6mm wide, margins flat or slightly recurved.   **Flowers:** terminal or axillary, with about 11 stamens on one side of 2 silky carpels.   **Flowering time:** September-November.   **Name:** *nitida* = Lat. lustrous.

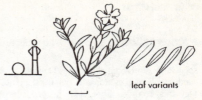

leaf variants

Hibbertia nitida

Hibbertia obtusifolia De Candolle

Grey Guinea Flower   **Ss**

A shrub to 60cm high, found in heath and woodland. All parts of the plant are covered in a layer of fine furry hairs.

Range: coast, ranges and inland areas of eastern mainland Australia. **Leaves:** soft, flat, blunt, usually spathulate (spoon-shaped) 10-30mm long. Stems and leaves greyish, finely felty.   **Flowers:** terminal or axillary, with 30-40 stamens completely surrounding 3 hairless carpels. **Flowering time:** spring.   **Name:** *obtusifolia* = blunt-leaved.

Hibbertia obtusifolia

Hibbertia pedunculata R. Brown ex De Candolle

Cumb

A small sprawling multi-stemmed shrub usually to 20cm high, found in open forest on clay soils. Its main local distribution was in the central clay suburbs from Yennora to Bexley, where it would by now have been destroyed by settlement. It still occurs rarely on the Cumberland Plain.

Range: coast, ranges and western slopes of eastern Australia.   **Leaves:** rough to touch due to fine stiff hairs, linear, margins recurved, 3-6mm long, 0.5mm wide, pointed.   **Flowers:** terminal, with 15-20 stamens completely surrounding 2 hairy carpels, flowers on stalks longer than the leaves.   **Flowering time:** spring.   **Name:** *pedunculata* = Lat. having peduncles (floral stalks).   **Similar species:** distinguished from *H.* sp. aff. *riparia* by the distinct floral stalks longer than the leaves and by the numerous stamens equally placed around the hairy carpels.

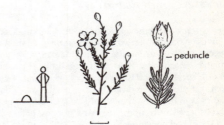

– peduncle

Hibbertia pedunculata

Hibbertia rufa Wakefield

Ss

A wiry sprawling shrub with stems to 40cm long. found in marshy sedgeland. It does not strictly occur in the area of this book, but deserves to be mentioned because it is often come across in mountain heaths, including southern parts of the Woronora Plateau.

Range: NSW coast and ranges (except the south coast), Qld and Vic. **Leaves:** rather triangular, distant on the stems, hairless, margins recurved, occasionally with a few small teeth.   **Flowers:** axillary; with 4 stamens, the filaments fused together, all on one side of 2 hairless carpels. **Flowering time:** summer.   **Name:** *rufa* = Lat. red, probably referring to the calyx.

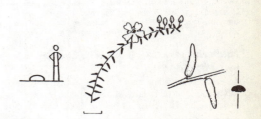

Hibbertia rufa

Hibbertia saligna R. Brown ex De Candolle

Tall Guinea Flower   **Ss**

A shrub 1-2m high with softly hairy branches and leaves. Found on alluvial soils in sheltered gullies in the Blue Mountains and foothills, also recorded from the Royal National Park.

Range: mainly restricted to the Blue Mountains (Glen Davis to Budawang Ranges).   **Leaves:** flat, furry on both surfaces, paler below, with leaf bases partly clasping the furry stems, margins entire or toothed, 20-110mm long, 4-15mm wide.   **Flowers:** terminal on short shoots, with 20-35 stamens completely surrounding 3 hairless carpels.   **Flowering time:** spring.   **Name:** *saligna* = Lat. willowy.

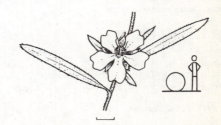

Hibbertia saligna

Hibbertia scandens
—See CLIMBERS.

Hibbertia serpyllifolia R. Brown ex De Candolle
Ss

A low sprawling or prostrate shrub with branches to 30cm long, found mainly in coastal heaths on sandstone. Rare in the Sydney area, recorded from sandy heath in the Royal National Park near Bundeena.

Range: coasts, ranges and inland parts of NSW, also Vic and Tas. **Leaves:** linear, 3-6mm long, mostly scabrous, blunt, margins revolute. **Flowers:** terminal, with 15-20 stamens completely surrounding 3 hairy carpels. **Flowering time:** spring. **Name:** *serpyllifolia* = Lat. with leaves like *Thymus serpyllum*, Creeping Thyme.

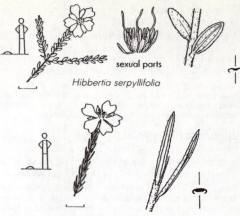

sexual parts

Hibbertia serpyllifolia

Hibbertia sp. aff. *serpyllifolia*
Ss

An unnamed species, close to *H. serpyllifolia*, has been collected from the Menai-Lucas Heights area. It has larger, longer leaves (8-10mm long) with sharp tips, and more numerous stamens (15-28).

Hibbertia sp. aff. *serpyllifolia*

Hibbertia sp. aff. *riparia*
Ss, Castl

An erect shrub 40-60cm high, found in heath and woodland on sandstone and shale. *H. riparia* is now recognised as a species confined to Tas and Vic, leaving one of Sydney's common *Hibbertia* for the time being without a name. *Hibbertia* sp. aff. *riparia* is a complex of intergrading forms which will probably be divided into a number of distinct varieties or subspecies. They share small, crowded, linear, scabrous leaves with strongly recurved margins, often with a thickened keel underneath.

Range: all states. **Leaves:** linear, rough to touch due to stiff hairs or leaf bases (a variable feature), often keeled below, with recurved margins, 8-10mm long, 0.5-2mm wide. **Flowers:** variable, typical form with 6-16 stamens completely surrounding 2 finely silky carpels. **Flowering time:** mostly September-November. **Name:** *riparia* = Lat. pertaining to creek banks. **Similar species:** *H. cistiflora*.

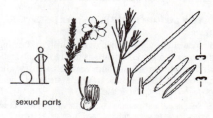

sexual parts

Hibbertia sp aff. *riparia*

Hibbertia virgata R. Brown ex De Candolle
ssp. *virgata* Ss

An erect or ascending shrub to 150cm high with slender stems and long thin leaves. An uncommon species found in damp coastal heath, e.g. La Perouse, Botany Bay swamps.

Range: widespread in southern Australia, including Tas. **Leaves:** hairless, erect, long and slender, margins tightly upcurved forming a groove on the upper surface, 7-25mm long, 0.5mm wide. **Flowers:** 10-12 stamens, completely surrounding 3 hairless carpels. **Flowering time:** spring. **Name:** *virgata* = Lat. twiggy.

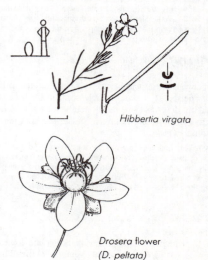

Hibbertia virgata

DROSERACEAE
Sundews
A family of herbs with about 100 species in 4 genera worldwide. Only *Drosera* occurs in Australia. The family includes *Dionaea*, the Venus' fly trap of North America.

• *Drosera* Linnaeus
Sundews
A cosmopolitan genus of small carnivorous herbs with about

Drosera flower
(*D. peltata*)

90 species, including 54 in Australia (42 in south-western WA). Droseras are remarkable for their pretty leaves covered in red glandular hairs, each tipped by a drop of clear sticky liquid, 'Jewelled with rubies small and bright, Each on a crimson stem, Upheld, to catch the chequer'd light'.[17]

They supplement their diet by consuming small insects

which become trapped in this sticky liquid. The leaves roll up and the insect is dissolved and digested, providing the plant with the nitrogen lacking in sandy soils. The flowers occur in erect racemes, which uncoil as they mature.

Name: *Drosera* = Gk. *droseros*, dewey, referring to the clear sticky drops of liquid on the hair-glands.

Drosera binata Labillardiere

Forked Sundew   **Ss**

An erect herb with a tuft of forked leaves, to 80cm tall, found in wet sunny heath. Occurs throughout the coastal strip, but not abundant. It was experimented upon by Charles Darwin as part of his extensive study of Sundews.

Range: NSW coast, Blue Mountains, southern tablelands, Qld, Vic, Tas and widespread in Asia.   **Leaves:** branched into 2, 4, or 8 slender segments, on tall stalks.   **Flowers:** WHITE, about 25mm wide; in a short cyme.   **Flowering time:** summer.   **Name:** *binata* = Lat. 2-fold.

Drosera burmanii Vahl

Burmann's Sundew   **Castl**

Similar to *D. spathulata*. A very rare species locally, recorded only from the Castlereagh woodlands.

Range: mainly on the central western and south-western slopes of NSW; also in Asia.   **Leaves:** in a dense rosette, about 30mm wide, more or less triangular, wedge-shaped, green (not red as in *D. spathulata*) **Flowers:** WHITE, and 5 entire styles (distinguish from *D. spathulata* which has 3-4 deeply divided styles).   **Flowering time:** spring and summer.   **Name:** *burmanii* = after Johannes Burmann (1707-79), the Dutch botanist who first illustrated this species, in his 1737 flora of Ceylon.

Drosera glanduligera Lehmann

Castl

A small herb to 10cm tall, similar to *D. spathulata*, but the flowers are red or orange and the flowering stem is covered in glandular hairs. Only recorded locally from the Castlereagh woodlands.

Range: mainly NSW western slopes; also Vic, SA and WA.   **Leaves:** to 15mm long, spoon-shaped.   **Flowers:** RED-ORANGE, calyx, stalks and stem with tiny scattered glandular hairs.   **Flowering time:** spring-summer.   **Name:** *glanduligera* = Gk. little gland bearing.

Drosera peltata Thunberg

Ss, Castl, Cumb

This species has 2 types of leaves: a rosette at the base of the plant (often withered or absent), and stalked semicircular leaves on a slim stem to about 20cm high. It occurs in sunny wet places.

There are 2 subspecies (or possibly a single variable species) and both are common. They are very similar and, unfortunately, require careful examination of the flowers to be distinguished.

• **ssp. *peltata*:** plants 5-17cm high.

Range: Sri Lanka, Nepal, South-east Asia to Japan, NG, Australia. **Flowers:** sepals 2-4mm long, outer surface hairy or hairless, margins fringed, less often irregularly toothed. Petals 5-6mm long. Unbranched basal part of style 0.1-0.2mm long, seeds about 0.5mm long.   **Name:** *peltata* = having the stalk attached to the centre of the leaf.

• **ssp. *auriculata*** (previously *D. auriculata*): plants 20-30cm high.

Range: eastern states and NZ.   **Flowers:** sepals 4-6mm long, hairless, margin irregularly toothed, petals 7-8mm long, unbranched basal part

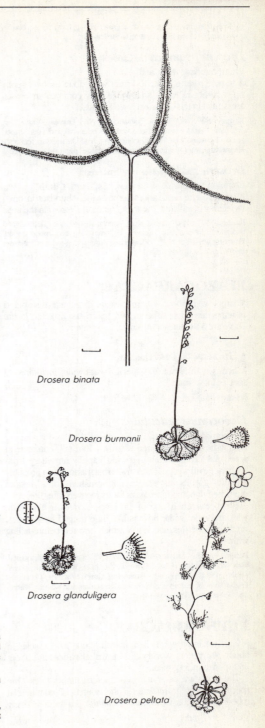

Drosera binata

Drosera burmanii

Drosera glanduligera

Drosera peltata

of style 0.3-0.5mm long. Seeds narrow, about 1mm long. **Name:** *auriculata* = Lat. ear-like, referring to the leaves.

Drosera pygmaea De Candolle

Pygmy Sundew **Ss, Castl**

A minute rosette herb, 10-12mm wide, found in wet sunny open heath, in sandy soil. Moderately common in coastal areas, also in the Castlereagh woodlands.

Range: NSW coast, Victoria, Tasmania and NZ. **Leaves:** 4-6mm long, red, numerous in a dense rosette, with a slender stalk and a cup-shaped apex. **Flowers:** WHITE, tiny, solitary, on thread-like stalks to 3cm high. **Flowering time:** spring-early summer. **Name:** *pygmaea* = Lat. pygmy.

Drosera spathulata Labillardière

Common Sundew, Rosy Sundew **Ss, Castl, Cumb**

A small rosette herb, about 30mm wide. Abundant in open wet sunny heathland. The most common *Drosera* in the area.

Range: NSW coastal areas, Blue Mountains, Qld, Vic, Tas, NZ and widespread in east Asia. **Leaves:** 10-20mm long, red, spoon-shaped. **Flowers:** WHITE or PINK, **Flowering time:** spring-summer. **Name:** *spathulata* = Lat. spoon-shaped.

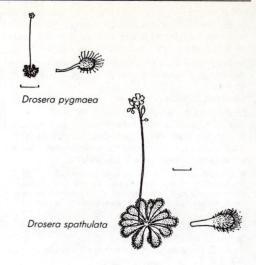

Drosera pygmaea

Drosera spathulata

ELAEOCARPACEAE

A family with about 350 species in 12 genera, distributed in temperate South America, NZ, South-east Asia and Japan. There are 33 species in Australia, in 5 genera.

• *Elaeocarpus* Linnaeus

A genus with about 200 species worldwide, including 20 species in Australia.

Name: *Elaeocarpus* = Gk. olive-fruit.

Elaeocarpus reticulatus Smith

Blueberry Ash **Ss**

A straight understorey tree usually 4-10m tall, common in woodland on sandstone, growing happily anywhere from stony ridges to wet gullies. A mycorrhizal association probably accounts for its success in impoverished soils. A stout elongated lignotuber accounts for its recovery after fire.

Blueberry Ash is one of the loveliest trees in the bush, with masses of white flowers like little fringed lampshades, pretty blue berries, and leaves which turn red before falling with age.

Range: NSW coast and ranges, Tas, Vic and Qld. **Leaves:** tough, toothed, with prominent net veins. **Flowers:** drooping, WHITE, with fringed petals, in axillary racemes. **Flowering time:** November-December. **Fruits:** shiny blue drupes, present through autumn and winter. **Name:** *reticulatus* = Lat. forming a network.

EUPHORBIACEAE

A large, mainly tropical family, with about 5000 species in about 300 genera worldwide. In Australia there are about 230 species in 53 genera.

The family includes many commercial timber trees. One species, *Hevea brasiliensis*, is the source of commercial rubber. Bitter Cassava, *Manihot esculenta*, is a staple in many tropical countries.

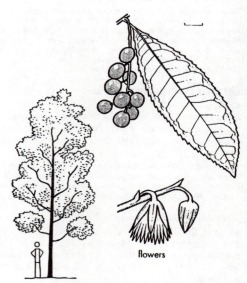

flowers

Elaeocarpus reticulatus

Most species are rainforest trees, the greatest Australian concentration being around the Atherton Tableland in north-eastern Qld.

The flowers are usually small and unisexual.

The leaves always have stipules: pairs of small scale-like appendages attached to the stem on either side of the leaf stalk. They serve to protect the leaf in its earliest bud stages. Often the stipules fall but a visible scar remains. Stipules are found in many families but they are especially distinctive of Euphorbiaceae.

The other distinctive feature is the fruit, which is typically ball-shaped and 3-chambered.

• *Amperea* Jussieu

An endemic genus with 6 species, 5 in south-western WA.

Name: *Amperea* = after Antoine Marie Ampère (1775-1836), professor of physics in Paris (the unit of electric current, the ampere, is named after him). He was an acquaintance of Antoine de Jussieu, who named the genus.

Amperea xiphoclada (Sieber ex Sprengel) Druce

Broom Spurge **Ss**
A wiry shrub to 60cm high, apparently leafless with several strongly ridged stems arising from a woody rootstock. A common species in woodland and dry heaths.

Range: NSW coast and ranges and all other states except WA and NT. **Leaves:** absent, apart from occasional small rudimentary leaves at the base of the stems. **Flowers:** tiny, almost microscopic, in small dense clusters with several male flowers surrounding a single female flower. **Flowering time:** spring.   **Name:** *xiphoclada* = Gk. sword-stemmed.

• *Baloghia*
—See RAINFOREST SPECIES.

• *Bertya* Planchon

An endemic genus of 20 species, all shrubs.

Name: *Bertya* = after Count Léonce de Lambertye, a French botanist and horticulturist.

Bertya brownii S. Moore

(previously *B. astrotricha*) **Ss**
A slender shrub to 2m, occasionally to 3m, with a dense felt of fine star-hairs on leaves and stems. Found in moist sheltered places in woodland. A locally uncommon species, found north of the harbour, e.g. Ku-ring-gai Chase NP (near Mt Colah) and Katandra Sanctuary at Mona Vale.

Range: NSW coastal districts. **Leaves:** flat, soft, rough-furry on both sides due to star-hairs, green above, white below. Tufts of star-hairs make the margins look somewhat toothed. **Flowers:** unisexual (plants monoecious), small, solitary, axillary, covered in tiny golden star-hairs. **Flowering time:** May-July.   **Name:** *brownii* = after Robert Brown (1773-1858), botanist on Matthew Flinders' 1801-03 circumnavigation of Australia.

Bertya pomaderroides F. Mueller

Hazel Bertya **Ss**
A shrub 1-1.5m high, often multi-stemmed, with stems and leaf undersides densely covered in fine star-hairs. Found in moist sheltered places in woodland. A locally uncommon species, restricted to valleys south of the harbour, e.g. in Royal National Park, Heathcote National Park, The Woolwash (Campbelltown).

Range: NSW coast and ranges south from Sydney. **Leaves:** small, fairly stiff, concave below; dull green, hairless above; pale or rusty below with a fine dense felt of star-hairs. **Flowers:** monoecious, YELLOWISH, small, solitary, axillary. **Flowering time:** spring (from June). **Name:** *pomaderroides* = Pomaderris-like.

• *Beyeria* Miquel (bi-EAR-ee-a)

An endemic genus with 14 species, all shrubs.

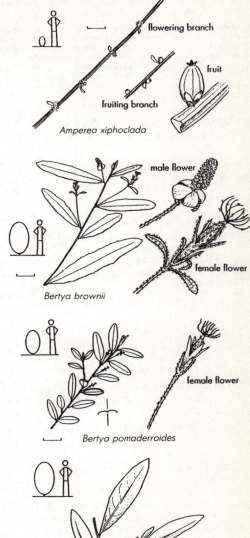

Amperea xiphoclada

flowering branch

fruiting branch

fruit

male flower

female flower

Bertya brownii

female flower

Bertya pomaderroides

Beyeria viscosa

Name: *Beyeria* = apparently after an obscure Dutch botanist named Beyer, who studied mosses and ferns in Denmark.

Beyeria viscosa (Labillardière) Miquel
Pink-wood **Ss, Cumb**
An erect shrub 1-2m high, found on dry rocky slopes in woodland. Recorded from a few sites in the area, e.g. upper Georges River (Basin Reserve), Nepean River (Maldon); and

occasionally on the Cumberland Plain and lower Blue Mountains. The woody blue-skinned fruits open explosively.

Range: NSW coast, ranges and inland areas, south from the Sydney region, also all states except SA and NT. **Leaves:** erect, slightly sticky, with obscure venation, hairless, pale beneath. **Flowers:** YELLOWISH, axillary, the males often in clusters on recurved peduncles, the females solitary. The flowers have 5 petals alternating with small glands. Male flowers have numerous stamens. The fruit is a green oval capsule about 8mm long, with 3 chambers. **Flowering time:** summer. **Name:** *viscosa* = sticky, referring to the leaves.

• *Breynia* J.R. & G. Forster (BRY-nee-a)

A genus of shrubs with about 25 species, including 2 endemic to Australia.

Name: *Breynia* = in honour of Jacob Breyn, a seventeenth century botanical author, resident in Danzig.

Breynia oblongifolia Jean Mueller

Breynia **Rf, Ss, Cumb**

An erect shrub 2-3m high with greyish-green leaves and red branchlets, common in rainforest margin and moist gullies, including creek banks on the Cumberland Plain. The pendant fruits resemble tiny apples.

Range: NSW coasts, Blue Mountains and some inland districts, and Qld. **Leaves:** olive green, rather dull, oval, thin and, fairly soft, 2-ranked on lateral branches (apparently pinnate). **Flowers:** tiny, reddish and drooping below the leaves. **Name:** *oblongifolia* = Lat. oblong-leaved.

• *Claoxylon*
—See RAINFOREST SPECIES.

• *Glochidion* J. R. & G. Forster (glo-KID-ee-on)

A genus of shrubs and trees with about 300 species, including 15 in Australia.

Name: *Glochidion* = Gk. *glochis*, a projecting point, from the stiffly projecting style.

Glochidion ferdinandi (Jean Mueller) F.M. Bailey

Cheese Tree **Rf, Ss**

A bushy shrub or tree usually 4-8m tall but occasionally 15-20m. A pioneer rainforest species that is often abundant in moist, sheltered woodlands and gullies, usually near the sea. It grows to be a large bushy tree in mature rainforests.

Range: coastal areas from the Illawarra through Qld to the Kimberleys in WA. **Leaves:** soft but firm, slightly accuminate, mostly hairless, old leaves discoloured purplish brown. The leaves appear pinnate as they are 2-ranked on short branchlets. **Flowers:** small, unisexual (plants monoecious). **Fruit:** about 15mm diameter, pale yellowish green, splitting at maturity to reveal several brilliant red seeds. **Name:** *ferdinandi* = in honour of Ferdinand von Mueller. The common name is an old children's name, because the fruits resemble tiny cheese rounds.

• *Micrantheum* Desfontaines

An endemic genus with 3 species, all small shrubs in eastern Australia.

Name: *Micrantheum* = Gk. tiny flower.

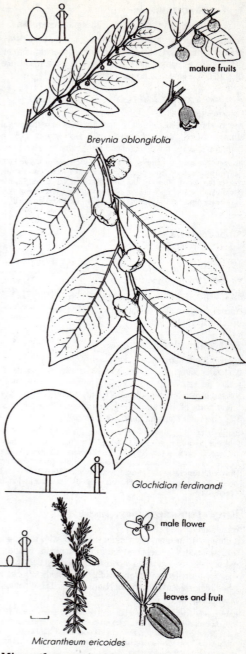

Breynia oblongifolia

Glochidion ferdinandi

male flower

leaves and fruit

Micrantheum ericoides

Micrantheum ericoides Desfontaines
Ss

Usually an obscure little shrub with stems 20-80 (rarely 150) cm high. Common in heath and woodland, usually in the shelter of other shrubs. The flowers are almost microscopic but the fruit are quite distinctive, red, ball-like, 6-7mm long.

Range: NSW coastal districts and Blue Mountains. **Leaves:** tiny and narrow, in whorls of 3 along a wiry stem. **Flowers:** just over 2mm wide, WHITE or pinkish, with 3 anthers. The stalk and calyx are red. **Name:** *ericoides* = *Erica*-like. *Erica* is the Heath or Heather of Europe.

Micrantheum hexandrum J. D. Hooker
Ss
An erect bushy shrub to about 2m high. Found in woodland, mainly on the banks of the Georges River, near Campbelltown.

Range: NSW ranges (mainly southern), Qld, Vic and Tas. **Leaves:** slender-oblong, in 3s. **Flowers:** tiny, WHITE, with 6 anthers and a long fine floral tube beneath the petals. **Flowering time:** spring. **Name:** *hexandrum* = Lat. 6-anthered.

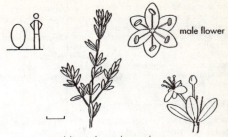
male flower

Micrantheum hexandrum

• *Monotaxis* Brongniart
An endemic genus of 11 species, most restricted to south-western WA.

Name: *Monotaxis* = Gk. single-arrangement, referring to the single row of stamens.

Monotaxis linifolia Brongniart
Ss
A tiny sprawling shrub with thin green stems to 30cm long arising from a thick woody base. Found in damp heath on sandstone. Uncommon or rare in the area.

Range: NSW coast and ranges south from the Sydney region. **Leaves:** tiny, with recurved margins, in whorls of 3. **Flowers:** tiny, GREENISH WHITE, several male flowers surrounding a single female flower. In the male flowers the anther cells are separated by long bar-like connectors. **Flowering time:** spring-summer. **Name:** *linifolia* = Lat. straight-leaved.

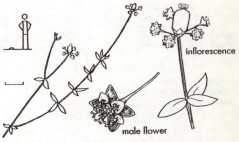
inflorescence

male flower

Monotaxis linifolia

• *Omalanthus* Jussieu
A genus of 35 species, including 3 in Australia.

Name: *Omalanthus* = Gk. *homalos*, smooth, *anthos*, flower, because the plants are hairless.

Omalanthus populifolius Graham
Bleeding Heart **Rf, Ss**
An attractive leafy shrub usually 2-4m high. An opportunistic species found in rainforest margins and gullies, frequently popping up as a weed in waste areas and gardens.

The common name is well deserved since the large heart-shaped leaves turn rich blood-red before falling.

Range: NSW coast and ranges, Lord Howe Island, Qld and NT. **Leaves:** thin, hairless, heart-shaped, arising from red stems, new leaves are subtended by very large soft pale stipules. **Flowers:** tiny, unisexual (plants monoecious), in dense slender terminal racemes. **Flowering time:** late spring. **Name:** *populifolius* = Poplar-leaved.

• *Phyllanthus* Linnaeus
A genus of small shrubs with about 600 species, including about 60 species in Australia.

Name: *Phyllanthus* = Gk. leaf-flower, as the flowers of some non-Australian species grow from the edges of leaf-like branches.

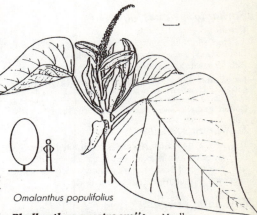
Omalanthus populifolius

Phyllanthus gasstroemii Jean Mueller
Spurge **Ss**
An open shrub 1-2m, occasionally to 3m, high with pale feathery foliage. Found in wetter woodland in sheltered alluvial valleys, mainly along the Georges and Nepean Rivers.

Range: NSW coast, ranges and inland slopes, and Qld. **Leaves:** soft, hairless, mostly 15mm long, not shiny, greyish-green, flat, thin-textured, 2-ranked on short branchlets (hence resembling pinnate leaves). **Flowers:** tiny, unisexual (plants dioecious), suspended on slender stalks below each leaf joint (the males often clustered, the females solitary). Male flowers in clusters of 3-4. Anther filaments joined together. Fruiting stalks 4-6mm long . **Flowering time:** spring-summer. **Name:** *gasstroemii* = of Gasstroem. The name is a misnomer. It was erroneously constructed from the name of the Swedish director of the board of commerce, S.C. Casström (1763-1827). The error was due to the fact that Casström habitually made a little slash at the bottom of the 'C' in his signature, making it appear a 'G'. Casström never visited Australia. Instead the type specimen was probably collected by Daniel Solander at Botany Bay. After Solander's early death, Casström acquired his herbarium. It eventually became part of the collection of the Swedish Museum of Natural History, where the Swiss botanist Jean Mueller described it many years later. **Similar species:** *P. gunnii*. Specimens with broad leaves are difficult to distinguish from *P. gunnii* without close examination of the male flowers.

Phyllanthus gunnii J.D. Hooker

An erect shrub 1-2m tall, found in wetter woodland on rocky slopes and river banks along the Nepean River, especially in the Douglas Park and Menangle areas.

Range: NSW coast, Blue Mountains, northern tablelands and inland areas, Qld, Vic and Tas. **Leaves:** 10-20mm long, slightly notched at the apex, generally similar to *P. gasstroemii*. **Flowers:** male flowers in clusters of 3-7, anther filaments free, slender. Fruiting stalks to 8mm long. **Flowering time:** spring-summer. **Name:** *gunnii* = after R.C. Gunn, who collected the type specimen in Tas. **Similar species:** *P. gasstroemii*.

Phyllanthus hirtellus F. Mueller ex Jean Mueller

(previously *P. thymoides*)
Thyme Spurge **Ss, Castl**
A distinctive miniature heath shrub, erect or sprawling, with a few wiry stems usually 20-30cm long. Common in woodland.

Range: NSW coast, ranges and inland areas, Vic and Qld. **Leaves:** tiny, under 8mm long, tough and shiny. **Flowers:** tiny, RED or CREAM, star-shaped, axillary, solitary. **Flowering time:** spring. **Name:** *hirtellus* = Lat. finely hairy

Phyllanthus similis Jean Mueller

Cumb
An erect shrub 20-50cm high, found along creeks on the Cumberland Plain and along the Nepean River (e.g. Douglas Park, Menangle). Not common.

Range: coast of NSW and Qld. **Leaves:** 10-20mm long (mostly 15mm), 6-10mm wide, on red striate stems. **Flowers:** male flowers in clusters of 2-3 on short stalks (1mm long). Fruiting stalks to 3mm long. **Flowering time:** summer. **Name:** *similis* = Lat. similar.

*Phyllanthus tenellus**

This species, to 45cm tall, resembles a miniature *P. gasstroemii* or *P. gunnii*. It occurs as a weed in gardens and disturbed land. A native of Madagascar, it is now widely naturalised in tropical and subtropical parts of the world.

Phyllanthus virgatus G. Forster

(includes *P. filicaulis* until this complex group can be better studied) **Cumb**
A prostrate to erect herb, sometimes woody, mostly 5-20cm

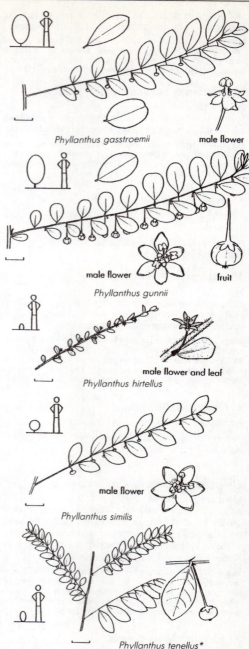

Phyllanthus gasstroemii   male flower

Phyllanthus gunnii

male flower   fruit

male flower and leaf

Phyllanthus hirtellus

male flower

Phyllanthus similis

Phyllanthus tenellus*

high, with many stems arising from a rootstock. Found in grassland on clay soils on the Cumberland Plain. Uncommon.

Range: NSW coast, ranges and inland areas, north from Sydney; also Qld. **Leaves:** narrow, mostly 5-10mm long. **Flowers:** mostly solitary. **Flowering time:** spring-summer. **Name:** *virgatus* = Lat. twiggy.

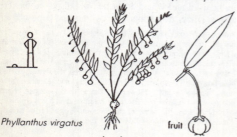

Phyllanthus virgatus   fruit

• *Poranthera* Rudge

A genus of small shrubs with 12 species; 10 endemic to Australia and 2 endemic to NZ.

Name: *Poranthera* = Gk. pore-anther, because the anther cells open through pores at their tips rather than splitting along their length as is usual in Angiosperms.

Poranthera corymbosa Brongniart
Ss

An erect shrub usually 30-80cm high, found in woodland and heath on sandstone. Its close resemblance to *Conospermum taxifolium* may be an example of convergent evolution.

Range: NSW coast and ranges, Qld and Vic. **Leaves:** densely spirally arranged on a single stem, fairly soft, often revolute. **Flowers:** WHITE, male and female intermingled (males more numerous) in a large terminal corymb of umbel-like racemes. **Flowering time:** spring **Name:** *corymbosa* = having corymbs, the inflorescence type.

Poranthera ericifolia Rudge
Ss

A small shrub 15-30cm high, found in woodland and heath on sandstone. It closely resembles *Conospermum ericifolium.*

Range: NSW coast and ranges. **Leaves:** tiny, crowded, with revolute margins. **Flowers:** tiny, WHITE, male and female together crowded in dense terminal corymbs. **Flowering time:** spring-summer. **Name:** *ericifolia* = *Erica*-leaved. *Erica* is the European Heath or Heather.

Poranthera microphylla Brongniart
Ss, Castl

A tiny annual herb to 10cm high with soft leaves and weak branches. Common, especially after wet winters, on the shady floors of woodlands. Its quick-flowering annual habit lets it survive in places where seasonal heat and dryness would normally exclude such a soft little herb.

Range: all parts of NSW except western plains, all states. **Leaves:** tiny, soft, hairless. **Flowers:** tiny, WHITE, in small leafy clusters at the end of stems. **Flowering time:** October-November. **Name:** *microphylla* = Lat. tiny-leaved.

• *Pseudanthus* Sieber ex Sprengel

An endemic genus of shrubs with 7 species.

Name: *Pseudanthus* = Gk. false-flower, because the cluster of flowers in the type species, *P. pimeleoides,* resemble a single showy flower.

Pseudanthus orientalis (Baillon) F. Mueller
(seu-DANTH-us) **Ss**

A low wiry shrub 20-30cm high with densely crowded leaves,

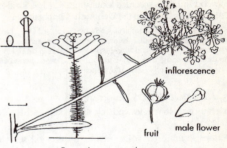

inflorescence

fruit

male flower

Poranthera corymbosa

male flower

Poranthera ericifolia

entire plant

inflorescence and leaves

Poranthera microphylla

found mainly in coastal heaths south of the harbour e.g. Maroubra, Kurnell, Royal National Park.

Range: Sydney area, NSW north coast and Qld. **Leaves:** there appear to be 2 forms; the common one with narrow (more or less 1.5mm wide), channelled leaves, found near the sea, and another with broad (more or less 3mm wide) flat leaves, often found away from the sea. The leaves are 6-8mm long in both forms. **Flowers:** terminal, tiny (petals 1-2mm long), WHITE. **Flowering time:** July-October. **Name:** *orientalis* = Eastern.

Pseudanthus pimeleoides Sieber ex Sprengel
Ss

An erect dense shrub to 1.5m high. Found along creek banks

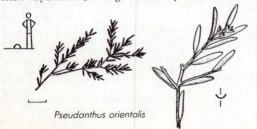

Pseudanthus orientalis

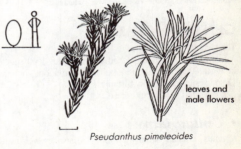

leaves and male flowers

Pseudanthus pimeleoides

in woodland. Only recorded locally from Royal National Park, the Woronora River and the Woolwash, Campbelltown.

Range: Sydney area, Blue Mountains, NSW north coast and Qld. **Leaves:** opposite, densely crowded, hairless, fairly stiff and sharply pointed. **Flowers:** WHITE, male and female crowded together in dense terminal heads. **Flowering time:** April to October. **Name:** *pimeleoides* = *Pimelea*-like, presumably due to the clustered flowers.

• *Ricinocarpos* Desfontaines

A genus with 16 species endemic to Australia and 1 in New Caledonia.

Name: *Ricinocarpos* = Lat. *ricinus*, a castor oil seed, Gk. *carpon*, a fruit, because the fruits resemble those of the Castor Oil plant, *Ricinus communis*.

Ricinocarpos pinifolius Desfontaines

(riss-in-o-CARP-us) Wedding Bush **Ss**
A soft erect shrub, usually 1.5m high, found in scattered colonies in woodland and heath. Moderately common in the area. The fragrance of the flowers resembles leatherwood honey.

Range: NSW coastal areas and southern tablelands, Qld, Vic and Tas. **Leaves:** fairly soft, erect, with recurved margins and soft points. **Flowers:** unisexual (plants monoecious), WHITE, with several male flowers surrounding a single female flower (female opening first). **Flowering time:** August-October. **Name:** *pinifolius* = Lat. Pine-leaved.

• *Ricinus* Linnaeus

A genus of tropical shrubs with 1 species naturalised in Australia.

Name: *Ricinus* = Lat. a tick, as the seeds resemble ticks.

*Ricinus communis** Linnaeus

Castor Oil Plant **Ss, Cumb**
A tall robust weedy plant to 3m high with broad palmate leaves and milky sap. Introduced from Asia or Africa and common in wastelands. A declared noxious weed in most areas.

The fruit contains castor oil which is a useful lubricant. In former times it was important for aero-engines. India was traditionally the main supplier, and in the early part of the century the United States had the largest processing industry. The plant also contains ricin, a highly poisonous substance, once used by Bulgarian KGB agents in assassinations!

Range: NSW coast and inland areas, all other states except NT, also Asia and Africa. **Leaves:** palmate, to 60cm diameter each with 7-9 lobes, toothed. **Flowers:** RED, unisexual (plants monoecious), in tall dense terminal racemes. **Name:** *communis* = Lat. common.

GENTIANACEAE

The Gentian family
A family mainly of annual herbs, with about 1000 species in about 80 genera, of cosmopolitan distribution. There are 12 species in 6 genera in Australia.

It is related to Menyanthaceae.

• *Centaurium* Hill

A genus of small herbs with about 50 species worldwide,

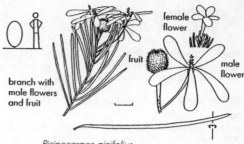

branch with male flowers and fruit

female flower

fruit

male flower

Ricinocarpos pinifolius

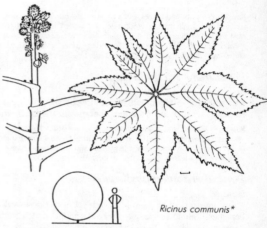

Ricinus communis*

including 1 native and 4 introduced species in Australia.

Name: *Centaurium* = Gk. called by Hippocrates after Chiron the centaur, who had a great knowledge of herbs, and was said to have used it to heal an arrow wound inflicted on his foot by Hercules.

Centaurium spicatum (Linnaeus) Fritsch

Australian Centaury **Cumb**
An erect herb 20-35cm, occasionally to 45cm high, with bright pink flowers. Uncommon, scattered in the area in moist sunny situations, but rarely on sandy soils. The problem with this little plant is that it is virtually indistinguishable from a common introduced weed, *C. tenuiflorum* (see below). It has medicinal properties. 'The plant is collected by the colonists, who consider it valuable in cases of dysentry and diarrhoea; it is also useful as a tonic and stomatic, like gentian (to which family it belongs); when required for medicinal purposes, it should be gathered in the spring season.'[18]

Range: NSW coast, inland areas, all other states, and occurring naturally in Europe. **Leaves:** opposite, soft, stalkless, hairless, rather variable in shape and size, to 3cm long, on square stems. **Flowers:** petals about 3mm long, RICH PINK, floral tube white, about 10mm long, sepals very narrow. **Flowering time:** summer. **Name:** *spicatum* = Lat. spike-bearing. **Similar species:** *Centaurium tenuiflorum**. Distinguish as follows. *C. tenuiflorum** has a well developed basal rosette (although it may wither with age), and the inflorescence is a complex cyme (ie. a cyme of cymes—2 secondary floral stems branching from the base of every flower: see illustration). *C. spicatum* has a basal rosette absent or poorly developed, and the inflorescence is a cyme of spikes (i.e. most flowers are spaced along unbranching stems: see illustration).

GERANIACEAE

A family of herbs and shrubs with about 600 species in 11 genera. In Australia there are 31 species in 3 genera.

The fruits adopt interesting seed-distribution mechanisms in the 3 local genera, based upon modifications of the styles, which elongate after fertilisation.

• *Erodium* L'Héritier ex Aiton

Heronsbills

A genus of annual or bi-annual herbs with about 90 species, including about 8 species in Australia. The flowers resemble those of *Geranium*, except the styles develop into stiff hairy awns which become curved or coiled at maturity, presumably to assist attachment to passing animals.

Name: *Erodium* = Gk. the classical name, from *erodios*, the heron (i.e. heron's bill).

Erodium crinitum Carolin

Blue Heronsbill, Blue Crowsfoot　**Cumb**

A weak sprawling or ascending herb with stems 30-60cm long. Scattered on the Cumberland Plain*. The fleshy roots were cooked and eaten by Aborigines.

Range: all parts of the state but uncommon on the coast; present in all other states.　**Leaves:** toothed, deeply incised, sometimes with 2 lobes at the base, soft.　**Flowers:** BLUE, in terminal umbels.　**Flowering time:** spring-early summer.　**Name:** *crinitum* = Lat. hairy.
* Since this species is abundant in western NSW, it might be thought to have been introduced to the coast, except that Robert Brown collected a specimen on the banks of the Nepean in 1802-05, before the mountains were crossed.
Note: 2 other Erodiums occur in the area.
• *E. cicutarium* (Linnaeus) L'Héritier ex Aiton. A weed introduced from western NSW, distinguished by having pinnate leaves with shallowly toothed leaflets.
• *E. moschatum*[*] (Linnaeus) L'Héritier ex Aiton. A weed introduced from the Mediterranean. It has pinnate leaves with deeply incised and toothed leaflets.

• *Geranium* Linnaeus

Cranesbills

A genus of herbs with about 400 species worldwide. There are about 13 species in Australia.

The local species are weak slender herbs with thick rootstocks. The fruit splits into 5 fruitlets which are raised upwards for distribution by the elongated styles which remain joined at the tip and curl up as the fruit matures. The roots of *G. homeanum* were roasted in ashes and eaten by Aborigines at Jervis Bay.

Name: *Geranium* = Gk. the classical name, from *geranos*, a crane (i.e. crane's bill).

Geranium homeanum Turczaninow

Northern Cranesbill　**Cumb, Ss (clay tops)**

A slender sprawling herb with stems to about 50cm long, found on clay soils on the Cumberland Plain and north of the harbour. Common in the Illawarra where it is occurs on the edges of rainforest.

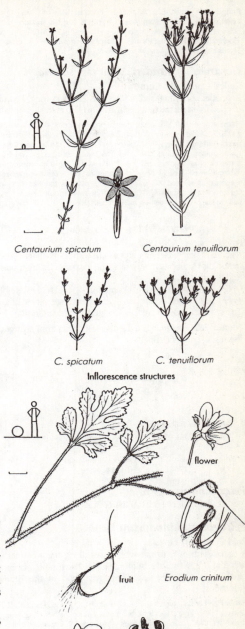

Centaurium spicatum　　　*Centaurium tenuiflorum*

C. spicatum　　　*C. tenuiflorum*

Inflorescence structures

flower

fruit　　*Erodium crinitum*

Geranium flower
(*G. solanderi*)

compound fruit with
fruitlets sprung

Range: NSW coast, Blue Mountains, northern tablelands and Qld.
Leaves: finely hairy, cut into broader segments than *G. solanderi*, often
purple below. **Flowers:** under 10mm wide, PALE PINK, in pairs.
Flowering time: spring-summer. **Name:** *homeanum* = Gk. similar.
Similar species: *G. solanderi.*

Geranium solanderi Carolin **var.** *solanderi*

Cutleaf Cranesbill **Cumb**

A slender sprawling herb with stems to 50cm long. Found
in open forest on the Cumberland Plain (also in the Illawarra).

Range: all parts of NSW except the far western plains, all other states,
and NZ. **Leaves:** deeply cut into lobes, hairy on both sides. **Flowers:**
mostly 12-18mm wide, PALE PINK to white, in pairs. **Flowering time:**
spring-summer. **Name:** *solanderi* = after Daniel Solander, the Swedish
naturalist who accompanied Joseph Banks on the *Endeavour*. He
afterwards lived in Banks' house as botanist-librarian. **Similar species:**
a cosmopolitan weed, *G. molle*, occurs in pastures and wasteland in
the area, but uncommonly. The beak of the fruits is only 5-6mm long
and the leaves are very densely hairy on both sides.

• *Pelargonium* L'Héritier ex Aiton

Storksbills

A genus of perennial herbs and shrubs with about 300 species,
including 13 species in Australia. The local species are robust
tufted herbs.

The common garden 'Geraniums' are cultivars of
Pelargonium species. The two local species are very similar.
The differing habitats are the best guides to identification.

Name: *Pelargonium* = Gk. the classical name, from *pelargos*,
the stork (i.e. stork's bill).

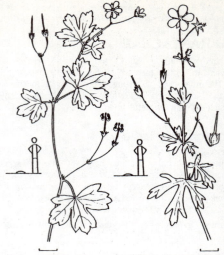

Geranium homeanum   Geranium solanderi
                                var. *solanderi*

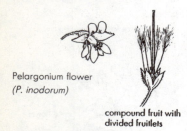

Pelargonium flower
(*P. inodorum*)

compound fruit with
divided fruitlets

Pelargonium australe

—See COASTAL AND ESTUARINE SPECIES.

Pelargonium inodorum Willdenow

Wild Geranium **Ss**

A tufted herb 6-40cm tall with leaves along the stem and
tufted at the base. Rare in the area, in shady moist places,
often on sandy river flats (more common in the Blue
Mountains).

Range: NSW coast, ranges and western slopes, Qld, Vic, Tas and NZ.
Leaves: blades from 2-5cm long, but reduced along the flowering stem,
slightly aromatic, covered in fine hairs. **Flowers:** PINK, to about 10mm
wide; in terminal umbels. Fertile stamens 3-5, calyx hairs long and soft.
Flowering time: spring to early summer. **Name:** *inodorum* = Lat.
scentless.

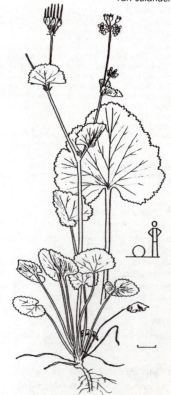

Pelargonium inodorum

GOODENIACEAE

A genus with 410 species in 17 genera worldwide. There are about 380 species in 16 genera in Australia.

The method of fertilisation is unusual. The flower mechanically compacts its pollen into a tight mass before squeezing it out onto the petals where it is held in place by stiff hairs. If the flower is not fertilised by a passing insect, its style will usually make contact with its own pollen still lying amongst the petal-hairs, and self-fertilise. This process occurs with slight variations amongst all the members of the family.

• *Dampiera* R. Brown

An endemic genus with 66 species, about 40 in south-western WA.

Name: *Dampiera* = in honour of William Dampier (1652-1715) the English buccaneer who visited the west coast of Australia in 1688 and 1699. He twice circumnavigated the world and collected plants in Australia, Brazil, Timor and NG. The blue flowers of a *Dampiera* caught his attention at Shark Bay, WA, and he took the first specimens back to Europe.

Dampiera purpurea R. Brown
Ss

An erect shrub usually 1-1.5m high, found in sheltered places in woodland on sandstone. Widespread but not common. The whole plant is cloaked in fine rusty star-hairs.

Range: NSW coast and ranges and Vic. **Leaves:** more or less round, rather thick, sometimes toothed. **Flowers:** DEEP MAUVE, in short axillary racemes. The calyces are covered in dense rusty wool. **Flowering time:** spring-summer. **Name:** *purpurea* = Lat. purple.

Dampiera scottiana F. Mueller
Ss (previously *D. rodwayana*)

A low greyish shrub to 50cm tall, covered in long grey hairs. A south coast species, only recently discovered in the Sydney area, in woodland in Marramarra National Park.

Range: Sydney area, south coast and tablelands. **Leaves:** lanceolate to linear-lanceolate, revolute, dull, more or less smooth above, with appressed close whitish felt below. The stems are densely covered in long grey hairs. **Flowers:** PURPLE, about 10mm long, the calyx and the central part of the petals are densely covered in long greyish hairs; flowers arranged a few together in short axillary racemes, only one opening at a time. **Flowering time:** spring. **Name:** *scottiana* = after Harriet Scott (1830-1907), one of the Scott sisters of Ash Island, Hunter River. Both were renowned naturalists and illustrators. She collected the type specimen.

Dampiera stricta (Smith) R. Brown
Ss

A small erect herb usually 20-40cm high, found in heath and woodland on sandy soils. A very abundant and widespread species in the area.

Range: NSW coast and ranges and Vic. **Leaves:** erect, thick, diamond-shaped (with teeth at the corners), usually rough to touch, hairless, arising from angular stems. **Flowers:** RICH MAUVE to BLUE. **Flowering time:** winter-summer (best in spring-early summer). **Name:** *stricta* = Lat. bound, referring to the leaves being held against the stem.

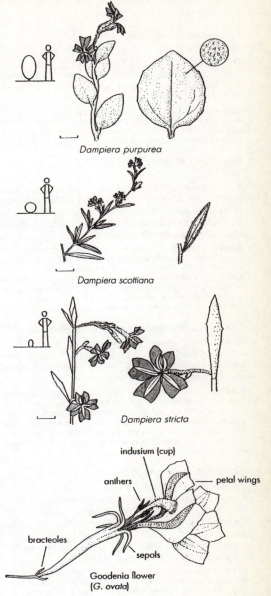

Dampiera purpurea

Dampiera scottiana

Dampiera stricta

indusium (cup)

anthers

petal wings

bracteoles

sepals

Goodenia flower
(*G. ovata*)

• *Goodenia* Smith

A genus with 170 species worldwide. There are 115-120 species distributed in south-western and south-eastern Australia.

Name: *Goodenia* = after the Reverend Dr Goodenough, Bishop of Carlisle, botanist and treasurer of the Linnean Society. He wrote on seaweeds and sedges. A. G. Hamilton wrote 'at first it was *Goodenoughia*, but even botanists could not put up with such a title'.[19]

Goodenia bellidifolia Smith
ssp. bellidifolia

Daisy-leaved Goodenia   **Ss, Castl, Cumb**
A small tufted herb with erect flower stalk to about 40cm high. Found in wet sunny heath on sandy soils, and in forests on clay soils. Common in the area.

Range: NSW coast and ranges.   **Leaves:** in a basal rosette, erect, glossy, rather thick, irregularly toothed or sometimes entire.   **Flowers:** YELLOW, sessile, in a tall leafless spike.   **Flowering time:** spring-summer. **Name:** *bellidifolia = Bellis*-leaved. *Bellis* are the original European daisies.

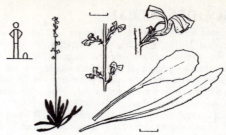

Goodenia bellidifolia ssp. *bellidifolia*

Goodenia dimorpha Maiden & Betche
Ss

A small tufted herb with erect flower stalk to about 40cm high, found in wet sunny heath on sandy soils. Fairly common in the Royal National Park but not found elsewhere in the area. Similar to *G. stelligera* except the flowers are stalked and arranged in a spreading panicle.

Range: restricted to the Sydney area and Blue Mountains (the Blue Mountains form has spoon shaped leaves).   **Leaves:** in a basal rosette, erect, slender, with a few teeth, glossy.   **Flowers:** YELLOW, in an erect panicle, with a fine cloak of tiny rusty star-hairs on the lower side (i.e. outside) of the corolla (visible with a hand lens).   **Flowering time:** spring-summer.   **Name:** *dimorpha* = Lat. 2-formed, referring to the different leaves in the coastal and mountain forms.

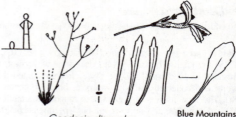

Goodenia dimorpha   **Blue Mountains form**

Goodenia hederacea Smith **var. hederacea**

Violet-leaved Goodenia   **Ss, Castl, Cumb**
A small perennial herb with a prostrate flowering stem extending from a small basal rosette. Found in sheltered places in forests on both sandy and clay soils. Common locally.

Range: Sydney area, south coast and Blue Mountains; also recorded from the north-western plains and Qld.   **Leaves:** spoon-shaped, erect, finely hairy; in a basal rosette and also along the prostrate flowering stem (but smaller).   **Flowers:** YELLOW, solitary, axillary, on long slender stalks. **Flowering time:** spring-summer.   **Name:** *hederacea = Hedera*-like. *Hedera* is a small genus of European woody vines; *H. helix* is English Ivy. Often called 'Ivy-leaved Goodenia'.

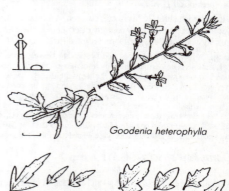

Goodenia hederacea var. *hederacea*

Goodenia heterophylla Smith

Variable-leaved Goodenia   **Ss**
A small ascending or sprawling shrub with stems 20-50cm long, found in woodland on sandstone, usually in dry, sheltered spots. Fairly common locally. There are 2 local subspecies:
• **ssp.** *heterophylla*, found mainly north of the harbour; and
• **ssp.** *eglandulosa*, found south of the harbour.

Range: NSW coastal areas and Blue Mountains.   **Leaves:** variably lobed and toothed, covered in fine hairs. The leaves of the 2 subspecies are similar, although those of ssp. *heterophylla* are consistently narrower (see illustration).   **Flowers:** YELLOW, axillary, on slender pedicels (floral stalks).   **Flowering time:** mainly spring-summer.   **Name:** *heterophylla* = Lat. different-leaved, referring to the variable leaves. *eglandulosa* = Lat. without glands, referring to the glandular hairs which are present on the flowers of ssp. *heterophylla*, but much reduced in frequency on this subspecies.

Goodenia heterophylla

ssp. *heterophylla*   ssp. *eglandulosa*

Goodenia ovata Smith

Hop-Goodenia **Ss**

An erect bushy shrub usually 1-1.5m high, found on better quality sandy soils, usually in sheltered gullies, often on the edges of rainforests. Fairly common in the area.

A. G. Hamilton noted that old Irish people called it 'Hunger-weed' and said that if you walked through it, you would get a good appetite.[20]

Range: widespread throughout eastern Australia, including the western slopes. **Leaves:** broad, thin, soft, glossy, hairless. **Flowers:** YELLOW, in short axillary racemes. **Flowering time:** spring-summer. **Name:** *ovata* = Lat. ovate, the leaf shape.

Goodenia paniculata Smith

Swamp Goodenia **Ss, Cumb, Castl, Aqu**

A small tufted herb with erect flower stalks to about 30cm high. Common in marshy meadows on the Cumberland Plain and also in open sandy heaths on coastal plateaus. Similar to *G. bellidifolia* except the flowers are arranged in a spreading panicle.

Range: NSW coastal areas, Blue Mountains, and Qld. **Leaves:** in a basal rosette, erect, irregularly toothed, glossy. **Flowers:** YELLOW, in an erect panicle, with a fine cloak of tiny red glandular-hairs on the outside of the corolla and the calyx (visible with a hand lens). **Flowering time:** spring-summer. **Name:** *paniculata* = Lat. having a panicle.

Goodenia stelligera R. Brown

Star-haired Goodenia **Ss**

A small tufted herb with erect flower stalks to about 30-50cm high. Found in wet sunny heath on sandy soils. Common in coastal heath.

J.H. Maiden called it 'Star-haired Goodenia', adding that he could 'never picture the majority of people adding the word *stelligera* to their vocabulary under any circumstances whatever.'[21]

Range: NSW coastal areas, northern tablelands and Qld. **Leaves:** very variable in size and shape, in a basal rosette, erect, slender, thick, irregularly toothed, glossy. **Flowers:** YELLOW, stalkless, in an erect spike (sometimes slightly branching), with a fine cloak of tiny rusty star-hairs on the lower side (i.e. outside) of the corolla (visible with a hand lens). **Flowering time:** spring-summer. **Name:** *stelligera* = Lat. starry, referring to the star-hairs on the corolla.

• *Scaevola* Linnaeus

(SEE-vo-la, or skee-VO-la)

A genus with about 80 species distributed widely in the tropics, extending across the Indian-Pacific region and, as seaside species, into the Caribbean and South Africa. There are about 50 species in Australia, found mainly in WA but present in all states.

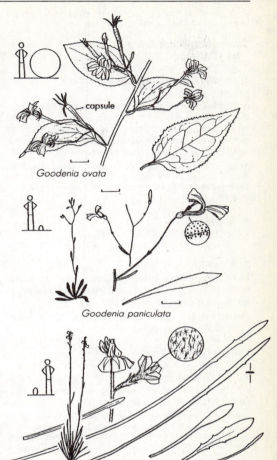

Goodenia ovata

Goodenia paniculata

Goodenia stelligera

Name: *Scaevola* = after Caius Mucius Scaevola, an ancient Roman hero, literally 'the left-handed one' (from Lat. *scaevus*, left), from the hand-shaped corolla of the flowers. He earned his name when captured during an Etruscan seige of Rome. He was threatened with torture but put his right hand into the fire to show his contempt for pain.

Scaevola albida (Smith) Druce

Cumb

A weakly ascending perennial herb, with many long stems to 30-50cm long. Found in open situations on clay soils on the Cumberland Plain, especially in the Camden-Campbelltown area. A fairly common species. The stems and floral parts are covered in tiny short bent hairs.

Range: coast, ranges and western slopes of NSW, Qld, Vic and SA. **Leaves:** small, thin, toothed. **Flowers:** MAUVE (drying blue), sessile (stalkless), solitary in the axils of the upper leaves. **Flowering time:** spring-late summer. **Name:** *albida* = Lat. *albi*, white. **Similar species:** *S. aemula* is a similar species found in inland NSW and north and south

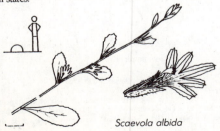

Scaevola albida

of the Sydney area. It can be distinguished by densely furry leaves and a dense mantle of long hairs on the stigmatic disc.

Scaevola calendulacea
—See COASTAL AND ESTUARINE SPECIES.

Scaevola ramosissima (Smith) Krause
Snake-flower **Ss**
A sprawling herbaceous scrambler, usually 50-100cm long. A beautiful and quite common species, found in woodland on sandstone. 'We always knew it as snake-flower when we were children, and there was a tradition amongst us that to eat the blossom was a certain antidote to snakebite.'[22]

Range: NSW coast and ranges, Qld and Vic. **Leaves:** rather thick, toothed, covered in stiff hairs. **Flowers:** large, BLUISH MAUVE. **Flowering time:** spring and summer. **Name:** *ramosissima* = Lat. much branched.

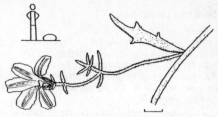

Scaevola ramosissima

• *Selliera*
—See COASTAL AND ESTUARINE SPECIES.

• *Velleia* Smith (VELL-ee-a)
An endemic genus of 20 species, found in all states. Similar to *Goodenia* except the calyx is surrounded by 3 broad bracts and the inflorescence is an extended cyme.

Name: *Velleia* = after Lieutenant-Colonel Thomas Velley (1748-1806), a British algologist.

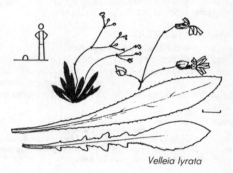

Velleia lyrata

Velleia lyrata R. Brown
Ss
A tufted herb with flowering stems 15-30cm high, found in wet open heath on sandstone. An uncommon species, confined to marshy coastal heaths.

Range: restricted to the Sydney area. **Leaves:** erect, spoon-shaped, toothed and sometimes lobed towards the base. **Flowers:** in an extended cyme, YELLOW, perianth 10-12mm long. **Flowering time:** spring-summer. **Name:** *lyrata* = lyre-shaped, referring to the leaves, but it's hard to see the allusion.

above   3 bracts

Velleia flower (V. lyrata)   below

GYROSTEMONACEAE

An endemic family of shrubs and small trees with 17 species in 4 genera, mainly in dry inland areas.

• *Didymotheca* J. D. Hooker
(diddy-mo-THEEK-a)
A genus of small shrubs with 4 species, distributed widely in inland Australia.

Name: *Didymotheca* = Gk. *didymos*, double, *theke*, capsule.

Didymotheca thesioides J. D. Hooker **Ss**
A slender erect shrub to 1m tall, irregularly present in woodland near the Georges River at Ingleburn, depending on recent fires. The seeds require burning for germination. The plant may be common after a fire but absent if burning has not occurred recently.

Range: across southern Australia, including Tas; rare in WA. **Leaves:** slender, 5-40cm long. **Flowers:** small, perianth reduced to a small cup;

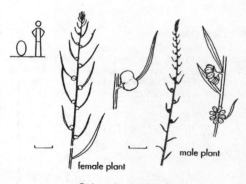

female plant   male plant

Didymotheca thesioides

the male consists of a ring of 8 stamens; the female of a 2-carpeled ovary, forming a flat, 2-chambered fruit. **Flowering time:** summer. **Name:** *thesioides* = Gk. *Thesium*-like. *Thesium* is a species in the Santalaceae family, with a similar habit.

HALORAGACEAE

A family of small shrubs and herbs, usually with tiny toothed leaves. One genus, *Myriophyllum*, is aquatic. There are about 120 species in 8 genera worldwide. Australia has about 90 species in 6 genera. The family has its centre of diversity in Australia, with some species extending through Asia as far as Japan, to New Guinea, the Pacific and NZ.

Haloragis and *Gonocarpus* are commonly known as Raspworts (pronounced rasp-werts).

• *Gonocarpus* Thunberg

Raspworts

A genus with 36 species, widely distributed from Japan to NZ. There are 31 Australia species distributed in all states with some extending through Asia and the Pacific. The flowers are tiny with 4 conspicuous hood-shaped petals.

Name: *Gonocarpus* = Gk. angle-fruit.

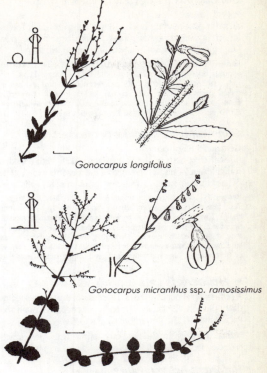

Gonocarpus longifolius

Gonocarpus longifolius (Schindler) Orchard

Ss Rare 3RC-
An erect shrub 35-100cm tall. Found in woodland on sandstone. A locally rare species recorded in the past from the Georges River and Nepean River (Douglas Park).

Range: Sydney area, Blue Mountains and northern tablelands. **Leaves:** oblong, covered in fine soft hairs, 15-25mm long, 3-6mm wide, serrated; arranged opposite or in whorls of 3, becoming alternate in the upper part. **Flowers:** GREENISH, petals 1.7-2.2 mm long. The fruit are often warty. **Flowering (and fruiting) time:** October-January. **Name:** *longifolia* = Lat. long-leaved.

Gonocarpus micranthus Thunberg ssp. *micranthus*

Ss, Castl
A creeping or ascending much-branched herb with branches about 10cm long, rooting from the stem nodes. Found in sunny marshy heath on sandy soil. Abundant in the area, especially in coastal heaths.

Range: all eastern states, NZ, NG, South-east Asia, China and Japan. **Leaves:** opposite, ovate, serrate, smooth (i.e. hairless), flat. **Flowers:** in more or less unbranched spikes; pendant, petals reddish 0.8-1.3mm long, hairless. **Flowering time:** December-February, fruiting from December-March. **Name:** *micranthus* = Lat. tiny-flowered.

Gonocarpus micranthus ssp. *ramosissimus*

Gonocarpus micranthus ssp. *micranthus*

Gonocarpus micranthus Thunberg ssp. *ramosissimus* Orchard

Ss, Castl
An erect much-branched herb 20-40cm tall. Found in sunny marshy heath on sandy soil. Uncommon in the area.

Range: NSW coast and ranges, north from Sydney. **Leaves:** as for ssp. *micranthus*. **Flowers:** in much branched spikes (branched 3 or 4 times); otherwise as for ssp. *micranthus*. **Flowering time:** October-March, fruiting from December-March. **Name:** *ramosissimus* = Lat. much branched.

Gonocarpus salsoloides

Reichenbach ex Sprengel

Nodding Raspwort **Ss Rare 3RCa**
An erect or ascending much-branched herb 15-40cm tall, found in swampy heath on sandy soil near the sea. Mainly recorded between La Perouse and North Head.

Gonocarpus salsoloides

Range: NSW coastal areas, mainly Sydney, but with a few recordings in other parts. **Leaves:** fleshy, cylindrical, 6-15mm long, hairless or scabrous. **Flowers:** in spikes; petals red-brown to yellowish 2.5-2.8mm long. **Flowering time:** June-October, fruiting July-January. **Name:** *salsoloides* = resembling *Salsola* (in the leaves), a genus in the family Chenopodiaceae.

Gonocarpus tetragynus Labillardière

Poverty Raspwort Ss, Castl

An erect or ascending herb 15-30cm tall with rough leaves, found in woodland in various soils. Rare in the area. Distinguish from *G. teucroides* mainly by the leaf shape.

Range: NSW coast, ranges and inland areas, Qld, Vic, SA and Tas. **Leaves:** opposite, lanceolate, serrate, scabrous, mostly 6-12mm long and 1.5-4.5mm wide, covered in fine dense hairs. **Flowers:** in terminal and axillary spikes; petals 2.4-2.8mm long, stigmas densely fringed. **Flowering time:** October to January (fruiting until April). **Name:** *tetragynus* = Gk. having 4 carpels (actually it has 1 carpel with 4 styles).

Gonocarpus teucrioides De Candolle

Germander Raspwort Ss

A small erect herb or shrub, usually to 40cm, with rounded rough leaves. Abundant throughout the area in a wide variety of habitats from heath to sheltered forest, in sandy soils.

Range: NSW coast and ranges, mainly south from Sydney, into Vic and Tas. **Leaves:** opposite, ovate, serrate, scabrous, mostly 7-15mm long and 5-13mm wide. **Flowers:** in long terminal and axillary spikes, opposite in the lower part, alternate in the upper part; petals 2.6-3.3mm long, stigmas densely fringed. **Flowering time:** September-February (fruiting also). **Name:** *teucroides* = resembling (in its leaves) *Teucrium*, or Germander, a large and widespread genus in the family Lamiaceae.

• *Haloragis* J. R. & G. Forster (hal-o-RAY-ghis)

A genus with about 29 species. There are 24 Australian species distributed in all states, with some extending through the Pacific and NZ. The flowers are similar to *Gonocarpus*.

Name: *Haloragis* = Gk. sea-berry, as the type species was collected beside the sea.

Haloragis heterophylla Brongniart

Variable Raspwort Cumb

An ascending annual or perennial herb, to 50cm tall, with rough stems and leaves, found in permanently moist swampy ground. Uncommon on the Cumberland Plain. Widespread in inland parts of eastern Australia.

Range: NSW coast, ranges and inland areas, Qld, Vic, SA and Tas. **Leaves:** opposite or alternate, sessile, slender, 15-30mm long, with 3 or more spreading lobes, scabrous. **Flowers:** in terminal and axillary spikes, petals 2.2-2.8mm long, styles hairless. **Name:** *heterophylla* = Lat. variable-leaved.

• *Haloragodendron* Orchard

A genus created in 1975 to include 5 Australian species, all endemic, distributed in NSW, Victoria and WA.

Name: *Haloragodendron* = Gk. *Haloragis*-tree.

Haloragodendron lucasii
(Maiden & Betche) Orchard

Endangered 2ECi

An erect shrub to 1m high with numerous 4-ranked, 4-winged branches. Apparently restricted to a small geographical area, possibly a single gully, in Davidson State Recreation Area near St Ives. It was not collected between 1926 and 1986 and was once thought to be extinct.

Range: restricted to a small area in Ku-ring-Gai Chase east of Hornsby. **Leaves:** opposite, four-ranked, sessile, slender, to 3cm long, hard, serrated. **Flowers:** in a terminal cyme, the individual racemes arising from the

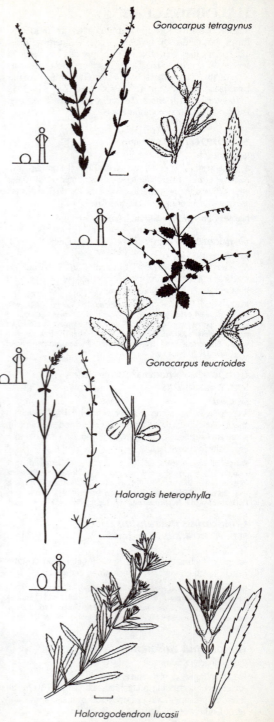

Gonocarpus tetragynus

Gonocarpus teucrioides

Haloragis heterophylla

Haloragodendron lucasii

axils of leaf-like bracts; more or less sessile, with 4 CREAMY-WHITE petals 9-12mm long, strongly twisted in bud and again after flowering; there are 8 yellow anthers and 4 styles. **Flowering time:** August-November, fruiting in October. **Name:** *lucasii* = after A.H.S. Lucas, the original collector, who found it 'in a wild gully near Gordon, Port Jackson, November, 1908'.[23]

• *Myriophyllum*
—See AQUATICS.

LAMIACEAE Labiatae

A family with about 3000 species in about 200 genera. There are about 250 Australian species in 38 genera.

Botany: They are usually fragrant herbs or shrubs with square stems and opposite or whorled leaves. The flowers are usually strongly irregular, usually with 2 lips.

Most species have aromatic leaves due to the presence of glands containing volatile oils. The fragrances are often strong and richly pleasant variations of mint or menthol. It would be surprising if some species were not used medicinally by local Aborigines for curing colds, skin irritations and for disinfection (as is one species in the Northern Territory), however there seem to be no records.

The family includes the exotic culinary plants Mint (*Mentha*), Rosemary (*Rosmarina*), Lavender (*Lavandula*), Sage (*Salvia*), Lemon Balm (*Melissa*), Majoram (*Origanum*) and the perfume plant Patchouli (*Pogostemon*).

The order Lamiales includes the families Lamiaceae, Verbenaceae and Boraginaceae.

Note: Lamiaceae is often hard to distinguish from Scrophulariaceae. The important distinction is the fruit; in Lamiaceae it is a 4-nut fruit, in Scrophulariaceae it is a capsule with many seeds.

• *Ajuga* Linnaeus (a-JOOG-a)

A genus with about 40 species, including 1-2 Australian species, distributed in all states except WA and NT.

Name: *Ajuga* = Lat. not yoked, i.e. unjoined, because the calyx teeth are not joined together into 2 lips.

Ajuga australis R. Brown

Bugle   **Cumb, Temp Rf, STRf margins**

An erect or ascending perennial herb, often purplish, 10-30cm high. Common in moist open forests on enriched soils, especially on the Cumberland Plain and rainforest margins. In Europe the bruised leaves and juice from the closely related species *A. reptans** were traditionally used as a treatment for skin wounds and sores.

Range: NSW coast, ranges and inland areas, Qld, Vic, Tas and SA. **Leaves:** opposite, bluntly toothed, dark green, usually with a strong purple tinge. **Flowers:** ranging from BLUE to PURPLE, upper lip inconspicuous; in sessile axillary cymes. **Flowering time:** summer. **Name:** *australis* = Lat. southern.

• *Hemigenia* R. Brown

An endemic genus with about 40 species distributed mainly in south-western WA. Two species occur in Qld and 2 in NSW.

Name: *Hemigenia* = Gk. half-offspring, since only 1 of each pair of anther cells is fertile.

Hemigenia cuneifolia Bentham

Broad-leaved Hemigenia   **Ss**

A slender erect shrub to 1m high, uncommon-rare in the area, locally restricted to the Georges River near Campbelltown. The flowers are smaller than *H. purpurea* and have 2 stamens and 2 staminodes (those of *H. purpurea* have 4 stamens).

Range: Georges River to Macleay River. **Leaves:** in whorls of 3 or 4, oblong to wedge shaped, 10-15mm long, contracted to a short stalk. **Flowers:** PALE MAUVE-BLUISH VIOLET, axillary, solitary. **Flowering time:** spring. **Name:** *cuneifolia* = Lat. wedge-shaped.

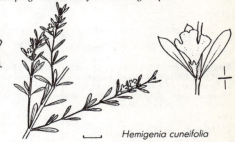

Hemigenia cuneifolia

Hemigenia purpurea R. Brown

Narrow-leaved Hemigenia   **Ss**

A slender erect shrub to 1m tall, found in open heath on sandstone. Common in the area.

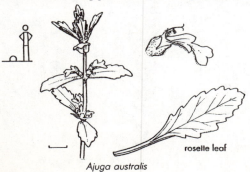

Ajuga australis

rosette leaf

Hemigenia purpurea

Range: restricted to the Sydney area and Blue Mountains. **Leaves:** linear-cylindrical, thick, finely hairy, channelled above, erect, often purple-tipped. **Flowers:** MAUVE to BLUISH, solitary, axillary. **Flowering time:** July-November. **Name:** *purpurea* = Lat. purple, referring to the flowers (and also the leaves).

• *Lycopus*
—See AQUATICS.

• *Mentha* Linnaeus
Mints

A genus with about 25 species worldwide. There are 6 species native to Australia. The genus includes European Mint.

Name: *Mentha* = the Latin name for mint.

Mentha saturejoides R. Brown
Creeping Mint, Native Pennyroyal **Cumb, Aqu**

A small slender plant to 15cm high and strongly aromatic. Found in open forest and marshy meadows on the Cumberland Plain. Uncommon to rare, mainly found in the Camden area. Colonists boiled the leaves as a tonic drink. Aborigines are also thought to have used it medicinally for colds.

Mentha saturejoides

Range: NSW coast and ranges north from Sydney, Qld and Vic. **Leaves:** entire or slightly toothed, stalked or almost sessile, rounded to oblong, 12-15mm long. **Flowers:** MAUVE to WHITE, in whorls of 4-8. **Flowering time:** spring-summer. **Name:** *saturejoides* = resembling *Satureja*, a genus in the same family.

• *Plectranthus* L'Héritier
Cockspur Flowers

A genus with about 250 species, including about 15 Australian species distributed in all mainland states, extending to South-east Asia and the Pacific.

Name: *Plectranthus* = Gk. cock's spur flower.

Plectranthus parviflorus Willdenow
Ss, Cumb, Temp Rf

A weakly erect perennial herb usually 30-60cm high. A hardy species found usually in moist sheltered situations, especially on rocky ground. Common in the area, mainly in gullies. The whole plant exudes a menthol fragrance. The flowers are sweetly scented.

Range: NSW coast, ranges and inland areas, Qld and Vic. **Leaves:** opposite, soft, slightly succulent, pubescent, toothed. **Flowers:** tiny, WHITE and BLUISH PURPLE, in short opposite cymes arranged in a long terminal spike. **Flowering time:** much of year. **Name:** *parviflorus* = Lat. small-flowered.

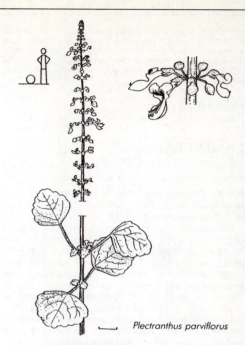

Plectranthus parviflorus

• *Prostanthera* Labillardière
Mint Bushes

An endemic genus with about 80 species, distributed in all states.

Name: *Prostanthera* = Gk. *prostheke*, an appendage, *anther*, anther, referring to the small spur-like appendages on the anthers.

Prostanthera densa A.A. Hamilton
Cliff Mintbush **Ss Vulnerable 3VCi**

An erect shrub, fairly compact and bushy, to 1m high, found in heath and sea coasts on sandstone. It occurs from Cronulla south into the Royal National Park.

Range: Sydney area, north coast, also separately on the central and north western slopes. **Leaves:** heart shaped or diamond shaped, densely and softly hairy. **Flowers:** MAUVE, delicate, large. **Flowering time:** spring. **Name:** *densa* = Lat. dense.

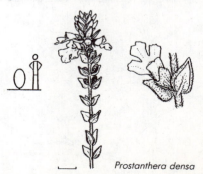

Prostanthera densa

Prostanthera denticulata R. Brown
Ss

A diffuse shrub with tangled twiggy branches, to 1.5m high. Locally distributed in moist woodland from Frenchs Forest to Newport and Cowan, on sandstone and Narrabeen Shales.

Range: NSW coast, scattered locations on the ranges and western slopes, and in Vic. **Leaves:** 5-12mm long, sparse on the stem, with recurved margins lined with a few obscure teeth. The stems are often scabrous. **Flowers:** in interrupted terminal heads **Flowering time:** winter-spring-autumn. **Name:** *denticulata* = Lat. finely toothed.

Prostanthera howelliae Blakely
Ss

An erect wiry shrub 0.5-1.5m high with finely scabrous leaves and stems. Found on sandy laterites in the Dural-Glenorie-Maroota area, and also recorded from the Lane Cove River near Gordon.

Range: restricted to the Sydney area and Blue Mountains. **Leaves:** opposite, 3-5mm long, blunt, with revolute margins. **Flowers:** DEEP PURPLE, solitary, axillary, calyx rough. **Flowering time:** spring. **Name:** *howelliae* = after Mrs T. J. Howell who accompanied Blakely on a collecting trip to Sackville Reach and Maroota in 1927, when the type specimen was found.

Prostanthera incana A. Cunningham
Velvet Mint-Bush **Ss**

A dense spreading much-branched shrub 1-1.5m high, densely hairy. Found in woodland in sheltered sandstone gullies. Uncommon in the area, restricted to the banks of the Nepean River (e.g. Douglas park area). The hairiness is not always as prominent as illustrated.

Range: NSW coast and ranges. **Leaves:** opposite, wrinkled, densely covered in pale hairs. **Flowers:** mauve, in short dense terminal racemes. **Flowering time:** spring. **Name:** *incana* = Lat. hoary with fine white hairs.

Prostanthera incisa Bentham
(including *P. sieberi*) **Ss**

An erect lightly foliaged shrub to 2m tall, found in moist sheltered forests, usually in gullies. The leaves are strongly aromatic.

Range: NSW coast north from Sydney, also Blue Mountains. **Leaves:** hairless, opposite, serrated, usually tapering into long stalks, thin, soft, oil glands visible. **Flowers:** DEEP MAUVE, solitary or in short racemes. **Flowering time:** spring. **Name:** *incisa* = Lat. cut, referring to the toothed leaves.

Prostanthera linearis R. Brown
Ss

A graceful shrub 1-3m high, found in moist sheltered valleys. Fairly common in the area.

Range: NSW coast and Blue Mountains and southern Qld. **Leaves:** opposite, narrow, blunt, more or less sessile, dark green, 12-25mm long. **Flowers:** WHITE to MAUVE, axillary or in terminal racemes, sometimes with yellow ochre spots on the throat. **Flowering time:** spring. **Name:** *linearis* = Lat. straight, referring to the leaves.

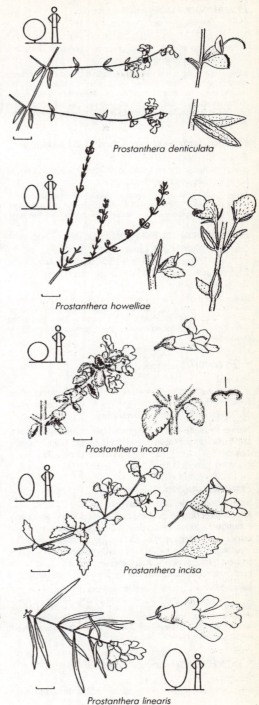

Prostanthera denticulata

Prostanthera howelliae

Prostanthera incana

Prostanthera incisa

Prostanthera linearis

Prostanthera ovalifolia R. Brown

Oval-leaf Mintbush **Ss**

An erect bushy shrub usually 2-2.5m tall. Found in sheltered valleys in the northern extreme of the area (north of Hornsby). A beautiful flowering species.

Range: NSW coast, ranges and inland districts, Qld and Vic. **Leaves:** opposite, soft, flat, very aromatic, on long stalks. **Flowers:** BLUISH MAUVE, dense in short terminal heads. **Flowering time:** spring. **Name:** *ovalifolia* = Lat. oval-leaved. **Note:** a narrow leaved form (illustrated) from the Hawkesbury area is liable to be separated in future as a sub-species.

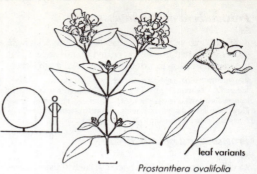

leaf variants

Prostanthera ovalifolia

Prostanthera saxicola R. Brown **var. *saxicola***

Slender Mint-bush **Ss**

A wiry prostrate shrub, found in sheltered woodland in the Georges River-Heathcote-Menai area.

Range: mainly NSW ranges. **Leaves:** opposite, finely scabrous, thick, crowded or sparse. **Flowers:** WHITE, with purple markings, about 8mm long. **Flowering time:** spring. **Name:** *saxicola* = Lat. rock-inhabiting.

Prostanthera scutellarioides (R. Brown) Briquet

Coast Mint-Bush **Castl, Cumb**

A lightly foliaged shrub 0.5-1.5m high, found in the Castlereagh woodlands, and also on lateritic outcrops on the Cumberland Plain.

Range: NSW coast and ranges from the Sydney area to Qld. **Leaves:** opposite, to 12mm long, smooth, not harsh, with strongly recurved margins. **Flowers:** PURPLE (deep lilac), scattered, axillary. **Flowering time:** spring. **Name:** *scutellarioides* = like *Scutellaria*, a genus in the same family.

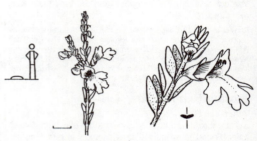

Prostanthera saxicola var. *saxicola*

• *Prunella* Linnaeus

Self-heal

A genus with about 7 species worldwide. It is uncertain whether the single native species is the same as one widespread in the northern hemisphere.

Name: *Prunella* = Lat. small plum; plum-coloured or brown; said to be from the German word for a disease (Bräune quinsy, 'the browns') which the plant was said to cure, hence the common name Self-heal.

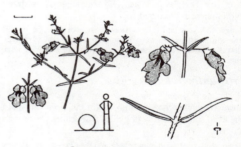

Prostanthera scutellarioides

Prunella vulgaris Linnaeus

Self-heal, Meadow Mint **Cumb, Ss**

A weak ascending or creeping herb to 40cm high. Moderately common in moist sheltered places in forests on enriched soils, e.g. Cumberland Plain and rainforest margins generally.

Aborigines in Vic applied the astringent leaves to wounds and cuts. In Europe the volatile essential oil is used as an expectorant, antispasmodic and for fever and rheumatism.

Range: NSW coast (mainly Sydney area), ranges and inland areas, Qld, Vic, Tas and SA; also possibly widespread in Europe. **Leaves:** opposite, soft, flat, dull, thin, finely hairy, stalked, entire or slightly toothed. **Flowers:** PURPLE, 12-16mm long; in a dense spike of whorls, 6 per whorl, each whorl sheltered by 2 broad bracts. **Flowering time:** summer. **Name:** *vulgaris* = Lat. common.

• *Scutellaria* Linnaeus (skew-tell-AIR-ee-a)

Skullcaps

A genus of about 300 species distributed worldwide. There

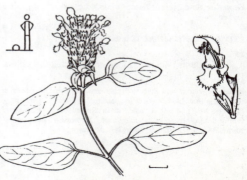

Prunella vulgaris

are 2 species endemic to Australia, distributed in all states except WA and NT.

Skullcap is an English name, dating from 1760, from the helmet-like calyx.

Name: *Scutellaria* = Lat. small dish, referring to the hollow pouch on the fruiting calyx.

Scutellaria humilis R. Brown

Cumb

A weak ascending herb 10-15cm tall. A rare species locally, recorded from the Cumberland Plain (e.g. woodland at Prospect Reservoir).

Range: NSW coast, ranges and inland areas, Qld, Vic and Tas.   **Leaves:** small, with shallow blunt lobes, 4-15mm long.   **Flowers:** small, WHITE, solitary, axillary, corolla about 5mm long.   **Name:** *humilis* = Lat. humble.

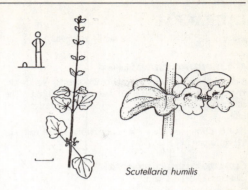

Scutellaria humilis

• *Teucrium* Linnaeus

Germanders

A genus with about 300 species, including 9-10 Australian species, distributed in all states. *Teucrium* has its main centre of diversity in China. The common name Germander is an old European name for a medicinal herb in this genus (*T. chamaedrys*), a corruption of a Greek word meaning ground-oak.

Name: *Teucrium* = after Teucer, first King of Troy; he was believed to have first used the plant medicinally; the name was used by Dioscorides in the first century AD.

Teucrium corymbosum R. Brown

Forest Germander **Ss**

An erect spreading lightly foliaged herb to 1m high. Found in sheltered forests. Rare (or possibly extinct) in the area, recorded in the past from the Royal National Park and Nepean River. The fine and fragile flowers seem out of place amongst the harsh sclerophyll shrubs.

Range: NSW coast, ranges and inland areas, also Qld, Vic, Tas and SA. **Leaves:** opposite, small (mostly 2-4cm long), thin, irregularly and deeply toothed and lobed, with recurved margins.   **Flowers:** small, WHITE, hand-shaped, in spreading axillary cymes, grading into a terminal panicle. **Flowering time:** spring-summer.   **Name:** *corymbosum* = Lat. having corymbs. The name is a misnomer since the inflorescence in no way resembles a corymb.

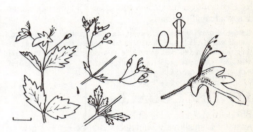

Teucrium corymbosum

• *Westringia* Smith

An endemic genus with about 25 species distributed in all states except NT. The flowers have only 2 stamens.

Name: *Westringia* = after Dr. Johan Petrus Westring (1753-1833), a Swedish writer on Lichens, who was also physician to the King of Sweden.

Westringia fruticosa

—See COASTAL AND ESTUARINE SPECIES.

Westringia longifolia R. Brown

Ss

A graceful erect shrub to 2m high, found in moist woodland along the Georges River between Ingleburn and Liverpool.

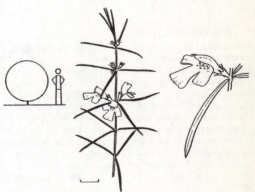

Westringia longifolia

Range: Restricted to southern parts of the Sydney region (Nattai River to Liverpool).   **Leaves:** in whorls of 3, linear, flat or recurved, more or less hairless.   **Flowers:** WHITE or MAUVE or pale pink, corolla about 12mm long.   **Flowering time:** much of the year (mainly summer and autumn).   **Name:** *longifolia* = Lat. long-leaved.

LAURACEAE

—See RAINFOREST SPECIES for family treatment.

• *Cinnamomum* Blume

A genus of tropical trees with about 250 species worldwide. There are 5 native species in Australian rainforests. The commercial cinnamon tree is *C. seylanicum*, a native of Sri Lanka.

Name: *Cinnamomum* = *kinnamomon* the Greek name of the cinnamon tree.

Cinnamomum camphora

(Linnaeus) Nees & Eberm.

Camphor Laurel

A large tree with dense bright green foliage. Common in gardens and parks, and a serious pest in bush areas. The crushed leaves have a lovely camphor fragrance. Introduced as a garden tree from China and Japan. The tiny white fruit is spread rapidly by birds.

Range: Sydney region, north coast, Queensland, Lord Howe Island, widespread in Asia. **Bark:** hard, fissured. **Leaves:** shiny, to about 8cm long, thin-textured, hairless, with 3 veins almost from the base. **Flowers:** WHITISH, tiny, numerous in open axillary panicles. **Name:** *camphora* = camphor, from the odour of the leaves.

LENTIBULARIACEAE

Bladderworts (pronounced bladder-werts)

A family of small herbs with about 280 species in 3 genera worldwide, mostly in the tropics and sub-tropics. There are about 58 species in 2 genera in Australia. All members of the family have roots or leaves which are adapted to capture and digest small water animals.

The family is related to Scrophulariaceae.

• *Utricularia* Linnaeus

A genus with over 200 species worldwide and 56 in Australia, mostly in tropical parts of the continent.

All are small carnivorous herbs with few or no green parts. Their nourishment is gained from microscopic water organisms captured by specialised leaves at the base of the plant. These are thread-like and lined with tiny bladders. Each bladder has a small entrance which is closed by a door with a triggering device, usually a tuft of hairs. When set, the trap is evacuated and under negative pressure, so that when the triggering device opens the door, the nearby water is sucked in, together with any organisms. The door rapidly shuts and the bladder proceeds to digest the organisms. It then resets itself.

Name: *Utricularia* = Lat. a little bladder or leather bottle.

Utricularia biloba R. Brown

Moth Bladderwort **Ss**

A wiry herb with small blue flowers on a stem 20-30cm tall. Found in mud at the edge of creeks and lagoons. Rare in the area, recorded from the Royal National Park (eg. Jibbon Lagoon).

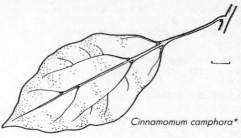

*Cinnamomum camphora**

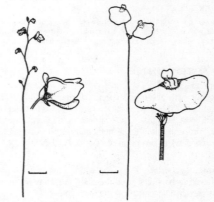

Utricularia biloba   *Utricularia dichotoma*

Range: NSW coasts north from Sydney. **Flowers:** several, BLUE, both lips 2-lobed, about 8mm long. **Flowering time:** summer. **Name:** *biloba* = Lat. 2-lobed.

Utricularia dichotoma Labillardière

Fairies' Aprons, Purple Bladderwort **Ss**

A wiry herb with 1 to a few pretty purple flowers on a stem to 40cm tall. Found in seepages in open heath country, especially beside paths. Common.

Range: all states except NT. **Flowers:** 2–several, DARK PURPLE, 12-22mm long; main lip with central 2-3 yellow/white ridges much more prominent than the purple side ridges; spur shorter than the main lip. **Flowering time:** August-April. **Name:** *dichotoma* = Gk. double-branching.

Utricularia gibba Linnaeus

Floating Bladderwort **Ss** (previously *U. exoleta*)

A small slender plant with butter yellow flowers, on fine stems to 8cm high. Found in wet mud or shallow water at

Utricularia bladders, showing trigger hairs

the edges of lagoons. Rare in the area. Recorded from Marley Lagoon in the Royal National Park, and Long Neck Lagoon and Cattai Creek in the north west of the area.

Range: coasts of NSW, Qld and NT. Sydney is its southern limit. **Leaves:** reduced to slender divided translucent filaments at the base of the plant, lined with tiny dark bladders. **Flowers:** 1–3, BUTTER YELLOW, 4–6mm wide. **Flowering time:** summer. **Name:** *gibba* = Lat. humped. **Similar species:** *U. aurea* is a similar small aquatic herb, but has bright yellow flowers and long highly divided leaves. It occurs to the north of Sydney.

Utricularia laterifolia R. Brown

Ss

A wiry herb with a few small purple flowers on a stem to 10cm tall. Found in seepages in open heath country, especially beside paths. Common.

Range: NSW coast, Blue Mountains, Vic and Tas. **Flowers:** PURPLE with a pale centre, about 8mm long, a few on a dark stem. **Flowering time:** summer. **Name:** *laterifolia* = side-leaved, reference obscure.

Utricularia uliginosa Vahl

Asian Bladderwort **Ss**

A wiry herb with a few pale blue flowers on a stem to 8cm tall. Found in wet mud or moss near creeks. A locally very rare species, recorded only from the Royal National Park.

Range: coastal parts of NSW, Qld, NT and NG; also widespread in Asia. **Leaves:** of 2 types; one green and broad, the other thread-like, with bladders. **Flowers:** 1-4, WHITISH to PALE BLUE, the broad lower lip 5-8mm wide; with large pale thin-textured sepals. **Flowering time:** summer. **Name:** *uliginosa* = Lat. growing in muddy places.

Utricularia uniflora R. Brown

Fairies Aprons, Purple Bladderwort **Ss**

A wiry herb with a single purple flower on a stem to 20cm high. Found in seepages in open heath country near the coast. Not often collected: its local abundance is unclear.

It resembles *U. dichotoma*: the main observable differences being the single flower and the equal prominence of the ridges on the main lip of the flower.

Range: coastal districts of eastern Australia. **Flower:** solitary, MAUVE or LILAC, 9-15mm long; main lip with central pair of yellow ridges about as prominent as the white side ridges: spur about as long as the main lip. **Flowering time:** August-May. **Name:** *uniflora* = Lat. single-flowered.

LINACEAE

A family of herbs and shrubs with about 300 species in 13 genera, mainly in temperate parts of the world. There are 3 native species in 2 genera in Australia.

Linum usitatissimum, Flax, was used in ancient Egypt to make linen cloth, ropes and nets. It is still widely grown for linen and linseed oil.

The family is closely related to Geraniaceae.

• *Linum* Linnaeus (LY-num)

A genus of herbs with about 230 species worldwide. There are 2 native species in Australia.

Name: *Linum* = Latin for Flax.

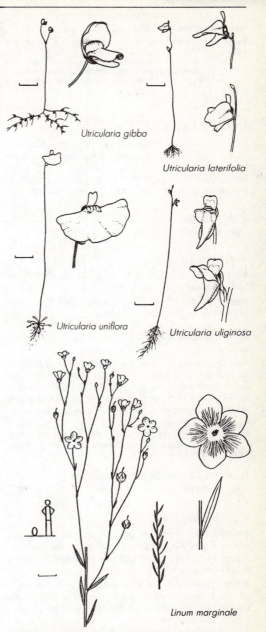

Utricularia gibba

Utricularia laterifolia

Utricularia uniflora

Utricularia uliginosa

Linum marginale

Linum marginale A. Cunningham ex Planchon

Native Flax **Ss (clay tops)**

A slender erect herb to 50cm tall, with delicate blue flowers, found in grasslands on clay soils. It was once common in the inner 'clay' suburbs, but settlement has restricted it to the northern suburbs, where it is very rare.

Aborigines were known to eat the seeds, which swell and become mucousy when wet.

Range: most temperate parts of Australia.   **Leaves:** small, thin-textured, stalkless, 1-2cm long.   **Flowers:** BLUE, on long fine stalks, with 5 sepals, 5 petals (8-12mm long), 5 stamens, a superior ovary with 5 chambers, and 5 styles.   **Flowering time:** spring.   **Fruits:** papery capsules about 5mm wide, with 10 seeds.   **Name:** *marginale* = Lat. pertaining to margins of creeks.

LOBELIACEAE

A family with about 1120 species in 29 genera, distributed on all continents but concentrated in the Americas. Australia has 50 species in 6 genera. Most are small blue flowered herbs. The flower shape and 'pollen-packing' method of fertilisation are virtually the same as for Goodeniaceae.

• *Hypsela*
—See AQUATICS.

• *Isotoma* Lindley
A genus with 10 species in Australia and 1 in Central and South America.

Name: *Isotoma* = Gk. *iso*, equal, *toma*, a cutting, referring to the equal length of the corolla lobes.

Isotoma axillaris Lindley
Ss

A small spreading herb, to 30cm high, with large beautiful sky-blue flowers. Found in open rocky places. A locally rare species recorded in the past from the Georges River area. More common in the Blue Mountains. It contains an irritant toxin—don't touch your eyes after touching the leaves.

Range: NSW coast, ranges and western slopes and plains, Qld and Vic.   **Leaves:** thin, toothed and deeply lobed.   **Flowers:** large, PALE BLUE, solitary, axillary, on long peduncles.   **Flowering time:** spring.   **Name:** *axillaris* = axillary, the position of the flowers.

Isotoma fluviatilis **ssp.** *fluviatilis*
—See AQUATICS.

• *Lobelia* Linnaeus
A cosmopolitan genus with over 300 species. There are 20 species in Australia, distributed in all states. The Australian species are shy herbs, often sheltering 'veil'd from the world, in nooks serene and lowly'.[24]

Name: *Lobelia* = in honour of Mathias de l'Obel (1538-1616), Flemish botanist, physician to King James I of England. He was the author of a Flemish herbal much used by Linnaeus.

Lobelia alata Labillardière
—See COASTAL AND ESTUARINE SPECIES.

Lobelia dentata Cavanilles
Ss

A small graceful herb to about 40cm high, found in sheltered forests and dense scrubs on sandy soils. Uncommon but fairly

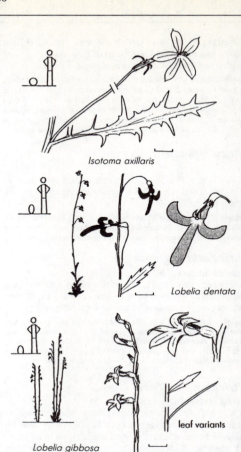

Isotoma axillaris

Lobelia dentata

Lobelia gibbosa

leaf variants

widespread in the area. The nodding flowers are very beautiful, with a rich electric blue colour.

Range: NSW coast and ranges and Qld.   **Leaves:** mostly clustered at the base of the stem, deeply toothed, thin, soft.   **Flowers:** RICH BLUE, in a slender erect raceme.   **Flowering time:** spring-summer.   **Name:** *dentata* = Lat. toothed.

Lobelia gibbosa Labillardière
Ss

An erect fleshy herb to 30-50cm high, found in open coastal heath on sandy soil. An uncommon species in the area. Recorded from Kurnell, Katandra Sanctuary, and Lane Cove Valley. The flowers are an intense blue-purple.

Range: NSW coast, ranges and western slopes, and all other states.   **Leaves:** variable, sometimes slender, linear, to 4mm wide.   **Flowers:** RICH BLUE-PURPLE, with thick petals, in a terminal 1-sided raceme on a thick reddish purple stem.   **Flowering time:** summer.   **Name:** *gibbosa* = Lat. humped, referring to the shape of the fruit capsule.   **Note:** It seems to have 2 forms: a small, semi-succulent form with linear leaves which die away at flowering time, found in exposed heath, and a tall, less succulent form with broad, toothed leaves, found in woodland. The heath form can survive long periods in dry conditions. (A broken stem left lying on a bench by the author continued to open new flowers for almost 3 weeks!)

Lobelia gracilis Andrews

Ss

An erect herb to 50cm high. Uncommon in the area, in damp shady spots in forests, scrubs and gullies. A beautiful species, with fragile, intense blue flowers.

Range: Sydney area, NSW north coast and Qld.   **Leaves:** soft, thin, lobed, hairless.   **Flowers:** small, RICH BLUE, on slender pedicels, all on one side of the stem.   **Flowering time:** late summer.   **Name:** *gracilis* = Lat. slender.

• *Pratia* Gaudichaud

A genus with 35 species in South America, tropical Africa and Asia, NZ and Australia. There are 13 Australian species, distributed in all states. All are small dioecious herbs.

Name: *Pratia* = in honour of Charles Louis Prat-Bernon, a midshipman on the *Uranie* on Freycinet's voyage of exploration; he died at sea soon after the expedition set sail in 1817.

Pratia purpurascens (R. Brown) Wimmer

White Root   **Ss, Castl, Cumb**

A weak herb to 15cm long. Common on moist forest floors on a variety of soils. The leaves are purple underneath. It has a large, succulent, white root, the juice of which was reputed to be a cure for snakebites.

Range: NSW coast and ranges, Vic and Qld.   **Leaves:** small, toothed, hairless, purple below.   **Flowers:** terminal, corolla WHITE, sometimes with pink lines, 8-10mm long. **Flowering time:** spring-summer.   **Name:** *purpurascens* = Lat. becoming purple.

LOGANIACEAE

A family with about 600 species in about 30 genera, distributed mainly in tropical parts of the world. There are about 80 species in 8 genera in Australia.

    A distinguishing feature is a thin flap of tissue joining the base of the opposite leaves, similar to the 'interpetiolar stipules' of Rubiaceae.

    The family has affinities with Scrophulariaceae, Apocynaceae and Rubiaceae. The tropical species *Strychnos nux-vomica* is the source of strychnine.

• *Logania* R. Brown (lo-GAIN-ee-a)

A genus of shrubs with about 30 species in Australia and a few in New Caledonia and NZ.

Name: *Logania* = after James Logan (1674-1751), an Irish immigrant to America who wrote on the sexuality of plants and eventually became Governor of Pennsylvania.

Logania albiflora (Andrews) Druce

Ss, Cumb

A graceful shrub usually 1.5 to 2m high with very sweetly scented flowers. Occasionally found in woodland on sandstone, prefering sheltered slopes and riverbanks.

Range: NSW coast and ranges, Vic and Qld.   **Leaves:** opposite, hairless, dull whitish below, variable in shape (see illustration), margins recurved, venation obscure. The leaf bases are joined by a raised ridge. The stems are square.   **Flowers:** about 2-3mm wide, WHITE, very sweet-fragrant;

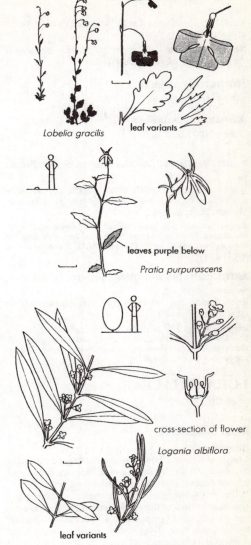

Lobelia gracilis   leaf variants

leaves purple below

Pratia purpurascens

cross-section of flower

Logania albiflora

leaf variants

in small racemes in the leaf-axils. **Flowering time:** spring.   **Name:** *albiflora* = Lat. white-flowered.

Logania pusilla R. Brown

Ss, Castl

A tiny shrub under 10cm tall, found in woodland on sandstone. Rare in the area, only found north of the harbour. Non-flowering specimens can only be distinguished from *Brunoniella pumilio* by the round fruits.

Range: coasts north from Sydney; also recorded from the southern tablelands, Qld and Vic.   **Leaves:** opposite, 5-20mm long, broad, with slightly recurved margins.   **Flowers:** WHITE, solitary, axillary, on very short stalks.   **Flowering time:** October.   **Name:** *pusilla* = Lat. very little.

• *Mitrasacme* Labillardière

Mitreworts
A mainly endemic genus of small herbs with about 40 species
in Australia.

Name: *Mitrasacme* = Gk. mitre-tip, from the similarity of
the corolla of *M. pilosa* to a bishop's mitre.

Mitrasacme alsinoides

—See AQUATICS.

Mitrasacme paludosa

—See AQUATICS.

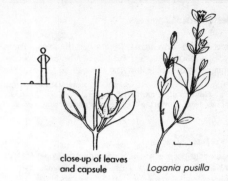

close-up of leaves
and capsule   *Logania pusilla*

• *Mitrasacme pilosa* Labillardière **var. *pilosa***

Ss
A small prostrate herb with stems 10-20cm long, found in
shady places on sandy soil. Rare in the area. Recorded from
Maddens Plains and Bulli tops.

Range: coast south from Sydney, Vic and Tas.   **Leaves:** opposite, flat,
thin-textured, 5-8mm long, hairless or only a few hairs at the base. The
stems are conspicuously hairy.   **Flowers:** WHITE.   **Name:** *pilosa* = Lat.
with long simple hairs.

Mitrasacme polymorpha R. Brown

Ss, Castl
A slender ascending herb 15-30cm tall. Very abundant in heath
on sandstone.

Range: NSW coast, Blue Mountains, southern tablelands, Qld, Vic and
NT. **Leaves:** 4-10mm long, narrow, with recurved margins, hairy.
Flowers: WHITE. **Flowering time:** spring-summer. **Name:**
polymorpha = Gk. many-shaped.

LORANTHACEAE

—See MISTLETOES.

MALVACEAE

Hibiscus, Mallows
A family with about 2000 species in about 85 genera. Australia
has about 160 species in 24 genera. Most are large-leafed
tropical shrubs with stellate hairs and fibrous stems.

The family includes the commercial cotton plant,
Gossypium hirsutum, the edible okra, *Hibiscus esculentus*,
and the cultivated garden hibiscus, *Hibiscus rosa-sinensis*.
Sturt's Desert Rose, *Gossypium sturtianum*, is the floral
emblem of the Northern Territory.

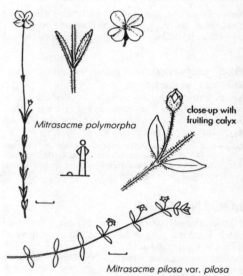

Mitrasacme polymorpha

close-up with
fruiting calyx

Mitrasacme pilosa var. pilosa

• *Abutilon* Miller

Lanterns, Chinese Lanterns
A genus of shrubs and trees with about 200 species, including
about 30 species in Australia.

Name: *Abutilon* = from the Arabic name for Mulberry, which
has similar leaves.

*Abutilon grandifolium** (Willdenow) Sweet

Ss
A spreading leafy shrub to 2m high which resembles *Lantana*

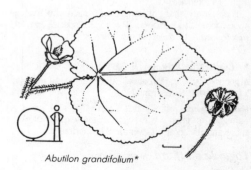

Abutilon grandifolium*

from a distance. Common on disturbed or waste ground near
water. Introduced from tropical America or Africa.

Range: from Nowra to Qld, in coastal areas. **Leaves:** large, more or
less ovate, furry (villous), dull green, crenate. **Flowers:** GOLDEN, about
2cm wide, axillary, sepals 8-10mm long. Capsule with 10 chambers,
densely hairy. **Flowering time:** most of year. **Name:** *grandifolium*
= Lat. large-leaved.

- **Gynatrix** Alefeld (jy-NAY-trix)

An endemic genus with a single species.

Name: *Gynatrix* = Gk. female-hair, i.e. hairy carpels.

Gynatrix pulchella (Willdenow) Alefeld

Hemp Bush   **Cumb**

A foul smelling shrub to 2m, occasionally to 4m, tall. Rare or extinct in the area. Recorded in the past from the Cumberland Plain, near streams (Nepean River, 1889 and South Creek near St Marys, 1928).

Range: scattered occurrences in NSW coast and ranges south from the Sydney area, and widely in Victoria. **Leaves:** soft, crenate, furry to feel above, pale below with a dense felt of star-hairs. **Flowers:** unisexual (plant dioecious), PALE GREENISH YELLOW, small, numerous in slender axillary panicles. **Flowering time:** August-October. **Name:** *pulchella* = Lat. beautiful.

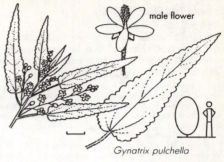

male flower

Gynatrix pulchella

- **Hibiscus** Linnaeus

A genus of trees, shrubs and herbs, with about 300 species widespread in the tropics and subtropics. There are about 35 species in Australia, in all mainland states.

Name: *Hibiscus* = from the Greek word for marsh mallow.

Hibiscus heterophyllus Ventenat
ssp. heterophyllus

Native Rosella

A shrub or small tree 3-8m tall with spectacular flowers and prickles on the stems. Found in moist forests along river banks and margins of rainforest. It once occurred along the Nepean River in western Sydney but has not been recorded in recent years. More common in forests in the southern Illawarra.

    The bark was used by Aborigines as an important source of fibre for rope, string and baskets.

Range: NSW coast north from Kiama, northern tablelands, also Queensland. **Leaves:** entire or 3-lobed (juveniles 3-5 lobed), finely toothed, 10-18cm long. **Flowers:** WHITE to PALE PINK, with DEEP RED centre, about 12cm wide, fragrant. The calyx is covered in dense stellate hairs. An epicalyx of 10 linear segments is present. **Flowering time:** mainly November-December. **Name:** *heterophyllus* = Lat. variable-leaved.

Hibiscus heterophyllus ssp. *heterophyllus*

- **Howittia** F. Mueller

An endemic genus with a single species.

Name: *Howittia* = after Dr Godfrey Howitt (1800-73), a Melbourne doctor, amateur botanist, and authority on insects.

Howittia trilocularis F. Mueller

Blue Howittia

A straggly shrub 2-4m tall, found in moist forests in valley floors and on rainforest edges. It occurs in valleys in the Blue Mountains, with a few old records in the Sydney area: Nepean River 1888, Hurstville 1893, Lane Cove River 1918.

Range: NSW coastal districts and Blue Mountains, and Vic. **Leaves:** 5-10cm long, soft, crenate, furry above, pale and densely woolly-felty below with star-hairs (also on stems). **Flowers:** PURPLISH BLUE, petals about 10mm long; solitary, axillary. **Name:** *trilocularis* = Lat. 3-chambered, referring to the fruits.

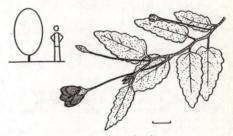

Howittia trilocularis

- **Pavonia** Cavanilles

A genus with about 200 species, including a single species naturalised in Australia.

Name: *Pavonia* = after José Antonio Pavón (1754-1840), Spanish botanist and traveller in South America, part-author of a flora of Peru and Chile.

*Pavonia hastata** Cavanilles

Pink Pavonia   **Ss, Cumb**

An erect shrub 1-2m tall with pretty pink flowers. Moderately common throughout the area, in moist open locations on enriched soils. A native of South America, long naturalised in the area*.

Range: scattered locations in NSW and Queensland, widespread in the tropics and sub-tropics.   **Leaves:** slightly stiff, to 35mm long, toothed, dull green, hairless or rough above, furry below with star-hairs.   **Flowers:** PINK with RED centres, to 3cm wide, solitary, axillary.   **Flowering time:** summer to late autumn.   **Name:** *hastata* = Lat. with spreading lobes at the base, of the leaves.

* It was first collected by Commerson in Argentina in 1767; the first collections in Australia were by Robert Brown on the Nepean and Hawkesbury Rivers (1802-05) and by Allan Cunningham on the Liverpool Plains (1817).

Pavonia hastata*

MELIACEAE

A mainly tropical family with about 600 species in 50 genera. There are about 34 species in 11 genera in Australia.

The family is related to Anarcardiaceae, Rutaceae and Sapindaceae. It includes the true Mahoganies, *Swietenia* genus, of South America.

• *Melia* Linnaeus

A genus of tropical trees with a single native species.

Name: *Melia* = the greek name of the Manna Ash, a species with similar leaves.

Melia azedarach Linnaeus
var. *australasica* (A. Juss.) C. De Candolle

White Cedar   **Cumb**

A small deciduous tree 3-8m high in this area, with bunches of yellow berries in the winter months. It was once apparently native along the banks of the Nepean, but became quickly cultivated, perhaps due to the European settlers' nostalgia for deciduous trees. 'On the banks of the Nepean, I saw almost the only deciduous native tree in the territory, namely, the white cedar (*Melia azedarach*), the common bead-tree of India, beautiful in itself, and congenial to me from that singularity'.[25]

It is now widespread in streets, gardens and a common weed on waste ground. The bark of the closely related Asian tree, *M. indica* (the Neem) was used for treating malaria before the advent of quinine.[26] The fruits are poisonous to people and stock.

Range: NSW coastal areas, Qld and WA. Now widespread as a shade tree in inland Australia.   **Leaves:** large and bipinnate, turning yellow before falling in winter.   **Flowers:** MAUVE, petals 8-10mm long, staminal filaments formed into a dark-coloured tube with 10 teeth; in large loose axillary panicles.   **Flowering time:** October-December.   **Name:** *Azedarach* = from *Azad-darakht*, the Persian name of the related Indian 'Neem' tree. Linneas conferred the name by mistake.

Melia azedarach var. australasica

• *Synoum*—see RAINFOREST SPECIES.

• *Toona*—see RAINFOREST SPECIES.

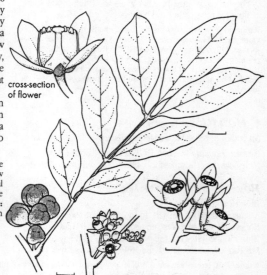

cross-section of flower

Synoum glandulosum

MYOPORACEAE

A family with about 215 species in 3 genera, distributed mainly in Australia, with some species on the islands of the southwest Pacific, Indian Ocean and West Indies. It includes *Eremophila*, a large genus with bright tubular flowers, which is abundant in the interior of Australia.

The family is related to Scrophulariaceae, Lamiaceae and Chloanthaceae.

Eremophila R. Brown
Poverty bushes
A genus of shrubs with 205 species in Australia and one in NZ. Mainly found in desert areas. Many have showy flowers and some are used as garden plants in drier areas.
Name: *eremophila* = Gk. desert-loving.

Eremophila debilis (Andrews) Chinnock

Amulla, Winter Apple **Cumb** (previously *Myoporum debile*)
A prostrate shrub with stems to 1m long, found uncommonly in marshy open forest on the Cumberland Plain (eg. Doonside, Mt Annan). According to the Cripps, the fruits are edible.
Range: mainly an inland species, also on the Cumberland Plain, NSW north coast and ranges, and Qld. **Leaves:** 5-8cm long, entire or toothed towards the tip and occasionally near the base, with recurved margins. **Flowers:** BLUE (PINK or MAUVE), 1-2 per axil. **Fruits:** 6-8mm wide, purplish and somewhat succulent (hence the common name Winter Apple). **Flowering time:** November-February. **Name:** *debilis* = Lat. weak.

• *Myoporum*
– See COASTAL AND ESTUARINE SPECIES.

MYRSINACEAE

A mainly tropical family with about 1000 species in 35 genera. There are 25 species in 7 genera in Australia. It is closely related to the herbaceous family Primulaceae.

• *Aegiceras*
—See COASTAL AND ESTUARINE SPECIES.

• *Rapanea* Aublet
A genus of trees and shrubs with about 200 species worldwide. There are about 10 species native in Australia.

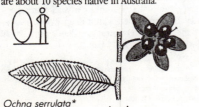

*Ochna serrulata**

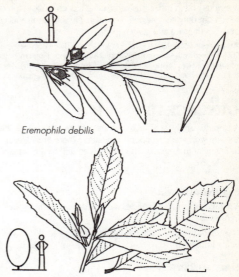

Eremophila debilis

Rapanea variabilis

This is one of the few genera of woody plants which are entirely self-fertilised: the flowers never open and the anthers release their pollen directly onto the mature stigmas. The tiny flowers are borne on old wood.
Name: *Rapanea* = from native name for the original type species in French Guiana (tropical America).

Rapanea howittiana
—See RAINFOREST SPECIES.

Rapanea variabilis (R Brown) Mez

Mutton Wood **Ss, Cumb**
A rather anonymous shrub usually 2-3m high. Found in sheltered forests or gullies. Common in the area.
Range: NSW coastal areas into Qld. **Leaves:** irregularly toothed (although sometimes barely so), tough, shiny on the upper surface. **Flowers:** PALE YELLOW, tiny, clustered on old wood. **Flowering time:** spring. **Name:** *variabilis* = Lat. variable, as it was not initially realised that *P. howittiana* was a separate species. Mutton Wood was a name used on the south coast, originating from a fancied resemblance to mutton fat.

OCHNACEAE

A tropical family of trees and shrubs with about 600 species in about 40 genera.

• *Ochna* Linnaeus
A genus with about 90 species, often cultivated.
Name: *Ochna* = from the Greek for pear tree.

*Ochna serrulata** (Hochstetter) Walpers
Ochna, Mickey Mouse Plant **Ss**
A tough weedy shrub with erect, wiry stems, about 1.5m high.

A serious pest in urban bushland, it has a deep woody taproot which can only be removed by poison. Originally introduced from South Africa as a garden plant.

Range: restricted to the Sydney region, and South Africa. **Leaves:** glossy, finely toothed, with numerous fine parallel lateral veins. **Flowers:** bright yellow, attractive. **Fruit:** a black 4-lobed berry, sitting on the fleshy red receptacle and calyx. **Name:** *serrulata* = Lat. with numerous tiny teeth.

OLACACEAE

A tropical family of shrubs and scramblers, with about 250 species worldwide in about 25 genera. There are 7 species in 2 genera in Australia. The family is related to the parasitic Santalaceae.

• *Olax* Linnaeus

A genus with about 55 species worldwide, including 5 species in Australia.

Name: *olax* = Lat. *aulax*, a furrow, refering to the flowers being furrowed.

Olax stricta R. Brown
Ss

A slender erect shrub to 1.5m high, with fleshy yellowish stems and leaves, found in heath and woodland on sandstone. Not common or abundant, but widely distributed in the area. The pale colour suggests that it may be a parasite on the roots of other plants.

Range: NSW coast, ranges and western slopes, also Qld and Vic. **Leaves:** smooth, hairless, soft, 2-ranked, usually pale and fleshy, stalkless, often on orange stems. **Flowers:** WHITE-YELLOWISH, with 2 stamens and 5 staminodes, the floral tube splits into 3 segments. The fruit is a fleshy berry. **Flowering time:** much of the year. **Name:** *stricta* = Lat. bundled, referring to the erect compact habit.

OLEACEAE

Olives

A family of shrubs, trees and climbers with about 650 species in 24 genera worldwide, especially in east and South-east Asia. There are about 30 species in 5 genera in Australia, including some of our worst introduced weeds.

The family includes the economically important Olive (*Olea europaea*), the European Ash (*Fraxinus*), Jasmin (*Jasminum*), Lilac (*Syringa*), and other ornamentals.

• *Ligustrum* Linnaeus (ly-GUST-rum)
Privetts

A genus of shrubs with about 50 species worldwide. There is a single native species in north-eastern Qld, and 3 introduced species.

Privetts are prodigious seed-producers and have tenacious woody root systems which are hard to eradicate.

Name: *Ligustrum* = the classical Latin name for one species.

Ligustrum lucidum Aiton
Large-leaved Privett **Ss, Cumb**

A tall shrub to 6m high with smooth grey bark. Introduced as a garden shrub from China and Japan, now a pest in bushland near habitation.

Range: NSW coast, Blue Mountains, southern tablelands, Qld, and widespread in east Asia. **Leaves:** opposite, hairless, to 12cm long, moderately thick and tough, glossy, always downcurving to the tip. **Flowers:** white, fragrant, in dense terminal pyramidal panicles. **Flowering time:** January-February. **Name:** *lucidum* = Lat. shining.

Ligustrum sinense Louriero
Privett **Ss, Cumb**

A dense leafy shrub usually 2-3m high, with smooth bark. A common weed in moist gullies near habitation. A single plant can produce 400,000 fruits per year, which are spread by birds. This, combined with a deep woody root system, make it the most serious threat to Sydney's native bushlands. Introduced from China and Japan.

Range: NSW coast, Blue Mountains, southern tablelands, Lord Howe Island, Qld and east Asia. **Leaves:** small, opposite, glossy, thin-textured, soft, 2-ranked on the branches. **Flowers:** WHITE, fragrant, in dense terminal pyramidal panicles. **Flowering time:** October-November. **Name:** *sinense* = Lat. Chinese.

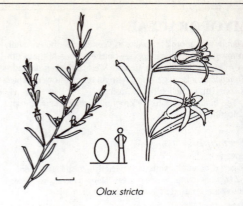

Olax stricta

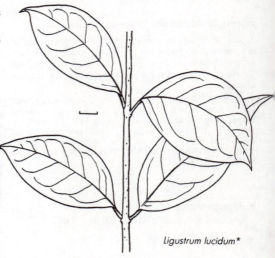

Ligustrum lucidum*

• *Notelaea* Ventenat (no-tel-EE-a)

Mock Olives, Native Olives

A genus with 7 species, endemic to eastern Australia. The flowers are YELLOWISH, small, in short geometric axillary cymes. Each flower has 2 pairs of pouch-like petals, each pair enclosing a single stamen. The petals are quickly deciduous, falling to reveal a superior ovary and a short 2-lobed stigma. The fruits are bitter blackish olive-like drupes, 10-15mm wide.

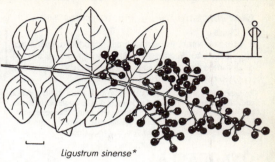

Name: *Notelaea* = Gk. *notos*, south, *elaia*, olive, i.e. the southern olive.

Note: all species have juvenile leaves which are larger, broader, and stiffer than adult leaves, with short stalks.

*Ligustrum sinense**

Notelaea longifolia Ventenat

Mock Olive **Ss, Cumb, Temp Rf**

A ubiquitous but rather anonymous shrub, usually 2-3m tall, common in moist sheltered situations on most soils. It survives fires and clearing by virtue of a deep stout lignotuber.

Range: NSW coast, Blue Mountains and northern tablelands. **Leaves:** opposite, variable depending on the age and habitat; hairless or covered in fine pale fur, firm to very harsh, dull olive-green colour. The lateral veins remain about the same width as they move from the mid-vein to the margin. **Flowers and fruit:** as per genus. **Name:** *longifolia* = Lat. long-leaved.

Notelaea ovata R. Brown

Mock Olive **Ss, Temp Rf**

An erect shrub usually 2-4m high, occasional found in wetter sclerophyll forests and rainforest edges. It is largely extinct in the area. Its main local range was in the inner southern suburbs and the Killara-Roseville-Lindfield area.

Range: NSW coast into Qld. **Leaves:** smaller and rounder than other species, mostly 3-7cm long, usually a dull olive colour, hard and leathery, very reticulate, wide at the base, with irregular margins. **Flowers and fruit:** as per genus. **Name:** *ovata* = Lat. oval.

Notelaea venosa

—See RAINFOREST SPECIES.

Notelaea longifolia

Notelaea flowers
(*N. longifolia*)

• *Olea* Linnaeus

A genus with about 20 species worldwide. Only 1 species is native to Australia, a rainforest tree in northern NSW and Qld.

Name: *Olea* = the Latin name for the Olive.

inflorescence   flower   cross-section

Leaf venation:

Notelaea ovata

N. longifolia   N. venosa

Olea europaea Linnaeus **ssp. *africana*** * Miller
Ss, Cumb

A spreading shrub, usually 3-6m tall, introduced from Africa as a hedge and ornamental plant, now common as a weed on disturbed ground. The abundant fruits and the deep woody root system make it difficult to eradicate.

Range: Sydney area and north coast, also widespread in north Africa and Asia. **Leaves:** opposite, rather leathery, dark green and shiny above, dull and pale green below, with recurved margins. **Flowers:** small, WHITE, in short axillary panicles. **Fruits:** black drupes 5-7mm wide. **Name:** *europaea* = Lat. European, *africana* = Lat. African.

ONAGRACEAE

A family with about 640 species in 18 genera, distributed widely in tropical and temperate parts of the world, with a centre of diversity in the temperate United States. There are about 19 species in 2 genera native to Australia.

The family includes *Fuschia*, pretty ornamental shrubs native to NZ, and the large American genus *Oenanthera*, Evening Primroses, now cosmopolitan weeds. Several species of *Oenanthera* are common weeds in the Sydney area.

The family is related to Myrtaceae.

• *Epilobium* Linnaeus
Willow Herbs

A genus with over 200 species worldwide, especially in the south-western United States. There are 15 species native to Australia, distributed mainly in temperate parts of the continent, and Tas.

Name: *Epilobium* = Gk. *epi*, upon, *lobos*, a pod, because the floral parts are supported upon the long pod-like ovary.

Epilobium billardieranum Séringe in De Candolle
ssp. *billardieranum*
—See AQUATICS.

Epilobium billardieranum ssp. *cinereum*
(A. Richard) Raven & Englehorn

Willow Herb **Ss, Cumb**

A small erect herb usually under 50cm high. Widely scattered but uncommon in the area. It prefers damp situations including disturbed and waste ground.

Range: coast, ranges and western slopes of NSW, all states, and NZ. **Leaves:** alternate, narrow, covered in a microscopic layer of fine grey hairs, erect, toothed, thin-textured, soft. **Flowers:** PINK. **Flowering time:** summer. **Name:** *cinereum* = Lat. ash-grey. **Similar species:** distinguish from *E. hirtigerum* by the sparse grey hairs, all alternate leaves, and small stature.

Epilobium hirtigerum A. Cunningham
Ss, Cumb

An erect herb usually 60-100cm tall, densely covered in grey hairs. This is the most common of the local species, widely distributed throughout the area. It prefers damp sunny places on disturbed sites.

Range: all parts of NSW, all other states, NZ, Indonesia and the Americas. **Leaves:** alternate above, opposite below, erect, soft, cloaked in a dense felt of fine grey hairs. **Flowers:** PINK or WHITE, solitary in the upper axils. **Flowering time:** summer. **Name:** *hirtigerum* = Lat. hairy. **Note:** The plant has a thick rootstock which appears to be edible.

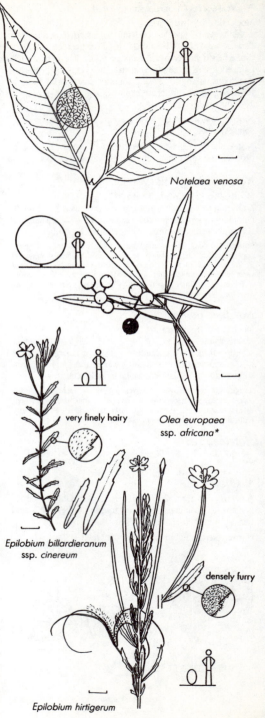

Notelaea venosa

very finely hairy

Olea europaea
ssp. *africana**

Epilobium billardieranum
ssp. *cinereum*

densely furry

Epilobium hirtigerum

• *Ludwigia*
—See AQUATICS.

OXALIDACEAE

A family with over 950 species, in 6 genera, mostly in South Africa, Central and South America. Only 1 genus occurs in Australia.

• *Oxalis* Linnaeus

A genus with about 800 species worldwide, including about 18 species in NSW; 5 native and 13 introduced. The leaves are edible, with a pleasant acid flavour, caused by oxalic acid, but they should not be eaten in large amounts. The small smooth seeds are released explosively from slits in the fruits. If mature green fruits are given a brief squeeze, they can put on quite a show!

The following species are very similar, and only practically distinguished by an examination of the stem hairs and roots.

Name: *Oxalis* = Gk. *oxys*, sharp, referring to the acid flavour.

Oxalis corniculata Linnaeus

Yellow Wood-sorrel   **Ss, Cumb**

A small weedy herb with weak stems 5-30cm long, with or without a tap root. Common throughout the area, in moist soils, including gardens. The hairs on the stems are spreading.

Range: all parts of Australia, also widespread in Asia and Africa.   **Leaves:** bright green, 3-foliate; leaflets finely hairy, variable in size.   **Flowers:** YELLOW, petals 3-12mm long, usually solitary.   **Flowering time:** much of the year.   **Fruit:** erect, cylindrical, usually on down-bent stalks, 8-16 long, 1.5-3mm wide.   **Name:** *corniculata* = Lat. having a little horn.

Oxalis perennans Haworth

Cumb, Castl

A small herb with weak stems 5-25cm long arising from a stout tap root. Uncommon, mainly on the Cumberland Plain. The hairs on the stems are bent upwards.

Range: widely scattered in coast, ranges and inland areas, NZ.   **Leaves:** variable in colour, 3-foliate; leaflets finely hairy, mostly 4-10mm long.   **Flowers:** 1-6 per inflorescence; petals YELLOW, 6-12mm long.   **Fruits:** erect, cylindrical, furry to almost hairless, 8-30mm long, 1.5-2.5mm wide.   **Name:** *perennans* = Lat. perennial.

Oxalis rubens Haworth

This species is similar to *O. perennans* but occurs on sand dunes beside the sea.
—See COASTAL AND ESTUARINE SPECIES.

PITTOSPORACEAE

A family with about 200 species in 9 genera. Its centre of distribution is Australia and South-east Asia, although some species are found in Africa.

• *Rhytidosporum*   F. Mueller ex J.D. Hooker

A genus with 4 species of small shrubs, endemic to eastern Australia.

Name: *rhytidosporum* = Gk. wrinkled-seed.

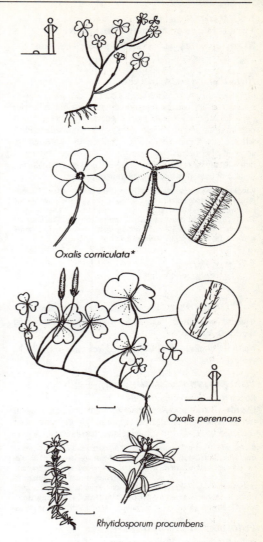

*Oxalis corniculata**

Oxalis perennans

Rhytidosporum procumbens

Rhytidosporum procumbens (W.J. Hooker) F. Mueller

Ss   (previously *Billardiera procumbens*)

A tiny shrub 10-25cm tall, erect or sometimes prostrate, often unbranched, with white star-like flowers. It occurs uncommonly in the area, mostly in damp sunny heath.

Range: coast and ranges in all eastern states.   **Leaves:** tiny, slender, soft, stalkless, crowded.   **Flowers:** WHITE, about 10mm wide. The fruits are similar to those of *Bursaria spinosa*.   **Flowering time:** spring.   **Name:** *procumbens* = Lat. lying down.

• *Billardiera*

– See CLIMBERS.

• *Bursaria* Cavanilles

A genus of shrubs or small trees with 6 species.

Name: *Bursaria* = Lat. purse-like or pouch-like, from the shape of the capsule.

Bursaria spinosa Cavanilles

Blackthorn, Kurwan **Cumb, Ss, Castl**

An erect shrub usually 2-3m, occasionally to 5m, tall, with light foliage and side-branches ending in thorns. It is opportunistic and highly successful on the Cumberland Plain where it now dominates the forest understorey over extensive areas. It also occurs near streams in sandstone country. A rather dreary plant most of the year but it puts on a magnificent display of fragrant white flowers in late summer.

Range: coasts, ranges and inland areas of all eastern states. **Leaves:** usually dull, thin-textured, soft, notched at the tip. The branches are lined with small rigid spines (actually new branchlets). **Flowers:** small, WHITE, fragrant, in dense pyramidal terminal panicles. The fruits are flat 2-chambered capsules. **Flowering time:** January-April. **Name:** *spinosa* = Lat. having spines. *Kurwan* is an Aboriginal name.

• *Citriobatus*

—See RAINFOREST SPECIES.

• *Pittosporum* Banks & Solander ex Gaertner

A genus with about 150 species worldwide and about 50 species in Australia.

Name: *Pittosporum* = Gk. resin-seed, referring to the sticky coating on the seeds.

Pittosporum revolutum Aiton

Rough-fruit Pittosporum **Rf, Ss**

Usually a rather anonymous shrub 1-3m high, although it can grow to be a small tree. Opportunistic in many moist sheltered situations, but less aggressive than its cousin below.

Range: NSW coast and ranges, also Vic, Qld. **Leaves:** dull, darkish green, ovate, undulating, rusty-felty when young, becoming hairless when old, usually appearing whorled on the stem. **Flowers:** YELLOW, fragrant, with down-curved petals; in terminal racemes of umbels. **Fruit:** an orange warty 4-ridged box about 3cm long, splitting to reveal a mass of sticky red seeds which are popular with birds. **Flowering time:** spring. **Name:** *revolutum* = Lat. curling down, referring to the petals.

Pittosporum undulatum Ventenat

Sweet Pittosporum, Wallundun-deyren **Rf, Ss**

A small tree, usually 3-10m high. Originally a scattered inhabitant of shady rainforest gullies, it is highly opportunistic and now aggressively colonises almost any moist shady location, especially in places affected by urban run-off.

Everyone either has or one day will have a Sweet Pittosporum in their backyard and it is a serious pest in urban bushland. On the positive side, there are a few weeks in September when streets and bush throughout Sydney are awash with its intoxicating fragrance, a delicious moment that punctuates the arrival of spring. The other thing in its favour is that it at least competes with Privet.

One of the best descriptions of Sweet Pittosporum comes from popular literature: ' . . . the most dominant odour in the cool evening air tonight, a strong, sickly-sweet odour

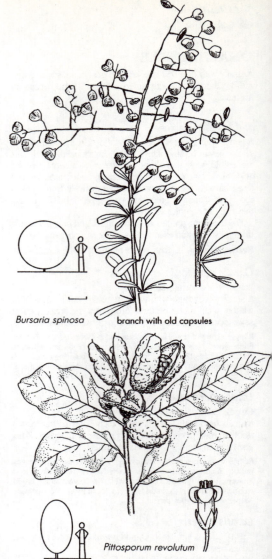

Bursaria spinosa   branch with old capsules

Pittosporum revolutum

not to every taste, is that of the native daphne, a species not native to Dog Rock, but one which has found the town so greatly to its liking it has come to dominate every ungrazed vacant block, every patch of virgin scrub, and all but the most carefully tended garden beds, whether of red basalt or black shale. Thriving best in the rainforest of the coastal escarpment,where it often attains a height of thirty-one feet, it flowers in September, producing in January a bountiful crop of small orange berries, each containing an abundance of sticky orange-red seeds, which when disseminated by the most numerous bird in Dog Rock, the pied currawong, have the capacity to colonize every plant community.'[28]

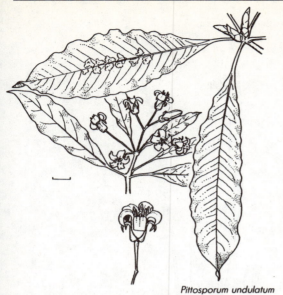

Pittosporum undulatum

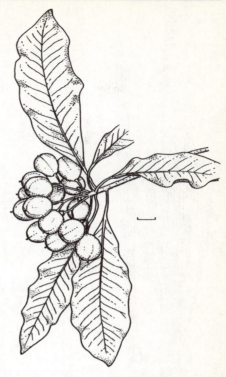

The seeds were ground as food by Aborigines in the Sydney region.

Range: widely distributed in coast and ranges in eastern Australia. **Leaves:** glossy above, thin, usually with wavy margins, best recognised by lines of brown blisters along the leaf surface (these are the excavations of tiny Pittosporum Leaf Miner grubs). **Flowers:** WHITE, very sweet-fragrant (resembling a mixture of jonquil and jasmin), in large terminal panicles of umbels. **Flowering time:** September-October. **Name:** *undulatum* = Lat. wavy, referring to the leaf margins. *Wallundun-deyren* is an Aboriginal name from the Illawarra. Other common names are Common Pittosporum, Native Daphne, Mock Orange and Native Laurel.

PLANTAGINACEAE

Plantains
A family of small tufted herbs with about 290 species in 3 genera, in temperate parts of both hemispheres.

A single genus occurs in Australia. The flowers are wind-pollinated (although some species appear to be adaptable to both states, depending on their habit). The leaves of some of the introduced species are edible.

The family has affinities with Scrophulariaceae and Lamiaceae.

• *Plantago* Linnaeus

A genus with about 280 species, including 24 native and 8 introduced in Australia.

Name: *Plantago* = the Latin name for these plants.

Plantago debilis R. Brown

Slender Plantain **Ss**
A small herb with spreading tufted leaves. Found in moist forests on sandstone and shale. Moderately common on the north shore.

Range: most parts of Australia. **Leaves:** 5-20cm long, covered in soft

furry hairs, with margins entire or toothed, 3-5 main veins. **Flowers:** in a dense slender spike on a scape 10-40cm tall. The scape is covered in soft white hairs. **Flowering time:** mainly summer. **Name:** *debilis* = Lat. feeble, weak.

Plantago gaudichaudii Barneoud

Cumb
A small plant with slender erect tufted leaves, found on clay soils on the Cumberland Plain.

Range: coast and ranges in all eastern states, including Tas. **Leaves:** 10-20cm long, about 15 times as long as broad, with a few teeth, and 3 main veins. **Flowers:** in a slender spike, not close together, on a scape to 20cm tall. The scape is covered in brownish hairs. **Flowering time:** September-April. **Name:** *gaudichaudii* = after Charles Gaudichaud, pharmacist and botanist on the Freycinet expedition which visited Shark Bay and Port Jackson in 1818-19. He collected the type specimen.

Plantago hispida

—See COASTAL AND ESTUARINE SPECIES.

Plantago varia R. Brown

Cumb
Very similar to *P. gaudichaudii*, but with wider leaves. It has been recorded a few times from near Richmond.

Range: NSW coast south from Sydney, NSW ranges, central and north western slopes, Vic and Tas. **Leaves:** 10-20cm long, 5-10 times as long as broad, slender, erect, covered in soft furry hairs, with 3-5 main veins, and scattered teeth. **Flowers:** in slender spikes, on scapes to 25cm long. The scapes are covered in whitish hairs. **Name:** *varia* = Lat. variable.

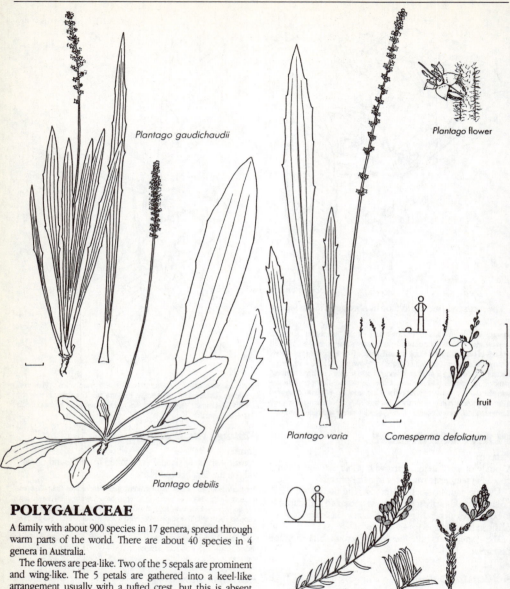

Plantago gaudichaudii

Plantago flower

Plantago debilis

Plantago varia

Comesperma defoliatum

fruit

Comesperma ericinum

POLYGALACEAE

A family with about 900 species in 17 genera, spread through warm parts of the world. There are about 40 species in 4 genera in Australia.

The flowers are pea-like. Two of the 5 sepals are prominent and wing-like. The 5 petals are gathered into a keel-like arrangement usually with a tufted crest, but this is absent in *Comesperma*. Pollination is presumably similar to that for pea flowers, with insects having to push aside the petals and penetrate into the keel.

Polygala myrtifolia is a South African species which is common in gardens.

The family is related to Tremandraceae.

• *Comesperma* Labillardière

An endemic genus of small shrubs or twiners with 24 species, distributed in all states.

Name: *Comesperma* = Gk. hair-seed, referring to tufts of hair on the seed.

Comesperma defoliatum F. Mueller

Fairies' Wings **Ss**

A small wiry leafless shrub to 50cm tall, arising from a thick rootstock. Found in moist situations in heathland. Rare in the area. Recorded from the Cowan area and Maddens Plains.

Range: coast and ranges in eastern Australia. **Leaves:** nil or present only as scales. **Flowers:** SKY BLUE (sometimes lilac). **Flowering time:** summer. **Name:** *defoliatum* = Lat. without leaves.

Comesperma ericinum De Candolle
Matchheads, Heath Milkwort   **Ss, Castl**
A slender erect shrub to 2m tall, abundant in heath and woodland on sandstone. A strikingly beautiful plant, easily recognised by the bright cluster of matchhead-like flower buds at the tips of the branches.

Range: coast and ranges of all eastern states. **Leaves:** fairly soft, crowded, flat or with recurved margins, variable according to habitat (a form with tiny leaves from coastal heath at north head is also illustrated). **Flowers:** RICH PINKISH PURPLE. **Flowering time:** spring. **Name:** *ericinum* = Heath-like.

Comesperma sphaerocarpum Steetz
Ss, Castl
A slender ascending plant with green stems to 10-30cm long arising from a thick rootstock. Found in heath and woodland on sandy soils. Fairly common in the area, but not in the Royal National Park. The only apparent difference between this and *C. defoliatum* is the fruit capsule, which lacks the long tapering base typical of the genus.
Range: NSW coast and ranges. **Leaves:** nil or present only as scales. **Flowers:** SKY BLUE to PURPLE-MAUVE, similar to *C. defoliatum*. **Flowering time:** summer (January). **Name:** *sphaerocarpum* = Gk. ball-fruit.

Comesperma volubile
—See CLIMBERS.

• *Polygala* Linnaeus
A genus of herbs and shrubs with 500-600 species worldwide, including about 15 species in Australia. The flowers are similar to *Comesperma*, except the 'keel' is tipped by a small crest-like tuft of hairs.

Name: *Polygala* = Gk. much-milk, as the ancients believed these plants promoted milk production in animals.

Polygala japonica Houttuyn
Dwarf Milkwort   **Cumb**
An inconspicuous shrublet with several erect stems under 20cm tall, arising from a thick rootstock. Uncommon in grassland on the Cumberland Plain.

Range: NSW coast, ranges and western slopes, Qld and Vic. **Leaves:** soft, hairless, thin-textured, with slightly recurved margins, sometimes opposite, 5-20mm long. **Flowers:** outer sepals 5-8mm long, MAUVE-PURPLE; in short lateral racemes. **Flowering time:** summer. **Name:** *japonica* = Japanese.

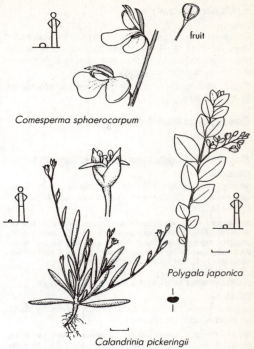

Comesperma sphaerocarpum

fruit

Polygala japonica

Calandrinia pickeringii

• *Calandrinia* Kunth
A genus with about 150 species, including about 40 species native to Australia.

Name: *Calandrinia* = after Jean-Louis Calandrini (1703-58), a Swiss mathematician, bureaucrat and botanist.

Calandrinia pickeringii A. Gray
Pink Purslane
A fragile herb to about 10cm high with succulent leaves and a thick taproot. Found on exposed barren rocks, its roots reaching into crevices. The whole plant may turn reddish and shrink during dry periods, swelling up again and greening when water becomes available. Widespread but uncommon.

Range: NSW coast and Qld. **Leaves:** thick, fleshy, to 35mm long, covered in tiny watery glands, giving a sheeny appearance. **Flowers:** PINK, with 4 petals, about 5mm long; in racemes. **Flowering time:** most of the year. **Name:** *pickeringii* = after Charles Pickering (1805-1878), naturalist on the United States Exploration Expedition 1838-42, under Charles Wilkes. He collected the type specimen from Sydney or the Illawarra in 1839.

PORTULACACEAE
A family of succulent herbs with about 580 species in 10 genera worldwide, mostly in the southern hemisphere. There are about 58 species in 5 or 6 genera in Australia.

The family is related to Caryophyllaceae and Aizoaceae.
Purslane or pigweed (*Portulaca oleraceae*), a prostrate plant with succulent leaves, is common as a weed in gardens and streets in Sydney. Aborigines in Central Australia eat it as a vegetable and grind the seeds into a damper.

PRIMULACEAE
—See COASTAL AND ESTUARINE SPECIES

RANUNCULACEAE
A family of herbs and climbers with about 1800 species worldwide, in 50 genera.
The family is very primitive, related to Menispermaceae.

• *Ranunculus* Linnaeus

Buttercups

A genus of marsh plants with about 400 species worldwide. There are about 35 species in Australia. All occur in marshy depressions and muddy ditches, although only *R. inundatus* is a truly aquatic species.

Name: *Ranunculus* = Lat. little frog, perhaps referring to its aquatic habitat.

Ranunculus inundatus

—See AQUATICS.

Ranunculus lappaceus Smith **var. *lappaceus***

Cumb, Ss

An erect plant 10-60cm tall, found in damp or marshy places on enriched soils. Common in the area, mainly on the Cumberland Plain.

Range: coast, ranges and western slopes in eastern Australia. **Leaves:** divided into 3 toothed lobes, softly hairy both sides. **Flowers:** YELLOW, 20-40mm wide, solitary. Fruits smooth with long hooked styles. **Flowering time:** spring-summer. **Name:** *lappaceus* = Lat. burr-like, referring to the hooked fruits.

Ranunculus plebeius R. Brown ex De Candolle

Cumb, Ss

An erect herb 50-100cm tall, found in damp or marshy places on enriched soils. Uncommon.

Range: NSW coast and ranges and Qld. **Leaves:** divided into 3 segments, all cut into sharply pointed lobes, softly hairy both sides. **Flowers:** YELLOW, under 12mm wide, in a leafy terminal panicle. Fruits smooth. **Flowering time:** summer. **Name:** *plebeius* = Lat. common.

Ranunculus sessiliflorus R. Brown ex De Candolle

Cumb

A small sprawling annual herb, found in moist situations. Rare in the area (Norton's Basin).

Range: widespread throughout the state; also all other states except NT. **Leaves:** 7-20mm wide, finely hairy. **Flowers:** YELLOW, about 2-4mm wide, axillary. The fruits are about 1mm long, covered in stiff microscopic hairs. **Flowering time:** spring. **Name:** *sessiliflorus* = Lat. stalkless flowers.

The following exotic species are included in order to prevent confusion with native species.

*Ranunculus muricatus** Linnaeus

Ss, Cumb

An erect herb in marshy ground. Common in the area. Introduced from the Mediterranean.

Range: scattered locations throughout the state; Vic, Europe. **Leaves:** divided into numerous pointed lobes, hairless. **Flowers:** YELLOW, 10-15mm wide, few in erect leafy panicles. Fruits to 5mm long, covered in stiff spines. **Flowering time:** spring. **Name:** *muricatus* = Lat. prickly, referring to the fruits.

*Ranunculus repens** Linnaeus

Ss, Cumb

An erect herb with creeping roots. Common in the area, in marshy places. Introduced from Europe. Perhaps the most common of the local species.

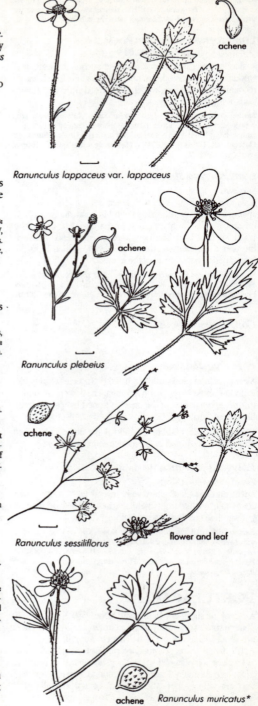

achene

Ranunculus lappaceus var. *lappaceus*

achene

Ranunculus plebeius

achene

Ranunculus sessiliflorus

flower and leaf

achene

Ranunculus muricatus*

Range: NSW coast and ranges, Vic, Tas and SA, Europe.   **Leaves:** divided into 3 toothed segments, not obviously hairy.   **Flowers:** YELLOW, 20-30mm wide, solitary on a long stalk. Fruits smooth.   **Flowering time:** spring-summer.   **Name:** *repens* = Lat. creeping.

Ranunculus sceleratus* Linnaeus

Poison Buttercup   **Ss, Cumb**

An erect herb in marshy ground. Uncommon in the area. Introduced from Europe.

Range: scattered locations throughout the state, Vic and Europe. **Leaves:** divided into segments and lobes which have blunt rounded tips. **Flowers:** YELLOW, under 10mm wide, on erect leafy panicles. The mature fruits aggregate into a vertically elongated cylindrical mass. Fruits smooth. **Flowering time:** spring-summer. **Name:** *sceleratus* = Lat. villanous, referring to its poisonous properties (it poisons stock).

RHAMNACEAE

A family with about 900 species in 58 genera. There are about 160 species in Australia, in 17 genera. The family is related to Vitaceae and Celastraceae.

• *Alphitonia*

—See RAINFOREST SPECIES.

• *Cryptandra* Smith

An endemic genus of small wiry heathy shrubs with about 40 species, distributed in all states except NT. The 5-pointed calyx is the most prominent feature of the flowers, completely surrounding the floral tube which is surmounted by 5 tiny hood-shaped petals, each enclosing an anther.

Name: *Cryptandra* = Gk. *kryptos*, hidden, *andros*, male, referring to the anthers being hidden by the hood-shaped petals.

Cryptandra amara Smith **var. amara**

Bitter Cryptandra   **Ss, Cumb**

An erect or sometimes sprawling shrub to 50cm tall, found in low open heath. Common in the area. It seems to prefer soils derived from laterites. Be careful not to confuse it with *Leucopogon microphylla*, another humble heath shrub.

Range: Sydney area, Blue Mountains, south coast and SA.   **Leaves:** tiny, about 2mm long, with recurved margins.   **Flowers:** clustered in terminal heads, 3-4mm long, covered outside in fine white felt. Smith compared them to 'little clusters of pearls'.   **Flowering time:** May-September. **Name:** *amara* = Lat. bitter, referring to the leaves. First Fleet surgeon John White sent the type specimen to James Smith who wrote 'Every part of this species is bitter, especially the leaves. The young twigs have the flavour of the [medicinal] Peruvian bark *Cinchona*, and it is much to be wished that this plant should be submitted to chemical and medical experiment.'

Cryptandra amara **var. longiflora**

F. Mueller ex Maiden & Betche

Cumb

Similar to the above except larger in all its parts. Recorded locally from the Glenfield area.

Range: restricted to scattered locations in the Sydney region.   **Leaves:** 3-4mm long. The branches often end in spines.   **Flowers:** 3-4mm long. **Name:** *longiflora* = Lat. long-flowered.

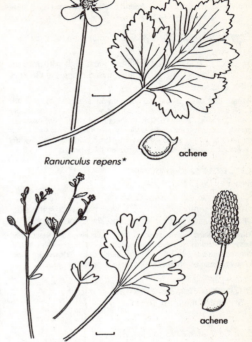

*Ranunculus repens**

achene

*Ranunculus sceleratus**

achene

Cryptandra amara var. amara

Cryptandra ericoides

Cryptandra ericoides Smith

Heath Cryptandra   **Ss**

An erect shrub to 50cm tall, found in open heath. Uncommon in the area.

Range: Sydney area and south coast.   **Leaves:** linear, 4-8mm long, with recurved margins, usually clustered.   **Flowers:** calyX WHITE covered in fine silky pubescence; in small terminal heads.   **Flowering time:** April-August.   **Name:** *ericoides* = *Erica*-like, referring to the leaves.

Cryptandra propinqua A. Cunningham ex Fenzl

Ss

An erect much-branched shrub to 50cm high with fragrant star-like flowers. Rare in the area, found along the Georges River near Revesby.

Range: NSW coast, ranges and some inland areas, Qld, Vic and WA. **Leaves:** about 2mm long (to 6mm) with recurved margins, usually broader than *C. amara.* **Flowers:** WHITE, about 7mm wide, calyx silky-hairy outside, with spreading segments joined into a tube which is surrounded by rows of brown bracts.   **Flowering time:** winter-spring.   **Name:** *propinqua* = allied, referring to its closeness to *C. amara.*

Cryptandra propinqua

Cryptandra spinescens

Sieber ex De Candolle

Spiny Cryptandra   **Cumb, Castl**

An untidy shrub to 50cm tall covered in short spiny side-branches, found on the Cumberland Plain. Uncommon.

Range: restricted to the Sydney area, Blue Mountains and western slopes. **Leaves:** round to elliptical, more or less flat.   **Flowers:** calyx WHITE covered with fine felt, 3-4mm long at fruiting stage.   **Flowering time:** August-September.   **Name:** *spinescens* = Lat. becoming spiny.

Cryptandra spinescens   **flower buds**

• *Emmenosperma*

—See RAINFOREST SPECIES.

• *Pomaderris* Labillardière

A genus of shrubs with about 40 species in Australia and a few in New Zealand.

Pomaderris are mostly tall shrubs of humid woodland, usually found in valleys away from the coast.

The flowers are small and numerous in dense panicles. The petals are absent in many species.

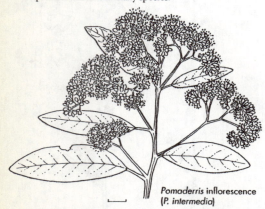

Pomaderris inflorescence
(P. intermedia)

Name: *Pomaderris* = Gk. *poma*, lid, *derris*, skin, referring to the membranous valve covering the capsule in some species.

Identification: *Pomaderris* is a difficult genus. Some species are very similar and can only be distinguished with a good

hand lens. Since the fingers can feel more than the eye can see, the furry feeling of some leaves is the easiest way to distinguish the presence of a layer of simple hairs, which is an important diagnostic feature.

Key to *Pomaderris*

A.   Leaves large (>5cm long).
  B.   Leaves toothed.
       = *P. aspera*
  *B.   Leaves not toothed.
    C.   Leaves with flat white felt below (not furry to feel), free simple hairs conspicuously present only on veins (flowers all yellow).
      D.   Petals present; leaves bluntly pointed.
           = *P. intermedia* or *P. elliptica**
      *D.   Petals absent; leaves sharply pointed.
           = *P. discolor*

* *P. elliptica* and *P. intermedia* can only be practically distinguished by the absence (*P. elliptica*) or presence (*P. intermedia*) of simple hairs on the undersurface veins. A hand lens or microscope are required to see them; the simple hairs are often rusty coloured, and clearly different from the flat white felty background.

    *C.   Leaves feel furry below due to a dense cloak of free simple hairs.
      E.   Leaves over 6cm long.
        F.   Leaves feel furry on both sides, flowers yellow.
             = *P. lanigera*
        *F.   Leaves only feel furry on one side, flowers cream.
             = *P. ferruginea*
      *E.   Leaves up to 6cm long.
        G.   Leaves with rounded tips, flowers yellow.
             = *P. vellea*

*G. Leaves small, flowers pale creamy-yellow, lacking petals.
= *P. ligustrina*

*A. Leaves small (<5cm long).

  H. Leaves all under 25mm long.
    = *P.* sp. aff. *phylicifolia*

  *H. Leaves up to 5cm long.

    I. Petals present, flowers yellow.
      = *P. andromedifolia*

    *I. Petals absent.

      J. Flowers pale yellow.
        = *P. ligustrina*

      *J. Flowers creamy white.

        K. Leaves smooth above.
          = *P. brunnea*

        *K. Leaves rough above.
          = *P. prunifolia**

* *P. prunifolia* was recorded in early times from Parramatta and Bankstown, but is certainly extinct there now. It has a scattered but widespread occurence in other parts of the state. The leaves have irregular margins and are conspicuously dotted below by single prominent rusty star-hairs on a field of pale silky star-hairs. It grows to about 2m.

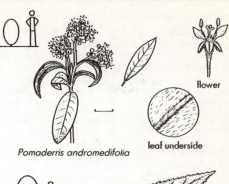

Pomaderris andromedifolia

flower

leaf underside

Pomaderris andromedifolia A. Cunningham

Ss

A shrub to 1.5m high, uncommon in the area. Recorded from Georges River near Campbelltown and the Woronora River, in moist sheltered valleys.

Range: NSW coast and ranges and Qld. **Leaves:** small (1-4cm long), lanceolate, margins slightly recurved; hairless above; grey with fine appressed silky hairs below. **Flowers:** YELLOW, with petals, floral tube silky. **Flowering time:** September-October. **Name:** *andromedifolia* = *Andromedia* leaved, *Andromedia* is a small genus of northern hemisphere shrubs in the Ericaceae family.

Pomaderris aspera Sieber ex De Candolle

Hazel Pomaderris **Ss**

An erect shrub to 3m or more, found in moist forest along streams in valleys. Uncommon in the area.

Range: mainly southern tablelands and Vic. **Leaves:** large (to 12cm), irregularly toothed; veins deeply impressed, furry to feel above; very densely covered in thick pale or rusty felt, rusty on veins below. **Flowers:** GREENISH with white filaments and pale yellow anthers, petals absent, floral tube with fine stellate hairs. **Flowering time:** October-November. **Name:** *aspera* = Lat. rough, referring to the furry leaves.

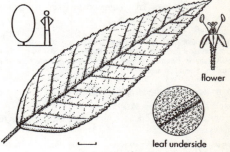

Pomaderris aspera

flower

leaf underside

Pomaderris brunnea Wakefield

Brown Pomaderris **Cumb Vulnerable 2V**

A shrub to 2m tall, uncommon in moist forests in the Camden-Elderslie area.

Range: restricted to the a few locations in the Sydney region. **Leaves:** 15-30cm long, with recurved margins; hairless above; furry with dense white silky hairs, becoming rusty on veins below. **Flowers:** CREAMY WHITE, lacking petals, floral tube silky-hairy. **Flowering time:** September-October. **Name:** *brunnea* = Lat. deep brown, referring to the rusty leaf hairs.

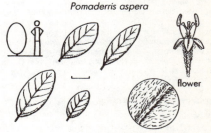

flower

leaf underside

Pomaderris brunnea

Pomaderris discolor (Ventenat) Poiret

Pomaderris **Ss**

An erect shrub to 3m, common in the area, in moist sheltered valleys on sandstone.

Range: Sydney area, Blue Mountains and north coast, also in eastern

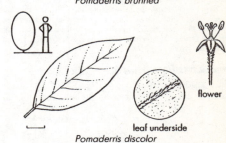

flower

leaf underside

Pomaderris discolor

Vic. **Leaves:** finely pointed; hairless above; whitish grey with a fine flat felt, veins grey and rusty below; margins slightly recurved. At high magnification there are sparse short simple hairs on the veins, arising from the background of flat felt. **Flowers:** CREAM to PALE YELLOW, petals (usually) absent, floral tube with fine white felt and slightly longer simple hairs. **Flowering time:** September-October. **Name:** *discolor* = Lat. differently coloured. **Similar species:** *P. intermedia* (distinguish by leaf tip shape), *P. elliptica* (distinguish by flowers).

Pomaderris elliptica Labillardière

Smooth Pomaderris **Ss**

An erect shrub to 3m, uncommon in the area, in moist sheltered valleys on sandstone. The leaves are dark green with veins obscure above.

Range: NSW coast and Blue Mountains. **Leaves:** mostly 5-6cm long; hairless, dark green, veins obscure above; whitish grey with a fine flat felt, veins grey and rusty below. At high magnitude no sparse simple hairs are visible on the veins. **Flowers:** YELLOW, with petals, style barely cleft, floral tube with fine flat felt. **Flowering time:** September-October. **Name:** *elliptica* = Lat. elliptical.

Pomaderris ferruginea Sieber ex Fenzl

Rusty Pomaderris **Ss**

A shrub to 4m high, fairly common north of the harbour, in moist sheltered valleys.

Range: NSW coast and Blue Mountains, also Qld and Vic. **Leaves:** 6-10cm long, lanceolate; hairless above; densely furry with silky white or rusty hairs on a flat white felt below. **Flowers:** CREAMY WHITE, with petals, floral tube with silvery silky hairs. **Flowering time:** September-October. **Name:** *ferruginea* = Lat. rusty.

Pomaderris intermedia Sieber

(previously *Pomaderris sieberiana*) **Ss**

An erect shrub to 3m, common in the area, in moist sheltered valleys on sandstone.

Range: Sydney area, south coast and NSW ranges and Vic. **Leaves:** not strongly pointed; mid-green, veins clearly impressed (compare to *P. elliptica* which has obscure veins), hairless (or rarely finely scabrous) above; whitish grey with a fine flat felt, veins grey and rusty below. At high magnification there are also sparse short simple hairs on the veins, arising from the background of flat felt. **Flowers:** pale YELLOW, petals present, style not deeply cleft, floral tube with fine white felt and single slightly longer simple hairs. **Flowering time:** September-October. **Name:** *intermedia* = Lat. in between, referring to its relationship to *P. discolor* and *P. elliptica.*

Pomaderris lanigera (Andrews) Sims

Woolly Pomaderris **Ss**

An erect shrub to 3m, common in the area, in moist sheltered valleys on sandstone.

Range: NSW coast and ranges, also Qld and Vic. **Leaves:** mostly 6-10cm long, rough with sparse tiny stiff hairs above; densely furry with curly silver-grey to rusty single hairs, on a background of whitish-grey felt below. **Flowers:** YELLOW, petals present, floral tube with silky silvery-grey hairs. **Flowering time:** August-September. **Name:** *lanigera* = Lat. woolly.

Pomaderris ligustrina Sieber ex De Candolle

Privett Pomaderris **Ss**

A shrub to 2m tall, uncommon in the area, mainly in the

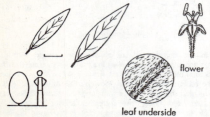

Pomaderris ligustrina

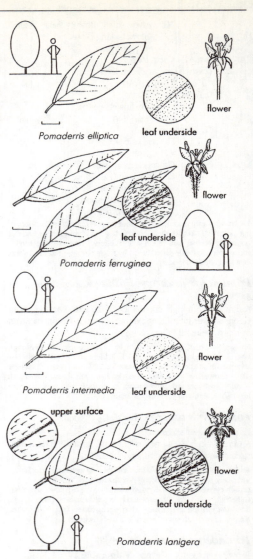

Pomaderris elliptica
leaf underside
flower

Pomaderris ferruginea
leaf underside
flower

Pomaderris intermedia
leaf underside
flower

upper surface
leaf underside
flower

Pomaderris lanigera

Georges River area (Campbelltown-Ingleburn). Found in moist sheltered forests and valleys.

Range: NSW coast and ranges, also Vic. **Leaves:** 25-40mm (60mm) long; hairless above; furry with dense grey or rusty silky hairs below. **Flowers:** CREAMY YELLOW, without petals, floral tube silky hairy. **Flowering time:** September-October. **Name:** *ligustrina* = resembling *Ligustrum sinense*, Privett.

Pomaderris sp. aff. phylicifolia

Slender Pomaderris **Ss**

An erect shrub to 3m high, found in woodland on sandstone. Rare in the area, restricted to the Barrenjoey Peninsula, Frenchs Forest and parts of the Woronora Plateau.

Range: restricted to a few locations in the Sydney region. **Leaves:** 10-15mm long, with strongly recurved margins; hairless above; densely covered in long silky hairs below. **Flowers:** PALE CREAMY-YELLOW, lacking petals, floral tube finely silky; in axillary panicles. **Flowering time:** September-October.

Pomaderris vellea Wakefield

Blue Pomaderris **Ss**

An erect shrub to 2m tall. Rare in the area, recorded from near the Georges River at Campbelltown.

Range: Sydney area, north coast and northern tablelands. **Leaves:** bluish, mostly 4-6cm long, with rounded tips and flat margins; furry to feel (covered in minute tangled hairs) above; furry with dense rusty curly hairs below. **Flowers:** YELLOW, petals present, floral tube with dense rusty hairs. **Flowering time:** September-October. **Name:** *vellea* = Lat. like vellum, referring to the fine soft texture of the leaves.

ROSACEAE

—See CLIMBERS for family treatment.

• *Acaena* Mutis ex Linnaeus

A genus of perennial herbs with about 100 species, including 5 in southern Australia. The mature fruit is enclosed in the hardened base of the flower, which develops a number of stiff slender prickles, barbed at the tip, which aggressively attach to the fur or clothing of passing animals.

Name: *Acaena* = Gk. *akaina*, a thorn.

Acaena novae-zelandiae Kirk

(previously *A. anserinifolia*)
Bidgy-widgy **Cumb**
An erect tufted herb to 25cm tall. Found in grassland and forests on the Cumberland Plain, and occasionally on better soils in other places.

Range: NSW coast and ranges, all eastern states, and NZ. **Leaves:** pinnate; the leaflets silky-hairy, toothed. **Flowers:** GREEN with RED prickles; in a terminal globular head. **Flowering time:** summer. **Name:** *novae-zelandiae* = Lat. New Zealand, where the type specimen was collected.

RUBIACEAE

A family with about 7000 species in about 100 genera worldwide. There are about 203 species in about 42 genera in Australia. A distinctive feature is the presence of interpetiolar stipules, which are pointed flaps of tissue joining the bases of the opposite leaf stalks. In *Asperula* and *Galium* the stipules mimic leaves.

The family includes Coffee (*Coffea arabica*) and Quinine (*Cinchona*). It is related to Loganiaceae and Caprifoliaceae.

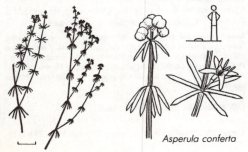

Asperula conferta

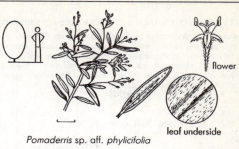

Pomaderris sp. aff. *phylicifolia*

flower

leaf underside

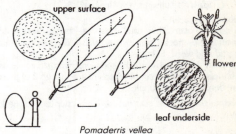

upper surface

leaf underside

flower

Pomaderris vellea

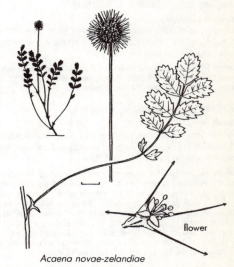

Acaena novae-zelandiae

flower

• *Asperula* Linnaeus

A genus of small weak herbs with about 216 species worldwide. There are 16 species endemic to Australia. The leaves occur in whorls of 6, although 4 of these 'leaves' are actually developed from stipules.

Name: *Asperula* = Lat. diminutive of rough, referring to the rough stems of some species.

Asperula conferta J. D. Hooker

Common Woodruff **Cumb**
A weak herb with stems to 30cm long, scrambling or forming mats in moist sheltered places. Scattered on clay soils on the Cumberland Plain. It was common in the last century

in the St Marys area, but is now much reduced by settlement.

Range: throughout eastern Australia. **Leaves:** glossy, in whorls of 5-6, 3-7mm long, hairless, with a distinct short point and a prominent mid-vein below, bent downwards when old. **Flowers:** WHITE, often pink-tinged, 3-5mm wide; in a short dense terminal cyme. **Flowering time:** September-November. **Name:** *conferta* = Lat. pressed together, referring to the old leaves being reflexed against the stem.

• *Coprosma*
—See COASTAL AND ESTUARINE SPECIES.

• *Galium* Linnaeus (GAY-lee-um)
Bedstraws

A cosmopolitan genus with about 400 species worldwide, including 6 species native to Australia. Three species are introduced weeds in lawns.

All are weak herbs, usually sprawling, with striate stems. The leaves usually occur in whorls of 4, although 2 of these are developed from stipules.

Name: *Galium* = Gk. *gala*, milk, as it was once used to curdle milk.

Galium binifolium N. A. Wakefield
Ss, Cumb (edges)

A weak tangled herb with stems to about 30cm long, found in moist sheltered forests and gullies. Uncommon, scattered in the area, but not near the sea.

Range: NSW coast, ranges and slopes, Vic and SA. **Leaves:** in pairs, usually bent downwards, 5-15mm long, hairless. **Flowers:** WHITE, in cymes. **Name:** *binifolium* = Lat. paired leaves.

Galium gaudichaudii De Candolle
Cumb

A short dense herb with many erect or ascending stems to 20cm tall. Uncommon in the area, in sheltered undergrowth in clay forests on the Cumberland Plain.

Range: Sydney area, NSW ranges and western slopes, and throughout southern Australia. **Leaves:** in whorls of 4, 3-6mm long, with finely scabrous revolute margins, on finely scabrous stems. **Flowers:** tiny, WHITE, in short dense axillary clusters. **Name:** *gaudichaudii* = after Charles Gaudichaud, pharmacist-botanist on the Freycinet expedition which stopped at Port Jackson in 1819. He collected the type specimen on his trip to Bathurst. Robert Brown had already collected it near Sydney in 1802-05, but he left it out of his 1810 *Prodromus*, so it was left to De Candolle to describe it, based on Gaudichaud's specimen.

Galium propinquum A. Cunningham
Ss

A prostrate tangled herb with stems to 30cm long. Uncommon

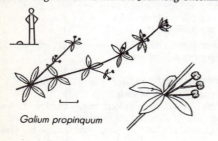

Galium propinquum

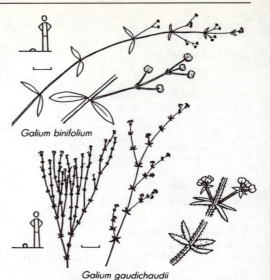

Galium binifolium

Galium gaudichaudii

to rare, scattered in the area in humid sheltered gullies on sandstone.

Range: NSW coast and ranges, Qld and Vic. **Leaves:** in whorls of 4, mostly 3-10mm long, thin-textured, hairless. **Flowers:** WHITE, mostly in pairs. **Flowering time:** summer. **Name:** *propinquum* = Lat. near, presumably referring to its relationship with other species.

• *Morinda*
—See CLIMBERS.

• *Opercularia* Gaertner

An endemic genus of slender shrubs with 15 species, distributed in all states. The leaves are opposite, usually scabrous and with a nasty odour like decaying flesh. The flowers are tiny in dense globular heads on long stalks. The calyces become united at fruiting time, forming a solid globular aggregate fruit, green or purplish. It consists of many capsules, each opening by a lid. The thick rootstock allows quick regeneration after fire.

Name: *Opercularia* = Lat. lidded, referring to the valved capsules.

Opercularia aspera Gaertner
Thin Stink Weed **Ss**

A wiry ascending shrub to 1m high, with an unpleasant odour. Common on sandstone, especially in rocky places.

Range: coast and ranges in eastern mainland Australia. **Leaves:** opposite, distant on a square stem, dull, rough to touch due to short stiff hairs. (Seacoast specimens have leaves covered in dense glossy wax.) **Flowers:** small in a dense cluster with united calyces. **Flowering time:** August-October. **Fruit:** a distinctive greenish globular head. **Name:** *aspera* = rough.

Opercularia diphylla Gaertner
Cumb

A weak shrub with ascending stems 20-30cm high. The main

local populations are on shale soils between Liverpool and Minto, but there are scattered occurrences on other parts of the Cumberland Plain. Easily recognised by the hairless leaves and stems.

Range: NSW coast, Blue Mountains, north western slopes and Qld. **Leaves:** hairless, fairly soft, variable in shape (see illustration). **Flowers:** in smaller heads than the other species, on short stalks. **Name:** *diphylla* = Gk. 2-leaved.

Opercularia hispida Sprengel
Ss

An erect or weakly ascending much-branched shrub to 40cm tall. Similar to *O. aspera*, except the leaves are densely covered in soft white hairs. Uncommon, locally restricted to the Hawkesbury River area, in rocky places on sandstone.

Range: NSW coast, ranges and western slopes, into Vic. **Leaves:** variable in shape, but always covered in dense soft white hairs. **Flowers:** similar to *O. aspera*, except densely hairy in the tube. **Flowering time:** spring. **Name:** *hispida* = Lat. roughly hairy.

Opercularia varia J. D. Hooker
Ss, Castl

An ascending shrub with many stems 10-30cm long. Moderately common north of the harbour near creeks in woodland. The leaves are scabrous and of 2 types: slender upper leaves and rounded basal leaves (although the basal leaves may be absent).

Range: coast and ranges in south-eastern Australia, including Tas and SA. **Leaves:** as above. **Flowers:** as for *O. aspera*, except there are usually a pair of small leaves attached to the base of the globular head. **Name:** *varia* = Lat. variable.

• *Pomax* Solander ex De Candolle (PO-max)

An endemic genus with a single species.

Name: *Pomax* = Gk. *poma*, a cover, *axon*, an axis, since a cover is formed over the capsule-like aggregate fruit.

Pomax umbellata (Gaertner) Solander ex A. Richard
Pomax **Ss, Castl**

A little spreading shrub 20-40cm high with a chandelier-like flower arrangement. Abundant in woodland on sandstone. One of the most common and widespread species in the area.

Range: all parts of Australia. **Leaves:** small, opposite, hairy, soft. **Flowers:** 2-3 united in small green cups formed by shared calyces; these are arranged in a distinctive terminal head, which persists (carrying the fruit) all year. **Flowering time:** spring-early summer. **Name:** *umbellata* = the inflorescence type, an umbel.

SANTALACEAE

A family with about 400 species in about 30 genera worldwide, widely distributed in tropical and temperate zones. In Australia there are 46 native species in 10 genera. The Australian species are mainly shrubs which are parasitic on the roots of other plants. Many are leafless (or rather the leaves are reduced to tiny scales). The fruits of most species are edible.

The family is closely related to Loranthaceae.

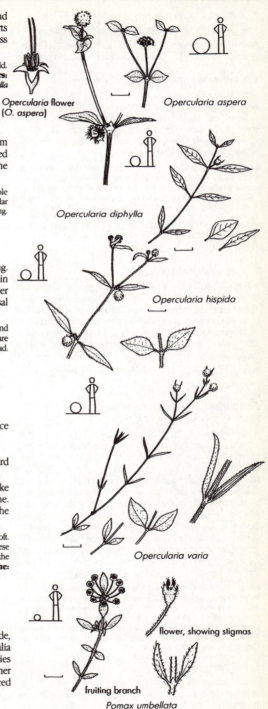

Opercularia flower (*O. aspera*)

Opercularia aspera

Opercularia diphylla

Opercularia hispida

Opercularia varia

flower, showing stigmas

fruiting branch

Pomax umbellata

• *Choretrum* R. Brown

An endemic genus of 6 species, distributed in all states.

Name: *Choretrum* = Gk. *choris*, apart, *etron*, abdomen, referring to a tiny gap between the receptacle and perianth.

Choretrum candollei F. Mueller ex Bentham

Snow Bush **Ss**

An erect shrub 30cm-2m high, found in heath and woodland in Royal National Park (uncommon), rare or absent in other parts of the area. The massed flowers exude an almost overpowering waxy-sweet fragrance. The fruits are sour but edible and were eaten by Aborigines.

Range: NSW coast, ranges and inland slopes and Qld. **Branchlets:** yellowish green, stiff, angular, with numerous ridges ending in tiny deciduous leaves. **Flowers:** WHITE, numerous in erect racemes at the ends of branches. **Flowering time:** spring-summer **Name:** *candollei* = after Swiss botanist, Augustin Pyramus de Candolle (1823-73). His immense *Prodromus Systematis Naturalis Regni Vegetabilis* included all the dicotyledons known at the time. The principals of nomenclature used in this work became the basis for the International Code of Botanical Nomenclature.

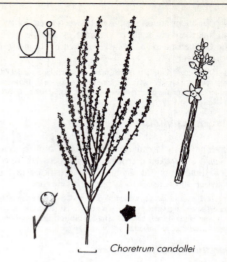

Choretrum candollei

• *Exocarpus* Labillardière

A genus of shrubs and small trees with 26 species, distributed in South-east Asia, New Caledonia, NZ, Hawaii and Australia. There are 10 Australian species, distributed in all states. The most distinctive feature is the flower stalk which becomes succulent and enlarged at fruiting time. This is an unusual strategy for convincing birds to distribute the seed in their droppings.

Name: *Exocarpus* = Gk. outside-seed, referring to the succulent stalk.

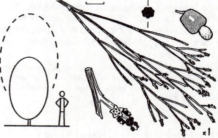

Exocarpus cupressiformis

Exocarpus cupressiformis Labillardière

Cherry Ballart **Ss, Castl, Cumb**

A tall shrub or small tree, usually 2-6m high, with dense drooping foliage, resembling a cypress. Common in woodland in many soil types, but not often on Hawkesbury sandstone. The fruit is hard and green and rests on a swollen RED stalk which is fleshy and edible when ripe, with a sweet flavour. The stalks were part of the diet of Aborigines in this area and also popular in colonial times. 'This is the poor little fruit of which so much has been written in English descriptions of the Australian flora. It has been likened to a cherry with the stone outside by some imaginative person.'[29] Another early commentator wrote 'Colonial children pick and eat these native cherries with avidity, as children will pick and eat any wild thing not especially nauseous.'[30]

Range: NSW coast, ranges and inland areas, Qld, Vic, SA and Tas. **Branchlets:** apparently leafless (leaves are tiny scales), erect when young, becoming drooping with age, finely ribbed. **Flowers:** tiny, YELLOW, in axillary spikes 3-5mm long, towards the ends of branches. **Flowering time:** December-May. **Names:** *cupressiformis* = Lat. cypress-shaped. *Ballart* or *Ballot* is an Aboriginal name, others are *Tchimmi-dillen* and *Coo-yie*, but none of these are local.

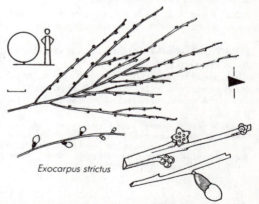

Exocarpus strictus

Exocarpus strictus R. Brown

Dwarf Currant **Ss**

An erect shrub usually about 2m high. Uncommon. Found in woodland on sandstone, eg. Heathcote National Park,

Georges River near Campbelltown and Bent's Basin. The swollen stalk is whitish at fruiting time. The plant resembles *Leptomeria acida*.

Range: NSW coast, ranges and inland areas, also Vic, Tas and SA. **Branchlets:** strongly angular, often glaucous, more or less erect, sparse compared to *E. cupressiformis*. **Flowers:** YELLOWISH-GREEN with yellow anthers, in small clusters which are sessile in the axils. **Flowering time:** spring. **Name:** *strictus* = Lat. bundled, probably referring to the tightly clustered flowers.

• *Leptomeria* R. Brown

An endemic genus with 17 species, all in southern Australia (12 in WA)

Name: *Leptomeria* = Gk. slender-part, referring to the branches.

Leptomeria acida R. Brown

Acid Drops, Native Currant **Ss, Cumb**
An erect shrub to 2m high, common in sheltered woodland. The succulent fruit were much consumed by local Aborigines. The botanist George Caley was grateful for the fruit on his attempt to cross the Blue Mountains in 1804: 'As a substitute for water, we made use of the native currant which we found to be in tolerable plenty in some places, upon the barren hilly ground, and with which in a great manner we alleviated our thirst.'[31]

The fruits are rich in vitamin C, equal per weight to an orange. They are best to eat when reddish, but rarely reach this state because they are almost always taken by birds before they ripen. Even when green they have pleasant acid flavour. They can also be used to make a jelly.

Range: from east Gippsland to south-eastern Qld, on coast and ranges. **Branchlets:** leafless, angular, stiff, erect-spreading. **Flowers:** RED, numerous in erect racemes 15-20mm long. **Flowering time:** summer. **Name:** *acida* = Lat. acidic.

Leptomeria acida

Omphacomeria acerba

Santalum obtusifolium

• *Omphacomeria* De Candolle

An endemic genus of 1 species.

Name: *Omphacomeria* = Gk. bitter-part, referring to the fruits.

Omphacomeria acerba (R. Brown) De Candolle

Leafless Sour-bush **Ss, Castl**
An erect wiry shrub 1-1.5m high, found in heath and woodland on sandy soils. Scattered in the area, but not common. The stems are cylindrical and strongly striate. The fruit are dull green, sometimes with purple markings, acidic, but edible.

Range: NSW coast and ranges south from the Hunter River into Vic. **Branchlets:** leafless, cylindrical, striate, dull green. **Flowers:** REDDISH, in small dense sessile clusters along the stems. **Flowering time:** spring. **Name:** *acerba* = Lat. sour, bitter.

• *Santalum* Linnaeus

A genus of shrubs and small trees, with 25 species in southeast Asia, Australia and the Pacific. Many have edible fruit (called quandongs in Australia). It includes the Sandalwood of commerce, *S. album*, which produces fragrant oil and timber. The 6 Australian species, distributed in all mainland states, include *S. acuminatum*, Sweet Quandong, which is an important food for Aborigines in inland Australia.

Name: *Santalum* = Gk. *santalon*, the sandal-wood tree.

Santalum obtusifolium R. Brown

Ss
An erect or straggling shrub 1-2m high with olive-like fruits. Found in valleys in wetter sclerophyll forest. Rare in the area. Recorded from Georges River at Casula, alluvial flats at Bent's Basin and Port Hacking near Audley. The fruits are just edible.

Range: NSW coast and Blue Mountains, Qld and Vic. **Leaves:** opposite, hairless; dark green and glossy above; dull, pale, almost glaucous, concave, below; with recurved margins. **Flowers:** DEEP CREAM inside, in short axillary cymes or racemes. **Fruits:** grape-purple, dull, 8-12mm wide, with a scar at the top. **Flowering time:** November. **Name:** *obtusifolium* = Lat. blunt-leaved.

SAPINDACEAE

A mainly tropical and subtropical family with about 2000 species in 150 genera worldwide, especially concentrated in tropical Asia and America. Australia has 190 species in 30 genera. The flowers are usually unisexual and inconspicuous. The family includes a number of tropical fruits including Lychee, Rambutan and Longan.

- ### *Alectryon*
—See RAINFOREST SPECIES.

- ### *Cupaniopsis*
—See COASTAL AND ESTUARINE SPECIES.

- ### *Diploglottis*
—See RAINFOREST SPECIES.

- ### *Dodonaea* Miller

Hop Bushes

A largely endemic genus of shrubs, with 68 species, including 61 in Australia, distributed in all states but concentrated in the tropical north.

The flowers are inconspicuous and unisexual, with male and female on different plants. There are no petals. The 8 stamens occur nakedly and often resemble the spokes of a wheel. The fruit are the most distinctive feature of the genus, having 3 or 4 broad wings. The leaves are often sticky to touch. Mrs Loudon, the esteemed author of the *The Ladies Flower Garden* thought they were 'ugly tropical shrubs of neither use nor beauty'.[32]

Name: *Dodonaea* = in honour of Rembert Dodoens (1517-85), author of *Stirpium Historae Pemptades*, a seminal work on herbal botany.

Dodonaea camfieldii Maiden & Betche

Ss

A prostrate or sprawling shrub, with branches usually less than 50cm long. The only specimens the author has seen were growing in a sunny rocky place on sandstone tops. A very uncommon plant, first collected in 1888. J.H. Maiden wrote that it was ' . . . not closely allied to any of the described species. The leaves have large groups of resin-secreting glands giving them a dotted appearance. Its growth resembles a good deal one of the smaller-leaved forms of *Grevillea sphacelata*, which is one of the plants with which it is associated'.[33]

Range: Nowra to near Gosford. **Leaves:** concave below, with prominent resin glands, sometimes slightly sticky. **Fruit:** green/dark brown. **Name:** *camfieldii* = in honour of Julius Henry Camfield, overseer of the Outer Domain, Sydney, and a keen botanical collector.

Dodonaea falcata West

(previously included in *Dodonaea filifolia*) **Castl**

A shrub to 1.5m high with very slender curved leaves. Found in open forest on sandy soil. Uncommon to rare in the area, now only found in the Castlereagh woodlands and Cumberland Plain. It once occurred at Rose Bay: 'Now, we are sorry to say, *D. filifolia* [sic] seems to be fast dying out in the Port Jackson district; hardly half a dozen plants could be found in 1896 in the same locality in which it abounded in 1883.'[34]

Range: coast and ranges of northern NSW, and extending down through the Putty area to western Sydney. **Leaves:** slender (<1mm wide), curved, channelled above, simple or slightly pinnate, covered in tiny sticky glands. **Fruit:** 4-winged. **Name:** *falcata* = Lat. sickle-shaped.

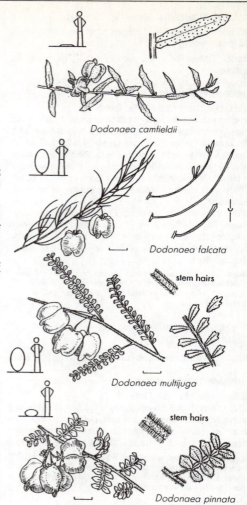

Dodonaea camtieldii

Dodonaea falcata

stem hairs

Dodonaea multijuga

stem hairs

Dodonaea pinnata

Dodonaea multijuga G. Don

Ss

An erect shrub 1-2m high, found in sheltered woodland on sandstone. Uncommon in the area. Restricted to the Woronora River, Georges River and Nepean River areas.

Range: NSW coastal areas, Blue Mountains and southern tablelands. **Leaves:** pinnate, with over 8-15 pairs of leaflets; leaflets mostly about 3mm, occasionally to 5mm, long, often prominently toothed at the tip, both opposite and alternately arranged on the rhachis. **Fruit:** 3-winged. **Name:** *multijuga* = Lat. many-paired.

Dodonaea pinnata Smith

Ss

A spreading shrub usually less than 1m high. Uncommon in woodland, often in rocky places. Locally restricted to Kuring-gai Chase National Park and also cliffs at Deep Creek, Narrabeen. The dense cloak of straight hairs on leaves and stems is an important feature to distinguish it from *D. multijuga*.

Range: restricted to the northern suburbs of Sydney, the Grose Valley and (especially) the Hawkesbury River area. **Leaves:** pinnate with 5-8, sometimes up to 14, pairs of leaflets, covered in fairly stiff hairs. Leaflets are sometimes slightly toothed, sometimes slightly sticky. **Fruit:** large, glossy, red or green. **Name:** *pinnata* = Lat. pinnate.

Dodonaea triquetra Wendland

Common Hop Bush **Ss, Cumb**

A soft leafy shrub to 2m high. Very common in forests, often in dense colonies, especially in disturbed areas and regrowth.

It was an important medicinal plant amongst Aborigines. The leaves were chewed for toothache, used as a poultice for stonefish and stingray wounds, and soaked in water and used as a sponge to relieve fever. A liquid made from soaking the roots was used for open cuts and sores.

The plant was also used by Europeans. The similarity of the fruit to that of *Humulus lupulus*, the hop, and the bitterness of the leaves, suggested it as a hop substitute and it was successfully used for beer making. The fruit was even used to raise yeast for bread-making in inland NSW.[35]

Range: NSW coast, Blue Mountains, Qld and Vic. **Leaves:** thin, soft, hairless, shining above, mid-green, with a bitter flavour. **Fruit:** green or reddish, with 3 wings, present in spring and summer. **Name:** *triquetra* = Lat. 3-cornered.

Dodonaea truncatiales F. Mueller
var. *truncatiales*

Ss

An erect shrub to 3m high, found in sheltered woodland. Locally uncommon, collected from Douglas Park on the Nepean River, but more common to the north and south of the area.

Range: NSW coast and Blue Mountains. **Leaves:** flat, with irregular margins, somwhat sticky, to 8cm long. **Fruit:** 4-lobed, with prominent projecting wings. **Name:** *truncatiales* = Lat. with a square end, as if cut off, referring to the fruit.

Dodonaea viscosa (Linnaeus) Jacquin
ssp. *angustifolia* Bentham

Ss

An erect shrub 2-3m high. Rare or absent in the area but common in the Illawarra and also present north of the Hawkesbury.

Range: NSW coast, ranges and inland areas, Qld and Vic. **Leaves:** similar to *D. truncatiales*. **Fruits:** small (under 10mm wide), mostly 4-lobed. **Name:** *viscosa* = Lat. sticky, *angustifolia* = Lat. narrow-leaved.

Dodonaea viscosa ssp. *cuneata* (Smith) West

Cumb

An erect or spreading shrub 1-3m high, common in open forest on clay soils on the Cumberland Plain.

Range: scattered distribution throughout eastern mainland Australia. **Leaves:** flat, sometimes slightly sticky, dotted with resin glands. **Fruit:** small, red or green. **Name:** *cuneata* = Lat. wedge-shaped.

• *Guioa*

—See RAINFOREST SPECIES.

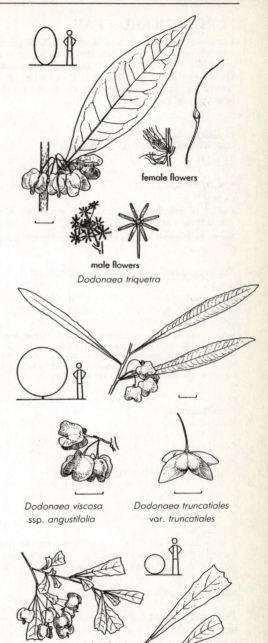

female flowers

male flowers

Dodonaea triquetra

Dodonaea viscosa ssp. *angustifolia*

Dodonaea truncatiales var. *truncatiales*

Dodonaea viscosa ssp. *cuneata*

SCROPHULARIACEAE

A family with 3000-5000 species worldwide in 220-250 genera, mainly herbs. There are 120 Australian native species in 24 genera. The leaves are mainly opposite, on square stems. The flowers have 2 lips. The family is closely related to Acanthaceae, Lentibulariaceae, Gesneriaceae and possibly Solanaceae and Plantaginaceae.

• *Bacopa*
—See COASTAL AND ESTUARINE SPECIES.

• *Euphrasia* Linnaeus
Eyebright
A genus of small herbs with about 170 species, including 18 in temperate Australia.
Name: *Euphrasia* = Gk. delight, from the attractive appearance of the flowers.

Euphrasia collina R. Brown **ssp. *speciosa***
Ss
An erect herb with wiry stems 30-50cm high. Locally restricted to the Helensburgh-Waterfall area, although it has not been collected for many years and may be extinct there.
Range: mainly NSW ranges. **Leaves:** small, erect, toothed, sessile. **Flowers:** DARK BLUE, very attractive. **Flowering time:** spring. **Name:** *collina* = Lat. pertaining to hills, *speciosa* = Lat. showy. **Note:** A closely related subspecies, **ssp. *paludosa***, has been recorded in the last century from Kurnell but appears to be now extinct there.

• *Gratiola*
—See AQUATICS.

• *Mimulus*
—See COASTAL AND ESTUARINE SPECIES.

• *Veronica* Linnaeus
Speedwells
A genus of small herbs with about 300 species, mainly in temperate parts of Europe and Asia. There are about 10 species native to Australia, distributed in southern parts of the continent.
Name: *Veronica* = in honour of Saint Veronica.

Veronica plebeia R. Brown
Ss, Cumb
A small prostrate shrub with stems usually to 40cm long. A pretty little shrub that's easily missed. Common in moist forest floors, gullies and valleys.
Range: NSW coast, ranges and inland areas, also all other states except NT and Tas. **Leaves:** opposite, toothed, thin, hairy. **Flowers:** small, PURPLE-BLUE, in axillary racemes. **Flowering time:** February-March. **Name:** *plebeia* = Lat. common. **Note:** the similar inland species *V. calycina*, was recorded at Helensburgh in 1888.

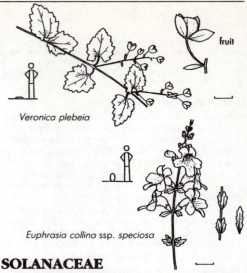

Veronica plebeia

Euphrasia collina ssp. *speciosa*

SOLANACEAE

A large family of herbs and shrubs with over 2000 species in about 90 genera, in all parts of the world. South America is the main centre of diversity, with secondary centres in Australia and Africa. There are about 117 species in about 24 genera in Australia, although only 94 species are native.

It is one of the world's most useful families of plants, including tomato (*Lycopersicon*), potato (*Solanum tuberosum*), capsicum and chilli peppers (*Capsicum*), paprika (*Capsicum annuum*), egg-plant (*Solanum melongena*), and tobacco (*Nicotiana*). The fruits of many native species were eaten by Aborigines. Some were chewed as narcotics (*Nicotiana, Duboisia*).

Most species contain alkaloids, some of which are powerful or poisonous drugs, e.g. *Datura*, mandrake, belladonna, *Stramonium, Hyoscyamus*. Two Australian species, *Solanum aviculare* and *S. laciniatum* are the basis of the steroid industry in the USSR.

Several small species of 'blackberry nightshades' are common weeds around Sydney. Their small black tomato-like fruits are sweet and tasty.

The family is most closely related to Scrophulariaceae.

• *Cyphanthera* Miers
An endemic genus with about 9 species, distributed in all states.
Name: *Cyphanthera* = Gk. bent flower.

Cyphanthera albicans (A. Cunn.) Miers
(previously *Anthoceris albicans*)
Grey Ray-flower **Ss**
A slender shrub to 2m tall, covered in dense greyish hairs. Found in woodland on sandstone. Locally restricted to the Nepean River at Douglas Park. The botanist Allan Cunningham described it as 'A shrub frequent upon Pine Hills in the interior, being a third and hitherto unpublished species of this interesting genus, originally discovered by me in 1817, and again seen in October 1822.'[36]

Range: inland NSW, occurring on the coast only at Douglas Park; also Qld and Vic. **Leaves:** 4-8mm long, round, densely covered in whitish furry hairs, with recurved margins. **Flowers:** WHITE with purple stripes, solitary, axillary. **Flowering time:** August-November. **Name:** *albicans* = Lat. white. **Note:** *C. scabrella*, a shrub to 2m with tiny scabrous leaves and yellowish green flowers, occurs in creeks running into the Nepean from the Blue Mountains.

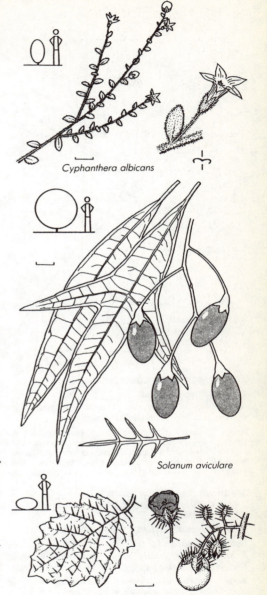

Cyphanthera albicans

• *Duboisia*
—See RAINFOREST SPECIES.

• *Physalis*
—See RAINFOREST SPECIES.

• *Solanum* Linnaeus (sol-AIN-um)

A cosmopolitan genus with over 1000 species, including 70-80 in Australia.

Name: *Solanum* = the name used by Pliny for *S. nigrum*, Black Nightshade.

Solanum aviculare G. Forster

Kangaroo Apple   **Rf margins**

An erect open shrub 2-3m tall, found in open places on the margins of rainforest, often near creeks. Fairly common in the Illawarra.

It contains solasodine, a steroid drug used in the manufacture of oral contraceptives. While most of the world relies on a substance produced from Wild Yams in Mexico, the Soviet Union cultivates it on a large scale, together with a related species, *S. laciniatum.*

Aborigines may have consumed the fruits after cooking. 'The aborigines were in the habit of eating the "bacca" or berry part of the kangaroo-apple, first burning off the skin which in a raw state would blister the mouth.'[37]

Range: widespread in eastern mainland Australia, also NG, NZ. **Leaves:** hairless, with distinct stalks 1-3cm long, satin, thin-textured, 10-20(30)cm long, entire or with 2-6 broad lobes. **Flowers:** PURPLE with yellow anthers, 2-3cm wide (but variable). **Flowering time:** summer. **Fruit:** egg-shaped, about 25mm long, changing from yellow to bright orange-red at maturity. **Name:** *aviculare* = Lat. little bird, referring to the wing-like leaves. The common name is from the resemblance of the leaves to the hind-feet of a kangaroo.

Solanum aviculare

Solanum campanulatum R. Brown

Cumb

A low spreading shrub to 1m tall, with a dense cloak of rather stout prickles on all parts. Uncommon. Mainly along the Nepean River south from Mulgoa, but also rarely scattered near the coast.

Range: Sydney area, north coast, northern tablelands and central western slopes. **Leaves:** broad, dark green, covered in stiff prickles, furry on both sides with brownish hairs (denser below), to about 12cm long. **Flowers:** PURPLE, numerous in lateral panicles, 20-30mm wide, distinctly bell-shaped. **Flowering time:** spring-summer. **Fruit:** yellowish, changing to brown and black, 20-25mm wide. **Name:** *campanulatum* = Lat. bell-like, referring to the flowers.

Solanum campanulatum

Solanum mauritianum • Scopoli

Wild Tobacco Tree   **Ss**

A tall open shrub with large greyish felty leaves, usually 3-4m high. Common in the area in wastelands and disturbed places in gullies. Introduced from tropical Asia.

The leaves smell of bitumen when crushed.

Range: NSW coast and Qld. **Leaves:** very large, grey-green, thickly covered in star-hairs on both sides, to 30cm long. **Flowers:** PURPLE in large terminal cymes. The flowers droop, but the fruits are erect. **Flowering time:** spring. **Name:** *mauritianum* = from Mauritania, the old name for western Morocco and Algeria, where the species was first collected.

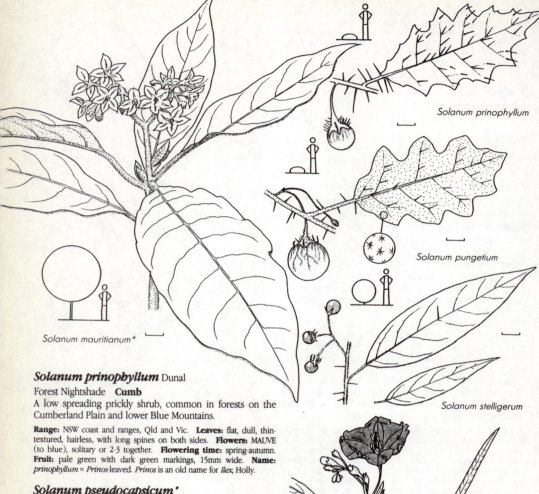

Solanum prinophyllum

Solanum pungetium

Solanum mauritianum*

Solanum stelligerum

Solanum prinophyllum Dunal

Forest Nightshade **Cumb**

A low spreading prickly shrub, common in forests on the Cumberland Plain and lower Blue Mountains.

Range: NSW coast and ranges, Qld and Vic. **Leaves:** flat, dull, thin-textured, hairless, with long spines on both sides. **Flowers:** MAUVE (to blue), solitary or 2-3 together. **Flowering time:** spring-autumn. **Fruit:** pale green with dark green markings, 15mm wide. **Name:** *prinophyllum = Prinos*-leaved. *Prinos* is an old name for *Ilex*, Holly.

Solanum pseudocapsicum*

—See RAINFOREST SPECIES.

Solanum pungetium R. Brown

Eastern Nightshade **Ss**

A low spreading prickly shrub. Uncommon in wetter sclerophyll forest near the coast. Common in the Illawarra.

Range: NSW coast and Blue Mountains. **Leaves:** flat, dull, thin-textured, covered in star-hairs on both sides, with long spines on both sides. **Flowers:** PURPLE (to blue), solitary or in racemes. **Flowering time:** spring-autumn. **Fruit:** pale green with dark green markings, 25-30mm wide. **Name:** *pungetium* = Lat. sharp.

Solanum stelligerum Smith

Devil's Needles **Ss**

A spreading shrub to 1.5m tall with scattered spines on the stems. Found in wetter sclerophyll forest in valleys in the Royal National Park. Also rarely in the Illawarra.

Solanum vescum

Range: NSW coast and Qld. **Leaves:** to 10cm long, more or less hairless and shiny above, densely pale-woolly below with star-hairs. Shiny brown spines are scattered on the stems and sometimes on the leaf mid-veins. **Flowers:** LILAC, a few in lateral racemes. **Fruit:** red, about 10mm wide.

Flowering time: spring. **Name:** *stelligerum* = Lat. star-bearing, referring to the cloak of star-hairs. **Similar species:** *S. brownii* occurs in the Illawarra and north of the Hawkesbury. It has larger, shallowly lobed leaves, which are furry on both sides.

Solanum vescum F. Mueller

Gunyang **Ss**

A bushy shrub to 1.5m tall, found in sandy soil in coastal forests, often near creeks or the sea. Uncommon, mainly recorded locally in the Waterfall area. Similar to *S. aviculare*, but the leaves are narrower, and stalkless, and the fruits are spherical, and green-white.

Range: all parts of eastern Australia. **Leaves:** hairless, stalkless, satin, thin-textured, 10-20cm, occasionally to 30cm, entire or with 2-4 slender lobes. **Flowers:** PURPLE with yellow anthers, very variable in size. The fruit is 20-25mm wide, green or whitish. **Flowering time:** spring. **Name:** *vescum* = Lat. little, weak (an inappropriate name).

STACKHOUSIACEAE

A mainly Australian family of herbs with 16 species in 3 genera.

• *Stackhousia* Smith

A genus with 14 species, 13 in Australia, 1 of which extends to South-east Asia and Micronesia, and 1 species in NZ.

The local species are small, graceful, attractively flowered herbs. The flowers are strongly fragrant at night and are pollinated by moths.

Name: *Stackhousia* = in honour of John Stackhouse, Cornish botanist and botanical artist who was especially interested in seaweeds.

Stackhousia monogyna Labillardière

(includes *S. maidenii*) **Ss**

A slender erect herb to 60cm tall, found in moist sheltered forest on various soils. Uncommon in the area.

Range: NSW coast, ranges and inland areas; widespread in eastern Australia. **Leaves:** thin, variable in shape but usually slender, mostly 1-2cm long. **Flowers:** WHITE, 5-8mm long, usually in a dense spike. **Flowering time:** summer. **Name:** *monogyna* = Gk. having a single carpel, a misnomer, since there are 3 fused carpels.

Stackhousia nuda Lindley

(includes *S. scoparia*) **Ss**

An erect leafless herb to 60cm tall. Uncommon to rare in the area, in wet open heath on sandstone. The brownish-yellow colour and lack of leaves suggests this species is saprophytic.

Range: coastal areas from eastern Vic to south-eastern Qld. **Leaves:** reduced to tiny scales. **Flowers:** GREENISH YELLOW, 2-3mm long, on brownish wiry branches. **Flowering time:** summer. **Name:** *nuda* = Lat. naked.

Stackhousia spathulata

—See COASTAL AND ESTUARINE SPECIES.

Stackhousia viminea Smith

Ss, Castl, Cumb

A slender erect herb to 70cm tall, found in heathland and moist pastures. Widespread and fairly common in the area.

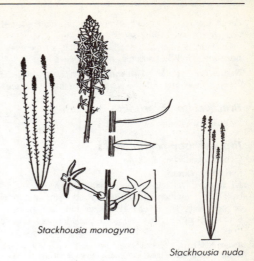

Stackhousia monogyna

Stackhousia nuda

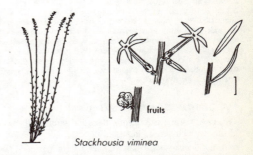

Stackhousia viminea

Range: NSW coast and ranges, Qld, Vic, NT and WA. **Leaves:** slender, 10-25mm long, mainly on the lower part of the stems. **Flowers:** YELLOW, about 4mm long. **Flowering time:** November-March. **Name:** *viminea* = Lat. of a *vimen*, a switch or twig, referring to the slender stems.

STERCULIACEAE

A large family with about 1200 species, in 70 genera, mainly distributed in the tropics and subtropics. There are 176 species in Australia, in 23 genera, present in all states.

The flowers of some local genera lack petals (*Lasiopetalum, Seringia, Brachychiton*). Some genera have stamens which open by pores at their tips. Staminodes (sterile stamens with a petal-like texture) are often present.

• *Brachychiton* Schott & Endlicher

(brack-ee-KY-tun)

A genus of mainly tropical trees with 30 species in Australia, distributed in all mainland states.

Aborigines used the inner bark of *Brachychiton* (and *Commersonia*) as a source of fibre for nets and twines. *Brachychiton* seeds were eaten raw or roasted, after removing the seed coats ('a nut of the highest quality' when roasted[38]). The seeds also make an acceptable coffee substitute when deeply roasted and ground. Flame Trees provide the largest and hence the best eating seeds.

Each carpel, when fertilised, develops into a large woody boat-shaped follicle, containing many large seeds.

Name: *Brachychiton* = Gk. *brachys*, short, *chiton*, an outer covering, referring to the loose outer covering of the seed.

Brachychiton acerifolius
—See RAINFORESTS.

Brachychiton populneum
(Schott & Endlicher) R. Brown

Kurrajong **Cumb**

An attractive symmetrical tree 10-20m tall with smooth grey bark. Fairly common on the Cumberland Plain, in dry clay or rocky soils. The inner bark was an important source of fibre for Aborigines. They also ate the yam-like roots of young trees.

Range: NSW coast, ranges and inland areas, and southern Qld, mainly on the western side of the Great Dividing Range. A popular street tree. **Leaves:** entire or 3(rarely 5)-lobed, hairless, fairly tough, 6-12cm long, shiny, slightly paler below, on long slender stalks, with a long drawn-out tip. Some trees are partly deciduous in early summer. **Flowers:** unisexual, CREAM, throat flecked with red and yellow, bell-shaped, 1-2cm wide, petals absent; in axillary panicles. **Fruit:** a boat-shaped woody follicle 4-7cm long. **Flowering time:** summer. **Name:** *populneum* = Poplar-like, from the similarity of the leaves to European Poplar species. 'Kurrajong' is a local Aboriginal name which seems to refer to the fibre, rather than the tree, since it is used for other fibre-producing species (e.g. *Hibiscus heterophyllus*).

• *Commersonia* J.R. & G. Forster
A mainly tropical genus of small trees and shrubs with about 13 species, including 12 in Australia.

Name: *Commersonia* = after Philibert Commerson (1728-1773), French botanist on the Bougainville expedition of 1766. He died during the voyage, so his many new species were named by others.

Commersonia fraseri J. Gay
Black-fellow's Hemp **Ss, Rf**

A leafy shrub or small tree mostly 3-6m tall, found in moist forest along the banks of the Nepean River, and rarely on the Hawkesbury River. It quickly colonises disturbed ground and also occurs on the edges of rainforest.

The inner bark was used by Aborigines as a source of fibre for nets and twine.

Range: mainly coastal districts north from Vic into Qld. **Leaves:** soft, thin, toothed, often lobed, often with many holes caused by insects, pale below with a layer of fine felt; on rusty felty stems. Juvenile leaves may be enormous, to 30cm long. **Flowers:** WHITE, 8-10mm wide, with broad sepals and slender petals almost lost amongst the numerous petal-like staminodes; in fairly dense axillary panicles. **Flowering time:** spring. **Fruit:** a capsule covered in long bristles. **Name:** *fraseri* = in honour of Charles Fraser, the first official superintendent of the Royal Botanic Gardens, Sydney.

• *Lasiopetalum* Smith
Rusty Petals

An endemic genus with 37 species, distributed in all states

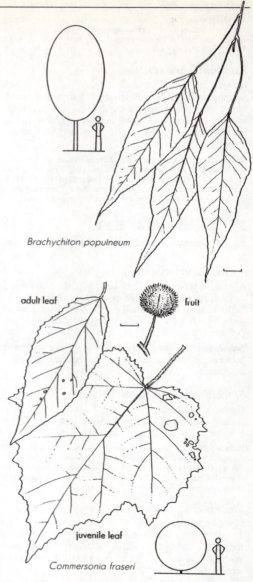

Brachychiton populneum

adult leaf   fruit

juvenile leaf

Commersonia fraseri

except NT, with the majority in south-western WA. The stamens open by pores at their tips.

Name: *Lasiopetalum* = Gk. woolly petals.

Lasiopetalum ferrugineum Smith
var. *ferrugineum*

Rusty Petals **Ss**

An erect rusty shrub to 1.5m high, common in woodland. The flowers appear to be permanently withered because of their rusty colour and shy drooping habit.

Range: NSW coast and Blue Mountains. **Leaves:** linear to lanceolate, dark green above, with recurved margins, densely covered below with rusty star-hairs on a background of fine pale star-hairs. The juvenile leaves are quite different, being broad and lobed at the base. **Flowers:** segments about 5mm long, densely rusty-hairy outside, pale inside with fine felt; in small dense cymes drooping beneath the leaves. **Flowering time:** spring. **Name:** *ferrugineum* = Lat. rust-coloured.

Lasiopetalum ferrugineum Smith
var. *cordatum* Bentham
Ss
An erect or spreading shrub to 1m tall. Basically a mountain species, but it occurs in Excelsior Park, Baulkham Hills. Differs from var. *ferrugineum* by having leaves which are heart-shaped at the base.

Name: *cordatum* = Lat. heart-shaped.

Lasiopetalum joyceae Blakely
Ss   Rare 2RC-
An erect shrub to 1.5m tall. Found in heath. Uncommon. Restricted to the northern parts of the area, e.g. Berowra, Ku-ring-gai Chase NP, Annangrove.

Range: restricted to the Sydney area.   **Leaves:** linear, otherwise similar to *L. ferrugineum*.   **Flowers:** segments 8-10mm long, FLESH-coloured to strongly RED, with a fine layer of star-hairs outside and apparently hairless inside. Similar to those of *L. rufum*, but more than twice as large.   **Flowering time:** spring.   **Name:** *joyceae* = named by William Blakely in memory of his adopted daughter, Joyce Blakely, 'who was the first to bring this beautiful species under my notice'.

Lasiopetalum macrophyllum Graham
(previously *L. dasyphyllum*)   **Ss**
A leafy shrub 1-2m high, found in moist sheltered gullies near streams. Uncommon to rare in the area, in gullies running into the Hawkesbury River (in Ku-ring-gai Chase and Marramarra National Parks); also Georges River (but more common in the Blue Mountains).

Range: NSW coast and ranges, Vic and Tas.   **Leaves:** large 8-12cm long, soft, untoothed, hairless above, with a dense layer of pale star-hairs below, and rusty veins.   **Flowers:** similar to *L. ferrugineum*, in dense head-like cymes, segments densely rusty-felty outside, pale green and hairless inside (this last feature is important to distinguish it from other species).   **Flowering time:** September-October.   **Name:** *macrophyllum* = Gk. large-leaved.

Lasiopetalum parviflorum Rudge
Cumb, Ss
An erect shrub 50-100cm high, found in open forest on clay soils on the Cumberland Plain and adjacent sandstone areas. Not common. Similar to *L. ferrugineum* var. *ferrugineum*, but smaller in all its parts.

Range: NSW coastal districts.   **Leaves:** linear, about 3mm wide (though occasionally similar in size and shape to *L. ferrugineum*). The juvenile

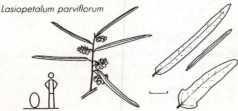

Lasiopetalum parviflorum

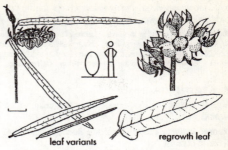

Lasiopetalum ferrugineum var. *ferrugineum*

leaf variants   regrowth leaf

Lasiopetalum ferrugineum var. *cordatum*

Lasiopetalum joyceae

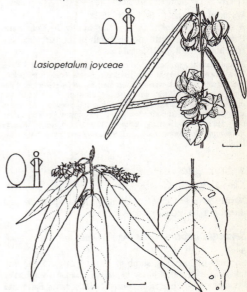

Lasiopetalum macrophyllum

leaves are broad and lobed.   **Flowers:** segments about 3mm long, pale-rusty hairy outside, pale and hairless inside.   **Flowering time:** October.   **Name:** *parviflorum* = Lat. small-flowered.

Lasiopetalum rufum R. Brown ex Bentham
Ss
A slender erect shrub to 1.5m high, found in heath and woodland on sandstone. Fairly common in the area. Similar

to *L. ferrugineum* var. *ferrugineum*, except the flowers are reddish and the leaves are always narrow.

Range: restricted to the Sydney area. **Leaves:** linear, otherwise similar to *L. ferrugineum.* **Flowers:** lobes about 5mm long, REDDISH or PINKISH on both sides, covered in fine hairs (both glandular and star-hairs). **Flowering time:** spring. **Name:** *rufum* = Lat. reddish.

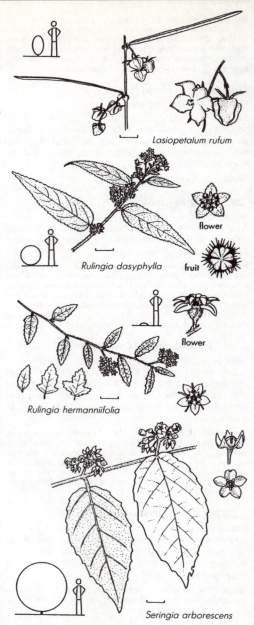

Lasiopetalum rufum

flower

Rulingia dasyphylla   *fruit*

flower

Rulingia hermanniifolia

Seringia arborescens

• *Rulingia* R. Brown

A genus with about 25 species, mainly Australian, with a few in Madagascar.

Name: *Rulingia* = after Dr Johann Rueling (born 1741), a German botanist.

Rulingia dasyphylla (Andrews) Sweet

(previously *R. pannosa*) Kerrawang **Ss**

An erect or low and spreading shrub 50cm-2m high, very hairy in all its parts. Found in sheltered woodland. Uncommon in the area, mainly on sandstone, but also on clay.

Range: NSW coast, ranges and western slopes, Qld and Vic. **Leaves:** 3-7cm long, toothed, deeply veined, hairy both sides. **Flowers:** similar to *R. hermaniifolia* except the petals and sepals are hairy and the white staminodes are curled up to enfold the anthers. The fruits are covered in rigid prickles. **Flowering time:** spring. **Name:** *dasyphylla* = Gk. thick-leaved. Kerrawang is an Aboriginal name of uncertain origin.

Rulingia hermanniifolia

(J. Gay ex De Candolle) Steetz

Wrinkled Kerrawang **Ss Rare 3RCa**

A small prostrate shrub with stems mostly 20-30cm long. Found in coastal heath, mainly south of the harbour. Very common in the Royal National Park.

Range: restricted to the Sydney area, and extending down the south coast. **Leaves:** 10-25mm long, wrinkled, crenate, finely hairy below, with or without lobes, with recurved margins. **Flowers:** about 4mm wide, in small cymes, with WHITE sepals and white petals (which are inconspicuous and folded back in the middle of the flower), red anthers and red staminodes (these are strangely shaped organs appearing below the stamens). **Flowering time:** spring (from July). **Name:** *hermanniifolia* = *Hermannia*-leaved. *Hermannia* is a genus in the same family.

• *Seringia* J. Gay (ser-INJ-ee-a)

A genus with 1 species.

Name: *Seringia* = after N. C. Séringe, a French professor and director of the botanic gardens at Lyons.

Seringia arborescens (Aiton) Druce

Ss

An erect or spreading shrub to 2-4m, occasionally to 8m, tall. Found in moist forest in valleys and on river banks. Uncommon in the area. Recorded from Norton's Basin and along the Hawkesbury River. The leaves closely resemble *Commersonia fraseri.*

Range: NSW coasts into Qld and NG. **Leaves:** 4-10cm long, drooping, soft, thin, toothed, pale below with a layer of fine pale or rusty felt. **Flowers:** segments about 4mm long, CREAM, finely felty both sides, petals absent; arranged in leaf-opposed or terminal cymes. **Flowering time:** spring-summer. **Name:** *arborescens* = Lat. tending to a tree.

STYLIDIACEAE

A family with 170 species in 6 genera mainly distributed in Australia, with a few species in east Asia (to India), NG, NZ and the southern tip of South America. Australia has 165 species in 5 genera, mainly concentrated in south-western WA, where over 100 endemic species exist.

• *Stylidium* Swartz & Willdenow

Trigger Plants

A genus of perennial herbs with about 136 species, distributed in all states and extending to South-east Asia and NZ.

Trigger plants are famous for their animated method of pollination. The style and 2 anthers are joined together in a tube which is elastic and sensitive. Normally it is bent back behind the flowers, but when the centre of the flower is touched by an insect, it flies upwards and strikes the insect like a little hammer, showering it with pollen. The column resets itself, usually within 20 minutes. The flowers are PINK, fading to mauve. They have 5 petals, 1 of which is inconspicuous.

Name: *Stylidium* = Gk. little-style.

Stylidium graminifolium Swartz ex Willdenow

Trigger Plant   **Ss, Castl, Cumb**

A tufted herb with grass-like leaves, found in moist forest situations. Common in the area, in sheltered forests on sandstone and clay soils, but not on Hawkesbury sandstone.

Range: NSW coast, ranges and western slopes, Qld, Vic, Tas and SA. **Leaves:** 1-2mm wide, erect, moderately stiff, variable in length.   **Flowers:** PINK, in a tall terminal spike.   **Flowering time:** August-January.   **Name:** *graminifolium* = Lat. grass-leaved. Often called 'Jack-in-the-box' in colonial times.   **Note:** this is a complex species with a variety of forms over its range.

Stylidium laricifolium A. Richard

Giant Trigger Plant   **Ss**

An erect herb, 20-120cm tall with more or less woody stems densely covered in short leaves. Fairly common in the area, in sheltered forests on sandstone.

Range: NSW coast and ranges, Qld and Vic.   **Leaves:** linear, soft, very dense on the stem.   **Flowers:** PINK, stalked, in a terminal panicle. **Flowering time:** spring.   **Name:** *laricifolium* = Lat. Larch-leaved.

Stylidium lineare Swartz

Heath Trigger Plant   **Ss**

A minute tufted herb 10-20cm, occasionally to 40cm, tall. Found in open sunny heath country, usually growing in moss on sandstone shelves, but sometimes in sheltered forest. Fairly common in the area.

Range: NSW coast and ranges south from Sydney.   **Leaves:** under 1mm wide, channelled above, mostly under 2cm long, in a dense tuft. **Flowers:** PINK, in a terminal spike, smaller than the other species.

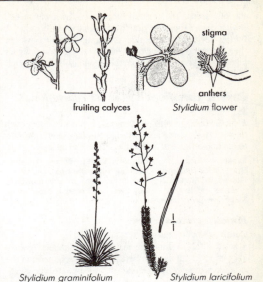

fruiting calyces   *Stylidium* flower   stigma   anthers

Stylidium graminifolium   *Stylidium laricifolium*

Flowering time: spring and summer.   **Name:** *lineare* = Lat. straight, referring to the narrow leaves.

Stylidium productum Hindmarsh & D. Blaxell

(previously included in *S. graminifolium*)

Trigger Plant   **Ss**

Similar to *S. graminifolium*, except the leaf tufts are located at the end of sprawling aerial stems. Fairly common in the area, but only on Hawkesbury sandstone. Young plants, whose stems have not yet elongated, can be hard to distinguish from *S. graminifolium**.

Range: restricted to the Sydney area.   **Leaves:** similar to *S. graminifolium*.   **Flowers:** as for *S. graminifolium*.   **Flowering time:** November-January.   **Name:** *productum* = Lat. elongated; referring to the elongated stem.

* If you have a microscope, *S. productum* has stomata in 2 rows, only on the leaf undersides, while *S. graminifolium* has stomata on both sides.

THYMELAEACEAE

A family of trees or shrubs with about 500 species in 45 genera, widely distributed in the tropics and temperate regions of the world. There are about 90 species in 8 genera in Australia. The family includes the sweet-smelling genus *Daphne*.

• *Pimelea* Banks & Solander ex Gaertner

Rice Flowers

A genus of shrubs with about 85 species worldwide. There are about 65 species in Australia, the remainder in NZ and extending through South-east Asia.

Judging by the white tubular flowers, the agents of pollination must be night-flying moths.

The bark is fibrous and very tough. Early settlers used it as a binding in place of twine.

Name: *Pimelea* = Gk. *pimele*, soft fat, probably referring to

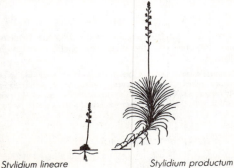

Stylidium lineare   *Stylidium productum*

the oily seeds. The humble Rice Flower narrowly missed having one of the most distinguished names in botany. J.R. Forster first described it under the name *Banksia*. However, the German botanist Gaertner realised this name was already taken and chose *Pimelea* from the unpublished manuscripts of Dr Solander.

Pimelea curviflora R. Brown ssp. *curviflora*

Ss

A small erect shrub to 30-50cm tall, found in undergrowth in woodland. A rare and endangered plant, occurring only to the immediate east and south of Frenchs Forest.

Range: restricted to the above area. **Leaves:** alternate, lanceolate, covered below (and on stems) with long hairs, and with recurved margins. **Flowers:** BROWN-GREEN sepals with red centres and a red tube which is curved and hairy; in axillary clusters. **Flowering time:** spring. **Name:** *curviflora* = Lat. curved-flowers.

Pimelea glauca R. Brown

Cumb (Not illustrated)

A small shrub to 1m high, mainly found amongst grasses in open forest on the Cumberland Plain. Uncommon in the area. It resembles *P. linifolia* except the leaves are blue-green.

Range: NSW coast, ranges and inland areas, Qld, Vic, Tas and SA. **Leaves:** blue-green, otherwise resembling those of *P. linifolia* **Flowers:** WHITE to CREAM, resembling those of *P. linifolia* except the inner bracts have hairy margins and the perianth tube is hairless at the base. **Name:** *glauca* = Lat. blue-green.

Pimelea latifolia R. Brown ssp. *hirsuta*

(Meisner) Threlfall **Ss**

A small erect shrub to 40cm tall, found amongst undergrowth in woodland. Rare or possibly extinct in the area. Recorded in the past from the western side of Pittwater.

Range: NSW coast and ranges. **Leaves:** alternate, small, elliptical, covered in long hairs. **Flowering time:** September-October. **Flowers:** GREENISH YELLOW, 4-8mm long. **Name:** *latifolia* = Lat. broad-leaved; *hirsuta* = Lat. hairy.

Pimelea ligustrina ssp. *hypericina*

—See RAINFOREST SPECIES.

Pimelea linifolia Smith ssp. *linifolia*

Rice Flower **Ss, Castl**

A small graceful shrub to 50cm high. Abundant throughout the area in sunny places in heath and woodland. Its common occurrence is due to a thick woody rootstock (lignotuber) which allows quick recovery from fire.

Range: NSW coast, ranges and inland areas, also Qld, Vic, Tas and SA. **Leaves:** opposite, 2-ranked, soft, thin, erect. **Flowers:** WHITE (sometimes pink), with orange anthers, softly hairy, especially at the base; in dense terminal heads protected in bud by 2 rows of leaf-like bracts, which remain visible below the flowering heads. **Flowering time:** most of the year. **Name:** *linifolia* = Lat. straight-leaved. Granny's Bonnet, Queen of the Bush, Tough Bark are some of the common names used in other states.

Pimelea spicata R. Brown

Cumb Endangered 3E

A small slender erect shrub 20-50cm tall, found amongst grasses in open forest on clay soils. A rare species. There

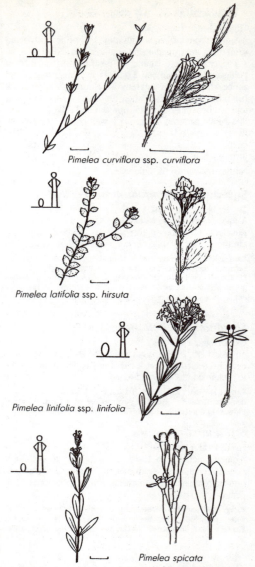

Pimelea curviflora ssp. *curviflora*

Pimelea latifolia ssp. *hirsuta*

Pimelea linifolia ssp. *linifolia*

Pimelea spicata

are only 2 known viable populations, one at Narellan Cemetery and Golfcourse and the other near Shellharbour in the Illawarra.

Range: restricted to the above locations (although once more widespread on the Cumberland Plain). **Leaves:** opposite, thin, soft, erect, hairless. **Flowers:** about 7mm long, in a short terminal spike, sepals WHITE with pink margins. **Flowering time:** summer. **Name:** *spicata* = having a spike.

• Wikstroemia Endlicher

A genus of shrubs with about 70 species distributed in China, Indo-China and the Pacific.

Wikstroemia is especially distinguished from *Pimelea* by the presence of 8 stamens.

Name: *Wikstroemia* = after Johan Emanuel Wikström (1789-1856), a Swedish botanist who did much work on this family.

Wikstroemia indica (Linnaeus) C. A. Meyer
Ss
An erect shrub to 1.5m high, found in woodland, in sheltered places near the sea. An uncommon species in the area, only recorded north of the harbour (e.g. Narrabeen, Hawkesbury). The fruit are shiny red drupes about 8mm wide.

Range: northern WA, NT, Qld and north coast of NSW. Sydney is its southern limit. **Leaves:** hairless, thin and soft, opposite, more or less flat. **Flowers:** GREEN, about 9mm long and 8mm wide, hairless, a few in a terminal head. **Flowering time:** summer. **Name:** *indica* = Lat. Indian (i.e. from the East Indies).

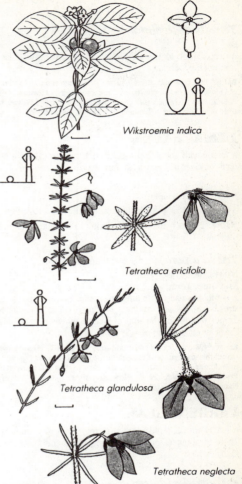

Wikstroemia indica

Tetratheca ericifolia

Tetratheca glandulosa

Tetratheca neglecta

TREMANDRACEAE

An endemic family with 43 species in 3 genera, mostly restricted to south-western WA.

• *Tetratheca* Smith
Black-eyed Susans
A genus of small heathy shrubs with rich purple flowers 'brightening and perfuming many a dreary waste of bush and scrub.'[38] There are 39 species, distributed in all states except NT.

Name: *Tetratheca* = Gk. *tetra*, four, *theke*, box, referring to the unusual 4-celled anthers. 'To this pretty genus, three species of which have been sent from New South Wales, we have given the name *Tetratheca*, on account of the curious structure of its antherae, each of which consists of four cells, communicating with one common tube, the excretory duct of the pollen.'[39]

Tetratheca ericifolia Smith
Ss
A small erect shrub to 50cm tall, common in heath and woodland north of the harbour.

Range: Woronora Plateau north to Myall Lakes, also a small population in the Blue Mountains. **Leaves:** in whorls of 3, rather blunt, linear, scabrous, with recurved minutely toothed margins. Stems with stiff appressed hairs. **Flowers:** ROSE-PURPLE, with hairless stalks, 2 ovules in each of 2 loci (i.e. 4 seeds). **Flowering time:** spring. **Name:** *ericifolia* = Lat. *Erica*-leaved. *Erica* is the European Heather.

Tetratheca glandulosa Smith
Ss Vulnerable 2VC-
A small erect or spreading shrub to 50cm high, found in heath and woodland north of the harbour.

Range: restricted to Sydney's north shore, and an area north of the Hawkesbury River. **Leaves:** opposite, linear, scabrous, with revolute, toothed margins. **Flowers:** ROSE-PURPLE, with small glandular hairs on the sepals and stalk. **Flowering time:** spring. **Name:** *glandulosa* = Lat. having glands, referring to the glandular hairs.

Tetratheca neglecta J. Thompson
Ss Rare 3RC-
An erect shrub 15-50cm high, found in heath and woodland

in the Royal National Park, Heathcote National Park and lower Georges River area.

Range: restricted to the above area and small populations in the southern Blue Mountains and on the plateau inland from Wollongong. **Leaves:** in whorls of 6, pointed, linear, with revolute margins. Stems without stiff appressed hairs. **Flowers:** ROSE-PURPLE, sepals hairless or glandular hairy, stalk hairless, 1 ovule in each of 2 loci (i.e. 2 seeds). **Flowering time:** spring. **Name:** *neglecta* = Lat. neglected (it was first recognised in 1976).

Tetratheca shiressii Blakely
Ss
A slender ascending shrub to 1m high, found in heath and woodland south from Botany Bay.

Range: there are 2 populations, one mainly in the Royal National Park, the other north of the Hawkesbury. **Leaves:** usually with 2 distinct types on each plant; one is broad, whorled, finely hairy, the other is linear, opposite, hairless, soft. **Flowers:** ROSE-PURPLE, sepals and stalk hairless. **Flowering time:** spring. **Name:** *shiressii* = named by W.F. Blakely in honour of his personal friend David Shiress (1862-1944), an accountant,

who accompanied him on many collecting trips in the Sydney area in
the 1920s.

Tetratheca thymifolia Smith

Ss

An erect shrub to 1m tall, common in heath and woodland
north of the harbour.

Range: NSW coast and ranges, Qld and Vic.   **Leaves:** broad, in whorls
of 4-6, with recurved margins, covered in scabrous hairs.   **Flowers:** ROSE-
PURPLE, with finely hairy (not glandular) sepals and stalk.   **Flowering
time:** June-November.   **Name:** *thymifolia* = Lat. Thyme-leaved.

ULMACEAE Elms

A family with about 200 species in 18 genera. There are 5
native species in 3 genera in Australia.

• *Trema* Loureiro

A genus with 15 species, including 2 species native to Australia.

Name: *Trema* = Gk. a hole, refering to the pitted stone of
the fruit.

Trema aspera (Brongniart) Blume

Native Peach, Poison Peach

Ss, Cumb, Temp Rf

A shrub or small tree 3-6m high, found in moist forests on
stream banks. Fairly common in the area. The fine-grained
timber, resembling the elms of Europe, was used in colonial
times for making gun-powder charcoal.

Range: NSW coast, ranges and inland areas, Qld and NT.   **Leaves:** two-
ranked, thin-textured, rough to touch, toothed.   **Flowers:** inconspicuous;
male, female, and bisexual flowers are mixed in short axillary racemes.
Fruit: a small black drupe.   **Flowering time:** November-February.
Name: *aspera* = Lat. rough.

VERBENACEAE

A family with about 3000 species in 75 genera worldwide.
There are about 62 species in 17 genera in Australia, including
many exotics.

• *Clerodendrum* Linnaeus

A genus with about 400 species worldwide, including 13
species native in Australia.

Name: *Clerodendron* = Gk. chance-tree, referring to the dicey
medicinal properties of certain species.

Clerodendrum tomentosum R. Brown

Hairy Clerodendrum   **Ss, Temp Rf**

A shrub 2-4m tall, found in moist gullies and rainforest
margins. The seeds are carried long distances by birds. Young
plants (easily recognised by their dark, soft, furry, slightly
lobed leaves) are a common sight in gullies and dense scrubs.
However, most fail before maturity, unless the situation is
suitably humid. Mature flowering plants are much less
common.

The agents of pollination are night flying moths. At fruiting
time the calyx becomes swollen, red and fleshy, holding the
large black shiny drupe in its centre.

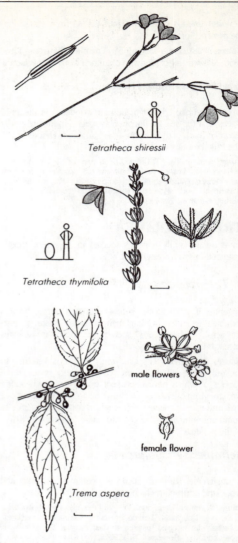

Tetratheca shiressii

Tetratheca thymifolia

male flowers

female flower

Trema aspera

Range: NSW coast and ranges, Qld and WA.   **Leaves:** opposite, dark
green; when young they are soft, thin, furry below and often with a
few shallow lobes; when adult the leaves are hairless, often glossy, thicker
and harsher.   **Flowers:** WHITE, with a long slim tube and 5 spreading
segments and 4 stamens on long filaments; arranged in dense terminal
corymbs.   **Flowering time:** October-November.   **Name:** *tomentosum*
= Lat. felty, referring to the furry undersides of new leaves.

• *Chloanthes* R. Brown

An endemic genus of 4 species; 1 in south-west WA, 1 in
the Blue Mountains, and 2 scattered in NSW and Qld.

Some authors place this genus in its own family—
Chloanthaceae.

Name: *Chloanthes* = Gk. grass-flower, from the greenish
flowers.

Note: Two other species occur just outside the area.
• *C. glandulosa:* found entirely in the Blue Mountains; leaves 5-7cm long, corolla greenish yellow.
• *C. parviflora:* found north-west and south of the Sydney area and widely scattered in NSW and Qld; recognised by the stamens and style being completely hidden in the pale mauve corolla.

Chloanthes stoechadis R. Brown

Ss

A straggling shrub with stems 30-60cm long and caterpillar-like leaves. Found in heath and woodland, scattered in the area, but only common in coastal heath (e.g. Royal National Park).

Range: NSW coast and ranges north from the Budawang Ranges; also north-western slopes, scattered in Qld and rare in WA. **Leaves:** opposite, dull, olive-green, ruggedly wrinkled, usually 1-4cm long, with stiff hairs above and densely white woolly hairs below. **Flowers:** GREENISH YELLOW, axillary, solitary, 20-35mm long. **Flowering time:** spring. **Name:** *stoechadis* = after *Lavandula stoechas*, French Lavender, from the similar leaves.

• *Lantana* Linnaeus

A genus of tropical shrubs native to South America and Africa, now cosmopolitan weeds. There are 3 species naturalised in Australia.

Name: *Lantana* = Lat. *lentus*, flexible, originally given to *Viburnum lantana*, the Pliant Mealy Tree.

*Lantana camara** Linnaeus

Lantana **Ss, Cumb**
A dense spreading shrub 2-4m high, with stiff prickly stems. Introduced from tropical South America as a garden plant and now a widespread and common pest, often forming dense thickets in disturbed areas. While undoubtedly a serious pest in most areas, there are some situations, especially around

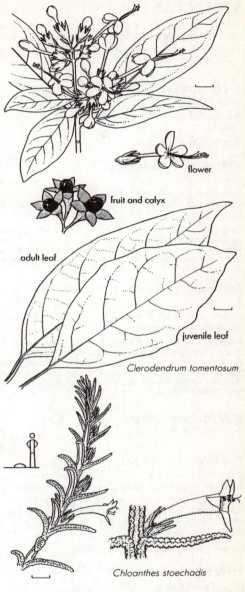

flower

fruit and calyx

adult leaf

juvenile leaf

Clerodendrum tomentosum

Chloanthes stoechadis

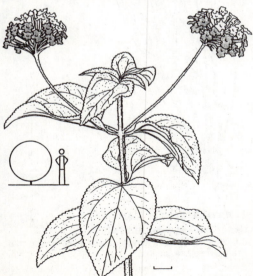

Lantana camara*

rainforests, when it is benevolent, forming protective barriers against incursions by humans, animals and herbaceous weeds.

Range: coastal NSW, Qld, NT, South America, and naturalised in many parts of the world **Leaves:** opposite, rough, soft, thin-textured, finely toothed, and with a distinctive odour. The weak branches are covered in short prickles. **Flowers:** very pretty, in dense mixed YELLOW-ORANGE-RED heads on long axillary stems. **Fruits:** grey or black fleshy spheres in a dense cluster, commonly believed to be poisonous, however the Cribbs report them to be edible with a pleasant flavour.[40] **Flowering time:** spring-summer. **Name:** *camara* = so called by the Tupian indians of the Amazon.

VIOLACEAE

A family of herbs, shrubs and a few climbers, with about 900 species in 22 genera, mainly in temperate regions of the world. Australia has about 26 species in 3 genera.

The family is related to Flacourtiaceae.

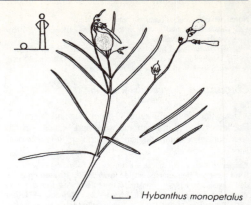

- ### *Hybanthus* Jacquin
Spade Flowers
A genus with about 150 species, including 10 in mainland Australia.

Name: *Hybanthus* = Gk. hump-flower.

Hybanthus monopetalus
(Roemer & Schultes) Domin

(previously *Hybanthus filiformis*) **Ss**
A small erect shrub 10-30cm tall, common in woodland, usually in rather sheltered sites.

Range: coast, ranges and inland areas throughout eastern mainland Australia. **Leaves:** upper ones opposite, lower ones alternate, 1-3mm wide, 10-60mm long, usually rather soft. **Flowers:** BLUE-MAUVE, few in a short terminal raceme. **Flowering time:** September-November. **Name:** *monopetalus* = Lat. single-petalled.

Hybanthus monopetalus

Hybanthus vernonii (F. Mueller) F. Mueller
Ss
A small erect shrub 30-50cm tall, common in woodland, usually in rather sheltered sites.

Range: coast and ranges south from Sydney into Victoria. **Leaves:** 1-3mm, occasionally to 5mm, wide, 20-40mm long, rather soft, generally broader and more crowded than *H. monopetalus.* **Flowers:** BLUE-MAUVE, solitary in the axils of leaves. **Flowering time:** September-December. **Name:** *vernonii* = after Mr W. Vernon, a Sydney horticulturist, who collected the type species.

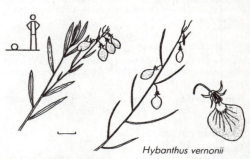

Hybanthus vernonii

- ### *Hymenanthera*
—See RAINFOREST SPECIES.

- ### *Viola* Linnaeus (VY-ola)
A genus of small herbs with about 450 species worldwide. There are 5 species to Australia, and 3 species naturalised, including *V. odorata,* the Sweet Violet of Europe, a plant much enjoyed for its scent. William Woolls considered our species 'destitute of scent', but A. G. Hamilton was able to detect some perfume on *V. hederacea.*

Name: *Viola* = the Latin name for the plants.

Viola betonicifolia Smith
Purple Violet **Cumb**
A small tufted herb, rare in the area, found mainly in moist shady pastures on the Cumberland Plain.

Range: coast, ranges and inland slopes throughout eastern Australia; also widespread in Asia. **Leaves:** usually erect, soft, toothed, arrow-head shaped. **Flowers:** RICH ROSE-PURPLE, with a white area at the centre. **Flowering time:** August-December. **Name:** *betonicifolia* = *Betonica*-leaved (a small genus in Lamiaceae).

Viola betonicifolia

Viola hederacea Labillardière
Native Violet **Ss, Temp Rf, STRf**
A pretty creeping herb, forming carpets in almost any moist shady place. Abundant locally.

Range: NSW coast and ranges (except the northern tablelands), Qld, Vic, Tas, SA and Malaya. **Leaves:** soft, toothed, hairless, paler below, mostly 1-3cm wide. **Flowers:** WHITE with PURPLE markings, petals 8-

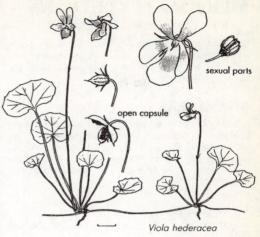

sexual parts

open capsule

Viola hederacea

10mm long. 'Although Australian violets are supposed to be scentless, this species is an exception, as on warm days, particularly when the air is moisture-laden, it has a very strong scent.'[41] **Flowering time:** densely in spring, but some flowers are present for much of the year. **Name:** *hederacea* = Ivy-like. *Hedera* is the Ivy genus (Araliaceae). **Similar species:** easily confused with *Dichondra repens*, Kidney Weed, a species in Convolvulaceae, but that never has toothed leaves.

Viola sieberana Sprengel

Tiny Violet **Ss**

A dwarf creeping herb, similar to *Viola hederacea*, except smaller in all its parts. It occurs in a wide range of habitat, from open moist heathland to rainforest margins. Locally restricted to the Royal National Park and Woronora Plateau.

Range: coastal areas south from Sydney, southern tablelands, Tas and SA. It is very common in Vic. **Leaves:** toothed, blades 10-15mm long, 10-20mm wide. **Flowers:** WHITE and PURPLE, petals about 5mm wide. **Flowering time:** September-December. **Name:** *sieberana* = after Franz Wilhelm Sieber of Prague, Bohemia, who collected extensively in Australia from 1819-23, spending 7 months in NSW. **Note:** There is a difference of opinion among botanists about whether this should be a subspecies of *V. hederacea*. The different leaf shape and chromosome number seem to support its separate status as a species.

VISCACEAE
—See MISTLETOES.

Viola sieberana

MONOCOTYLEDONS

Monocotyledons are a major division of flowering plants, characterised by the embryo having a single cotyledon (seed leaf). Most are herbs with leaves with parallel veins and flowering parts in 3s.

AGAVACEAE

A family of large perennial herbs with about 670 species in 20 genera, widespread in the tropics and sub-tropics. There are 7 species in Australia, in 5 genera, including *Cordyline*, *Dracaena* (the tropical Dragon's Blood Tree), *Agave* (introduced from the Americas) and *Phormium* (the Flax plant of NZ).

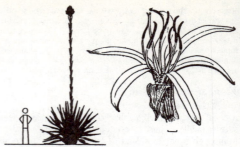

Doryanthes excelsa (large illustration on p. 2)

• *Doryanthes* Correa

An endemic genus with 3 species, restricted to NSW and Qld.

Name: *Doryanthes* = Gk. spear-flower.

Doryanthes excelsa Correa

Gymea Lily **Ss** (See page 2 for large illustration)
A colossal leafy herb with stiff flowering stem 3-4m tall bearing a dense cluster of large red flowers. Common around Sydney in rocky woodland. One of the most beautiful and striking flowering plants in the area. The stems and roots were consumed by Aborigines. 'These (flowering) stems are roasted and eaten by the Aborigines, who cut them for this purpose, when they are about a foot and a half high, and thicker than a man's arm. The Blacks also roast the roots and make them into a sort of cake, which they eat cold.'[1]

Range: NSW coast north from Sydney to Qld.   **Leaves:** erect, tufted, 1-2m long, to 10cm wide, thick and fleshy, fibrous.   **Flowers:** succulent, RED, about 10cm long, protected by deep red bracts in a tightly clustered head usually 30-40cm wide. Each flower contains a deep pool of clear sweet nectar.   **Flowering time:** June-September.   **Name:** *excelsa* = Lat. exceptional. Gymea was an Aboriginal name for this plant.

COMMELINACEAE

Dayflowers
A family with about 700 species in about 50 genera, mainly in the tropics. There are 29 species in 8 genera in Australia. Most are herbs with creeping, rooting stems. The flowers, with 3 fragile petals, only last 1 day. The stamens of the local native genera are unusual: instead of the usual 6, there are 3 fertile stamens and 2 small infertile stamens (staminodes), except for *Murdannia* which has 3 of each.

• *Aneilema*

—See RAINFOREST SPECIES.

• *Commelina* Linnaeus

A genus with about 230 species worldwide, and about 7 species in Australia.

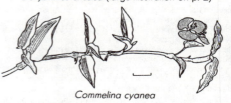

Commelina cyanea

Name: *Commelina*, after Johan and Caspar Commelin, seventeenth century Dutch botanists.

Commelina cyanea R. Brown

Creeping Christian, Scurvy Weed
Ss, Cumb, Temp Rf
A weak creeping herb with fragile blue flowers, common throughout the area in moist shady places. Sometimes a weed in gardens. When not flowering it is very similar to *Tradescantia albiflora* (Wandering Jew) but always has smaller, less crowded leaves. The young shoots can be cooked as a green vegetable.

Range: NSW coast and ranges, and Qld.   **Leaves:** soft, crisp and watery, usually folded and with wavy margins, arising from a closed sheath at the base, mostly 2-4cm long.   **Flowers:** about 15mm wide, fragile, RICH BLUE, with yellow anthers, a few arising from a folded green spathe.   **Flowering time:** warmer months of the year.   **Name:** *cyanea* = Lat. a rich mid-blue.

• *Murdannia* Royle

A genus of herbs with about 50 species widespread in the tropics. There are about 6 species in Australia, distributed in WA, NT, Qld and NSW.

Name: *Murdannia* = after Murdan Ali, an Indian plant collector and keeper of a herbarium at Saharunpore, northern India.

Murdannia graminea (R. Brown) Bruckner

Blue Murdannia **Cumb, Castl**
A grass-like herb to 50cm tall, found in marshy meadows in the Richmond district. The Cribbs note that although there is no record of the roots being used by Aborigines, they appear to be edible raw or cooked without any unpleasant flavour.[2]

Range: NSW coast and ranges and inland slopes north from Sydney, Qld, NT and WA.   **Leaves:** 3-6mm wide, to about 10cm long, grass-like. **Flowers:** fragile, MAUVE-PINK, 15-20mm wide, numerous in an open terminal panicle. **Flowering time:** summer. **Name:** *graminea* = Lat. grassy.

• *Pollia*
—See RAINFOREST SPECIES.

• *Tradescantia* Linnaeus
A genus of creeping herbs widespread in the Americas. One species is naturalised in Australia. *Tradescantia* are called Spiderworts in Britain because if the leaves are broken and the 2 parts drawn slowly away thread-like spiral vessels are visible, resembling a spider web.

Name: *Tradescantia* = after John Tradescant (died 1638), an English traveller and gardener.

*Tradescantia albiflora** Kunth
Wandering Jew, Creeping Christian
Ss, Cumb, Temp Rf
A weak but vigorously spreading creeping herb with white flowers. Widespread throughout the area in moist sheltered places. It is very intrusive in bush gullies near habitation, often swamping native vegetation. Common in gardens. A native of South America.

Range: NSW coast and Blue Mountains, Vic and South America. **Leaves:** soft, crisp and watery, rather oblong. **Flowers:** WHITE, fragile, in terminal clusters protected by broad leafy spathes. **Flowering time:** warmer months of the year. **Name:** *albiflora* = Lat. white flower.

ERIOCAULACEAE
Pipeworts
A family of about 1200 species in 12 genera worldwide, especially concentrated in tropical America. There are 20 species in a single genus in Australia.

• *Eriocaulon* Linnaeus
A genus with about 200 species widespread in the tropics and subtropics, including 20 species in Australia, distributed in all states except SA and Tas, with 4 species extending into tropical Asia.

Name: *Eriocaulon* = Gk. woolly-stem (but not on our species).

Eriocaulon scariosum Smith
Common Pipewort　**Cumb, Ss**
An unusual little herb with a tuft of short leaves and greyish ball-like flower heads on slender stalks 10-18cm tall. Found in sunny ground in marshy meadows and on creek banks, usually on richer soils. Uncommon but widely recorded in the area.

Range: NSW coast and ranges, Qld, Vic and NT. **Leaves:** to 4cm long, about 2.5mm wide, broad and sheathing at the base, tapering to the tip. **Flowers:** unisexual, in a greyish white globular head, the lower rows female, the upper rows male, all concealed by overlapping hairy scale bracts. **Flowering time:** spring-summer. **Name:** *scariosum* = Lat. dry and membranous, referring to the scale-bracts.

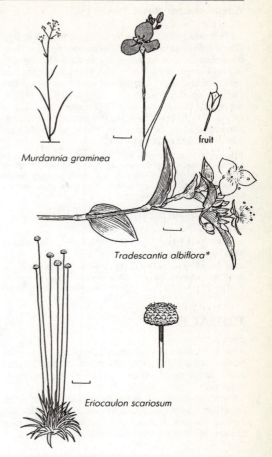

Murdannia graminea

fruit

Tradescantia albiflora*

Eriocaulon scariosum

HAEMODORACEAE
A family of herbs with about 100 species in 14 genera worldwide, including about 84 Australian species in 7 genera. All Australian genera except *Haemodorum* are restricted to south-west WA. The family includes *Anigozanthos* and *Macropidia*, the Kangaroo Paws of WA.

• *Haemodorum* Smith
A genus of perennial herbs with 21 species. Australia has 20 species, distributed in all states except Tas and SA. One species occurs in NG.

The roots are a brilliant orange-red colour. The leaves die off in late summer, but the distinctive dead black inflorescences remain stiffly erect until the following year. The method of pollination is a mystery since the black flowers seem to lack any means of attracting insects, and yet are not self-pollinated.

Name: *Haemodorum* = Gk. blood-gift, from the beautiful orange-red colour in the stem and roots.

Haemodorum corymbosum Vahl

Blood Root **Ss, Castl**

An erect tufted herb to about 50cm high, with black flowers. Common in moist open heath. The itinerant preacher James Backhouse found Aborigines eating the roots of this species in King George Sound, WA, in 1837. He wrote 'Among their articles of food is the long bulb *Haemodorum teretifolium* [sic], which they call Mean; and poor fare, it truly is, occasioning their tongues to crack grievously: it is prepared for eating by being roasted, and beaten up with the earth, from the inside of the nest of the White Ant, or with a red substance, found on burnt ground.'[3]

Range: Sydney area, south coast, Blue Mountains and southern tablelands. **Leaves:** cylindrical, smooth, somewhat fleshy. **Flowers:** REDDISH BLACK, in dense racemes arranged in a closely branched panicle. **Flowering time:** November. **Name:** *corymbosum* = Lat. having a corymb (a corymbose panicle).

Haemodorum planifolium R. Brown

Blood Root **Ss**

An erect herb 1-1.5m high with black flowers. Common in woodland, often on rocky sites.

Range: NSW coast and ranges, and Qld. **Leaves:** somewhat fleshy, more or less flat. **Flowers:** REDDISH BLACK, in dense racemes arranged on a tall widely branching panicle. **Flowering time:** October. **Name:** *planifolium* = Lat. flat-leaved.

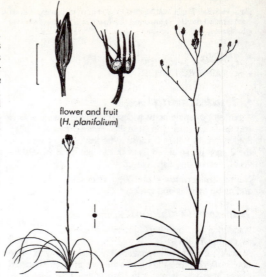

flower and fruit
(*H. planifolium*)

Haemodorum corymbosum   *Haemodorum planifolium*

IRIDACEAE

Irises, Patersonias

A family of tufted herbs with about 1800 species in 70 genera worldwide, especially concentrated in South Africa and Central and South America. There are 21 species in 7 genera native to Australia.

Many exotic members of the family have large attractive flowers and are popular garden plants. Some exotics, e.g. *Freesia, Watsonia, Romulea, Homeria, Ixia, Watsonia,* have become naturalised in urban bushland around Sydney.

Patersonia glabrata

• ***Libertia***—See RAINFOREST SPECIES.

• ***Patersonia*** R. Brown

A genus of grass-like herbs with tough, stiff leaves and large purple flowers which are fragile and short-lived. 'One, the most beautiful, was something like a small iris, of a pure ultra-marine blue, with smaller petals in the centre, most delicately pencilled; but ere I had gathered it five minutes, it had withered away, and I never could bring one home to make a drawing from. Surely it must have been some sensitive little fay, who, charmed into the form of a flower, might not bear the touch of a mortal hand!'[4]

There are about 18 species, mostly restricted to south-west WA, with a handful in eastern Australia, NG and South-east Asia.

Name: *Patersonia* = after Lieutenant-Colonel William Paterson (1755-1810) of the NSW Corps. He was appointed Lieutenant Governor of NSW in 1800, during which time he was wounded in a duel and took part in the Rum Rebellion. He was interested in botany, sent specimens to Joseph Banks, and administered Australia's first horticultural garden at Parramatta.

Patersonia glabrata R. Brown

Leafy Purple Flag **Ss**

A tufted herb with large purple flowers and stiff grass-like leaves to 20cm long, borne on a sprawling aerial stem. Common in heath and woodland on sandstone. Young plants, whose stems have not yet elongated, can only be distinguished from *P. sericea* by the hairless spathes. The old leaves curl prettily on the stem and often turn an attractive bronze colour.

Range: NSW coast and ranges, Qld and Vic. **Leaves:** 1.5-3mm wide, stiff, more or less erect. **Flowers:** PURPLE, 4-6cm wide, borne in a stiff more or less hairless spathe. **Flowering time:** September. **Name:** *glabrata* = Lat. hairless.

Patersonia longifolia R. Brown

Dwarf Purple Flag **Ss**

An erect tufted herb with stiff grass-like leaves and purple flowers. Found in heath and woodland on sandstone. Uncommon, occurring only north of the Harbour, e.g. Muogamarra Nature Reserve.

Range: NSW coast, Blue Mountains, southern tablelands and Vic.
Leaves: 1-2mm wide, often twisted. **Flowers:** PURPLE, borne in a short
woolly-hairy spathe. **Flowering time:** spring. **Name:** *longifolia* = Lat.
long-leaved.

Patersonia sericea R. Brown ex Ker

Silky Purple Flag **Ss, Castl**
A tufted herb with large purple flowers and stiff grass-like
leaves 25-40cm long. Common in heath and woodland on
sandstone.

Range: NSW coast, ranges and some inland slopes, Qld and Vic. **Leaves:**
3-5mm wide, stiff, erect. **Flowers:** PURPLE, 4-6cm wide, borne in a
stiff spathe covered in short silky hairs. **Flowering time:** September.
Name: *sericea* = Lat. silky.

Patersonia sp. aff. *fragilis*

Short Purple Flag **Ss**
An erect tufted herb with stiff grass-like leaves and small
purple flowers. Rare in the area. Recorded at Deep Creek,
Narrabeen. Distinguish from other species by the narrow
leaves and slender hairless spathe.

Range: NSW coast. **Leaves:** erect, 2-3mm wide, about 25cm long,
sometimes twisted. **Flowers:** PURPLE, 2-3cm wide, borne in a slender
hairless spathe. **Flowering time:** spring.

• *Watsonia* Millet

A genus of South African *Gladiolus*-like herbs with 9 species
introduced in Australia.

Name: *Watsonia* = after Sir William Watson (1715-1787),
an English botanist.

*Watsonia meriana** (Linnaeus) Millet
cultivar *Bulbillifera*

Wild Watsonia, Bugle Lily **Ss** (previously *W. angusta*?)
An erect perennial herb with flowering stem to 2m high. A
garden escape introduced from South Africa, now a serious
pest in urban bushland, forming dense colonies. The species
is a sterile hybrid which reproduces aggressively from brown
globular cormils which develop in clusters along the scape.

Range: NSW coast, South Africa. **Leaves:** strap-like, to 80cm long and
4cm wide. **Flowers:** APRICOT RED, drooping from a tall scape to 2m
high. **Flowering time:** October-December. **Name:** after Madame
Merian, possibly an 18th century plant enthusiast.

LILIACEAE

Lilies
A family of tufted perennial herbs with about 4000 species
in about 280 genera worldwide. In Australia there are about
266 species in 66 genera (202 species in 30 genera are native).

Most species (except *Crinum* and *Dianella*) are small herbs
that die back to underground tubers in winter.

Aborigines in other parts of Australia are recorded to have
consumed the roots of *Wurmbea, Bulbine bulbosa, Caesia
parviflora*, and *Arthropodium*, amongst other species.

There has always been disagreement about the boundaries
of this family, but extreme positions are now being taken
by the *Flora of Australia* (as followed here) and the *Flora
of NSW*. The latter creates several new families, while Liliaceae
itself is reduced to the single exotic genus *Lilium*, as follows.[5]

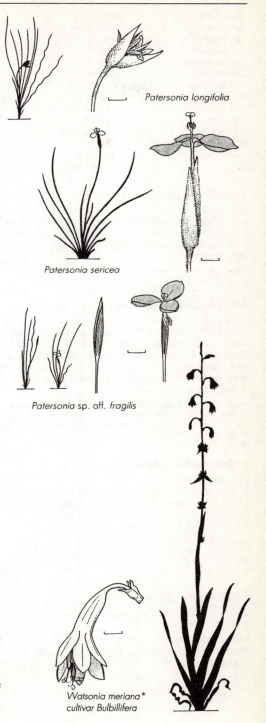

Patersonia longifolia

Patersonia sericea

Patersonia sp. aff. *fragilis*

Watsonia meriana *
cultivar Bulbillifera

Amaryllidaceae
  Crinum
Asparagaceae
  Myrsiphyllum
  Protasparagus
Blandfordiacea
  Blandfordia
Phormiaceae
  Dianella
  Stypandra
  Thelionema
Asphodeliaceae
  Bulbine

Anthericaceae
  Laxmannia
  Sowerbaea
  Caesia
  Tricoryne
  Thysantos
  Dichopogon
Hypoxidaceae
  Hypoxis
Uvulariaceae
  Schelhammera
Colchicaceae
  Wurmbea
  Burchardia

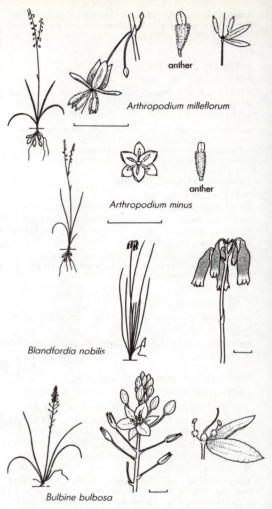

anther

Arthropodium milleflorum

anther

Arthropodium minus

Blandfordia nobilis

Bulbine bulbosa

• *Arthropodium* R. Brown

Vanilla Lilies

A genus of tufted herbs with 8 species worldwide. There are 4 species in Australia. The flowers do not twist after flowering. The dividing line between the 2 local species seems rather vague.

Name: *Arthropodium* = Gk. jointed foot, referring to the jointed pedicels.

Arthropodium milleflorum (Red.) Macbride

Pale Vanilla Lily **Cumb**

An erect grass-like herb 20-100cm high with small pale flowers with purple markings. Moderately common in the area, mainly in clay soils on the Cumberland Plain, in grassland. The roots (which are swollen only at the tips) are succulent and probably edible. Distinguish from *A. minus* by having 2 or more flowers at each node on the stem.

Range: NSW coast, ranges and inland areas, Qld, Vic, Tas and SA. **Leaves:** mostly 8-15mm wide. **Flowers:** 8-18mm wide, pedicels 8-15mm long, anthers 1-2mm long; usually 2-3 arising together on the flowering stem, anther filaments bearded. **Flowering time:** November-February. **Name:** *milleflorum* = Lat. thousand-flowered.

Arthropodium minus R. Brown

Small Vanilla Lily **Cumb**

An erect grass-like herb 20-50cm tall with tiny pale flowers with purple markings. Rare in the area, found in grassland on the Cumberland Plain. The roots (which are swollen right up to the base of the plant) are succulent and probably edible.

Range: NSW coast, ranges and inland areas, Qld, Vic, Tas and SA. **Leaves:** 3-5 mm wide. **Flowers:** 6-12mm wide, mostly solitary, anthers 0.5-1mm long, anther filaments bearded. **Flowering time:** August-December. **Name:** *minus* = Lat. lesser.

• *Blandfordia* Smith

An endemic genus of tufted herbs with 4 species, restricted to eastern Australia.

Name: *Blandfordia* = after George Spencer-Churchill, Marquis of Blandford, the fifth Duke of Marlborough, who kept a famous garden.

Blandfordia nobilis Smith

Christmas Bells **Ss**

An erect tufted herb with slender leaves and large bright bell-flowers. Common in moist open heath on sandstone. One of the most beautiful and popular of our local flowers. 'People who never go into the bush from one year's end to another come out at this time in search of the bells . . . For of all the flowers that grow there are none so dear to the heart of a Sydney-sider . . . '[6]

Range: Sydney area, south coast and southern tablelands. **Leaves:** 2-4mm wide. **Flowers:** tubular, ORANGE-RED becoming yellow at the tips. **Flowering time:** summer. **Fruit:** a large winged capsule, held erect. **Name:** *nobilis* = Lat. famous.

• *Bulbine* Willdenow (BULB-in-ee)

A genus of tufted herbs with about 50 species worldwide,

mainly in Africa. There are 5 Australian species, distributed in all states. The bulb is reported to be edible.

Name: *Bulbine* = Lat. bulbine, a name used by Pliny for a certain lily-plant, from Gk. *bolbos*, a bulb.

Bulbine bulbosa (R. Brown) Haworth

Golden Lily, Bulbine Lily **Cumb, Castl, Ss**
An erect tufted herb with succulent leaves and bright yellow flowers. Moderately common on clay soils on the Cumberland Plain, growing amongst grasses.

Range: Sydney area, north coast, ranges and inland areas, Qld, Vic, Tas and SA. **Leaves:** thick, succulent, about 5mm wide. **Flowers:** YELLOW, numerous in an unbranched raceme. **Flowering time:** spring. **Name:** *bulbosa* = Lat. having a bulb.

• *Burchardia* R. Brown

An endemic genus with 5 species, distributed in all states.

Name: *Burchardia* = after Johann H. Burckhard (1784-1817), a Swiss traveller.

Burchardia umbellata R. Brown

Milkmaids **Ss, Castl**
An erect tufted herb 20-70cm high, with a small cluster of attractive white flowers. Common in heath and woodland. The flowers are sweet honey scented. Aborigines are reported to have eaten the bulb.

Range: NSW coast, Blue Mountains, southern tablelands and southern inland slopes, and in all other states. **Leaves:** few, slender. **Flowers:** WHITE with dark purple ovaries and anthers, in a small terminal cluster. The ovaries are 3-winged and so is the fruiting capsule. **Flowering time:** spring. **Name:** *umbellata* = having an umbel.

• *Caesia* R. Brown (SEE-zee-a)

Grass Lilies
A genus of about 11 species, distributed in NG, South Africa and Australia. There are 8 Australian species, distributed in all states. The flowers twist after flowering.

Name: *Caesia* = after Frederico Cesi (Caesius in Latin), a seventeenth century Italian naturalist, the first to discover the purpose of fern spores.

Note: The distinction between the 2 varieties here is unclear and seems to depend mainly on flower colour.

Caesia parviflora R. Brown **var. *parviflora***

Pale Grass-lily **Ss, Cumb**
An erect grass-like herb to 50cm tall, found in moist dense undergrowth, usually with grasses. Common in the area on many soil types. The bulbs may be edible.

Range: NSW coast, Blue Mountains, all other states except SA and NT. **Leaves:** 3-4mm wide, to 30cm long. **Flowers:** 12-18mm wide, WHITISH with grey or purplish stripes, filaments greenish white; numerous on a tall raceme. **Flowering time:** spring-summer. **Name:** *parviflora* = Lat. small-flowered.

Caesia parviflora var. *vittata*

(R. Brown) R. Henderson

Blue Grass Lily **Ss, Castl**
An erect grass-like herb to 50cm tall, found in moist dense

Burchardia umbellata

Caesia parviflora var. parviflora

Caesia parviflora var. vittata

undergrowth, usually with grasses. Common in the area on many soil types. The bulbs may be edible.

Range: NSW coast, ranges and some inland areas, all states. **Leaves:** over 8mm wide. **Flowers:** 12-18mm wide, BLUE (pale to dark), filaments divided into blue and white lengths; numerous on a tall raceme. **Flowering time:** spring-summer. **Name:** *vittata* = Lat. ribbony.

• *Crinum*
—See COASTAL AND ESTUARINE SPECIES.

• *Dianella* Lamark

Flax-lilies
A genus of tufted herbs with 25-30 species worldwide, distributed in south-eastern Africa, South-east Asia, Hawaii, Pacific Islands, Australia and NZ. There are 15 species in Australia, distributed in all states.

Their rich blue flowers are a common sight in woodlands in spring and summer. The perianth segments are usually recurved backwards and the anthers are bright yellow. The

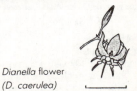

Dianella flower
(*D. caerulea*)

fruit is a rich purple berry. The leaves are notable for their conspicuous sheathing bases.

Thrips (small flower-eating insects) commonly induce bizarre floral malformations, known as 'double flowers', where the sexual parts become petaloid.

Name: *Dianella* = diminutive of Diana, the virgin huntress, the presiding genius of woods. The type specimen was collected on the island of Mauritius and labelled simply 'Diana' by the French botanist-explorer Commerson.

Dianella caerulea Sims **var. *caerula***

Blue Flax Lily   **Ss**
A tufted herb to 50cm tall found in woodland on sandstone. Uncommon in the area.

Range: from south-eastern Qld to Tas.   **Leaves:** hard, stiff, glossy, to about 20mm wide, 30-50cm long, with tiny scattered teeth on margins and keel.   **Flowers:** RICH BLUE with yellow anthers.   **Flowering time:** September-November.   **Name:** *caerula* = Lat. a rich blue.

Dianella caerulea Sims
var. *producta* R. Henderson

Blue Flax Lily   **Ss**
The most common *Dianella* in the area. Similar to var. *caerulea* except the leaf tufts are borne on elongated aerial stems lined with brown bracts and the whole plant is usually sprawling. Often there are 2 tufts per stem.

Name: *producta* = Lat. extended, referring to the aerial stems.

Dianella congesta
—See COASTAL AND ESTUARINE SPECIES.

Dianella longifolia R. Brown **var. *longifolia***
Ss, Castl, Cumb

An erect tufted herb to 80cm high. Found on clay and sandstone soils, on the Cumberland Plain and the north shore (Berowra Creek and Bobbin Head).

Range: NSW coast, ranges and inland areas, and all states except NT.   **Leaves:** grey-green, 20-40cm long, 4-12mm wide, often with scattered teeth on margins and keel.   **Flowers:** PALE BLUE.   **Flowering time:** spring-summer.   **Name:** *longifolia* = Lat. long-leaved.

Dianella prunina R. Henderson
Ss

An erect tufted herb resembling *D. caerulea*, except the leaves and stalks are purplish with a strong blue-grey bloom. Found in heath and woodland on sandstone. Uncommon in the area, occurring on the north shore.

Range: Sydney region and Blue Mountains.   **Leaves:** 40-60cm long, to 35mm wide, like *D. caerulea* but larger in all respects, not toothed.   **Flowers:** inner perianth whorl BLUE, outer whorl blue with a grey central stripe; on an inflorescence 50-100cm tall.   **Flowering time:** spring.   **Name:** *prunina* = Lat. plum-coloured, 'referring to the overall appearance of the plants', although the glaucous bloom is the most conspicuous feature.

Dianella revoluta R. Brown

Mauve Flax Lily   **Ss, Castl, Cumb**
An erect tufted herb to 1m tall. Not very common in the area, on both clay and sandstone, mainly on the north shore.

Range: NSW coast and ranges, and all states.   **Leaves:** to 70cm long,

Dianella caerulea
var. *caerula*

Dianella caerulea
var. *producta*

Dianella longifolia
var. *longifolia*

Dianella prunina

Dianella revoluta

to 20mm wide, with in-rolled (revolute) margins **Flowers:** MAUVE to BLUE with yellow filaments. **Flowering time:** November-December. **Name:** *revoluta* = Lat. revolute.

• *Dichopogon* Kunth

A genus with 5 species, distributed in all states. One species extends to NG. Included in *Arthropodium* by some botanists.

Name: *Dichopogon* = Gk. double-beard, because the anthers have 2 tiny beard-like appendages.

Dichopogon fimbriatus R. Brown

Nodding Chocolate Lily, Grass Lily **Cumb**
An erect grass-like herb with purple flowers on a stem 50-80cm high. Found uncommonly on the Cumberland Plain, in open forest and grasslands. The swollen succulent roots may be edible. The name Chocolate Lily comes from the chocolate scented flowers.

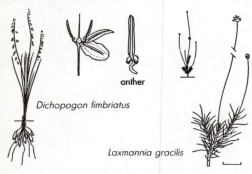

anther

Dichopogon fimbriatus

Laxmannia gracilis

Range: Sydney area, NSW ranges and inland areas, Qld, Vic and SA. **Leaves:** numerous, slender, 3-5mm wide, surrounded with a tuft of dense fibres at the base (the remains of leaves). **Flowers:** BLUE-PURPLE, about 20mm wide, pendant, in groups of 3-4 , mostly falling to one side of the stem, anthers purple, anther filaments hairless. The fruiting capsules are mostly erect. **Flowering time:** September-November. **Name:** *fimbriatus* = Lat. fringed, referring to the fibres at the base of the plant.

• *Hypoxis* Linnaeus

A genus with about 150 species distributed in America, Africa, east Asia and Australia. There are about 10 species native to Australia, distributed in all states. Often placed in a separate family, Hypoxidaceae, on account of its inferior ovary.

Name: *Hypoxis* = Gk. *hyp*, under, *oxys*, sharp, referring to the contraction at the base of the capsule.

Hypoxis hygrometrica

Hypoxis hygrometrica Labillardière

Yellow-stars **Ss, Castl**
A small opportunistic herb to 25cm high, common in many habitats, usually with grasses. The name *hygrometrica* refers to the fine long hairs that cover the plant. It means the same

as *hydroscopic*, that is, water-responsive: in dry conditions the hairs twist, in moist conditions they uncoil again. No one has suggested what advantage this gives the plant.

Range: NSW coast, ranges and inland areas, Qld, Vic and Tas. **Leaves:** slender, linear, sprinkled with long hairs. **Flowers:** YELLOW, solitary or in short racemes, terminal. **Flowering time:** spring, summer and autumn. **Name:** *hygrometrica* = Gk. responding to water by changing shape.

• *Laxmannia* R. Brown

Wire-lilies
An endemic genus with about 13 species, distributed in all states. The majority are restricted to south-western WA.

Name: *Laxmannia* = after Erich Laxmann, an eighteenth century professor at St Petersburg, Russia, who wrote on Siberian botany.

Laxmannia gracilis R. Brown

Slender Wire-lily **Ss, Castl**
A small herb 5-30cm high, with numerous small leaves on short stiff stems, and tiny flowers clustered at the end of tall wiry thread-like peduncles. Common in heath and woodland. Widely scattered through the area in many soil types.

Range: NSW coast, ranges and some inland areas, Qld and Vic. **Leaves:** linear, varying in crowding and length according to the degree of exposure of the habitat. **Flowers:** tiny, the outer whorl translucent and membranous, the inner whorl PINK, arranged in small dense heads surrounded by membranous bracts. **Flowering time:** spring. **Name:** *gracilis* = Lat. slender or slight.

• *Myrsiphyllum* Willdenow

A genus with 12 species, all native to South Africa. There are 3 naturalised species in Australia.

Name: *Myrsiphyllum* = Gk. Myrtle-leaf.

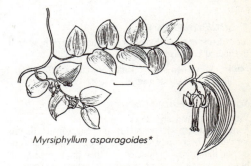

*Myrsiphyllum asparagoides**

*Myrsiphyllum asparagoides**
(Linnaeus) Willdenow

A dense scrambling herbaceous plant with twining stems to 1m or more long. A serious weed in bushland, especially in gullies. Introduced from South Africa.

Range: Sydney area, Vic, SA and South Africa. **Cladodes:** broad, flat, smooth. **Flowers:** WHITE, about 8mm long, solitary or a few, in the axils of cladodes. **Fruit:** a succulent red berry with 1-3 seeds. **Name:** *asparagoides* = *Asparagus*-like.

• *Protasparagus* Oberm

A genus with about 100 species in Africa and Asia, including 4 naturalised and 1 native species in Australia. The leaves are reduced to fine scales at the base of clusters of leaf-like cladodes.

Name: *Protasparagus* = Gk. first-*Asparagus*, since it is more primitive. *Aspharagos* is the Greek word for a shoot.

*Protasparagus aethiopicus** (Linnaeus) Oberm.
Asparagus Fern (previously *P. densiflorus**)
A dense scrambling herb with stiff stems to about 1m long. Originally a native of Cape Province and Natal, South Africa, it was introduced as an indoor pot plant and is now a serious pest in urban bushland, mainly in shady places.

Range: Sydney area, NSW north coast, Lord Howe Island and South Africa. **Cladodes:** about 2mm wide, flat; the main stem has a stiff prickle below each branch. **Flowers:** WHITE, about 4mm long, numerous in axillary racemes. **Fruit:** a succulent red berry with a single seed. **Name:** *aethiopicus* = Lat. Ethiopian.

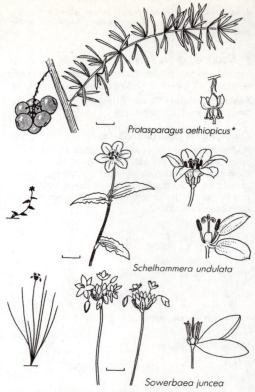

Protasparagus aethiopicus *

Schelhammera undulata

Sowerbaea juncea

• *Schelhammera* R. Brown

An endemic genus of 3 species, distributed in the eastern mainland states.

Name: *Schelhammera* = after G. C. Schelhammer (1649-1716), a German professor of medicine.

Schelhammera undulata R. Brown
Lilac Lily **Ss**
A small erect or sprawling herb with dainty pink flowers and leaves that arise alternately on the stem. Somewhat uncommon, scattered through the area in moist shady places in woodland, on sandstone, usually near the coast.

Range: NSW coast, Qld and Vic. **Leaves:** soft, with wavy margins and about 5 main parallel veins. **Flowers:** BRIGHT PINK, with dark purple anthers, solitary, terminal. **Flowering time:** spring. **Name:** *undulata* = Lat. wavy.

• *Sowerbaea* Smith

An endemic genus of 5 species found in swampy heathland, distributed in all states except SA.

Name: *Sowerbaea* = after James Sowerby (1757-1822), a prolific English botanical artist.

Sowerbaea juncea Smith
Vanilla Plant, Rush Lily **Ss**
A small erect herb with pretty clusters of fragile mauve flowers surrounded by a cup of membranous bracts, from which one by one they arise, briefly open and then droop their lovely heads. Found in moist open heath on sandstone. Common in the area.

Range: NSW coast, Blue Mountains and southern tablelands, Qld and Vic. **Leaves:** slender (1mm wide), 20-50 cm long. **Flowers:** MAUVE with yellow stamens, set in dense terminal umbels. There are only 3 stamens, alternating with 3 staminodes. **Flowering time:** spring. **Name:** *juncea* = Lat. sedgey.

• *Stypandra* R. Brown

An endemic genus with one species.

Name: *Stypandra* = Gk. *stype*, the coarse fibre of hemp or flax, *andros*, male, referring to the woolly stamens.

Stypandra glauca R. Brown
Nodding Blue Lily **Ss**
An erect herb 1-1.5m high with leaves in an unusual fishbone arrangement. Found in moist places in woodland on sandstone. Uncommon in the area; recorded along the Georges River (Campbelltown to Macquarie Fields), Nepean River (Menangle Bridge, Bents Basin) and near Sackville; more common in the Blue Mountains.

Range: NSW coast, ranges and inland areas; also distributed widely in temperate mainland Australia and possibly New Caledonia. **Leaves:** thin, soft, light green, with closed sheaths at the base, 2-ranked on the stem. **Flowers:** BLUE-MAUVE, with yellow stamens. **Flowering time:** mainly spring (but some present for most of the year). **Name:** *glauca* = Lat. grey-green, reference obscure.

• *Thelionema* R. Henderson

An endemic genus with 3 species, distributed in south-eastern Australia.

Name: *Thelionema* = Gk. female-thread, referring to the slender style.

Thelionema caespitosa (R. Brown) R. Henderson

(previously *Stypandra caespitosa*)
Tufted Blue Lily **Ss, Castl**
An erect tufted herb with blue flowers. Rare in the area since it has been eradicated from most of its local range in the now densely settled inner suburbs. It still occurs occasionally in coastal heath.

Range: NSW coast, Blue Mountains and southern tablelands, Qld, Vic and Tas. **Leaves:** 5-8mm wide, 30-40cm long. **Flowers:** RICH BLUE with yellow anthers, numerous in a branched inflorescence. **Flowering time:** spring-summer. **Name:** *caespitosa* = Lat. tufted.

Thelionema umbellata (R. Brown) R. Henderson

(previously *Stypandra umbellata*) **Ss**
A slender tufted herb with white flowers. Found in coastal heath on sandstone. Fairly common in the area.

Range: Sydney area, south coast and Blue Mountains. **Leaves:** slender, 3-5mm wide, under 30cm long. **Flowers:** WHITE with yellow anthers, few in the inflorescence. **Flowering time:** spring-summer. **Name:** *umbellata* = Lat. having umbels (a misnomer, as the inflorescence is a cyme).

• *Thysanotus* R. Brown

Fringe Lilies
A genus of herbs with 49 species distributed mainly in Australia with a few in Asia. The majority restricted to south-western WA. Each pretty lilac flower 'opens only after rain, once, and never blows again.'[7]

Name: *Thysanotus* = Gk. fringed.

Thysanotus juncifolius (Salisbury) Willis & Court

Fringe Lily **Ss**
An ascending or sprawling herb with stems to 50cm long. Basal leaves are absent but there are small green leaves along the lower stems. Common in moist heath, usually amongst dense undergrowth.

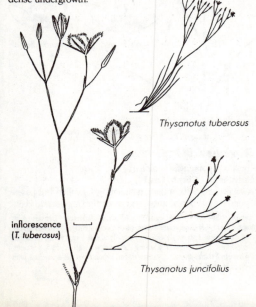

inflorescence
(*T. tuberosus*)

Thysanotus tuberosus

Thysanotus juncifolius

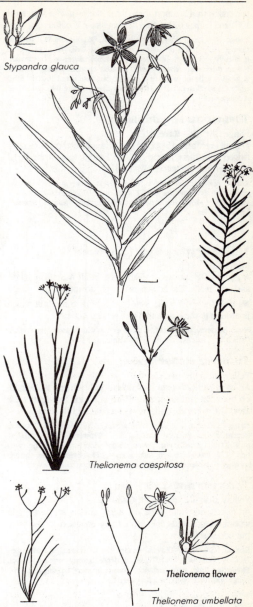

Stypandra glauca

Thelionema caespitosa

Thelionema flower

Thelionema umbellata

Range: NSW coast, Blue Mountains, Vic and SA. **Leaves:** absent or short and withered. **Flowers:** MAUVE, with outer (unfringed) segments 1.5-2mm wide, on a much-branched inflorescence. **Flowering time:** spring-summer. **Name:** *juncifolius* = Lat. rush-leaved.

Thysanotus tuberosus R. Brown

Fringe Lily **Ss, Castl**
An ascending or sprawling herb with stems to 50cm long. Found in moist heath and woodland, usually amongst dense

undergrowth. Common throughout the area in a variety of soils and habitats. The crisp tuberous root is edible.

Range: NSW coast, ranges and inland areas, Qld, Vic and SA. **Leaves:** slender, more or less cylindrical. **Flowers:** MAUVE. The inflorescence is usually not much branched. **Flowering time:** spring-summer. **Name:** *tuberosus* = having tubers. **Similar species:** Distinguish from *T. juncifolius* by the presence of conspicuous basal leaves 10-20cm long, while the small stem leaves (where branches join) are thin and almost membranous.

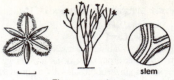

Thysanotus virgatus   stem

Thysanotus virgatus Brittan

Fringe Lily   **Ss**   **Rare 3RC-**
A small erect herb 15-30cm high, distinguished by its roughly ridged branchlets. Found only on lateritic tops in the Royal National Park (Heathcote-Waterfall).

Range: restricted to the Royal National Park. **Leaves:** absent or short and withered. **Flowers:** MAUVE, with outer (unfringed) segments 3-4mm wide. **Flowering time:** September-January. **Name:** *virgatus* = Lat. twiggy.

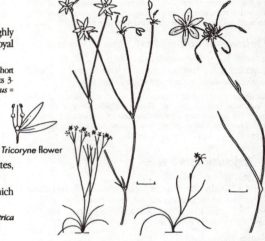

Tricoryne flower

Tricoryne elatior   *Tricoryne simplex*

• *Tricoryne* R. Brown (tri-co-RY-nee)

Rush Lilies
A genus of 8 species, 7 distributed in all Australian states, and one in NG. The flowers twist after flowering.

Name: *Tricoryne* = Gk. 3-clubs, referring to the fruit which is divided to the base into 3 one-seeded nutlets.

Note: Be careful not to confuse these species with *Hypoxis hygrometrica* (which lacks hair tufts on the anther filaments).

Tricoryne elatior R. Brown

Yellow Rush-lily   **Ss, Cumb**
An erect herb 20-40cm high, found in heath and woodland, on both clay and sandy soils. Fairly common throughout the area. The stems are dull, grey-green and slightly striate.

Range: NSW coast, ranges and inland areas, Qld, Vic, SA and WA. **Leaves:** slender, may be absent at flowering time. **Flowers:** BRIGHT YELLOW to WHITE, in small umbels, about 15mm wide; terminal at the many tips of a much-branched inflorescence. **Flowering time:** spring-summer. **Name:** *elatior* = Lat. taller, in comparison to *T. simplex*.

Tricoryne simplex R. Brown

Yellow Rush-lily   **Ss, Castl, Cumb**
An ascending herb 10-25cm high, found in heath and woodland on sandstone. Moderately common in the area, but not near the sea.

Range: NSW coast. **Leaves:** slender, flat or channelled. **Flowers:** BRIGHT YELLOW to WHITE, in a dense solitary terminal umbel. **Flowering time:** spring-summer. **Name:** *simplex* = Lat. simple, i.e. not compound, referring to the inflorescence.

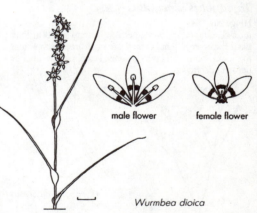

male flower   female flower

Wurmbea dioica

• *Wurmbea* Thunberg

A genus of small herbs with about 30 species worldwide. There are about 19 Australian species and the remainder are African.

Name: *Wurmbea* = after F. van Wurmb, a Dutch merchant in Batavia (Jakarta). Like several of the early wealthy Dutch merchants in the Far East, he was a strong supporter of natural history and an amateur botanist.

Wurmbea dioica F. Mueller

(previously *Anguillaria dioica*)
Early Nancy   **Cumb, Castl**
A small herb 5-30cm high, with strongly swollen leaf bases. Found uncommonly, amongst grass, on the Cumberland Plain.

Range: NSW coast, ranges and inland areas, all states. **Leaves:** 3, at least 2 with very dilated leaf bases, blades very slender. **Flowers:** star-like, unisexual (plants dioecious); usually about 8mm wide, on a zig-zag peduncle, WHITE with a strong dark purple band on each segment. **Flowering time:** spring. **Name:** *dioica* = dioecious, i.e. unisexual, with the sexes on different plants.

ORCHIDS

ORCHIDACEAE

The world's largest family of flowering plants, with 20 000-35 000 species distributed in all continents except Antarctica, but most especially in the tropics. Australia has about 1000 species in 107 genera.

Orchids constitute about 10% of the world's flowering species. They are about 5% of Australia's flora and about 10% of the native species of the Sydney area. Despite this high percentage they often seem to be completely absent from the bush. Reasons for this are shy and retiring habits, long periods of dormancy, dependence on fire of some species for flowering, a tendency to form small widely separated populations, grazing by sheep and rabbits, and overcollecting.

Uses: Australian terrestrial Orchids generally produce edible tubers and many genera were important sources of nourishment for Aborigines. The tubers of some genera, especially *Diuris*, were eagerly consumed by European children in the last century.

Orchids produce only one industrial substance, vanilla (from the fruit pods of *Vanilla fragrans*, a climbing orchid from tropical America). However orchids themselves are a major commodity in the horticultural trade, because of their beautiful flowers.

Flower structure: Orchids are closely related to Lilies, but their sexual organs are more highly evolved. Put simply: one petal has developed into the labellum or 'tongue', a specialised organ which acts as an attractor and landing pad for insects; meanwhile the sexual organs have become fused into a single organ called the *column*. The male part has been reduced to a single anther located at the top of the column (beneath a short cap). Each of the four anther cells produces a congealed mass of pollen called a *pollinium*. As the anther matures, the walls of the anther sac become fragile and open at the slightest touch, releasing the pollinia. Beneath the anther is a new organ called the rostellum. This produces a sticky liquid to help the pollen adher to passing insects. Beneath the rostellum is the stigma, in the form of a broad sticky plate. The *ovary* is located beneath the flower (i.e. it is inferior) and contains many thousands (or millions) of ovules.

Most species are pollinated by insects but some have developed techniques of self-pollination whereby the pollen fall naturally onto the stigma. Others are apomictic, i.e. producing seeds without any pollination, e.g. some *Microtis* species.

The most interesting aspect of orchids is the remarkable and varied range of strategies used to attract and exploit insects as agents of cross-pollination. These are described (if known) in the descriptions below.

Life-cycle: Most local species are deciduous, that is, the flowers and leaves die back in the heat of summer and the plant is reduced to an underground tuber until the following year when autumn rains promote the growth of new leaves. In most species the flowers develop in spring.

Fire is an important aspect of growth. Many species will flower poorly or not at all without the stimulus of hot summer fires (though this is not true of species favouring dark moist scrubs and swampy sites, e.g. *Corybas, Acianthus*). The absence of hot summer fires may partly account for the disappearance of many species from Sydney's bush reserves.

Many orchids form a replacement tuber each year to take the place of the parent tuber. Many take this one step further by forming additional daughter tubers at the end of long fleshy horizontal roots. In this way new plants are formed by vegetative reproduction. Such species (e.g. *Pterostylis, Acianthus, Corybas*) tend to form dense colonies.

Orchids and fungi: Orchids, like many other groups of plants, are dependent on relationships with thread-like fungi for their nourishment. In the early stages of seed development, before photosynthesis begins, fungal infection is essential to supply the developing plants with nourishment. Once the plant matures, the fungal filaments become localised in the roots and take part in the supply and processing of nutrients. Some species have taken this to its logical extreme and become saprophytes. These have ceased their own respiration and, lacking chlorophyll, are totally dependent on fungi for their nourishment (e.g. *Gastrodia, Dipodium, Erythrorchis*).

Names: The names are accurate as at June 1990. The family is in a fluid state and there are likely to be many changes in future.

I am especially indebted to Leo Cady and Ron Tunstall for assistance with this family.

TERRESTRIAL ORCHIDS

• *Acianthus* R. Brown

A genus of small terrestrial orchids with about 20 species distributed in Australia, NZ, New Caledonia and the Solomon Islands. There are about 10 Australian species.

They are often exceedingly obscure, preferring dark moist conditions beneath shrubs or bracken, but once recognised the distinctive heart-shaped leaves are easy to spot. One species, *A. fornicatus*, is easily the most abundant orchid in the area.

The flowers are very small and purplish, with several on a stem 10-20cm high. The labellum has 2 tiny glands that secrete nectar to attract small gnats as pollinators. While the level of fertilisation is very low, vegetative reproduction is aggressive, resulting in dense colonies.

The leaves of the local species are heart-shaped, purple beneath, 20-40mm long, and held horizontally near to the ground.

Name: *Acianthus* = Gk. *acis*, a point, *anthos*, a flower, referring to the finely pointed flower segments.

Acianthus caudatus R. Brown

Ss

A rare species in the area, mainly recorded from the lower north shore.

Range: NSW coastal areas north from Sydney and Blue Mountains (common), Vic, Tas and SA. **Flowers:** with fine segments up to 30mm long. **Flowering time:** August (later than the rest of the genus). **Name:** *caudatus* = tailed, refers to long petals and sepals.

Acianthus exsertus R. Brown

Gnat Orchid **Ss**

An uncommon species widely scattered in the area. It may be found together with *A. fornicatus*. The 2 species are very similar.

Range: NSW coast, ranges and inland areas, also all other states except WA, NT. **Flowers:** similar to *A. fornicatus* except the dorsal sepal is more slender (to 3mm) and does not completely hood the column, and the petals are flexed backwards. **Flowering time:** mostly July (occasionally from April). **Name:** *exsertus* = protruding, referring to the labellum. **Note:** an unnamed species, close to *A. exsertus*, has been recently collected from the Helensburg area. It has smaller segments and more numerous flowers, growing densely on the stem.

Acianthus fornicatus R. Brown

Pixie Orchid **Ss**

An exceedingly common orchid, present in sandstone bushland throughout the area.

Range: NSW coast, ranges and inland areas, and Qld. **Flowers:** with transparent strongly hooded dorsal sepal, segments about 10mm long and 5-7mm wide. **Flowering time:** March-August. **Name:** *fornicatus* = Lat. hooded, refers to the arched dorsal sepal.

Acianthus reniformis

—see *Cyrtostylis reniformis*.

• *Arthrochilus* F. Mueller

A genus of small terrestrial orchids consisting of about six species. All are found in Australia and 2 extend to NG.

Name: *Arthrochilus* = Gk. *arthros*, jointed, *cheilos*, lip, referring to the hinged labellum.

Arthrochilus irritabilis F. Mueller **Ss**

A small dull-coloured orchid found in woodland on sandstone. Rare in the area, only recorded north of the harbour.

This is one of the more bizarre members of the family. The labellum resembles an insect and it appears the method of pollination is pseudo-copulation with small male wasps. The wasps are attracted by chemicals exuded by glands in the labellum. The labellum is loosely hinged and when the wasp alights its weight causes it to swing down against the column where it may come into contact with the pollinia or stigmatic disc. Despite the name the labellum is not really irritable, although it can easily be moved by the wind.

As the flowers are small and inconspicuous it can be difficult to find.

Range: NSW coast north from Sydney, and Qld. **Leaves:** ground-hugging, to 8cm long, few in a rosette. **Flowers:** 3-20, GREENISH or REDDISH, small, segments about 5mm long; labellum hammer shaped, with long red or purple hairs, the tip notched and covered in shiny glands. **Flowering time:** January-April. **Name:** *irritabilis* = Lat. sensitive.

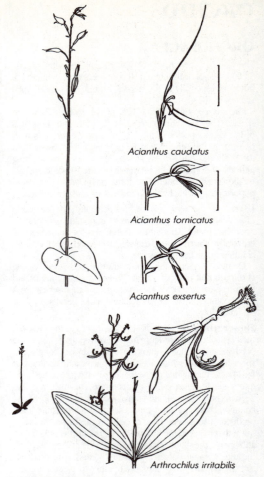

Acianthus caudatus

Acianthus fornicatus

Acianthus exsertus

Arthrochilus irritabilis

• *Burnettia* Lindley

A genus with a single endemic species.

Name: *Burnettia* = after Gilbert T. Burnett, first Professor of Botany in King's College, London.

Burnettia cuneata Lindley

Lizard Orchid **Ss**

Found in swampy sedgelands on heathy tops. It is rarely seen except after fires, because it is hidden by dense marsh vegetation. Found locally on Maddens Plains.

Range: southern NSW, Vic and Tas. **Leaves:** reduced to sheathing scales, fleshy and purplish-brown. **Flowers:** 1-7, about 25mm wide, PINK or WHITE inside, greenish-brown or purplish-brown outside with darker veins, fleshy and brittle. **Flowering time:** September-December. **Name:** *cuneata* = wedge-shaped.

• *Caladenia* R. Brown

Lady's Fingers

A genus of terrestrial orchids with about 120 species, all

endemic to Australia except for a handful in NZ and the Pacific Islands. Its best development is in the south-west of Western Australia. *Caladenia* are deciduous and die back in summer.

Most local species are pollinated by small bees or flies. The labellum is hinged and its action assists pollination. 'On one occasion I had the pleasure of seeing *Caladenia* [*catenata*] actually fertilized by an insect. A flower was observed to tremble, and on examination it was found that a fly had alighted upon its labellum, was by its spring carried against the stigma and adhering to it struggled violently to escape, and thereby withdrew the pollen-masses from the anther and smeared them over the stigma.'[10]

Name: *Caladenia* = Gk. beautiful glands, referring to the attractive calli (stalked projections which line the labellum).

The genus is divided into 2 groups: small-flowered species (Lady's Fingers), and large-flowered species (Spider Orchids).

1. **Small-flowered** *Caladenia*
Lady's Fingers

Caladenia alata R. Brown
Orange-tip Caladenia **Ss** (Not illustrated)
Found in woodland on sandstone, or on moss in heathland. A rare and little known species, although widespread and sometimes locally common on the south coast. It has been collected from the Cataract Dam Road and may be in the Royal National Park. Similar to *C. carnea*, but the flowers are tiny and short-lived, and there are 2 prominent stalked calli at the base of the labellum.

Range: coastal parts of south-eastern Australia. **Leaf:** to 6cm, slender, sparsely hairy. **Flowers:** 1 or 2, WHITE, about 10mm wide, perianth segments to 3mm long, dorsal sepal erect, labellum yellow or orange tipped, with 2 rows of yellow calli; on a stem to 10cm tall which is thin, wiry and sparsely hairy. **Flowering time:** August-October. **Name:** *alata* = Lat. winged. **Note:** The Sydney species has been confused with *C. aurantiaca*, a species of southern NSW and Vic.

Caladenia caerulea R. Brown
Blue Caladenia **Ss**
Found in forest and scrubs. Uncommon in the area (e.g. Castle Hill, Woronora River). Very similar to *C. carnea* but readily distinguished by the blue colour. Fitzgerald noted '. . . sparsely distributed . . . generally found on the flat tops of hills of ironstone and gravel'.

Range: NSW coast, ranges and inland areas, Qld, Vic, Tas. **Leaf:** to 7cm, narrow (to 5mm wide), sparsely hairy. **Flower:** about 25mm wide, SKY BLUE, segments covered outside with tiny purple glands; dorsal sepal erect, labellum with dark bands, and 2 rows of yellow clubbed calli. Flower stem to 15cm high. **Flowering time:** August-September. **Name:** *caerulea* = Lat. sky-blue.

Caladenia carnea R. Brown
Pink Fingers **Ss**
Found in shady places in forest and scrubs but also in sunny places on tops. It may hybridise with *C. catenata*.

Range: NSW coast, ranges and inland areas, Qld, Vic, Tas, SA, also NZ, New Caledonia, Indonesia and Malaysia. **Leaf:** to 15cm, narrow (4mm wide), sparsely hairy. **Flowers:** 1-3, 20-30mm wide, segments to 20mm long, PINK but also sometimes WHITE, the outside greenish or pink

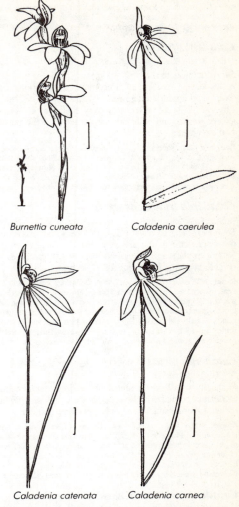

Burnettia cuneata   Caladenia caerulea

Caladenia catenata   Caladenia carnea

with glandular hairs, dorsal sepal erect, labellum with conspicuous red tiger-stripes, calli in 2 rows (sometimes 2 extra part rows present). Flower stem to 20cm tall, thin, sparsely glandular-hairy. **Flowering time:** August-December. **Name:** *carnea* = Lat. fleshy, referring to the pink colour. **Note:** there are a number of unnamed, poorly known species, close to *C. carnea*, in the area.

Caladenia catenata (Smith) Druce
(previously *C. alba*)
White Fingers **Ss**
Occurs in colonies in shady places in forests and scrubs on sandy soil. Distinguish from the closely related *C. carnea* by the absence of red bars on the labellum and column. Probably the most common *Caladenia* in the area, often in numerous colonies.

Range: coastal parts of NSW, Qld, Vic. **Leaf:** to 12cm tall, narrow (4mm wide), sparsely hairy. **Flowers:** 1 or 2, WHITE to PINK, about 30mm wide, dorsal sepal erect, labellum orange-tipped, calli clubbed, yellow to white, in 2 rows. Flower stem to 20cm tall, wiry, hairy. **Flowering time:** April-October. **Name:** *catenata* = Lat. chain-like (referring to the calli). **Note:** this was previously well known as *C. alba.* The type specimen was collected by Surgeon White at Port Jackson in about 1795.

Caladenia fuscata

(H. G. Reichenbach) M. Clements & D. Jones

Ss (not illustrated)

A slender species 15cm tall. Uncommon to rare in the area, mainly collected from sandstone woodland near the Nepean River in the south of the area. Very similar to *C. carnea*, except smaller and with furry brown hairs on the outside of the segments.

Range: an inland species only occurring east of the ranges in the Sydney area, also Qld, Vic, Tas and NZ. **Flower:** very pale PINK, about 10mm across. Flower stem dark brown, to 10cm tall. **Flowering time:** September-October. **Name:** *fuscata* = Lat. darkened. **Note:** Local specimens were previously confused with *Caladenia carnea* var. *minor.*

Caladenia iridescens Rogers

Bronze Caladenia **Ss**

Found in sheltered moist places in forests and scrubs near the coast. Rare in the area, e.g. Elanora Heights on the Narrabeen plateau, and Royal National Park. It can be easily confused with the more common *C. testacea.*

Range: NSW coast and ranges south from the Sydney area, Vic and Tas. **Leaf:** to 10cm, slender, with scattered hairs. **Flowers:** 1-4, about 18mm across, DARK RED, PURPLISH to GREENISH, often with iridescent golden tints. Segments about 10mm long, the outer surface covered in purple glands. Dorsal sepal hooded. Flower stem to 15cm, thin and wiry with scattered glandular hairs, usually purplish. **Flowering time:** September-November. **Name:** *iridescens* = Lat. with a rainbow-like play of colours.

Caladenia picta (Nicholls) M. Clements & D. Jones

Ss (not illustrated)

Found in woodland on sandstone or deep coastal sands. Moderately common in the area. Similar to *C. catenata* but earlier flowering and with a brightly coloured column.

Range: Sydney region, south coast. **Leaves:** to 8cm long, slender, sparsely hairy. **Flowers:** 1-2, WHITE, to 30mm wide, column with broad red and green bands, labellum orange-tipped, with prominent blunt teeth on the margin of the curled frontal lobe, and calli in 2 rows to the base of the curled lobe. Flower stem 15cm tall, very wiry, hairy. **Flowering time:** May-July. **Name:** *picta* = Lat. coloured, painted.

Caladenia testacea R. Brown

Honey Caladenia **Ss**

Uncommon north of the harbour, rare in the Royal National Park, but may be locally common after fires. The flowers are honey scented.

Range: NSW coasts, Blue Mountains, Vic and Tas. **Leaf:** to 20cm tall, narrow, sparsely hairy. **Flowers:** 1-6, YELLOW, BROWNISH or GREENISH-YELLOW, about 18mm wide, segments about 6.5-8mm long, with dark tips, outside with dense glandular hairs; labellum whitish with purple tip; calli in four rows. Flowers several on a stem to 15-25cm tall. **Flowering time:** September-October. **Name:** *testacea* = brick coloured, referring to the crowded calli.

2. Large-flowered Caladenia

Spider Orchids

These have relatively dull-coloured flowers with long thin filamentous segments. The sepals (and often petals) end in

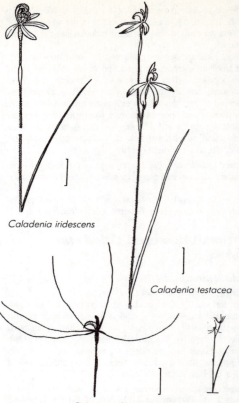

Caladenia iridescens

Caladenia testacea

Caladenia filamentosa

a prominent structure called a club. This consists of a mass of glands which produce sexual attractants appealing to pollinating insects. The leaf is broad and hairy.

Note: 2 other spider orchids were previously recorded in the area but are now extinct:

C. dilatata R. Brown (Gladesville-Cooks River);

C. fitzgeraldii Rupp (Gladesville)

Caladenia filamentosa R. Brown

Daddy Long Legs **Ss**

Rare or now extinct in the area. Recorded from Campbelltown (1950) Manly (1898) and Como (1912).

Range: scattered populations in widespread parts of the state, also all other states except NT. **Leaf:** to 18cm long, narrow (3mm wide), densely hairy (both simple and glandular). **Flowers:** 1-4, about 80mm wide, DEEP RED, segments 55-70mm long, initially flat, then very fine and densely covered in glandular hairs; dorsal sepal erect, labellum pale, with darker veins, recurved, with short calli on the margins towards the tip and 2 rows of fleshy flattened calli along the centre. Stems 15-20cm tall. **Flowering time:** July-November **Name:** *filamentosa* = Lat. thread-like, referring to the perianth segments.

Caladenia tessellata Fitzgerald

Ss Vulnerable 3V

Found in sheltered moist places in forests and scrubs,

especially in stony laterites on coastal tops. It occurs in the Woronora River area, also uncommonly north of the harbour (e.g. Middle Harbour, Berowra). It is usually only seen after fire.

Range: Sydney area, southern coast and ranges and Vic.   **Leaf:** to 6cm, narrow (5mm wide), sparsely hairy.   **Flowers:** 1-2, CREAM or PALE YELLOW, to 30mm wide, long, with reddish stripes and slender glandular tips; labellum heart-shaped, yellowish with darker streaks, thick glandular margins and four rows of dark calli. Stems to 15-30cm tall.   **Flowering time:** September-October.   **Name:** *tessellata* = Lat. formed of a mosaic of small squares or cubes, referring to the labellum calli.

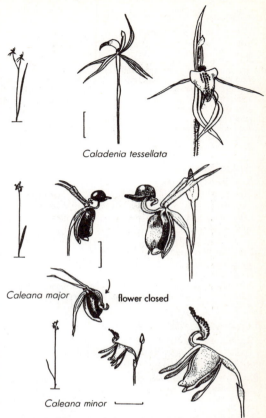
Caladenia tessellata

• *Caleana* R. Brown

A genus with 5 species, one extending to NZ.

Name: *Caleana* = in honour of George Caley (1770-1829), Joseph Banks' botanical collector in NSW from 1800-1810. It seems appropriate that so irritable a species should be named after a botanist of whom Joseph Banks once said 'had he been borne a gentleman he would long ago have been shot in a duel'. The common name of Duck Orchid is well deserved since the flowers closely resemble a duck in flight.

Caleana major A. Gray

Large Duck Orchid   **Ss**

A small, inconspicuous terrestrial orchid with a remarkable floral structure. Found in exposed sunny places on sandstone tops. An uncommon species in the area.

R. D. Fitzgerald wrote 'with its red-brown leaf, wiry stem, red-brown flowers, peculiarity of form, resembling in body, wings and head, a large ant, and its power of suddenly curling its neck and hiding its head within its body, it seems to depart from the vegetable world to join the insect world.'[11]

The duck-bill-shaped labellum is so sensitive that the slightest touch by an insect causes it to spring down, trapping the insect into the body of the column with the sticky disc and pollinia. The usual method of pollination is pseudo-copulation with male sawflies, but the method of attraction is not known.

Range: NSW coast and ranges, Qld, Vic, Tas and SA.   **Leaf:** to 10cm long, reddish, spotted.   **Flowers:** 2-4 on a thin stem to 40cm high; upside down; REDDISH-BROWN, segments to 15mm long; labellum deep red, shaped like a duck bill and attached by a sensitive strap.   **Flowering time:** October-December.   **Name:** *major* = Lat. greater.

Caleana minor R. Brown

Small Duck Orchid   **Ss**

A small orchid to 18cm tall with 1-4 small dull-coloured flowers, similar in shape and function to *Caleana major*.

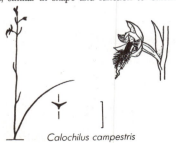
Calochilus campestris

Caleana major   **flower closed**

Caleana minor ⊢———⊣

Found in heath and woodland, in semi-shade, often near the base of Eucalypts. Uncommon.

Range: NSW coast and ranges, also all states except WA, NT and NZ. **Flowers:** small, upside down, segments REDDISH GREEN, about 8mm long, similar to *Caleana major* except the labellum is prominently covered in shiny black glands and the column is set at a right angle to the ovary. **Flowering time:** November-January.   **Name:** *minor* = Lat. lesser.

• *Calochilus* R. Brown

Bearded Orchids, Beardies

A genus of terrestrial orchids with 11 species: 10 in Australia, one of which extends to NG and 2 of which extend to NZ; the other species occurs in New Caledonia.

The richly coloured beards make this one of the more remarkable of the local genera. 'Next in beauty and singularity I place the strange form to which I have given the name Satyr Orchis; as, to my fancy, the bearded lip, and the 2 horn-like upcurving sepals, not inaptly image the grotesque attributes of those sylvan monsters.'[12]

Pollination is by pseudo-copulation with male Scollid wasps. In the absence of insect pollination the flowers self-pollinate.

Name: *Calochilus* = Gk. *kalos*, beautiful, *cheilos*, lip, referring to the gorgeously bearded labellum.

Calochilus campestris R. Brown

Copper Beard Orchid **Ss, Castl**
Found in heath and woodland. Moderately common in the area.

Range: NSW coast, ranges and inland areas, all other states except NT. **Leaf:** 3-sided in cross-section (but not sharply angled as in the other species), to 10mm wide. **Flowers:** about 20mm long, PALE GREEN with purple markings, several on an often greyish stem; labellum with 2 smooth blue plates on its upper part and dense thick purple-red hairs on the lower part, ending in a short undulating tail to 5mm long (often recurved out of sight or hidden by hairs); 2 dark glands are visible on either side of the column base. **Flowering time:** October. **Name:** *campestris* = Lat. pertaining to fields.

Calochilus gracillimus Rupp

Late Beard Orchid **Ss**
Found in sheltered woodland, not on marshy sites. Uncommon in the area. It is best distinguished from the other species by its late flowering time. It is closely related to *C. robertsonii*.

The type specimen was collected by the Reverend Rupp near Woy Woy on Christmas Day 1933.

Range: from the Sydney area to southern Qld. **Leaf:** 5-8mm wide, reddish at the base. **Flowers:** about 30mm wide, GREEN with REDDISH or PURPLISH stripes; labellum with coarse purple or bronze hairs and a tail to 25mm long. **Flowering time:** December-January. **Name:** *gracillimus* = Lat. very weak.

Calochilus paludosus R. Brown

Red Beardie **Ss, Castl**
Found in moist heath and woodland. Moderately common in the area.

Range: NSW coast and ranges, Qld, Vic, Tas, SA and NZ. **Leaf:** about 5mm wide, 3-sided. **Flowers:** about 30mm long, PALLID GREEN or REDDISH with purple veins, several on an often grey-green stem; labellum densely covered in long thick red hairs and drawn out to a long slender hairless tail (to 14mm long), lacking frontal glands. **Flowering time:** October. **Name:** *paludosus* = Lat. pertaining to marshes (an inappropriate name as it also commonly grows on well drained ground).

Calochilus robertsonii Bentham

Purple Beard Orchid **Ss**
Found in heath and woodland. Uncommon in the area. The most spectacular of the local species.

Range: NSW coast and ranges, all other states except NT, also NZ. **Leaf:** fleshy, 3-sided in cross-section, to 8mm wide. **Flowers:** about 35mm long, GREEN with red or purple stripes; the labellum densely covered in the upper part with purple-red glands and in the lower part with long thick purple-red hairs, ending in a slender tail to 10mm long. **Flowering time:** October. **Name:** *robertsonii* = after J. G. Robertson, the original collector.

• *Chiloglottis* R. Brown

Bird Orchids
A genus of small terrestrial orchids with about 15 species in Australia and NZ. They have paired leaves at the base of the plant and a small solitary flower on a short stem. Pollination is by pseudo-copulation with wasps. The stem elongates after fertilisation to as much as 20cm tall, to help disperse the seeds.

All the local species are very similar and need careful attention to the arrangement of calli on the labellum for identification.

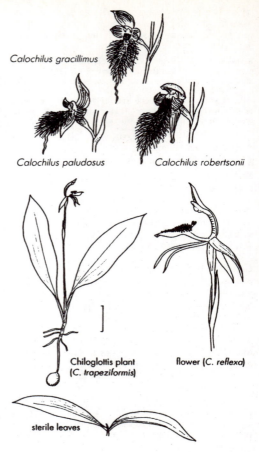

Calochilus gracillimus

Calochilus paludosus   Calochilus robertsonii

Chiloglottis plant
(C. trapeziformis)

flower (C. reflexa)

sterile leaves

Name: *Chiloglottis* = Gk. *chielos*, lip, *glottis*, tongue, referring to the shape of the labellum.

Chiloglottis diphylla R. Brown

Ant Orchid, Autumn Bird Orchid **Ss**
A small orchid to 10cm tall. Found in sheltered damp places in gullies on sandstone. Common in the area, often in dense colonies. It has generally been confused with the larger flowered *C. reflexa*, but is now regarded as a separate species.

Range: endemic to the Sydney area. **Leaves:** similar to *Chiloglottis formicifera*. **Flowers:** GREENISH BRONZE to purplish; segments to 16mm long; labellum to 9mm long, curled down on the edges, diamond shaped, pinkish with a blackish point, a large notched gland at the base, and numerous other dark glands, both with and without stalks. **Flowering time:** March-May. **Name:** *diphylla* = Gk. 2-leaved.

Chiloglottis formicifera R. D. Fitzgerald

Ant Orchid **Ss**
A small orchid to 10cm tall, found in sheltered damp places in gullies on sandstone. A moderately common species south of the harbour, it forms dense colonies. It can be easily confused with *Chiloglottis reflexa*, but is distinguished by the labellum.

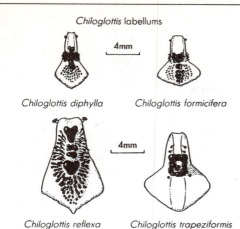

Chiloglottis labellums

4mm

Chiloglottis diphylla   Chiloglottis formicifera

4mm

Chiloglottis reflexa   Chiloglottis trapeziformis

Range: NSW coast north from Sydney, and Qld. **Leaves:** in a pair, to 3-6cm long, up to 25mm wide, with wavy margins. **Flowers:** GREEN with BROWN markings (or all brown); segments about 10mm long; labellum with broad black shiny calli, a few stalked calli are also present. **Flowering time:** September-November. **Name:** *formicifera* = Lat. ant-carrying, in reference to the appearance of the labellum.

Chiloglottis reflexa (Labillardière) Druce

Ant Orchid **Ss**

A small orchid 4-12cm high. Found in sheltered damp places in gullies on sandstone. Uncommon to rare in the area.

Range: NSW coast and ranges, also Qld, Vic, Tas and SA. **Leaves:** similar to *C. formicifera*. **Flower:** GREENISH BROWN to PURPLE, segments to 20mm long; the labellum is more or less flat, largely covered with shiny black and red calli, some small and stalked, others larger and club-shaped. There is one large black notched callus at the rear of the labellum. **Flowering time:** February-May (or much of the year, according to some authors). **Name:** *reflexa* = bent backwards, probably referring to the petals.

Chiloglottis trapeziformis Fitzgerald

Broad-lip Bird Orchid **Ss**

A small orchid to 8cm tall. The type specimen is from Liverpool but the species is probably now rare in the area.

Range: coast and ranges in south-eastern Australia. **Leaves:** similar to *C. formicifera*. **Flower:** BROWNISH GREEN to REDDISH, segments to 15mm long; labellum to 12mm long and 7mm wide, diamond shaped, with a prominent central group of stalkless black calli. **Flowering time:** September-November. **Name:** *trapeziformis* = Lat. trapezium-shaped.

• *Corybas* Salisbury

Helmet Orchids, Red Helmets

A genus of terrestrial orchids with about 100 species widely distributed through northern India, southern China, South-east Asia, Polynesia, Australia and NZ. There are 15 species in Australia. These obscure but remarkable little orchids are always found in moist dark places in scrub or forest where sandy soils have been enriched by leaf mould.

The common method of spreading is vegetative, by producing new tubers at the end of horizontal roots. Hence they usually grow in dense colonies. Pollination is apparently by gnats; it may be that the flowers mimic certain fungi which are part of the life cycle of fungus gnats. Following fertilisation

the ovary is often raised by a surprising growth of the flower stem, sometimes by as much as 30cm.

Name: *Corybas* = after a Corybant or wild dancing priest of the goddess Cybele in Phrygia. It bears no apparent relationship to the orchid. It was given in 1807 by the English botanist Richard Salisbury in most improper circumstances: Robert Brown had collected a species in eastern Australia and coined the very apt name *Corysanthes* (Gk: *corys*, helmet, *anthos*, flower). Ferdinand Bauer had illustrated it. Before Brown could publish the name, however, Salisbury had pirated the genus under his name of *Corybas* by compiling an inaccurate description from his memory of Bauer's plate. Because of the rules of priority, Salisbury's name is accepted.[13]

Corybas aconitiflorus Salisbury

Cradle Orchid **Ss**

Found in moist dark places in scrub and forest on sandy soils. Moderately common on both sides of the harbour.

Range: Sydney area, south coast, Blue Mountains, NSW north coast, Qld, Vic and Tas. **Leaf:** to 35mm long, heart-shaped, DARK GREEN above, PURPLISH below. **Flower:** to 30mm long, PURPLISH, the hooded dorsal sepal dominates the flower, completely covering the other parts. **Flowering time:** May-June. **Name:** *aconitiflorus* = flower like *Aconitum* (poisonous plants of the Crowsfoot family).

Corybas fimbriatus (R. Brown) H. G. Reichenbach

Fringed Helmet Orchid **Ss**

Found in moist dark places in scrub and forests on sandy soils. Mainly a near-coastal species which is common in the Royal National Park but rare north of the harbour. Distinguish from *C. pruinosus* by the lack of calli on the surface of the labellum. The explorer Dr Ludwig Leichhardt collected a specimen in 'Sidney at the rocks near Farm Cove. May 1842'.[14]

Range: NSW coast and ranges, also Qld, Vic, Tas. **Leaf:** more or less circular, green on both sides. **Flower:** to 30mm long, DARK RED, hooded, labellum circular, with strongly toothed, incurved margins. **Flowering time:** May-July. **Name:** *fimbriatus* = Lat. fringed.

Corybas fordhamii (Rupp) Rupp

Banded Helmet Orchid **Ss**

A tiny species, uncommon and rarely seen, found in dense

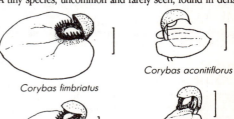

Corybas fimbriatus

Corybas aconitiflorus

Corybas pruinosus

Corybas undulatus

Corybas fordhamii

Corybas unguiculatus

heathy sedgelands. Recorded from Maddens Plains on the Woronora Plateau. It is usually only visible after fire has razed the sedges. Even then it can only be seen by bending down and closely scrutinising the ground.

Range: coastal parts of eastern mainland Australia and NZ. **Leaves:** heart-shaped, to 20mm long, green both sides, held above the soil. **Flowers:** about 14mm long, REDDISH PURPLE with white markings, much narrower than other species. **Flowering time:** July-August. **Name:** *fordhamii* = after F. Fordham, the initial collector.

Corybas pruinosus

(R. Cunningham) H. G. Reichenbach

Toothed Helmet Orchid **Ss**

Found in moist dark places in scrub and forest on sandy soils. Moderately common north of the harbour, rare in the Royal National Park.

Range: NSW coast. **Leaf:** to 30mm long, more or less circular, green both sides. **Flowers:** to 20mm long, GREYISH/PURPLE; labellum about 10mm wide, purple, circular, with a rounded central dome surrounded by numerous pointed protuberances (calli) and with toothed margins. **Flowering time:** April-June. **Name:** *pruinosus* = frosty or waxy, refering to the grey-green leaf underside.

Corybas undulatus (R. Cunningham) Rupp & Nicholls

Tailed Helmet Orchid **Ss**

Found in moist dark places in scrub and forests on sandy soils. Mainly found north of the harbour, also in Royal National Park. An uncommon species, but it can be locally common after fires. The leaves can be very small on species growing in open country.

Range: NSW coast and Qld. **Leaf:** 5-20mm long, heart-shaped, grey-green above, reddish below. **Flowers:** to 15mm long, DARK RED, hooded; labellum broad, with a white central area encircled by numerous red protuberances, margins finely toothed, with a short tail at the tip. **Flowering time:** May-June. **Name:** *undulatus* = Lat. wavy.

Corybas unguiculatus (R. Brown) H. G. Reichenbach

Pelicans, Small Helmet Orchid **Ss**

Found in moist dark places in scrub and forest on sandy soils. Uncommon in the Royal National Park, rare north of the harbour.

Range: Sydney area, northern tablelands, Vic, Tas, SA and NZ. **Leaf:** to 30mm long, heart-shaped, grey-green above, red beneath. **Flowers:** to 15mm long, DARK RED to PURPLE BLACK, hooded; labellum broad with a white central area and finely toothed margins. **Flowering time:** June. **Name:** *unguiculatus* = Lat. clawed.

• Cryptostylis R. Brown

A genus of terrestrial orchids with about 20 species distributed in Australia, South-east Asia and the Pacific. There are 5 species in Australia, with one extending to NZ.

The plants can be recognised when not flowering by the single erect leathery leaf which does not die back in winter. The exception is the rare species *C. hunteriana* which is a leafless saprophyte.

Each plant has several spidery flowers on a stem 20-40cm high. The flowers are upside down with conspicuous colourful labellums. The other segments are reduced to slender green arms, serving as insect guides.

The genus is remarkable for the method of pollination

Cryptostylis erecta

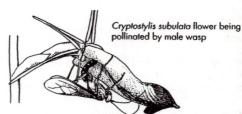

Cryptostylis subulata flower being pollinated by male wasp

by 'pseudo-copulation' with male wasps (*Lissopimpla* genus) which are attracted by a special scent.

The plants usually form small dense colonies in sandy soils in moderately shady locations.

Name: *Cryptostylis* = Gk. *crypto*, to conceal, *stylos*, a style or column.

Cryptostylis erecta R. Brown

Hooded Orchid **Ss**

A common species in the area, in sandy soils in heath and woodland.

Range: NSW coast and Blue Mountains, Qld and Vic. **Leaf:** erect, leathery, lanceolate, 8-15cm long, purplish below. **Flowers:** labellum pale with conspicuous RED veins, erect, forming a large hood. **Flowering time:** November-December. **Name:** *erecta* = Lat. erect, referring to the labellum.

Cryptostylis hunteriana Nicholls
Ss Vulnerable 3VC-
A very rare species, collected in the past from the Ku-ring-gai area and recently from near Campbelltown, on sandstone. A saprophyte.

Range: NSW coastal areas south from the Hawkesbury and eastern Vic. **Leaf:** none. **Flowers:** labellum erect, about 30mm long, densely covered in short dark RED glandular hairs and with red-black markings, the edges rolled upwards. **Flowering time:** December-February. **Name:** *hunteriana* = in honour of W. Hunter, a surveyor in the Orbost district, who collected the original specimens.

Cryptostylis leptochila F. Mueller
A rare species in the area, not found near the coast unless at high altitude. It is found on Maddens Plains, in Heathcote National Park and the Royal National Park.

Range: NSW coast and ranges, also Qld, Vic and Tas. **Leaf:** ovate, leathery, purplish below, to 10cm long. **Flowers:** labellum erect, to 20mm long, densely covered in soft short RED hairs, the margins rolled back and the tip often reflexed, with a black raised central ridge and black swollen markings (calli). **Flowering time:** December-February. **Name:** *leptochila* = Gk. slender lip.

Cryptostylis subulata
(Labillardière) H. G. Reichenbach

Large Tongue Orchid, Duck Orchid **Ss**
A common species in the area, in sandy soils in heath and woodland.

Range: NSW coast and ranges, Qld, Vic, Tas and SA. **Leaf:** erect, leathery, lanceolate, 8-15cm long, yellowish-green on both surfaces. **Flowers:** labellum about 22-30mm long, YELLOWISH-GREEN, RED towards the tip, edges folded upwards, with a conspicuous dark red projection below the tip. **Flowering time:** October-March. **Name:** *subulata* = Lat. awl-shaped. 'Duck' as the labellum somewhat resembles a duck's bill.

• *Cyrtostylis* R. Brown
A genus of small terrestrial orchids with 4 Australian species and one in NZ.
It is closely related to *Acianthus*, and included in that genus by many authors. The comments are the same as for *Acianthus*.

Name: *Cyrtostylis* = Gk. *cyrtos*, curved, *stylos*, a style or column.

Cyrtostylis reniformis R. Brown
(previously *Acianthus reniformis*)
Mosquito orchid **Ss**
A rare species in the area, mainly found north of the harbour. Occurs in dark shady places beneath bracken or shrubs, in sandy soils.

Range: NSW coast and ranges, all eastern states and NZ. **Leaf:** heart-shaped, grey-green above, paler and watery-crystalline beneath, 20-40mm long, held horizontal near to the ground. **Flowers:** EARTHY RED, segments to 8mm long, the labellum is conspicuous (with 2 tiny nectar glands visible near the joint). **Flowering time:** July-August. **Name:** *reniformis* = Lat. kidney-shaped, referring to the leaves.

• *Dipodium* R. Brown
A genus of terrestrial orchids with about 25 species, distributed in Malaysia, NG, the Pacific, and Australia. There are 8 species in Australia, 6 of which are leafless saprophytes.

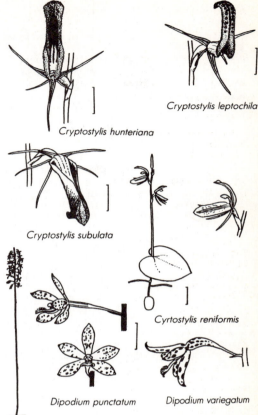

Cryptostylis hunteriana

Cryptostylis leptochila

Cryptostylis subulata

Cyrtostylis reniformis

Dipodium punctatum

Dipodium variegatum

Name: *Dipodium* = Gk. *di*, 2, *podion*, a little foot, referring to the 2 stalks on the anther cells.

Dipodium punctatum (Smith) R. Brown
Hyacinth Orchid **Ss**
Leafless saprophytic orchid with bright pink flowers on a dark purplish fleshy stem 40-80cm high. It prefers dry sandy soils in coastal forests. A very beautiful orchid which is quite common in the area. R. D. Fitzgerald wrote that it is 'frequently to be seen in the hands of Christmas holiday-makers, who cannot fail to notice its spike of spotted flowers growing leafless from the baked ground, at the foot of some gnarled gum tree—almost the only flower in that dry season, and all the more remarkable for the specially barren situation it elects to grow in'.[15]

Range: NSW coast; mainly from the Sydney area to Ulladulla. **Leaf:** none. **Flowers:** 10-50 in a raceme, BRIGHT PINK with dark spots, 10-30mm wide; labellum hairy. **Flowering time:** December-April. **Name:** *punctatum* = Lat. dotted. Two other common names were Plum Pudding Flower and Dragon's Head. **Note:** Some confusion surrounds the exact identity of the local species. It seems that the common coastal form with curled back perianth segments is a separate unnamed species (proper *D. punctatum* has cupped segments). A very dark purple form from Thornleigh, and elsewhere in NSW, is probably another unnamed species.

Dipodium variegatum M. Clements & D. Jones

Ss (not illustrated)

Very similar to *D. punctatum*, with which it often grows. Although only described in 1987, it is common in the area in sandy coastal forests. It differs from *D. punctatum* by the green stems, small leaf at the base, densely hairy patch on labellum, and a spotted and humped ovary.

Range: coastal parts of eastern Vic, NSW and Qld. **Flowers:** PALE PINK with purple spots extending to the ovary, which is humped. **Name:** *variegatum* = Lat. variegated.

• *Diuris* Smith

Double Tails

A genus of terrestrial orchids with about 40 species, concentrated in south-east and south-west Australia. All the species are Australian except for one endemic to Timor.

The usual habitat is open grassland or grassy understory in forest. All the local species occur on the Cumberland Plain. They are uncommon on sandstone.

Pollination is by native bees. The flowers mimic pea flowers which usually attract the same insects. The plants are deciduous, dying away in summer.

The edible tubers were consumed by Aborigines. Fitzgerald described them as 'sweet, mawkish, with a slight taste of raw potato.'[16] They were popular with European children in colonial times who knew them as 'boyams' or 'yams'. An observer in 1832 noted that they could readily recognise their favourite 'boyams' among the specimens he collected. Fitzgerald, in the 1870s, complained that one species was becoming rare around Sydney because of the activities of children.

Identification can be difficult because the species are often very similar (and variation within each species may be wide). Natural hybrids are common.

Name: *Diuris* = Gk. 2-tailed.

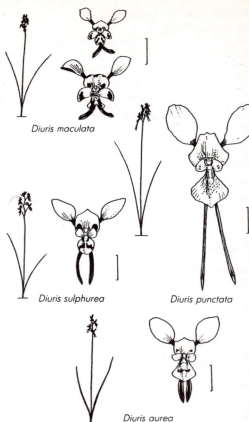

Diuris maculata

Diuris sulphurea

Diuris punctata

Diuris aurea

Diuris aurea Smith

Golden Donkey Orchid **Cumb, Ss**

Found in colonies in forests on clay soils on the Cumberland Plain and also on sandstone. Probably the most common *Diuris* in the area.

Range: Sydney region and NSW north coast. **Leaves:** 2, grass-like to 20cm long. **Flowers:** 2-5, about 35mm across, GOLDEN with DARK BROWN MARKINGS, with a raised plate (callus) on the labellum. Flower stems to 30-40cm high. **Flowering time:** August-October **Name:** *aurea* = Lat. golden. **Note:** *D. aurea* and *D. sulphurea* are very similar species. The most practical distinctions in the field are the colour and labellum plates; *D. sulphurea* is a pure sulphur yellow and lacks a raised labellum plate; *D. aurea* is a golden or canary yellow and has a plate.

Diuris maculata Smith

Spotted Double Tail, Leopard Orchid **Cumb, Ss**

Found in grassland and open forest in clay soils. Fairly common in the area. The earliest *Diuris* to flower.

Range: all states except WA and NT. **Leaves:** to 20cm tall, channelled, 2-3 per plant. **Flowers:** 2-8, about 30mm wide, YELLOW, strongly spotted with dark brown (especially on rear surfaces). The lateral sepals cross in front of the flower. Flowering stem to 20-30cm tall. **Flowering time:** July-November. **Name:** *maculata* = Lat. spotted.

Diuris punctata R. Brown

Purple Donkey Orchid **Cumb, Ss**

Found in grassland and open forest in clay soils on the Cumberland Plain. Uncommon to rare in the area.

Range: NSW coast, ranges and inland areas, Vic, SA and Qld. **Leaves:** 2, grass-like, to 25cm long. **Flowers:** 2-10, about 60mm wide, PINK-PURPLE, often with darker markings. Flower stem to 50cm tall. **Flowering time:** September-December. **Name:** *punctata* = Lat. dotted.

Diuris sulphurea R. Brown

Tiger Orchid **Cumb, Ss**

In colonies on drier clay soils of the Cumberland Plain, uncommon on sandstone.

Range: all states except WA and NT. **Leaves:** usually 2, 20-50cm long, grass-like. Slightly scented. **Flowers:** 2-7, about 30mm wide, SULPHUR-YELLOW with strong brown markings, lacking a callus on the labellum. Flower stem to 50cm tall. **Flowering time:** August-November. **Name:** *sulphurea* = Lat. sulphurous.

• *Eriochilus* R. Brown

A genus of small terrestrial orchids with about 6 species, all endemic to Australia. Pollination is by small bees.

Name: *Eriochilus* = Gk. *erion*, wool, *cheilos*, a lip.

Eriochilus autumnalis R. Brown

Parson's Bands **Ss, Castl**
Found in damp sandy soil in open heath and woodland.
A fairly common species in the area.

Range: NSW coast, ranges and inland areas, also all states except WA
and NT. **Leaf:** small, hairy, heart-shaped, 10-15mm long, dark green,
purple below, often incompletely developed at flowering time.
Flowers: 1-3 on thin, wiry, hairy stems up to 12cm high; lateral sepals
prominent, WHITISH, to 10mm long; the other segments small, green;
labellum recurved, cream with small purple spots, covered in short stiff
hairs. **Flowering time:** March-May. **Name:** *autumnalis* = Lat. autumn
flowering.

Eriochilus cucullatus

(Labillardière) H. G. Reichenbach

Parson's Bands **Ss, Castl** (not illustrated)
Found in damp sandy soil in thick forest. A more robust
species than the preceding. Uncommon in the area, e.g. Royal
National Park.

Range: NSW coast, ranges and inland areas, also all states except WA
and NT. **Leaf:** shiny, ovate, 10-30mm long, pale green. **Flowers:** 1-
3 on glandular-hairy stems up to 25cm high; lateral sepals prominent,
WHITISH PINK, to 17mm long; otherwise similar to *E. autumnalis.*
Flowering time: March-May. **Name:** *cucullatus* = hooded.

• *Erythrorchis* Garay

A genus of climbing orchids with 3 species widely distributed
from Japan to Australia. There is one species in Australia.
The genus was previously known as *Galeola.*

Name: *Erythrorchis* = Gk. *erythros*, red, *orchis*, orchid, since
it dries deep red.

Erythrorchis cassythoides

(A. Cunningham ex Lindley) Garay

Bootlace Orchid, Climbing Orchid **Ss**
A leafless climbing saprophytic orchid with stems 0.5-5m long.
Usually found in sunny places in woodland or in the margins
of rainforest. Uncommon in the area, on sandstone. It can
be very hard to spot and plants may not appear in some
years. It climbs by means of short stiff, hooked roots.
Pollination is by small native bees attracted by the perfume
of the flowers.

Range: NSW coast and ranges north from the Illawarra, also Qld. **Leaves:**
none. **Flowers:** segments 12-18mm long, BROWN and YELLOW, fleshy,
brittle; labellum white with wavy margins, hairy; in short panicles spaced
along the stems. **Flowering time:** September-November. **Name:**
cassythoides = resembling *Cassytha*, a genus of leafless climbing plants
in Lauraceae.

• *Gastrodia* R. Brown

A genus of terrestrial saprophytic orchids with about 20 species
widely distributed from India to NZ. There are 2 Australian
species.

Name: *Gastrodia* = Gk. *gaster*, a stomach, from the inflated
appearance of the flowers.

Gastrodia sesamoides R. Brown

Native Potato **Ss**
A leafless orchid with a fleshy brown stem to 90cm tall, carrying

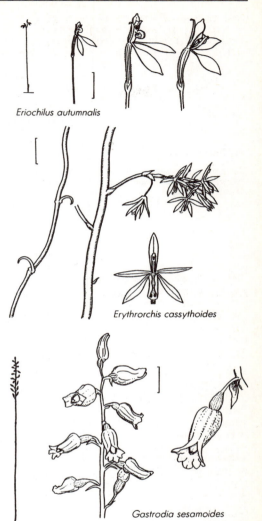

Eriochilus autumnalis

Erythrorchis cassythoides

Gastrodia sesamoides

numerous brown and white flowers. Found in moist sheltered
places in forests where there is plenty of leaf litter and
decaying plant matter. It is a very uncommon species in the
area.

How this leafless plant supplies itself with nourishment
was long a mystery. It had generally been supposed that it
was a parasite on the roots of other plants, however the Sydney
botanist J. McLuckie in 1923 found that the tuberous root
was inhabited by both a fungus and a bacteria. The fungus
inhabits the superficial cells of the root and the fungal
filaments replace the root hairs in supplying soil nutrients
to the plant. Unlike other root fungi, however, the fungus
does not synthesise nitrogen for the plant. Instead this
function is performed by the bacteria which pervade the root.

The tubers were roasted and eaten by Aborigines in Victoria

and Tasmania. Daniel Bunce, a botanical traveller, tasted them while travelling with Aborigines in the Dandenongs in the 1850s. He found them ' . . . especially plentiful, large, and well-flavoured.'[17] The flavour has been described as resembling beetroot but watery and insipid.

The flowers produce a strong sweet perfume on warm days. Pollination is by a small native bee which enters to collect a starch-rich false pollen from the labellum.

Range: NSW coast, ranges and western slopes, and all other states except NT; also NZ. **Leaf:** none. **Flowers:** numerous, PALE CINNAMON BROWN with a WHITE interior, 15-20mm long, upside down; the segments are fused to form a sac. **Flowering time:** August-January. **Name:** *sesamoides* = resembling the sesame plant. **Note:** it is likely that this is an unnamed species. True *G. sesamoides* is probably a slender pretzel-like plant to 40cm tall, with small orange-brown flowers; collected in the past from Sydney but now rare or locally extinct. It occured in woodland on deep coastal sands.

• *Genoplesium* R. Brown

(previously included in *Prasophyllum*)
Midge Orchids
A genus with about 30 species, mostly endemic to Australia. All are small slender plants with dense racemes of tiny flowers. They are probably the most obscure and difficult to detect plants in the area because they are inconspicuous and grass-like and often grow in dense sedgeland.

The flowering stem is contained in the hollow cylindrical leaf, and emerges through a slit near the tip. The labellum of some species is hinged and trembles at the slightest touch or breeze.

Pollination is by tiny ferment flies (such as the fruit fly *Drosophila*) which are attracted by the sweet perfume and dark-coloured flowers.

It is closely related to *Prasophyllum* and was until recently included in that genus.[18]

Name: *Genoplesium* = Gk. near-race, referring to its closeness to *Prasophyllum*.

Genoplesium baueri R. Brown

Ss   Rare 3RC-
A saprophyte. Found in shady places in woodland. Abundant where it occurs, mainly north of the harbour; rare in the Royal National Park.

Range: Sydney area and south coast. **Leaf:** to 12cm long, the free part to 25mm long, fleshy, brittle. **Flowers:** about 10mm across, with widely spreading wing-like lateral sepals, RED AND GREEN, OR ALL RED; labellum dark red, thick and fleshy, bent sharply upwards; 2-6 flowers in a spike to 30mm long. **Flowering time:** January-May. **Name:** *Baueri* = after Ferdinand Bauer, renowned botanical artist on Flinders' 1801-03 voyage of exploration around Australia.

Genoplesium filiforme

(Fitzgerald) D. Jones & M. Clements
Ss
Very uncommon in the area. Found in woodland, among shrubs and in mossy depressions on sandstone rocks.

Range: Sydney area, NSW north coast. **Leaf:** to 25cm long, the free part about 20mm long. **Flowers:** about 5mm wide, nodding, GREEN with PURPLISH-RED markings, petals and labellum with microscopically hairy margins; labellum purplish-red with a prominent callus; about 8 well spaced flowers in a spike about 20mm long. **Flowering time:** January-April. **Name:** *filiforme* = Lat. thread-like

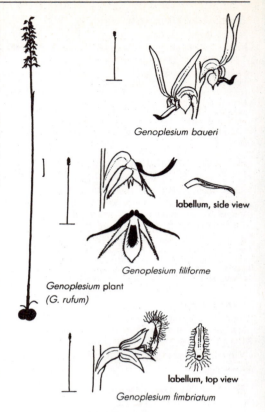

Genoplesium baueri

labellum, side view

Genoplesium filiforme

Genoplesium plant (*G. rufum*)

labellum, top view

Genoplesium fimbriatum

Genoplesium fimbriatum

(R. Brown) D. Jones & M. Clements
Ss
Found in marshy places in open woodland and in mossy depressions on sandstone rocks. The most common Midge Orchid in the area; abundant on the north shore; also present in Heathcote National Park and Royal National Park.

The flowers have a lemon perfume in warm weather. The labellum trembles to the touch. 'After a careful examination, I came to the conclusion that the most probable method in which this interesting little orchid becomes impregnated is by a very minute insect alighting on the under surface of the labellum and following it up to the flower, the lip giving way to its pressure upwards (by being lifted on the hinge) should the visitor be too large.'[19]

Range: NSW coast and ranges. **Leaf:** to 25cm long, the free part about 20mm long. **Flowers:** about 5mm across, PALE with RED STRIPES; labellum pale red or cream, covered in hairs; 5-30 tiny flowers in a dense spike to 7cm long. **Flowering time:** March-April. **Name:** *fimbriatum* = Lat. fringed.

Genoplesium nudiscapum

(J. D. Hooker) D. Jones & M. Clements
Dense Midge Orchid   **Ss**
Found in woodland in sandy soil. Present in the Royal National Park and uncommon north of the harbour.

Range: Sydney area, Blue Mountains, south coast and southern tablelands; Vic and Qld. **Leaf:** to 10cm long, slender, the free part (to 15mm long) jutting out at an angle to the stem like a tail (a useful identifying feature). **Flowers:** about 4mm wide, nodding, hairless, changing colour with aging, from GREEN to PURPLE to YELLOW, labellum oblong, similarly coloured; 15-40 flowers in a dense spike to 20mm long. The sepals and petals are tipped with microscopic glands. **Flowering time:** February-March. **Name:** *nudiscapum* = Lat. naked-stemmed.

Genoplesium pumilum

(J. D. Hooker) D. Jones & M. Clements

Gold/Green Midge Orchid   **Ss**

Found in woodland, coastal scrubs and mossy depressions on sandstone rocks. A moderately common species, found on both sides of the harbour.

Range: Sydney area, Blue Mountains, Vic, Qld and NZ.   **Leaf:** to 20cm long, slender, the free part to 20mm long.   **Flowers:** about 3mm across, hairless, nodding, GREEN, with bright red markings (other species have purple markings, not red), rarely found open; 8-15 flowers in a spike to 25mm long. The sepals and petals are tipped with microscopic glands. **Flowering time:** February-May.   **Name:** *pumilum* = Lat. low, dwarf.

Genoplesium rufum

(R. Brown) D. Jones & M. Clements

Red Midge Orchid   **Ss**

Found in woodland. Widely distributed but uncommon in the area.

Range: restricted to the Sydney area and Blue Mountains.   **Leaf:** to 20cm long, the free part about 25mm long.   **Flowers:** 2.5-4mm wide, nodding, LIGHT RED, petals and sepals with thickened red margins, not opening widely, labellum smooth, yellowish at the base with thickened red margins; 10-20 flowers in a fairly open spike to 30mm long.   **Flowering time:** January-May.   **Name:** *rufum* = Lat. red.

Genoplesium woollsii

(F. Mueller) D. Jones & M. Clements

Ss

Found in open forest on sandy soil and in mossy depressions on sandstone rocks. Uncommon in the area and mainly found on the north shore (Chatswood; Asquith; Lane Cove). Very similar to *G. filiforme*. To distinguish them a hand-lens is needed to examine the labellum callus (the central fleshy swelling): that of *P. filiforme* is conspicuous, while that of *P. woollsii* is inconspicuous and deeply channelled.

Range: Sydney area and southern tablelands.   **Leaf:** to 25cm long, free part 20-30mm long.   **Flowers:** about 4mm across, PURPLE with GREEN MARKINGS, nodding, very dense on the scape, the margins of the sepals and labellum are lined with microscopic hairs (a useful identifying feature).   **Flowering time:** February-May.   **Name:** *Woollsii* = after William Woolls, a clergyman, teacher, and amateur botanist, one of the most influential figures in nineteenth century NSW botany.

• Glossodia R. Brown

Waxlips

A genus of terrestrial orchids with 2 species, both endemic to eastern Australia. It is distinguished from *Caladenia* by the presence of a prominent callus arising at the base of the labellum.

William Woolls wrote that they 'enliven the face of nature in early spring . . . During the latest season I noticed hundreds of these beautiful flowers born, as it were, "to blush unseen" amidst the thick scrub . . . '[20]

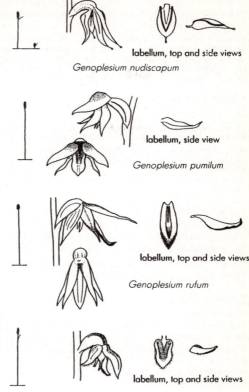

labellum, top and side views

Genoplesium nudiscapum

labellum, side view

Genoplesium pumilum

labellum, top and side views

Genoplesium rufum

labellum, top and side views

Genoplesium woollsii

Fitzgerald noted a feature not mentioned by later authors: 'The agents of fertilization appear to be large flies that lighting upon the labellum are pressed by its spring action against the anther and stigma.'[21]

Name: *Glossodia* = Gk. *glossodes*, tongue-like, from the tongue-like calli at the base of the labellum (Woolls' mistranslation 'tongue-tooth' also seems quite appropriate).

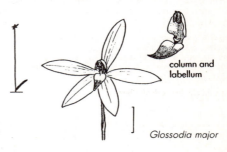

column and labellum

Glossodia major

Glossodia major R. Brown

Wax Lip Orchid   **Ss**

Found in woodland on sandstone. A moderately common

species in the area. Fitzgerald noted that the leaf has a sweet perfume, especially when bruised, and that the odour is long retained by the dried plant.

Range: NSW coast, ranges and inland areas, also all other states except WA and NT. **Leaf:** to 20cm long, oblong, hairy. **Flowers:** 40-60mm wide, ROSE-PURPLE; labellum heart-shaped, divided into a white base and purple tip; labellum callus with notched yellow apex. **Flowering time:** July-September. **Name:** *major* = Lat. greater.

Glossodia minor R. Brown

Ss

Found in heath and woodland on sandstone. A common species in the area, often locally abundant in spring.

Range: NSW coastal areas and Qld. **Leaf:** 10-30mm long, broad, ground-hugging, hairy. **Flower:** about 20mm wide, ROSE-PURPLE; labellum heart-shaped; labellum callus divided in 2 parallel parts, curved forwards, each with dark club-like tips. **Flowering time:** September (a little in advance of *G. major*). **Name:** *minor* = Lat. lesser.

• *Lyperanthus* R. Brown

Beak Orchids

A genus of terrestial orchids with about 5 species. Four are found in Australia; the other occurs in NZ and New Caledonia.

Name: *Lyperanthus* = Gk. *hyperos*, sad or mournful, *anthos*, flower, referring to the gloomy colour of the flowers.

Lyperanthus nigricans R. Brown

Redbeaks **Ss**

Found in heath and woodland on sandstone, especially in sunny coastal heath. A common but very shy species. It rarely flowers except after summer fires, when it can be locally abundant.

Pollination is by a native bee which forces a passage between the labellum and column.

Range: NSW coast, also Vic, Tas, SA and WA. **Leaf:** heart-shaped to oval, ground-hugging, fleshy, to 10cm long. **Flowers:** few to several on a fleshy stem 12-20cm high; WHITE with RED STRIPES, each protected by a conspicuous rusty-coloured bract. **Flowering time:** August-September. **Name:** *nigricans* = Lat. becoming black, since the plant turns a deep black colour when dried.

Lyperanthus suaveolens R. Brown

Brown Beaks **Ss**

Found in heath and woodland on sandstone. A moderately common species in the area. The spidery flowers resemble small horned beasts. They are strongly fragrant, but only on warm sunny days.

Range: NSW coast, Blue Mountains, Qld, Vic and Tas. **Leaf:** narrow, stiff, leathery, erect, pale on the inside, 12-26cm long. **Flowers:** 2-6, RED-BROWN to YELLOWISH GREEN, segments 20-30mm long. **Flowering time:** August-October. **Name:** *suaveolens* = Lat. sweet smelling.

• *Microtis* R. Brown

Onion, Ear or Mignonette Orchids

A genus of terrestrial orchids with 9 species, 8 in Australia (2 of which extend into Asia) and 1 endemic to NZ.

The plants are 20-40cm high, with a single slender cylindrical leaf from which the flowering stem emerges via a slit. The tiny green flowers are about 6mm long and as many as 40 may be arranged spirally in an often dense spike.

column and labellum

Glossodia minor

Lyperanthus nigricans

Lyperanthus suaveolens

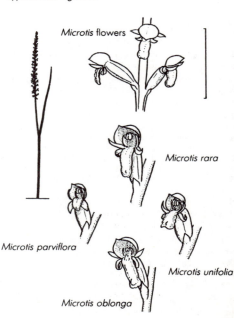

Microtis flowers

Microtis rara

Microtis parviflora

Microtis unifolia

Microtis oblonga

They are usually found in moist sunny depressions, swampy areas and grasslands in high rainfall areas; on clays, alluviums and sandy soils. They are very hard to spot because of their inconspicuous shape and colouring.

Pollination is by a range of small insects. *Microtis parviflora* has been observed to be pollinated by 3 species of small black ants. Plants are also spread by vegetative reproduction.

The local species are closely related and can be difficult to distinguish. The best guide is to compare the length of the labellum to the ovary.

The genus is closely allied to *Prasophyllum.*

Name: *Microtis* = Gk. *micros*, tiny, *otis*, an ear, referring to the tiny appendages on each side of the column which resemble ears.

Microtis oblonga Rogers

Ss, Cumb

Found in marshy heath and sedgelands. Fairly common in the area, but only flowering after fire. Some authors consider that it is the same as *M. rara.*

Range: widespread in south-eastern Australia. **Leaf:** similar to *M. rara.* **Flowers:** similar to *M. rara*, except larger and with the labellum closely pressed against the ovary. **Name:** *oblonga* = Lat. oblong, referring to the labellum.

Microtis parviflora R. Brown

Slender Onion Orchid **Ss, Cumb**

Found in moist low-lying areas in open forest and grassland. Found north of the harbour, but uncommon.

Range: NSW coast and ranges, and all states except WA and NT; also NZ and New Caledonia. **Flowers:** GREEN or YELLOWISH GREEN; labellum to 2mm long, more or less heart shaped, bent downwards, with or without a tiny callus at the tip; in a dense spike. **Flowering time:** September-October **Name:** *parviflora* = Lat. small-leaved.

Microtis rara R. Brown

Scented Onion Orchid, Sweet Onion Orchid **Ss, Cumb**

Mainly found amongst grass woodland near the coast. Uncommon, scattered through the area. The flowers have a sweet scent in warm weather.

Distinguished from the closely related *M. unifolia* by the more slender habit, the flowers prominently stalked and more distantly spaced, and the longer labellum and more slender ovary.

Range: NSW coast and ranges, all other states except NT. **Flowers:** GREEN, labellum to 5mm long, about as long as the ovary, bent downwards, narrowing about half way, notched at the tip, with a callus; in an open spike. **Flowering time:** October-November. **Name:** *rara* = Lat. rare.

Microtis unifolia (J. R. Forster) H. G. Reichenbach

Common Onion Orchid **Ss, Cumb**

Usually found in patches in swampy ground on many soil types. The flowers are fragrant in warm weather. Uncommon in the area, occuring north of Botany Bay.

Range: NSW coast, ranges and inland areas and all other states except NT, also NZ, New Caledonia, Indonesia, the Phillipines, Japan and China. **Flowers:** GREEN, labellum to 2.5mm long, about half the length of the ovary, oblong, often curled, notched at the apex, with a callus near the tip; in a dense spike. **Flowering time:** October-November. **Name:** *unifolia* = Lat. one-leafed.

Orthoceras strictum

• *Orthoceras* R. Brown

A terrestrial genus with one species, closely related to *Diuris.*

Name: *Orthoceras* = Gk. upright-horn, referring to the lateral sepals.

Orthoceras strictum R. Brown

Bird's Mouth Orchid, Horned Orchid **Ss**

Found mainly in open marshy sites with sedges, making it difficult to see. Occurs mainly north of the harbour; rare in the Royal National Park (more common in the Blue Mountains). It is entirely self-pollinating. Fitzgerald wrote: '*Orthoceras strictum* is by no means an attractive species— there is nothing either in colour or form to please the eye.'[22]

Range: NSW coast and ranges, also Qld, Vic, Tas, SA, NG, NZ and New Caledonia. **Leaves:** 2-5, to 30cm tall, erect, slender, grass-like. **Flowers:** 1-9 on a stem to 50cm high, about 10mm wide, YELLOWISH GREEN to DEEP BROWN, strongly hooded, with slender erect lateral sepals. **Flowering time:** November-January (mostly December). **Name:** *strictum* = Lat. erect.

• *Prasophyllum* R. Brown

Leek Orchids

A mainly endemic genus with about 45 species, with its centre of distribution in south-eastern Australia, particularly around Sydney, the Blue Mountains and nearby areas. 2 species extend to NZ.

All are terrestrial orchids with single erect leaves which sheath the flowering stem for much of its length. The leaves die off and the plants are dormant during summer. The flowers are upside down on the stem, usually crowded in erect racemes.

Fire is important to stimulate the flowering of most species and some may only be seen following hot summer fires. The lack of hot fires probably helps account for their rarity in suburban bushlands (rabbits and the loss of pollinators are other factors).

Most species prefer open locations in wet soils in heath and woodland. The flowers of the local species are pollinated by insects, usually small flies and beetles, attracted by nectar and scent.

Name: *Prasophyllum* = Gk. leek-leaf.

Prasophyllum australe R. Brown

Ss

Found in sedge mashes. Mainly a mountain species. It frequently reproduces by growing daughter tubers at the end of short horizontal roots (the only local *Prasophyllum* to do so). The flowers are very fragrant. It is closely related to *P. elatum*; the main observable difference being the sharply bent labellum.

Range: NSW coast and Blue Mountains, also all other states except NT. **Leaf:** to 75cm long, the free part to 30cm long, usually reddened at the base. **Flowers:** about 15mm wide, WHITE with REDDISH BROWN and GREEN stripes and markings; labellum reflexed, white, very rumpled; ovary erect against the stem: 15-60 flowers in a dense spike to 25cm long. **Flowering time:** September. **Name:** *australe* = Lat. southern.

Prasophyllum brevilabre (Lindley) J. D. Hooker

Ss

Found on moist heath and sedgeland near the coast. Moderately common in coastal heaths, mainly south of the harbour.

Range: NSW coast, ranges and some inland areas, also Qld, Vic and Tas. **Leaf:** to 35cm long, the free part to 8cm long, slender, fleshy. **Flowers:** about 10mm wide, GREEN with DARK RED markings or dark purplish green; labellum white, bent back sharply in the middle through 180°, with rumpled margins; 8-32 flowers on a spike to 20cm tall. **Flowering time:** August-January. **Name:** *brevilabre* = Lat. short lip i.e. labellum.

Prasophyllum elatum R. Brown

Tall Leek Orchid **Ss**

Usually in marshy heath but also in dry forest, in small groups. The flowers are fragrant. It is the commonest *Prasophyllum* in the area and the tallest orchid in Australia.

Range: NSW coast and Blue Mountains, also all states except NT. **Leaf:** 50-120cm long, stout, fleshy, GREEN to DARK PURPLE, the free part to 20cm long. **Flowers:** about 16mm wide, from pale green to almost black; labellum white; ovaries appressed against the stem; 15-60 flowers in a spike to 40cm long. **Flowering time:** August. **Name:** *elatum* = Lat. tall.

Prasophyllum flavum R. Brown

Yellow Leek Orchid **Ss**

A saprophytic species with yellowish flowers and brownish stem. It grows near decaying wood in dense moist undergrowth on sandstone, often in disturbed ground beside tracks, where timber has been buried. Occurs in the Royal National Park and on the north shore. The flowers are similar to *P. australe* except yellowish, and the labellum is less reflexed and pointed. It has a strong unpleasant smell like rancid olive oil.

Range: NSW coast and ranges, Qld, Vic and Tas. **Leaf:** to 60cm long, the free part absent or to 25mm long. **Flowers:** about 10mm wide, YELLOW or YELLOWISH GREEN, sometimes with reddish brown markings; ovaries closely appressed to the stem; labellum gently curved upwards, green with white or cream rumpled margins; 6-50 flowers in a crowded spike to 20cm long. **Flowering time:** October-February (mostly about Christmas). **Name:** *flavum* = Lat. yellow.

Prasophyllum odoratum R. Rogers

Ss

A tall species, to 25-70cm high, mainly found in coastal heaths. Flowers have a strong sweet fragrance. Closely related to *P.*

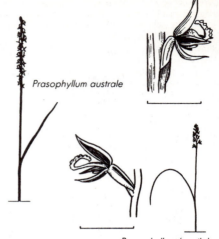

Prasophyllum australe

Prasophyllum brevilabre

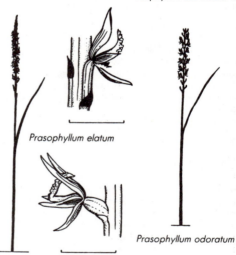

Prasophyllum elatum

Prasophyllum odoratum

patens; distinguish by reflexed labellum and scent.

Range: NSW coast, ranges and inland areas, also all states except NT. **Leaf:** to 70cm long, the free part to 20mm. **Flowers:** 10-15mm wide, GREEN and WHITE or with reddish stripes, on thick projecting ovaries; labellum white, with rumpled margins, sharply bent below the middle, with the tip projecting through the lateral sepals; 10-40 flowers. **Flowering time:** August-February. **Name:** *odoratum* = Lat. sweet smelling.

Prasophyllum patens R. Brown

Broad-lip Leek Orchid **Ss**

Mainly in coastal scrubs and heathlands. Uncommon. Flowers scentless.

Range: Sydney area, north coast, northern tablelands and Blue Mountains, Qld, Vic, Tas and SA. **Leaf:** to 30cm long, the free part to 15cm long, often withered at flowering time. **Flowers:** about 13mm wide, GREEN and WHITE or sometimes pinkish, with thick projecting ovaries; labellum bent upwards at the middle, white or pink, with rumpled margins; 15-50 flowers in a spike of variable density. **Flowering time:** September-December. **Name:** *patens* = Lat. spreading.

Prasophyllum striatum R. Brown

Striped Leek Orchid **Ss**
Found in sedge marshes. Moderately common in the area. The flowers have a foul musty odour, possibly to attract flies and blowflies.

Range: Sydney area, south coast and Blue Mountains. **Leaf:** to 30cm tall, free part up to 10cm long, very slender. **Flowers:** about 7mm wide, not opening widely, WHITE or GREENISH with conspicuous brown or purple stripes, 2–10 flowers in a spike to 5cm long. The sepals are tipped with tiny glands. **Flowering time:** April. **Name:** *striatum* = Lat. striped.

• *Pterostylis* R. Brown

Greenhoods
A genus of terrestrial orchids with about 120 species, mostly in Australia, but also in NZ, NG and New Caledonia. Most species are in south-eastern Australia.

Greenhoods are notable for their sensitive tongues, which withdraw at the slightest touch. 'So lifelike is it, that the first observation of a spike . . . with all its little tongues protruding and rapidly drawn in on the slightest touch, is certainly very startling and impressive.'[23]

Greenhoods usually grow in colonies which spread by the development of new tubers at the end of horizontal roots. The stem and leaves are deciduous and die back in summer or during drought. The leaves of all species (except *P. plumosa*) are very similar.

The method of pollination is ingenious. Small insects are attracted to the flower by nectar glands at the base of the labellum. The labellum is hinged at its base by an elastic strap (often called a claw) which when tripped causes the labellum to spring against the column, trapping the insect inside the hood. The hood (or galea) is formed by the dorsal sepal and petals. It prevents any method of escape except by climbing up through the column. As the insect does so it rubs against the sticky rostellum, receiving a spot of glue, and then past the anther where it collects the loose pollinia. It then travels to another greenhood, and while repeating the process, rubs off some of the pollen. The agents of pollination appear to be gnats, or sometimes small flies or mosquitoes.

Name: *Pterostylis* = Gk *pteron*, wing, *stylos*, style, referring to the winged column.

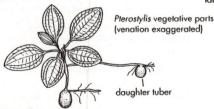

Pterostylis vegetative parts (venation exaggerated)

daughter tuber

Pterostylis acuminata R. Brown

Sharp Greenhood **Ss**
Found in colonies in sheltered sandy soil, mainly on

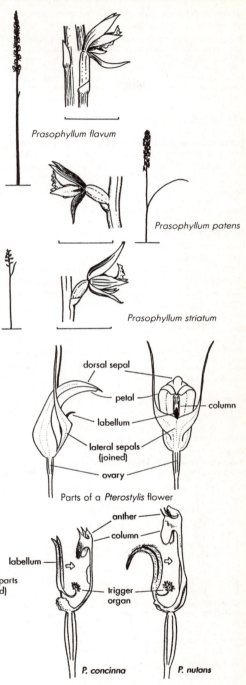

Prasophyllum flavum

Prasophyllum patens

Prasophyllum striatum

dorsal sepal

petal

labellum

column

lateral sepals (joined)

ovary

Parts of a *Pterostylis* flower

anther

column

labellum

trigger organ

P. concinna   *P. nutans*

Pterostylis pollination mechanisms

sandstone, rarely on shale. A fairly common species in the area, mainly north of the harbour.

Range: north from the Sydney region into Qld. **Leaves:** 3-5 in a tight basal rosette, oblong. **Flowers:** solitary, about 30mm long, often slightly nodding, GREEN and WHITE with a reddish brown tip, lateral sepals with points about 25mm long; the labellum is curved downwards. Flowering stem 15-25cm tall, leafless. **Flowering time:** April-May. **Name:** *acuminata* = drawn out into a long sharp point, referring to the labellum.

Pterostylis alveata Garnet
Ss

Found in colonies in sheltered wetter woodland. Uncommon to rare in the area, e.g. Waterfall, Royal National Park. It is very similar to *P. obtusa* except the flower is smaller and the lip on the mouth is blunt, not sharp as in that species.

Range: coastal parts of NSW and Vic. **Leaves:** several along the stem, rosette absent at flowering time. **Flowers:** 10-12mm long, GREEN; labellum pointed. **Name:** *alveata* = Lat. beehive-like.

Pterostylis baptistii R. D. Fitzgerald

King Greenhood **Ss**

Forms colonies in rainforest gullies. Locally rare, e.g. Narrabeen and La Perouse. It has the largest flower of any *Pterostylis.* There are 2 forms: one is a magnificent solitary plant to 60cm tall, with flowers 50-60mm long; the other occurs in colonies, is 20-30cm tall and has flowers 40-50mm long.

Range: NSW coasts, Qld and Vic. **Leaves:** 4-8 in a basal rosette, with curly margins, dark green, with short stalks. **Flowers:** solitary, very large, TRANSLUCENT WHITE with GREEN and BROWN colouring, hood gently curving, lateral sepals bent backwards. Flower stems leafless. **Flowering time:** September-October. **Name:** *baptistii* = after John Baptist, the original collector.

Pterostylis bicolor M. Clements & D. Jones

Midget Greenhood **Cumb**

Found in open forest on the Cumberland Plain (in clay soils or stony laterite). Usually solitary. Fairly common.

Range: NSW coast, ranges and inland areas, Qld and Vic. **Leaves:** 6-12 in an overlapping basal rosette, sessile, dark green, there are also numerous closely sheathing stem leaves **Flowers:** 15-25, each to 8mm

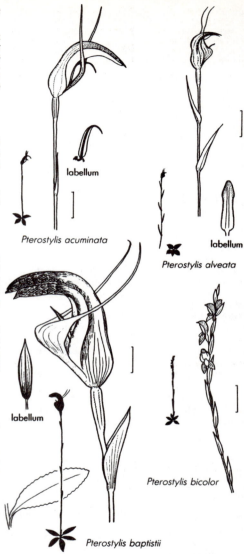

Pterostylis acuminata

labellum

Pterostylis alveata

labellum

labellum

Pterostylis bicolor

labellum

Pterostylis baptistii

long, GREEN or YELLOWISH, with hood bent forwards; lateral sepals concave, 6mm long, united for most of their length, blunt. Flower stem to 30cm, with sheathing leaves. **Flowering time:** September-December. **Name:** *bicolor* = Lat. 2-coloured. **Note:** this species has generally been confused with the inland species *P. mutica* in the past.

Pterostylis concinna R. Brown

Trim Greenhood **Ss**

Found in dense colonies on mossy rocks and damp leaf litter in sheltered forests and scrubs. A very common species in the area.

Range: NSW coastal areas and Blue Mountains, Vic, Tas and SA. **Leaves:** 4-6 in a basal rosette, thin. **Flowers:** solitary, to 15mm long,

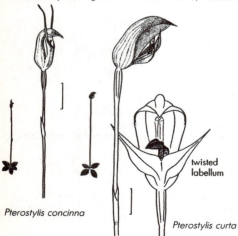

Pterostylis concinna

twisted labellum

Pterostylis curta

TRANSLUCENT with STRONG GREEN STRIPES and RED markings around the mouth; hood curving forward in its upper part, with a point about 3mm long; lateral sepals embracing the hood with points about 20mm long, labellum only slightly curved, largely hidden. **Flowering time:** July. **Name:** *concinna* = Lat. neat, trim, referring to its habit.

Pterostylis curta R. Brown
Brown Nose, Blunt Greenhood   **Ss**
Solitary or in colonies in moist forests and on creek banks. Common in the area.

Range: NSW coast, ranges and inland areas, also Qld, Vic, Tas and SA. **Leaves:** 2-6 in a basal rosette, stalked. **Flowers:** solitary, to 35mm long, WHITE with GREEN STRIPES and green and brown colouring; hood bent forward on its upper half. Flowering stem to 20cm high, leafless. **Flowering time:** July-September. **Name:** *curta* = Lat. short, referring to the labellum.

Pterostylis daintreana F. Mueller ex Bentham
Daintrey's Greenhood   **Ss**
Found as solitary specimens in shallow soil in the shadow of shrubs. An uncommon species, only recorded locally in the Royal National Park (Helensburg area).

Range: Sydney area and NSW south coast, also separately in southern Qld. **Leaves:** 5-8 in a basal rosette, dark green, stalked, sometimes finely toothed. **Flowers:** 3-10, to 6-8mm long, TRANSLUCENT with GREEN stripes, hood downcurved, hood and lateral sepals with thread-like points about 4mm long. Flowering stem to 30cm tall, leafless. **Flowering time:** April-July. **Name:** *daintreana* = in honour of Edwin Daintrey (1814-1887), who first identified the species at Sugar Works Bay, Sydney. He was a Sydney solicitor, amateur botanist and founding member of the Linnaean Society of NSW.

Pterostylis erecta Hunt
Upright Maroonhood   **Ss**
Found in sheltered woodland near the coast. A common

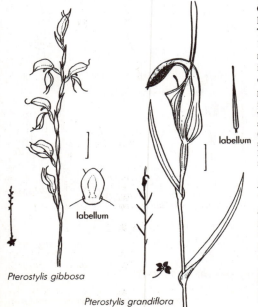

Pterostylis gibbosa

labellum

Pterostylis grandiflora

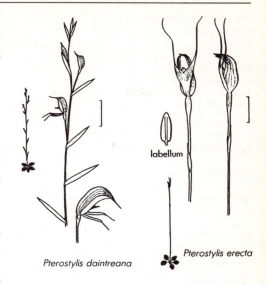

labellum

Pterostylis daintreana

labellum

Pterostylis erecta

species. Easily distinguished by the flower being very flattened in frontal view.

Range: coastal areas from southern NSW to south-east Qld. **Leaves:** in a basal rosette. **Flower:** solitary, GREENISH BROWN to DARK CHOCOLATE BROWN, or reddish at the tip, about 15mm long, narrow. The hood points upwards. Flowering stem 15-30cm long. **Flowering time:** August-September. **Name:** *erecta* = Lat. erect, referring to the flowers. **Note:** it is similar to *P. pedunculata*, but that species has relatively bulbous flowers. The 2 can be found growing together.

Pterostylis gibbosa R. Brown
Cumb Endangered 2E
Found in grassy understories of open forest on clay soils. This is a very rare species, collected by Robert Brown in 1809 south-west of Parramatta. Another collection was made near Woronora in 1949. The only currently known population is near Yallah in the Illawarra where it is threatened by loss of habitat.

Range: restricted to the Sydney area and the Illawarra. **Leaves:** 4-7 in a basal rosette. **Flowers:** 2-7, 14mm long, GREEN and translucent white, shiny or waxy; hood with a 2mm filiform tip; lateral sepals reflexed against the ovary, wider than the hood, with 3mm points; labellum very dark, oblong, fleshy, channelled, with a pair of long slender spines and a few lesser spines located near the base. Flowering stem to 40cm tall. **Flowering time:** September-October. **Name:** *gibbosa* = Lat. pouched, referring to the whole flower.

Pterostylis sp. aff. *gibbosa*
'Sydney plains rufa'   **Ss** (not illustrated)
A rare species thought extinct but recently rediscovered in gullies along the Georges River (Campbelltown-Ingleburn) and at Douglas Park. Found in shallow sandy soils in open places on sandstone ledges. It is threatened by proposed developments along the Georges River.

Range: restricted to the above areas. **Leaves:** similar to *P. gibbosa*. **Flowers:** RED-BROWN and TRANSLUCENT WHITE, with longer points than *P. gibbosa*. **Flowering time:** September-October (a few weeks later than *P. gibbosa*).

Pterostylis grandiflora R. Brown

Cobra Greenhood, Superb Greenhood **Ss**
A most spectacular species, found in moist sheltered forests. Common in the area. Distinguished from similar large-flowered species by the broad dark petals (on either side of the hood) and blunt labellum.

Range: NSW coast, Blue Mountains, Qld, Vic and Tas. **Leaves:** 3-5 small leaves in a basal rosette, usually absent at flowering time, 6-9 sheathing stem leaves. **Flowers:** solitary, to 35mm long, GREEN and WHITE in the body, strongly RED-BROWN and GREEN in the hood; the hood curves strongly downwards, the lateral sepals have erect slender points to 5cm tall. Flowering stem to 25cm tall, with sheathing leaves. **Flowering time:** May-August. **Name:** *grandiflora* = Lat. large-flowered.

Pterostylis longifolia R. Brown

Ss
Found as scattered individuals in the litter of moist sheltered woodland. Moderately common in the area.

Range: NSW coast and ranges, also Qld, Vic, Tas and SA. **Leaves:** dark green, 3-6, small (to 3.5cm), in a basal rosette, plus 5-8 longer (to 10cm) stem leaves. **Flowers:** up to 12, to 15mm long, GREEN and WHITE (often brown-tipped); the labellum is short, protruding from the flower, with 3 lobes, an upturned tip and a covering of pimple-like projections; the lateral sepals are down-flexed and joined together for half their length. Flowering stem leafy, 20-30cm, occasionally to 60cm, long. **Flowering time:** April-October. **Name:** *longifolia* = Lat. long-leaved.

Pterostylis nutans R. Brown

Nodding Greenhood, Parrot's Beak Orchid **Ss**
Found in dense colonies in damp leaf litter in sheltered forests and scrubs. A very common species in the area, even in rapidly changing urban gullies.

Range: NSW coast and ranges, Qld, Vic, Tas, SA and NZ. **Leaves:** 3-6 leaves in a basal rosette, often with curly margins. **Flowers:** solitary, to 25mm long, TRANSLUCENT with GREEN stripes and markings, hood curved forward in an arc, so that the opening faces the ground; the labellum is curved downwards. Flowering stem 10-30cm tall, leafless. **Flowering time:** June-July. **Name:** *nutans* = Lat. nodding.

Pterostylis obtusa R. Brown

Blunt-tongue Greenhood **Ss**
Found in colonies in moist sheltered gullies and scrubs. Uncommon.

Range: NSW coast and ranges, Qld, Vic, Tas and SA. **Leaves:** 3-6 in a basal rosette, with curly margins, also 3-5 spreading stem leaves. **Flowers:** solitary, to 28mm long, TRANSLUCENT WHITE with GREEN stripes and brown colouring, hood curving gradually downward to the tip; lateral sepals embracing the hood, with points about 25mm long, labellum hidden. Flowering stem to 25cm tall, leafy. **Flowering time:** February-June. **Name:** *obtusa* = Lat. blunt, referring to the labellum.

Pterostylis ophioglossa R. Brown
ssp. *ophioglossa*

Snake-tongue Greenhood **Ss, Cumb**
Found in moist sheltered places in forests and scrubs. Uncommon or rare, but widespread in the area, e.g. Rookwood Cemetery (on clay), Castlereagh State Forest (on sand).

Range: NSW coast, south-eastern Qld and New Caledonia. **Leaves:** 4-6 in a basal rosette, dull green, stalked, with acuminate tips. **Flowers:** solitary, to 30mm long, WHITE with RED-BROWN or GREEN markings; the hood is swollen near the base, then curving downwards in its upper part; the lateral sepals have long slender points to 30mm long; the labellum is notched at the tip. Flowering stem to 25cm high. **Flowering time:**

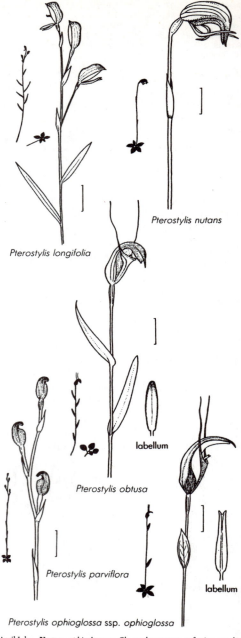

Pterostylis nutans

Pterostylis longifolia

labellum

Pterostylis obtusa

Pterostylis parviflora

labellum

Pterostylis ophioglossa ssp. *ophioglossa*

April-July. **Name:** *ophioglossa* = Gk. snake-tongue, referring to the notched labellum.

Pterostylis parviflora R. Brown

Baby Greenhood **Ss**
An uncommon species in the area, flowering after fires in

wet coastal heaths. Solitary or in diffuse colonies. There are 2 forms: a green form found throughout the area on sandy soils, with only about 4 flowers; and a larger brown form found in sunny wet heath near the coast, with up to 12 flowers (and a stale pungent smell).

Range: NSW coast and ranges, Qld, Vic, Tas and SA. **Leaves:** 3-10 in a tight rosette with wide stalks, up to 4 rosettes together on a single plant (but these may be absent at flowering time). **Flowers:** 1-12, to 10mm long, GREEN and WHITE or GREEN and BROWN, with erect lateral sepals closely embracing the hood, the free points very short (about 3mm). Flowering stem to 40cm tall, with several closely sheathing leaves. **Flowering time:** autumn. **Name:** *parviflora* = Lat. small-flowered.

Pterostylis pedoglossa R. D. Fitzgerald

Prawn Greenhood **Ss**
Found in colonies in sandy soil in the shelter of dense coastal scrubs. An uncommon species in the area, found south of the harbour.

Range: Sydney area, Blue Mountains, south coast, Vic and Tas. **Leaves:** 3-6 in a basal rosette, with prominent stalks. **Flowers:** solitary, to 15mm long, with TRANSLUCENT WHITE and GREEN stripes at the base, green or brown at the tip. Hood curving forward with a long thread-like point, lateral sepals also with long thread-like tips and closely embracing the hood. Flowering stem to 15cm tall, leafless. **Flowering time:** April-June. **Name:** Lat. *pedoglossa*, with a foot-like tongue.

Pterostylis pedunculata R. Brown

Little Red Riding Hood **Ss**
Forms large, dense colonies in ferny gullies. Easily recognised by the reddish flower. Uncommon, scattered in the area.

Range: NSW coast and ranges, Vic, Tas and SA. **Leaves:** 4-6 in a basal rosette, on long stalks, with prominent veins and a blunt tip. **Flowers:** solitary, to 15-20mm long, GREEN and WHITE at the base and REDDISH-BROWN in the upper parts, lateral sepals with long slender points to 30mm long. Flowering stem 15-25cm long, leafless. **Flowering time:** September (August-October). **Name:** *pedunculata* = having a stalk (peduncle) on the flower. **Note:** don't confuse this with *P. erecta*, a similar species distinguished by a very narrow flower.

Pterostylis plumosa Cady

Bearded Greenhood **Ss**
A rare species in the area, recorded from coastal scrubs, e.g. Maroubra, Kurnell.

Range: southern and central NSW ranges and slopes, on the coast in the Sydney area, Vic, Tas, SA and NZ. **Leaves:** 10-20 in a crowded basal rosette which extends up the stem for some distance, pale or yellowish, drawn out to a long point at the tip. **Flowers:** solitary, GREEN, to 15-25mm long, easily recognised by the long protruding labellum covered with long yellow hairs and ending in a dark knob. Stems 10-15cm high. **Flowering time:** October-November. **Name:** *plumosa* = Lat. plumed, feathery.

Pterostylis reflexa R. Brown

Dainty Greenhood **Ss**
Found in colonies on moist sheltered slopes in woodland. Usually not near the coast (e.g. Campbelltown area).

Range: NSW coast, ranges and inland areas, and Qld. **Leaves:** 4-6 in a basal rosette, with short stalks, (may be absent at flowering time), also 4-6 closely sheathing stem-leaves. **Flowers:** solitary, to 30mm long, TRANSLUCENT WHITE with DARK-GREEN stripes and brown markings; hood swollen at the base, then curving forward with a point about 6mm long; lateral sepals with points about 30mm long. Flowering stem to 25cm tall, with sheathing leaves. **Flowering time:** March-May. **Name:** *reflexa* = Lat. bent backwards.

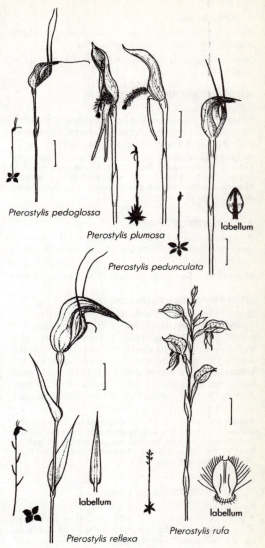

Pterostylis pedoglossa

Pterostylis plumosa

Pterostylis pedunculata

labellum

labellum

labellum

Pterostylis reflexa

Pterostylis rufa

Pterostylis rufa R. Brown

Rusty Hood **Cumb**
Found in woodland amongst grasses, on clay soils. Locally common after fires on the Cumberland Plain. Much reduced since earlier times by clearing.

Range: NSW coast and ranges, Qld, Vic, Tas and SA. **Leaves:** 5-12 crowded in a basal rosette, also several closely sheathing stem bracts present. **Flowers:** 1-10 (15), to 14mm long, usually REDDISH BROWN, somewhat nodding; hood with a short point about 2mm long; lateral sepals (about as wide as the hood), partly concave, tapering into points about 3mm long, curved outward; labellum fleshy, reddish brown, with numerous white spines. Flowering stem to 15cm long, slender, with closely sheathing leaves. **Flowering time:** September-December. **Name:** *rufa* = Lat. reddish.

• *Rimacola* Rupp

A genus with one terrestrial species restricted to south-eastern Australia. It is closely related to *Lyperanthus*.

Name: *Rimacola* = Lat. *rima*, a cleft or fissure, *cola*, an inhabitant.

Rimacola elliptica (R. Brown) Rupp

Green Rock Orchid   **Ss**

Found in wet dripping crevices and ledges in sandstone cliffs, often near waterfalls. An uncommon species, found north of the harbour and rarely in the Royal National Park.

Range: restricted to the Sydney area and Blue Mountains.   **Leaves:** few to several, broad, stalked.   **Flowers:** 6-15, in a drooping or arching raceme; GREEN, facing forward, with reddish-brown markings. **Flowering time:** November-January (mostly December).   **Name:** *elliptica* = elliptic, of the leaves.

• *Spiranthes* Richards

A genus of terrestrial orchids with about 25 species in temperate North and South America and Africa. There is 1 species in Australia.

Name: *Spiranthes* = Gk. *speira*, spiral, twisted, *anthos*, a flower.

Spiranthes sinensis (Persoon) Ames

Austral Ladies Tresses   **Cumb, Ss**

A very pretty evergreen terrestrial orchid 20-45cm high, with a dense spiral of tiny pink and white flowers. Most common in marshy meadows on the Cumberland Plain, but widely scattered throughout the area. Fitzgerald thought it was self-pollinating but it is now believed that pollination is by small native bees attracted by 2 glands at the base of the labellum. A single plant may produce 400 000 seeds although many are sterile.[24]

Range: NSW coast and ranges, and widespread in Asia, NG and NZ. **Leaves:** 3-5, erect, to 16cm long, to 10mm wide, sometimes absent at flowering time.   **Flowers:** tiny, dense in a spiral arrangement; segments BRIGHT PINK, labellum WHITE.   **Flowering time:** October-March. **Name:** *sinensis* = from China.

• *Thelymitra* G & J. R. Forster

Sun Orchids

A genus of terrestrial orchids with about 45 species, about 37 in Australia and the remainder in NG, New Caledonia and the Phillipines. Their best development is in the south-east and south-west of the continent.

They are the most spectacular orchids in the area, growing in sunny places in heath and woodland. The flowers only open widely in strong sunlight—on cloudy days they remain closed. All species have a single erect basal leaf which is thick and fleshy. The flowering stem may be 60cm or more high.

Pollination is by small native bees although some species are self-pollinating (the self-pollinating species remain closed except on very hot humid days). The flower mimics *Patersonia* (Native Iris). All species flower in spring and may hybridise with each other.

Name: *Thelymitra* = Gk. female hat, referring to the hooded column in many species.

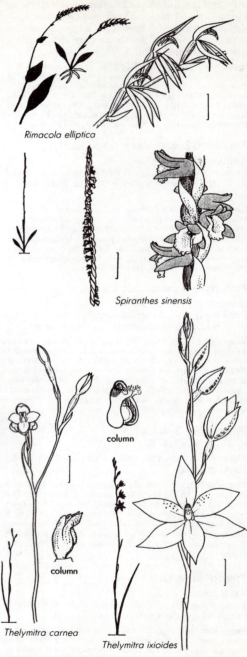

Rimacola elliptica

Spiranthes sinensis

column

column

Thelymitra carnea

Thelymitra ixioides

Thelymitra carnea R. Brown

Pink Sun Orchid   **Ss, Cumb**

Found in moist or mossy soils in sunny heathland. Occurs in coastal heath at La Perouse, on tops in Ku-ring-gai Chase

National Park, Heathcote National Park, and rarely in Royal National Park (also recorded from Rookwood Cemetery). Moderately common in the area.

The flowers are almost always closed, and only open on very hot, humid days.

Range: NSW coast and ranges, all states, NZ. **Leaf:** to 15cm long, 3mm wide, cylindrical or channelled. **Flowers:** 1-4, about 14mm wide, BRIGHT PINK (yellow populations sometimes occur); segments not fully opening, to 7mm long, broad; column to 4mm long, cream to reddish, hoodless, lacking hair tufts. Flowering stems to 35cm tall. **Flowering time:** September-October. **Name:** *carnea* = Lat. fleshy.

Thelymitra circumsepta Fitzgerald
Ss

Found in sunny places on wet sandy or muddy soils, generally at higher altitudes. Locally recorded from tops on the Appin-Heathcote road. It flowers much later than the other species. Since the flowers only open on very humid days, it is probably self-pollinating.

Range: NSW coast and ranges, Vic. **Leaf:** to 20cm long and 12mm wide, thick, leathery, ribbed, channelled, dark green. **Flowers:** 3-10, BLUE, greenish-white or mauve, 20-25mm wide, rarely opening; the column is unusual, with fringed accessory lobes on each side above, 2 side brushes, and a third brush arising from the front. Flowering stem 40-60cm tall. **Flowering time:** December—January. **Name:** *circumsepta* = Lat. partitioned all round.

Thelymitra ixioides Swartz

Spotted Sun Orchid, Blue Sun Orchid   **Ss**
Found in sunny places in heath and woodland. Abundant on the north shore, less common south of the harbour. This is the commonest *Thelymitra* in the area.

Range: most parts of Australia, NZ, New Caledonia. **Leaf:** to 20cm long, 10mm wide, channelled and ribbed, fleshy when new. **Flowers:** 3-9, segments BLUE (sometimes purple) 16-22mm long, marked with dark spots; column 5mm high, bluish, the back densely covered with rows of coloured finger-like glands, with 2 extra orange lobes on top and arms ending in tufts of white hairs. Flowering stems grow to 60cm tall. **Flowering time:** August. **Name:** *ixioides* = *Ixia*-like. *Ixia* is a genus of blue-flowered South African Irises, sometimes called Corn Lilies.

Thelymitra malvina

M. Clements, D. Jones & B. Molloy   **Ss**
Found in dense forests, often near the coast. Fairly common in the area. Closely related to *T. nuda*, it is distinguished by the yellow column hood and erect, mauve hair-tufts (as opposed to spreading, white brushlike tufts of *T. nuda*).

Range: coast south from the Sydney area, Vic and NZ. **Leaf:** 10-20cm long, dark-green, channelled. **Flowers:** 6-15, 20-25mm wide, BLUE to MAUVE; column about 5mm long, white or bluish, upper lobe hooded, deeply divided, column arms more or less erect with a dense erect tuft (not a spreading brush as in *T. nuda*) of mauve or pink hairs. Flowering stem to 60cm tall. **Flowering time:** November-January. **Name:** *malvina* = mauve, referring to the hair-tufts. **Note:** this new species has generally been confused with *T. nuda* in the past.

Thelymitra media R. Brown
Ss

Found in heath and woodland. An uncommon species in the area, e.g. Heathcote National Park, Royal National Park. Resembles *T. ixioides*. At best it is a magnificent plant, but the local form is small and few-flowered.

Range: coast and ranges in eastern Australia. **Leaf:** to 30cm long, 18mm

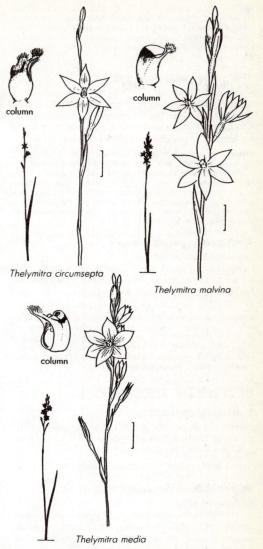

Thelymitra circumsepta

Thelymitra malvina

Thelymitra media

wide, channelled, thick and fleshy when new, ribbed. **Flowers:** 5-25, about 20mm wide, segments DEEP BLUE with darker lines, to 17mm long, moderately fleshy; column to 6mm long, cream to bluish, marked with a dark collar-like band, surmounted with blunt accessory lobes and tufts of white hairs on the column arms. Flowering stems usually to 40cm tall. **Flowering time:** October. **Name:** *media* = Lat. intermediate, referring to its relationships.

Thelymitra nuda R. Brown

Scented Sun Orchid   **Ss**   (not illustrated)
Found in heath and woodland. Uncommon (mainly a western slopes species). It is closely related to *T. pauciflora*, but the flowers are larger and open freely.

Range: all states except Tas and NT. **Leaf:** 10-30cm long, 6-20mm wide, often lax, channelled inside, deeply ribbed outside. **Flowers:** 2-20, BLUE (or mauve), 20-40mm wide; segments to 20mm long; column about 6mm long, white or bluish, upper lobe hooded, deeply divided, column arms pointing forwards with a brush of white hairs. Flowering stems to 60cm tall, stout. **Flowering time:** August-September. **Name:** *nuda* = Lat. naked.

Thelymitra pauciflora R. Brown

Slender Sun Orchid **Ss**

Found in moist places in heath and woodland. Moderately common in the area. The flowers open rarely, only on hot, humid days. Distinguished from *T. nuda* by the hair-tufts being erect, not spreading, and flowers opening poorly.

Range: NSW coast and ranges, all other states, and NZ. **Leaf:** to 5-20cm long, 20mm wide, thick, fleshy, channelled, ribbed. **Flowers:** few, small, 10-20mm wide, BLUE, segments not widely spreading, to 10mm long; column to 5mm high, white or bluish, with yellow and brown hood at the back, the arms erect, ending in white hairs. Flowering stem to 50cm tall. **Flowering time:** September-October. **Name:** *pauciflora* = Lat. few-flowered. **Note:** a form from Kurnell with exceptionally large leaves is probably an unnamed species.

Thelymitra venosa R. Brown

Large-veined Sun Orchid **Ss**

Found in sunny places in wet sandy soil or mud. Basically a Blue Mountains species, but it occurs beside creeks on Maddens Plains. The flowers open wide and remain open even at night.

Range: restricted to the Sydney area and Blue Mountains. **Leaf:** to 30cm long and 7mm wide, thick, fleshy, channelled, ribbed. **Flowers:** 1-6, about 5cm wide, DARK BLUE with darker veins. The lower petal is differentiated into a simple labellum. The column has 2 erect twisted arms, lacking hair tufts. Flowering stem 40-60cm tall. **Flowering time:** October-December. **Name:** *venosa* = Lat. veined.

EPIPHYTIC ORCHIDS

• Bulbophyllum Thouars

A genus of with over 900 species distributed widely around the world. There are over 600 species in NG. Australia has 26 species, mainly in tropical Qld.

Name: *bulbophyllum* = Gk. *bulbos*, a bulb, *phyllon*, a leaf.

Bulbophyllum exiguum F. Mueller

Ss, Temp Rf, STRf

An epiphytic orchid with small globular pseudobulbs which are pale green and deeply grooved. It forms dense spreading masses on rocks near streams in humid rainforest gullies. A rare species in the area (e.g. Waterfall), more common in the Blue Mountains. Pollination is by small flies.

Range: NSW coast, Blue Mountains and Qld. **Leaves:** one per pseudobulb, tiny, thin but tough. **Flowers:** tiny, 1-5 in a slim raceme, GREENISH to CREAM, about 10mm wide; labellum fleshy, yellow. **Flowering time:** April-May. **Name:** *exiguum* = Lat. small, insignificant, referring to the habit.

Bulbophyllum minutissimum F. Mueller

Ss, Temp Rf, STRf

This rare species is the world's smallest orchid. It has tiny pseudobulbs 2-3mm long and looks more like an encrusting lichen than an orchid. It was first discovered in 1849 by a certain Archdeacon King 'at the back of the old mill, in the

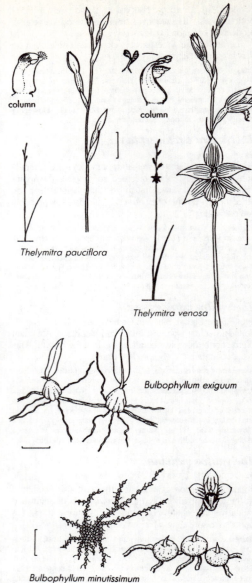

column

column

Thelymitra pauciflora

Thelymitra venosa

Bulbophyllum exiguum

Bulbophyllum minutissimum

gully, then in a state of nature, leading down from Woollahra to Rushcutters Bay.'[25] It was not recorded again until found at Ballina in the 1870s but it has since been found in rainforest gullies both north and south of Sydney. Although not recorded from Sydney this century it is likely that specimens may still exist on old fig trees around Sydney harbour, where they are easily confused with lichens.

Range: coastal areas from Nowra to central Qld. **Leaves:** about 1mm long, scale-like, often shed early, arising from circular flattened hollow pseudobulbs 2-3mm wide. **Flowers:** solitary, about 5mm wide, REDDISH with darker stripes, on a thread-like stem to 3mm long. **Flowering time:** October-November. **Name:** *minutissimum* = Lat. extremely small.

Bulbophyllum shepherdii F. Mueller

(previously *B. crassifolium*)
Wheatgrain Bulbophyllum **Ss, Temp Rf, STRf**
An epiphytic orchid forming densely packed clumps on rocks and trees. Rare in the area. Found near streams in deep rainforest gullies in the Royal National Park. The thickness of the leaves varies according to the humidity of the position. Pollination is by small flies.

Range: NSW coast and ranges, and Qld. **Leaves:** thick, fleshy, moderately tough, smooth, deeply grooved on the upper surface, to 40mm long and to 8mm wide, arising from inconspicuous pseudobulbs. **Flowers:** small, to 5mm long, located at the base of the leaves, WHITE with YELLOW tips; labellum red-orange. **Flowering time:** spring-summer. **Name:** *shepherdii* = after T. W. Shepherd, the original collector.

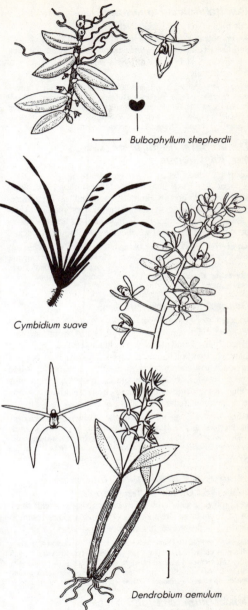

Bulbophyllum shepherdii

• *Cymbidium* Swartz

A genus of epiphytic or terrestrial orchids with about 50 species distributed in India, Madagascar, China, Japan, South-east Asia, NG and Australia. There are 3 species in Australia. Some exotic species are highly prized for cultivation and have been extensively hybridised.

Name: *Cymbidium* = Gk. a small boat, referring to the small boat-shaped hollow found in the labellum of some species.

Cymbidium suave R. Brown

Snake Flower **Ss, Temp Rf**
An epiphytic orchid forming large grass-like clumps in the arms of trees, usually high above the ground. Its roots may penetrate for many metres into the rotten heart wood. The usual hosts are Eucalypts growing in humid valleys. It is fairly common in the area.
   Pollination is by native bees. The flowers are highly fragrant.

Range: NSW coastal areas, Blue Mountains, northern inland slopes and Qld. **Leaves:** 4-8, to 35cm long, to 20mm wide, thin, erect or arching. **Flowers:** often very numerous, GREEN, 20-30mm wide, crowded in a pendulous raceme; labellum yellowish with red markings. **Name:** *suave* = Lat. sweet, referring to the fragrant flowers.

Cymbidium suave

• *Dendrobium* Swartz

A huge genus of epiphytes with over 1400 species distributed throughout Asia. There are about 60 Australian species with the majority in tropical Qld, the number reducing progressively southwards, with only one in Tas. A distinctive feature in many species is the thickened water-storing stem (pseudobulb) surmounted by stiff leaves. In other species the leaves themselves are thickened into distinctive fleshy organs. The inverted flowers are strongly fragrant.

Name: *Dendrobium* = Gk. *dendron*, a tree, *bios*, life, i.e. tree-living, referring to the epiphytic habit.

Dendrobium aemulum R. Brown

Ironbark orchid, White Feather Orchid
Ss, Temp Rf, STRf
An epiphytic orchid with cylindrical pseudobulbs to 20cm long by 8mm wide. Found on rocks and rainforest trees in deep gullies. Rare in the area, e.g. Royal National Park. In

Dendrobium aemulum

other parts of the state it is often found on Ironbark trees, hence the common name. According to A. G. Hamilton, it is very sweet scented, but gives out its odour at night only, suggesting pollination by night-flying insects.[26]

Range: NSW coastal areas and Qld. **Leaves:** 2-4, thick and tough. **Flowers:** 2-12 on a raceme to 10cm long, WHITE, segments to 25mm long. **Flowering time:** August-October. **Name:** *aemulum* = Lat. allied, because of its similarity to other species.

Dendrobium cucumerinum Macleay ex Lindley

Cucumber Orchid, Gherkin Orchid **Ss**

An epiphytic orchid found spreading on the limbs of River She Oaks (*Casuarina cunninghamiana*). Rare in the area, e.g. Georges River near Campbelltown. Mainly a species of mountain valleys.

Range: Blue Mountains to Bunya Bunya Mountains in Qld. **Leaves:** stout, stiff, shaped like gherkins. **Flowers:** 2-10 in a raceme; CREAM to GREENISH WHITE with purplish stripes, segments to 20mm long, twisted; labellum pale, with crinkled margins. **Flowering time:** November-February. **Name:** *cucumerinum* = Lat. like a cucumber.

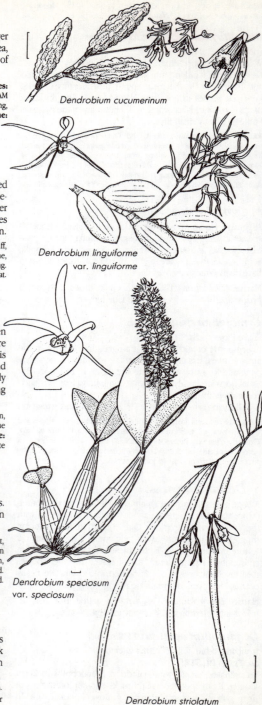

Dendrobium cucumerinum

Dendrobium linguiforme Swartz
var. *linguiforme*

Tongue Orchid **Ss**

A remarkably hardy little rock-orchid, common on exposed sandstone cliffs and also in moist mossy gullies. The tongue-like leaves are able to store water in their pith-like inner tissues; in dry weather the furrows deepen and the leaves become purplish; in wet weather they swell and green again.

Range: NSW coast and ranges, Qld and New Caledonia. **Leaves:** stiff, tough, flattened, often deeply furrowed. **Flowers:** up to 20 in a raceme, WHITE, fragrant, with slender curved segments 15-20mm long. **Flowering time:** September-October. **Name:** *linguiforme* = Lat. tongue-shaped.

Dendrobium linguiforme
var. linguiforme

Dendrobium speciosum Smith

Rock Lily, Rock Orchid **Ss**

A spectacular epiphytic orchid with stout swollen pseudobulbs, found in clumps on cliffs and rock ledges where there is plenty of light and air (not usually on trees this far south). An uncommon species in the area, mostly found on the Hawkesbury and Illawarra escarpments. It frequently suffers at the hands of collectors. The flowers have a strong sweet perfume in the full heat of day.

Range: NSW coast, Blue Mountains and Vic. **Leaves:** 2-5 on each stem, thick, stiff and tough. **Flowers:** very numerous in an arching raceme to 45cm long; WHITE to YELLOW; segments fleshy. **Flowering time:** September-October. **Name:** *speciosum* = Lat. showy. **Note:** A poor rate of reproduction accounts for the rarity of young plants.[27]

Dendrobium striolatum H. G. Reichenbach

Streaked Rock Orchid **Ss, Temp Rf, STRf**

An epiphytic orchid growing in dense masses on cliff faces. An uncommon or rare species in the area, though common nearby. The flowers are fragrant in warm weather.

Range: south from the Hunter Valley into Vic and Tas. **Leaves:** pendant, cylindrical, curved, stiff, with shallow grooves, 6-11cm long, about 3mm wide. **Flowers:** 1-3 in short racemes; CREAM to YELLOW or greenish, with REDDISH stripes, up to 20mm long; labellum white, crinkled. **Flowering time:** September. **Name:** *striolatum* = Lat. finely ridged.

Dendrobium speciosum
var. speciosum

Dendrobium teretifolium R. Brown

Pencil Orchid, Rat's Tail Orchid
Ss, Temp Rf

An epiphytic orchid with long pendulous leaves and masses of spidery white flowers. It usually grows on Swamp Oak (*Casuarina glauca*) and less commonly on rocks. Uncommon in the area (e.g. Audley, Royal National Park).

Range: NSW coast. **Leaves:** pendulous, cylindrical, smooth, usually 20-30cm long. **Flowers:** 8-15 per raceme, strongly fragrant, WHITE or

Dendrobium striolatum

CREAM, with short red or purple stripes near the base; the labellum is cream with red spots and sinuous margins, drawn out to a fine point. **Flowering time:** July-August. **Name:** *teretifolium* = Lat. cylindrical-leaved.

Dendrobium tetragonum A. Cunningham

Spider Orchid **Ss, Temp Rf**

An epiphytic orchid with four-sided pseudobulbs and beautiful starry flowers, found on rainforest trees and rocks in deep humid coastal gullies. A rare species in the area, e.g. Royal National Park.

Range: coastal areas north from the Illawarra into southern Qld. **Leaves:** 2-5, thin but hard. **Flowers:** 1-5 in a short raceme, YELLOWISH with RED-BROWN margins; labellum cream with red or purple markings. **Flowering time:** October. **Name:** *tetragonum* = 4-angled, referring to the stems.

• *Liparis* Richard

A genus of epiphytic or terrestrial orchids with about 250 species, of cosmopolitan distribution. There are 10 species in Australia, mostly in tropical areas.

Name: *Liparis* = Gk. *liparos*, oily, greasy or smooth, referring to the leaves of some species.

Liparis reflexa (R. Brown) Lindley

Tom Cats, Onion Orchid **Ss, Temp Rf**

An epiphyte forming dense clumps on rocks near creeks in humid gullies. Uncommon in the area. Mainly found in Heathcote and Royal National Parks. Pollination is by flies attracted to the urine-like odour of the flowers. The odour also accounts for the common name.

Range: NSW coast, Blue Mountains and Qld. **Leaves:** light green, 1-3, fairly soft, 10-30cm long, arising from a fleshy globular pseudobulb. **Flowers:** 5-30 on a raceme to 30cm long; GREENISH to YELLOWISH; segments and labellum about 10mm long. **Flowering time:** February-June. **Name:** *reflexa* = bent backwards, referring to the labellum.

• *Papillilabium* Dockrill

A genus with a single species.

Name: *Papillilabium* = Lat. *papillatus*, having papillae (pimples), *labium*, a lip.

Papillilabium beckleri

(F. Mueller ex Bentham) Dockrill **STRf**

A small epiphytic orchid, found on small branches of shrubs. A rare species, known locally only from deep rainforest gullies in the Royal National Park.

Range: coastal areas from Sydney to southern Qld. **Leaves:** 2-6, to 5cm long, often slightly sickle-shaped. **Flowers:** 2-8 in a raceme up to 40mm long; about 4mm wide; segments spreading, PALE with REDDISH-BROWN markings; labellum about 4mm long, greenish white. **Flowering time:** September-October. **Name:** *beckleri* = after Dr H. Beckler, the original collector.

• *Plectorrhiza* Dockrill

A genus of epiphytic orchids with 3 species, 2 in mainland Australia and 1 on Lord Howe Island.

Name: *Plectorrhiza* = Gk. *plectos*, plaited, twisted, *rhizos*, a root, referring to its tangled habit.

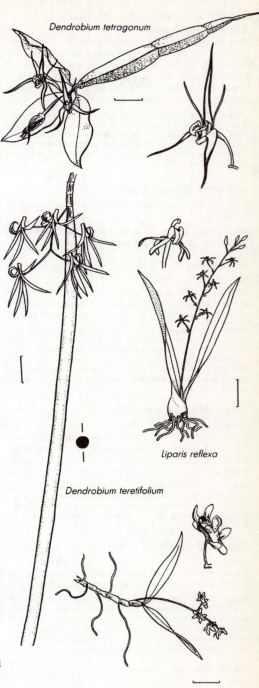

Dendrobium tetragonum

Liparis reflexa

Dendrobium teretifolium

Papillilabium beckleri

Plectorrhiza tridentata (Lindley) Dockrill

Tangle Orchid   **Temp Rf, STRf**

An inconspicuous epiphytic orchid dangling from the smallest branches of shrubs in humid rainforest gullies. The orchid itself hangs in mid-air and has only the most tenuous connection to is host via a few of its tangled roots. It is rare locally, e.g. Royal National Park, Berowra Creek. The usual host is Water Gum (*Tristaniopsis laurina*).

Range: NSW coast and Blue Mountains, Qld and Vic. **Leaves:** small, 4-10cm long, pointed, firm, often curled downwards. **Flowers:** small, about 4mm wide, GREEN and BROWN; labellum white, conspicuously 3-lobed, descending into a dark-coloured pouch. **Flowering time:** September-November. **Name:** *tridentata* = Lat. 3-toothed, referring to the shape of the labellum.

• *Sarcochilus* R. Brown

A genus of epiphytic orchids with 12 out of 13 species endemic to Australia.

Name: *Sarcochilus* = Gk. *sarcos*, fleshy, *cheilos*, lip, referring to the fleshy labellum of some species.

Sarcochilus australis (Lindley) Reichenbach

Butterfly Orchid   **STRf**

A small epiphytic orchid found on limbs of rainforest trees in deep humid gullies. A rare species locally, scattered in rainforest gullies north of the harbour. The flowers are fragrant.

Range: NSW coastal areas, Vic and Tas. **Leaves:** 3-7cm long, 3-10 on a short stem, slightly twisted, leathery, sickle-shaped, to 14mm wide. **Flowers:** 5-14 in a raceme; PALE BROWN to YELLOW-GREEN, about 15mm wide; segments narrow, spoon-shaped, somewhat fleshy; labellum white with purple and yellow markings, with a deep pointed pouch and strongly lined sides. **Flowering time:** October-December. **Name:** *australis* = Lat. southern.

Sarcochilus falcatus R. Brown

Orange Blossom Orchid   **STRf**

A small epiphytic orchid found on trees in rainforest. It does not seem to have been collected in the Royal National Park, but since it is present in the Illawarra it is likely to be found in the area. The flowers are highly fragrant.

Range: east coast of Australia. **Leaves:** 3-8, 8-16cm long, 10-20mm wide, mostly curved, pale green to yellowish, tough. **Flowers:** 3-12, CREAM to WHITE, about 30mm wide; the labellum is white with yellow or orange markings. **Flowering time:** June-October. **Name:** *falcatus* = Lat. sickle-shaped.

Sarcochilus hillii (F. Mueller) F. Mueller

STRf

A small epiphytic orchid found on rainforest trees in humid gullies. A rare species in the area but widely scattered.

Range: NSW coast and Qld (Nowra to Rockhampton). **Leaves:** 2-10 on a short stem, 3-6cm long, narrow (3mm wide), drooping, fleshy, often spotted. **Flowers:** crystalline WHITE (sometimes slightly pink or with yellowish markings), about 10mm wide; segments slightly cupped; labellum white with yellow callus, hairy. **Flowering time:** December. **Name:** *hillii* = after Walter Hill, the original collector.

Sarcochilus olivaceus Lindley

STRf

A small epiphytic orchid found on limbs of rainforest trees and rocks in deep humid gullies. A rare species locally,

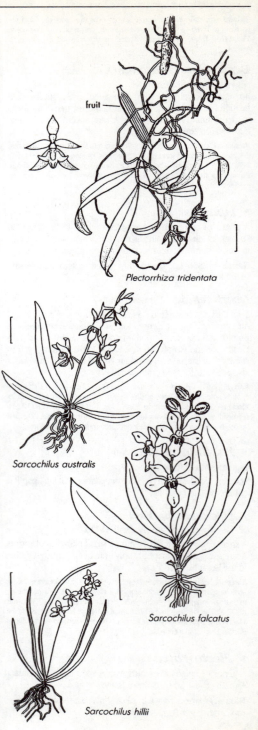

fruit

Plectorrhiza tridentata

Sarcochilus australis

Sarcochilus falcatus

Sarcochilus hillii

restricted to the Royal National Park. The flowers are fragrant.

Range: NSW coast, Blue Mountains and Qld.   **Leaves:** 2-8, stiff, thin, 5-15cm long, broad (to 40mm wide).   **Flowers:** 2-12, OLIVE GREEN to YELLOW GREEN, about 20mm wide; segments somewhat thick, spoon-shaped, narrowed at the base; labellum white with red markings. **Flowering time:** October-November.   **Name:** *olivaceus* = Lat. olive green.

POACEAE Grasses

A family with about 10 000 species in 620-650 genera worldwide. There are about 1230 species in 220 genera in Australia (although over 300 species and 66 genera are introduced).

Grasses are economically very important since they provide all the world's cereal crops (Wheat, Rice, Maize, Barley, Oats, Sorghum, Rye and Millet), and form the grasslands which are the basis of grazing agriculture. They also have more specialised uses: Bamboos are the fundamental building material in Asia. Sugarcane is the major source of sugar, as well as producing fibreboard, paper, and motor spirit (mainly in Brazil). Other species produce useful oils.

Extensive clearing, sowing of introduced species and grazing by sheep and cattle have destroyed much of Australia's native grasslands. Because native grasses cannot compete with exotic species in fertilised pastures, most grasslands near the coast are now dominated by exotic species.

Anatomy: Grasses have a highly specialised structure with its own terminology. A hand lens is essential for examination of the fine features of the floral parts.

A grass plant usually consists of a tuft of leaves arising from a stem which elongates at flowering time. As new stems arise from axillary buds *tufts* or *tussocks* are formed. Some grasses spread by underground stems called *rhizomes*. Many grasses are annuals and reproduce from seed. Others are perennials, and re-grow each year from the base. Most grasses are wind-pollinated or self-pollinating.

Leaves: these consist of 2 parts; a cylindrical *sheath* (usually split down one side), surrounding the stem, and a *blade*. A tongue-like flap of transparent tissue or ring of hairs, called a *ligule*, arises from the junction of the sheath and blade.

Spikelets: the inflorescence of a grass is usually a *panicle* divided into units called *spikelets*. Each spikelet usually consists of 2 bracts, called *glumes*, enclosing one or more *florets*. Often the glumes are prominent features of the spikelets and their character is useful in identification.

Florets: each *floret* consists of a flower contained within 2 other bracts. The outer bract, facing away from the axis and enclosing the other parts, is called the *lemma*. The inner one is called the *palea*. The lemma is often armed with one or more long awns that are important identification features.

The perianth of a grass flower is reduced to 2 or 3 small fleshy structures (lodicles) at the base of the ovary. The ovary is single-chambered, with a single ovule, and has 2 styles near the tip. There are 1-6 (usually 3) stamens. In many species the ovary is missing in some florets (= *male florets*), or the lemma and palea are empty (= *sterile florets*).

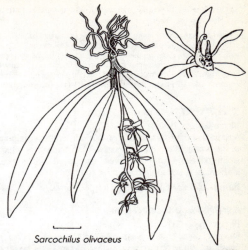

Sarcochilus olivaceus

Further reading: For reasons of space it is not possible to include all the local native grasses. For a thorough guide to the native and exotic grasses of the area the best identification guide is *Grasses of New South Wales*, by Wheeler, Jacobs and Norton,[28] which should be available in most local libraries.

• *Ancistrachne* S.T. Blake (an-sis-TRAC-nee)

A genus with 3 species, 2 in Australia and one in the Phillipines.
Name: *Ancistrachne* = Gk. hooked-scale.

Ancistrachne maidenii (A.A. Hamilton) Vickery
Poorly known 2KC-
A small sprawling or creeping grass, found on moist creek banks. A very rare species, only known from a few collections

Ancistrachne maidenii

along Berowra Creek, Cowan Creek and a nearby part of the Hawkesbury River.

Range: restricted to the above area. **Leaves:** grey-green, hairless, 10-40mm long, thin-textured. **Panicle:** slender, spike-like, mostly 20-25mm long. **Spikelets:** about 2mm long, lower glume tiny or absent, upper glume and lower lemma similar, green, covered in microscopic curved hairs. Upper (inner) lemma with a tiny projecting green point. **Name:** *maidenii* = after J.H. Maiden, director of the Royal Botanic Gardens, Sydney.

• *Agrostis* Linnaeus

Blown Grasses, Bents

A genus with 150-200 species, distributed in temperate regions of the world. There are 21 species in Australia, 5 of which are introduced. 3 native and several introduced species occur in the area; *A. avenacea* is the most common.

Name: *Agrostis* = Gk. a name for a type of grass.

Agrostis avenacea Gmelin

Blown Grass **Ss**

An erect annual grass to 80cm tall, common, usually in damp places on sandy or clay soils. Called Blown Grass because the dead inflorescences break off as single units. They can be blown for large distances, and often pile up around fences and other obstacles.

Range: most parts of all states; also NZ, Pacific Islands and the Americas. **Leaf:** slender, to 25cm long, usually about 2mm wide, scabrous in one direction. There is a conspicuous membranous ligule. **Panicle:** in its early stages is a dense spray in the protection of a leaf (illustrated), but later open and spreading (not illustrated). **Spikelets:** 2-4mm long, usually greenish (sometimes straw-coloured or purple-tinged); glumes are scabrous, about 3.5mm long; the enclosed lemma has a conspicuous twisted and bent awn about 4mm long. **Name:** *avenacea* = like *Avena*, Oats.

• *Ammophila*

—See COASTAL AND ESTUARINE SPECIES.

• *Anisopogon* R. Brown (an-iss-o-PO-gon)

An endemic genus with a single species.

Name: *Anisopogon* = Gk. *anisos*, unequal, *pogon*, a beard (awn).

Anisopogon avenaceus R. Brown

Oat Speargrass **Ss**

A tall graceful grass with stems to 1.5m tall, common in woodland and heath on sandstone. Easily recognised by the long distinctive spikelets. Even after the florets have fallen the persistent papery glumes make identification easy.

Range: coasts and ranges in eastern temperate mainland Australia. **Leaves:** sparse, inrolled, with a tiny fringed ligule. **Panicle:** open, with large nodding spikelets. **Spikelets:** with glumes 3-5cm long and papery at maturity; lemma with 3 rigid awns, 1 much longer than the others (5-8cm), twisted and bent. **Name:** *avenaceus* = Oat-like.

• *Aristida* Linnaeus (a-RIS-tid-a)

A genus with about 300 species worldwide. There are about 60 native species in Australia and 5 in the Sydney area.

The genus is easily recognised by the distinctive 3-branched awns.

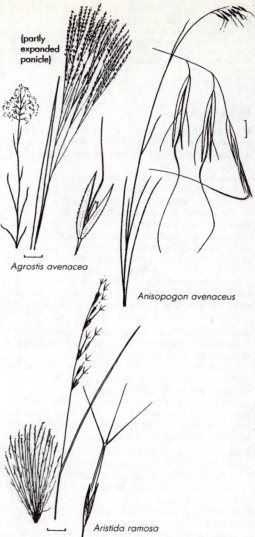

(partly expanded panicle)

Agrostis avenacea

Anisopogon avenaceus

Aristida ramosa

Name: *Aristida* = Lat. bristle or awn.

Aristida ramosa R. Brown

Three-awn Speargrass **Ss, Castl**

A slender grass with greyish-green stems 20-60cm high, often forming dense clumps. Common in heath and woodland. Distinguished by its spike-like panicle.

Range: NSW coast, ranges and inland districts, Qld and NT. **Leaves:** slender, inconspicuous, often inrolled. **Panicle:** to about 18cm long, spike-like and erect. **Spikelets:** lemma 7-8mm long, circular in cross-section, purple when new, without a groove, bearing a 3-branched awn. **Flowering time:** summer-autumn. **Name:** *ramosa* = Lat. twiggy. **Note:** *A. calycina* is a less common species, very similar to *A. ramosa*, except the margins of the awned lemma are inrolled, forming a deep vertical groove.

Aristida vagans Cavanilles
Three-awn Speargrass **Ss, Castl**
A slender grass 20-50cm tall, common in heath and woodland.
Distinguished from the other local species by its spreading
panicle.
Range: NSW coast, ranges and some inland districts. **Leaves:** slender,
often inrolled. **Panicle:** to about 18cm long, becoming open and much-
branched. **Spikelets:** lemma 7-10mm long, circular in cross-section,
without a groove, bearing a 3-branched awn. **Flowering time:** summer-
autumn. **Name:** *vagans* = Lat. wandering.

Aristida warburgii Mez
Ss, Castl
A slender grass 40-80cm tall, found in heath and woodland.
Uncommon in the area. Distinguished from the other species
by the florets being twisted just below the awns.
Range: Sydney area, Blue Mountains, north coast and Qld. **Leaves:**
slender, often inrolled. **Spikelets:** the lemma apex is twisted below
the unequal branches (see illustration). **Flowering time:** summer.
Name: *warburgii* = after Otto Warburg (1859-1938), a German botanist.

• *Austrofestuca*
— See COASTAL AND ESTUARINE SPECIES.

• *Cymbopogon* Sprengel (sim-bo-PO-gon)
A genus of about 40 species, mainly in tropical and subtropical
parts of the world. There are 9 species in Australia and a
single species in the Sydney area. The genus is characterised
by having racemes in reflexing pairs along the stem.

   The Asian species *C. nardus* is the source of Citronella
oil. Another Asian species, *C. citrinus*, is Lemon Grass.

Name: *cymbopogon* = Gk. hollow-beard.

Cymbopogon refractus (R. Brown) A. Camus
Barbed-wire Grass **Ss, Cumb**
A tufted grass with tall wiry stems, moderately common in
woodland on sandstone, especially in stony areas, and on
laterites on the Cumberland Plain.

Range: most parts of NSW, Qld, Vic and NT. **Leaves:** green, about
30cm long at the base of the plant, aromatic when crushed, with a
conspicuous jagged ligule. **Spikelets:** arranged in short paired racemes,
which bend downwards (reflex) upon maturity. **Name:** *refractus* = Lat.
bent backward.

• *Cynodon* Richard (SY-no-don)
Couch Grasses
A genus with about 8 species in warm parts of the world
and a single native species in the Sydney area.

Name: *Cynodon* = Gk. dog's tooth (it is actually known as
Dog's Tooth Grass in some countries, although why is not
obvious. Clothes line grass might be a better name).

Cynodon dactylon (Linnaeus) Persoon
Common Couch **Ss, Castl, Cumb**
A low greyish green grass with short leaves arising from
creeping stems, common in many moist bush situations. It
is also common in streets and wastelands. J.H. Maiden called
it 'the chief grass of our lawns'[29] and thought it 'one of the

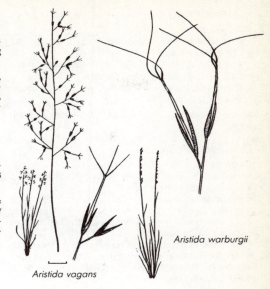

Aristida warburgii

Aristida vagans

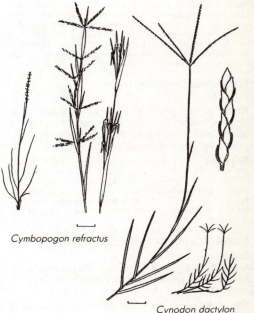

Cymbopogon refractus

Cynodon dactylon

best all-round Australian fodder grasses'.[30] It is not clear
whether it is a native or an introduced species. Robert Brown
collected it around Sydney in 1804, so if introduced it must
have followed closely upon European settlement.

Range: all parts of Australia, also world-wide. **Leaves:** 2-ranked, flat,
dull, with scabrous edges, slender, 3-10cm long. **Panicle:** an antenna-
like arrangement of usually 4-5 narrow spikes. **Spikelets:** 2-2.5mm long,
overlapping in 2 rows on the underside of the rhachis. **Name:** *dactylon*
= Gk. *dactylos*, a finger, referring to the finger-like spikes.

• *Danthonia* Lamark & De Candolle

Wallaby Grasses

A genus with about 150 species worldwide. There are about 33 species in Australia.

A magnifying glass is needed for identification as the lemmas are often the only useful distinguishing features.

About 14 native species occur in the area, the most common of which is *D. tenuior*.

Name: *Danthonia* = after Etienne Danthoine, a French botanist.

Danthonia linkii Kunth

Cumb

An erect grass 50-80cm high, fairly common in western Sydney. Two varieties occur in the area:

• **var. *linkii*:** distinguished by having only a single loose twist at the base of the awn. Found mainly along the Nepean River in the south-west of the area, but also scattered elsewhere on clay soils.

• **var. *fulva*** Vickery: distinguished by having the awn tightly twisted for 3-4mm at the base. Often a more robust plant with broader leaves. Somewhat less common than var. *linkii*. Scattered on clay soils.

Range: NSW coast, ranges and western slopes, except for northern inland parts; also Vic. **Spikelets:** glumes with purple margins, lemma about 12mm long (including bristled lobes), evenly covered in long silky hairs (i.e. not in 3 separate rows), with lobes twice as long as the lower body, central awn bent below the middle, about 15mm long. **Name:** *linkii* = after the German botanist H.F. Link, who described this species under the name *Avena bipartita* in 1827.

Danthonia longifolia R. Brown

Cumb, Ss

An erect grass forming clumps 30-60cm (usually about 40cm) high. Not common in the area, Once abundant on clay soils near the coast, has now mostly disappeared from its previous range in the inner suburbs. Still common in the Illawarra.

Range: NSW coast, ranges and some inland areas, Qld, Vic and Tas. **Leaves:** slender, about 2mm wide, about as long as the panicle, dull grey-green, becoming inrolled. **Panicle:** dense, straw coloured, rather feathery. **Spikelets:** lemma about 9mm long (including bristled lobes), with a row of long silky hairs below the lobes, and fine hairs on the rest of the body, awn bent, about 9mm long. **Name:** *longifolia* = Lat. long-leaved.

Danthonia pilosa R. Brown **var. *pilosa***

Cumb, Ss

A slender erect grass to 30cm high. Not common. Found in various soils, generally near the coast. The fine leaves are conspicuously hairy.

Range: NSW coast and ranges, except north coast, some inland areas, all states and NZ. **Leaves:** 1-2mm wide, to 15cm long, finely hairy,. **Spikelets:** glumes purple tinged, lemma about 13mm long (including bristled lobes), often purplish, hairless except for a tuft at the base; awn straight, about 16mm long, the bristles at the end of the lobes about 6mm long. **Name:** *pilosa* = softly hairy.

Danthonia racemosa R. Brown **var. *racemosa***

Cumb

An erect grass 40-80cm high, usually with long fine leaves. Common on clay soils on the Cumberland Plain. The spikelets

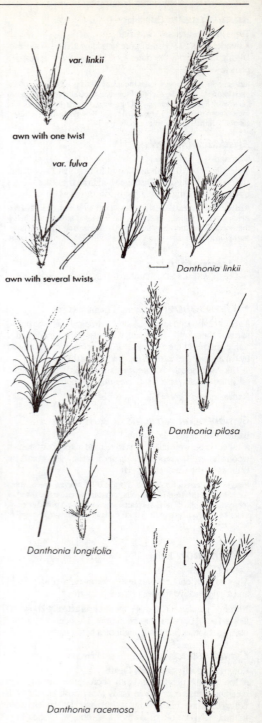

var. *linkii*

awn with one twist

var. *fulva*

awn with several twists

Danthonia linkii

Danthonia pilosa

Danthonia longifolia

Danthonia racemosa

lack the conspicuous silky hairs of other species.

Range: all except arid parts of the continent, also NZ. **Leaves:** slender, 1-2mm long. **Spikelets:** lemma about 13mm long (including bristled lobes), almost hairless, with a bristle about 12mm long, the bristles at the end of the lobes are about 3mm long. **Name:** *racemosa* = Lat. having racemes.

Danthonia tenuior (Steudel) Conert

Cumb, Ss

An erect grass usually with slender stems 50-70cm high, not forming clumps. Common on the sandy and clay soils.

Range: NSW coast, ranges and western slopes, Qld, Vic, SA and NZ. **Leaves:** about 1.5mm wide, dull green, inrolled, not densely tufted. **Panicle:** straw coloured, with few spikelets. **Spikelets:** pale green (straw-coloured when old) with purple tinged margins; lemma with 3 dense rows of hairs, the lemma about 10-12mm long (including bristled lobes), the body of the lemma 3.5mm long, the lemma awns do not exceed the glumes. **Name:** *tenuior* = Lat. thin.

• *Deyeuxia* Clarke ex Beauvois

(de-YOOX-ee-a)

A genus with about 29 native species in Australia, related to *Agrostis* and *Dichelachne*.

There are 2 fairly common native species in the area, and 2 other species occurring only rarely.

Name: *Deyeuxia* = after N. Deyeux, a professor of medicine in Paris.

Deyeuxia decipiens (R. Brown) Vickery

Reed Bent Grass **Ss**

An erect grass 45-100cm tall. Fairly common in heath and woodland on sandstone.

Range: NSW coast and ranges south from Sydney, Vic and Tas. **Leaves:** slender. **Panicle:** open, nodding, divided into branches separated by bare stems. **Spikelets:** 2-3mm long, green or purplish. The lemma awn is almost invisible to the naked eye. **Name:** *decipiens* = deceptive.

Deyeuxia quadriseta (Labillardière) Bentham

Reed Bent Grass **Ss**

A slender perennial grass to 1m tall, with a dense cylindrical green panicle. Fairly common in the area on moister soils in woodland on sandstone.

Range: widespread in southern parts of the continent, and NZ. **Leaves:** short, flat or slightly inrolled. **Panicle:** dense, green, cylindrical, to 8cm long, on a scabrous stem; glumes translucent green. **Spikelets:** the enclosed lemma with a short bent awn (2-3mm long) inserted on its lower half. **Name:** *quadriseta* = Gk. referring to 4 teeth at the tip of the lemma.

• *Dichelachne* Endlicher (di-kel-ACK-nee)

Plume Grasses

A genus with 3 species endemic to Australia, NZ and the Pacific.

Name: *Dichelachne* = Gk. cleft-glume, referring to the lemma which has 2 lobes on either side of the awn.

Dichelachne crinita (Linnaeus) J. D. Hooker

Longhair Plume Grass **Ss**

A graceful erect grass 70-100cm high, with a dense plume-like panicle. Common on sandy soils near the sea.

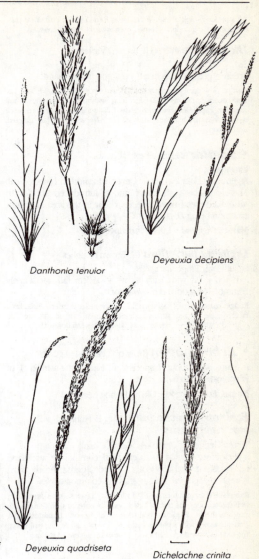

Danthonia tenuior

Deyeuxia decipiens

Deyeuxia quadriseta

Dichelachne crinita

Range: NSW coast and ranges, except the south coast, central and south western slopes, all states except NT; also NZ and Pacific Islands. **Leaves:** few, grey-green, under 20cm long, without a conspicuous tuft at the base. **Spikelets:** awns 20-50mm long, silvery-green. The awns are dense, completely concealing the spikelets. **Name:** *crinita* = Lat. hairy.

Dichelachne micrantha (Cavanilles) Domin

Shorthair Plume Grass **Ss, Castl, Cumb**

A graceful slender grass 50-80cm high, with a dense plume-like panicle. Common in woodland on sandstone and laterites.

Range: most parts of NSW, all states except NT, NZ and NG. **Leaves:** few, short, slender, grey-green, often rough. **Spikelets:** each with 2 slender glumes; the lemma is armed with a long bent and twisted awn

8-25mm long, dark coloured. The awns form a dense cylindrical mass concealing the spikelets. **Name:** *micrantha* = Gk small-flowered.

Dichelachne rara (R. Brown) Vickery

Ss

An erect grass 70-100cm tall, common in woodland.

Range: NSW coast and ranges, south western plains, Qld, Vic and Tas. **Leaves:** few, pale green, 20-40cm long, without a conspicuous tuft at the base. **Spikelets:** greenish, awns 7-20mm long. The inflorescence is loose with bare branches clearly visible. **Name:** *rara* = Lat. scattered, uncommon.

• *Digitaria* Heister ex Fabricius

Fingergrasses

A genus of about 200 species, mainly tropical and subtropical. There are about 40 native and 8 introduced species in Australia. Several native species occur in the area, the most common being *D. parviflora.*

Name: *Digitaria* = Lat. *digitus*, finger.

Digitaria parviflora (R. Brown) Hughes

Smallflower Fingergrass **Ss**

A tufted grass with leafy stems 45-150cm tall. Moderately common in woodland on sandstone.

Range: coastal parts of NSW and Qld. **Leaves:** flat, slender. **Spikelets:** more or less hairless, striate, dark, about 2mm long, all on one side of slender wavy axes. **Name:** *parviflora* = Lat. small-flowered.

• *Echinopogon* Beauvois (ek-ino-PO-gon)

A genus with about 7 species, all found in Australia, 1 of which extends to NZ.

Name: *Echinopogon* = Gk. hedgehog-beard.

Echinopogon caespitosus C. E. Hubbard var. *caespitosus*

Tufted Hedgehog Grass **Ss, Castl, Cumb**

A slender erect grass 60-100cm high, common in woodland on sandstone and clay soils. Its short, dense, bristly head is easily recognised and suggests the common name.

Range: NSW coast and ranges, Qld and NG. **Leaves:** flat, 3-4mm wide, well spaced along the stem which is sparsely covered with fine whitish glandular hairs. **Panicle:** short, dense, pale green. **Spikelets:** with 2 equal glumes with scabrous backs, enclosing a single bisexual floret. The lemma has a long green awn. **Name:** *caespitosus* = Lat. tufted

• *Entolasia* Stapf

A genus with about 5 species, in tropical Africa and Australia. There are 3 species in Australia, all of which occur in the Sydney area.

Name: *Entolasia* = Gk. inside-hairy, referring to the hairy lemma, which distinguishes it from other 'panic' grasses such as *Panicum* and *Digitaria.*

Entolasia marginata (R. Brown) Hughes

Ss, Cumb

A sprawling grass with broad, short, flat, dull stem-leaves. Common in forests on sandstone or shale, usually in cooler, sheltered locations.

Dichelachne micrantha

Dichelachne rara

Echinopogon caespitosus
var. caespitosus

Digitaria parviflora

Range: NSW coast and ranges, Vic, Qld and NG. **Leaves:** flat, well-developed, under 20cm long, dull, rather greyish green, usually hairless, but some hairy forms occur. **Panicle:** short, with wavy branches lying loosely against or slightly away from the central axis. **Spikelets:** 2.5-4mm long. **Name:** *marginata* = Lat. drawing attention to the pale vein-like margins of the leaves.

Entolasia stricta (R. Brown) Hughes

Ss

A wiry grass, usually in a dense spreading tuft. Common in woodland on sandstone, usually amongst rocks. The leaves are shorter, narrower and harsher than those of *E. marginata.*

Range: NSW coast and ranges, Qld and NG. **Leaves:** incurved or inrolled. Often, but not always, there are dense tufts of short leaves along the stems. The leaves and stems are finely rough to touch. **Panicle:** similar to *E. marginata.* **Name:** *stricta* = Lat. bundled. **Similar species:** *E. whiteana* is similar to *E. marginata* in habit, but has spikelets 4-6mm long.

• *Eragrostis* Wolf

Love Grasses

A genus with about 300 species worldwide, including about 55 species in Australia, 13 of which are introduced. There are 6 native and several introduced species in the area. The most common is *E. brownii.*

The grain of some species is collected and made into damper flour by Aborigines in Central Australia.

Name: *Eragrostis* = Gk. love-grass.

Eragrostis brownii Nees ex Steudel

Brown's Love Grass **Ss**

An ascending or sprawling grass to 30cm long, very common in woodland on sandstone.

Range: most parts of mainland Australia, South-east Asia and Pacific Islands. **Leaves:** dull green, 1-2mm wide. **Panicle:** on a slender axis to 30cm long. **Spikelets:** pale and tinged with purple. **Name:** *brownii* = after Robert Brown (1773-1858), botanist on Matthew Flinders' 1801-03 circumnavigation of Australia.

• *Eriochloa* Kunth (er-e-o-CLO-a)

A genus of tropical and sub-tropical grasses with about 20 species worldwide. There are 6 species in Australia, and 2 in the area.

Name: *Eriochloa* = Gk. wool-grass.

Eriochloa pseudoacrotricha

(Stapf ex Thellung) J.M. Blake

Early Spring Grass **Cumb**

A grass 60-100cm tall, common on clay soils on the Cumberland Plain.

Range: common in inland NSW, with only scattered occurrences on the coast and ranges, also all other mainland states. **Leaves:** tufted, light green, with a hairy ligule. **Panicle:** with branches 3-5cm long. **Spikelets:** with a single finely silky-hairy glume, drawn out to a fine point, 4.5-6mm long. **Name:** *pseudoacrotricha* (pronounced seu-do-ak-ro-TRICK-a) = Gk. false-*Acrotricha.* **Other species:** *E. procera:* spikelets under 4mm long. An annual grass 25-70cm tall. Occurs on the Cumberland Plain.

• *Festuca* = *Austrofestuca*
—See COASTAL AND ESTUARINE SPECIES.

• *Hemarthria* R. Brown

A genus of about 8 species, with one in Australia.

Name: *Hemarthria* = Gk. half-joint.

Entolasia marginata

Entolasia stricta

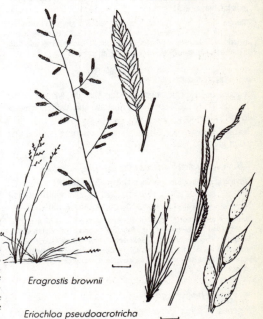

Eragrostis brownii

Eriochloa pseudoacrotricha

Hemarthria uncinata R. Brown

Mat Grass **Ss, Cumb, Aqu**

A creeping grass with bright green leaves and ascending stems, 30-80cm tall, usually forming dense colonies on marshy ground. The flowering spike at first sight appears to be a bare length of stem.

Range: most parts of all states. **Leaves:** to 25cm long, hairless.

Panicle: a slender cylindrical spike. **Spikelets:** with prominent green glumes which are partly sunk into hollows in the axis. **Flowering time:** summer. **Name:** *uncinata* = hooked, reference obscure.

• *Imperata* Cyrillo

A genus with about 10 species in warm and tropical regions of the world. There is a single species in Australia.

Name: *Imperata* = after Ferrante Imperata, a Neapolitan botanist of the sixteenth century.

Imperata cylindrica Beauvois **var. major**
(Nees) C. E. Hubbard

Blady Grass **Ss, Cumb, Castl**
An erect grass to 1m tall, easily recognised by its broad erect leaves and feathery-silky inflorescence. Abundant throughout the area. A hardy species, with tough fibrous leaves. It regenerates rapidly after clearing and fire due to its long rhizomes. Before the introduction of exotic pastures it was a principal native pasture species, both here and in Asia. The strong broad leaves were often used in thatching in Australia in the early days, and are still used for this purpose in India and the Malaysia. The Cribbs write that the 'underground shoots are fibrous but pleasant to chew; they contain both starch and sugar, and are something like a poor man's sugarcane'.[31]

Range: most parts of Australia, Europe, Asia and Africa. **Leaves:** 50-80cm long, 5-10mm wide, erect, with a ligule of hairs. **Panicle:** dense, cylindrical, spike-like. **Spikelets:** with a plume of long silvery-silky hairs at the base. **Name:** *cylindrica* = Lat. cylindrical.

Hemarthria uncinata   Imperata cylindrica var. major

• *Microlaena* R. Brown

A genus of 10 species, distributed in Australia, NZ and Pacific Islands. There are 2 species in Australia and a single species in the Sydney area.

Name: *Microlaena* = Gk. micro-cloak, referring to the 2 tiny outer glumes.

Microlaena stipoides (Labillardière) R. Brown

Weeping Grass, Meadow Rice Grass **Ss, Cumb**
A small slender grass, 15-70cm high, usually with nodding spikelets. Common in woodland on sandstone and clay.

Range: wetter temperate parts of all states except NT; also NZ and some Pacific Islands. **Leaves:** short, flat, thin, smooth or slightly hairy. **Panicle:** delicate, narrow. **Spikelets:** with glumes reduced to insignificant scales; the dominant parts of the spikelet are 2 sterile lemmas armed with long rough awns, enclosing an unawned fertile floret. **Name:** *stipoides* = like a *Stipa* grass.

• *Oplismenus* Beauvois

A genus of about 15 species found in most temperate and tropical parts of the world. There are 5 Australian species, 2 of which occur in the area.

Name: *Oplismenus* = Gk. armed, referring to the awned spikelets.

Microlaena stipoides

Oplismenus aemulus

Oplismenus aemulus (R. Brown) Kunth

Basket Grass **Temp Rf, STRf, Ss**
A small weak grass with sprawling or ascending stems and short broad leaves. It is common in shady places on forest floors, especially in wetter woodland and rainforest.

Range: NSW coast, Blue Mountains, western slopes, Qld, Vic and NG. **Leaves:** short and broad, less than 7 times as long as broad, with wavy margins. **Panicle:** slender, with 1-sided spike-like racemes (to 35mm long) with overlapping spikelets. **Spikelets:** with 2 hairy glumes, the

lower with a red awn. At flowering time a bright red stigma is visible.
Name: *aemulus* = Lat. allied, referring to its closeness to other species.

Oplismenus imbecillis (R. Brown) Roemer & Schultes

Basket Grass **Temp Rf, STRf, Ss**

A very similar species to the preceding, only readily distinguished by the more slender leaf proportions. Also common in shady places.

Range: mainly coastal parts of NSW; also Qld, Vic, NT and NG. **Leaves:** similar to *O. aemulus*, except more than 10 times longer than wide. **Panicle:** similar to *O. aemulus*, but with shorter racemes (under 15mm long). **Name:** *imbecillis* = Lat. weak.

• *Panicum* Linnaeus

A genus with over 300 species, mainly in tropical and subtropical parts of the world. The seeds of some species were used by Aborigines for food. There are 5 native species in the area, of which the most common is *P. simile*.

Name: *Panicum* = the Latin name for Millet.

Panicum simile Domin

Two Colour Panic **Ss, Castl**

A slender erect grass 30-45cm tall, with dull green leaves. Fairly common in woodland and heath on sandstone.

Range: NSW coast and ranges, Qld and Vic. **Leaves:** 1-1.5mm wide, often incurled, dull, smooth. **Panicle:** open, about 10cm long, with fine slightly zig-zag branches. **Spikelets:** pale or purple, 2-3mm long. **Name:** *simile* = Lat. similar, to other species.

• *Paspalidium* Stapf

A genus of about 30 species worldwide, with 23 in Australia. There are 6 native species in the area, the most common being *P. radiatum*.

Name: *Paspalidium* = from *Paspalum*, a closely related genus.

Paspalidium radiatum Vickery

Ss, Castl

A densely tufted grass 30-40cm tall, moderately common in woodland on sandstone.

Range: coasts of NSW and Qld. **Leaves:** 1-3mm wide, to 18cm long. **Panicle:** consisting of racemes on hairless stems. **Spikelets:** 1.5-2mm long, stalkless, overlapping, often purplish. **Flowering time:** summer. **Name:** *radiatum* = Lat. radiating.

• *Phragmites*—See AQUATICS.

• *Plinthanthesis* Steudel

An endemic genus with 3 species, carved out of *Danthonia* in 1972. A single species occurs in the area.

Name: *Plinthanthesis* = Gk. plinth-opposite, referring to a mistaken belief about the position of the lemma awn.

Plinthanthesis paradoxa (R. Brown) S.T.Blake

(previously *Danthonia paradoxa*) **Ss**

A grass 50-70cm tall, with long fine leaves. Fairly common on moist sandy soils in coastal areas. Closely related to *Danthonia*, now placed in a separate genus.

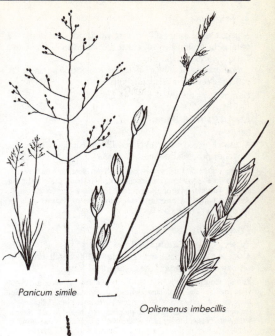

Panicum simile

Oplismenus imbecillis

Paspalidium radiatum

Plinthanthesis paradoxa

Range: NSW coast and ranges south from Sydney. **Leaves:** flat or inrolled. **Spikelets:** lemmas well spaced and clearly separate within the glumes, about 5mm long, with fine short hairs on the lower part, awn about 1mm long, bent. Glumes always with purple colouring. **Name:** *paradoxa* = Lat. something unexpected, as it is not typical for a *Danthonia*, in which genus it was previously placed.

• *Poa* Linnaeus

A genus with about 200 species worldwide and about 40 species in Australia, 6 of which are introduced. There are 7 native species in the area.

Poa grasses usually form dense tussocks. The spikelets consist of several overlapping florets.

Name: *Poa* = the Greek word for grass.

Poa affinis R. Brown
Ss

A tussock grass, with panicle 60-120cm tall, fairly common in woodland on sandstone.

Range: restricted to the Sydney area and Blue Mountains. **Leaves:** 1-5mm wide, 10-30cm long, rough below; occurring both basally and along stems. **Panicle:** more or less open, with leafy stems. **Spikelets:** small, about 2mm long. **Flowering time:** early summer. **Name:** *affinis* = Lat. similar (to other species).

Poa labillardieri Steudel
Tussock Grass   **Cumb, Castl**

A dense tussock grass, with panicle 60-100cm tall, common on clay on drier parts of the Cumberland Plain.

Range: most parts of NSW, Qld, Vic, SA and Tas. **Leaves:** to 3.5mm wide, to 80cm long, mainly basal, dull grey-green, rough below. **Panicle:** more open than the preceding, with few leaves on the stem. **Spikelets:** strongly compressed, greenish-purplish 2.5-4mm long.. **Name:** *labillardieri* = after Labillardière, who collected it on his visit to Tasmania in 1791.

Poa poiformis

A dense tussock grass, common on seacoasts and beside estuaries.

—See SEACOAST AND ESTUARINE SPECIES.

• *Spinifex*

—See COASTAL AND ESTUARINE SPECIES.

• *Sporobolus*

—See COASTAL AND ESTUARINE SPECIES.

• *Stipa* Linnaeus
Speargrasses

A genus of over 300 species mainly in temperate areas. There are 60 native and several introduced species in Australia. *Stipa* grasses are distinguished by their long, twisted and bent awns.

There are 8 species in the area, all native, of which *S. pubescens* is the most common.

Name: *Stipa* = Gk. word for fibre.

Stipa mollis R. Brown
Ss, Sal

A slender grass to 1m high, similar to *S. pubescens*, except the awn is lined with a spiral of dense spreading white hairs. Found in heathy woodland, generally near the coast, also on sand dunes.

Range: Sydney region, south coast, NSW ranges, Vic, Tas, SA and WA. **Name:** *mollis* = Lat. soft.

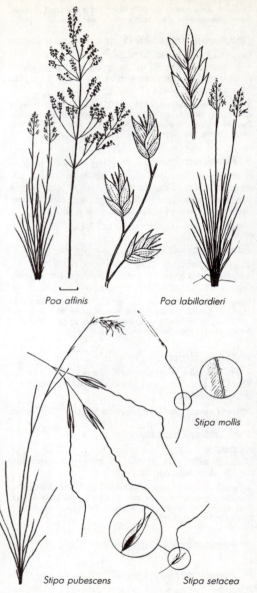

Poa affinis

Poa labillardieri

Stipa mollis

Stipa pubescens

Stipa setacea

Stipa pubescens R. Brown
Tall Speargrass   **Ss**

A tufted grass to 1m tall, fairly common in woodland on sandy or rocky soils. The twisted awns often curl the mature inflorecence into a tight bundle.

Range: NSW coast and ranges, and Qld. **Leaves:** 20-30cm long, inrolled, the upper surface is finely scabrous. **Panicle:** spreading, to 30cm long. **Spikelets:** glumes 15-25mm long and slightly unequal; the lemma is covered in soft appressed hairs and surmounted by a twisted awn 6-

9cm long, with 1 or 2 conspicuous bends. **Name:** *pubescens* = softly hairy.

Stipa setacea R. Brown
Cumb

A slender grass to 80cm high. Not common. Found in clay soils on the Cumberland Plain.

Range: mainly in inland parts of Australia. The Cumberland Plain is its only location near the coast. **Leaves:** leaves <1mm wide, cylindrical. **Spikelets:** awn 2-4cm long, transparent glumes very unequal. **Name:** *setacea* = Lat. bristly, referring to the leaves.

• *Themeda* Forskal

A genus with 16 species worldwide, and 3 in Australia, distributed in all states. A single species occurs in the area.

Name: *Themeda* = uncertain derivation, but probably from an Arabic word.

Themeda australis (R. Brown) Stapf
Kangaroo Grass **Ss, Castl, Cumb**

A grass with a tuft of slender light green leaves and a long wiry flowering stem to about 1m high. Easily recognised by its distinctive brown and purplish spikelet clusters. A common species on all soil types. Kangaroo grass is one of the most widely distributed grasses in Australia, once a dominant tussock over wide areas of grassland and woodland, now frequently out-competed by introduced grasses.

Range: most parts of all states. **Leaves:** slender, with prominent mid-ribs. **Panicle:** each branch bears 2 or more dense clusters of spikelets held in a pair of pointed leafy bracts. Each cluster has several sterile spikelets and a single fertile spikelet with a long dark awn 4-6cm long. **Name:** *australis* = Lat. southern

• *Zoysia*
—See COASTAL AND ESTUARINE SPECIES.

XANTHORRHOEACEAE

A family of tufted perennial herbs with about 75 species in 9 genera. Australia has about 70 species in 9 genera, distributed in all states.

• *Lomandra* Labillardière

A genus of small stiff grass-like herbs with about 40 species, distributed in all states, NG, and New Caledonia. The tiny yellow flowers are unisexual and dioecious. The flowers are arranged in wiry inflorescences whose shape is an important guide for identification. Generally the plants are hard to tell from a grass except when flowering.

Name: *Lomandra* = Gk. *loma*, edge, *andros*, male, referring to the bordered anthers of some species.

Lomandra brevis Lee
Ss

A small grass-like herb with erect green leaves, usually about 15mm long, found in moist open heathland. Fairly common in the area.

Themeda australis

Range: restricted to the central coast area around Sydney. **Leaves:** inrolled, to 20cm long, about 1mm wide, with pointed tips. **Flowers:** solitary, on short, slightly branched racemes. **Name:** *brevis* = Lat. brief.

Lomandra confertifolia (F. M. Bailey) Fahn
ssp. *rubiginosa* Lee
Ss

A small grass-like herb with slender leaves 30-50cm long, often occurring in large dense tufts. Found in heath and woodland on sandstone, usually in drier locations. Uncommon in the area. Easily distinguished by the floral bracts

Range: NSW coast and Blue Mountains. **Leaves:** glaucous, concave to inrolled, 1-1.5mm wide, 20-30cm long, toothed at the tip, with many interwoven reddish shreds at the base. **Flowers:** about 3mm long, inner whorl YELLOW, outer whorl deep reddish brown; in small clusters, with conspicuous chaffy bracts. **Flowering time:** early spring. **Name:** *confertifolia* = Lat. leaves pressed together, *rubiginosa* = Lat. rusty, referring to the outer perianth whorl.

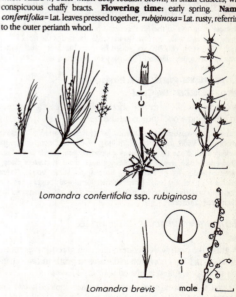

Lomandra confertifolia ssp. *rubiginosa*

Lomandra brevis   male

Lomandra cylindrica Lee

Ss, Castl

An erect grass-like herb to 50cm tall with almost cylindrical leaves. Found in heath and woodland. Not common in the area.

Range: Sydney area, Blue Mountains, and coast and ranges into Vic. **Leaves:** few per shoot, cylindrical or with one side flattened, 1-2mm wide, often twisted, lacking teeth at the tips. **Flowers:** small, solitary, in a short, slightly branched raceme. **Flowering time:** spring. **Name:** *cylindrica* = Lat. round in cross-section.

Lomandra filiformis ssp. *coriacea* Lee

Ss, Castl

A small grass-like herb with stiff leathery leaves, usually sprawling. Uncommon in the area, in heath and woodland.

Range: NSW coast, ranges and western slopes; also Vic. **Leaves:** 3-4 (2-5)mm wide, thick, stiff, dull, flat, toothed at the tip, with scabrous margins. **Flowers:** solitary, more or less sessile, in short; slightly branched racemes. **Flowering time:** spring. **Name:** *coriacea* = Lat. hard and leathery, referring to the leaves.

Lomandra filiformis (Thunberg) J. Brittan ssp. *filiformis*

Ss

A grass-like herb with very slender inrolled green leaves about 0.5mm wide, mostly 10-30cm tall. Common in the area in woodland on sandstone.

Range: NSW coast, ranges and inland areas, Qld and Vic. **Leaves:** inrolled, erect or curling, pale and shredding at the base, mostly toothed at the tip. **Flowers:** in racemes or panicles 5-18cm long (the female smaller), male flowers 1-2.5mm long, female flowers 2-3mm long. **Name:** *filiformis* = Lat. thread-leaved.

Lomandra fluviatilis (R. Brown) Lee

Ss Rare 3RC-

A grass-like herb to 50cm tall found in dense clumps in dry rocky creek beds. Common in the area.

Range: restricted to the NSW central coast around Sydney. **Leaves:** shiny, 1(-2)mm wide, concave (to inrolled), toothed at the tip, 25-50cm long. **Flowers:** YELLOW, subtended by sharp bracts; in small clusters on a slender spike. **Name:** *fluviatilis* = Lat. pertaining to rivers.

Lomandra glauca (R. Brown) Ewart ssp. *glauca* **Ss, Castl**

A small grass-like herb with short blue-green leaves. Common in heath and woodland on sandstone.

Range: NSW coast, ranges and central western slopes and Vic. **Leaves:** about 1mm wide, mostly 10-25mm long, blue-green, more or less flat, lacking teeth at the tip, with many interwoven pale shreds at the base. **Flowers:** sessile, female in a solitary cluster, male in clusters along a raceme to 12cm long. **Flowering time:** spring (from June). **Name:** *glauca* = Lat. blue-green. **Note:** distinct forms with bright-green (i.e. non-glaucous) leaves occur in some places (e.g. ridges near Audley, Heathcote Creek area).

Lomandra gracilis (R. Brown) Lee

Ss

A grass-like herb with slender erect dull green leaves mostly 30-40cm tall. Very common in the area in heath and woodland on sandstone. Often confused with *L. filiformis.*

Range: Sydney area, north coast and northern tablelands into Qld. **Leaves:** about 1.5mm wide, not toothed at the tip, slightly concave.

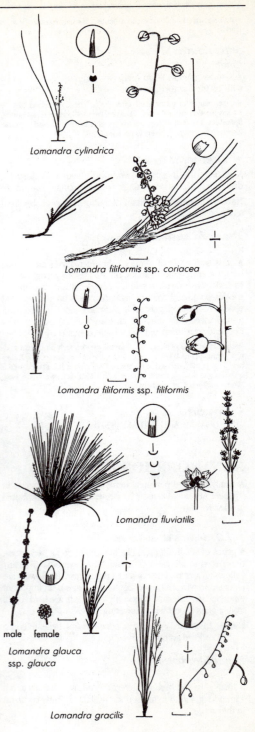

Lomandra cylindrica

Lomandra filiformis ssp. coriacea

Lomandra filiformis ssp. filiformis

Lomandra fluviatilis

male   female

Lomandra glauca ssp. glauca

Lomandra gracilis

Flowers: solitary, 1-2mm long, with slender stalks; arranged in a slender panicle. **Flowering time:** October-November. **Name:** *gracilis* = Lat. slender.

Lomandra longifolia Labillardière

Mat Rush   **Ss, Cumb, Castl, Sal**

A large tufted herb with tough strap-like leaves usually about 50cm long. Very common in the area in a wide range of habitats. The flowers exude a heavy lacquer scent which often pervades wide areas. The flowers were eaten by Aborigines. The Cribbs say their taste resembles fresh fragrant green peas.[32] The white succulent leaf bases are also pleasant to eat (choose new leaves as the old ones are impossible to pull out). The strong fibrous leaves were used by Aborigines to make net bags.

Range: NSW coast, ranges and western slopes, Qld, Vic, Tas and SA. **Leaves:** shiny, up to 1m long, with a prominently toothed tip. **Flowers:** sessile, in clusters on a prickly much-branched inflorescence **Flowering time:** September-November. **Name:** *longifolia* = Lat. long-leaved.

Lomandra micrantha (Endlicher) Ewart
ssp. *tuberculata*   Ss

An erect grass-like herb, with more or less revolute leaves and scabrous inflorescence branches. Found in woodland, with a preference for cool damp habitats. Uncommon in the area.

Range: Sydney area, Blue Mountains and ranges south to Vic; also Tas and SA. **Leaves:** 30-50cm long, 1-2mm wide, more or less revolute (often appearing square when dried), not toothed at the tip. **Flowers:** female about 5mm long, in a panicle or raceme; male 2-3mm wide (bell shaped), in a broad panicle, the inflorescence branches conspicuously scabrous. **Flowering time:** April-June. **Name:** *micrantha* = Gk. small-flowered.

Lomandra multiflora (R. Brown) J. Brittan

Ss, Castl

A grass-like herb with flowers in dense clusters. Common in the area in heath and woodland on sandstone. The strong fibrous leaves were used by Aborigines to make net bags.

Range: NSW coast, ranges and inland areas and all states except Tas. **Leaves:** 2.5-5mm (most 2.5-3mm) wide, 30-50cm long, more or less concave, not toothed at the tip. **Flowers:** female flowers 3-4mm long, stalkless; male flowers 2-3mm long, on stalks 8-10mm long; arranged in clusters in a panicle or raceme. **Flowering time:** spring. **Name:** *multiflora* = Lat. many-flowered.

Lomandra obliqua (Thunberg) Macbride

Fish Bones   **Ss**

A small, stiff, sprawling herb with 2-ranked leaves. Common in heath and woodland.

Range: NSW coast and ranges and Qld. **Leaves:** short, glaucous, twisted, not toothed at the tip. **Flowers:** sessile, in clusters. **Name:** *obliqua* = Lat. asymmetrical, referring to the leaves.

• *Xanthorrhoea* Smith

Grass-trees

An endemic genus with 15 species, distributed in all states. One of the most interesting and distinctive of Australia plants, and one of the most useful. Grass-trees have a short trunk (which may be underground), a large crown of slender arching leaves, and a dense spike of white flowers on a tall stout scape.

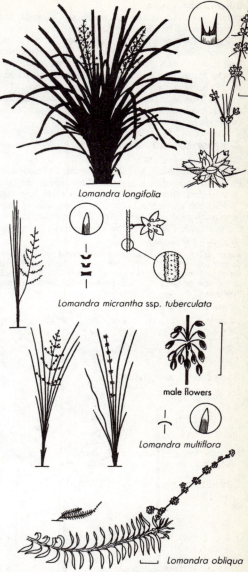

Lomandra longifolia

Lomandra micrantha ssp. *tuberculata*

male flowers

Lomandra multiflora

Lomandra obliqua

The flowers produce a great deal of nectar, which can often be licked off. Aborigines soaked the flowers in water to make a sweet drink, fresh or slightly fermented. In the Sydney area the stalks were used for spear shafts, and the resin as a glue to make weapons and tools. The resin was collected as a powder by beating the leaf bases. It can also be easily found in the trunks of old dead burnt stumps where it forms congealed masses.

The flowering period is short and not necessarily annual.

Name: *Xanthorrhoea* = Gk. *xanthos*, yellow, *rheo*, to flow, referring to the resin.

Other nearby species:
- North of the Hawkesbury: *X. media* ssp. *latifolia*, has a short trunk and broader nearly flat leaves.
- North of the Hawkesbury: *X. macronema*, lacks a trunk, has short spikes on very slender scapes, and a perianth and long stamens which are spreading (rather than recurved as in other species), the leaves are triangular, with several deep grooves between the ribs and very scabrous margins.
- In the Blue Mountains: *X. australis* ssp. *australis*, has an aerial trunk, distinctly triangular leaves, and a stout spike (with light brown bracts) on a short scape.

Xanthorrhoea arborea R. Brown

Broadleaf Grass-tree **Ss**

A grass-tree to 4m tall, with an aerial trunk. The trunk may be very short in some specimens; check beneath the skirt of old leaves. Found in sheltered valleys north from Port Hacking. Fairly common in the area, but populations have been much reduced by settlement. They were abundant in the small valleys around Sydney Cove and can be seen in many early paintings.

Range: Sydney area and Blue Mountains. **Aerial trunk:** present. **Leaves:** broad (5-8mm), flattish, often dull or slightly bluish-green. **Spike:** long (the longest of local species), stout, nearly equal in length to the scape (about 1-2m). **Name:** *arborea* = Lat. tree-like, referring to its trunk.

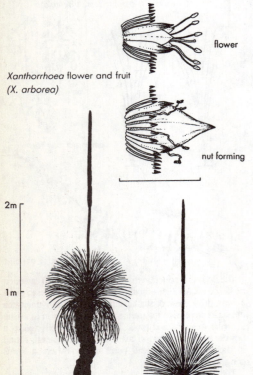

flower

nut forming

Xanthorrhoea flower and fruit
(*X. arborea*)

Xanthorrhoea media R. Brown **ssp.** *media*

Forest Grass-tree **Ss**

A grass-tree to 2.5m tall, common in the area, in heath and woodland. It is very similar to *X. resinosa* and *X. arborea*.

Range: Sydney area and Blue Mountains (Picton to Wyong). **Aerial trunk:** absent. **Leaves:** narrow, glossy, usually 3mm or less wide, triangular to quadrangular in cross-section. **Spikes:** dark brown, very variable in size (30-80cm long), on a much longer scape (90-200cm long); bracts glabrous or shortly ciliate, short, pointed. **Name:** *media* = Lat. middle, referring to its taxonomic position.

Xanthorrhoea minor R. Brown

Ss, Castl

A grass-tree to 1m tall, found in boggy open heathland. Fairly common on the coastal plateaus. Despite its size it is closely related to *X. media**.

Range: Sydney sandstones and north coast, SA, Vic and Tas. **Aerial trunk:** absent, but with a usually much-branched subterranean trunk which produces a number of spikes at flowering time. **Leaves:** triangular, often concave above, 2-2.5mm broad and 1mm thick. **Spikes:** short (often 5-12cm long), slender (5-10mm wide), on slender scapes 25-50cm long and 2-5mm wide. The flowers are larger than those of any other species except *X. macronema*. **Name:** *minor* = Lat. lesser.
* Hybrids intergrading towards *X. media* ssp. *media* occur in northern parts of the area.

Xanthorrhoea resinosa Persoon
ssp. *resinosa* **Ss**

A grass-tree to 2.5m tall. Fairly common in the area, mainly in moist heathland. Easily recognised by its densely furry spike.

Range: coast and ranges from eastern Vic to southern Qld. **Aerial trunk:** absent (or a few inches high). **Leaves:** thick, triangular or quadrangular, 3-3.5mm wide. **Spike:** shorter than the scape, stout, densely furry due to felty bracts. **Name:** *resinosa* = having resin.

2m

1m

Xanthorrhoea arborea   *Xanthorrhoea media* ssp. *media*   *Xanthorrhoea minor*   *Xanthorrhoea resinosa*

XYRIDACEAE

A family with about 270 species in 4 genera, widespread in the tropics and subtropics, with a few species extending into temperate regions. Only *Xyris* occurs in Australia, the other genera are confined to the Americas.

• *Xyris* Linnaeus (ZY-ris)

Yellow-eye

A genus with about 250 species, including about 19 in Australia. All are slender erect herbs 1-1.5m high, with tufted leaves and a wiry stem bearing a tight head of delicate yellow flowers protected by dark overlapping bracts.

Name: *Xyris* = Gk. cutting knife or shears, from the sword-shaped leaves.

Xyris complanata R. Brown

Feathered Yellow-eye **Ss, Cumb**

An erect sedge-like herb to 60cm tall. Uncommon in the area (Castlereagh woodlands, Narrabeen Lake, Kurnell) in marshy sedgeland.

Range: coast and western slopes north from the Sydney area, Qld, NT, WA and extending into tropical Asia. **Leaves:** 5-30cm long, 1-3mm wide, flat, with paler, often scabrous margins. **Flowers:** YELLOW, several arising from a head 10-25mm long; bracts uniform in colour; scape flattened, to 60cm long, with rough ribs running along its edges. **Flowering time:** summer. **Name:** *complanata* = Lat. flattened, referring to the scape.

Xyris gracilis R. Brown

Slender Yellow-eye **Ss**

An erect sedge-like herb to 60cm tall, found in marshy sedgeland on the coastal plateaus. There are 2 subspecies in the area:

• **ssp. *gracilis*:** recorded locally only from the Hawkesbury River area.

Range: Blue Mountains, coast and ranges south from Botany Bay, into Vic. **Leaves:** up to 2mm wide, 3-30cm long, with pale scabrous margins. **Flowers:** YELLOW, 1-4 per head, surrounded by 6-14 bracts; heads 6-8mm long; scape to 60cm long, 0.5-1mm wide, cylindrical, smooth. **Flowering time:** summer. **Name:** *gracilis* = Lat. slender.

• **ssp. *laxa*** O.D. Evans: perhaps the most common *Xyris* in the area, especially abundant in the Royal National Park. North of the harbour it intergrades with ssp. *gracilis*.

Range: Hawkesbury River to Jervis Bay. **Leaves:** 2-5mm wide, 3-30cm long, with pale scabrous edges. **Flowers:** YELLOW, 8-12 per head, surrounded by 18-28 bracts; heads about 10mm long; scapes to 60cm long, 1-2mm wide. **Flowering time:** summer. **Name:** *laxa* = Lat. slack, referring to the 2 lowest bracts, which are long (3-13mm) and hang loosely, compared to ssp. *gracilis* where the lowest bracts are short (3mm) and appressed.

Xyris juncea R. Brown

Dwarf Yellow-eye **Ss**

An erect sedge-like herb to 30cm tall. A dwarf species, rare in the area (recorded only just north of Waterfall station), in marshy sedgeland.

Range: NSW coast and ranges, southern Qld and eastern Vic. **Leaves:** 2-20cm long, up to 1mm wide, compressed cylindrical to almost flat, blunt tipped. **Flowers:** YELLOW; heads globular 4-8mm long; scapes very slim, 7-30cm tall, 0.3-1mm wide, cylindrical or slightly angular. **Flowering time:** summer. **Name:** *juncea* = Lat. sedgey.

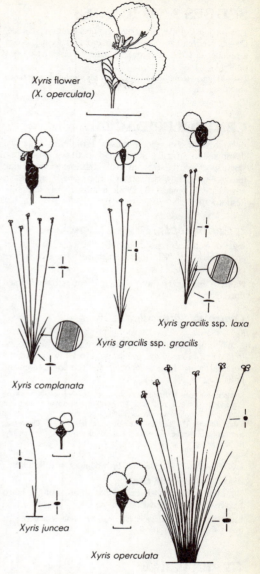

Xyris flower
(*X. operculata*)

Xyris gracilis ssp. *laxa*

Xyris gracilis ssp. *gracilis*

Xyris complanata

Xyris juncea

Xyris operculata

Xyris operculata Labillardière

Tall Yellow-eye **Ss**

An erect sedge-like herb to 1m tall. Common in the area, in marshy sedgelands on the coastal plateaus.

Range: NSW coast and ranges (but absent from the Blue Mountains), Qld, Vic, SA and Tas. **Leaves:** 20-60cm long, to 1mm wide, rigid, more or less cylindrical. **Flowers:** YELLOW; heads 10-15mm long, usually tapering gradually to the scape, bracts usually in 5 vertical ranks; scapes 30-100cm long, 1-1.5mm wide, cylindrical. **Flowering time:** summer. **Name:** *operculata* = Lat. lidded, referring to the hardened tip of the fruiting capsule, which fails to divide when the capsule splits, and is often cast off like a lid.

SEDGES AND RUSHES

This section includes the related families Centrolepidaceae, Cyperaceae, Juncaceae, and Restionaceae. For reasons of space a number of locally uncommon or rare species have been omitted.

I would like to thank Van Klaphake for his invaluable assistance with this group.

Centrolepis fascicularis

Centrolepis strigosa

CENTROLEPIDACEAE

A family with about 36 species worldwide, in 3 genera, distributed in Australia, NG, NZ and South-east Asia, with a single species on the southern tip of South America (indicating the family's Gondwanan origin). There are 29 species in Australia in 3 genera. The family is most closely related to Restionaceae.

• *Centrolepis* Labillardière (sen-TROL-e-pis)

A genus with 21 species in Australia, distributed in all states, and extending to NG, NZ and South-east Asia. Two species occur in the area.

Name: *Centrolepis* = Gk. spur-scale, referring to the pointed floral bracts.

Centrolepis fascicularis Labillardière
Ss

A miniscule grass-like annual herb to a few cm high, found in open moist sandy soil and moss on rocks. Fairly common but rarely noticed due to its small size. The flowers are wind pollinated.

Range: NSW coast and ranges, all states and South-east Asia. **Leaves:** tiny and slender, in a small tuft. **Flowers:** tiny, bisexual, with a single stamen; in 2 rows in a spikelet clustered between 2 green bracts on a short stiff stalk. The bracts have long drawn out tips (awns). **Flowering time:** spring. **Name:** *fascicularis* = Lat. bundled, referring (presumably) to the flowers.

Centrolepis strigosa (R. Brown) Roemer & Schultes

Hairy Centrolepis　**Ss, Castl**
Similar to *C. fascicularis*, except that the awns on the bracts are very short or absent. Uncommon.

Range: NSW coast and ranges, all states, NZ. **Name:** *strigosa* = Lat. beset with bristles or stiff hairs.

Baumea acuta

CYPERACEAE

Sedges
A family of herbs with about 4000 species worldwide, in about 90 genera. There are about 650 species in 47 genera in Australia including many introduced species. Most are adapted to marshy sunny conditions, although some grow in dry forest or rainforest.

The leaves may be prominent or reduced to sheaths. The flowers are bisexual or unisexual, with no perianth (or the perianth may be reduced to bristles or scales). There are 1-3 stamens and a superior single-chambered ovary with one ovule. The fruit is a small capsule, usually called a 'nut'.

• *Baumea* Boeckeler (BO-me-a)

Twig-rushes
A genus with about 30 species, including about 15 in Australia, and 10 in the Sydney area.

Name: *Baumea* = after E. F. Antoine Baumé (1728-1804), professor of chemistry and apothecary, in Paris.

Baumea acuta (Labillardière) Palla

Pale Twig-rush　**Ss, Cumb, Castl**
A small erect sedge 20-50cm tall, arising from spreading rhizomes. The flat twisted leaves are characteristic. Common on sandy soils near the coast, also at Richmond.

Range: coastal parts of southern Australia. **Leaves:** 1.5-2mm wide, flat, stiff, twisted, strongly erect. **Panicle:** zig-zag, arising from conspicuous stem-bracts. **Name:** *acuta* = Lat. pointed, referring to the leaves.

Baumea articulata (R. Brown) S.T. Blake

Jointed Twig-rush **Ss, Cumb**

A stout sedge 1-2m tall, growing in swamps. Uncommon in the area. Easily recognised by its thick, hollow, chambered leaves. The inflorescence is large and drooping. A very attractive species.

Range: NSW coast, Qld, Vic, SA, WA, NZ, NG and New Caledonia. **Leaves:** up to 10mm wide at the base, tapering to a fine tip, chambered, shiny, mid-green. **Panicles:** large, dense, drooping, willowy. **Name:** *articulata* = Lat. jointed, referring to the chambered leaves.

Baumea juncea (R. Brown) Palla

Ss, Sal

A slender erect sedge to 1m tall, arising from spreading rhizomes and often covering quite extensive areas. Common in the area. Easily recognised by its grey-green leaves and small inflorescence. It commonly grows in slightly salty environments near the sea, though not directly in salt-marsh.

Range: coastal parts of southern Australia; also NZ and New Caledonia. **Leaves:** reduced to several sheaths along the stem which is grey-green, cylindrical, 1-2mm wide. **Panicle:** small (under 3cm long), arising from inconspicuous stem-bracts. **Name:** *juncea* = Lat. rush-like.

Baumea nuda (Steudel) S.T. Blake

Ss

A slender erect sedge, in small dense clumps 50-70cm tall. Occasional in marshy sandy soil.

Range: Sydney area and Blue Mountains, Qld, NZ, NG and New Caledonia. **Leaves:** cylindrical, 0.5mm wide. **Panicle:** small (under 3cm long), zig-zag; spikelets few, arising from small sheathing stem bracts; the glumes have green keels. **Name:** *nuda* = Lat. naked.

Baumea rubiginosa (Sprengel) Boeckeler

Soft Twig-rush **Ss**

An erect sedge to 1m tall with spreading rhizomes, common

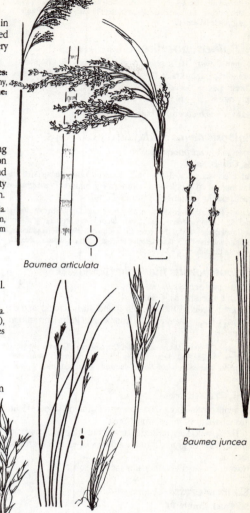

Baumea articulata

Baumea juncea

Baumea nuda

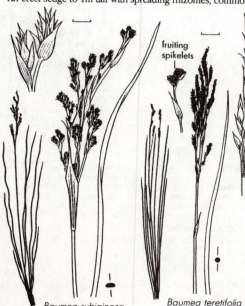

fruiting spikelets

Baumea rubiginosa

Baumea teretifolia

in marshy sandy soils. Distinguished by the compressed strongly erect leaves and clusters of spikelets.

Range: NSW coast and ranges, Qld, SA, WA, NT, NZ, New Caledonia and South-east Asia. **Leaves:** 4-5mm wide, compressed, often slightly twisted. **Panicle:** large (over 10cm long), arising from conspicuous stem bracts. All glumes have finely hairy margins. **Name:** *rubiginosa* = reddish.

Baumea teretifolia (R. Brown) Palla

Wrinkle-nut Twig-rush **Ss**

An erect sedge to 1m tall, fairly common in swampy ground on sandy soils. Similar to *B. rubiginosa* but recognised by the cylindrical or slightly angular leaves and very erect rather dense inflorescence.

Range: coast of NSW and Qld; also NZ, NG. **Leaves:** cylindrical or slightly angular, about 3mm wide. **Panicles:** large (mostly 5-10cm long) and fairly dense, arising from conspicuous stem-bracts. **Name:** *teretifolia* = Lat. cylindrical-leaved.

• *Bolboschoenus* (Ascherson) Palla

A genus with 16 species worldwide, on all continents, including 3 in Australia. It was previously included in *Scirpus*. Three species occur in the area, but one, *B. medianus*, is very rare.

Name: *Bolboschoenus* = bulb-*Schoenus*.

Bolboschoenus caldwellii (V.J. Cook) Soják

(previously *Scirpus caldwellii*)
Ss, Cumb, Sal
An erect sedge 50-100cm tall, found along creeks and in swamps, often in brackish conditions e.g. inland of *Phragmites* reeds on the margins of estuaries. Common.

Range: NSW coast, inland parts of NSW, widespread in southern Australia and NZ. **Leaves:** erect, 3-6mm wide. Stem leaves are usually absent on small plants, so that they resemble a *Cyperus*. **Spikelets:** globular, 5-7mm diameter. Main stalk triangular in cross-section. **Name:** *caldwellii* = after A.C. Caldwell, a NZ collector.

Bolboschoenus fluviatilis (Torrey) Soják

(previously *Scirpus fluviatilis*)
Marsh Clubrush **Ss, Cumb**
An erect sedge 50-100cm tall, found along creeks and in swamps. Found mainly on the Cumberland Plain. Uncommon in the area.

Range: NSW coast, Murray River and Queensland. **Leaves:** weeping, 8-12mm wide. **Spikelets:** globular, 5-7mm diameter. Main stalk triangular in cross-section. **Name:** *fluviatilis* = Lat. pertaining to rivers.

• *Carex* Linnaeus

A genus with about 200 species, including about 45 in Australia, and 10 in the Sydney area.

The spikelets are unisexual, each consisting of a tiny bract and a modified glume forming a flask-shaped utricle around the nut.
Name: *Carex* = the Latin name for sedges.

Carex appressa R. Brown

Ss, Castl, Cumb, Rf
A graceful sedge 70-100cm tall, with narrow densely tufted bright green leaves. Common in a range of habitats, from moist rainforest floors to open swamps with standing water.

Range: most parts of NSW, all states, NG, NZ and New Caledonia. **Leaves:** mostly 3-4mm wide, shiny, fairly tough, finely raspy on margins, channelled or V-shaped in cross-section, up to 120cm long in rainforests. **Spikelets:** numerous, apparently spiralling up the panicle, but in fact sessile along closely appressed lateral branches. Panicle 10-30cm long. Stem sharply triangular. **Name:** *appressa* = Lat. pressed down, referring to the spikelets.

Carex inversa R. Brown

Ss, Cumb, Castl
A weak grass-like herb with a slender lax stem 10-50cm long. Found in wetter woodland or grassland and often in lawns. Common.

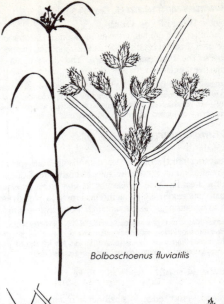

Bolboschoenus fluviatilis

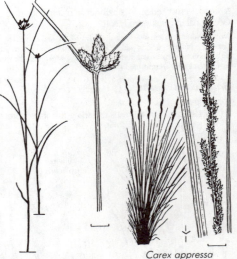

Bolboschoenus caldwellii

Carex appressa

Range: most parts of NSW, all states and NZ. **Leaves:** 1-1.5mm wide, channelled, very slightly rough to feel (microscopic teeth present). **Spikelets:** green, in spikes about 10mm long, with 2-3 leaf-like bracts at the base. The stem is triangular, about 0.5mm wide. **Name:** *inversa* = Lat. inverted, reference obscure.

Carex pumila

—See COASTAL AND ESTUARINE SPECIES.

• *Caustis* R. Brown (c-AUST-iss)

An endemic genus with 9 species, including 3 in the Sydney area.

Name: *Caustis* = Gk. burnt, from the appearance of the sheathing leaves.

Caustis flexuosa R. Brown

Old Man's Beard, Curly Wigs **Ss**
An erect sedge 60-120cm tall, with masses of curly branchlets. Common in dry soils in woodland on sandstone.

Range: NSW coast and ranges (except the north coast), Qld and Vic. **Leaves:** reduced to dark brown sheaths along the stems. **Spikelets:** bisexual, slender, about 7mm long, at the ends of the curly branchlets. **Name:** *flexuosa* = Lat. curly.

Caustis pentandra R. Brown
Ss
An erect sedge to 2m tall with all branches straight or very slightly wavy. It forms large dense clumps. Common in dry sandy heath. The stems are shiny, light green and quite stout at the base.

Range: NSW coast, Blue Mountains and all states. **Leaves:** reduced to dark brown sheaths along the stems. **Spikelets:** about 15mm long (together with subtending bract), held close against the stems. **Name:** *pentandra* = Gk. 5 stamens (compared to *C. flexuosa* which has 3 stamens).

Caustis recurvata Sprengel **var. recurvata**
Ss
An erect sedge to 80cm tall, found in dry sandy soil in heathy country. Once widely distributed in coastal heaths in southern Sydney, but now only known from an area near the Wattamolla turnoff in the Royal National Park, where it is common. Distinguished by having 2 types of stems: straight stems (with male flowers), and stems with densely curly branchlets (with female flowers).

Range: NSW coast, Blue Mountains and Qld. **Leaves:** reduced to dark brown sheaths along the stems. **Spikelets:** male under 10mm long (together with bract which almost hides it), in dense erect panicles; female shorter, solitary at the tips of curly stem segments. **Name:** *recurvata* = Lat. bent backward, referring to the curly branchlets.

Caustis recurvata **var. birsuta** Kükenthal
Ss
An erect sedge to 60cm tall. A rare species, known only from the Royal National Park where it is locally common in the Audley-Wattamolla area (with var. *recurvata*). Similar to var. *recurvata* but the male panicle is denser and all stems and spikelets are covered in microscopic hairs.

Range: restricted to the Royal National Park. **Name:** *birsuta* = Lat. hairy.

• *Chorizandra* R. Brown (cor-iz-AND-ra)
Bristle-rush
A genus with 6 species, 5 endemic to Australia. 2 species occur in the area.

Name: *Chorizandra* = Gk. separate flowers, referring to the separate male and female flowers of some species.

Chorizandra cymbaria R. Brown

Heron Bristle-rush **Ss**
An erect rush with stems 50-150cm tall, arising from spreading rhizomes. It occurs on marshy ground and in standing water in swamps and streams. Uncommon, but more frequent near the coast.

Range: NSW coast, southern tablelands, Blue Mountains, Qld, Vic, Tas, WA and New Caledonia. **Leaves:** 2-3mm wide, chambered in the upper part, slightly glaucous, to 150cm tall, usually longer than the stems. **Spikelet:** plate-like, within the broad base of the terminal leaf-like bract. The stems are similar to the leaves. **Name:** *cymbaria* = Gk. boat-like, referring to the inflorescence bract.

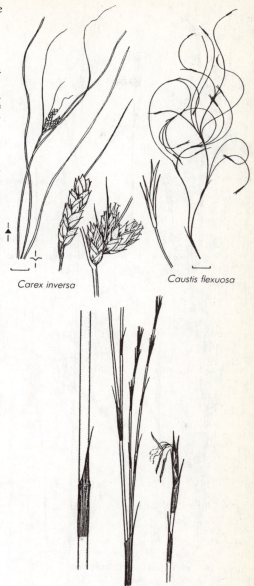

Carex inversa

Caustis flexuosa

Caustis pentandra

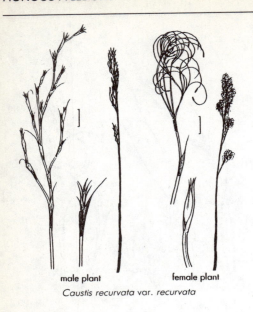

male plant   female plant

Caustis recurvata var. *recurvata*

male plant   female plant

Caustis recurvata var. *hirsuta*

Chorizandra sphaerocephala R. Brown

Round-headed Bristle-rush **Ss**

An erect rush with stems 50-100cm tall, arising from spreading rhizomes. Much less common than *C. cymbaria*, but found in similar habitats.

Range: NSW coast, Blue Mountains, Qld and Vic. **Leaves:** 2-3mm wide, chambered, slightly glaucous, to 100cm tall, usually longer than the stems. **Spikelets:** spherical. The stems are similar to the leaves. **Name:** *sphaerocephala* = Gk. spherical-head.

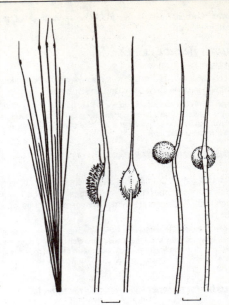

Chorizandra cymbaria   *Chorizandra sphaerocephala*

• *Cladium* P. Brown (CLAY-dee-um)

A genus with 2-4 species worldwide, including 1 species in Australia.

Name: *Cladium* = Gk. *kladion*, a small branch, refering to the branching inflorescence.

Cladium procerum S.T. Blake

Leafy Twig-rush **Ss**

An erect leafy sedge 1-1.5m high. Found on the edges of freshwater swamps on the coast. Uncommon, e.g. Marley Lagoon in the Royal National Park, Kurnell and Wondabyne.

Range: coasts of all mainland states. **Leaves:** 7-9mm wide, saw toothed on margins and mid-vein below, arising in dense clusters from nodes along stout, hollow, cylindrical stems. **Spikelets:** red-brown, very numerous, in dense corymb-like panicles subtended by long leafy bracts. **Flowering time:** summer. **Name:** *procerum* = Gk. front horn.

• *Cyathochaeta* Nees (sy-ay-tho-KEET-a)

An endemic genus with 4 species, including 1 in the Sydney area.

Name: *Cyathochaeta* = Gk. cup-bristle, referring to the perianth, which, like many genera in this family, is reduced to bristles.

Cyathochaeta diandra (R. Brown) Nees

Ss, Castl

An tough erect grass-like sedge, forming small clumps to over 80cm tall. Fairly common in dry sandy soils, especially near the coast. It flowers only sporadically, especially after fire, so identification often depends on the leaves alone, which can be recognised by their stiff, twisted character.

Range: Sydney area, north coast and Qld. **Leaves:** shorter than the stems, thick, stiff, dull-green, striate, often twisted, 1-2mm wide, upper part compressed, lower part triangular. **Spikelets:** about 15mm long, pale brown-orange, in a leaning open panicle. The stems are cylindrical or slightly flattened. **Name:** *diandra* = Gk. 2-flowered (each spike has 1 bisexual and 1 male flower).

• *Cyperus* Linnaeus (sy-per-us)

Sedges

A genus with about 600 species, including about 100 native to Australia. There are 16 native and several introduced species in the area.

C. polystachyos is probably the most common native species in the area, especially in streets and parks. *C. papyrus*, a species of the Nile and other African rivers, and the source of Papyrus paper, is often planted in gardens.

Name: *Cyperus* = from *kypeiros*, the Greek name for a sedge.

Cyperus brevifolius (Rottboel) Hasskard

Mullumbimby Couch   **Ss, Cumb**

An erect sedge 10-60cm tall, common in marshy ground throughout the area, including wet lawns.

Range: coastal parts of eastern mainland Australia, Africa, America and Asia. **Leaves:** 1-2mm wide, channelled, 10-30cm long. **Spikelets:** numerous, green, in an ovoid head. **Name:** *brevifolius* = short-leaved. **Note:** the introduced species *C. sesquiflorus** is almost identical, and also common in lawns. It is distinguished by its whitish or very pale green head.

Cyperus congestus* Vahl

Ss, Cumb

A robust sedge mostly 40-60cm tall. Common as a weed in waste places.

Range: scattered locations in the southern mainland states, Mediterranean and South Africa. **Leaves:** to 5mm wide. **Spikelets:** delicate, red-brown, about 10mm long. **Name:** *congestus* = Lat. crowded.

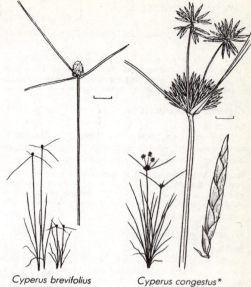

Cyperus brevifolius   Cyperus congestus*

Cyperus difformis Linnaeus

Ss, Cumb

An erect sedge 30-50cm tall, found in marshy disturbed places, especially in the western suburbs. Easily recognised by its tiny black spikelets with almost round glumes.

Range: most parts of the state, except the Blue Mountains; also all other states and widespread in the tropics. **Leaves:** channelled, 3-5mm wide. **Spikelets:** small (4-8mm long), with blunt, dark purplish brown glumes (0.75mm long); arranged in dense globular heads on short stalks. The stem is sharply triangular. **Name:** *difformis* = Lat. deformed, referring to the unusual blunt glumes.

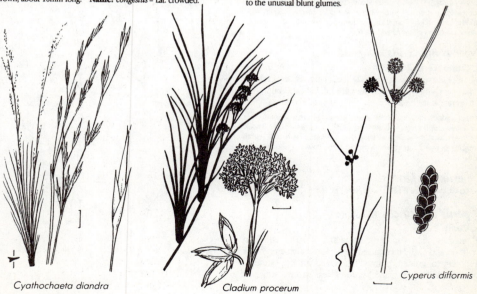

Cyathochaeta diandra   Cladium procerum   Cyperus difformis

*Cyperus eragrostis** Lamark

A robust sedge forming dense clumps 40-100cm high in ditches and marshy wastes. Introduced from South America. Common.

Range: Sydney area, north coast, Queensland, and widespread in tropical parts of the world.   **Leaves:** 3-4mm wide.   **Spikelets:** 2.5-3mm wide, green, becoming brown when old, in a spreading inflorescence consisting of dense balls of 50-100 spikelets.   **Name:** *eragrostis* = Gk. loving grass.

Cyperus flaccidus R. Brown

Cumb, Ss

A sedge with erect stems 3-15cm high, fairly common in wet clay soils on the Cumberland Plain. The stems are usually flaccid, with the inflorescence flattened on one plane.

Range: Sydney area, north coast, northern tablelands, Qld, Vic and NT.   **Leaves:** 3-4mm, often longer than the stem.   **Spikelets:** 3-5 per cluster; pale green, mostly about 5mm long, with spreading or recurved tips and sharply ridged green keels. Stem sharply triangular.   **Name:** *flaccidus* = Lat. soft.

Cyperus gracilis R. Brown

Ss, Cumb

A small sedge 10-20cm tall, fairly common in moist clay soils on the Cumberland Plain, but also in disturbed sandy locations. Often in lawns.

Range: NSW coast, ranges, and certain inland areas, Qld, New Caledonia and Hawaii.   **Leaves:** about 1mm wide, flat, shorter than the stems.   **Spikelets:** 7-10mm long, green; in clusters of 4-6. The glumes have 2-3 veins on each face.   **Name:** *gracilis* = Lat. slender.

Cyperus haspan Linnaeus

Ss, Castl, Cumb

An erect sedge 30-40cm tall, found in damp ground and ditches, mainly on the Cumberland Plain. An uncommon species.

Range: mainly in northern Australia; Sydney is its southern limit; also widespread in tropical parts of the world.   **Leaves:** 1-2mm wide.   **Spikelets:** red, mostly 5-6mm long, in clusters borne on slender branches.   **Name:** *haspan* = Persian name for a sedge.

Cyperus imbecillis R. Brown

Ss, Cumb, Temp Rf, STRf

A slender lax sedge with stems 20-50cm long, usually in dense sprawling clumps. Found in sheltered forests and rainforest. Not common in the area.

Range: Sydney area and NSW north coast.   **Leaves:** 2-3mm wide, channelled.   **Spikelets:** 4-10mm long, usually 1-3 together on 1-3 stalks of various lengths (some stalkless), green, glumes with tips slightly spreading outwards. Stems about 1mm wide.   **Name:** *imbecillis* = Lat. weak.

Cyperus laevigatus

—See COASTAL AND ESTUARINE SPECIES.

Cyperus polystachyos Rottboell

Ss, Cumb

An erect sedge with clustered stems 40-70cm tall. Very common and easily recognised by its dense clustered heads of green to golden pointed spikelets. An opportunistic coloniser of ditches, marshy ground near streams, edges of

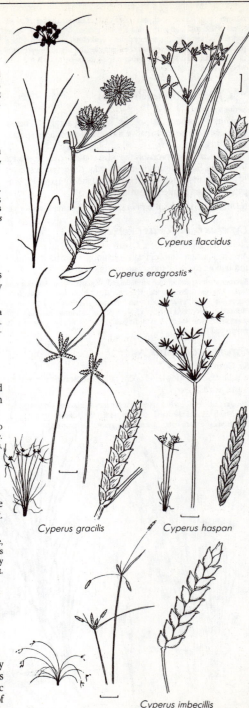

Cyperus flaccidus

Cyperus eragrostis*

Cyperus gracilis   Cyperus haspan

Cyperus imbecillis

swamps, footpaths, parks, and roadsides. Some botanists doubt whether it is native.

Range: mainly coastal parts of NSW, Vic, Qld, NT and WA; also widespread in the tropics. **Leaves:** flat, about 3mm wide. **Spikelets:** erect, mostly about 12-16mm long, green, becoming golden and copper-red. Stem triangular. **Name:** *polystachyos* = Gk. many-spiked (literally, many ears of corn).

*Cyperus rotundus** Linnaeus

Nut-grass **Ss, Cumb**

A sedge to 40cm tall (to 70cm in gardens), forming dense colonies on moist ground, spreading by creeping rhizomes. Despite its small size, Nut-grass is a very tough species: 'I have seen it come through 2 inches of blue-metal asphalt, which contained no visible crack.'[36] The roots have been found 10m underground. The purplish tubers are edible and were roasted by Aborigines in some areas.

Range: a cosmopolitan weed, native to temperate and tropical parts of Australia, but introduced to most places where it is now found. **Leaves:** glossy mid-green, channelled, 3-5mm wide. **Spikelets:** 10-30mm long, arranged pinnately, glumes shiny red-brown. Stem strongly triangular. **Name:** *rotundus* = Lat. rounded, referring to the nut.

Cyperus sanguinolentus Vahl

Ss, Cumb

An erect sedge, solitary or tufted 40cm high. Common in damp grasslands and disturbed marshy areas.

Range: coast and ranges in eastern mainland Australia, also widespread in tropical parts of Asia and Africa. **Leaves:** 3-4mm wide. **Spikelets:** very dark, several arranged pinnately in close clusters; glumes blackish-red with pale yellow margins. Stems angular. **Name:** *sanguinolentus* = Lat. blood-nut, from the colour of the seed.

Cyperus tenellus Carl von Linné

Ss, Castl

A diminutive sedge 3-10cm tall with very slender stems and leaves, densely tufted. Found sporadically in marshes near the coast. Also at Agnes Banks and Menangle Park.

Range: Sydney area, Blue Mountains, south-western slopes, all southern states, NZ and South Africa. **Leaves:** under 0.5mm wide. **Spikelets:** 3 (sometimes 1 or 2) per head, with short subtending bracts. **Name:** *tenellus* = Lat. delicate.

Cyperus tetraphyllus R. Brown

Ss, Temp Rf, STRf

An erect sedge 30-60cm tall, found in shady rainforests, including littoral rainforest.

Range: Sydney area, north coast and ranges, into Qld. **Leaves:** light to dark green, 3-5mm wide, channelled. **Spikelets:** 10-18mm long, dark brown; arranged in sessile and stalked clusters. Stem sharply triangular. **Name:** *tetraphyllus* = Lat. 4-leaved, reference obscure.

• *Eleocharis* R. Brown (eel-ee-0-KAR-is)

Spike-rushes

A genus of marsh herbs with about 200 species, including 28 in Australia, and 10 in the Sydney area.
The stems are hollow (chambered in *E. sphacelata*) and the leaves are reduced to scales at the base.

Name: *Eleocharis* = Gk. *helos*, marsh, *charis*, delight.

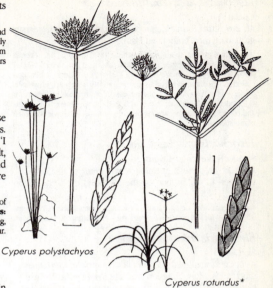

Cyperus polystachyos

Cyperus rotundus*

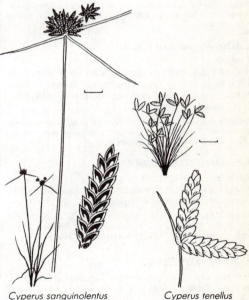

Cyperus sanguinolentus   Cyperus tenellus

Eleocharis cylindrostachys Boeckeler

Cumb

An erect rush forming dense clumps 40-60cm tall. Fairly common in marshes on the Cumberland Plain.

Range: Sydney area, south coast and tablelands, Qld and New Caledonia. **Stems:** 2-3mm wide. **Spikelets:** 15-30mm long, 3-4mm wide. **Name:** *cylindrostachys* = Lat. cylindrical ear of corn.

Eleocharis dietrichiana Boeckeler

Cumb

An erect rush forming clumps 20-40cm tall. Rare in marshy ground on the Cumberland Plain.

Range: Sydney area, south coast, southern tablelands and Qld. **Stems:** ribbed, about 1mm wide. **Spikelets:** about 10mm long. **Name:** *dietrichiana* = after Amalie Dietrich (1821-1891), a German botanical collector. This diminutive fearless woman travelled widely in Qld, virtually alone, in the years 1863-72. She amassed a remarkable collection for G.J. Godeffroy, a Hamburg trader, who sold the specimens to botanists and collectors in Europe. Among her collections was the type specimen of this species.

Eleocharis gracilis R. Brown

Slender Spike-rush   **Cumb, Ss**

A small erect rush forming small clumps 10-25cm tall. Common in wet ground on the coast and the Cumberland Plain.

Range: coast and ranges throughout eastern Australia and NZ. **Stem:** 0.5-1.5mm wide. **Spikelets:** 5-9mm long. **Name:** *gracilis* = Lat. slender.

Eleocharis minuta Boeckeler

Ss, Castl

A common small rush 3-20cm tall, forming clumps in marshy sandy soils. More common near the sea (e.g. La Perouse to Marley Beach) but also occurring on the Cumberland Plain.

Range: Sydney area, south coast, Qld, Vic, East Africa and Madagascar. **Stems:** 1mm wide or less. **Spikelets:** 2-3mm long. **Name:** *minuta* = Lat. very small.

Eleocharis pusilla R. Brown

Cumb

A slender rush forming clumps typically about 20cm high. Uncommon in the area, in scattered marshes on the Cumberland Plains. Best recognised by the very slender stems, usually about 0.5mm wide.

Range: widespread in NSW (except the south coast), all states except WA, also in NZ. **Stems:** <1mm wide, 5-35cm long. **Spikelets:** 2-4 (7)mm long. **Name:** *pusilla* = Lat. very little.

Eleocharis sphacelata R. Brown

Tall Spike-rush   **Ss, Cumb**

A large rush to 2m tall, forming extensive colonies in standing water. Common throughout the area.

Range: NSW coast, ranges and inland areas, Qld, Tas, SA, WA, NZ and NG. **Stems:** about 10mm wide, hollow, chambered. **Spikelets:** 5-10cm long. **Name:** *sphacelata* = Lat. withered, reference obscure.

• *Fimbristylis* Vahl

A genus with about 300 species, including about 85 in Australia. There are 5 species in the area, but 4 of these are uncommon or rare.

Name: *Fimbristylis* = Lat. fringed-style.

Fimbristylis dichotoma (Linnaeus) Vahl

Ss, Castl, Cumb

A small erect sedge 30-50cm tall, common in many habitats and soils.

Range: NSW coast, also widespread in warm parts of the world. **Leaves:**

Cyperus tetraphyllus

Eleocharis cylindrostachys

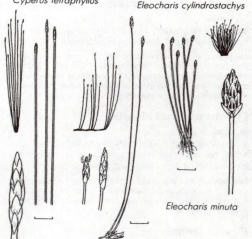

Eleocharis minuta

Eleocharis gracilis

Eleocharis dietrichiana

dull green, sometimes slightly greyish, more or less 0.5mm wide, flat, channelled. **Spikelets:** about 4mm long, short, with several flowers surrounded by shiny red-brown bracts, on long stalks; arranged in an irregular terminal umbel. **Name:** *dichotoma* = Gk. 2-branching. **Note:** *F. ferruginea* is a similar species, found growing in saline swamps (e.g. at Towra Point). It is stouter and has spikelets 8-14mm long in a more compact umbel.

• *Gahnia* G. & J.R. Forster (GAHN-ee-a)

Saw Sedge, Sword Grass

A genus of large leafy sedges forming tussocks on moist or marshy ground. There are about 30 species distributed in Asia and the Pacific, including about 23 in Australia, and 8 in the Sydney area. The sharply serrated leaves are an obvious distinguishing feature. The French botanist Labillardière gave one the first accounts of these plants which he found in Tasmanian coastal marshes in 1793: ' . . . we attempted to make our way across some of the marshes, in order to get onto ground that has acquired a more solid consistence from the roots of the plants; but a species of *sclerya*, which grows to the height of 6 or eight feet, cut our hands and faces with its leaves in such a manner that we were obliged to desist from our attempt.'[37]

Name: *Gahnia* = after Dr Henry Gahn, a Swedish botanist and friend of Linnaeus.

Gahnia aspera (R. Brown) Sprengel
Ss

A small tufted sedge 40-60cm high, common in sandy soils enriched with clay.

Range: NSW coast, Blue Mountains, northern tablelands and slopes, Qld, South-east Asia and Polynesia. **Leaves:** rough on the underside, about 10mm wide (at the middle). **Spikelets:** 6-8mm long, in narrow panicles shorter than the leaves. The nut is shiny, yellowish to bright red-brown, 4-6mm long. **Name:** *aspera* = Lat. rough, referring to the microscopically rough spikelet glumes.

Gahnia clarkei Benl
Ss

A tall leafy sedge to 2.5m high, often forming dense thickets on marshy sites and creek banks. Common in the area. Distinguish from *G. sieberana* by the numerous small bracts on the lower half of the spikelet and the leaves being shiny green on both sides (leaves of *G. sieberana* are blue-green on one side).

Eleocharis sphacelata

Eleocharis pusilla

Fimbristylis dichotoma

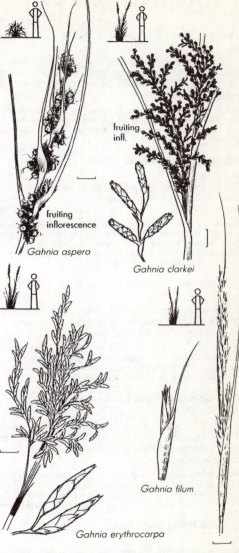

Gahnia aspera

fruiting inflorescence

fruiting infl.

Gahnia clarkei

Gahnia filum

Gahnia erythrocarpa

Range: NSW coast, Blue Mountains, Qld, Vic and SA. **Leaves:** rough on the upper side, about 10-15mm wide (at the middle). **Spikelets:** 4-6mm long, almost black. The nut is shiny red-brown at maturity, about 3mm long. **Name:** *clarkei* = after C.B. Clarke, (1832-1906), a British botanist who worked on South African plants.

Gahnia erythrocarpa R. Brown
Ss

A tall leafy sedge to 2m, preferring dry sites on hillsides. Moderately common in the area. Distinguish from *G. sieberana* by having large spikelets (over 10mm long).

Range: restricted to the Sydney area. **Leaves:** rough on the upper side, about 10mm wide (at the middle). **Spikelets:** almost black. The nut is shiny and bright red-brown, about 5mm long. **Name:** *erythrocarpa* = Gk. red-fruit.

Gahnia filum (Labillardière) F. Mueller

Ss

A tall leafy sedge to 2m high, found on the edges of swamps. Rare. Only recently discovered in the Sydney area, at Mill Creek and Salt Pan Creek on the Georges River, near the edge of salt-marsh.

Range: Sydney area, south coast, Vic, SA and Tas. **Leaves:** smooth on the underside. **Spikelets:** in a slim pale panicle; each almost enclosed in a broad bract with wide translucent margins. **Name:** *filum* = Lat. a thread.

Gahnia melanocarpa R. Brown

Ss

A tall leafy sedge 1-2m high. Relatively common, in wetter sclerophyll forest and the margins of rainforest. The main identification feature is the shiny black nut.

Range: NSW coast, Blue Mountains, Qld and Vic. **Leaves:** smooth on both sides, about 10mm wide (at the middle). **Spikelets:** 3-4mm long, partly concealed by shiny red-brown bracts; the upper glumes round-tipped; in a narrow panicle, under 3cm wide. The nut is black and shiny. **Name:** *melanocarpa* = Gk. black-fruit.

Gahnia microstachya Bentham

Ss

A leafy sedge to 1m tall, more slender than the other local species. Found on drier sites on sandy soil. Rare, mainly on southern parts of the Woronora Plateau.

Range: Sydney area, NSW ranges and Vic. **Leaves:** smooth on both sides, about 2-3mm wide, mostly inrolled. **Spikelets:** very small, 2-3mm long, well spaced along the panicle branches. Inflorescence about as tall as the basal leaves. **Name:** *microstachya* = Lat. small ear.

Gahnia radula (R. Brown) Bentham

Ss

A leafy sedge to 1m tall, on hillsides in woodland where there is a clay influence. Sporadically distributed in the area but not uncommon. It spreads by long rhizomes, with leaves arising in distant tufts.

Range: Sydney area, south coast, Vic, Tas and SA. **Leaves:** under 8mm wide. **Spikelets:** about 6mm long, very narrow (<1mm wide), dark grey, almost enclosed in the basal glume; in a dense blackish panicle. The nut is almost black, about 2mm long. **Name:** *radula* = Lat. a scraper.

Gahnia sieberana Kunth

Ss, Cumb

A tall leafy sedge 2m or more high, found in dense thickets on marshy sandy soils. Very common near the coast but rare on the Cumberland Plain. The blue-green leaf underside is a useful distinguishing feature.

Range: coast and ranges in eastern Australia. **Leaves:** rough on the upper side, about 10-15mm wide (at the middle). The blue-green underside is distinctive. **Spikelets:** dark brown to blackish, 4-7mm long, with glumes fewer than 10, the lowest ones mostly more than half as long as the spikelet; in a dense blackish panicle. Nut bright red, about 3mm long. **Name:** *sieberana* = after Franz Wilhelm Sieber of Prague, Bohemia, who collected extensively in Australia from 1819-23.

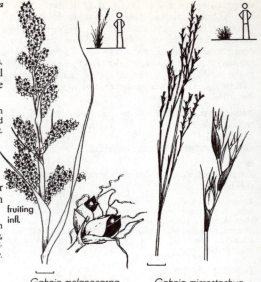

fruiting infl.

Gahnia melanocarpa   *Gahnia microstachya*

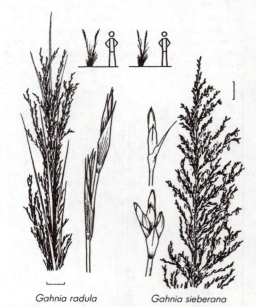

Gahnia radula   *Gahnia sieberana*

Gahnia subaequiglumis S.T. Blake

Ss

A leafy sedge to 1m or more high occurring in open ground on the edges of swamps. Locally rare, recorded from the Royal National Park and Woronora Plateau.

Range: Sydney area, south coast, NSW ranges, Qld, Vic and Tas. **Leaves:** almost smooth on the upper side. **Spikelets:** almost enclosed in broad bracts (3-4 spikelets per bract); in tight panicles slightly shorter than the leaves. **Name:** *subaequiglumis* = Lat. almost equal glumes.

• *Gymnoschoenus* J.D. Hooker

(jim-no-SKEEN-us)

An endemic genus with 2 species, including 1 in the Sydney area.

Name: *Gymnoschoenus* = Gk. naked-rush.

Gymnoschoenus sphaerocephalus

(R. Brown) J. D. Hooker

Button Grass   **Ss**

A sedge with spherical heads on graceful stems to over 2m tall, forming extensive colonies in wet heath country. Locally restricted to the Woronora Plateau (especially Maddens Plains) and La Perouse.

Range: Sydney area, south coast, NSW ranges, Vic, SA and Tas (where it forms extensive Button Grass plains).   **Leaves:** stiff, usually channelled, much shorter than the stem.   **Spikelets:** numerous in dense globular heads to 15mm wide.   **Name:** *sphaerocephalus* = Gk. spherical head.

• *Isolepis* R. Brown

A genus with 70 species worldwide (on all continents, especially east and south Africa and Australia), including 28 in Australia, and 7 in the Sydney area. The spikelets resemble those of *Cyperus*, except the florets are arranged spirally, instead of in 2 rows.

Name: *Isolepis* = Gk. equal scale.

Note: *Isolepis* results from the division of the old genus *Scirpus* into 5 genera, all of which occur in Australia.

Isolepis cernua

—See COASTAL AND ESTUARINE SPECIES.

Isolepis fluitans Linnaeus

(previously *Scirpus fluitans*)

Ss, Cumb, Aqu

This species has 2 quite different habits. When submerged it is a slender grass-like herb with long flaccid underwater stems and emergent spikelets. However, when growing on mud it forms small erect clumps 3-12cm high depending on conditions. These clumps often coalesce into extensive mats. Uncommon in the area. Recorded from Nepean River, Cataract River, Cooks River.

Range: Sydney area, south coast, southern and northern tablelands, Vic, Tas, SA, WA, NZ, Europe, Asia and Africa.   **Leaves:** about 0.5mm wide, flat, 2-15cm long.   **Spikelets:** 3-4mm long, surrounded by 2 green bracts.
Name: *fluitans* = Lat. floating.

Isolepis nodosus

—See COASTAL AND ESTUARINE SPECIES.

Isolepsis inundatus R. Brown

(previously *Scirpus inundatus*)

Ss, Castl, Aqu

A small tufted sedge, 5-30cm tall, rather commonly distributed in damp places.

Range: NSW coast and ranges, all states, South-east Asia, NZ and South America.   **Leaves:** reduced to red sheaths at the base of the stems.
Spikelets: (1) 2-several, mostly 2-3mm wide; glumes pale, with reddish brown central strip. The stems are cylindrical, under 1mm wide.   **Name:** *inundatus* = Lat. inundated.

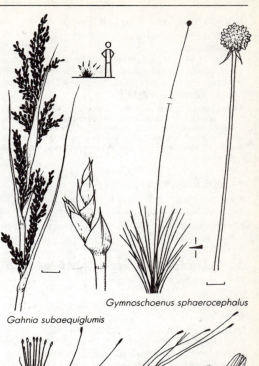

Gymnoschoenus sphaerocephalus

Gahnia subaequiglumis

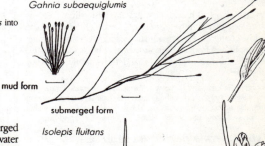

mud form

submerged form

Isolepis fluitans

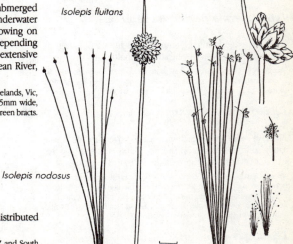

Isolepis nodosus

Isolepsis inundatus

*Isolepis prolifer** (Rottboell) R. Brown

(previously *Scirpus prolifera*)

Ss, Cumb, Aqu

A sedge to 50cm high, forming dense colonies in ditches, edges of dams, and disturbed marshland. A distinctive feature is the proliferation of new plants from the ends of the stems. A native of South Africa.

Range: Sydney area, south coast, Blue Mountains, Vic, WA, NZ and South Africa. **Leaves:** reduced to sheaths at the base of the stems. **Spikelets:** variable in number and size (3-10mm long), in radiating heads. The stems are about 2mm wide, erect or arching, bright green, smooth, rounded, slightly compressed and easily crushed. **Name:** *prolifer* = Lat. proliferating.

• *Lepidosperma* Labillardière

A genus with about 50 species worldwide, including 40 species in Australia and 12 species in the Sydney area.

Name: *Lepidosperma* = Gk. scale-seed, referring to the scales surrounding the nut.

1. Cylindrical-leaved *Lepidosperma*

These are known as Rapier-sedges.

Lepidosperma filiforme Labillardière

Ss

An erect sedge 60-100cm tall, with stems arising from creeping rhizomes. Found in wet sandy soils, generally in woodland. Fairly common, recorded mainly south of the harbour. Distinguished from *L. flexuosum* by the inflorescence being a spike, instead of a panicle, and the strongly spreading rhizome.

Range: NSW coast and ranges, Vic, Tas and NZ. **Leaves:** shorter than the stems, 1-2mm, occasionally to 3mm wide. **Spikelets:** outer bracts grey, in a zig-zag spike 5-10cm long. The stems are cylindrical or slightly compressed, about 1mm wide. **Name:** *filiforme* = Lat. thread-like.

Lepidosperma flexuosum Labillardière

Ss

An erect sedge forming clumps 60-100cm tall. Common in wet sandy soils, especially heath communities.

Range: NSW coast. **Leaves:** very short, about 1mm wide. **Spikelets:** 7-9mm long with grey outer-bracts; in a zig-zag panicle; on cylindrical stems about 1mm wide. **Name:** *flexuosum* = Lat. flexible.

Lepidosperma forsythii A.A. Hamilton

Ss

An erect sedge forming clumps usually over 1m tall in wet sandy soil. An uncommon species, found only south of the harbour (mainly in swamps on the Woronora Plateau).

Range: coast south from Sydney, and Vic. **Leaves:** shorter than stems or reduced to sheaths. **Spikelets:** with outer bracts grey, 11-15mm long; in a distinctive zig-zag arrangement. The stems are 1-2mm wide, cylindrical or slightly flattened. **Name:** *forsythii* = after William Forsythe, who first collected this species in Centennial Park in 1897.

Lepidosperma neesii Kunth

Ss

An erect sedge 40-50cm tall with stems arising from spreading rhizomes. Uncommon in moist sandy soil.

Isolepis prolifer*   Lepidosperma filiforme

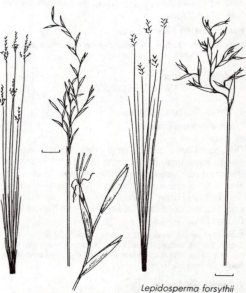

Lepidosperma flexuosum   Lepidosperma forsythii

Range: NSW coast, Blue Mountains and Vic. **Leaves:** shorter or longer than the stems, 1-2mm wide, flattened, stiff, more or less square, channelled, often twisted. **Spikelets:** with dark brown bracts, in short dense compact panicles, 3-4cm long. The stems are more or less square, about 1mm wide. **Name:** *neesii* = after Christian Gottfried Nees von Esenbeck (1776-1858), a professor of botany at Breslau who named many Australian plants.

Lepidosperma urophorum Wakefield

Ss

An erect sedge forming clumps 40-100cm tall, found in wet

sandy soil. Uncommon. Distinguished from *L. flexuosum* by the panicle branches being straight, not zig-zag.

Range: NSW coast, Blue Mountains and Vic. **Leaves:** very short or reduced to scales. **Spikelets:** outer bracts grey, in a narrow spike or panicle 5-8cm long. Stems cylindrical or slightly flattened, about 1mm wide. **Name:** *urophorum* = Gk. tail-bearing, referring to the slender inflorescence.

2. Flat-leaved *Lepidosperma*

These are known as Sword-sedges.

Key

A. Growing in sedge swamps.
    B. Leaves and stems hollow or pithy.
        = *L. longitudinale* (rare)
    *B. Leaves and stems solid.
        = *L. limicola*
*A. Growing in woodland or gullies.
    C. Panicles very compound, drooping.
        = *L. elatius* (rare)*
    *C. Panicles erect.
        D. Leaves 3-5mm or more wide.
            E. Leaf margins and bases exuding sticky resin.
                = *L. viscidum*
            *E. Leaf margins not sticky.
                F. Spikelets dense, obscuring the secondary inflorescence branches.
                    = *L. concavuum*
                *F. Spikelets not dense, not obscuring the secondary inflorescence branches.
                    = *L. laterale*
        *D. Leaves 2-3mm wide (spikelets not as numerous as in other species).
            = *L. lineare*

* *L. elatius* is not described here. In the Sydney area it has only been recorded at Katandra Sanctuary. It grows in dense clumps, with stems up to 2m high. The drooping panicles are distinctive.

Lepidosperma concavuum R. Brown

(includes those local specimens previously placed in *L. squamatum*)
A leafy sedge to 60cm tall, found in woodland on sandstone. Common. Distinguish from *L. laterale* by the density of the spikelets (see illustration).

Range: coast and ranges in eastern Australia. **Leaves:** 3-8mm wide, to 60cm long, flat or concave on one side. The bases of the leaves are usually yellowish-brown. **Panicle:** 4-10cm long, dense (spikelets obscure the secondary branches). **Name:** *concavuum* = Lat. concave, referring to the leaves (but not a consistent feature). **Similar species:** *L. laterale*. Small specimens of *L. laterale* can only be practically distinguished by the density of the inflorescences. To be safe, it is best to examine populations, rather than individuals.

Lepidosperma laterale R. Brown

Ss

A leafy sedge of variable dimensions, with leaves and stem 50-100cm or more high. Found in woodland on sandstone. Common.

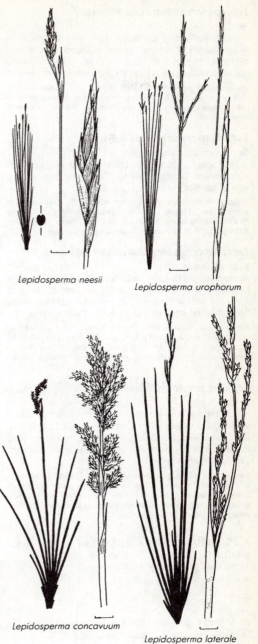

Lepidosperma neesii

Lepidosperma urophorum

Lepidosperma concavuum

Lepidosperma laterale

Range: all except arid parts of the continent. **Leaves:** 3-5mm wide (sometimes wider). **Panicle:** 6-20cm long, spikelets not dense (secondary inflorescence branches exposed). The bases of the leaves are usually orange-reddish. **Name:** *laterale* = Lat. pertaining to the sides. **Similar species:** *L. concavuum* (see note on preceding species).

Lepidosperma limicola N. Wakefield

Ss

A sedge with only a few leaves, 120-150cm tall, found in sedge swamps. Common on the Woronora Plateau (e.g. Maddens Plains, with Button Grass, *Gymnoschoenus sphaerocephalus*), but not recorded elsewhere in the area.

Range: Sydney area, north coast, NSW ranges and Vic. **Leaves:** 4-7mm wide, solid. **Panicle:** 7-15cm long. Spikelets densely clustered. Stems solid. **Name:** *limicola* = Lat. mud-dwelling. **Similar species:** *L. longitudinale*.

Lepidosperma gunnii Boeck

Ss (previously *L. lineare*)

A leafy sedge 40-50cm high, found in heath and woodland on sandstone. Common. Distinguished by its small size and slender leaves.

Range: coast and ranges of south-eastern Australia. The Sydney area is its northern limit. **Leaves:** 2-3mm wide; usually shorter than the stem. **Panicle:** spikelets sparse, on a stem 1-3mm wide. **Name:** *gunnii* = after R.C. Gunn (1808-1881), renowned Tasmanian plant collector.

Lepidosperma longitudinale Labillardière

Ss (not illustrated)

An erect sedge with leaves and stem 1-2m tall, found in sedge swamps usually in dense pure stands. Rare in the area. Recorded from La Perouse, Marley swamps and Moorebank. The leaves and stems are hollow or filled with soft pith.

Range: coastal parts of all states. **Leaves:** about 10mm wide, tips drawn out into long slender curved points, convex on both sides. **Panicle:** 12-25cm long. Spikelets very densely clustered and spreading, giving a prickly appearance. **Name:** *longitudinale* = Lat. long. **Similar species:** *L. limicola*.

Lepidosperma viscidum R. Brown

Ss

An erect sedge with leaves and stem to 60cm high, found in woodland on sandstone. Common. Similar to *L. laterale* or *L. concavuum*, but distinguished by the sticky clear resin exuding from the base and margins of the leaves and stem (it turns red upon drying).

Range: coast and ranges in eastern Australia. **Leaves:** 3-6mm wide, to 60cm long. **Panicle:** 7-15cm long. Spikelets usually not densely clustered. **Name:** *viscidum* = Lat. sticky (from *viscum*, the Latin name for the mistletoe, named on account of the stickiness of its berries). **Note:** closely related to *L. concavuum*.

• *Ptilothrix* (R. Brown) K.L. Wilson
ty-lo-THRIX (previously *Ptilanthelium*)

An endemic genus with a single species.

Name: *Ptilothrix* = Gk. feather-hair.

Ptilothrix deusta (R.Brown) K.L. Wilson
Ss, Castl (previously *Ptilanthelium deustum*)

An erect sedge 30-60cm tall, common in wet sandy soil, usually in heath communities.

Range: NSW coast and ranges, into Qld. **Leaves:** channelled, 1-1.5mm wide, 10-30cm long. **Spikelets:** numerous, in a dense head 12-20mm long, surrounded by 2 blackish bracts, with broad transparent margins and long green tips. **Name:** *deusta* = Lat. burnt.

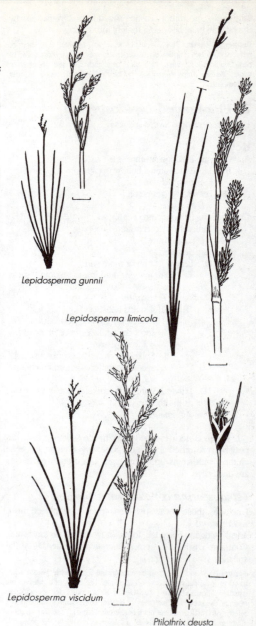

Lepidosperma gunnii

Lepidosperma limicola

Lepidosperma viscidum

Ptilothrix deusta

• *Schoenoplectus* Valla

A genus with about 60 species, including 11 in Australia. It was formerly included in the large genus *Scirpus*. A total of 4 species occur in the area although only 2 are relatively common.

Name: *Schoenoplectus* = Gk. twisted rush.

Schoenoplectus mucronatus

(Linnaeus) Palla ex Kerner

(previously *Scirpus mucronatus*)   **Cumb, Ss**
An erect sedge 40-70cm tall forming clumps in shallow fresh
water and on creek banks. Common on western parts of the
Cumberland Plain, rare near the coast.

Range: Sydney area, northern coast and ranges, widespread in northern
Australia, Asia and Europe.   **Leaves:** reduced to sheaths at the base of
the flowering stems.   **Spikelets:** brown, ovoid, 8-12mm long, in a cluster.
The flowering stem is acutely 3-angled.   **Name:** *mucronatus* = Lat. tipped
with a small point.

Schoenoplectus validus (Vahl) A. & D. Löve

(previously *Scirpus validus*)
River Club-rush   **Cumb, Ss**
An erect rush 1.5m or more high, forming dense stands on
the edges of freshwater streams. Fairly common in the area.
The bluish green stems are filled with a spongy pith with
many tiny air pockets. The young white underground roots
are edible after boiling.[38]

Range: widespread in NSW (except the Blue Mountains), also in NZ,
New Caledonia and the Americas.   **Leaves:** reduced to a sheath at the
base of the flowering stalk.   **Spikelets:** rusty-brown, cylindrical, mostly
3-4mm wide, 8-12mm long. The blue-green stems are quite stout at the
base, 12-15mm wide.   **Name:** *validus* = Lat. strong, robust.

• *Schoenus* Linnaeus (SKEEN-us)

Bog-rushes
A genus with about 100 species, including 85 in Australia,
and 12 in the Sydney area.

Name: *Schoenus* = Gk. *schoinos*, the ancient name for a type
of rush.

Schoenus apogon Roemer & Schultes

Fluke Bogrush   **Ss, Castl**
An erect sedge 12-25cm tall, forming dense soft clumps in
open wet sandy soils. Common in the area.

Range: most parts of NSW, all eastern states, and NZ.   **Leaves:** flat leaves
are present along the stems and at the base of the plant, each leaf has
a conspicuous sheathing red-brown base (a useful identifying feature).
Spikelets: 2-3mm long, shiny dark red-brown to blackish; shortly stalked,
in small dense clusters, subtended by short leaves.   **Name:** *apogon* =
Gk. unbearded.

Schoenus brevifolius R. Brown

Ss
An erect sedge forming spreading stands of wiry flexible stems
40-70cm tall. Found in open wet sandy ground. A very
common species in heath communities.

Range: NSW coast, Blue Mountains, Qld, Vic, Tas, WA, NZ and New
Caledonia.   **Leaves:** reduced to short projections 5-15mm long, arising
from dark shiny sheaths at the base of the stems.   **Spikelets:** 7-12mm
long, stalked, shiny red-brown, in slender panicles 10-20cm long, the
panicle branches appressed to the stem. Glumes with microscopically
woolly margins.   **Name:** *brevifolius* = Lat. short-leaved.

Schoenus ericetorum R. Brown

Ss, Castl
A small sedge, growing in tufts 20-30cm high, with blackish
spikelets. Common in dry sandy soils.

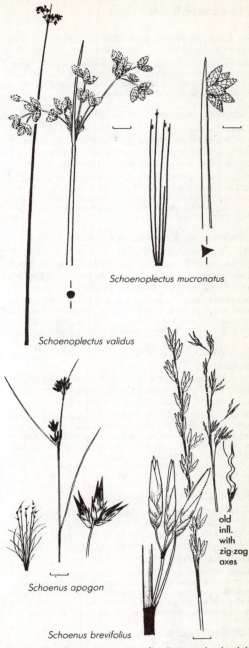

Schoenoplectus mucronatus

Schoenoplectus validus

old
infl.
with
zig-zag
axes

Schoenus apogon

Schoenus brevifolius

Range: coast and ranges in eastern Australia.   **Leaves:** reduced to dark
purple-red sheaths at the base.   **Spikelets:** 6-9, dark red-brown to
blackish, the margins of the glumes densely lined with woolly white
hairs; arranged in short dense terminal clusters. The stems are under
1mm wide, channelled, cylindrical.   **Name:** *ericetorum* = Lat. inhabiting
heaths.

Schoenus imberbis R. Brown

Ss

A small sedge, growing in tufts 20-40cm high, with blackish spikelets. Common in dry sandy soils.

Range: Sydney area, south coast, Blue Mountains and Vic. **Leaves:** reduced to dark red sheaths at the base. **Spikelets:** 10–30, very dark, in dense clusters; stems under 1mm wide, channelled, cylindrical, smooth or scabrous. **Name:** *imberbis* = Lat. beardless.

Schoenus maschalinus Roemer & Schultes

Dwarf Bog-rush **Ss**

An inconspicuous creeping grass-like herb with stems 10-20cm long, occurring in marshy heath and in muddy soil on the edges of streams and ponds. Uncommon.

Range: NSW coast, Blue Mountains, northern tablelands, all states, NZ and South-east Asia. **Leaves:** flat, usually under 1mm wide, with sheathing bases, at intervals along the prostrate stems. **Spikelets:** about 2mm long, stalked, pale, 2-3 per axil. **Name:** *maschalinus* = Lat. with axils (literally armpits).

Schoenus melanostachys R. Brown

Ss

An erect sedge forming tall dense graceful clumps 60-200cm high. Common in wet sandy soils. Distinguished by its long (often weeping) stems and black spikelets.

Range: NSW coast and ranges, also Vic, Qld and South-east Asia. **Leaves:** reduced to dark scales at the base of the stems. **Spikelets:** black, about 8mm long. The glumes have microscopically woolly margins. The stems are 1-1.5mm wide. **Name:** *melanostachys* = Gk. black ear of corn.

Schoenus moorei Bentham

Ss, Castl

An erect sedge forming dense clumps 10-30cm tall. Common in dry sandy soils. The stems are flat, covered in microscopic stiff hairs, with many dark shreds at the base.

Range: coast and ranges north from the Woronora Plateau; also inland NSW. **Leaves:** flat, hispid, almost thread-like, basal, about as long as the stems **Spikelets:** stalkless, pale with reddish tips, each subtended by a broad blackish bract with translucent edges; in small dense panicles. Each panicle is subtended by a stem bract which may be extended into a long slender leaf. **Name:** *moorei* = after Charles Moore, director of the Royal Botanic Gardens, Sydney, 1848-1896.

Schoenus nitens (R. Brown) Poiret

Shiny Bogrush **Ss**

A small erect sedge 15-35cm tall, resembling a *Cyperus* or *Isolepis*. Found rarely in damp sandy soil close to the coast (probably restricted to Cape Banks). It spreads by a rhizome and does not form dense clumps.

Range: NSW coast, northern tablelands, Qld, Vic, Tas, SA, NG, NZ and South America. **Leaves:** 3-8mm long, cylindrical, less than 1mm wide. **Spikelets:** about 3mm long, shiny red-brown, stalkless, a few in a small cluster, with a single green bract appearing to continue the stem. The stem is cylindrical, under 1mm wide. **Name:** *nitens* = Lat. shining.

Schoenus pachylepis S. T. Blake

Ss

An erect sedge to 60cm tall, uncommon in dry sandy soil near the coast, mainly in heath communities.

Range: NSW coast, Blue Mountains, northern tablelands and Qld. **Leaves:** reduced to sheaths. **Spikelets:** usually solitary, blackish, 12-16mm long; stems 1-1.5mm wide, cylindrical. **Name:** *pachylepis* = Gk. thick-scale.

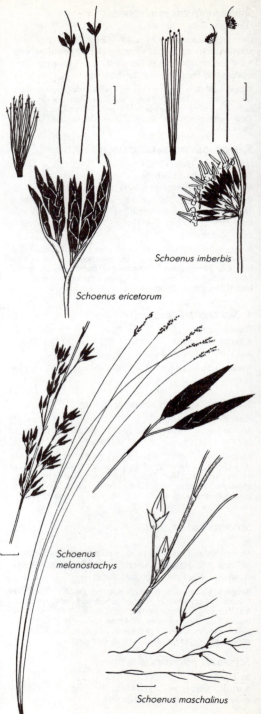

Schoenus imberbis

Schoenus ericetorum

Schoenus melanostachys

Schoenus maschalinus

Schoenus paludosus (R. Brown) Poiret

Ss

An erect sedge to 25cm tall with prominent slender leaves near the base. Common in moist sandy soils near the coast, mainly in heath communities.

Range: NSW coast, Blue Mountains and Qld. **Leaves:** flat, 1mm or less wide, arising from sheathing bases, numerous at the base of the plant, and also along the stems. **Spikelets:** about 4mm long, shiny red-brown, stalked, numerous in long open panicles, on a cylindrical stem. **Name:** *paludosus* = Lat. pertaining to swamps.

Schoenus turbinatus (R. Brown) Poiret

Ss

An erect sedge to 40cm tall, found uncommonly in dry sandy soil (e.g. Kurnell, Royal National Park, Heathcote National Park).

Range: NSW coast, Blue Mountains, Vic and Tas. **Leaves:** 10-15cm long, channelled, appearing cylindrical, very slender, under 1mm wide. **Spikelets:** in a compact terminal cluster, surrounded by long slender brownish bracts. **Name:** *turbinatus* = Lat. like a spinning top.

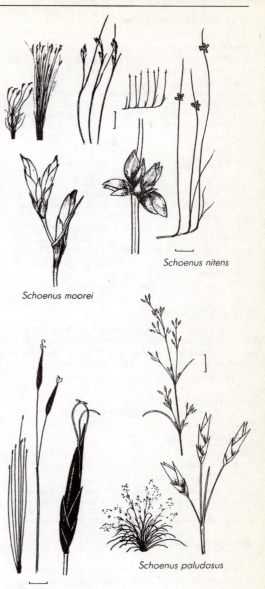

Schoenus nitens

Schoenus moorei

Schoenus turbinatus

Tetraria capillaris

Schoenus pachylepis

Schoenus paludosus

• *Scirpus*
—See *Bolboschoenus, Isolepis, Schoenoplectus*

• *Tetraria* Beauvois (tet-rair-ee-a)

A genus with about 38 species worldwide, distributed in Africa, Borneo and Australia, where there are 6 species.

Name: *Tetraria* = Gk. *tetra*, 4, since the flowers have 4 stamens.

Tetraria capillaris (F. Mueller) J.M. Black

Hair-sedge, Bristle Twig-rush **Ss**
A fine-stemmed sedge 25-60cm high, forming small clumps. Moderately common, in heath and woodland, mainly on the Woronora Plateau.

Range: coasts of all states except the NT; also NZ. **Leaves:** reduced to reddish-brown sheaths at the base of the stems. **Spikelets:** about 3mm long, dark brown, small, often on reflexed stalks. **Name:** *capillaris* = Lat. hair. **Note:** There appear to be two forms, one with stems about 0.25mm wide and 20-30cm high, and one with stems about 1mm wide and 40-60cm high.

• *Tricostularia* Nees

A genus with 6 species, all Australian (1 extends to NG), including a single species in the Sydney area.

Name: *Tricostularia* = Lat. 3-ribbed, referring to the nut.

Tricostularia pauciflora

(F. Mueller) Bentham

Needle Bogrush   **Ss**

A tufted sedge forming erect or leaning clumps 30-50cm tall. Common on sandy soils.

Range: NSW coast, Blue Mountains, Vic and Tas.   **Leaves:** reduced to sheaths at the base of the stem.   **Spikelets:** solitary or a few in a terminal cluster, about 3mm long, consisting of a single flower surrounded by shiny red-brown bracts. Stems cylindrical, 1mm or less wide.   **Name:** *pauciflora* = Lat. few-flowered.

JUNCACEAE

A family of grass or sedge-like herbs with about 400 species in 8 genera occurring worldwide but rarely in the tropics. There are about 75 species (including 20 introduced) in 2 genera in Australia. All occur in marshy situations.

The inflorescence is compound, made of panicles or heads. The wind-pollinated flowers are small and bisexual. There are 6 membranous perianth segments, 3-6 stamens. The ovary is 1-3 chambered, with 3-many ovules. There is a single style, with 3 stigmas. The fruit is a capsule.

The family is closely related to Restionaceae.

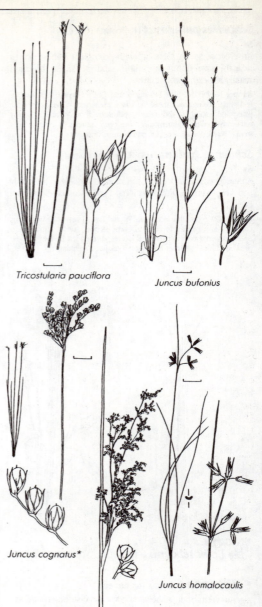

Tricostularia pauciflora

Juncus bufonius

Juncus cognatus*

Juncus continuus

Juncus homalocaulis

• *Juncus* Linnaeus (JUNK-us)

A genus with about 44 native species in Australia, including about 16 native and many introduced in the Sydney area.

The small seeds become gelatinous on exposure to moisture, allowing them to stick to passing animals.

Name: *Juncus* = Lat. the classical name for bulrush.

Juncus acutus

—See COASTAL AND ESTUARINE SPECIES.

Juncus bufonius Linnaeus

Ss, Cumb

A slender annual herb 20-40cm tall, common in open wet places and on disturbed sites.

Range: most parts of Australia. A cosmopolitan weed.   **Leaves:** fine, flat, about 0.5mm wide.   **Panicles:** flowers located at distant intervals along the stem and at branching points; perianth segments 2-4mm long, membranous.   **Name:** *bufonius* = from Lat. *bufo*, a frog, allusion obscure.

*Juncus cognatus** Kunth

Ss

An erect rush 40-50cm tall, common along tracks in woodland, in moist sandy soil. Easily recognised by its small stature and relatively large capsules. A native of temperate South America.

Range: NSW coast and Blue Mountains, NZ and South America.   **Leaves:** slender, under 1mm wide, compressed cylindrical, shorter than the stems.   **Panicle:** to 4cm long, with shiny pale brown spikelets about 3mm long, evenly spaced along the branches.   **Name:** *cognatus* = Lat. allied.

Juncus continuus L. Johnson

Ss, Castl

An erect rush forming clumps 60-100cm tall, found in ditches and edges of marshes on sandy soil. Common. Recognised by the yellow-brown bases of the stem sheaths, unbroken stem pith, and yellow-green stems 2-4mm wide.

Range: most parts of eastern Australia, NZ and Norfolk Island.   **Leaves:** reduced to sheaths at the base of the stems.   **Panicles:** pale brown; on stiff shiny green to yellow-green stems 2-3.5mm wide, yellow-brown to brown at the base; stamens usually 3, outer perianth segments 1.5-2.5mm long. The stems have continuous pith.   **Name:** *continuus* = Lat. referring to the continuous pith.   **Similar species:** *J. pallidus*.

Juncus homalocaulis F. Mueller ex Bentham

Cumb, Ss

An erect rush 15-25cm high, found in moist grassland on the Cumberland Plain. Common.

Range: most parts of NSW, Qld, Vic, SA, WA and NZ. **Leaves:** slender, about 1mm wide, convex. **Spikelets:** shiny, green, about 5mm long. **Name:** *homalocaulis* = Gk. even-stem.

Juncus kraussii

A tall robust rush forming dense clumps in saltmarsh communities.
—See COASTAL AND ESTUARINE SPECIES.

Juncus pallidus R. Brown

Pale Rush　**Ss**

A stout rush forming dense clumps usually 1-1.5m tall. Found close to the sea, in freshwater swamps and marshy ground. Locally common from Malabar to Royal National Park and Helensburgh, especially around Botany Bay (e.g. La Perouse, Towra Point, Kurnell). Recognised by the thick blue-green stems and the large erect capsules.

Range: southern coasts of the continent and NZ. **Leaves:** reduced to long sheaths at the base of the stems. **Panicles:** strongly ascending, on stiff stems 2.5-4mm wide at top, 7mm at base. The stems have continuous pith. **Spikelets:** densely clustered, stamens 6, outer perianth segments usually 3-4mm long. **Name:** *pallidus* = Lat. pale. **Similar species:** *J. continuus.*

Juncus planifolius R. Brown

Broad-leaf Rush　**Ss, Castl**

A species with broad grassy leaves, very common in the area on wet sandy ground.

Range: most parts of all states, also NZ, Chile and Hawaii. **Leaves:** flat, thin-textured, 3-12mm wide, 6-24cm long. **Panicle:** flowers in clusters of 4-10, arranged in a usually open panicle on a stem 10-40cm tall. The perianth segments are red-brown, 1.5-2mm long. The capsule is rounded at the top and about the same length as the perianth segments. **Name:** *planifolius* = Lat. broad-leaved. **Similar species:** *J. prismatocarpus.*

Juncus prismatocarpus R. Brown

Branching Rush　**Ss, Castl**

A rush with grass-like leaves, common in wet sandy ground.

Range: most parts of all states, Mauritius, NG and NZ. **Leaves:** flattened, hollow, chambered, although the internal partitions are often partly formed. **Panicle:** flowers in clusters of 2-6, in an open panicle on stems 20-40cm tall. The perianth segments are slender, green (straw-coloured when old), 2.5-3mm long. The capsule is sharply pointed, triangular in cross-section, and much longer than the perianth segments. **Name:** *prismatocarpus* = Lat. prism-fruit, referring to the capsule which is sharply triangular in cross-section. **Similar species:** *J. planifolius.*

Juncus subsecundus Wakefield

Finger Rush　**Ss, Castl, Cumb**

A rush forming loose clumps 40-70cm tall. Common in the area, mainly on the Cumberland Plain, on damp soils. Recognised by its slender blue-green stems which are strongly erect and not densely tufted.

Range: most parts of all states and NZ. **Leaves:** reduced to sheaths. **Panicle:** flowers not numerous, in a small erect panicle, on stems 0.7-1.5mm wide (with internal pith separated by small hollows). **Name:**

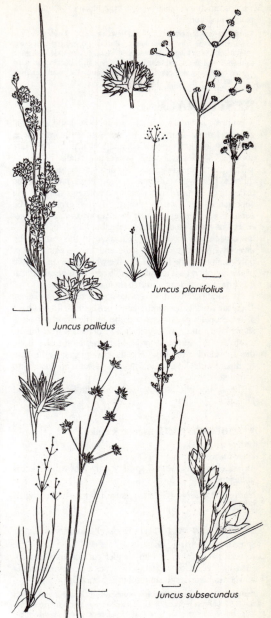

Juncus planifolius

Juncus pallidus

Juncus subsecundus

Juncus prismatocarpus

subsecundus = Lat. almost on one side, referring to the position of the flowers.

Juncus usitatus L. Johnson

Common Rush　**Ss, Cumb**

A gracefully arching rush forming dense clumps to 1m tall.

Very common in a range of soils from moist to swampy sites, mainly in disturbed areas.

Range: all parts of most states, NZ and New Caledonia. **Leaves:** reduced to sheaths at the base of the stems. **Panicle:** open; capsules blunt, pale, about 1.5mm long; on arching, shiny stems 1-2mm wide, dark green to slightly blue-green, red-brown at base. The pith is discontinuous, i.e. broken by distinct air pockets. **Name:** *usitatus* = Lat. usual, common.

RESTIONACEAE

A family of sedge-like plants with about 400 species in 30 genera, mainly distributed in the southern hemisphere, especially in south-western WA and South Africa. There are about 115 species in about 20 genera in Australia.

The plants are dioecious, i.e. different sexes occur on different plants. In some genera, especially *Leptocarpus*, the male and female plants are completely different in appearance. J.H. Maiden wrote 'If the expression be admissible, one might say that the Restionaceae are the most dioecious plants in the whole vegetable kingdom, or rather the dioecism is most strongly marked in this family. The diversity of structure in the male and female plants is not only confined to the flowers, but the whole male and female plants are often (not always) so different in appearance that it is extremely difficult to match them correctly.'[39]

The wind-pollinated flowers are aggregated into spikelets. There are usually 6 perianth segments. The male flowers have 3, occasionally 6, stamens and the female flowers have a single ovary and a style with 3(2-1) branches. The fruit is a capsule. The leaves are reduced to sheathing scales along the stems and at the base. The sheaths are split to the base (compare with Cyperaceae where the sheaths are fused into complete tubes).

The family is closely related to Centrolepidaceae and Juncaceae.

• *Empodisma* L. Johnson & Cutler
(em-po-DIZ-ma)
Rope-rushes
An endemic genus with 2 species, only 1 of which occurs in the area.
Name: *Empodisma* = Gk. a hindrance, referring to the tangled foliage.

Empodisma minus (J.D. Hooker) L. Johnson & Cutler
Spreading Rope-rush **Ss**
A weak perennial herb with slender curvaceous stems 20-50cm long, often forming tangled masses. It occurs commonly in wet heathlands and damp spots in woodland.
Range: NSW coast and ranges, also widespread in eastern Australia, Tas and NZ. **Leaves:** reduced to sheaths with narrow pointed tips, 1-3mm long; the slender tips are bent sharply outwards or downwards; there is a tuft of woolly hairs in the throat of the sheath. **Spikelets:** inconspicuous, solitary and stalkless; largely hidden by the sheathing bracts. Female with 1 flower, male with several. **Name:** *minus* = Lat. lesser.

• *Hypolaena* R. Brown (hy-po-LEEN-a)
An endemic genus with 4 species, including 1 species in the Sydney area.

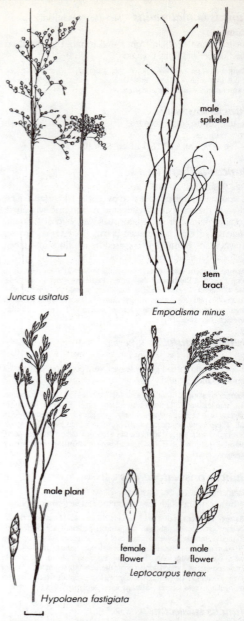

Juncus usitatus

male spikelet

stem bract

Empodisma minus

male plant

female flower

male flower

Leptocarpus tenax

Hypolaena fastigiata

Name: *Hypolaena* = Gk. under-cloak, referring perhaps to the layer of fine hairs on the plant.

Hypolaena fastigiata R. Brown
Tassel Rope-rush **Ss**
A sedge 30-60cm tall, with many erect curvaceous stems, easily distinguished from *Leptocarpus tenax* by the grey stems. Sporadic and often locally common in wet coastal heath from

Malabar to the Royal National Park. It was once quite common in the eastern suburbs.

Range: NSW coast, Blue Mountains and all states. **Spikelets:** deep-brown; male spikelets 4-7mm long, stalked, fairly numerous in terminal panicles; female spikelets usually solitary, stalkless, at the tips of the branchlets. The stems are covered in fine white hairs. **Name:** *fastigiata* = Lat. bundled.

• *Leptocarpus* R. Brown

Twine-rushes

An endemic genus with 24 species, including 1 species in the area.

Name: *Leptocarpus* = Gk. slender-fruit.

Leptocarpus tenax (Labillardière) R. Brown

Ss

A rush with erect, dull green stems 40-70cm tall, common in wet sandy heath. The male and female plants are completely different in appearance.

Range: NSW coast, Blue Mountains, northern tablelands and all states. **Spikelets:** rich-brown; male plants: spikelets 2-4mm long, very numerous in a dense dangling panicle at the tip of the stem; female plants: spikelets few, about 12mm long, bright red-brown, strongly erect. **Name:** *tenax* = Lat. holding fast.

• *Lepyrodia* R. Brown (lep-ee-RO-dee-a)

Scale-rushes

A genus with about 18 species, including 16 in Australia and 4 in the Sydney area. The female and male plants are similar in appearance.

Name: *Lepyrodia* = having husks, referring to the membranous inflorescence bracts.

Lepyrodia anarthria F. Mueller ex Bentham

Ss

An erect rush to 80cm high with very slender stems lacking bracts and joints. Locally rare, in coastal heaths. Recorded from Malabar, Uloola Swamp, Bulli Pass.

Range: NSW ranges, and coast south from Sydney; also Qld and Vic. **Leaves:** reduced to sheaths at the base. **Panicle:** mostly to 25mm long, on very slender stems (under 1mm wide), lacking bracts. **Spikelets:** each protected by a transparent bract. **Name:** *anarthria* = Gk. without joints.

Lepyrodia gracilis R. Brown

Slender Scale-rush **Ss**

A rush with slender stems 30-50cm high. Locally rare, in damp sandy soil along creeks (e.g. Woronora River), but more common in Blue Mountains. Easily recognised by the small, free spikelets.

Range: Sydney area, Blue Mountains and southern tablelands. **Spikelets:** perianth segments unequal, 2mm long or shorter, not protected by large bracts. The stems are often much branched, about 1mm wide on the upper parts. **Name:** *gracilis* = Lat. slender.

Lepyrodia muelleri Bentham

Ss, Castl

An erect rush usually about 50cm high, found in wet ground in heathland. Common in the Castlereagh woodlands, uncommon in coastal heaths.

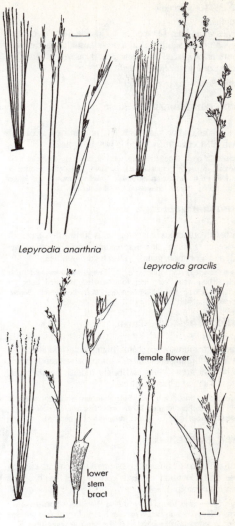

Lepyrodia anarthria

Lepyrodia gracilis

female flower

lower stem bract

Lepyrodia muelleri

Lepyrodia scariosa

Range: NSW coast, Blue Mountains, Vic, Tas and SA. **Leaves:** reduced to short sheaths at the base. **Panicle:** on a stem lined with appressed bracts, each bract with a ragged translucent upper margin and a long slender projecting point. **Spikelets:** protected by transparent bracts. **Name:** *muelleri* = after Ferdinand von Mueller.

Lepyrodia scariosa R. Brown

Ss, Castl

A variable rush 30-80cm tall, easily recognised by the large outward-arching stem bracts which are dull brown outside, almost silvery inside, and become pale and thin-textured in the panicle. An abundant species in wet heathland.

Range: NSW coast and ranges, and Qld. **Spikelets:** pale brown, subtended by almost translucent bracts; in a narrow panicle. **Name:** *scariosa* = Lat. membranous, scar-like, referring to the floral bracts.

• *Restio* Rottboell

Cord-rushes

A genus with about 120 species worldwide. Since true *Restio* only occurs in South Africa, the 36 Australia species will eventually be placed in 2 new genera, as yet unnamed. 6 species occur in the Sydney area

Name: *Restio* = Lat. rope-maker.

Restio complanatus R. Brown

Ss

A weakly ascending rush with flat, unbranched stems 30-100cm tall. Occasionally found in wet sandy heath.

Range: NSW coast, Blue Mountains, Qld, Vic and Tas.   **Spikelets:** not numerous, in narrow terminal panicles. Male plants with spikelets 5-7mm long on thread-like stalks; female spikelets narrower and longer than the males.   **Name:** *complanatus* = Lat. flattened.

Restio dimorphus R. Brown

Ss

A rush with numerous branching stems 30-100cm tall, usually curvaceous, forming dense spreading tufts. Found in wet sandy soil. Common, mainly in heath communities.

Range: restricted to the Sydney area.   **Spikelets:** with 6 segments; male spikelets about 4mm long, numerous, stalkless, scattered along the branchlets; female spikelets resembling male but fewer. **Name:** *dimorphus* = Lat. with 2 forms.

Restio fastigiatus R. Brown

Tassel Rush   **Ss**

A rush with numerous graceful, highly branched stems 30-100cm tall, forming erect tufts. Common in wet sandy heath. The brilliant green stems and bright reddish brown bracts make this a most attractive species.

Range: Sydney area, south coast, Blue Mountains, southern tablelands and Qld.   **Spikelets:** appressed to the branchlets; male about 4mm long, female similar but stalked.   **Name:** *fastigiatus* = Lat. bundled.

Restio gracilis R. Brown

Ss

A rush with slender unbranched stems 30-100cm tall, forming dense tufts. Common in heath communities south of the harbour, in wet sandy soil.

Range: Sydney area, south coast and Blue Mountains.   **Spikelets:** red-brown; male spikelets in narrow panicles 8-15cm long; female spikelets smaller, in narrow panicles 2-4cm long. The stems are about 1mm wide. **Name:** *gracilis* = Lat. slender.

Restio tetraphyllus Labillardière
ssp. *meiostachyus* L. Johnson & O.D. Evans

Ss

An elegant rush to 1.2m tall. The straight stems are lined with dense tufts of green thread-like branchlets. Found in sheltered marshy sites near the coast, usually in deep sands. Uncommon in the area. There are good stands in Scarborough Park, Kogarah and at Narrabeen Lake.

Range: NSW coast and Qld.   **Spikelets:** shiny, reddish; in a narrow terminal panicle.   **Name:** *tetraphyllus* = Gk. 4-leaved, *meiostachyus* = Gk. smaller spikelet.

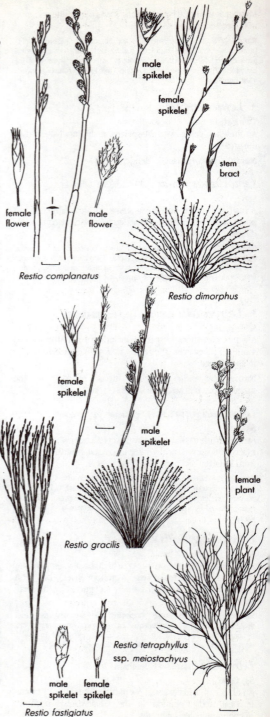

male spikelet

female spikelet

stem bract

female flower

male flower

Restio complanatus

Restio dimorphus

female spikelet

male spikelet

female plant

Restio gracilis

Restio tetraphyllus ssp. *meiostachyus*

male spikelet

female spikelet

Restio fastigiatus

PRIMITIVE PLANTS

These are remnants of floras which dominated world vegetation before the rise of flowering plants. Ferns are the most successful survivors from those earlier times, however a number of other interesting groups occur in the area. The following classes of primitive plants occur in the Sydney area.

Seedless plants

Psilopsida	Fork ferns
Lycopsida	Clubmosses
Filicopsida	Ferns

Seed plants

Cycadopsida	Cycads
Coniferopsida	Conifers

(Cycads and Conifers have been usually referred to as Gymnospermae, however they are now regarded as distinct evolutionary lines.)

PSILOPSIDA Fork ferns

These are direct descendants of the earliest land plants. Their fossilised relatives date back 410 million years, to late Silurian times.

The spore-producing organs (sporangia) are joined into fused organs called synangia. These are located in the joints of simple leaves or bract-like projections. There is a much-branched rhizome, but true roots are absent; the plants rely on mycorrhizal fungi for nourishment.

The class Psilopsida consists of a single family.

PSILOTACEAE

A family with 2 genera.

• *Psilotum* Sweet

A genus with 3 species, 2 found in Australia.

Name: *Psilotum* = Gk. naked.

Psilotum nudum (Linnaeus) Beauvois

Skeleton Fork-fern **Ss**

A plant with brittle leafless much-forked stems 10-50cm long. Widespread but rather uncommon, in crevices in wet sandstone cliff faces (some can be seen on the rock face in the Sydney Opera House carpark).

One commentator described it as 'a little bushy evergreen herbaceous plant of no beauty' with 'no merit except as an object of curiosity . . .'[1]

The upright branching stem lacks the moisture conducting vessels found in higher plants.

Range: Australia-wide (except Tas and SA), and worldwide, especially in the tropics. **Stems:** erect, stiff, green, strongly ridged. **Synangia:** yellow, located along the stem in the axils of short 2-pronged projections. **Name:** *nudum* = Lat. naked.

• *Tmesipteris* Bernhardi

A genus of about 10 species, 6 found in Australia. *Tmesipteris* is more advanced than *Psilotum*, since it possesses leaves.

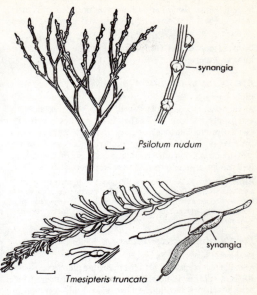

Psilotum nudum

Tmesipteris truncata

synangia

synangia

Tmesipteris truncata R. Brown

STRf

A small sprawling plant, with stems 10-30cm long, found on mossy rocks in subtropical rainforest. Uncommon.

Range: mainly in coastal districts in NSW and Qld. **Leaves:** forked into 2 flat segments, the mid-veins ending in fine points. **Synangia:** in the forks of each leaf, consisting of 2 chambers, pointed at each end. **Name:** *truncata* = Lat. cut off abruptly, probably referring to the leaf tips.

LYCOPSIDA Clubmosses

Clubmosses are vascular plants which reproduce sexually by spores. The oldest fossils date from the early Devonian, 395 million years ago. Unlike ferns, which bear their sporangia on the undersides of well developed leaves, clubmosses bear sporangia in the axils of rudimentary leaves.

LYCOPODIACEAE

Clubmosses

A family with 3 genera. The fertile (sporangia producing) leaves are shaped differently from sterile leaves and crowded into cone-like heads.

• *Lycopodium* Linnaeus

Clubmosses

A genus with about 100 species, widespread especially in tropical parts of the world, including about 15 species in Australia.

Lycopodium has an interesting economic history. The spores are highly inflammable and were used to produce explosive lighting effects in the theatre, a function now performed by magnesium powder. 'It is rather interesting to know that the first internal combustion engine was invented by Sadi Carnot, the father of the former president of France. At the Great Exhibition of 1852, he showed an engine driven by the explosion of *Lycopodium*.'[2]

Name: *Lycopodium* = Gk. wolf-foot, from the stems of some European species.

Lycopodium cernuum Linnaeus
Cliff Clubmoss   **Ss**
A vigorous creeping plant with wiry stems scrambling extensively on rock faces. The final branches are highly divided, resembling little pine trees. The fertile terminal cones are erect or daintily drooping. An uncommon species in the area, found only on railway cuttings between Heathcote and Helensburg, at Meadowbank and at Peats Ferry.

Range: common in the tropics and sub-tropics of Australia (the Sydney area is the southern limit); also widespread in tropical parts of the world. **Leaves:** slender, free from the stem, hooked upwards. **Sporangia:** in terminal cones, with spirally arranged fertile leaves. **Name:** *cernuum* = Lat. nodding or drooping.

Lycopodium deuterodensum Herter
Mountain Clubmoss   **Ss**
A small erect plant, resembling a miniature pine tree, usually 20-30cm tall, but sometimes much taller, with many more branches than shown in the illustration. Fairly common in wet sandy soil in sunny locations.

Range: widespread in coast and ranges in eastern Australia, NZ, New Caledonia and Norfolk Island. **Leaves:** scale-like, shiny, green. **Sporangia:** in terminal cones, with numerous scaly fertile leaves. **Name:** *deuterodensum* = Gk. secondary, Lat. dense, perhaps referring to the numerous secondary branches.

Lycopodium laterale R. Brown
Marsh Clubmoss   **Ss**
An erect plant to 20cm tall, with few branches. Found in permanently marshy sandy heath. Uncommon-rare in the area: northern suburbs and Woronora Plateau (Maddens Plains).

Range: coast and ranges in eastern Australia, also NZ, New Caledonia and the Chatham Islands. **Leaves:** slender, free from the stem, hooked upwards. **Sporangia:** in lateral cones, with fertile leaves in 4 rows. **Name:** *laterale* = Lat. on the side.

SELAGINELLACEAE

A family with a single genus. The sporangia are produced in the axils of the upper leaves, but these do not differ in shape from the lower non-fertile leaves.

• *Selaginella* Beauvois
Ss, Cumb
A genus with about 700 species worldwide, and 12 in Australia.

Name: *Selaginella* = from *selago*, the Latin name for the plant.

Selaginella uliginosa (Labillardière) Spring
Ss, Cumb
A plant under 10cm tall, with rather stiff branching stems. Very abundant in wet and sandy soil, in sunny locations.

Range: coastal ranges and inland parts of all states. **Leaves:** scale-like, spreading, in 4 rows. **Sporangia:** in the axils of the upper leaves. **Name:** *uliginosa* = Lat. swampy.

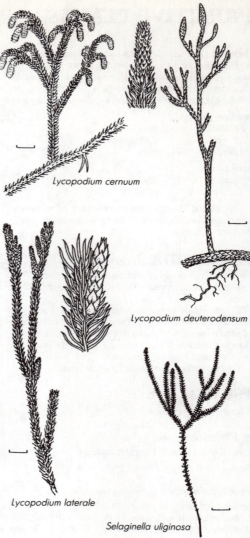

Lycopodium cernuum

Lycopodium deuterodensum

Lycopodium laterale

Selaginella uliginosa

FILICOPSIDA Ferns

Ferns are vascular plants which reproduce sexually by spores. They pre-date seed-bearing plants, the earliest fossils dating from late Devonian times about 370 million years ago.

Ferns are usually found in wet conditions, since moisture is necessary for ferilisation.

Worldwide there are 40-77 families, over 350 genera and over 9000 species. Australia has about 32 families, 115 genera and about 400 species.

The 2-phase life-cycle of ferns
Each fern passes through a life-cycle consisting of 2 separate plants.

Prothallus (or gametophyte): an independent plant consisting of a delicate tissue 1 cell thick and less than 10mm wide. It grows from a spore without any fertilisation taking place. The prothallus contains the fern's sexual organs and is haploid, i.e. has a single set of chromosomes. The male organs produce mobile sperm which swim to fertilise the ovum of the female organ. The fertilised ovum then grows into the mature sporophyte phase and the prothallus dies.

Sporophyte: the spore-producing phase which has a fully developed rhizome and leaves i.e. what we usually think of as a fern. It is diploid, i.e. has 2 sets of chromosomes.

The local ferns should present few identification problems, except for the various lacy ferns, a key for which appears below.

Key to ferns with much-divided (lacy) fronds

A. Trunk present.
    B. Fronds thin textured.
        = CYATHEACEAE: *Cyathea* spp.,
        DICKSONIACEAE: *Dicksonia antarctica*
    *B. Fronds tough and leathery (trunk poorly developed).
        = OSMUNDACEAE: *Todea barbara*
*A. Trunk absent.
    C. Fronds densely tufted.
        D. Segments tough, divided once.
            = OSMUNDACEAE: *Todea barbara*
        *D. Segments soft, some divided twice.
            = PTERIDACEAE: *Pteris tremula*
        **D. Segments tough, axis and stalk covered in conspicuous scales.
            = DRYOPTERIDACEAE:
            Polystichum australiense
    *C. Fronds not tufted.
        E. Fronds arising from a projecting rhizome which is thick and densely hairy (usually in rock crevices).
            = DAVALLIACEAE: *Davallia pyxidata*
        *E. Rhizome underground.
            F. Fronds branches opposite.
                G. Robust fern with tough leaves.
                    = DENNSTAEDTIACEAE:
                    Pteridium esculentum
                *G. Small fern with soft leaves.
                    = DENNSTAEDTIACEAE:
                    Hypolepis muelleri
            *F. Frond branches alternate (at least in the upper part of the axis).
                H. Axis densely covered in very short curly hairs (segments very thin-textured).
                    = DRYOPTERIDACEAE:
                    Lastreopsis spp.
                *H. Axis and stalk hairless or with long spreading hairs.
                  = DICKSONIACEAE:
                  Calochlaena dubia

ADIANTACEAE

A family with a single genus.

• *Adiantum* Linnaeus

Maidenhair Ferns

A genus with 150-200 species, distributed worldwide. Australia has 9 species. Distinctive features are the kidney-shaped sori and dark polished wiry stems.

Name: *Adiantum* = Gk. literally, not to wet. Pliny wrote 'in vain you plunge *Adiantum* in water: it always remains dry.'[3]

Adiantum aetbiopicum Linnaeus

Common Maidenhair Fern   **Ss, Temp Rf, STRf**

A delicate fern 15-40cm high, common in wet shady places, especially along creek banks. Usually occurs in dense colonies.

Range: NSW coast and ranges, all states, worldwide. **Rhizome:** creeping, much-branched, covered with papery scales. **Sterile fronds:** with delicate light green segments 3-8mm long. **Fertile fronds:** with smaller segments. **Sori:** large, kidney-shaped, 1-7 per segment. **Name:** *aetbiopicum* = Lat. from Ethiopia, where the type specimen was collected.

Adiantum formosum R. Brown

Giant Maindenhair   **STRf**

A handsome erect fern to over 1m high, common in rainforest and wetter woodland, especially near streams. Especially abundant in subtropical rainforest. In 1914 A.G. Hamilton noted that 'This fern is gathered in quantities, tied in bundles and exported to Germany, where it is dyed with an anilin green and re-exported to Australia for decorative purposes'.[4]

Range: NSW coast and ranges except the southern tablelands, also Qld, Vic and NZ. **Rhizome:** long-creeping, deeply buried. **Sterile fronds:** segments 5-15mm long, dark green, upper margin lobed and often toothed, terminal segments very much smaller than the basal segments. **Fertile fronds:** similar. **Sori:** small, 5-9 per segment, in shallow

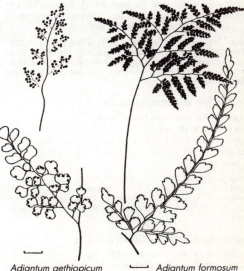

Adiantum aethiopicum   *Adiantum formosum*

depressions in the lobes of the segments. **Name:** *formosum* = Lat. beautiful. W.J. Hooker wrote 'Although a pretty fern, it must be allowed that it hardly deserved the pompous specific name..'[5] **Similar species:** *A. silvaticum*, occurs in rainforest valleys in the higher Blue Mountains. It is best distinguished by having terminal segments about the same size as the basal segments on each branch.

Adiantum bispidulum Swartz

Rough Maidenhair Fern **Ss, Temp Rf, STRf**
An erect fern to 50cm high, found in wetter woodland and rainforest margins, on creek banks and amongst rocks. Not common in the area.

Range: NSW coast and ranges except the southern tablelands, Qld, Vic, NT, NZ, Pacific Islands, South-east Asia and Africa. **Rhizome:** short-creeping, covered with dark brown scales. **Sterile fronds:** with tough segments 5-13mm long, on a rough black stem. **Fertile fronds:** with smaller segments. **Sori:** small, 6-14 close together on the upper edges. **Name:** *bispidulum* = Lat. rough.

ASPLENIACEAE

A family with about 750 species in 6 genera worldwide. There are 28 species in 2 genera in Australia.

• Asplenium Linnaeus

A genus with about 700 species worldwide. There are 29 species in Australia

Name: *Asplenium* = from Gk. spleen. Some species were known as Spleenworts and believed to be remedies for diseases of the spleen.

Asplenium australasicum

(J. Smith) W.J. Hooker

Bird's Nest Fern **Temp Rf, STRf**
A spectacular epiphytic fern with long tough radiating leaves, found in the branches of trees along creeks and in rainforests. Uncommon in the area. The early Sydney botanist William Woolls wrote 'as a caution to fern gatherers, sometimes a species of black snake coils itself up in the centre.'[6]

Range: NSW coast and ranges except for the southern tablelands, also Qld, Vic and Pacific Islands. **Rhizome:** erect, stout. **Fronds:** 60-80cm long, 10-20cm wide, tough, bright green. **Sori:** numerous, linear, about 1mm wide, 40-60mm long, along the frond veins. **Name:** *australasicum* = Lat. Australasian.

Asplenium difforme R. Brown

(previously *A. obtusatum* var. *difforme*)
Shore Spleenwort **Sal**
A short tough fern, found on rocks under the influence of sea spray. A rare species in the area: only recorded from La Perouse.

Range: La Perouse, NSW north coast, Qld, Norfolk Island, NZ, Pacific Islands and Pacific Coast of the Americas. **Rhizome:** stout, erect, densely covered with long dark scales. **Fronds:** thick, fleshy, often brittle. **Sori:** linear, covered by a flap of tissue. **Name:** *difforme* = Lat. irregular in shape.

Asplenium flabellifolium Cavanilles

Necklace Fern **Ss, Temp Rf, STRf**
A small weak fern with trailing fronds 10-20cm long, common in moist sheltered situations.

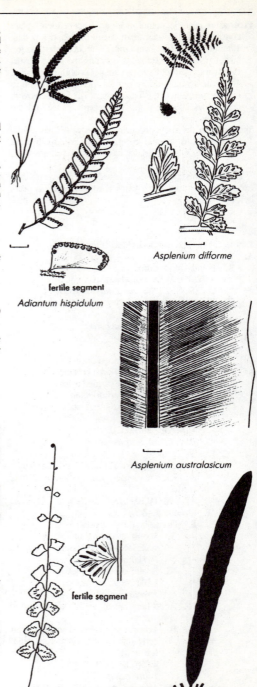

Asplenium difforme

fertile segment

Adiantum hispidulum

Asplenium australasicum

fertile segment

Asplenium flabellifolium

Range: NSW coast, ranges and western slopes, Qld, Vic, Tas and NZ. **Rhizome:** short, erect with dark scales. **Fronds:** decumbent; segments fan-shaped, soft, thin-textured; stalk green. **Sori:** 2-5mm long, a few per segment. **Name:** *flabellifolium* = Lat. fan-leaved.

AZOLLACEAE

Tiny plants floating in freshwater steams and ponds.
—See AQUATICS.

BLECHNACEAE

A family with about 220 species in 8 genera worldwide. There are 28 species in 4 genera in Australia.

• *Blechnum* Linnaeus

A genus with over 200 species worldwide, including 18 species in Australia.

In all *Blechnum* species the sori form 2 bands on either side of the mid-vein, protected by narrow membranous indusia which open towards the mid-vein.

Name: *Blechnum* = the Greek name for a type of fern.

Blechnum ambiguum (Presl) Kaulfuss ex C. Christens

Temp Rf

A fern with fronds 30-50cm long, found on wet rocks in sandstone gullies. Common.

Range: NSW south coast, Sydney area, Blue Mountains and Qld. **Rhizome:** short to medium creeping, covered in pale to red-brown scales **Sterile fronds:** pale to dark green, usually drooping, finely toothed, often more or less lobed at the base; the axis often sparsely scaly; segments not becoming much shorter towards the base of the axis. **Fertile fronds:** with narrow segments. **Name:** *ambiguum* = Lat. uncertain. **Similar species:** *B. camfieldii.*

Blechnum camfieldii Tindale

Ss

A fern with light-green leathery fronds 50-100cm long. Fairly common, usually beside creeks.

Range: NSW coast north from Clyde Mountain and Qld. **Rhizome:** short-creeping, covered with brown scales. **Sterile fronds:** light green, leathery, finely toothed; the axis sometimes scaly; the stalk covered at the base with dense brown scales; segments much shorter at the base of the axis. New growth is pink or bronze. **Fertile fronds:** with narrow segments. **Name:** *camfieldii* = in honour of Julius Henry Camfield (1852-1916), a gardener at the Royal Botanic Gardens, Sydney, for 34 years.

Blechnum cartilagineum Swartz

Gristle Fern **Ss**

A robust harsh fern forming tufts to 60-100cm high. Common in wetter sclerophyll forest and edges of rainforest. The fronds are rosy pink when young.

Range: NSW coast and ranges except the northern tablelands, also Qld, Vic, Tas and South-east Asia. **Rhizome:** short-creeping. **Sterile fronds:** segments attached to the axis along the full length of a broad base, finely toothed; stalk with black scales. **Fertile fronds:** with slightly narrower segments. **Name:** *cartilagineum* = Lat. gristly, firm and tough.

Blechnum indicum N.L. Burman

Swamp Water Fern, Bungwall Fern **Aqu**

An erect fern 50-150cm high, forming dense colonies in

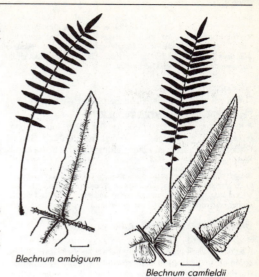

Blechnum ambiguum

Blechnum camfieldii

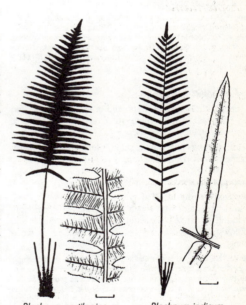

Blechnum cartilagineum   *Blechnum indicum*

freshwater swamps near the coast. It was once plentiful around Botany Bay but is now uncommon. Recent recordings have been from Deep Creek at Narrabeen, Narrabeen Lake, Kurnell, East Lakes Golf Course, Maroubra Bay, and Scarborough Park at Kogarah.

The starchy rhizome was once roasted as a staple food by Aborigines in coastal NSW. The dark outer layer can be easily broken away, revealing the white starchy centre. It would have been an important food for Aborigines around Botany Bay.

Range: NSW coast north from Jervis Bay, also Qld, NT, South-east Asia, Polynesia and Central America. **Rhizome:** erect, with a pithy centre. **Sterile fronds:** clustered, shiny, segments finely toothed, distinctly stalked. **Fertile fronds:** with slightly smaller segments. **Name:** *indicum* = Lat. Indian (i.e. from the East Indies). Bungwall is an Aboriginal name, probably from around Morton Bay.

Blechnum nudum

(Labillardière) Mettenius ex Luerssen

Fishbone Water Fern   **STRf, Temp Rf**

A tufted fern with erect fronds to 60cm high, found along creek banks. Uncommon. Recorded from Galston Gorge, Otford, Cataract Dam, and Lady Carrington Drive in the Royal National Park.

Range: coast and ranges in eastern Australia. **Rhizome:** short-creeping to erect with dark shiny scales. **Sterile fronds:** segments fairly rigid 4-12cm long, not toothed; the axis is dark and shiny. **Fertile fronds:** shorter, with narrow segments. **Name:** *nudum* = Lat. naked.

Blechnum patersonii (R. Brown) Mettenius

Strap Water Fern   **STRf**

A fern with dark green, leathery fronds 20-50cm long. Fairly common in subtropical rainforest in the northern Illawarra, usually amongst rocks along creeks. May be present in the Royal National Park.

Range: NSW coast and ranges except the northern tablelands, Qld, Vic, Tas, south-west Pacific and South-east Asia. **Rhizome:** erect, with brown shiny scales. **Sterile fronds:** erect or drooping, entire or variously lobed, 10-25mm wide. **Fertile fronds:** with slender segments. **Name:** *Patersonii* = after Lieutenant-colonel William Paterson (1755-1810) of the NSW Corps.

• *Doodia* R. Brown

A genus with 11 species distributed in Asia, Australasia and the Hawaiian Islands. There are 6 species in Australia, distributed in the eastern states.

Name: *Doodia* = after Samuel Doody (1656-1706), an English botanist who specialised in ferns.

Doodia aspera R. Brown

Rasp Fern   **Temp Rf, STRf**

A small erect fern with rough harsh fronds 20-40cm high. Found in extensive colonies in shady places in gullies and rainforest. Common in the area. The fronds are pink when young.

Range: NSW coast and ranges, Qld and Vic. **Rhizome:** short-creeping, covered in black scales. **Sterile fronds:** harsh, leathery and rough to touch when mature; segments to 6cm long. **Fertile fronds:** similar. **Sori:** circular, in 1 or 2 rows on each side of the mid-vein. **Name:** *aspera* = Lat. rough.

Doodia caudata (Cavanilles) R. Brown
var. *caudata*

Ss, Temp Rf

A fern with erect or drooping fronds 15-30cm long. Fairly common in moist sheltered situations in gullies and rainforest, especially on the north shore.

Range: coast and ranges in eastern Australia, also Norfolk Island, NZ and New Caledonia. **Rhizome:** short-creeping, covered with dark scales. **Sterile fronds:** divided into segments except at the tip, at least several segments stalked; segments varying from very thin-textured to almost

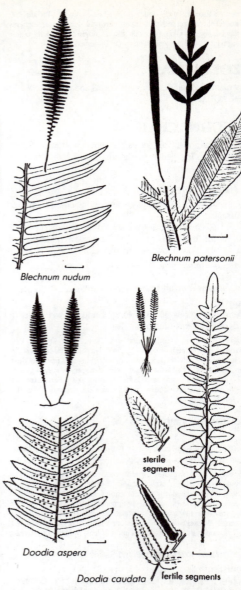

Blechnum nudum

Blechnum patersonii

Doodia aspera

sterile segment

Doodia caudata   fertile segments

leathery. **Fertile fronds:** very slender. **Sori:** in 1 row on each side of the midrib but joining together with age. **Name:** *caudata* = Lat. stalked. **Note:** var. *laminosa* occurs just outside the area: its fronds are undivided except for a few pairs of segments at the base.

CYATHEACEAE

A family with 2 genera and 250 species. There are 11 species in a single genera in Australia. Their most obvious feature is a woody trunk or caudex. This is hard on the outside with a pithy soft centre partly made of masses of tough aerial roots. In Qld and Vic, Aborigines roasted and consumed the young fronds as a tonic after sickness

• *Cyathea* Smith

Treeferns
A genus with over 600 species worldwide, including 11 species in Australia.

Name: *Cyathea* = Gk. cup-shaped, from the cup-shaped indusia.

Cyathea cooperi (W.D. Hooker ex F. Mueller) Domin

Straw Treefern **Temp Rf, STRf**
A treefern usually 2.5-6m high (to 12m). Common in the area, in gullies and rainforests, particularly on the north shore.

Range: coast and ranges in eastern Australia. **Trunk:** to 15cm wide. Stalks: yellowish to brown, with warty projections; the scales at the base of the stalk are of 2 kinds: one kind is pale (straw-like) and 20-50mm long, the other is red-brown and 5-15mm long. **Name:** *cooperi* = after Sir Daniel Cooper, first Speaker of the NSW Legislative Assembly, 1856-60.

Cyathea leichhardtiana (F. Mueller) Copeland

Prickly Treefern **Temp Rf, STRf**
A treefern usually 1-7m high. Uncommon in the area, in subtropical rainforest in the Royal National Park and Illawarra.

Range: coast of NSW and Qld. **Trunk:** 5-15cm wide, covered with prickly persistent stalk bases. **Stalks:** with sharp spines to 4mm long; the scales at the base of the stalk are very pale, to 6cm long and 1mm wide. **Name:** *leichhardtiana* = after the explorer Ludwig Leichhardt who was also a keen botanical collector.

Cyathea australis (R. Brown) Domin

Rough Treefern **Temp Rf, STRf**
A treefern usually 2.5-6m high (to 20m). Fairly common in deep gullies and rainforests.

Range: coast and ranges in eastern Australia. **Trunk:** 16-40cm wide. Stalk: with harsh warty projections; the scales at the base of the stalk are shiny, red-brown, stiff and often twisted, 2-5cm long. **Name:** *australis* = Lat. southern.

DAVALLIACEAE

A family with about 200 species in about 12 genera, mainly in tropical parts of the world. There are 17 species in 6 genera in Australia.

• *Arthropteris* J. Smith ex J.D. Hooker

A genus of ferns with about 20 species in tropical and temperate parts of Europe, Asia, Africa and Australia.

Name: *Arthropteris* = Gk. jointed wing.

Arthropteris tenella (J.R. Forster) J. Smith

STRf
A fern climbing on trees and rocks, with a long wiry rhizome. Common in subtropical rainforest in the Royal National Park and Illawarra.

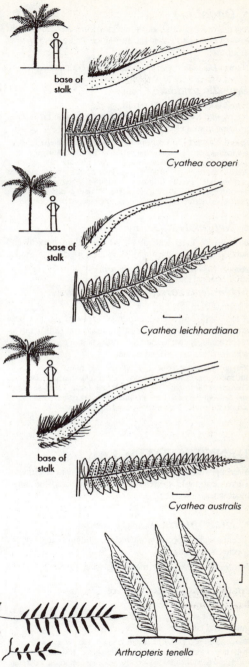

base of stalk

Cyathea cooperi

base of stalk

Cyathea leichhardtiana

base of stalk

Cyathea australis

Arthropteris tenella

Range: NSW coast and ranges except the southern tablelands, also Qld, Norfolk Island and NZ. **Rhizome:** very long-creeping, stiff, densely covered with brown scales. **Fronds:** mostly 15-30cm long. **Sori:** circular. **Name:** *tenella* = Lat. delicate.

• *Davallia* J. Smith

A genus of ferns with about 40 species distributed from south-eastern Europe to Polynesia, and Africa. There are 3 species in Australia.

Name: *Davallia* = after E. Davall, a Swiss botanist.

Davallia pyxidata Cavanilles

Hare's Foot Fern **Ss, Temp Rf**

A fern with tough shiny fronds and long exposed rhizomes, growing from rock crevices. Fairly common.

Range: NSW coast and ranges except the southern tablelands, also a few locations on the western slopes, Qld, Vic and Tas. **Rhizome:** long-creeping, about 12mm wide, densely covered with fine hair-like scales. **Sterile fronds:** mostly 30-60cm long, glossy green, segments triangular, deeply lobed. **Fertile fronds:** with narrower segments. **Sori:** near the margins, partly sunken in the surface. **Name:** *pyxidata* = from Gk. *pyxis*, a box, refering to the sori being partly enveloped by the leaf surface.

• *Nephrolepis* Schott

A genus of ferns with about 30 species in tropical and subtropical parts of the world. There are 6 species in Australia.

Name: *Nephrolepis* = Gk. kidney-scale.

*Nephrolepis cordifolia** (Linnaeus) Presl

Fishbone Fern **Ss**

A fern with narrow erect fronds, often spreading over large areas. Common in many moist locations, e.g. cliffs, gardens, creek banks. Native to the NSW north coast. A garden escapee widely naturalised around Sydney.

Range: NSW north coast, Qld, NT and widespread in the tropics. **Rhizome:** erect, covered with scales. The roots often bear globular tubers. **Fronds:** to 75cm long, yellowish green; on a scaly stalk. **Sori:** half-way between the margin and the midvein; partly covered by a kidney-shaped indusium. **Name:** *cordifolia* = Lat. heart-leaved.

DENNSTAEDTIACEAE

A family with about 200 species in 12 genera worldwide. There are about 12 species in 6 genera in Australia, distributed in all states.

• *Histiopteris* (Agardh) J. Smith

A genus with 7 species worldwide, including a single native species in Australia.

Name: *Histiopteris* = Gk. membrane-wing.

Histiopteris incisa (Thunberg) J. Smith

Batswing Fern **Ss, Temp Rf**

A fern with soft pale green fronds 1-2m long. Common in gullies and cliff lines.

Range: coast and ranges in eastern Australia; also NT and widespread in the tropics and temperate southern hemisphere. **Rhizome:** 2-7mm wide, covered with narrow red-brown to golden-brown scales, about 5mm long. **Sterile fronds:** hairless, pale green, soft, bluish-green on lower surface, all segments with rounded lobes; stalk hairless, dark at base, paler above. **Sori:** marginal. **Name:** *incisa* = Lat. incised, referring to the deeply lobed segments.

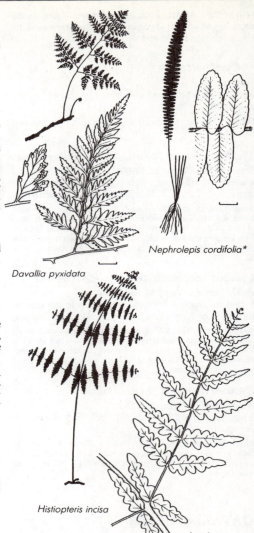

*Nephrolepis cordifolia**

Davallia pyxidata

Histiopteris incisa

• *Hypolepis* Berhhardt

A genus with about 50 species, mainly in tropical and southern temperate areas. There are about 6 species in Australia, distributed in the eastern states.

Name: *Hypolepis* = Gk. under-scale.

Hypolepis muelleri N. A. Wakefield

Harsh Ground Fern **Ss**

An erect fern 30-100cm high, found along creeks and swamps in woodland. Common. Despite its common name it has soft fronds. The branches are more widely spaced than in similar species and the axis is slightly rough to touch.

Range: NSW coast and ranges, except the northwern tablelands; also Qld, Vic and Tas. **Rhizome:** long-creeping, 1-3mm wide, with short stiff dark brown hairs mainly on new parts. **Fronds:** dark green, thin-textured, soft, both surfaces with scattered stiff hairs; the axis is rough to touch due to tiny stiff hairs; branches opposite; the stalk smooth or with scattered hairs with raised bases. **Sori:** originating away from the margin, lacking protective indusium. **Name:** *muelleri* = in honour of the pioneering botanist Ferdinand von Mueller (1825-96).

• *Pteridium* Gleditsch ex Scopoli

A genus with 7 species worldwide, including 3 in Australia. Many botanists believe there is only a single species, which would make it the most widespread plant on the planet.

Name: *Pteridium* = Gk. little wing.

Pteridium esculentum (J.G. Forster) Cockayne

Bracken   **Ss, Cumb, Castl**
An erect fern with harsh stiff fronds 1-1.5m high. Adundant throughout the area, in dense colonies on disturbed ground and moist forest situations. It is able to grow in drier and sunnier places than most other ferns.

The rhizomes were a staple of NSW coastal Aborigines. In October 1788, William Bradley wrote 'The fern and some other roots they prepare by moistening and beating between 2 stones a considerable time . . . '[7] In 1834 the Quaker preacher James Backhouse saw Tasmanian Aborigines 'roast this root in the ashes, peel off its black skin with their teeth, and eat it with their roasted kangaroo, &c. in the same manner as Europeans eat bread.'[8] Aborigines in other parts of Australia used the juicy young stems, well rubbed in, to relieve insect bites.

Before European arrival, Bracken probably had a minor ecological role. However the removal of the forest canopy allowed it to spread rapidly, developing into aggressive colonies. Frequent burning and grazing also benefited Bracken by removal of competitors.

Range: most parts of Australia (except dry inland areas and NT); also NZ and Pacific Islands. **Rhizome:** very long-creeping, densely covered with dark red-brown hairs. **Fronds:** segments narrow, stiff, lobed only at base, with recurved margins. **Stalks:** red-brown, rough due to tiny tubercles. **Sori:** continuous beneath the margins, protected by an indusium. **Name:** *esculentum* = Lat. edible.

DICKSONIACEAE

A family with 6 genera and about 50 species in tropical and southern temperate parts of the world. Australia has 2 genera and 5 species distributed in the eastern states.

• *Calochaena* M. Turner & R. White

A genus with 5 species, including 2 in eastern Australia. Previously included in *Culcita.*

Name: *Calochlaena* = Gk. beauty-cloak.

Calochlaena dubia (R.T. Brown) M. Turner & R. White

(previously *Culcita dubia*)
False Bracken Fern   **Ss**
A graceful, light green fern to 1.5m high, forming dense colonies on sandy soils. Abundant in moist forests and valleys.

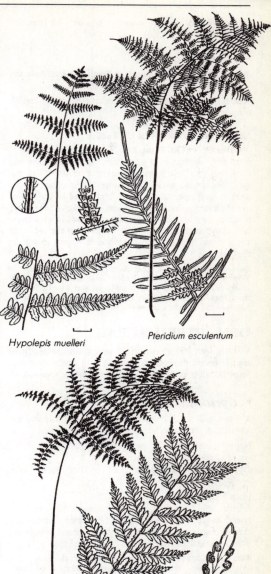

Hypolepis muelleri   Pteridium esculentum

Calochlaena dubia

Similar to Bracken Fern, but softer and with alternate frond branches.

Range: coasts and ranges in eastern Australia. **Rhizome:** stout, covered with soft white pale and dark brown hairs. **Fronds:** lacy, 40-150cm high, erect with drooping tips; axis alternately branching, with a broad central channel. **Stalk:** yellow or brown, darker at the base, densely hairy to almost hairless. **Sori:** small, circular, each covered by a recurved marginal lobe. **Name:** *dubia* = Lat. doubtful. **Similar species:**

Hypolepis muelleri, Pteridium esculentum (Bracken); but these have opposite-branching fronds.

• *Dicksonia* L'Héritier

A genus with about 25 species in South-east Asia, Australia, Polynesia, Mexico, South America and St Helena.

Name: *Dicksonia* = after James Dickson (1737?-1822), English botanist.

Dicksonia antarctica Labillardière

Soft Treefern   **STRf, Temp Rf**

A treefern usually up to 4.5m high. Found in gullies and rainforests. Rare near Sydney, more common in the Illawarra. James Backhouse wrote: 'The native Blacks of the colony used to split open about a foot and a half of the top of the trunk of the Common Tree-fern, and take out the heart, in substance resembling a Swedish turnip, and of the thickness of a man's arm. This they either roasted in the ashes, or ate as bread; but it is too bitter and astringent to suit an Engish palate.'[9]

Range: coast and ranges in eastern Australia.   **Trunk:** thick, usually to 30cm wide.   **Fronds:** surfaces leathery, dark glossy green.   **Stalk:** smooth except for a dense clump of red-brown hairs at the base.   **Sori:** about 1mm diameter, bead-like, marginal.   **Name:** *antarctica* = Lat. opposite-Arctic, i.e. in far southern regions.

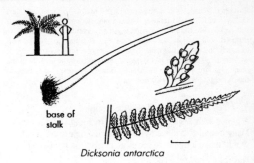

base of
stalk

Dicksonia antarctica

DRYOPTERIDACEAE

A family with 750 species in 20 genera worldwide. There are 27 species in 6 genera distributed in eastern Australia. Some botanists place the genera in the family Aspidiaceae.

• *Cyrtomium* Presl

A genus with about 25 species, native to east Asia and the Americas. A single species is naturalised in Australia.

Name: *Cyrtomium* = Gk. *kyrtos*, curved.

Cyrtomium falcatum (Carl von Linné) Presl
cv 'Rochfordii'

Holly Fern   **Sal**

A harsh tufted fern with thick shiny fronds 30-50cm long. Found in crevices of seacliffs around Sydney harbour and nearby coast, e.g. Bondi. A cultivar, originating in Japan, introduced as a garden plant and now naturalised.

Range: Japan, Sydney, Brisbane and SA.   **Rhizome:** short, covered in broad loose scales.   **Fronds:** tough, coarsely toothed and lobed.   **Sori:** circular, evenly spread over the lower surface.   **Name:** *falcatum* = Lat. sickle-shaped.

• *Lastreopsis* Ching

Shield Ferns

A genus with about 36 species distributed in the tropics and southern temperate regions. There are 14 species in Australia.

Name: *Lastreopsis* = to distinguish it from a related genus, *Lastrea*.

Cyrtomium falcatum * cv 'Rochfordii'

Lastreopsis decomposita (R. Brown) Tindale

Trim Shield Fern   **Temp Rf, STRf**

A fern with broad lacy fronds 50-90cm long, found in deep sandstone gullies and subtropical rainforest north from Mt Kembla. Often in large colonies. Common.

Range: NSW coast and ranges except for the southern tablelands; Qld and Vic.   **Rhizome:** short-creeping, thick, densely or sparsely covered in reddish scales.   **Fronds:** segments thin-textured, grey-green, densely hairy. Secondary branches opposite, but segments arranged alternately; the axis densely covered in short hairs.   **Stalk:** densely hairy, with a single conspicuous groove on the upper surface, cloaked with dark scales at the base.   **Sori:** circular.   **Name:** *decomposita* = Lat. compounded more than once, refering to the segments.

Lastreopsis microsora (Endlicher) Tindale
ssp. *microsora*

Creeping Shield Fern   **STRf**

A tufted fern with broad lacy fronds 40-90cm long, found in subtropical rainforest in the Royal National Park and Illawarra. Fairly common.

Range: NSW coast and ranges except for the southern tablelands, Qld, Vic and NZ. **Rhizome:** long-creeping, covered in brown scales. **Fronds:** segments soft, thin-textured, shiny; axis and veins finely hairy. **Stalk:** not conspicuously hairy, 2-3 grooves on the upper surface, but no single prominent groove as in *L. decomposita*, slightly scaly or naked at the base. **Sori:** circular. **Name:** *microsora* = Lat. tiny sori.

• *Polystichum* Roth

A genus with over 175 species worldwide. Australia has 4 species, found in the eastern states.

Name: *Polystichum* = Gk. many-flowered.

Polystichum australiense Tindale

STRf, Temp Rf

A tufted fern 40-80cm long with tough shiny fronds and prominently scaly stalks. Most common in subtropical rainforest, but occasionally in sandstone gullies, mainly in the Royal National Park and Illawarra.

Range: NSW coast, Blue Mountains and central western slopes. **Rhizome:** erect, thick, covered with broad scales. **Fronds:** leathery, axis scaly. **Stalk:** densely covered in broad shiny scales. **Sori:** circular. **Name:** *australiense* = Lat. Australian.

GLEICHENIACEAE

A family with 5 genera and about 150 species in tropical and temperate regions. There are 11 species in 4 genera in Australia.

• *Gleichenia* Smith

Coral Ferns

A genus with about 10 species in tropical and southern subtropical parts of the world. There are 6 species in Australia.

James Backhouse noted that prisoners in Macquarie Harbour in Tasmania used the stems for making bird cages.[10] William Woolls wrote that 'when tied in bundles and suspended from the ceiling, it may be usefully employed as a resting place for flies.'[11]

Name: *Gleichenia* = after W.F. von Gleichen (1717-83), a German botanist who specialised in microscopic studies.

Gleichenia dicarpa R. Brown

Pouched Coral Fern **Ss**

A scrambling fern forming dense entanglements in sunny moist sites, especially in swampy heathlands. Common. The British botanist W.J. Hooker wrote 'There is not perhaps among the whole range of the ferns, one which, as grown in the Royal Gardens of Kew, with its tender feathery drooping branchlets, is more admired for its graceful form, than the present.'[12]

Range: coast and ranges in eastern Australia, NZ, NG, New Caledonia and the Philipines. **Rhizome:** long creeping, slender, dark and wiry, covered with scales. **Fronds:** segments 1-1.5mm long, pale green below.

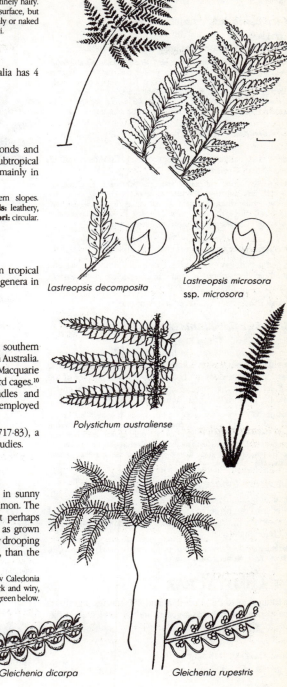

Lastreopsis decomposita

Lastreopsis microsora
ssp. *microsora*

Polystichum australiense

Gleichenia microphylla

Gleichenia dicarpa

Gleichenia rupestris

Stalk: stalk finely hairy, forked several times, to 2m long. **Sori:** composed of 2 sporangia, contained within the pouch-like underside of the segments. **Name:** *dicarpa* = Gk. 2-fruited.

Gleichenia microphylla R. Brown

Coral Fern **Ss**

Habit and habitat as for the preceding. Uncommon.

Range: NSW coast and Blue Mountains, all other states, NZ and South-east Asia. **Rhizome:** long creeping, slender, dark and wiry. **Fronds:** segments 1-2mm long, dark green above, pale green below. **Stalk:** covered in fine star-hairs, forked several times, to 2m long. **Sori:** composed of 3-4 sporangia, located on the flat or slightly concave underside of the segments. **Name:** *microphylla* = Lat. tiny-leaved.

Gleichenia rupestris R. Brown

Coral Fern **Ss**

Habit and habitat as for the preceding. Common, though less so than *G. dicarpa*.

Range: NSW coast and ranges, and Qld. **Rhizome:** long-creeping, slender, dark and wiry. **Fronds:** segments 2-4mm long, blue-green below. **Stalk:** hairless, forked several times, to 2m long. **Sori:** composed of 3-4 sporangia, located on the flat or slightly concave underside of the segments. **Name:** *rupestris* = Lat. rocky.

• *Sticherus* Presl

A genus with over 90 species widespread in the tropics and southern hemisphere. Australia has 3 species, in the eastern states.

Name: *Sticherus* = Gk. *sticho*, a row or line.

Sticherus flabellatus (R. Brown) St. John

Umbrella Fern **Temp Rf, Ss**

An erect fern to about 1m high, forming large colonies in moist sheltered sites in gullies and rainforest. Common. 'The Fernery of Kew does not boast a more lovely species of the family of ferns than the present: the colour is a lively green, and the ramification [branching] is particularly graceful.'[13]

Range: NSW coast and ranges except the northern tablelands, Qld, Vic, NZ and New Caledonia. **Rhizome:** long-creeping, wiry, covered in brown scales. **Fronds:** divided into 1-2 pairs of axes, each branched once or twice, segments finely toothed. **Stalks:** green or brown, smooth. **Sori:** numerous, in a single row on each side of the midvein. **Name:** *flabellatus* = Lat. fan-like.

Sticherus lobatus Wakefield

Spreading Shield Fern **Temp Rf, Ss**

Similar to the preceding, except there are additional lobed segments at the base of the branches. Uncommon but widely scattered in the area.

Range: NSW coast and ranges except the northern tablelands; also Qld, Vic and Tas. **Name:** *lobatus* = Lat. lobed.

GRAMMITACEAE

A family with about 15 genera and 450 species, mainly in the tropics. Australia has 4 genera and 18 species, all in the eastern states.

• *Grammitis* Swartz

A genus with about 160 species ranging from the tropics

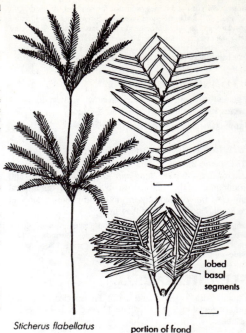

Sticherus flabellatus　　portion of frond

lobed basal segments

Sticherus lobatus

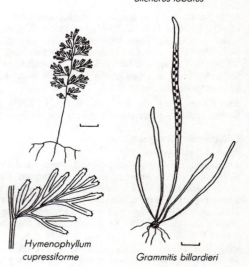

Hymenophyllum cupressiforme

Grammitis billardieri

to southern cool-temperate regions. Australia has 9 species in the eastern states.

Name: *Grammitis* = Gk. *Gramma*, a line, refering to the sori being in rows.

Grammitis billardieri Willdenow

Finger Fern **STRf**

A tiny epiphytic fern with slender dark green fronds, usually found amongst mosses on wet rocks in creeks. Common in subtropical rainforest and occasional in deep sandstone gullies.

Range: coast and ranges in eastern Australia, and NZ. **Rhizome:** erect, short, covered with papery scales. **Fronds:** 5-15cm long, leathery, dark green, margins often undulating. **Sori:** in a row on each side of the mid-vein. **Name:** *billardieri* = after James Julian la Billardiere (Labillardière), botanist on the 1791-93 French expedition in search of La Pérouse, under D'Entrecastaux. He collected the type specimen in Tas.

HYMENOPHYLLACEAE

Filmy Ferns

A family with about 42 genera and 600 species worldwide. Australia has 12 genera and 41 species.

The Filmy Ferns have fronds 1 cell thick and are able to take up water as a liquid or vapour from the atmosphere. They are limited to permanently wet or misty areas and usually grow as epiphytes on rocks, tree trunks or treeferns. Their usual associates are mosses and liverworts, and some species are easily confused with mosses.

• *Hymenophyllum* Smith

A genus with about 300 species worldwide, including 13 Australian species, distributed in the eastern states.

Name: *Hymenophyllum* = Gk. membrane-leaf.

Hymenophyllum cupressiforme Labillardière

Common Filmy Fern **Temp Rf, STRf**

A tiny delicate fern with fronds 2-9cm long, found in dense masses on wet rocks and tree trunks in rainforests and gullies. Often abundant along creeks in subtropical rainforest.

Range: coast and ranges in eastern Australia. **Rhizome:** long-creeping, fine, hairless. **Fronds:** pinnate, translucent, finely toothed. **Sori:** contained in a cup-shaped indusium, borne on the upper sides of the segments. **Name:** *cupressiforme* = Lat. Cypress-shaped.

LINDSAEACEAE

A family with about 200 species in 6 genera. Australia has a single genus.

• *Lindsaea* Dryander (lind-see-a)

A genus with about 200 species worldwide, including 14 in Australia.

Name: *Lindsaea* = after John Lindley (d. 1803), a surgeon of Jamaica, who wrote on ferns.

Lindsaea linearis Swartz

Screw Fern **Ss, Castl**

A slender erect fern 15-40cm high, common in wet sunny heath and woodland.

Range: coast and ranges in eastern Australia, all states except NT; also NZ and New Caledonia. **Rhizome:** short-creeping, covered with golden

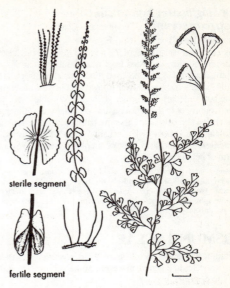

sterile segment

fertile segment

Lindsaea linearis   *Lindsaea microphylla*

brown scales. **Sterile fronds:** segments 8-14mm wide, flat. **Stalk:** dark, shiny. **Fertile fronds:** longer; segments 4-9mm wide, margins curled to protect the sori. **Sori:** in a band a short distance from the outer margin, protected by a membranous narrow flap-like indusium. **Name:** *linearis* = Lat. straight. **Similar species:** *Asplenium flabellifolium.*

Lindsaea microphylla Swartz

Lacy Wedge Fern **Ss**

A delicate erect fern mostly 20-40cm high. Common in moist or dry sandy soils, especially in partly sheltered spots beside tracks in woodland. It favours disturbed sites.

Range: coast and ranges in eastern mainland Australia. **Rhizome:** creeping, covered in narrow golden to reddish scales. **Sterile fronds:** fan-shaped, soft. **Stalk:** short, straw-coloured, darker at base. **Fertile fronds:** similar. **Sori:** generally divided into 2 parts, on the outer margin of the final segments, protected by a pale thin indusium. **Name:** *microphylla* = Lat. tiny-leaved.

MARSILEACEAE

A family of clover-leaved plants floating in ponds or in marshy situations.
—See AQUATICS.

OPHIOGLOSSACEAE

A family with about 55 species in 3 genera worldwide. Australia has 10 species in 3 genera.

• *Ophioglossum* Linnaeus

A genus with about 30 species worldwide, including 7 species in Australia.

Name: *Ophioglossum* = Gk. serpent tongue.

Ophioglossum lusitanicum Linnaeus
ssp. *coriaceum* (A. Cunningham) Clausen

Austral Adder's Tongue   **Cumb**

An erect fern usually 5-8cm high, found in damp open sites. Rare in the area. Recorded from near Casula, and at Costers Point, Royal National Park. Used medicinally in Europe. 'The little Adder's Tongue was well known to collectors of simples [herbal remedies] in former days as a valuable medicine for wounds, or in their own quaint vocabulary, as a vulnerary. Gerard, Culpepper and other herbalists give directions for making the "green oyl of charity" from it. I was quite intertested to find it in a list of simples issued by a Sydney firm of herb-doctors . . .'[14]

Range: most parts of Australia, worldwide.   **Rhizome:** short, erect, slightly tuberous.   **Sterile frond:** elliptic, 10-50mm long, 12-10mm wide. **Fertile frond:** slender, erect, spike-like.   **Sporangia:** large, in 2 rows, at the apex of a long stalk.   **Name:** *lusitanicum* = Lat. from western Spain, or Portugal.

Ophioglossum lusitanicum ssp. *coriaceum*

Todea barbara

Dictymia brownii

Microsorum scandens

OSMUNDACEAE

A family with about 15 species in 3 genera worldwide. There are 2 species in 2 genera in eastern Australia.

• *Todea* Willdenow

A genus with 2 species, distributed in tropical and subtropical parts of the world. There is a single species in Australia. **Name:** *Todea* = after Rev. Henry Julius Tode, a clergyman of Mecklenberg (1733-97), author of *Fungi Mecklenbergenses Selecti*, 1790.

Todea barbara (Linnaeus) T. Moore

King Fern   **Ss, Temp Rf**

A large tufted fern usually 1.5-2m tall, with a short trunk at the base, forming dense clumps beside creeks and in wetter woodland. Common.

Range: NSW coast and ranges, north and central western slopes, all eastern states, NZ and South Africa.   **Fronds:** tough, shiny, 50-250cm long. **Sporangia:** dark brown, usually covering the lower half of the undersurface of the pinnae.   **Name:** *barbara* = Lat. foreign.

POLYPODIACEAE

A family, mainly of epiphtyic ferns, with about 50 genera and about 1000 species worldwide. There are 10 genera and about 26 species in Australia.

• *Dictymia* J. Smith

A genus with 4 species, distributed in South-east Asia, Australasia and the Pacific.

Name: *Dictymia* = Gk. *dictyo*, net.

Dictymia brownii (Wikström) Copeland

Temp Rf

An epiphytic fern with thick leathery erect fronds mostly 30-40cm long. Found on rocks along creeks in deep shady gullies. Uncommon in the area. Recorded from Mill Creek near Wisemans Ferry, Cowan Creek, and Otford (but not from the Illawarra).

Range: coastal areas north from Sydney, Blue Mountains and southern tablelands; also Qld.   **Rhizome:** long-creeping, covered in club-shaped scales. **Fronds:** tough, thick and leathery, mostly 8-10mm wide. **Sori:** large, oval, in 2 rows, alternate on each side of the mid-vein. **Name:** *brownii* = after Robert Brown (1773-1858), botanist on Matthew Flinders' 1801-03 circumnavigation of Australia.

• *Microsorum* Link

A genus with about 60 species, distributed in Asia, South-east Asia and the Pacific. Australia has 6 species distributed in the eastern states and NT.

Name: *Microsorum* = Lat. tiny sori.

Microsorum scandens (J.G. Forster) Tindale

Fragrant Fern **STRf**

An attractive epiphytic fern forming dense colonies on rocks and trees. Common in subtropical rainforest. The fresh leaves have a musky fragrance.

Range: coast and ranges in eastern Australia, also NZ. **Rhizome:** very long-creeping, tough and wiry, covered in persistent scales. **Fronds:** thin-textured, dark green, 20-50cm long, entire or pinnately lobed. **Sori:** 1-3mm wide, in 2 rows on either side of the mid-vein. **Name:** *scandens* = Lat. climbing.

• *Platycerium* Desvaux

A genus with 15 species, widespread in the tropics and sub-tropics, including 3 species in Australia, distributed in Qld and NSW.

Name: *Platycerium* = Gk. broad honeycomb.

Platycerium bifurcatum (Cavanilles) C. Christens **ssp.** *bifurcatum*

Elk Horn **Temp Rf, STRf**

A large epiphytic fern, found on tree branches overhanging streams, usually in rainforests. Uncommon in the area. Recorded from Lady Carrington Drive, Royal National Park.

It is a highly specialised fern which forms its own self-contained nutrient system. The upper leaves are a good litter-collecting device. They are replaced about once per year and collapse inwards, compressing the litter. The roots of the fern eventually grow into this humus and are protected from drying winds. New plants grow from the base of the fern, so that clusters of plants form around tree branches.

Range: coastal NSW, Qld and NG. **Sterile fronds:** known as 'nest leaves', 12-30cm wide, erect, papery, overlapping, green becoming brown with age. **Fertile fronds:** drooping, divided, 25-90cm long. **Sporangia:** in masses, covering most of the lower frond segments. **Name:** *bifurcatum* = Lat. 2-forked.

• *Pyrrosia* Mirbel

A genus with about 100 species worldwide, mainly in Asia and South-east Asia, extending to Africa, Australia and NZ. There are 5 species in Australia, distributed in NSW and Qld.

Name: *Pyrrosia* = from Gk. red, tawny.

Pyrrosia rupestris (R. Brown) Ching

Rock Felt-fern, Robber Fern **Temp Rf, STRf**

An epiphytic fern easily recognised by its thick leathery leaves. It grows on rocks and trees in rainforests and moist gullies. Common.

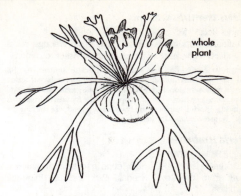

whole plant

Platycerium bifurcatum ssp. *bifurcatum*

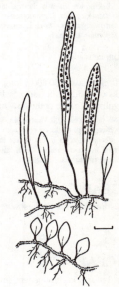

Pyrrosia rupestris

Range: NSW coast, ranges and some inland areas, Qld and New Caledonia. **Rhizome:** long-creeping, branched, covered in papery reddish brown scales. **Sterile fronds:** more or less circular, 1.5-4cm long. **Fertile fronds:** elongated, 4-10cm long. **Sori:** circular, covering most of the lower surface, growing together with age. **Name:** *rupestris* = Lat. rocky.

PTERIDACEAE

A family with over 250 species in tropical and subtropical parts of the world. There are 10 species in 2 genera in Australia.

• *Pteris* Linnaeus

A genus with about 250 species worldwide, including 8 species in Australia.

Name: *Pteris* = Gk. fern, from *pteron*, feather or wing.

Pteris tremula R. Brown

Tender Brake   **Ss**

A tufted fern mostly 50-120cm high, found amongst rocks in gullies and moist cliff-faces. A common visitor to gardens.

Range: widespread on coasts and ranges in eastern Australia; also NZ and Fiji.   **Rhizome:** tufted, erect, covered with narrow brown scales. **Sterile fronds:** hairless, highly divided, lacy, pale green.   **Stalk:** brown, shiny, with a deep narrow central groove.   **Fertile fronds:** with narrower segments.   **Sori:** linear, not joined between segments, nor reaching the tips.   **Name:** *tremula* = Lat. trembling.

Pteris umbrosa R. Brown

Jungle Brake   **STRf**

A dark green fern 40-80cm high, found in subtropical rainforest south from the Royal National Park and the Illawarra. Common.

Range: NSW coast, Blue Mountains, Qld and Vic.   **Rhizome:** short-creeping, with narrow dark brown scales at the tip.   **Sterile fronds:** tough, erect, pinnate, 40-80cm long, with finely toothed or entire margins. **Fertile fronds:** with narrow segments.   **Sori:** linear, continuous along the margins.   **Name:** *umbrosa* = Lat. shady.

Pteris vittata Linnaeus

Chinese Brake

A harsh fern with fronds mostly 30-80cm long, common as an epiphyte in walls of buildings in inner Sydney suburbs. Also occasional in gullies. A native of the NSW north coast.

Range: Sydney area, NSW north coast, Qld, Vic, NT, WA, Asia and tropical Africa.   **Rhizome:** short-creeping, thick, covered with papery scales. **Fronds:** mid to dark green, segments 6-10m wide.   **Stalk:** brown at the base, densely covered in papery scales.   **Sori:** linear, continuous along the margins.   **Name:** *vittata* = Lat. ribbony.

SALVINIACEAE

Small floating plants forming mats in freshwater streams or ponds.
—See AQUATICS.

SCHIZAEACEAE

A family with about 140 species in 4 genera, in tropical and temperate parts of the world.

• *Cheilanthes* Swartz

A genus with over 150 species, almost worldwide. There are about 16 species in Australia.

Name: *Cheilanthes* = Gk. lip-flower.

Cheilanthes distans (R. Brown) Mettenius

Bristly Cloak Fern   **Ss**

A small harsh fern forming dense tufts, often with a shrivelled rusty-woolly appearance. Uncommon, on dry rocky ground throughout the area.

Range: widespread in Australia; also NZ and New Caledonia.   **Rhizome:** short, densely covered with pointed scales.   **Sterile fronds:** to 30cm high; upper surface sparsely hairy with whitish hairs, lower surface with scales; on a shiny dark stalk covered in hair-like brown scales.   **Fertile fronds:** similar.   **Sori:** more or less circular, at the ends of veins, often joining together.   **Name:** *distans* = Lat. separated.

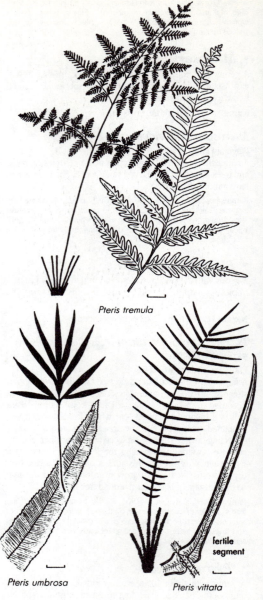

Pteris tremula

Pteris umbrosa

fertile segment

Pteris vittata

Cheilanthes sieberi Kunze **ssp.** *sieberi*

Mulga Fern **Cumb, Castl, Ss**

A small harsh fern, often with a shrivelled appearance. Common on dry clay soils and in thin soil on rock ledges on sandstone.

Range: widespread in Australia; also NZ and New Caledonia. **Rhizome:** short, densely covered with pointed entire scales. **Sterile fronds:** more or less hairless, usually 15-25cm high; on a shiny dark stalk. **Fertile fronds:** similar. **Sori:** more or less circular, at the ends of veins, separate. **Name:** *sieberi* = after Franz Wilhelm Sieber of Prague, Bohemia, who collected extensively in Australia from 1819-23.

• *Schizaea* Smith

Comb Ferns

A genus with about 30 species including 4 species in Australia. The spore-bearing segments are arranged in unusual comb-like heads at the tip of slender erect stems. The early collector William Woolls wrote 'It is a singular looking plant, with its fructification at the extremity of the leafless stems, and has so little resemblance to ordinary ferns, that persons unaccustomed to the examination of such plants, might easily pass it by as if it were a tuft of some grassy plant in a decaying state'.[15]

Name: *Schizaea* = Gk. *schizein*, to cleave.

Schizaea bifida Willdenow

Forked Comb Fern **Ss**

An erect fern mostly 25-35cm high, found in heath and woodland. Fairly common.

Range: NSW coast and ranges except Blue Mountains, eastern Australian states, NZ and New Caledonia. **Sterile fronds:** resembling the stalk of a fertile frond, but shorter. **Fertile fronds:** about 1mm wide, clustered, mostly 10-35cm high, undivided, or divided 1-2 times. Fertile portion 10-20mm long. **Name:** *bifida* = Lat. 2-split.

Schizaea dichotoma (Linnaeus) Smith

Branched Comb Fern **Ss**

An erect fern mostly 20-40cm high, found in heath and woodland. Uncommon.

Range: NSW coast north from Jervis Bay, Qld, NT, WA, South-east Asia, Pacific and Madagascar. **Sterile fronds:** 15-30cm long, regularly divided into over 20 segments, 1-1.5mm wide. **Fertile fronds:** slightly flattened, longer than the sterile fronds, divided 3-6 times. Fertile portions 10-15mm long. **Name:** *dichotoma* = Gk. 2-cut.

Schizaea rupestris R. Brown

Ss

A fern with drooping fronds to 12cm long, often forming matted masses on wet shadowy rocks under cliffs and waterfalls. Uncommon. William Woolls described it as a 'very diminutive plant, generally growing on the caudices of *Todea barbara*, or amongst mosses on some moist rock by the side of a creek.'[16]

Range: coast and ranges from Gosford south to the Budawang Mountains. **Sterile fronds:** 1-2.5mm wide, undivided, smooth and glossy. **Fertile fronds:** longer, narrower and less common than sterile fronds. **Name:** *rupestris* = Lat. pertaining to rocks.

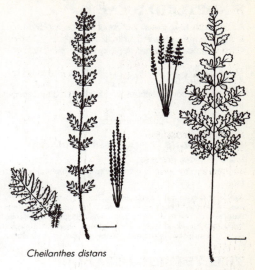

Cheilanthes distans

Cheilanthes sieberi ssp. *sieberi*

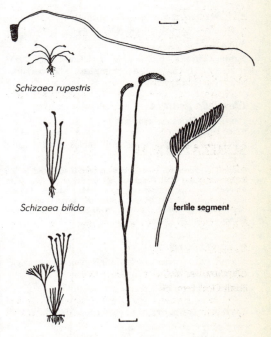

Schizaea rupestris

Schizaea bifida

Schizaea dichotoma

fertile segment

SINOPTERIDACEAE

A family with 12-16 genera and about 300 species, distributed in America, Africa, Asia and Australia.
Often included in Adiantaceae.

• *Pellaea* Link

A genus with about 40 species worldwide including 2 species in Australia.

Name: *Pellaea* = Gk. dark-coloured.

Pellaea falcata (R. Brown) Fée **ssp. *falcata***

Sickle Fern **Ss, Temp Rf**
An erect fern to 60cm tall, common in rainforest and open forest.

Range: NSW coast and ranges, Qld, Vic, Tas, NZ, New Caledonia and Asia. **Rhizome:** long-creeping, covered in narrow, dark scales. **Fronds:** 20-60cm long; segments 2-6cm long, light green, tough, shiny. **Stalk:** dark, covered with narrow spreading scales. **Sori:** forming a band about 1mm wide next to the margin. **Name:** *falcata* = Lat. sickle-shaped.

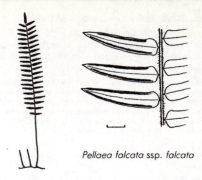

Pellaea falcata ssp. falcata

THELYPTERIDACEAE

A family with up to 1000 species in 28 genera, mainly in tropical regions. Australia has about 22 species in 10 genera, distributed in all states except NT.

• *Christella* Léveillé emend Holttum

A genus with over 50 species worldwide, including 5 in eastern Australia.

Name: *Christella* = probably after K.H. Christ (1833-1933), professor of Botany in Basel, Switzerland, who specialised in ferns and plant geography.

Christella dentata (Forsskal) Brownsey & Jermy
(previously *Cyclosorus nymphalis*)
STRf, Temp Rf
A fern 40-80cm high forming small clumps on creek banks in or near rainforest. Moderately common.

Range: NSW coast north of Mt Cambewarra (near Nowra), Qld, SA, WA, Pacific Islands and tropical and subtropical parts of Asia and Africa. **Rhizome:** short-creeping, covered with dark red-brown scales. **Fronds:** dull, papery, with hairs on the veins. **Stalk:** pale brown to mid-brown, densely covered in short fine hairs. **Sori:** small, circular, in rows. **Name:** *dentata* = Lat. toothed.

• *Cyclosorus* Link

A genus with 3 species worldwide, including a single species native to Australia.

Name: *Cyclosorus* = Gk. circular-sorus.

Cyclosorus interruptus (Willdenow) H. Itô
(previously *C. gongylodes*) **Aqu**
An erect fern to 50-150cm high, occurring as clumps in

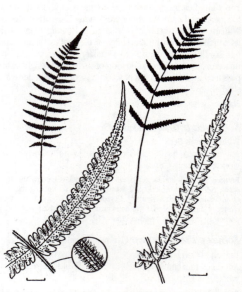

Christella dentata   *Cyclosorus interruptus*

freshwater swamps. Banks and Solander collected it around Botany Bay in 1770. By 1956 its local population was apparently reduced to a single clump in marsh at Scarborough Park, Kogarah. Fortunately this has flourished and there are now several plants growing there amongst *Blechnum indicum*.

The rhizome is reported to be edible.

Range: NSW coast north from Sydney, Qld, NT, WA, NZ and widespread in the tropics. **Rhizome:** long-creeping, sparsely covered in scales. **Fronds:** leathery, lower segments not much reduced in size. **Stalk:** dark at the base, pale and pinkish above. **Sori:** forming a row around the margin, protected by a hairy indusium. **Name:** *interruptus* = Lat. interrupted, referring to the sori.

CYCADOPSIDA Cycads

Cycads reproduce sexually from spores. They have woody, often underground, stems and palm-like leaves. Together with conifers they dominated world vegetation from about 200 to 80 million years ago.

ZAMIACEAE

One of the 3 relict families of cycads. There are about 80 species remaining in 8 genera worldwide, including 17 species in 3 genera in Australia.

Range: NSW coast. **Leaves:** pinnate, the leaflets tough, thick, sharply pointed. **Sexual organs:** large male and female cones form on different plants every 2 or more years. The female cone is a spectacular sight when mature, like a huge pineapple, with swollen red seeds appearing from behind stiff protective bracts. **Name:** *communis* = Lat. common.

Macrozamia spiralis (Salisbury) Miquel

Castl, Ss

A tufted fern-like plant with spiky leaves 40-120cm long. Found in the Castlereagh woodlands, and a few other spots in the area (e.g. Wallacia, and Picnic Point on the Georges River).

Range: largely restricted to the Sydney area and Blue Mountains. **Leaves:** pinnate, conspicuously twisted; the leaflets tough, thick, sharply pointed. **Sexual organs:** similar to *M. communis*, but smaller. **Name:** *spiralis* = Lat. spiral, referring to the twisted leaves.

Macrozamia communis

Macrozamia spiralis

• *Macrozamia* Miquel

An endemic genus with about 14 species.

Name: *Macrozamia* = Gk. large *Zamia*, a genus in the same family.

Macrozamia communis L. Johnson

Burrawang **Ss**

A large tufted fern-like plant with spiky leaves to 2m long, found in woodland on sandy soils. Widespread but not common in the area.

The fleshy red seeds are rich in starch and were a staple food for Aborigines. They need careful preparation by slicing and soaking to remove toxins. Ignorance of these methods resulted in sickness amongst early explorers and settlers. Because of bad effects on stock, landowners exterminated the plant in many areas. The starch-rich underground stems were exploited commercially before World War II for laundry starch and paste.

CONIFEROPSIDA Conifers

Conifers are trees or shrubs which do not form flowers, but reproduce sexually by seeds that are naked, that, is, not borne within an ovary.

Conifers once dominated the planet, but are now largely restricted to the northern hemisphere due to the advance of the more adaptable angiosperms. The earliest fossils date from the Jurassic period, about 200 million years ago.

CUPRESSACEAE

Cypresses, Native Pines

A family of evergreen trees and shrubs with 140 species worldwide, in 18 genera. There are 17 Australian species in 3 genera. The leaves are tiny and scale-like. The male cones are small and inconspicuous. The female cones are larger, with several broad valve-like scales, bearing the seeds.

• *Callitris* Ventenat

A genus with 15 species endemic to Australia and one in
New Caledonia. These are the only native mainland trees
with woody Gymnosperm-type cones. Their tiny leaves are
arranged in whorls of 3.

Name: *Callitris* = Gk. *kalos,* beauty.

Callitris muelleri (Parlatore) F. Mueller

Mueller's Cypress **Ss**
A shrub or small tree 3-8m tall, common on rocky gully sides
on the sandstone plateaus.

Range: Sydney area, south coast and Blue Mountains.   **Leaves:** appressed
to the branchlets, keeled in the back. Smaller branches not drooping.
Female cones: about 3cm diameter; the scales smoothly rounded, with
only a tiny point near the top.   **Name:** *muelleri* = after Ferdinand Mueller.

Callitris rhomboidea R. Brown ex A. & L.C. Richard

(previously *C. cupressiformis*)
Port Jackson Cypress **Ss**
A slender shrub or small tree, 3-6m tall, common in rocky
gully sides on the sandstone plateaus.

Range: coast and ranges in eastern Australia.   **Leaves:** similar to *C.
muelleri,* but slightly thinner. Smaller branches drooping. **Female
cones:** about 2cm wide, the scales strongly projecting, sometimes almost
conical.   **Name:** *rhomboidea* = Lat. shaped like a spinning top, referring
to the scales.

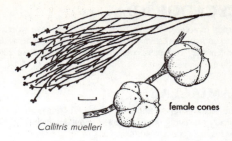

female cones

Callitris muelleri

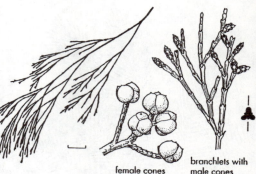

female cones

branchlets with
male cones

Callitris rhomboidea

PODOCARPACEAE

A family of trees and shrubs with about 140 species in 7
genera, mainly distributed in the southern hemisphere. There
are 13 species in 4 genera in Australia. This is an old Gondwana
family represented by many magnificent tree species,
especially in NZ and the Pacific.

• *Podocarpus* L'Héritier

A genus with about 100 species worldwide, including 6
species in Australia.

Name: *Podocarpus* = Gk. foot-fruit, drawing attention to the
swollen seed receptacles.

Podocarpus spinulosus (Smith) R. Brown ex Mirbel

Plum Pine **Ss**
A straggling shrub with branches to about 1m long, widely
scattered in woodland in gullies, but not common. The male
and female organs are on different plants. The seeds are borne
on swollen fleshy receptacles that are attractive to birds and
edible to humans, but rather lacking in flavour.

Range: NSW coast (Ulladulla to Woy Woy) and Blue Mountains.   **Leaves:**
3-6cm long, thick, stiff, sharply pointed.   **Male cones:** cylindrical, densely
clustered.   **Female organs:** seeds borne nakedly on receptacles which
become swollen, purple-black and succulent.   **Name:** *spinulosus* = Lat.
spiny.

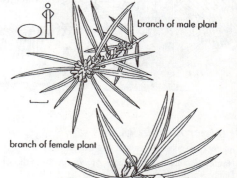

branch of male plant

branch of female plant

seed and
receptacle

Podocarpus spinulosus

SEPARATE GROUPS

For ease of identification the following 6 groups of plants have been collected into separate sections based on obvious characteristcs of habit or environment.

CLIMBERS

This section includes climbers, twiners and scramblers; plants which rely on other plants to support their relatively weak stems.

Key to climbers

Leaves apparently absent .... **Group 1**
Leaves compound .... **Group 2**
Leaves opposite .... **Group 3**
Leaves alternate .... **Group 4**

> **How to use the key**
> Work your way through by making successive choices: either A or *A, then B or *B etc..

Group 1 Leaves apparently absent.

A. Petals 3, flowers barely opening. CASSYTHACEAE:*Cassytha* 329
***A.** Petals 5, flowers opening freely. CUSCUTACEAE:*Cuscuta* 332

Group 2 Leaves compound.

A. Stems and leaves lined with thorns. ROSACEAE:*Rubus* 340
***A.** Plants lacking thorns.
>   **B.** Tenrils present. VITACEAE 342
>   ***B.** Tenrils absent.
>>   **C.** Leaflets arranged palmately (radiating from a single point). CONVOLVULACEAE:*Ipomoea cairica* 397
>>   ***C.** Leaflets arranged pinnately.
>>>   **D.** Leaflets 5-7. BIGNONIACEAE: *Pandorea* 328
>>>   ***D.** Leaflets 3.
>>>>   **E.** Leaf stalks long and twining. RANUNCULUS:*Clematis* 339
>>>>   ***E.** Leaf stalks short and straight. FABACEAE 333

Group 3 Leaves opposite.

A. Leaves toothed. CUNONIACEAE: *Aphanopetalum* 332
***A.** Leaves untoothed.
>   **B.** Three parallel veins conspicuous. SMILACACEAE:*Pipogonum* 344
>   ***B.** Leaves otherwise.
>>   **C.** Leaves covered in star-hairs. MONIMIACEAE:*Palmeria* 336
>>   ***C.** Leaves otherwise.
>>>   **D.** Leaves with prominent domatia. RUBIACEAE:*Morinda* 341
>>>   ***D.** Leaves otherwise.
>>>>   **E.** Net veins prominent. FABACEAE:*Oxylobium* 335
>>>>   ***E.** Net veins visible but not raised.
>>>>>   **F.** Scrambler on fences and disturbed ground. CAPRIFOLIACEAE:*Lonicera* 329
>>>>>   ***F.** Climbers.
>>>>>>   **G.** Stamens free from style. APOCYNACEAE 325
>>>>>>   ***G.** Stamens and style unified in a complex hollow structure. ASCLEPIDACEAE 326

Group 4 Leaves alternate

A. Leaves toothed.

    B. Thorny climber: ROSACEAE: *Rubus* 340

    ***B.** Thorns absent.

        C. Tendrils present. VITACEAE: *Cissus* 342

        ***C.** Tentrils absent.

            D. Leaves almost round, soft. ASTERACEAE:*Senecio mikanioides* 328

            ***D.** Leaves longer than wide.

                E. Leaves thin-textuired and harsh. MORACEAE:*Malaisia* 337

                ***E.** Leaves soft-textured. DILLENIACEAE: *Hibbertia* 332

***A.** Leaves untoothed.

    F. Leaves with all veins parallel.

        G. Leaves ending with long fibrous tenril. FLAGELLARIACEAE 343

        ***G.** Leaves otherwise.

            H. Leaves grouped on short side-branches, appearing pinnate. PHILESIACEAE 343

            ***H.** Leaves on main stem. SMILACEAE 344

    ***F.** Leaves with lateral veins.

        I. Leaves lobed.

            J. Low twiner on grasses and shrubs. CONVOLVULACEAE:*Convolvulus* 330

            ***J.** Robust climbers.

                K. Lobes blunt. PASSIFLORACEAE 337

                ***K.** Lobes pointed. CONVOLVULACEAE: *Ipomoea indica* 330

        ***I.** Leaves not lobed.

            L. Leaves heart-shaped or arrow-head shaped.

                M. Margins crenate or finely undulating. POLYGONACEAE:*Muehlenbeckia* 339

                ***M.** Leaf margins even.

                    N. Flowers large and conspicuous. CONVOLVULACEAE 330

                    ***N.** Flowers tiny, fleshy, about 4mm wide. MENISPERMACEAE.*Sarcopetalum* 336

            ***L.** Leaves otherwise.

                O. Leaves under 35mm long. Twiners.

                    P. Stems herbaceous. POLYGALACEAE: *Comesperma* 338

                    ***P.** Stems fine and woody. PITTOSPORACEAE:*Billardiera* 338

                ***O.** Leaves over 35mm long.

                    Q. Leaves with pointed tips.

                        R. Stem attached to lower surface of leaf.
                          MENISPERACEAE:*Stephania* 336

                      ***R.** Stem attached to base of leaf.

                          S. 5-7 main veins arising from near the base. Robust rainforest climber. PIPERACEAE 338

                        ***S.** Leaves otherwise.

                              T. Leaves <5cm long. AMARANTHACEAE: *Deeringia* 325

                              ***T.** Leaves >5cm long.

                                  U. Leaves with small stipule-like segments on the stalk. FABACEAE:*Hardenbergia* 335

                                  ***U.** Leaves otherwise. DILLENIACEAE: *Hibbertia scandens* 332

                  ***Q.** Leaves with tips rounded or notched.

                    V. Tips notched. CONVOLVULACEAE: *Ipomoea brasiliensis* (see Seacoast and estuarine species) 397

                    ***V.** Tips rounded. Large leaves with strong venation. MENISPERMACEAE:*Legnephora* 336

• DICOTYLEDONS

AMARANTHACEAE

• *Deeringia* R. Brown

A genus of climbers with about 12 species, including 2 species in Australia.

Name: *Deeringia* = after Georg Karl Deering, a medical doctor in England, who wrote on Nottinghamshire plants.

Deeringia amaranthoides (Lamarck) Merril

Deeringia **Temp Rf**

A woody climber or scrambler, 2-4m tall, found in rainforest in the Royal National Park, where it is rare (e.g. Werong Beach).

Range: NSW coast and ranges, Qld, widespread in New Guinea, South-east Asia and China. **Leaves:** dark olive green, hairless, thin-textured, 3-10cm long. **Flowers:** bisexual, GREEN, with white anthers; in slender terminal and axillary spikes 5-20cm long, often gracefully arching. **Flowering time:** summer. **Fruit:** a succulent RED berry. **Name:** *amaranthoides* = *Amaranthus*-like.

APOCYNACEAE

A family with about 1500 species in about 180 genera worldwide, mainly in the tropics. Most species have a milky latex in the stems and leaves. The flowers are fragrant.

The family includes several decorative species, including Oleander (*Nerium*) and Frangipani (*Plumeria*). It is closely related to Asclepidaceae.

• *Melodinus* G. & J. R. Forster

A genus of climbers with about 50 species worldwide, including 2 species in Australia.

Name: *Melodinus* = Gk. *melon*, apple, *dinein*, to twist, because the fruit resembles an apple, and the plant is a twiner.

Melodinus australis (F. Mueller) Pierre

Southern Melodinus **STRf**

A climber with stems to several metres long. Found in subtropical rainforest in the Royal National Park and the Illawarra, but uncommon.

Range: NSW coast north from the Illawarra north; also Qld. **Leaves:** opposite, 5-10cm long, thin-textured, hairless, almost stalkless, usually dark-green above. **Flowers:** YELLOW, small, in axillary cymes.

Deeringia amaranthoides

Flowering time: late summer. **Fruit:** a large ovoid orange-red berry, 4-5cm long, filled with large seeds. **Name:** *australis* = Lat. southern.

• *Parsonsia* R. Brown

A genus of climbers with about 100 species worldwide, including about 20 species in Australia.

Name: after James Parsons (1705-70), a London doctor who wrote on botanical subjects.

Parsonsia straminea (R. Brown) F. Mueller var. *straminea*

Monkey Rope, Common Silkpod

STRf, Temp Rf

A robust rainforest climber with woody stems many metres long, climbing by adventitious roots. Very common in subtropical rainforest in the Royal National Park, also on *Casuarina glauca* in estuaries. Old specimens in rainforest develop thick, fantastically convoluted trunks. The juvenile and adult plants are so different as to appear to be two quite different species. The juveniles are miniature creepers with tiny soft leaves, purple beneath, while the adults are robust climbers.

Range: NSW coast and Blue Mountains and Qld. **Leaves:** juvenile leaves: soft, opposite 10-15mm long, heart-shaped at the base, purple beneath.

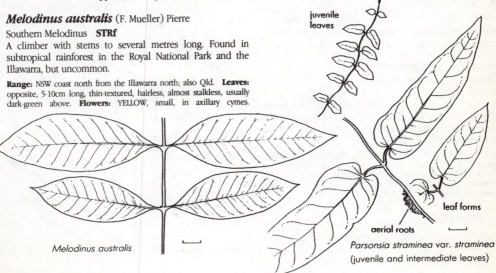

Melodinus australis

juvenile leaves

leaf forms

aerial roots

Parsonsia straminea var. *straminea*
(juvenile and intermediate leaves)

Adult leaves: opposite, hairless, tough, thick, shiny above, dull below, with strong reticulation, old leaves dark green, with undulate margins. **Flowers:** CREAM/PALE PINK, numerous in dense cymes. **Flowering time:** summer. **Fruit:** long green finger-like pods containing numerous seeds, each with a tuft of silky hairs. **Name:** *straminea* = Lat. chaffy, straw-coloured, reference obscure.

ASCLEPIADACEAE

A family with about 2000 species in about 250 genera worldwide. In Australia there are about 75 species in 19 genera.

The flowers have all sexual parts joined together in a complex hollow structure known as a gynostemium, whose passageways are specialised for penetration by certain insects, notably butterflies. The fruit is a follicle, splitting longitudinally to reveal numerous seeds with tufts of silky hairs for wind dispersal.

All the local species are woody climbers with milky sap.

• *Araujia* Brotero

A genus of South American climbers with a single species naturalised in coastal NSW.

Name: *Araujia* = after Antonia de Araujo de Acebedo, a Portugese statesman.

*Araujia hortorum** Fournier

Moth Plant   **Ss, Cumb**

A robust climber, whose greyish leaves and large swollen fruit grace just about every vacant lot or fence in Sydney. Often a pest in bushlands. Introduced from South America. All parts are filled with a sticky white milk

Range: NSW coasts, South America. **Leaves:** opposite, dark green, shiny above, dull pale grey-green below. **Flowers:** WHITE, CREAM (occasionally pinkish). **Fruit:** swollen grey-green, 8-10cm long, filled with seeds, each with a tuft of silky hairs. **Name:** *hortorum* = Lat. of gardens.

• *Leichhardtia* R. Brown

A genus of climbers with about 5 species in Australia.

Name: *Leichhardtia* = After Ludwig Leichhardt (1813-48), famous German explorer of northern Australia.

Leichhardtia leptophylla
(F. Mueller ex Bentham) Bullock

Cumb

A twiner with slender leaves on stems to a few metres long. Rare in the area. Recorded in the past from a few sites on clay soils on the Cumberland Plain. The only recent recording is from Lansdowne Park, Bankstown.

Range: Sydney area, NSW north-western slopes and Qld. **Leaves:** opposite, slender, thin but firm-textured, 4-10cm long, veins not conspicuous, margins recurved. **Flowers:** the corolla forms an urn-shaped cup with 5 small lobes; flowers arranged in small axillary cymes. **Name:** *leptophylla* = Gk. thin-leaved.

• *Marsdenia* R. Brown

A genus of climbers with 20-30 species, including 15 species in Australia.

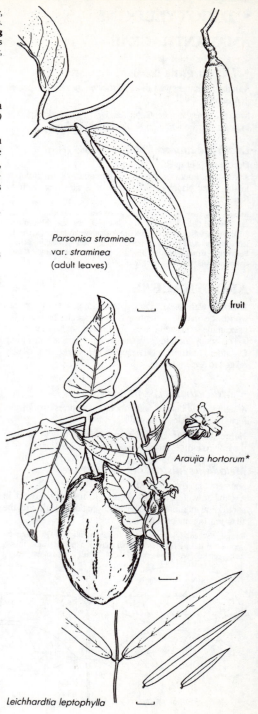

Parsonsia straminea
var. *straminea*
(adult leaves)

fruit

Araujia hortorum*

Leichhardtia leptophylla

Name: *Marsdenia* = after William Marsden (1754-1836), an Irish-born Secretary of the Admiralty who collected plants in Sumatra.

Marsdenia flavescens A. Cunningham

Hairy Milk Vine, Yellow Milk Vine, Native Potatoe
STRf margins

A climber with stems to several metres long. Found in rainforest in the Royal National Park. The flowers have a rich honey scent and produce much nectar. A. G. Hamilton recommended them as an ideal lure for butterfly hunters. Captain Hunter found the roots being consumed by Aborigines on the Hawkesbury River in 1788. 'It had much the appearance of horseradish and had a sweetish taste, and having swallowed a small quantity, it occasioned violent spasms, cramps in the bowels, and sickness in the stomach.'[1]

Range: NSW coast and Blue Mountains. **Leaves:** opposite, fairly soft, glossy and more or less hairless above, yellowish green, dull, densely furry below and on stems (sometimes hairs absent), venation not prominent below. Note the abruptly acuminate tips. Its hairiness may not be immediately visible but the leaf undersides and stems are obviously furry to touch. **Flowers:** PALE YELLOW, about 3mm wide. **Flowering time:** summer. **Fruit:** slender, finger-like, about 5cm long. **Name:** *flavescens* = Lat. becoming yellow, referring to the flowers.

Marsdenia rostrata R. Brown

Common Milk Vine **STRf**

A robust climber in rainforest, found locally in the Royal National Park. It often develops thick woody stems (e.g. over 4cm wide).

Range: NSW coast and ranges, Lord Howe Island, Vic and Qld. **Leaves:** opposite, hairless, often undulate, thin, soft. **Flowers:** YELLOWISH, about 6mm wide, numerous in dense simple umbels. **Flowering time:** spring-summer. **Fruit:** broad, about 5cm long and 2.5cm wide. **Name:** *rostrata* = Lat. beaked, referring to the long beak-like stigmatic head.

Marsdenia suaveolens R. Brown

Sweet-scented Doubah **STRf, Temp Rf, Ss**

A slender climber in rainforest and gullies, or a short shrubby plant in woodland valleys (both forms are illustrated). Uncommon in the area.

Range: NSW coast and Blue Mountains. **Leaves:** opposite, dull olive green above (in the woodland form), pale below with a dull waxy texture, not thick, smooth and hairless both sides, margins recurved, stems finely pubescent. **Flowers:** WHITE-CREAM; in short, dense, axillary umbels. **Flowering time:** summer. **Fruit:** slender, 5-10cm long. **Name:** *suaveolens* = Lat. sweet, referring to the fragrant flowers.

• *Tylophora* R. Brown

A genus of climbers with about 50 species, including 11 in Australia.

Name: *Tylophora* = Gk. *tylos*, knot or knob, *phoros*, bearing, from the 5 raised swollen knobs surrounding the sexual parts.

Tylophora barbata R. Brown

Temp Rf, Ss

A small scrambling twiner, sometimes climbing, abundant in moist undergrowth in gullies and beside streams. Very common but rarely seen in flower.

Range: NSW coast, Blue Mountains, and southern ranges and Vic.

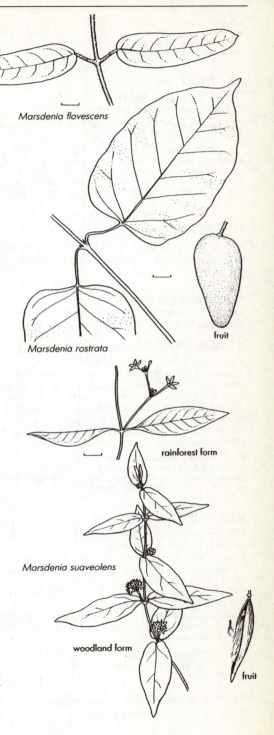

Marsdenia flavescens

fruit

Marsdenia rostrata

rainforest form

Marsdenia suaveolens

woodland form

fruit

Leaves: opposite, hairless, thick, soft, with recurved margins, glossy above. **Flowers:** DEEP DULL RED, about 7mm wide, on slender stalks, in axillary compound umbels. **Flowering time:** summer. **Name:** *barbata* = Lat. bearded, presumably referring to the seeds.

ASTERACEAE

*Senecio mikanioides** Otto ex Walpers

Cape Ivy **Ss, Temp Rf, STRf (margins)**

A robust scrambling herbaceous climber, common in deep moist gullies and rainforests. Introduced from South Africa.

Range: coast and ranges of NSW, Vic and South Africa. **Leaves:** soft, hairless. **Flower-heads:** numerous in dense terminal corymbs, disc flowers GOLDEN YELLOW, ray flowers absent. **Flowering time:** spring and summer. **Name:** *mikanioides* = like *Mikania*, a genus of tropical American vines in the same family.

BASELLACEAE

A family with 15-20 species in 4 genera, native to warmer parts of Asia and the Americas. A single species is introduced into Australia.

• *Anredera* Antoine L. de Jussieu

A genus with 5-10 species native to the southern United States, West Indies, South America and Galapagos Islands.

*Anredera cordifolia** (Tenore) Steen

Madeira Vine, Lamb's Tails **Ss, Cumb**

A vigorous herbaceous vine forming dense masses on other vegetation. Common in waste ground and urban bush gullies where it is a serious pest. A native of South America, it was introduced into NSW as a creeper. The numerous tubers along the stems are the only means of reproduction since there is no evidence that fruit are produced in Australia. The leaves and tubers are eaten in Mexico and southern Europe.

Range: NSW coast, recently recorded from a number of inland districts. **Leaves:** soft, thick, fleshy and heart-shaped. **Flowers:** small, CREAM, fragrant and numerous in dense drooping racemes. **Flowering time:** early April. **Name:** *cordifolia* = Lat. heart-leaved.

BIGNONIACEAE

A mainly tropical family of woody plants, with about 800 species in 120 genera, especially in the Americas. There are 9 species in 5 genera in Australia.

The family is related to Gesneriaceae and Scrophulariaceae.

• *Pandorea* Spach

A genus of climbers, some shrubby, with 6 species in Southeast Asia, Australia and New Caledonia. There are 4 species native to Australia.

Name: *Pandorea* = After Pandora, in Greek mythology the name of the first mortal woman, on whom all the gods bestowed gifts.

Pandorea pandorana (Andrews) Steenis

Wonga-Wonga Vine **Ss, Temp Rf, STRf**

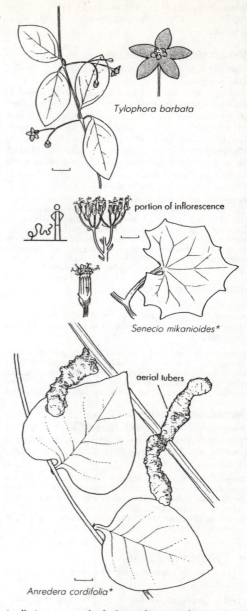

Tylophora barbata

portion of inflorescence

Senecio mikanioides*

aerial tubers

Anredera cordifolia*

A tall vigorous woody climber with spectacular cascades of flowers in spring. Common in many situations. Judith Wright called it 'my white waterfall' in her poem *Wonga Vine*.

Range: coast, ranges and inland slopes in eastern mainland Australia, also NG and the Molucca Islands. **Leaves:** pinnate with 3-7 leaflets; leaflets thick, glossy, hairless. The juvenile leaves are rather ferny looking, with small, soft, toothed leaflets. **Flowers:** WHITE with purple markings, in large drooping masses. **Flowering time:** spring. **Name:** *pandorana* = a double commemoration of Pandora.

CAPRIFOLIACEAE
• *Lonicera* Linnaeus

A genus of climbers and shrubs with 200 species worldwide, mainly in the northern hemisphere. There are 2 species naturalised in Australia.

Name: *Lonicera* = after Adam Lonicera (1526-89), a German botanist.

*Lonicera japonica** Thunberg
Japanese Honeysuckle **Ss, Cumb**
An attractive scrambler, very abundant in disturbed bushland, on fences and in wastelands. One can easily suck honey from the base of the flowers. Originally a native of China and Japan, introduced as a garden plant, and now widely naturalised.

Range: NSW coast and ranges, eastern Asia. **Leaves:** opposite, hairless, tough (the juvenile leaves are coarsely toothed). **Flowers:** mixed PALE ORANGE and WHITE on each plant, beautifully fragrant, with a honey nectar. **Name:** *japonica* = Japanese.

CASSYTHACEAE

A family with a single genus, related to Lauraceae, and often included in that family.

• *Cassytha* Linneaus (cas-SY-tha)
Devil's Twine, Devil's Guts

A genus of hemi-parasitic, apparently leafless vines with 17 species, widely distributed but mainly in warm parts of the world. There are 14 species in Australia, mainly in south-western WA.

Devil's Twine is a parasite which forms dense tangled masses on host plants. The term 'hemi-parasite' is used because it begins life by drawing nourishment from the earth and only becomes parasitic after contacting another plant. It attacks any host, even itself, absorbing sap by specialised parasitic roots called haustoria.

A. G. Hamilton described its growth: 'When the seed germinates, it sends up a bright green thread-like shoot, which swings round and round till it comes in contact with some living plant—it is not particular what kind—it coils around this, haustoria are formed, and as soon as it has begun to draw sap from the host, the lower part of the shoot dies off and the plant becomes a holo-parasite. In the early stages the shoot contains chlorophyll, but later, is entirely without it.'[3]

The small pendant fruits are one of the most abundant and tasty morsels in the bush, being sweet and mucousy.

Leaves are present as tiny scales. The flowers are tiny and WHITE to YELLOWISH, arising on a short spike (sometimes branched).

Name: *Cassytha* = from *kasytas*, the Greek name of a parasitic plant, probably Dodder (*Cuscata*). 'Devil's Twine' is a sanitised version of the colonial name 'Devil's Guts'.

Cassytha glabella R. Brown
Slender Devil's Twine **Ss, Cumb, Castl**
A common species in heath and woodland, easily

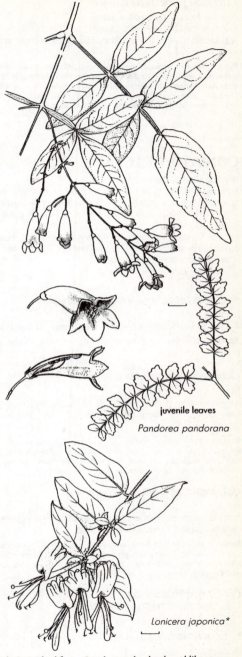

juvenile leaves
Pandorea pandorana

*Lonicera japonica**

distinguished from *C. pubescens* by the thread-like stems.

Range: NSW coast, Blue Mountains, all states. **Stems:** very slender; 0.4-0.6(-1)mm wide. **Fruit:** green, smooth, often with red markings. **Name:** *glabella* = Lat. hairless.

Cassytha pubescens R. Brown,

(now includes *Cassytha paniculata*)
Common Devil's Twine **Ss, Cumb**
A common species in woodland. The stems become very
warty when old.

Range: NSW coast, ranges and some inland areas, all other states. **Fruit:**
green, smooth or with 6 longitudinal veins, hairless or covered in fine
short hairs, or sometimes densely felty. **Name:** *pubescens* = Lat. with
fine hairs. **Note:** the forms with hairless, ribbed capsules until recently
were considered to be a separate species, *C. paniculata.*

CONVOLVULACEAE

Morning Glories, Bindweeds
A family of climbers and twiners with about 1650 species
in about 55 genera mainly in tropical and subtropical parts
of the world. There are about 100 species in about 18 genera
in Australia.

Some native *Ipomoea* have swollen roots which were
consumed by Aborigines. The Sweet Potato (*Ipomoea batatas*)
is an important tropical food crop.

The family is related to Solanaceae.

• *Calystegia* R. Brown (cal-ee-STEE-jee-a)

Bindweeds
A genus with about 30 species, including 3 native to Australia.
Name: *Calystegia* = Gk. calyx-covering, referring to the 2
enclosing bracteoles.

Calystegia marginata R. Brown

Ss
A vigorous twiner, with slender tangled stems to several metres
long. Found in deep gullies and rainforest margins.
Uncommon in the area.

Range: NSW coast, Blue Mountains, Qld, Vic. **Leaves:** soft, thin-textured,
hairless, with pointed basal lobes, very variable in size. **Flowers:** WHITE
with pink markings, 15-20mm long. **Flowering time:** summer.
Name: *marginata* = Lat. pertaining to margins (of rainforests?).

Calystegia sepium (Linnaeus) R. Brown

Ss
A scrambling twiner, forming dense tangled masses in swampy
disturbed areas. Uncommon near Sydney.

Range: coasts north from the Shoalhaven River, Qld and NT. **Leaves:**
soft, thin-textured, hairless, with pointed basal lobes. **Flowers:** PINK
with white stripes, 4-7cm long. **Flowering time:** summer. **Name:**
sepium = Lat. pertaining to hedges.

Calystegia soldanella

—See COASTAL AND ESTUARINE SPECIES.

• *Convolvulus* Linnaeus

Bindweeds
A genus of twiners with about 250 species, including 3 native
to Australia, distributed in all states.

Name: *Convolvulus* = Lat. little twiner

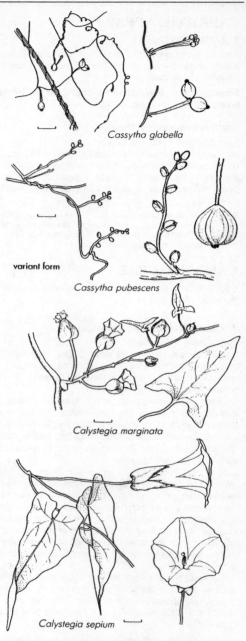

Cassytha glabella

variant form

Cassytha pubescens

Calystegia marginata

Calystegia sepium

Convolvulus erubescens Sims

Australian Bindweed, Blushing Bindweed
Cumb
A pretty twiner with stems to 80cm long. Found uncommonly
in dry grasslands or open forests on clay soils. 'In the same
barren spots, too, I found a likeness of another old friend,

the small meadow convolvulus, the new one being far brighter in hue than the sly, mischievous little sprite that frisks over our English fields, and baffles the sagacity of the neatest farmer when he strives to exclude it. The garb of my new friend is veritable couleur de rose . . . '4

NSW Aborigines drank a decoction of the plant for indigestion, stomach ache and diarrhoea.

Range: all parts of Australia. **Leaves:** distinctively lobed (see illustration), finely hairy. **Flowers:** PINK, 6-20mm wide. The 5 sepals are equal in size and overlapping. **Flowering time:** spring-summer. **Name:** *erubescens* = Lat. becoming red. Bindweed is a old English name for related species which infest meadows and crops. **Similar species:** Be careful to distinguish it from the more common introduced *C. arvensis*, which is hairless and has blunt sepals.

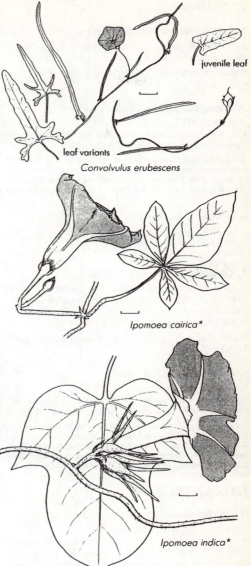

juvenile leaf

leaf variants

Convolvulus erubescens

• *Ipomoea* Linnaeus (i-po-ME-a)

A genus of climbers and twiners with about 500 species, including about 45 native and introduced species in Australia.

Name: *Ipomoea* = Gk. worm-like.

Ipomoea brasiliensis
—See COASTAL AND ESTUARINE SPECIES.

*Ipomoea cairica**
—See COASTAL AND ESTUARINE SPECIES.

*Ipomoea indica** (N. L. Burman) Merrill
Morning Glory **Ss, Cumb**

A vigorous scrambling herbaceous climber, common on fences and in waste areas. Easily recognised by the large heart-shaped leaves and spectacular blue or purple flowers. Introduced as a garden plant from the tropics.

Range: coastal areas north from Sydney, into Qld and NT. **Flowers:** BLUE (or bluish-purple), about 8cm wide. The sepals are 14-25mm long. **Flowering time:** spring. **Name:** *indica* = Indian. **Similar species:** *I. purpurea**, is a less common weed, similar to *I. indica*, except the leaves are smaller and the flowers are pink-purple and smaller. The best identifying feature is the sepals which are under 10-15mm long.

Ipomoea cairica*

• *Polymeria* R. Brown

A genus with about 10 species worldwide, including 6 endemic species in Australia.

Name: *Polymeria* = Gk. many-parted, referring to the several-branched style.

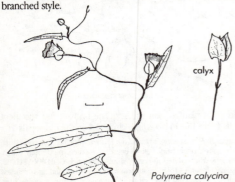

calyx

Polymeria calycina

Ipomoea indica*

Polymeria calycina R. Brown
Swamp Bindweed **Cumb, Ss**

A prostate or twining herb with slender stems to about 50cm long. Found in grassland and open forest on clay soils, or in marshy places.

Range: NSW coasts and Qld. **Leaves:** 2-5cm long, with 2 backward-pointing lobes at the base, usually hairless. **Flowers:** PINK, funnel shaped, about 10mm long. The stigmas have 6 lobes. The calyx has 2 large heart-shaped sepals enveloping 3 smaller sepals. **Flowering time:** spring-summer-early autumn. **Name:** *calycina* = Gk. drawing attention to the prominent calyx lobes.

CUNONIACEAE

• *Aphanopetalum* Endlicher

An endemic genus of rainforest climbers with 2 species: 1 in eastern Australia and the other in south-western WA.

Name: *Aphanopetalum* = Gk. invisible-petals; they are indeed very obscure.

Aphanopetalum resinosum Endlicher

Gum Vine **STRf**

A woody climber found in subtropical rainforest in the Royal National Park. Also common in the Illawarra.

Range: NSW coast and ranges, and Qld. **Leaves:** opposite, glossy both sides, toothed, thin-textured, firm, hairless. **Flowers:** GREEN, with 4 prominent sepals, 4 microscopic petals, and 8 stamens; in axillary cymes. **Flowering time:** mainly October. **Name:** *resinosum* = Lat. having resin.

CUSCUTACEAE

A family of parasitic twiners, with a single genus. Often included in Convolvulaceae.

• *Cuscuta* Linnaeus (cus-KEW-ta)

A genus of twiners with about 170 species worldwide, including 7 species native, and 5 introduced into Australia. *Cuscuta* are selective parasites on *Persicaria* species (see AQUATICS: Polygonaceae).

Name: *Cuscuta* = the medieval Latin name, from the Arabic *keshut.*

Cuscuta campestris • Yuncker

Dodder **Ss, Cumb**

A leafless twiner, parasitic on *Persicaria* (Polygonaceae). Uncommon in the area. Introduced from America.

Range: a cosmopolitan weed; in Australia it occurs in the Sydney area, NSW north coast, inland NSW, Qld and Vic. **Flowers:** WHITE, in dense sessile clusters. **Name:** *campestris* = Lat. pertaining to fields. **Note:** the local species was previously thought to be the native *C. australis,* but that only occurs on the north coast and northern tablelands in NSW.

DILLENIACEAE

Hibbertia dentata R. Brown ex De Candolle

Twining Guinea Flower **Ss, Temp Rf**

A shy scrambling vine with toothed leaves, moderately common in sheltered gullies on sandstone and clay soils. A really beautiful species. 'So often does it display its flaunting beauty in our hedges that, perhaps, the appellation of the hedge pride might suit it.'[5]

Range: NSW coast, Blue Mountains, Qld, Vic. **Leaves:** sparsely toothed, often purplish, distant on the stem. **Flowers:** YELLOW, with 30 or more stamens completely surrounding 3 hairless carpels. **Flowering time:** spring and early summer. **Name:** *dentata* = Lat. toothed.

Hibbertia scandens (Willdenow) Gilg

Golden Guinea Flower **Ss, Temp Rf**

A vigorous scrambler with dense foliage. One of our most spectacular native flowers. Common and widespread in the area, preferring sunny places on better soils. It is salt resistant

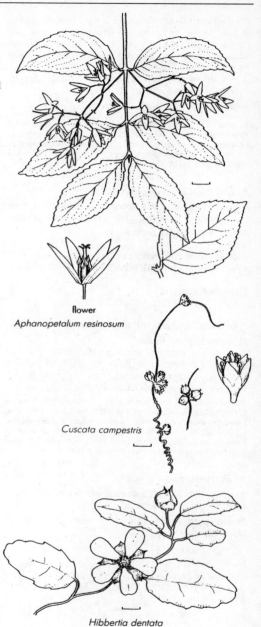

flower

Aphanopetalum resinosum

Cuscata campestris

Hibbertia dentata

and often planted near the sea. The brilliant red succulent fruits (attractive to birds) are clustered on the old sepals.

Range: NSW coast, ranges north from Sydney, into Qld. **Leaves:** large, shiny above, often hairy below, entire or toothed, moderately tough. New growth is covered in cotton wool. **Flowers:** GOLDEN YELLOW, to 9cm wide, with 30 or more stamens completely surrounding 3-7 hairless carpels. **Flowering time:** spring and summer. **Name:** *scandens* = Lat. climbing.

FABACEAE

• *Desmodium* Desvaux

A pantropical genus of about 450 species, with 37 in Australia.

The distinctive pods break easily into segments and are adapted for travel. William Woolls wrote ' . . . it is almost impossible to walk in the bush during the summer months without finding some of the joints adhering to the clothes. This arises from the circumstance of the pods being covered with minute hooked bristles.'[6]

Name: *Desmodium* = Gk. *desmos*, a bond or ligament, referring to joints in pods; or *desmodion*, a little chain, also referring to the pods.

Desmodium brachypodum A. Gray
Ss

A scrambling plant with ascending stems, hairless or nearly so. Found in wetter sheltered forests. Uncommon.

Range: NSW coast, north from Sydney into Qld and NG; also in Vic. **Leaflets:** 3; 2-6cm long, hairless, soft, thin-textured. **Flowers:** tiny, PINK, in axillary or terminal racemes. **Flowering time:** much of the year. **Name:** *brachypodum* = Gk. short-pod.

Desmodium rhytidophyllum Mueller
Ss

A scrambling or prostrate plant, rusty-hairy or felty all over, with stems mostly under 50cm long. Found in wetter sheltered forests. Uncommon.

Range: NSW coast into Qld. **Leaflets:** 3; 2-6cm long, softly furry both sides, soft-textured. **Flowers:** tiny, PINK, in axillary and terminal racemes. **Flowering time:** much of the year. **Name:** *rhytidophyllum* = Gk. wrinkle-leaved. **Similar species:** *Kennedia rubicunda*.

Desmodium varians Endlicher
Ss, Cumb

A humble prostate creeper, hairless or nearly so, found in grasslands and sheltered wetter forests.

Range: NSW coast, ranges and inland districts, Qld, Vic and Tas. **Leaflets:** 3, less than 25mm long. **Flowers:** tiny, PINK, in terminal racemes. **Flowering time:** much of the year. **Name:** *varians* = Lat. variable, referring to the habit and leaves.

• *Dipogon* Liebm.

A genus of African climbers, with 1 species naturalised in mainland Australia.

Name: *Dipogon* = double-bearded, referring to lines of stiff hairs on each side of the style. These collect and retain the pollen as it falls from the anthers, presumably aiding in self-fertilisation.

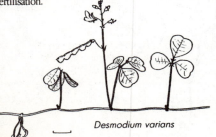

Desmodium varians

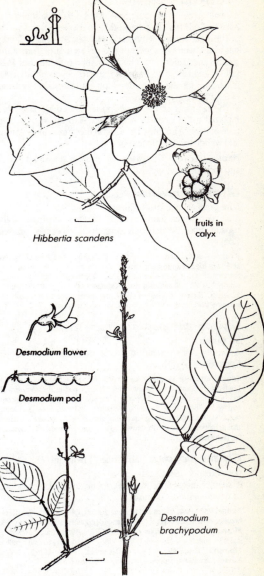

Hibbertia scandens

fruits in calyx

Desmodium flower

Desmodium pod

Desmodium brachypodum

Desmodium rhytidophyllum

Dipogon lignosus • (Linnaeus) Verdc.
Ss, Cumb

A beautiful flowering climber with diamond shaped leaflets and bright pink flowers. Introduced as a garden plant and now found wild near habitation.

Range: all states except Tas. **Leaflets:** 3, diamond-shaped, thin, soft, hairless. **Flowers:** bright PINK, fading to mauve, on long slender stalks; in short dense racemes. **Flowering time:** spring. **Name:** *lignosus* = Lat. woody.

• *Glycine* Linnaeus (Glis-I-nee)

A small genus of climbing peas distributed in Australia and Asia. Australia has 14 of the world's 16 species.

The most famous member is *G. max*, the Soya Bean, China's gift to the world; a source of protein for a large part of the world's population, and a trade commodity worth over $A20 billion annually. The Australian species represent a crucial gene pool for the future development of resistant varieties of Soya Bean.

The tap-roots of the local species are edible and were reported to be eaten by Aborigines. They are supposed to taste of licorice but the Cribbs found them 'extremely fibrous and without noticeable flavour'.[7]

Name: *Glycine* = Gk. *glykys*, sweet, from the sweet leaves and roots of some species.

Glycine clandestina Wendland

Love Creeper **Ss, Castl, Cumb**

A slender twiner, found in moist situations on better soils, usually amongst dense undergrowth, especially grasses. Common.

Range: coast and ranges of NSW; Qld, Vic and Tas. **Leaflets:** elongated, 20-58mm long, 1-2mm wide (note the absence of an extra segment on the central leaflet stalk—see illustration). **Flowers:** variable in colour, mainly MAUVE. **Flowering time:** October-December. **Pods:** with 9-12 seeds. **Name:** *clandestina* = hidden, referring to the flowers, probably meaning that they are often hidden amongst other plants.

Glycine microphylla (Bentham) Tindale

Ss, Cumb

A slender twiner, found in similar situations to the above. Common.

Range: extensive in south-eastern Australia, including Tas and Qld. **Leaflets:** 15-50mm long, 3-6mm wide (first formed leaflets very broad, can be confused with *G. tabacina*). **Flowers:** variable in colour, mostly MAUVE, 4-7mm long (excluding stalks); inflorescences 30-70mm, occasionally to 100mm, long (including main stalk). **Flowering time:** mainly spring-summer. **Pods:** with 3-6 seeds. **Name:** *microphylla* = Lat. small-leaved.

Glycine tabacina (Labillardière) Bentham

Love Creeper **Ss, Cumb**

A slender trailer (not twining), found in similar situations to *G. clandestina*. Common.

Range: NSW coast, ranges and western districts, Qld and Vic. **Leaflets:** broader than other species; width:length proportions greater than 1:3. **Flowers:** variable in colour, mostly MAUVE, 6-10mm long (excluding stalks); inflorescences 80-250mm long (including main stalk). **Flowering time:** mostly October-December. **Pods:** with 3-6 seeds. **Name:** *tabacina* = of tobacco, referring to the leaf colour.

• *Hardenbergia* Bentham

An endemic genus of 3 species, distributed in all states.

Name: *Hardenbergia* = in honour of Frances or Franziska, Countess of Hardenberg, sister of Baron Huegel (1795-1870). While he toured in Australia and the Phillipines she cared for his specimens in Germany.

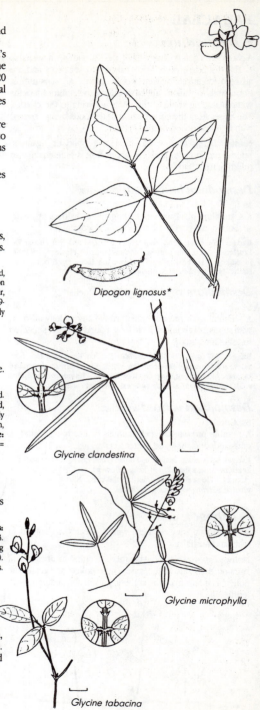

Dipogon lignosus *

Glycine clandestina

Glycine microphylla

Glycine tabacina

Hardenbergia violacea (Schneevoogt) Stearn

Hardenbergia, False Sarsaparilla **Ss, Cumb, Castl**

An attractive scrambler or twiner with rich purple pea-flowers 'sprawling over stones and bare earth in a glorious flush of rosy purple'.[8] Common in woodland, often seen growing as a scrambler on bare roadsides.

The leaves can be boiled to make a slightly sweet and reasonably pleasant tea.

Range: all states except WA, in coast and mountain areas. **Leaves:** 4-15cm long, narrow-oblong to heart-shaped, with prominent network veins, tough and stiff. Where the plant grows in an exposed place, the leaves stand erect in the heat of day and return to horizontal in the evening. **Flowers:** PURPLE with pale yellow centres, small, in axillary racemes. **Flowering time:** spring (finished by mid-October). **Name:** *violacea* = Violet-like, referring to the flowers.

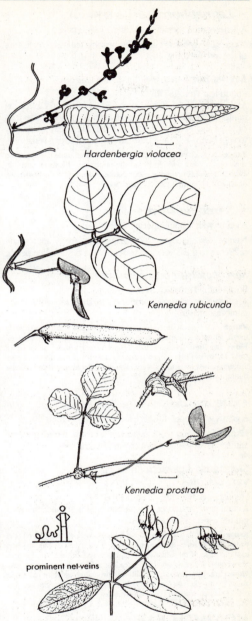

Hardenbergia violacea

Kennedia rubicunda

Kennedia prostrata

prominent net-veins

Oxylobium scandens var. scandens

• *Kennedia* Ventenat

An endemic genus with 15 species of climbers, found in all states.

Name: *Kennedia* = after Mr John Kennedy, a botanically minded nurseryman of the firm of Lee and Kennedy, at Hammersmith, near London. In the early nineteenth century his nursery was the main centre for the propagation and sale of Australian plants to British collectors.

Kennedia prostrata R. Brown ex Aiton

Running Postman **Ss**

A prostrate creeping plant with stems usually 50-100cm long. Found in sunny places in heath and woodland. Uncommon in the Sydney area. The flowers are a bright post box red.

Range: NSW coastal districts and southern ranges into Vic, Tas and SA. **Leaflets:** 3, with wavy margins, grey-hairy below, with broad stipules 4-8mm long, arising from finely grey-hairy stems. **Flowers:** bright RED. The flower stalk is encircled near the base by a distinctive broad pointed bracteole 4-10mm wide. **Flowering time:** spring. **Name:** *prostrata* = Lat. lying down.

Kennedia rubicunda (Schneevoogt) Ventenat

Dusky Coral Pea **Ss, Cumb**

A robust twiner with large red pea-flowers and stems several metres long. Abundant in a wide variety of sunny places.

Aborigines sucked nectar from the flowers and used the stems as a string for securing objects.

Range: NSW coast, Blue Mountains, Qld and Vic. **Leaflets:** 3, variable in size and shape, narrow-oblong to oval, rusty-hairy below. **Flowers:** RED with black markings, rather like a Sturt's Desert Pea. **Flowering time:** spring and summer. **Name:** *rubicunda* = Lat. ruby-red.

Oxylobium scandens (Smith) Bentham var. *scandens*

Cumb

A scrambling or climbing shrub found in forests on clay soils. Not common locally.

Range: NSW coast and Qld. **Leaves:** very blunt, with a small point, prominent net veins and recurved margins. The stems are cylindrical. **Flowers:** PALE ORANGE, in small cymes in the axils, or terminal. **Flowering time:** most of the year. **Name:** *scandens* = Lat. climbing.

MENISPERMACEAE

A family of woody rainforest climbers with about 350 species in 65 genera, distributed widely in the tropics. There are 21 species in 12 genera in Australia. All species are dioecious with insignificant flowers often growing on old woody stems.

• *Legnephora* Miers (leg-NEFF-or-a)

A genus with 3 species, including 1 in Australia.

Name: *Legnephora* = Gk. border-bearing, referring to a feature of the fruit anatomy.

Legnephora moorei (F. Mueller) Miers

Round-leaf Vine **STRf**

A tall vigorous rainforest climber, fairly common in subtropical rainforest in the Royal National Park. It grows in the tops of trees and is rarely visible, but the fallen leaves are easy to spot because of their unusual shape and strong venation.

Range: NSW coastal areas and Qld. **Leaves:** rounded, with strong venation, to 20cm wide, paler on the underside. **Flowers:** small, in cymes. **Flowering time:** summer. **Name:** *moorei* = after Charles Moore, director of the Royal Botanic Gardens, Sydney, 1848-96.

• *Sarcopetalum* F. Mueller

A genus with a single species.

Name: *Sarcopetalum* = Gk. flesh-petals, a very appropriate reference to the colour and texture of the tiny swollen petals.

Sarcopetalum harveyanum F. Mueller

Pearl Vine **Temp Rf, STRf**

A climber or scrambler, common in sheltered gullies and rainforest margins.

Range: NSW coastal areas, Vic and Qld. **Leaves:** heart-shaped, fairly tough, glossy, on long stiff stalks, hairless. **Flowers:** tiny, in racemes. **Flowering time:** spring-summer. **Name:** *harveyanum* = in honour of Dr W. H. Harvey (1811-66), professor of botany at Trinity College, Dublin, a distinguished collector of algae, who worked with Ferdinand Mueller during a visit to Australia.

• *Stephania* Loureiro (steff-AIN-ee-a)

A genus with about 40 species, including 3 in Australia.

Name: *Stephania* = Gk. *stephanos*, a crown, referring to the anthers being joined into a crown-like structure.

Stephania japonica (Thunberg) Miers var. *discolor*

Stephania, Snake Vine **Temp Rf, STRf**

A climber or scrambler, common in rainforests and sheltered gullies, especially near the sea.

Range: NSW coast and ranges north from the Sydney area, Qld, NT and widespread in Asia. **Leaves:** heart-shaped, peltate (i.e. stalk attached to the middle of the leaf surface), firm-textured, but not stiff, hairless. **Flowers:** GREENISH, small, in spreading axillary compound umbels. **Flowering time:** summer. **Fruit:** a shiny yellow-orange or red drupe about 5mm wide. **Name:** *japonica* = Japanese, as the species was first collected there, *discolor* = paler on one side.

MONIMIACEAE

• *Palmeria* F. Mueller (pah-MEER-ee-a)

A genus with about 20 species in South-east Asia and Australia, where there are 3 endemic species.

Name: *Palmeria* = after Sir James Palmer (1803-1871), businessman, pastoralist and first president of the Vic Legislative Council.

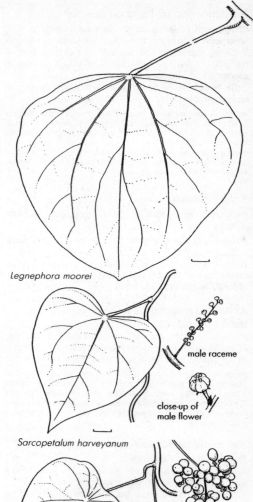

Legnephora moorei

male raceme

close-up of male flower

Sarcopetalum harveyanum

fruits

Stephania japonica var. discolor

Palmeria scandens F. Mueller

Anchor Vine **STRf**

A rainforest climber, sometimes appearing shrubby when young. Common in subtropical rainforest in the Royal National Park. Also occasionally recorded from sandstone gullies in other parts of the area (e.g. Toongabbie).

It climbs by means of leading stems equipped with short hook-like side-branches*. The flowers have a strong sweet smell and appear to be pollinated by small pollen-eating beetles.

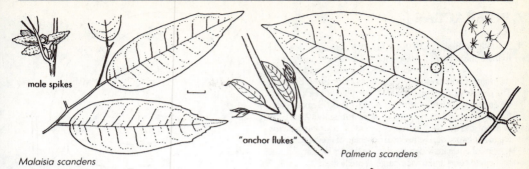

male spikes

"anchor flukes"

Malaisia scandens

Palmeria scandens

Range: NSW coastal areas and Qld. **Leaves:** opposite, broad, flat, paper-textured, rough on both sides due to small stiff star-hairs. **Flowers:** unisexual (dioecious), WHITE-PALE GREEN, female flowers spherical, about 3mm wide, with a small orifice; male flowers cup-shaped, about 10mm wide. **Flowering time:** winter. **Name:** *scandens* = Lat. climbing.

* '*Palmeria* is remarkable as an example of a rare climbing method. The plant sends up tall, naked shoots, eight to ten feet long. At the nodes, short branches develop in the form of an anchor fluke, and as the tall, flexible shoot sways about in the wind, the flukes catch over some neighbouring branch and hold tightly. One interesting little point is the thickening of the fluke where it joins the stem; just where the strain will be greatest, it is reinforced.'[9]

MORACEAE

• *Malaisia* Blanco (mal-AYZ-ee-a)

A genus with a single species.

Name: *Malaisia* = from Malaysia, where it was first collected.

Malaisia scandens (Loureiro) Planchon

Burny Vine, Crow Ash **STRf**
A robust climber with woody stems, found in subtropical rainforest in the Royal National Park and the Illawarra. Its climbing equipment consists of long cane-like leading stems, densely cloaked with stiff hairs. The hairs are bent downward and help support the stem wherever it touches another plant (it is impossible to slide one's fingers up the stem!).

Range: NSW coast, Lord Howe Island, Qld, NT, Malaysia, east Asia, and the Pacific. **Leaves:** 8-12cm long, alternate, two-ranked, spreading, fairly thick, tough, stiff, glossy, usually toothed on the upper half, dark-green above, satin and paler below. **Flowers:** unisexual (dioecious), tiny, axillary, the males in cylindrical spikes 4-12mm long, the female in cauliflower-like heads 3-4mm wide. **Flowering time:** winter (or irregularly). **Name:** *scandens* = Lat. climbing.

PASSIFLORACEAE

Passion flowers, Passionfruits
A family of climbers with over 500 species in 12 genera, mainly in tropical South America and Africa. There are 14 species in 2 genera in Australia.
  Passiflora edulis*, the commercial Black Passionfruit, is naturalised in Sydney bushland.

• *Passiflora* Linnaeus

A genus with about 370 species (350 in the Americas),

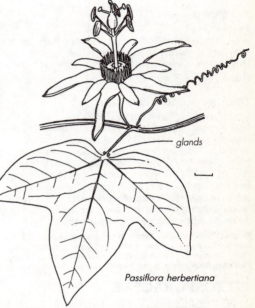

glands

Passiflora herbertiana

including 3 native species and 7 naturalised American Passionfruits in Australia.

Name: *Passiflora* = Lat. passion-flower, from the resemblance of the sexual parts to the shape of a crucifix.

Passiflora herbertiana Ker

Ss
A vigorous climber with stems to many metres long. Found in wetter sclerophyll forest in gullies. Rare in the area. Recorded in the past from the Hacking River, Lane Cover River, and the Nepean River at Douglas Park. More common in the Blue Mountains and north of the Hawkesbury.

Range: NSW coast and ranges, except the southern tablelands, and Qld. **Flowers:** GREENISH-WHITE to YELLOW-ORANGE. **Flowering time:** spring-early summer. **Name:** *herbertiana* = after the family name of Lord Carnarvon, in whose garden the type specimen was raised, from seeds sent to England by the exploring botanist Allan Cunningham. **Note:** *P. cinnabarina* is a very similar species, much less common, whose most obvious difference is the colour of the flower, a brilliant red. It has been recorded a number of times in the Illawarra. The leaves are similar but lack glands.

PIPERACEAE

Peppers

A family with about 2100 species in 5 genera, widespread in the tropics. There are 9 species in 2 genera in Australia.

The plants contain volatile oils and resins which make them an important source of food flavours and medicines. The drupes of *Piper nigrum* are the source of black pepper. *Piper betle* supplies the leaves in which the betel nut (a palm nut) is wrapped before being chewed throughout Asia, parts of Africa and the West Indies. The roots of *Piper methysticum* are made into Kava, the national beverage of Polynesia. Other species of *Piper* are widely used in the tropics for fish poisons, snake-bite cures and a wide range of medicines.

• *Piper* Linnaeus

Peppers

A genus with about 2000 species, including 8 species in rainforests in eastern Australia. They climb by means of clusters of short aerial roots which grasp the limbs of trees.

Name: *Piper* = the Latin name for pepper.

Piper novae-hollandiae Miquel

Giant Pepper Vine, Native Pepper **STRf**

A tall vigorous climber found in subtropical rainforest in the Royal National Park, where it is fairly common. It has medicinal properties. The plant was chewed by Aborigines for sore gums. Queensland's famous medical investigator, Dr Joseph Bancroft, found it an excellent stimulant tonic to the mucous membrane, and used it in the treatment of gonorrhoea. The active principle, which Bancroft extracted with ether, has a "warm, aromatic, pleasant taste, and a benumbing effect on the tongue, when applied to it in minute quantity".[10]

Range: NSW coast and Qld. **Leaves:** glossy, dark green, somewhat thick, hairless. **Flowers:** male flowers small, in a dense cylindrical spike, female flowers ovoid. **Fruits:** red, in dense clusters, in January-February. **Flowering time:** spring. **Name:** *novae-hollandiae* = New Holland.

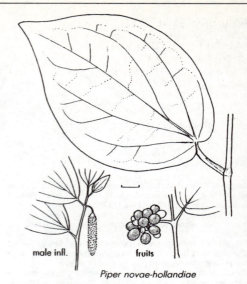

male infl.　　fruits

Piper novae-hollandiae

PITTOSPORACEAE

• *Billardiera* Smith

An endemic genus of climbers with 9 species, about half restricted to south-western WA.

Name: *Billardiera* = in honour of James Julian la Billardiere (known as Labillardière), botanist on the 1791-93 French expedition in search of La Pérouse, under D'Entrecastaux. He made extensive collections at Cape Leeuwin (WA) and in Tas.

Billardiera scandens Smith

Apple Berry, Dumplings **Ss, Castl, Cumb**

A slender climber or scrambler with stems to about 3m long. Common in woodland. The fruits are edible and their reputation as a tasty delight is well deserved, although the denizens of the bush leave little for humans to enjoy. Note: they are really horrible to eat unless purple.

Range: coast and ranges of all eastern states. **Leaves:** soft, often furry, pale green, undulate. **Flowers:** CREAM, drooping, solitary, terminal. **Flowering time:** spring. **Fruit:** green, becoming purple when ripe, to 3cm long, furry. **Name:** *scandens* = Lat. climbing.

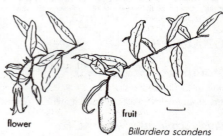

flower　　fruit

Billardiera scandens

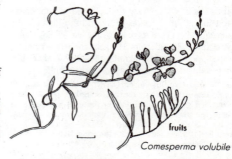

fruits

Comesperma volubile

POLYGALACEAE

Comesperma volubile Labillardière

Love creeper **Ss**

A pretty slender twiner with tangled green stems. Widespread in heath and woodland, but not common in the area. It is called Love Creeper because 'it ties itself up in true lovers' knots'.[11]

Range: coast and ranges in all eastern states. **Leaves:** soft, flat, often with irregular margins, to 3cm long. **Flowers:** RICH PINKISH PURPLE. **Flowering time:** spring. **Name:** *volubile* = Lat. twining.

POLYGONACEAE

• *Muehlenbeckia* Meisner

Lignums

A genus of small climbers or shrubs with 15 species in Australia, NZ, NG and South America. There are 10 species in Australia, distributed in all states.

Name: *Muehlenbeckia* = after Henri Gustav Muehlenbeck (1798-1845), a French physician and botanical collector. Lignum is usually Latin for wood, but in this case it is a corruption of *Polygonum*, in which genus the species were previously placed.

Muehlenbeckia gracillima Meisner

Slender Lignum **Ss**

A slender twiner, found in wetter sclerophyll forest and gullies. Uncommon in the area.

Range: NSW coast, Blue Mountains and Qld. **Leaves:** soft, thin-textured, with finely undulating crenate margins, to 7cm long. **Flowers:** GREENISH, about 4mm wide, in axillary racemes. **Flowering time:** summer. **Name:** *gracillima* = Lat. slender.

RANUNCULACEAE

• *Clematis* Linnaeus

A genus of climbers with about 250 species, including 4 species endemic to Australia. The abundant cascades of white flowers in spring are a beautiful sight. Both Aborigines and early colonists used the crushed leaves to cure headaches by inhaling the strong and sharp aroma. The Cribbs explain the effect '. . . an unexpected burning sensation in the nasal passages. Headaches are forgotten as the patient wonders whether the top of his head has blown off.'[12]

The fruits form a spidery aggregate, each with a long hairy tail (formed from the persistent style).

Note that the juvenile leaves are very different; consisting of a single large dark green leaflet, with pale markings around the veins.

Name: *Clematis* = Gk. diminutive of *klema*, a vine branch.

Clematis aristata R. Brown ex De Candolle

Old Man's Beard, Traveller's Joy **Ss, Cumb**

A vigorous twining climber with masses of white flowers in spring. Common in sandstone gullies, and in forests on the Cumberland Plain.

Range: NSW coast and ranges, Vic, Tas and WA. **Leaves:** opposite, 3-foliate; the leaflets toothed, with 3 parallel veins. **Flowers:** WHITE, 35-50mm wide, anthers tipped by a slender appendage longer than the anther; in large, tumbling cymes. **Flowering time:** October-November. **Name:** *aristata* = Lat. bearing a fine bristle, referring to the anther appendage.

Clematis glycinoides De Candolle

Forest Clematis, Old Man's Beard **Ss, Cumb**

Similar to *C. aristata*, except the leaves lack teeth and the anthers have a short inconspicuous appendage. Common in the area, in similar habitats.

Range: NSW coast and ranges, Vic and Tas. **Leaves:** similar to *C. aristata* except toothless, or with a single tooth near the base, smaller and thinner.

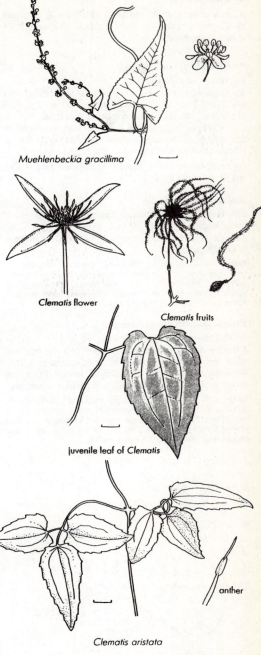

Muehlenbeckia gracillima

Clematis flower

Clematis fruits

juvenile leaf of *Clematis*

anther

Clematis aristata

Flowers: 25-40mm wide, similar to *C. aristata*, except for the short anther appendage. **Flowering time:** August-October. **Name:** *glycinoides* = resembling *Glycine*, a small pea climber.

ROSACEAE

A family of trees, shrubs and herbs with about 3370 species in 122 genera worldwide. There are about 65 species in 24 genera in Australia.

• *Rubus* Linnaeus

Raspberries, Blackberries

A genus of thorny vines and scramblers with about 250 species worldwide. There are 15 species in Australia, only about 7 of which are native, distributed in the eastern states.

The fruits are aggregates of succulent drupelets. All native and introduced species are edible. Some are not as tasty as others, but all are worth trying.

Name: *Rubus* = the Latin name for the blackberry, from *ruber*, red, the colour of the fruit.

Rubus hillii F. Mueller

Broad-leaved Bramble, Molucca Bramble, Native Raspberry   **STRf**

A robust climber with long thorny stems. Found in rainforest in Royal National Park.

Range: NSW coasts, also Vic, Qld and SA.   **Leaves:** simple, satin and finely hairy above with impressed veins, rusty-felty below, with 2 lobes at the base.   **Flowers:** PINK, in a terminal raceme.   **Flowering time:** summer.   **Name:** *hillii* = after a Reverend Hill, who sent the type specimen to Mueller, from the Brisbane River.

Rubus parvifolius Linnaeus

Native Rasberry   **Temp Rf, Ss**

A small scrambler with stems to a metre or more long, and white leaf undersides. Found in moist forests in valleys. Uncommon in the area (e.g. Royal National Park), but common in the Illawarra and valleys in the Blue Mountains.

Range: coast, ranges and inland slopes throughout eastern Australia, including Tas and SA; also widespread in eastern Asia.   **Leaves:** pinnate, with 3 (rarely 5) leaflets, with deeply impressed veins above and a layer of white felt below.   **Flowers:** PINK, in terminal panicles.   **Flowering time:** spring.   **Name:** *parvifolius* = Lat. small-leaved.

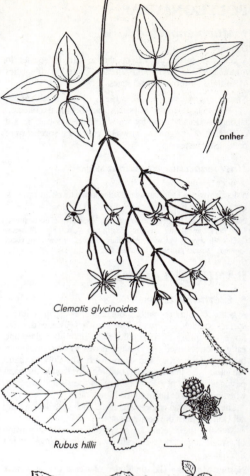

anther

Clematis glycinoides

Rubus hillii

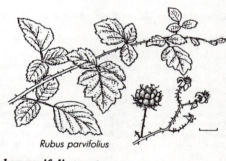

Rubus parvifolius

Rubus rosifolius

Rubus rosifolius Smith

Temp Rf, Ss

A weak ascending shrub, forming dense thickets in sunny places in gullies, usually near rainforest. Uncommon locally, mainly in the Royal National Park. One of the best eating of the native species.

Range: NSW coast and ranges, Tas, SA, Vic and Qld.   **Leaves:** pinnate, with usually 7 leaflets, thin, soft, light-green, finely hairy, green on both surfaces. **Flowers:** WHITE, terminal. **Flowering time:** spring-summer. **Name:** *rosifolius* = rose-leaved

Rubus sp. aff. *moorei*

Bush Lawyer   **STRf**
A robust thorny climber. Found in rainforest in Royal National Park.

Range: NSW coastal areas and Qld. **Leaves:** compound, with 5 leaflets, arranged palmately. **Flowers:** WHITE, in short axillary racemes. **Flowering time:** spring-summer. **Name:** *moorei* = after Charles Moore, director of the Royal Botanic Gardens, Sydney, 1848-96.

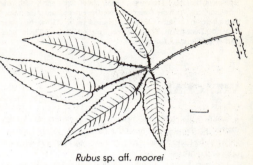

Rubus sp. aff. moorei

Rubus ulmifolius* Schott

Blackberry   **Ss, Cumb**
A scrambling vine with stout thorny branches ('canes'), forming dense thickets. A nasty pest in pastures, wastelands, and disturbed bushland throughout eastern Australia, very hard to eradicate due to its deep woody root system. Originally a native of Europe (where it is deciduous, although here it is evergreen). Now a declared noxious weed in most states. The seeds are spread by birds.

It was first recorded in Australia in 1843. In 1863, Dr Bennet, President of the NSW Acclimatization Society, recommended that members of the society busy themselves with planting blackberries to prepare for the arrival of the curassow (a South American bird, almost as big as a turkey, which thrived on them).

The fruits (in January-February) are edible and much collected for jams and pies. Harvesting of wild blackberries was a local industry. As recently as 1914, A. G. Hamilton reported that 80-100 tons were sent to Sydney jam factories from Bulli alone.

Range: NSW coast and ranges, and Vic. **Leaves:** dark green, dull above, pale bluish below, toothed, with sharp recurved thorns on the mid-vein below, extending down to the branches. **Flowers:** WHITE, in terminal panicles. **Flowering time:** November-January. **Name:** *ulmifolius* = Elm-leaved. **Note:** *'Rubus fruticosus'* is a broad title for many introduced species of blackberries, some of which are extremely difficult to distinguish. Fortunately it is enough to know that *R. ulmifolius* is by far the most locally predominant of these species.

RUBIACEAE

• *Morinda* Linnaeus

A mainly tropical genus of climbers with about 80 species, including 6 species in Australia, distributed in the eastern mainland states.

Name: *Morinda* = Lat. *morus*, mulberry, *indicus*, Indian i.e. Indian Mulberry.

Morinda jasminoides A. Cunningham

Jasmine Morinda   **STRF, Temp Rf**
A scrambling climber in rainforest and humid gullies with stems to a few metres long. Not common, but widespread in the area. It well deserves its name 'jasmin-like' not only from the tumbling masses of soft leaves but also from the gentle orange-blossom fragrance of the flowers.

The leaves have conspicuous domatia. The fruit is edible when soft, with, a 'rotten cheese flavour'.[13]

Range: NSW coast and ranges, and Qld. **Leaves:** opposite, 2-ranked (appearing pinnate), glossy above, duller below, thin-textured, flat, with

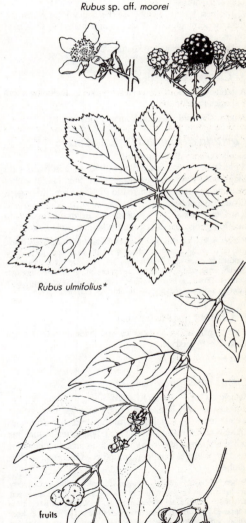

Rubus ulmifolius *

fruits

Morinda jasminoides   inflorescence

prominent domatia. **Flowers:** CREAM, about 8mm wide, with large orange anthers; 3 or more flowers clustered together, joined at the ovaries; each cluster on a stalk, usually in terminal pairs. **Flowering time:** November-December. **Fruit:** an orange aggregate, 10-12mm wide. **Name:** *jasminoides* = Jasmin-like.

VITACEAE

Grapes

A family with about 700 species in 12 genera worldwide, mainly in the tropics. Australia has about 34 species in 5 genera. Most species are perennial woody climbers with leaf-opposed tendrils.

The best known member of the family is *Vitis vinifera*, the European cultivated grape, an important crop since early times.

The family is related to Rhamnaceae.

• *Cayratia* A. L. de Jussieu

A genus with about 45 species worldwide, including about 8 species in Australia.

Name: *Cayratia* = derived from an Indian name.

Cayratia clematidea (F. Mueller) Domin

Slender Grape   **STRf margins**

A plucky herbaceous scrambler, with stems mostly under 1m long, found on the edges of rainforest or in humid gullies near the sea. Locally restricted to the Royal and Ku-ring-gai Chase National Parks.

It forms a large tuber beneath the ground from which a new foliage sprouts each spring and dies away in autumn.

Range: NSW coast and Qld. **Leaves:** compound, the leaflets fleshy, soft, dull, usually sparsely sprinkled with soft short hairs. Each leaf is opposed by either tendrils or flowers. The stems are striate. **Flowers:** GREEN, small, with 4 petals, in dense axillary cymes. **Flowering time:** summer. **Fruit:** a berry, 5-6mm wide. **Name:** *clematidea* = like *Clematis*, a climber with slightly similar leaves, in Ranunculaceae.

• *Cissus* Linnaeus (SISS-us)

A genus with about 350 species worldwide, including about 18 species in Australia.

Name: *Cissus* = Gk. *kissos,* ivy.

Cissus antarctica Ventenat

Kangaroo Grape   **Temp Rf, STRf**

A robust woody climber with stems to a few metres long. Locally restricted to rainforest in the Royal and Kuring-gai Chase National Parks. The fruit is edible when mature, but rather acid. Aborigines used the stems as an aid for climbing trees by placing a long loop around both the trunk and the climber.

Range: NSW coasts and Qld. **Leaves:** grey-green or dark green, glossy, grey-hairy above, densely rusty-felty below, toothed on the upper part, fairly tough. Domatia are present in the underside vein axils. Each leaf is opposed by either tendrils or flowers. **Flowers:** GREENISH, in dense axillary cymes. **Flowering time:** summer. **Fruit:** glossy black berries, about 10mm wide. **Name:** *antarctica* = Lat. opposite the north pole, i.e. connected with far southern regions.

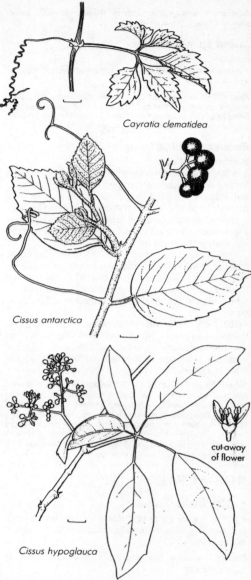

Cayratia clematidea

Cissus antarctica

Cissus hypoglauca

cut-away of flower

Cissus hypoglauca A. Gray

Water Vine, Native Grape   **Ss, Temp Rf, STRf**

A robust woody vine with stems to several metres long. Common in humid places near the sea and in rainforest.

The black grapes can be sweet and refreshing to eat, but are more often astringent. They were consumed by Aborigines and used by early settlers to make jam or jelly. They have much mucous, and have been used medicinally, e.g. as a gargle for a sore throat.

The woody stem may grow to thigh-width in rainforest:

'Sometimes these huge cables reach from the top of one tree to another at some distance, the slack hanging within a few feet of the ground and providing a natural swing where one can sit and enjoy a rest and a pipe after lunch in the brush.'[14]

A short length of stem cut at both ends is a source of drinking water, hence the common name.

Range: NSW coast and ranges, Qld and Vic. **Leaves:** compound, with 5 leaflets palmately arranged; the leaflets are waxy, fairly tough, irregularly toothed on the upper half or sometimes entire, pale on the undersurface. Each leaf is opposed by either tendrils or flowers. **Flowers:** small, BRIGHT YELLOW, in dense cymes. **Flowering time:** summer. **Name:** *hypoglauca* = Gk. not quite blue-green, referring to the leaf undersides.

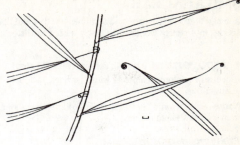
Flagellaria indica

• MONOCOTYLEDONS

FLAGELLARIACEAE

A small, mainly tropical, family of robust reed-like herbs and climbers, with 7 species, including a single species in Australia.

• *Flagellaria* Linnaeus

A small genus of cane-like climbers with one species in Australia.

Name: *Flagellaria* = Lat. *flagellum*, a whip.

Flagellaria indica Linnaeus

Whip Vine, Supplejack, Twining Bamboo   **STRf**
A climber with strong cane-like stems 10m or more long, reaching to the tops of trees. Rare in the area. Restricted to subtropical rainforest in the Royal National Park. It supports itself with stiff tendrils formed from coiled leaf tips. Aborigines in Arnhem land use thin strips of stem to bind baskets and sew together sections of the hulls of bark canoes. It also was used medicinally in northern NSW and Qld: the astringent leaves were used to heal wounds, the tips were applied to sore eyes, and it was also used as a contraceptive.

Range: coastal rainforests from north-western WA through Qld to NSW; also tropical Africa, India, South-east Asia, Taiwan and Polynesia. The Sydney area is the southern limit. **Leaves:** to 30cm long, the bases form closed sheaths around the stem and the tips are drawn out to slender but extremely tough coiling projections. **Flowers:** tiny, membranous, bisexual, in a broad much-branched terminal panicle. **Flowering time:** summer. **Name:** *indica* = Lat. pertaining to India.

PHILESIACEAE

A family of shrubs and climbers with 12 species in 6 genera worldwide, mainly in South America and Australasia.

• *Eustrephus* R. Brown

A genus of climbers with a single species.

Name: *Eustrephus* = Gk. well-twined, plaited.

Eustrephus latifolius R. Brown

Wombat Berry   **Temp Rf, Ss**
A climber with striate green stems usually several metres long. Common in the area in moist sheltered forests and rainforest gullies. The fruits are edible succulent orange berries. The

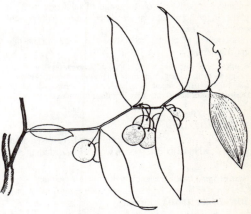
Eustrephus latifolius

plant produces a cluster of crisp white tuberous roots which are edible raw.

Range: NSW coast and ranges, Qld, Vic, NG, New Caledonia and the Loyalty Islands. **Leaves:** thin, flexible, with numerous parallel veins, usually several on short lateral zig-zag branchlets. **Flowers:** WHITE-PURPLE, drooping, with fringed petals, lily-like, in clusters in the leaf-joints. **Flowering time:** spring. **Name:** *latifolius* = Lat. broad-leaved.

• *Geitonoplesium* A. Cunningham ex J.D. Hooker
(guy-ton-o-PLEEZ-ee-um)

A genus with a single species.

Name: *Geitonoplesium* = Gk. *geiton*, neighbour, *plesios*, near, from its closeness to the genus *Luzuriaga*.

Geitonoplesium cymosum
A. Cunningham ex W. J. Hooker

Scrambling Lily   **Temp Rf, Ss**
A climber with striate green stems tangling over trees and shrubs in sheltered forests and rainforest gullies. Common in the area.

Range: NSW coast and ranges, South-east Asia and New Caledonia. **Leaves:** 5-8cm long, dull green, rather stiff, with a raised central vein. **Flowers:** WHITE to purplish green, with yellow anthers. **Flowering time:** spring. **Name:** *cymosum* = Lat. having cymes.

SMILACACEAE

A family of woody climbers and scramblers, with about 250 species in 4 genera worldwide. Closely related to Liliaceae.

• *Ripogonum* J. R. & G. Forster (ry-po-GO-num)

A genus of rainforest climbers, with 7 species, including 5 in Australia.

Name: *Ripogonum* = Gk. *rhips*, wickerwork, *gonia*, a joint, from the many-jointed stems.

Ripogonum album R. Brown

White Supplejack **Temp Rf**
A robust rainforest climber, usually forming dense entanglements. Found on the edge of rainforest in deep gullies in the Royal National Park. Prickles are usually present on the larger branches.

Aborigines in coastal NSW used the stems for making crayfish traps.

Range: coastal rainforests from Vic to Qld. **Leaves:** opposite, tough, mostly about 10cm long,, with about 5 longitudinal veins. **Flowers:** GREENISH WHITE, bisexual, in axillary racemes. **Fruit:** red globular berries. **Name:** *album* = Lat. white, referring to the flowers.

• *Smilax* Linnaeus

A genus of shrubby climbers with tendrils (evolved from stipules), with about 250 species worldwide, including 3 in Australia.

Name: *Smilax* = the ancient Greek name for the plant.

Smilax australis R. Brown

Temp Rf, STRf
A robust thorny climber, common in subtropical rainforest. The green stems are as strong as rope and usually scattered with sharp thorns. It can form treacherous entanglements. 'A specimen of *Smilax* assisted much to render the thickets of this vale the more intricate . . . ' wrote Allan Cunningham in 1817.[15]

Range: NSW coast and ranges, Qld, Vic and Tas. **Leaves:** large (5-10cm long), tough and stiff, with 5 longitudinal veins, with a pair of tendrils at the base. **Flowering time:** spring. **Name:** *australis* = Lat. southern.

Smilax glyciphylla Smith

Native Sarsaparilla, Sweet Tea **Ss**
A small scrambler with wiry stems, very common in woodland and heath. It was the most famous bush tea of early colonial times.

A few boiled leaves in a pot produce a pleasant bitter-sweet brew. Local Aborigines sucked the leaves, perhaps medicinally. They yield a refreshing bitter flavour.

The first fleeters called it 'sweet tea' and believed it to be a good tonic and effective against scurvy. Captain Tench described it as 'a vegetable creeper found growing on the rocks, which yields, on infusion in hot water, a sweet astringent taste, whence it deserves its name: to its virtues the healthy state of the soldiery and convicts may be greatly attributed. It was drank universally' (1793).[16] William Woolls wrote

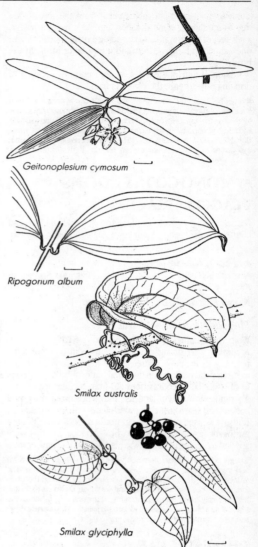

Geitonoplesium cymosum

Ripogonum album

Smilax australis

Smilax glyciphylla

'Excellent sarsaparilla may be obtained from it, and a few years since it was an article of export from this colony. Why it has ceased to be exported, I [am] not aware, nor can I say why so much foreign sarsaparilla is imported into the colony, when *smilax* exists in great abundance amongst us. Competent judges in England have pronounced the colonial sarsaparilla "excellent," and I have been informed that Dr Greenup, one of the most eminent medical men in the colony, regards it as a most useful medicine'.[17]

Range: NSW coast and northern tablelands, also Qld. **Leaves:** tough and stiff, with three parallel veins and a pair of short tendrils at the base of each stalk. **Flowers:** tiny, yellowish, unisexual (dioecious), in terminal umbels. **Flowering time:** spring-summer. **Fruits:** bunches of black glossy berries, in winter. **Name:** *glyciphylla* = Gk. sweet-leaved.

MISTLETOES

Mistletoes are parasitic shrubs, which draw part of their nourishment from the sap of host trees.

LORANTHACEAE

Mistletoes

A family of parasitic shrubs with about 950 species in about 65 genera, mainly distributed in the tropics and southern temperate parts of the world. Australia has 70 species in 12 genera.

The fruits are edible when ripe, with a sticky, gelatinous, glucose-rich pulp around a single seed. They are popular with birds, especially honeyeaters and mistletoe birds. The stickyness helps the seeds to adhere to the branches of trees when the birds are finished with them.

The leaves are dull and fleshy and often mimic the shape of the hosts. Sometimes the mimicry is so close that they are almost impossible to detect (e.g. *Amyema cambagei* on *Casuarina glauca*). The large red flowers are a conspicuous and beautiful sight. 'The Bastard Box is frequently much encumbered with the twining adhering *Loranthus auranticus* which "Scorning the soil, aloft she springs, Shakes her red plumes and clasps her golden wings".' wrote Allan Cunningham in 1817.

The flowers are arranged, usually in 3s, in geometrical cymes.

The family is of Gondwanan origin, related to the root-parasitic families Santalaceae and Olacaceae.

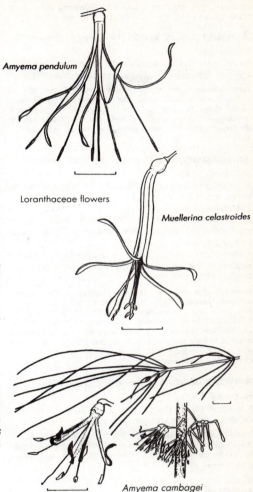

Amyema pendulum

Loranthaceae flowers

Muellerina celastroides

Amyema cambagei

• *Amyema* Tieghem (ay-me-EE-ma)

A genus with about 100 species, in Australia, south-east Asia and the western Pacific. There are about 36 species in Australia.

Name: *Amyema* = Gk. *a*, not, *myeo*, I point out anew, since until Tiegham's splitting of the huge old genus *Loranthus* in 1894, the divisions in the genus had not been pointed out.

Amyema cambagei (Blakely) Danser

She-oak Mistletoe **Cumb**

A mistletoe with ascending stems usually under 40cm long, found along the Nepean and Hawkesbury Rivers. Moderately common but almost impossible to detect unless flowering because the leaves so closely resemble the *Casuarina* host. The mimicry is so successful that it was not collected by a botanist until 1906.

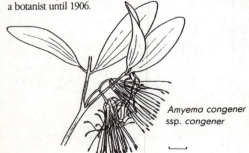

Amyema congener
ssp. congener

Hosts: *Casuarina glauca, Casuarina cunninghamiana*. **Range:** coast and ranges from the ACT to Cairns. **Leaves:** cylindrical, fleshy, drooping, soft, 6-15cm long, 1-1.3mm in diameter. **Flowers:** about 20mm long, PINK and finely felty outside, DEEP RED inside, in 3-flowered cymes. **Flowering time:** autumn-summer. **Name:** *cambagei* = after R. H. Cambage (1857-1928), surveyor with the Department of Mines, one time president of the Linnaean Society of NSW and of the Royal Society of NSW.

Amyema congener (Sieber ex Schultes & son) Tieghem **ssp.** *congener*

Ss

A mistletoe with erect or spreading stems to about 50cm long. Common in the area.

Hosts: many species, especially *Casuarina littoralis*, but not *Eucalyptus*. **Range:** from Merimbula, NSW, to the Torres Straight Islands, mainly in coastal districts. **Leaves:** to 6cm long, opposite, thick, fleshy, yellowish. **Flowers:** 25-30mm long, very attractive, with narrow recurved GREEN

petals and bright RED anthers and style. **Flowering time:** spring.
Name: *congener* = Lat. allied, i.e. closely related to other species.

Amyema gaudichaudii (De Candolle) Tieghem
Cumb, Castl

A mistletoe with erect stems usually under 40cm long. Fairly
common in swampy woodland on the Cumberland Plain.

Host: *Melaleuca decora* **Range:** Illawarra to Hunter River in NSW and
Darling Downs in Qld. **Leaves:** small (20-35mm long), erect, fleshy,
blunt. **Flowers:** small (7-10mm long), RED, erect. **Name:**
gaudichaudii = after Charles Gaudichaud, pharmacist and botanist on
the Freycinet expedition which visited Shark Bay and Port Jackson in
1818-19.

Amyema miquelii (Lehmann ex Miquel) Tieghem
Ss, Cumb

A mistletoe with drooping stems to 1.5m long. Uncommon
in the area
There are 2 forms:
• The 'type' form, found on *Eucalyptus* on the clay soils of
the Cumberland Plain, has glaucous leaves and large flowers
(2-3cm long).
• The 'Sydney' form, found on *Eucalyptus* on Sydney
sandstones, has green leaves and small flowers (15-18mm
long).

Hosts: *Eucalyptus* species. **Range:** widespread on the Australian
mainland. **Leaves:** drooping, fleshy, curved, 10-15cm long. **Flowers:**
RED, to 3cm long. **Name:** *miquelii* = after Freidrich Miquel (1811-71),
a Dutch Botanist who specialised in several families with Australian
species. **Note:** a guide to distinguish this species from *A. pendulum*
is that all its flowers have stalks, while the middle flower in each cyme
of *A. pendulum* is stalkless. The leaves are usually narrower and more
curved than *A. pendulum*.

Amyema pendulum (Sieber ex Sprengel) Tieghem
Ss, Cumb

A mistletoe with drooping stems to 1.5m long. Common in
the area, in both clay and sandstone areas.

Hosts: *Eucalyptus* species. **Range:** widespread in eastern Australia on
coasts, ranges and inland areas. **Leaves:** opposite, thick, fleshy, drooping,
10-20cm long, somewhat curved. **Flowers:** RED, 3-4cm long. **Name:**
pendulum = Lat. drooping.

• *Amylotheca* Tieghem

A genus with 5 species distributed in NG, South-east Asia
and eastern Australia. There are 2 Australian species.

Name: *Amylotheca* = Lat. *amylum*, starch, *theca*, case, referring
to the starchy fruits.

Amylotheca dictyophleba (F. Mueller) Tieghem
STRf

A spreading or drooping mistletoe with rounded fleshy leaves.
Rare in the area, restricted to rainforests in the Royal National
Park and Illawarra.

Hosts: various rainforest trees, and *Banksia integrifolia* in littoral
rainforest. **Range:** Illawarra to Cape York and NG. **Leaves:** opposite,
thick, to 5-8cm long, elliptical to orbicular. **Flowers:** 28-38mm long,
ORANGE-RED, tube joined for about two-thirds of its length and slightly
swollen in the middle, lobes bent backwards. **Name:** *dictyophleba* =
Gk. net-veined, as the leaf reticulation is often prominent.

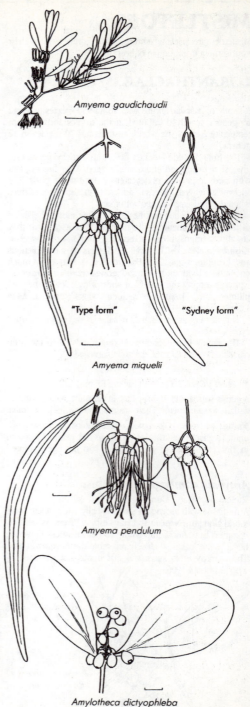

Amyema gaudichaudii

"Type form"   "Sydney form"

Amyema miquelii

Amyema pendulum

Amylotheca dictyophleba

• *Dendrophthoe* Martius (den-drof-THO-ee)

A genus with about 30 species distributed widely from tropical Africa to Australia, where there are 6 species.

Name: *Dendrophthoe* = Gk. *dendron*, tree, *phthienin*, to wither, i.e. what a mistletoe does to its host.

Dendrophthoe vitellina (F. Mueller) Tieghem
Ss

A mistletoe with drooping to spreading stems usually under 1m long. Common in the area.

Hosts: many hosts, but mainly *Eucalyptus* and other *Myrtaceae.* **Range:** coast and ranges from Mallacoota, Vic to the Atherton Tableland in Qld. **Leaves:** alternate, 8-14cm long, thick and fleshy, often grey-green. **Flowers:** 25-50mm long, YELLOW to RED. **Name:** *vitellina* = Lat. *vitellus,* the yolk of an egg, allusion obscure.

• *Muellerina* Tieghem

An endemic genus with 4 species, mainly in south-eastern Australia. This is one of the most primitive of the local Mistletoe genera.

Name: *Muellerina* = after Ferdinand Mueller (1825-96).

Muellerina celastroides

(Sieber ex Schultes & son) Tieghem **Ss**

A mistletoe with erect branches to 1m long. Common in the area.

Hosts: many species, especially *Banksia integrifolia*, but not *Eucalyptus.* **Range:** coasts and ranges from eastern Vic to Noosa in Qld. **Leaves:** opposite, thick, fleshy, spreading-erect, rather similar to *Amyema congener.* **Flowers:** PALE PINKISH YELLOW outside, with DEEP RED anthers; 25-30mm long. **Name:** *celastroides* = *Celastrus*-like.

Muellerina eucalyptoides (De Candolle) Barlow
Ss

A mistletoe with drooping stems to 1.5m long. Common in the area.

Hosts: *Eucalyptus* species, but also other hosts, including exotics. **Range:** NSW coast, ranges and western slopes, also Qld, Vic and SA. **Leaves:** drooping, thick, fleshy, mostly 6-12cm long, not strongly curved. **Flowers:** GREENISH YELLOW outside, RED inside with red anthers, 30-40cm long. **Name:** *eucalyptoides* = *Eucalyptus*-like.

VISCACEAE

A family of semi-parasitic shrubs growing in the branches of trees, with about 400 species in 7 genera, mainly tropical. In Australia there are 14 species in 3 genera, 7 of which extend to NG and South-east Asia.

The family was previously placed in Loranthaceae, but is now recognised as separate on account of its unisexual flowers and single perianth whorl.

Viscum album is the traditional European Mistletoe, the subject of much folklore and mythology.

Korthalsella rubra (Tieghem) Engler
ssp. *rubra* (previously *K. japonica* in part)

Jointed Mistletoe **STRf**

A very strange little plant with erect, flattened, ribbed stems

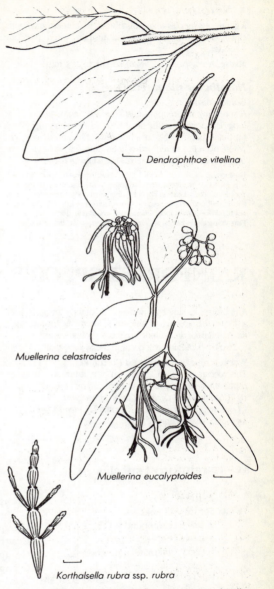

Dendrophthoe vitellina

Muellerina celastroides

Muellerina eucalyptoides

Korthalsella rubra ssp. *rubra*

usually 10-16cm tall, apparently leafless. A rare species locally, found on rainforest trees in the Royal National Park.

The fruits are explosive, releasing tiny projectile-shaped seeds.

Hosts: various rainforest species. **Range:** coast and ranges from eastern Vic to Cape York Peninsula, also Lord Howe Island and NG. **Leaves:** rudimentary, forming a border less than 1mm high around the flowers. **Flowers:** unisexual, tiny, about 0.5mm long, numerous (10-80 per cluster), developing successively in 2-5 rows, male flowers few; in clusters on either side of the stem joints. **Name:** *rubra* = Lat. red, referring to the single row of red hairs between the flowers.

• *Notothixos* Oliver

A genus of 8 species widely distributed in southern and South-east Asia, NG, the Solomons and Australia, where there are 4 species.

Name: *Notothixos* = Gk. *notos*, southern, *ixos*, mistletoe.

Notothixos subaureus Oliver

Golden Mistletoe

A spreading or drooping mistletoe with stems under 50cm long. Uncommon in the area. It could be called piggy-back mistletoe because its only hosts are other mistletoes. The whole plant is covered with a fine yellow felt, which is dense on new parts and well deserves the name 'golden'.

Hosts: other mistletoes (family Loranthaceae), except in north Qld where it is found on rainforest trees. **Range:** from eastern Vic to the Cape York Peninsula. **Leaves:** opposite, about 3cm long, thick, glossy green above, dull and yellow below. **Flowers:** covered in YELLOW felt, in tiny hand-like clusters about 4mm across, arranged in short terminal cymes. **Flowering time:** summer. **Name:** *subaureus* = Lat. almost golden.

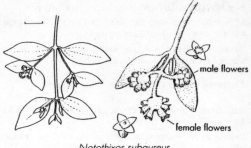

male flowers

female flowers

Notothixos subaureus

RAINFOREST SPECIES

A rainforest is, simply, any closed or canopy forest. In such a forest the crowns of the trees intertwine producing a darkened floor with a much reduced ground cover.

Two types of rainforest occur in the Sydney area.

Warm temperate rainforest (Temp Rf)
This occurs in deep gullies in the sandstone plateaus, especially near the sea. It is a simple community, dominated by Coachwood (*Ceratopetalum apetalum*), Water Gum (*Tristaniopsis laurina*), and Lillypilly (*Acmena smithii*), with a ground cover mainly of ferns.

Subtropical rainforest (STRf)
This is restricted to a few deep gullies in the Royal National Park where Narrabeen shales outcrop, producing rich, water-retentive clay soils (the southern part of Lady Carrington Drive has good examples). It is a very complex community, with dozens of tree species intermixed in the canopy. Many vines are also present.

The subtropical rainforests of the Royal National Park are the northern outliers of extensive subtropical rainforests in the Illawarra.

Key to rainforest species

Herbs. .... **Group 1**
Shrubs and trees.
• Leaves compound..................................**Group 2**
• Leaves opposite ....**Group 3**
• Leaves alternate, untoothed ....**Group 4**
• Leaves alternate, toothed........................**Group 5**
Palm ....ARECACEAE: *Livistona*

> **How to use the key**
> Work your way through by making successive choices: either A or *A, then B or *B etc.. Where numbers occur (eg. H1, H2, H3) check each one.

Group 1 Herbs

A. Leaves basal, strap-like. Monocotyledons.
    B. Leaves over 100cm long. ARACEAE:*Gymnostachys* 383
    ***B.** Leaves under 60cm long. IRIDACEAE:*Libertia* 385
***A.** Leaves on stems.
    C1. Leaves whorled. PIPERACEAE: *Peperomia* 373
    C2. Leaves opposite.

D. Leaves toothed.

    E1. Leaves hairless. ASTERACEAE: *Ageratina* 130

    E2. Leaves with stinging hairs. URTICACEAE: *Urtica* 382

    E3. Leaves with soft hairs. Epiphyte on rocks and trees. GESNERIACEAE:*Fieldia* 361

*D. Leaves untoothed.

    F. Leaves <12mm long. CARYOPHYLLACEAE: *Stellaria* 355

    *F. Leaves >20mm long. ACANTHACEAE: *Pseuderanthemum* 123

C3. Leaves alternate.

    G. Leaves toothed.

        H1. Groundcover with rounded leaves. VIOLACEAE: *Viola hederacea* 224

        H2. Assymetrical leaves. URTICACEAE: *Elatostema* 381

        H3. Otherwise.

            I. Leaves narrow. ASTERACEAE: *Senecio* 353

            *I. Leaves broad. SOLANACEAE: *Physalis* 378

    *G. Leaves untoothed.

        J. Leaves with parallel veins. COMMELINACEAE 384

        *J. Leaves 2-forked. TMESIPTERIS (see Primitive plants: PSILOPSIDA) 303

Group 2 Shrubs and trees with compound leaves.

A. Leaves 3-foliate. RUTACEAE: *Melicope* 376

*A. Otherwise.

    B. Leaves bipinnate.

        C. Leaflets opposite. ARALIACEAE: *Polyscias* 352

        *C. Leaflets mainly alternate. MIMOSACEAE: *Pararchidendron* 365

    *B. Leaves pinnate.

        D. Leaves opposite.

            E. Plants hairless, leaflets toothed. CAPRIFOLIACEAE: *Sambucus* 354

            *E. Plant hairy, leaflets untoothed. EUCRYPHIACEAE: *Eucryphia* 358

        *D. Leaves alternate.

            F. Leaflets with domatia.

                G. Leaflets 12-18. MELIACEAE: *Toona* 364

                *G. Leaflets 4-10.

                    H. Odd number of leaflets. MELIACEAE: *Synoum* 364

                    *H. Even number of leaflets. ANARCARDIACEAE: *Euroschinus* 352

            *F. Leaflets lacking domatia.

                I. >20 leaflets. ARALIACEAE: *Polyscias murrayi* 353

                I. <20 leaflets.

                    J. Leaflets <2.5cm, long. EUPHORBIACEAE: *Breynia* (leaves only appear compound) 166

                    *J. Leaflets over 6cm long.   166

                        K. Leaflets 6-12cm long:

                            L. Leaflets green below. SAPINDACEAE: *Alectryon* 376

                            *L. Leaflets with a pallid waxy surface below. SAPINDACEAE: *Guioa* 377

                      *K. Leaflets >15cm long: SAPINDACEAE: *Diploglottis* 377

Group 3 Shrubs or trees with opposite leaves.

A. Leaves toothed.

    B1. Teeth very blunt (crenate). CELASTRACEAE:*Cassine* 355

    B2. Teeth with stiff drawn out points. GROSSULARIACEAE:*Polyosma* 361

    B3. Teeth otherwise.

        C. Leaf stiff and leathery with strong net-veins. MONIMIACEAE:*Wilkiea* 366

*C. Leaves otherwise.

　D. Leaves irregularly toothed. MONIMIACEAE: *Hedycarya* 366

　*D. Leaves regularly saw-toothed.

　　E. Leaves white below. CUNONIACEAE: *Callicoma* 157

　　*E. Leaves green below.

　　　F. Leaves with a joint between the stalk and blade: CUNONIACEAE:*Ceratopetalum* 356

　　　*F. Leaves otherwise.

　　　　G. Stalk <5mm long. ATHEROSPERMATACEAE:*Doryphora* 353

　　　　*G. Stalk >10mm long. CUNONIACEAE: *Schizomeria* 356

*A. Leaves untoothed.

　H. Leaves with translucent oil-dots.

　　I. Leaves with a joint between the stalk and the blade. RUTACEAE:*Acronychia* 375 *Sarcomelicope* 376

　　*I. Leaves otherwise: MYRTACEAE 369

　*H. Leaves lacking oil dots.

　　J. Stiff leaves with a short abrupt apex. EUPHORBIACEAE:*Baloghia* 358

　　*J. Leaves otherwise.

　　　K. Leaves <7cm long. THYMELIACEAE:*Pimelea ligustrina* 380

　　　*K. Leaves otherwise.

　　　　L. Leaves with prominent venation. OLEACEAE:*Notelaea* 192, 372

　　　　*L. Leaves with venation visible but not prominent. RHAMNACEAE:*Emmenosperma* 375

Group 4 Shrubs and trees with alternate leaves. Leaves not toothed.

A. Leaves with parallel veins.

　B. 7+ main veins. EPACRIDACEAE: *Trochocarpa* 358

　*B. 2-5 main veins. MIMOSACEAE. *Acacia binervia, A. implexa, A. longifolia, A. maidenii* 365

*A. Leaves with lateral veins.

　C. At least some leaves with angular margins. FLACOURTIACEAE:*Scolopia* 360

　*C. All leaves with smooth margins.

　　D. At least some adult leaves deeply lobed.

　　　E. Lobes blunt. STERCULIACEAE: *Brachychiton* 379

　　　*E. Lobes pointed. SOLANACEAE: *Solanum* 213

　　*D. Leaves not lobed.

　　　F. Stems armed with stout thorns. Shrub. MORACEAE:*Maclura* 368

　　　*F. Stems without thorns.

　　　G1. Leaf blades broad at the base. WINTERACEAE:*Tasmannia* 382

　　　G2. Bark corky.

　　　　H1. Leaves broadest in upper part. SOLANACEAE:*Duboisia* 378

　　　　H2. Leaves broadest at the middle. MYOPORACEAE:*Myoporum* 400

　　　　H3. Leaves with yellow central vein: LAURACEAE:*Endiandra* 363

　　　G3. Translucent oil dots in leaves.

　　　　I. Leaves broadest above the middle. Oil dots just visible MYRTACEAE: *Tristaniopsis* 371

　　　　*I. Leaves broadest at the middle. RUTACEAE:*Geijera* 375

　　　G4. Leaves with conspicuous domatia in vein angles. ICACINACEAE:*Pennantia* 362

　　　G5. Leaf stalks exude white milky latex when broken.

　　　　J. Large tree with buttresses or small tree with coalesced roots. MORACEAE:*Ficus* 366

　　　　*J. Otherwise: SAPOTACEAE: *Planchonella* 377

G6. Leaves with yellow central vein. Slightly aromatic when crushed.
LAURACEAE:*Cryptocarya* 363

G7. Leaves strongly 2-ranked, often appearing pinnate. Stems often noticeably zig-zag.
K1. Leaves grey-green. EUPHORBIACEAE: *Breynia* 166
K2. Leaves dark-green, glossy, thickish. Shrub. EUPOMATIACEAE:*Eupomatia* 360
K3. Leaves yellowish below. EBENACEAE:*Diospyros* 357
K4. Leaves mid-green above, slightly paler below, shiny, not thick.
EUHORBIACAE:*Glochidion* 166

G8. Leaves white below. RHAMNACEAE:*Alphitonia* 374

G9. Side-veins running almost parallel to main vein. PROTEACEAE:*Stenocarpus* 374

G10. Leaves heart shaped. EUPHORBIACEAE: *Omalanthus* 167

G11. Leaves over 15cm long, green both sides.
L. Leaves glossy, dark green, hairless. NYCAGINACEAE:*Pisonia* 372
*L. Leaves dull, dark-green, covered in fine hairs below. SAPINDACEAE:*Diploglottis*
(juvenile leaves) 377

G12. Leaves at ends of branchlets apparently whorled. PITTOSPORACEAE 196

G13. Leaves covered with tiny red glands below. Small tree usually around cliffs.
GROSSULARIACEAE:*Quintinia* 362

G14. Large shrub. Leaves 5-10cm long, glossy, tough, slightly thick. Teeth usually
present on some leaves. MYSINACEAE:*Rapanea howittiana* 369

G15. Small shrub, leaves thin-textured, 5-10cm ling, shiny.
SOLANACEAE:*Solanum pseudocapsicum* 379

Group 5 Leaves toothed.

A. Leaves <4cm long, shrubs.
 B. Leaves more or less oval. PITTOSPORACEAE:*Citriobatus* 373
 *B. Leaves lance-shaped. VIOLACEAE: *Hymenanthera* 382
*A. Leaves >4cm long.
 C. Leaves >15cm long, covered with stringing hairs. URTICACEAE:*Dendrocnide* 381
 *C. Leaves otherwise.
  D. Leaf blade broad at the base. ELAEOCARPACEAE:*Sloanea* 357
  *D. Leaf blade tapering to the base.
   E. Leaves firm and leathery.
    F. Leaves 10-12cm long. SYMPLOCACEAE: *Symplocos* 380
    *F. Leaves under 10cm long. MYRSINACEAE: *Rapanea* 369
   *E. Leaves thin textured, not leathery.
    G. Leaves with a group of tiny glands on the stalk at the junction with the leaf blade.
    EUPHORBIACEAE:*Claoxylon* 358
    *G. Glands absent.
     H. Leaves widest in the upper half. GROSSULARIACEAE:*Abrophyllum* 361
     *H. Leaves widest in the middle.
      I. Leaves >10cm long. BORAGINACEAE:*Ehretia* 354
      *I. Leaves <6cm long. MORACEAE: *Streblus* 368

• DICOTYLEDONS

ACANTHACEAE

• *Pseuderanthemum variabile*

STRf, Temp Rf, Ss

A small herb with pink flowers. Common on dark rainforest floors.

—See LESSER FAMILIES: Acanthaceae.

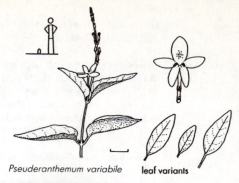

Pseuderanthemum variabile   leaf variants

ANARCARDIACEAE

A family with about 600 species in about 70 genera in tropical and temperate parts of the world. There are 10 species in 9 genera native to Australia.

The family includes *Schinus areira**, the Pepper Tree, a common sight in inland NSW, *Anarcardium occidentale*, the Cashew tree, a native of tropical America, *Mangifera indica*, the Mango, and *Pistacia vera*, the Pistachio nut. Oriental lacquer comes from the sap of *Rhus vernicifera*.

The family is related to Sapindaceae.

• *Euroschinus* J. D. Hooker (yoo-ro-SKY-nus)

A genus with 6 species: 4 in New Caledonia, 1 in NG, and 1 in Australia.

Name: *Euroschinus* = Gk *euros*, the south-east wind, *Schinus*, a related genus, i.e. the *Schinus* of south-eastern Australia.

Euroschinus falcata J. D. Hooker **var.** *falcata*

Ribbonwood, Brush Cudgerie   **STRf**

A small tree 10-20m tall, uncommon in subtropical rainforest in the Royal National Park. Common in the Illawarra.

Range: from Jervis Bay to the Endeavour River in Qld.   **Leaves:** pinnate, leaflets 4-10, asymmetrical, glossy, hairless, moderately thick and tough, with domatia. The branches exude a clear sap when cut.   **Flowers:** PINK with cream margins, small (petals 2mm long), unisexual, numerous in panicles.   **Flowering time:** summer.   **Fruit:** small black drupes.   **Name:** *falcata* = Lat. sickle-shaped, referring to the asymmetrical leaves.   **Similar species:** *Toona ciliata* (MELIACEAE).

ARALIACEAE

Polyscias elegans (C. Moore & F. Mueller) Harms (polly-SY-as)

Silver Basswood, Celerywood   **Temp Rf, STRf**

An erect shrub or small tree 3-8m tall, found in humid woodland and rainforest, nearly always near the sea. Uncommon to rare in the area (e.g. Clark Island in Sydney Harbour, Royal National Park).

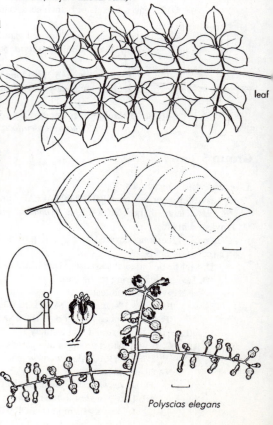

leaf

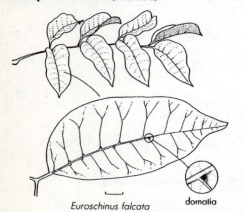

Euroschinus falcata   domatia

Polyscias elegans

It has the largest leaf area of any local species; some of the bipinnate leaves measure 100cm long and 50cm wide! The common name is from the fresh celery-like fragrance of the crushed leaves and bark.

Range: coastal rainforests from Jervis Bay to Qld and NG. **Leaves:** bipinnate, 80-100cm long, spreading or slightly drooping; leaflets mostly about 10cm long, hairless, not thick, soft, more or less flat, somewhat glossy above, dull below. **Flowers:** with DARK RED petals and white anthers, about 8mm wide when open, numerous in a large terminal pyramidal panicle, the branches of which are covered in fine pale brown felt. **Flowering time:** February-March **Name:** *elegans* = Lat. ornamental.

Polyscias murrayi (F. Mueller) Harms

Pencil Cedar, Umbrella Tree **STRf**

A medium-sized tree 8-15m tall, found on the edges of subtropical rainforest in the Royal National Park. Easily recognised by its ornamental appearance: a tall straight trunk with smooth grey bark, unbranched for most of its length, supporting a symmetrical umbrella-like crown of long pinnate leaves. Young trees are unbranched, possibly giving rise to the common name 'Pencil Cedar'.

Range: NSW coast and ranges, Vic, Qld. **Leaves:** pinnate, adult leaves with 15-18 pairs of leaflets and a terminal leaflet (juvenile leaves with extra pairs of leaflets); leaflets soft, smooth, hairless, thin-textured, entire or finely toothed, lacking domatia (not that this description will do you any good, since it is impossible to get to the leaves without a ladder). **Flowers:** similar to *P. elegans.* **Flowering time:** February-March. **Name:** *murrayi* = after a Reverend Murray who sent the type specimen to Ferdinand Mueller.

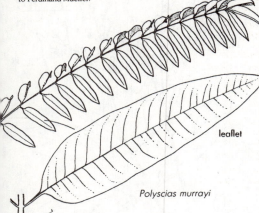

leaflet

Polyscias murrayi

ASTERACEAE

The introduced species *Ageratina riparia**, Mist Weed, has spread widely in rainforests, especially along streams where it often forms dense masses.
—See LESSER FAMILIES.

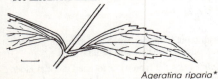

Ageratina riparia*

Senecio linearifolius A. Richard

Fireweed Groundsel **STRf**

A strongly smelling erect perennial herb usually about 1.5m high, found on the margins of subtropical rainforest and as a weed on richer soils.

Range: NSW coast and ranges and some inland districts, Vic and Tas. **Leaves:** numerous, toothed, aromatic. **Flower heads:** numerous in a terminal corymb, ray flowers YELLOW, disc flowers YELLOW. **Flowering time:** most of the year. **Name:** *linearifolius* = Lat. straight leaved.

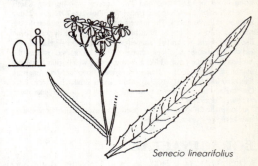

Senecio linearifolius

ATHEROSPERMATACEAE

A small family of rainforest trees with 12 species in 5 genera worldwide, distributed in Australasia and Chile. There are 8 species in 4 genera in Australia. The genera are often placed in the family Monimiaceae.

• Doryphora Endlicher

A genus of rainforest trees with 2 species, one widespread in eastern Australia, and the other, *D. aromatica*, restricted to the Atherton Tableland.

Name: *Doryphora* = Gk. spear-carrier, referring to the prominent spear-like anther appendages.

Doryphora sassafras Endlicher

Sassafras **STRf**

A medium to tall tree 20-40m high, with dense dark foliage. Common in subtropical rainforest in the Royal National Park and the Illawarra, and a dominant species in high altitude

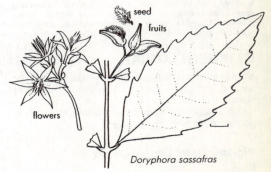

seed

fruits

flowers

Doryphora sassafras

temperate rainforests in mountain areas. Easily recognised by its dark green, shiny, coarsely toothed leaves.

All parts of the tree have a spicy smell. The bark was used as a tea substitute in early times*. A remarkable fact about the mighty Sassafras is that it depends on the humble mosquito for its pollination. In spring great numbers of mosquitoes and crane flies ('giant mosquitoes') are attracted to the flowers. Male mosquitoes are nectar-eaters and in their struggle to feed they pollinate the flowers.

Range: NSW coast and ranges, and Qld. **Leaves:** opposite, shiny, tough, more or less flat, coarsely toothed, hairless. **Flowers:** WHITE, 15-25mm wide; in axillary clusters. The flowers have a highly unusual structure; with 6 anthers opening by little lids and surmounted by long spear-like appendages, 6 similarly shaped staminodes, and several carpels. **Flowering time:** August-September. **Fruit:** contained within the swollen floral tube (shaped like a curved bottle) which splits to release numerous plumed seeds. **Name:** *sassafras* = from the North American *Sassafras albidum* (LAURACEAE), which has a similar fragrance. Peter Cunningham in 1827 seems to record *Kalang* as an Aboriginal name from the Sydney area.
* Although the Cribbs warn that it contains the toxic alkaloid doryphorine and should be used with caution.[1]

BORAGINACEAE

A family with about 2400 species in 113 genera distributed worldwide. In Australia there are about 90 species in 23 genera.

• *Ehretia* R. Brown (air-EE-she-a)

A genus of shrubs and trees with about 50 species worldwide. There are 6 species in Australia.

Name: *Ehretia* = after Georg Dionysius Ehret (1705-70), a German botanical illustrator living in England.

Ehretia acuminata R. Brown

Koda **STRf**

A medium sized tree, semi-deciduous, 15-30m tall, found scattered in subtropical rainforest in the Royal National Park and Illawarra, especially near creeks. It bears masses of succulent red drupes which seem edible. In India the unripe fruit is pickled as a relish.

Range: NSW coast north from Bega, Qld, India, Japan and the Phillipines. **Leaves:** dark-green above, satin, hairless, thin, shallowly toothed, with prominent veins. Tiny domatia often present. **Flowers:** WHITE, shortly tubular, with 5 spreading lobes, 5 stamens alternating with the lobes, and a superior ovary; numerous in axillary panicles. **Flowering time:** summer. **Fruit:** an orange drupe, in late summer. **Name:** *acuminata* = Lat. drawn out to a point, referring to the leaves. Koda is an Indian name.

CAPRIFOLIACEAE

A family with about 500 species in 13 genera, mainly in the northern hemisphere. There are 5 species in 3 genera in Australia.

Only *Sambucus* occurs naturally in Australia. Some authors place in its own family, Sambucaceae.

• *Sambucus* Linnaeus (sam-BEW-cus)

Elders

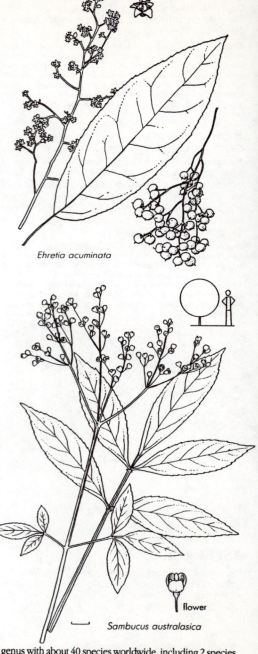

Ehretia acuminata

flower

Sambucus australasica

A genus with about 40 species worldwide, including 2 species in eastern Australia. Both have small edible fruits.

Name: *Sambucus* = the Latin name for the European Elder, *Sambucus nigra*, which is naturalised in eastern Australia.

Sambucus australasica (Lindley) Fritsch

Native Elder, Yellow Elderberry **STRf**
A spreading shrub 2-4m tall. Found in light-breaks in subtropical rainforest in the Royal National Park and Illawarra. The flowers have a heavy sweet scent, like lacquer or Tarzan's Grip.

Range: NSW coast and ranges, Vic and Qld. **Leaves:** opposite, pinnate, with 5 leaflets, held parallel to the ground; leaflets soft, thin-textured, to 10cm long, toothed, hairless, glossy above. A small gland is visible at the base of each leaflet. **Flowers:** CREAMY YELLOW, 2-3mm wide, numerous in a large terminal panicle. **Flowering time:** December-February. **Fruit:** yellow drupes. **Name:** *australasica* = Lat. Australian.

CARYOPHYLLACEAE

A family of small herbs, with about 2000 species in about 80 genera worldwide, especially in temperate areas of the northern hemisphere. There are about 34 native species in 7 genera in Australia, plus a host of introduced species. The best known member is *Dianthus caryophyllus*, the Carnation.

The family is related to Chenopodiaceae, Aizoaceae and Phytolaccaceae.

• *Stellaria* Linnaeus

A genus of herbs with about 120 species worldwide, including about 6 species native to Australia.

The introduced species *S. media* (Chickweed) is a common weed in gardens, and an excellent, though little recognised, salad vegetable.

The 5 petals are deeply incised, giving the appearance of 10 petals.

Name: *Stellaria* = Lat. starry.

Stellaria flaccida W. J. Hooker

Forest Starwort **STRf, Temp Rf**
A small weak herb with tangled stems, often forming a dense ground cover. Abundant on the edges of rainforest in the Royal National Park and Illawarra.

Range: coast and ranges throughout NSW, Qld, Vic, Tas and SA. **Leaves:** opposite, crisp, hairless. **Flowers:** WHITE. **Flowering time:** summer. **Name:** *flaccida* = Lat. flaccid, weak.

CELASTRACEAE

A family of trees and shrubs with about 800 species in 50 genera. There are 34 species in 14 genera in Australia.

• *Cassine* Linnaeus (CASS-in-ee)

A genus of trees and shrubs with about 80 species, widespread in the tropics and subtropics, mostly in the Americas. There are 2 species in Australia.

Name: *Cassine* = a name given by Florida indians to a plant once in this genus, but now placed in *Ilex* (Aquifoliaceae).

Cassine australis (Ventenat) Kunze
var. *australis*

(previously *Elaeodendron australe*)
Red-fruited Olive Plum **STRf**

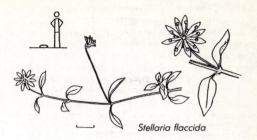

Stellaria flaccida

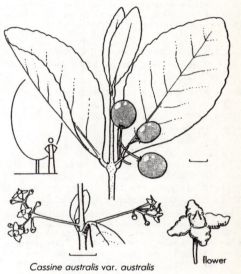

Cassine australis var. australis

flower

A small tree 6-10m tall. Common in subtropical rainforest in the Royal National Park and Illawarra. Easily recognised by its broad, rather fleshy leaves and bright orange fruit.

Range: Batemans Bay to Central Qld, in coastal rainforests. **Leaves:** opposite, rather thick and fleshy, with crenate margins, hairless. **Flowers:** tiny, GREEN, in axillary cymes. **Flowering time:** October-November. **Fruit:** a large orange drupe. **Name:** *australis* = Lat. southern.

CUNONIACEAE

A family with about 250 species in 26 genera. There are about 19 species in Australia in 14 genera.

It is a mainly southern hemisphere family, related to Pittosporaceae. Some authors include it in Saxifragaceae.

Aphanopetalum resinosum STRf
—See CLIMBERS: Cunoniaceae.

Callicoma serratifolia

Temp Rf, STRf, Ss
A large shrub or small tree with large coarsely toothed leaves, white below. Common in rainforest.
—See LESSER FAMILIES: Cunoniaceae.

Ceratopetalum apetalum D. Don

Coachwood, Boola **Temp Rf, STRf**

A medium-sized rainforest tree 10-25m high, with smooth, mottled bark, found along creeks in deep sandstone gullies, usually with Lillipilly and Water Gum. Very common in the area. In former times it was an important timber for coaches and buggies. During World War II it provided the butts for all rifles made in Australia.

Range: NSW coast from Bateman's Bay to Qld. **Bark:** pale grey, smooth, with multicoloured lichen patches. **Leaves:** 1-foliate, large, opposite, tough and stiff, toothed. In open sites the leaves may be as small as 6cm long. **Flowers:** small and WHITE, lacking petals, numerous in axillary panicles. **Flowering time:** November. **Name:** *apetalum* = Lat. without petals. Boola is an Aboriginal name from the Illawarra. Also known as Lightwood in colonial times.

• *Schizomeria* D. Don (skiz-o-MEER-ee-a)

A genus of rainforest trees with about 18 species, including 2 species in Australia.

Name: *Schizomeria* = Gk. cut-part, referring to the incised petals.

Schizomeria ovata D. Don

Crab Apple, White Cherry, Snowberry
Temp Rf, STRf

A tree to 15m (25m in northern NSW) with dense foliage, found in or near rainforest gullies. Scattered throughout the area, but not common. The common name Crab Apple is from the acid, astringent taste of the fleshy white fruit.

Range: from Narooma to north Qld. **Leaves:** opposite, rather tough but not thick, toothed, glossy, hairless. **Bark:** grey, smooth to wrinkled. Can be confused with Coachwood. Buttresses may be well developed on this species. **Flowers:** tiny, numerous, WHITE. **Flowering time:** September-November. **Fruit:** a white or yellowish globular drupe, 10-15mm wide. **Name:** *ovata* = Lat. oval-shaped, referring to the leaves.

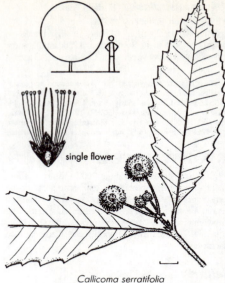

single flower

Callicoma serratifolia

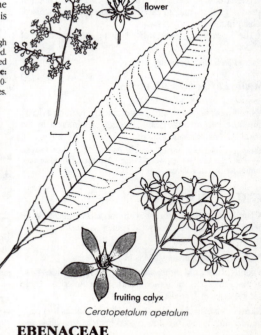

flower

fruiting calyx

Ceratopetalum apetalum

flower

Schizomeria ovata

EBENACEAE

A family of rainforest trees and shrubs with about 500 species in 2 genera, widespread in the tropics. There is a single genus in Australia. The majority of species are in Africa and Madagascar.

The family is related to Sapotaceae and Symplocaceae and includes the Persimmon (*Diospyros kaki*), although this is just one of many species with edible fruit. Several species in Sri Lanka and Madagascar produce the commercial black ebony timber.

• *Diospyros* Linnaeus (di-OS-pi-ros)

A genus with over 400 species, including about 15 species in Australia.

Name: *Diospyros* = Gk. godly wheat, i.e. food of the gods, referring to the edible fruits.

Diospyros australis (R. Brown) Hiern

Black Plum **STRf**

A small-medium rainforest tree, usually 6-15m tall, found in subtropical rainforest in the Royal National Park and Illawarra. The fruits are not especially edible, being slimy but bitter.

Range: NSW coast from Batemans Bay into Qld. **Leaves:** tough, thickish, more or less oblong, dark green above, blunt, hairless. The undersurface is very distinctive, with a dull waxy lustre, pale yellowish green, and barely visible veins. **Flowers:** unisexual (plants dioecious), WHITE, with 4 petals, in short axillary clusters. The male flowers have numerous stamens. **Flowering time:** December. **Fruit:** a shiny black berry. **Name:** *australis* = Lat. southern.

Diospyros pentamera F. Mueller

Myrtle Ebony, Black Myrtle **STRf**

A small tree, 3-18m high, occurring in subtropical rainforest. Uncommon in the Royal National Park, more common in the Illawarra.

Range: NSW coast from Batemans Bay into Qld. **Leaves:** similar to *D. australis*, except lanceolate (lance-head shaped) in outline, often rather small (under 5cm long, but sometimes to 10cm). **Flowers:** PINK to WHITE, with 5 petals. **Name:** *pentamera* = Gk. 5-segmented, referring to the flowers.

ELAEOCARPACEAE

• *Sloanea* Linnaeus

A genus with about 120 species, including 4 species in Australia.

Name: *Sloanea* = after Sir Hans Sloane (1660-1753), an aristocratic collector and patron who was the principal founder of the British Museum, and also President of the Royal Society, succeeding Isaac Newton.

Sloanea australis (Bentham) F. Mueller

Maiden's Blush **STRf**

A small rainforest tree usually 2-6m high with large handsome leaves. Found in subtropical rainforest on the banks of creeks, in the Royal National Park and Illawarra. The broad, toothed leaves are easily recognised by their distinctive bases.

Range: NSW coastal rainforests north from Batemans Bay into Qld. **Leaves:** large (10-30cm long), shiny, hairless, thin-textured, firm (fairly stiff), flat, toothed. **Flowers:** CREAM, about 20mm wide; axillary, solitary or in racemes. **Flowering time:** October-November. **Fruit:** large capsules densely covered with short stiff hairs. **Name:** *australis* = Lat. southern. The common name arises from the pink blush of the timber (the new leaves are also pink).

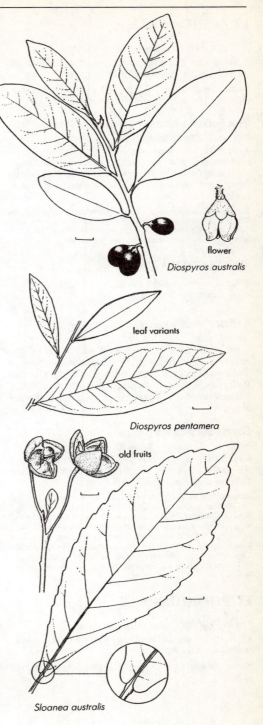

flower

Diospyros australis

leaf variants

Diospyros pentamera

old fruits

Sloanea australis

EPACRIDACEAE

• *Trochocarpa* R. Brown (tro-co-CARP-a)

A genus with 6 species in eastern Australia and others extending to the island chains north of Australia.

Name: *Trochocarpa* = Gk. *trochos*, a wheel, *karpos*, fruit, referring to the fruit which is a 10-stoned berry.

Trochocarpa laurina R. Brown

Tree Heath   **Temp Rf, STRf, Ss**

A large shrub or small tree, 3-6m high, found in humid rainforest gullies in the coastal plateaus. It is the largest member of the family. The new leaves are very ornamental, forming red drooping umbrella-like clusters at the tips of branches.

Range: NSW coastal districts from the Sydney area to Qld.   **Leaves:** shiny, with 5-7 major parallel veins.   **Flowers:** WHITE; in terminal spikes 2-4cm long.   **Flowering time:** January-February.   **Fruit:** a dark blue berry, 6-8mm diameter.   **Name:** *laurina* = like a Laurel.

EUCRYPHIACEAE

A family with a single genus, related to Cunoniaceae, Hypericaceae, and Rosaceae.

• *Eucryphia* Cavanilles (yoo-CRIFF-ee-a)

Leatherwoods

A genus of shrubs and small trees with 5 species. The distribution clearly betrays its Gondwanaland origin; 1 species in eastern Australia, 2 in Tas, and 2 in southern Chile. One Tas species, *E. lucida*, is the source of Leatherwood Honey.
Name: *Eucryphia* = Gk. well-covered, referring to the cap-like calyx.

Eucryphia moorei F. Mueller

Pinkwood, Plumwood   **Temp Rf**

A small rainforest tree usually 2-10m tall. Rare in the Royal National Park, more common along the Illawarra escarpment. The large white flowers are sweetly fragrant.

Range: NSW coast and ranges south from the Royal National Park into Vic.   **Leaves:** opposite, pinnate, fairly tough, almost hairless above, white-felty below, smelling of oil when crushed   **Flowers:** WHITE, 25-30mm wide, solitary or a few together in the upper axils. The sepals are joined into a cap which falls away as the flower opens.   **Fruit:** a woody or leathery capsule, opening by boat-shaped valves, each of which contains a few winged seeds.   **Flowering time:** late summer.   **Name:** *moorei* = after Charles Moore, director of the Royal Botanic Gardens, Sydney, from 1848-96.

EUPHORBIACEAE

• *Baloghia* Endlicher (bal-OAG-ee-a)

A genus of tropical shrubs and trees with 4 species in eastern Australian rainforests.

Name: *Baloghia* = after Dr Joseph Balogh, a German botanical author.

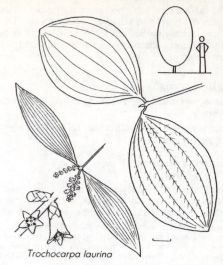

Trochocarpa laurina

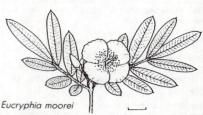

Eucryphia moorei

Baloghia inophylla (G. Forster) P. S. Green

(previously *B. lucida*)
Brush Bloodwood   **STRf**

A small tree usually 6-10 high with dense dark-green foliage, common in subtropical rainforest in the Royal National Park and Illawarra. The woody fruits open explosively.

Range: NSW coast, Qld and Lord Howe Island.   **Leaves:** opposite, leathery, broad, with abrupt accuminate tips and recurved margins.   **Flowers:** unisexual (plants monoecious), with thick waxy PINKISH petals, male and female on separate branches.   **Flowering time:** September-October.   **Name:** *inophylla* = Gk. fibrous-leaved.

Breynia oblongifolia

Ss, Cumb, STRf, Temp Rf

A shrub to 2m, with dull greyish leaves, common in moist gullies, rainforest edges and near streams.
—See LESSER FAMILIES: Euphorbiaceae.

• *Claoxylon* Jussieu

A genus of tropical shrubs with about 80 species, including 3 endemic in Australia.

Name: *Claoxylon* = Gk. *klao*, to break, *xylon*, wood, because the wood is brittle.

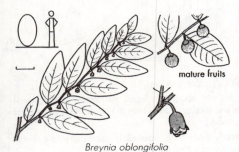

Baloghia inophylla

Breynia oblongifolia

mature fruits

Glochidion ferdinandi

Ss, Temp Rf, STRf margins

A leafy shrub or small tree, common in moist gullies and rainforest.
—See LESSER FAMILIES: Euphorbiaceae.

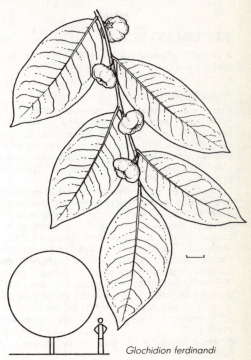

Glochidion ferdinandi

Claoxylon australe Baillon

Brittlewood **STRf**

A broad-leaved shrub usually 1.5-2m high, found in the understorey of subtropical rainforest and occasionally in coastal rainforest gullies. The leaves have a number of tiny glands at the junction of the blade and stalk.

Range: NSW coastal districts north from Bermagui, and Qld. **Leaves:** thin, soft, toothed, drooping in hot weather, often finely hairy when young. **Flowers:** unisexual (plants monoecious), GREENISH, in axillary racemes. The anthers open through pores at their tips. **Flowering time:** summer. **Name:** *australe* = Lat. southern.

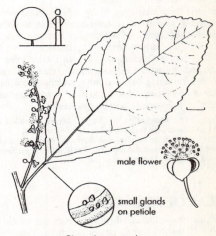

male flower

small glands on petiole

Claoxylon australe

Omalanthus populifolius

Ss, Temp Rf margins

A tall shrub with large heart-shaped leaves, common on the edges of rainforests.
—See LESSER FAMILIES: Euphorbiaceae.

Omalanthus populifolius R

EUPOMATIACEAE

A primitive angiosperm family, with 2 relict species in rainforests.

• *Eupomatia* R. Brown (yoo-po-MAY-ti-a)

A genus with 2 species, found in eastern Australia.

The flowers are large and unusual. The perianth is fused into a lid which covers the flower in bud (like *Eucalyptus*), there are 2-3 rings of many stamens, and several rings of petal-like staminodes, surrounding a central disc containing numerous stigmas. The ovaries are sunken in the pulpy body of the flower.

The plants are entirely dependent on a small weevil beetle for pollination. Large numbers of weevils are attracted to the strong rich and penetrating scent 'with reminiscences of pineapple, mango and decaying fish' according to A. G. Hamilton. They voraciously consume the dense palisade of staminodes which separate the anthers from the central disc. Once the palisade is breached, the scrambling weevils transfer pollen to the stigmas which lie on the surface of the disc. 'The flower opens in the morning and closes about 5.30 on the same day. The ring of staminodes and stamens drops off entire the same night or early next day, resembling small sea-anemones . . . All the plants in the area flowered within a week . . .'[2]

Name: *Eupomatia* = Gk. well-covered, referring to the perianth lid.

Eupomatia laurina R. Brown

Bolwarra, Native Guava   **STRf**

An erect shrub with a few fleshy arching stems, eventually becoming a small tree to 6m tall. Found in rainforest on enriched soils. Restricted to subtropical rainforest in the Royal National Park. Fairly common in the Illawarra.

The fruits are pleasant to eat, with a clear sweet pulp surrounding many seeds. Aborigines used the bark as a source of fibre for fishing lines and string, soaking it in a 'tan' (of *Acacia* or *Persoonia* bark) and then twisting the strands together in the sap of *Eucalyptus gummifera*.

Range: NSW coast and ranges, Vic, Qld, NG.   **Leaves:** two-ranked, glossy, dark-green, somewhat thick and fleshy, more or less oblong.   **Flowers:** WHITE-CREAM, solitary, axillary or on old wood.   **Flowering time:** very brief, for a few days around new year.   **Fruit:** yellow to purplish when ripe, 2-3cm wide.   **Name:** *laurina* = Laurel-like.

FLACOURTIACEAE

A mainly tropical family of rainforest trees and shrubs, with about 1300 species in 89 genera worldwide. There are 17 species in 8 genera in Australia.

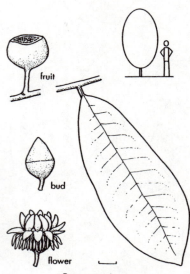

Eupomatia laurina

• *Scolopia* Schreber

A genus with about 37 species, distributed in subtropical Africa and southern Asia. There is a single endemic species in Australia.

Name: *Scolopia* = Gk. pointed, because the young shoots can be armed with axillary thorns.

Scolopia braunii (Klotzsch) Sleumer

Scolopia, Flintwood   **STRf**

A small tree mostly 3-8m tall, found scattered in subtropical rainforest in the Royal National Park and Illawarra. The common name comes from the timber which is hard and difficult to cut.

Range: Jervis Bay to Cape York.   **Leaves:** shiny, rather thick, tough, hairless, mostly with an angular outline, especially when young.   **Flowers:** WHITE, about 5mm wide, scented, with numerous stamens; in short axillary racemes.   **Flowering time:** spring.   **Fruit:** a globular berry, about 10mm wide, dark-red, turning black.   **Name:** *braunii* = after Robert Brown.

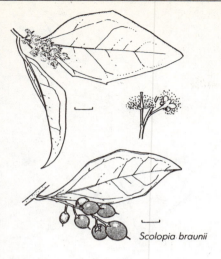

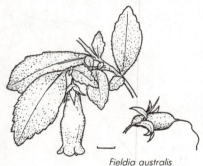

Scolopia braunii

Fieldia australis

Range: NSW coast and ranges, Vic (where it is common on tree ferns) and Qld. **Leaves:** opposite in unequal pairs, thin, rusty-furry on both sides, satin and dotted with hair bases above, more densely furry below. **Flowers:** WHITE, large, pendulous, axillary, solitary. The calyx is protected by a pair of bracts. **Flowering time:** summer. **Fruit:** a crisp succulent white berry. **Name:** *australis* = Lat. southern.

GROSSULARIACEAE

A family of shrubs and trees with less than 350 species in about 25 genera worldwide. There are about 20 species in 8 genera in Australia.

The family includes *Ribes* (gooseberries and currants). Some authors include it within Saxifragaceae or Escalloniaceae.

• *Abrophyllum* J. D. Hooker ex Bentham

An endemic genus with 2 species of rainforest trees in eastern Australia.

Name: *Abrophyllum* = Gk. delicate leaf.

Abrophyllum ornans

(F. Mueller) J. D. Hooker ex Bentham

STRf

An elegant shrub or small tree 3-8m tall, found in subtropical rainforest in the Royal National Park, where it is uncommon or rare, and in the Illawarra.

Range: from the Illawarra to southern Qld. **Leaves:** large (10-20cm long), very soft and thin, irregularly toothed on the upper part, veins impressed above and prominent below. **Flowers:** small, GREENISH YELLOW, petals about 4mm long; in terminal and axillary umbrella-like panicles. **Flowering time:** summer. **Fruit:** small dark-purple berries, forming dangling grape-like clusters in June. **Name:** *ornans* = Lat. beautiful.

GESNERIACEAE

A family of rainforest herbs or shrubs, mainly tropical, with about 2000 species in 120 genera worldwide. In Australia there are 6 species in 6 genera.

The family is closely related to Scrophulariaceae, and considered by some botanists to be its tropical counterpart.

• *Fieldia* A. Cunningham

An endemic genus of small rainforest herbs with a single species.

Name: after Judge Baron Field (1786-1846), first judge of the NSW Supreme Court. He was an enthusiastic observer of the new continent and published the first book of poetry in Australia, all his own work (see *Epacris longiflora*).

Fieldia australis A. Cunningham

Fieldia **STRf**

A weak herb with stems usually 20-40cm long, found as an epiphyte on rocks or tree-ferns in humid gullies in subtropical rainforest. Only recorded in the Illawarra, but may be present in the Royal National Park.

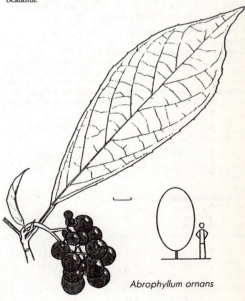

Abrophyllum ornans

• *Polyosma* Blume (polly-OZ-ma)

A genus of rainforest trees with about 60 species, including 7 species in Australia.

Name: *Polyosma* = Gk. much-odour, referring to the strong fragrance of some species.

Polyosma cunninghamii J. J. Bennett

Featherwood **STRf**

A small tree 6-10m tall found in subtropical rainforest in the Royal National Park and Illawarra.

Range: from Cambewarra Mountain near Nowra to southern Qld.
Leaves: opposite, glossy both sides, with scattered stiff projecting teeth, hairless, thin-textured, veins obscure above, clearly visible below.
Flowers: tubular, WHITE to creamy-green, 10-12mm long, with 4 spreading star-like tips, very fragrant. **Flowering time:** April-October.
Fruit: a glossy green ovoid berry, strongly ribbed, resembling those of Doryphora sassafras. **Name:** *cunninghamii* = after Allan Cunningham (1791-1839), pioneering botanist-explorer of inland NSW.

fruits

Polyosma cunninghamii

• *Quintinia* A. de Candolle

A genus of rainforest trees with about 20 species, including 4 species in Australia.

Name: after Jean de la Quintinie (1626-88), a lawyer and well-known horticulturist. He was appointed director-general of the royal vegetable gardens of Louis XIV.

Quintinia sieberi A. de Candolle

Rough Possumwood **STRf**

A small tree, usually 4-8m tall, found in rainforest, usually associated with gully-sides and escarpments. On the north coast it usually begins its life as an epiphyte on tree ferns, but in the Royal National Park and the Illawarra it grows in crevices on cliffs, often on sheer rock faces. Perhaps its aversion to the earth accounts for its common name.

Range: NSW coast and ranges north from the Budawangs, into Qld.
Leaves: hairless, thickish, 7-15cm long, with recurved margins and short accuminate tips. The stalks are usually thick and red. The leaf undersides, stalks and new stems are covered with microscopic red glands. **Flowers:** WHITE, about 10mm wide, fragrant; in large dense terminal panicles.
Flowering time: spring (October-November). **Fruit:** a small capsule.
Name: *sieberi* = after Franz Wilhelm Sieber of Prague, Bohemia, who collected extensively in Australia from 1819-23, spending 7 months in NSW.

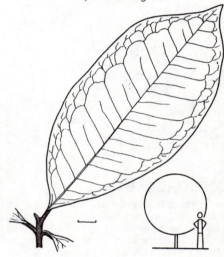

Quintinia sieberi

ICACINACEAE

A family of trees and shrubs with over 400 species in 56 genera, mainly in the tropics. There are 7 species in 6 genera in Australia.

• *Pennantia* J. R. & G. Forster

A genus with 3 species distributed in eastern Australia, Norfolk Island and NZ.
There is a single endemic species in Australia.

Name: *Pennantia* = after Thomas Pennant (1726-98), zoologist and traveller.

Pennantia cunninghamii Meirs

Brown Beech **STRf**

A small rainforest tree 3-6m tall (although it grows to a tall

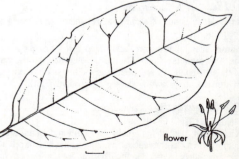

flower

Pennantia cunninghamii

tree in northern Qld). Found in deep gullies in subtropical rainforest, usually near streams. Uncommon in the Royal National Park, but common in the Illawarra. The glossy leaves are easily recognised by the prominent bulbous domatia in the forks of the lateral veins.

Range: from Clyde Mountain, NSW, to the Atherton Tableland in northern Qld. **Leaves:** large (8-14cm long), glossy on both sides, thin-textured, firm, with wavy margins and prominent domatia. **Flowers:** unisexual, WHITE, in dense panicles which are terminal or in the upper axils. **Flowering time:** November-January. **Fruit:** a succulent black berry 12-15mm long, with astringent flavour; in February. **Name:** *cunninghamii* = in honour of Allan Cunningham, pioneering botanical explorer of inland NSW. The wood resembles English Beech.

LAURACEAE

Laurels

A family of rainforest trees with 2000-2500 species in about 30 genera worldwide. There are about 90 species in 8 genera in Australia.

The leaves have microscopic oil dots, giving a pleasant odour when crushed.

The Laurel family is related to the primitive families Monimiaceae and Atherospermataceae. Some authors include the parasitic climber *Cassytha* (see Cassythaceae).

It includes the exotic commercial species Avocado (*Persea americana*) and Bay Laurel (*Laurus nobilis*). Many species produce commercial timbers.

Note: a useful identification feature is the strong pale yellow central vein on the leaves of all local species.

• *Cryptocarya* R. Brown

A genus of rainforest trees with 200-250 species, including 34 species native in Australia.

Name: *Cryptocarya* = Gk. hidden-nut, referring to the fruit being concealed by the old perianth.

Cryptocarya glaucescens R. Brown

Brown Beech, She Beech, Jackwood, Native Laurel, Oorawang
STRf, Temp Rf

A medium sized tree, 15-30m high, abundant in subtropical rainforest in the Royal National Park and Illawarra. Also sometimes found in sandstone gullies near the sea. Easily distinguished from the following species by the bluish-green undersurface of the leaves.

Range: coastal areas from Mt Dromedary into Qld. **Bark:** grey-smooth on young trees; thick, fissured, fibrous and red on old trees. **Leaves:** alternate, tough, shiny, concave and bluish-green below, with strong yellow mid-vein above. Crushed leaves have a faint pleasant oily fragrance. **Flowers:** PALE GREEN, tiny (about 5mm wide); numerous in dense terminal and axillary panicles. **Flowering time:** spring. **Fruit:** a shiny, black, compressed, globular drupe, about 20mm wide. **Name:** *glaucescens* = Lat. glaucous, blue-green, referring to pale undersides of leaves. *Oorawang* is an Aboriginal name from the Illawarra.

Cryptocarya microneura R. Brown

Murrogun **STRf**

A medium-tall tree 15-30m high, uncommon in subtropical rainforest in the Royal National Park, but more common in the Illawarra. It is very similar to *Cryptocarya glaucescens* and the two species often occur together.

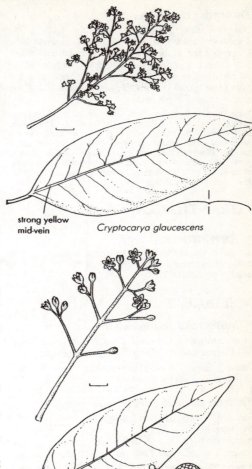

strong yellow mid-vein — *Cryptocarya glaucescens*

conspicuous net veins — *Cryptocarya microneura*

strong yellow mid-vein

Range: from Batemans Bay into Qld. **Leaves:** alternate, fairly thick, tough, shiny, *not bluish-green below*, tapering to a blunt point, fragrant when crushed, with strong yellow mid-vein. **Flowers:** about 8mm wide, in large terminal panicles, longer than the leaves. The panicle branches are densely white-pubescent, so much so that the whole tree can turn whitish at flowering time. **Flowering time:** November. **Fruit:** a black drupe, 12-16mm wide. **Name:** *microneura* = Gk. small-veined, referring to the conspicuous net-veins in the leaves.

• *Endiandra* R. Brown

A genus of rainforest trees with about 80 species worldwide, including 33 species in Australia.

Name: *Endiandra* = Gk. inner-anthers, because there are 3 stamens in each of 2 whorls, but only the inner whorl is fertile.

Endiandra sieberi Nees

Corkwood   **STRf, Temp Rf**

A medium-sized tree 20-30m high, with thick corky bark. Uncommon-rare in the area, in rainforests, often in gullies near the sea. It prefers sandy soils and sometimes occurs on the edges of wet Eucalypt woodland. The fruit is too large to be spread by birds; perhaps possums and gliders are the means of distribution.

Range: from Nowra to Qld.   **Bark:** pale, corky, deeply fissured, hard. **Leaves:** 5-9cm long, alternate, tough, glossy, drawn out to a blunt point, barely aromatic, with strong yellow mid-vein. In fact similar to *Cryptocarya microneura* except smaller.   **Flowers:** small, WHITISH, in axillary panicles.   **Flowering time:** early spring.   **Fruit:** a shiny deep blue or purple drupe 20-25mm long.   **Name:** *sieberi* = after Franz Wilhelm Sieber of Prague, Bohemia, who collected extensively in Australia from 1819-23.

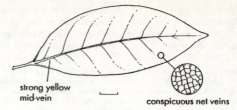

strong yellow mid-vein

conspicuous net veins

Endiandra sieberi

LORANTHACEAE Mistletoes

• *Amylotheca*

A rare species, restricted to rainforest, including littoral rainforest (where *Banksia integrifolia* is its most common host). —See MISTLETOES.

MELIACEAE

• *Synoum* A. Jussieu (sin-O-um)

An endemic genus of trees with 1 species in eastern Australia, and 1 on the Atherton Tableland in north-eastern Qld

Name: *Synoum* = Gk. joined egg, referring to the seeds joined in pairs in each ovary chamber.

Synoum glandulosum (Smith) A. Jussieu

Scentless Rosewood, Bastard Rosewood
Ss, Temp Rf

A leafy shrub 1.5-3m high in this area, common in moist sheltered gullies. A useful indicator of rainforest conditions.

Range: NSW coastal areas, and Qld.   **Leaves:** with 5-7, occasionally 9, leaflets, glossy, hairless, rather thick, with hairy domatia.   **Flowers:** CREAMY WHITE, petals tinged with pink, rather stiff and waxy, stamens 10, filaments united in a tube, rather stiff and waxy.   **Flowering time:** summer.   **Fruits:** attractive RED capsules, 2-3cm wide and 3-lobed, in spring.   **Name:** *glandulosum* = Lat. having glands, referring to the domatia.

cross-section of flower

Synoum glandulosum

• *Toona* M. Roemer

A genus of largely tropical trees with about 15 species, including a single species in Australia.

Name: *Toona* = from Toon, an Indian name for a tree in this genus.

Toona ciliata M. Roemer

(previously *Toona australis*)
Red Cedar   **STRf**

A medium to tall deciduous tree 20-40m high, found in subtropical rainforest in the Royal National Park (Lady Carrington Drive has many fine old specimens), and Illawarra.

The rich red colour and fine woodworking qualities make

domatia

old fruits

Toona ciliata

Red Cedar a premium furniture timber. It was heavily cut and almost wiped out in the last century. The crash of 1893 ruined the Cedar trade and its international position was taken by American Redwoods. Populations have now recovered in many places, especially the Illawarra, where it is almost common in remnant rainforests.

Easily spotted at a distance by yellow leaves in mid-winter, tangled skeletal branches in late winter, and rosy new leaves in early summer.[3]

Range: Ulladulla to the Atherton Tableland. **Bark:** pale, scaly. **Leaves:** pinnate, the leaflets usually 14-16, thin-textured, shiny both sides, flat, soft, with domatia. **Flowers:** small, 5-6mm long, WHITE-pinkish, with 5 stamens; in a long open drooping pyramidal panicle. **Flowering time:** October-November (with new leaves). **Fruit:** brown woody capsules. **Name:** *ciliata* = Lat. fringed. **Similar species:** *Euroschinus falcata* (ANARCARDIACEAE), and *Ailanthus altissima**, Tree of Heaven, (Simaroubaceae). The last species is an exotic tree found in old gardens, and now becoming a pest in gullies, especially in mountain areas. It has similar pinnate leaves, but the leaflets lack domatia and have prominent gland-bearing lobes near the base.

MIMOSACEAE

Acacia binervata

A. binervata

Two-veined Hickory **Ss, Temp Rf**
A dense leafy shrub or small tree 3-8m tall, common on the edges of rainforest.
—See MAJOR FAMILIES: Mimosaceae.

Acacia maidenii F. Mueller

Hickory, Sally, Maiden's Wattle **Ss, Temp Rf**
A slender, graceful shrub or tree to 12m high, found in gullies near the coast, usually associated with rainforest, e.g. Royal National Park.

Range: Illawarra to southern Qld, in coastal areas, also a few rare occurrences in coastal Vic. **Phyllodes:** drooping, gently curved, gradually tapering at both ends, 8-15mm, occasionally to 20mm, wide, with 2 main veins (one more prominent than the other) and many tiny parallel veins. **Flower-heads:** PALE YELLOW, in cylindrical heads. **Flowering time:** autumn and winter. **Name:** *maidenii* = in honour of J.H. Maiden (1859-1925), Government Botanist and long-time Director of the Royal Botanic Gardens, Sydney. **Similar species:** *A. implexa* (more than 2 main veins), *A. longifolia* (phyllodes never loosely drooping).

Acacia implexa

Acacia implexa

Ss, Temp Rf margins
A leafy shrub or small tree 3-8m tall, common on the edges of rainforest.
—See MAJOR FAMILIES: Mimosaceae.

Acacia longifolia

Acacia longifolia

Sydney Golden Wattle **Ss, Temp Rf margins**
A shrub or small tree 3-5m tall, common on the edges of rainforest.
—See MAJOR FAMILIES: Mimosaceae.

• Pararchidendron Kosterm.

A genus with a single species. There are 4 varieties, 1 of which occurs in eastern Australia, the others occur in south-east Asia

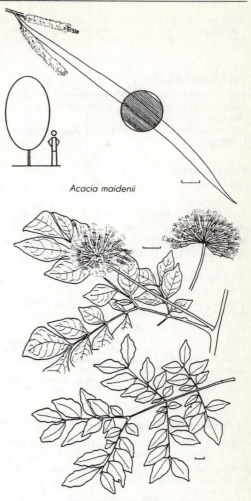

Acacia maidenii

Pararchidendron pruinosum

Name: *Pararchidendron* = Gk. beside-*Archidendron*, i.e. similar but different to *Archidendron*, a related genus.

Pararchidendron pruinosum (Bentham) Nielsen

(previously *Abarema sapindoides, Pithecellobium pruinosum*)
Snow Wood **STRf**
An attractive small tree, usually 4-8m high, found in subtropical rainforest in the Royal National Park and the Illawarra, where it is uncommon.

Snow Wood resembles an ancestral wattle. It is easy to see how the large bipinnate leaves and globular flower heads could be related to those of modern wattles.

Range: Illawarra to the Atherton Tableland in Qld, NG and Asia. **Leaves:** bipinnate, 20-50cm long with a single gland near the base of the rhachis; leaflets more or less rhomboid, thin, hairless, soft, undulate. **Flowers:**

CREAM becoming ORANGE, stalked, in dense globular heads on long peduncles, paired in the axils. **Flowering time:** December. **Fruit:** a large pod, curling after opening. **Name:** *pruinosum* = Lat. covered in whitish dust.

MONIMIACEAE

A family of rainforest trees and shrubs with about 150 species worldwide, in 20 genera. There are 18 species in Australia, in 8 genera.

It is an ancient family, related to Magnoliaceae and Lauraceae.

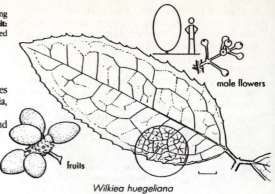

male flowers

fruits

Wilkiea huegeliana

• *Palmeria*
—See CLIMBERS.

• *Wilkiea* F. Mueller

An endemic genus of 6 species.

Name: *Wilkiea* = after David E. Wilkie, Vice-President of the Philosophical Society of Vic (later the Royal Society of Vic).

Wilkiea huegeliana (Tulasne) A. de Candolle

Wilkiea **STRf**

A shrub 2-4m tall (rarely a small tree), with amazingly stiff and leathery leaves. Common in subtropical rainforest in the Royal National Park and Illawarra.

Range: NSW coastal areas and Qld. **Leaves:** opposite, fairly thick, stiff, shiny or dull, concave below, coarsely toothed, with raised net-veins on both surfaces, finely hairy all over. **Flowers:** unisexual (plants dioecious), YELLOW, spherical, 3-4mm wide, in short racemes. **Flowering time:** summer (November). **Name:** *huegeliana* = after Baron Carl von Huegel or Hügel (1795-1870), an Austrian traveller and botanist, who collected in WA in 1833.

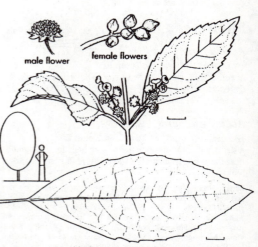

male flower   female flowers

Hedycarya angustifolia

• *Hedycarya* J. R. & G. Forster

A genus of tropical shrubs and trees with about 25 species, including 2 species in Australia.

Name: *Hedycarya* = Gk. sweet-nut, as the fruits resemble the common Mulberry.

Hedycarya angustifolia A. Cunningham

Native Mulberry **STRf**

A shrub or small tree usually 2-4m, occasionally to 8m, tall. Found on the edges of subtropical rainforest in the Royal National Park and Illawarra.

Range: coastal districts from Bass Straight to Qld; common in Vic rainforests. **Leaves:** opposite, shiny, mid-green, 4-10cm long, toothed. Microscopic oil dots are present, giving the leaves a pleasant aroma when crushed. **Flowers:** unisexual (plants dioecious), YELLOWISH, in axillary racemes; the floral tube is flat or slightly cup-shaped, with 8 (6-10) pointed segments, carrying many stamens or carpels. **Flowering time:** early spring. **Fruit:** an aggregate of 10-20 yellow fleshy drupes. **Name:** *angustifolia* = Lat. narrow-leaved.

MORACEAE

A family of trees and climbers with about 1400 species in 53 genera, widely distributed in the tropics. There are about 47 species in 7 genera in Australia.

The family is related to Urticaceae, which also has fleshy aggregate fruits. It includes the edible Fig (*Ficus carica*), Mulberry, (*Morus nigra* and *Morus alba*), Breadfruit (*Artocarpus communis*), Jackfruit (*Artocarpus beterophyllus*), and *F. elastica*, the source of India rubber before Para Rubber (*Hevea*) came into use.

Figs were eaten by Aborigines in many parts of Australia.

• *Ficus* Linnaeus (FY-cus)

A genus of rainforest trees (or climbers), often with immense buttressed roots, with about 1000 species widely distributed in Europe and Asia. There are 42 species in Australia.

The fig is not the fruit, but the entire inflorescence! Its hollow interior is lined with hundreds of tiny unisexual flowers (the male near the opening, the female deeper inside). At the tip is an entrance used by tiny female wasps (family Agaonidae) which are the agents of pollination. The females are attracted by wingless male wasps which spend their entire life cycle inside the fig. Each species of fig is

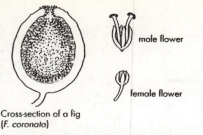

Cross-section of a fig
(*F. coronata*)

male flower

female flower

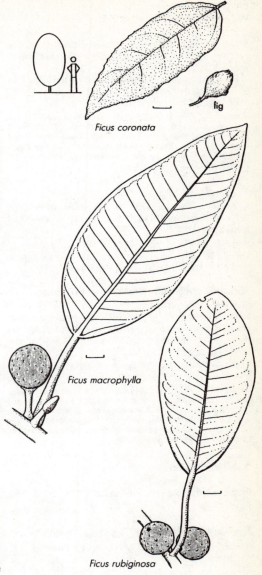

Ficus coronata

fig

Ficus macrophylla

Ficus rubiginosa

dependent on a single species of wasp for its fertilisation.

The leaves exude a thick milky sap which contains rubber. A distinctive feature is the long fleshy stipules rolled around each leaf bud, which fall when the leaf opens.

Buttressed species such as *F. superba* and *F. macrophylla* are known as 'strangler figs'. After they commence their lives as seedlings in the branches of another tree, 'they send roots down to the ground which, in their course, adhere to the tree . . . Those that reach the ground thicken rapidly, still spreading themselves upon the face of the foster-tree, which, at length, is completely encased. These gigantic parasites rear their towering heads above all the other trees . . .'[4]

Name: *Ficus* = Latin name for Fig (the English word is derived from *Ficus* via the French name).

Ficus coronata Spin

Sandpaper Fig   **STRf, Temp Rf**

A straggly small tree usually 3-4m tall, common on creek banks in subtropical rainforest.

The leaves are so rough that they can be used to smooth timber. 'They make a good substitute for sandpaper and will polish bone or ivory' wrote A. G. Hamilton.[5]

Range: NSW coast and ranges, Vic, Qld and NT.   **Leaves:** 7-15cm, roughly scabrous on upper surface.   **Figs:** covered in short stiff hairs, 10-30mm wide, often growing from the trunk.   **Figs ripen:** January-June.   **Name:** *coronata* = Lat. crowned, referring to the circlet of pointed segments around the entrance to the fig.

Ficus macrophylla Desfontaines ex Persoon

Moreton Bay Fig   **STRf**

A colossal tree with an immense buttressed trunk, usually 30-50m tall, found in subtropical rainforest. Its spreading crown emerges above the canopy of other trees. Common in the Illawarra, and occasional in the Royal National Park.

Range: Illawarra and NSW north coast, and Qld.   **Leaves:** large (10-25cm long), glossy, thick, smooth both sides, rusty underneath (with microscopic felt).   **Figs:** 18-25mm, stalked, in pairs, yellow, becoming purple when ripe.   **Figs ripen:** much of the year.   **Name:** *macrophylla* = Gk. large-leaved.

Ficus rubiginosa Desfontaines ex Ventenat

Port Jackson Fig, Rusty Fig, Dthaaman

Temp Rf, Ss

A small tree, 4-10m high. Common around Sydney on the sides of gullies. It begins life as an epiphyte in crevices on sandstone cliffs, eventually enveloping the rock in a massive system of coalesced roots. Distinguished from similar fig species by the rusty leaf undersides and absence of buttresses on the trunk.

The figs were eaten by Sydney Aborigines. They are still popular with birds, bats, and flying foxes, which may be heard squabbling in the trees after dark.

Range: coast and ranges from Bateman's Bay north into Qld.   **Leaves:** usually but not always with a furry layer of rusty coloured hairs on the lower surface (always on young leaves), fairly thick and tough, with recurved margins. Note the thick stalks.   **Figs:** 12-20mm diameter, in pairs, purple with warty markings.   **Fruit ripen:** February-July.   **Name:** *rubigosa* = reddish brown, from the leaf undersides. *Dthaaman* is an Aboriginal name from the Sydney area.

Ficus superba Miquel
var. *henneana* (Miquel) Corner

Deciduous Fig   **STRf**

A large tree with an immense buttressed trunk. Deciduous in winter. Common in subtropical rainforest in the Illawarra, less so in the Royal National Park.

The pallid stipules from new growth cloak the forest floor in November; they have a delicious acid flavour and while not exactly edible are pleasant to chew.

Range: from the Illawarra to Qld and NT.   **Leaves:** deciduous, 7-14cm long, green underneath, with long slender leaf stalks (by comparison, those of *F. rubiginosa* are at least 3mm wide).   **Figs:** on stalks 4-6mm long, 25-30mm wide, green-yellow turning dark purple.   **Figs ripen:** December-June.   **Name:** *superba* = Lat. excelling, *henneana* = Lat. brownish-red.

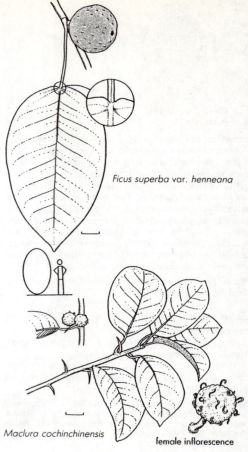

Ficus superba var. henneana

• *Maclura* Nuttall

A genus of shrubs with 12 species, widespread in the tropics, including 1 species native to Australia and 1 introduced species.

Name: *Maclura* = after William Maclure, a scientific philosopher, who made great contributions to geology in the United States in the late 1700s and early 1800s.

Maclura cochinchinensis (Loureiro) Corner

Cockspur Thorn   **STRf**

A weedy-looking shrub 2-3m tall with graceful cane-like branches, easily recognised by its cruel thorns. Found on the edges of rainforest. Uncommon in the Royal National Park, more common in the Illawarra.

The fruits are edible when ripe, juicy, with a pleasant, sweet flavour.

Range: NSW coastal areas, Qld and south-east Asia.   **Leaves:** 4-8cm long, oval, dull, flat, with a sharp woody thorn in each axil.   **Flowers:** unisexual (plants dioecious), in YELLOW globular clusters, 3-8mm wide, paired in the axils.   **Flowering time:** early summer.   **Aggregate fruit:** orange, 12-16mm wide, ripens mid-late summer.   **Name:** *cochinchinensis* = from Cochinchina, an old name for Indo-China.

Maclura cochinchinensis

female inflorescence

• *Streblus* Burton

A genus with 25 species mainly in southern Asia and the Pacific, including 2 species in Australia.

Name: *Streblus* = Gk. twisted, from the twisted branches.

Streblus brunonianus (Endlicher) F. Mueller

Whalebone Tree, Axe-handle Wood, Grey Handlewood, Waddywood, Ragwood
STRf

Usually a small tree, 4-8m tall, found in subtropical rainforest in the Royal National Park. The trunk is marked with distinctive horizontal rows of wart-like lenticels (breathing pores). An interesting feature is the sprung anther filaments which, when released, fling the pollen away from the flower in explosive bursts.

Range: NSW coastal areas, Blue Mountain and Qld.   **Leaves:** thin, tough, shiny above, irregularly toothed on the upper half. The juvenile leaves (rarely seen) are very long and slender, with 2 short lobes at the base.   **Flowers:** unisexual (plants monoecious), the males in long spikes 15-40mm long, the females in very short spikes with a few flowers.   **Fruit:** a yellow berry about 5mm long.   **Flowering time:** October-February.

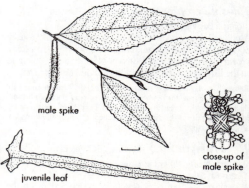

male spike

juvenile leaf

close-up of male spike

Streblus brunonianus

Name: *brunonianus* = after Robert Brown, renowned early botanist in New South Wales. The origin of the common name Whalebone Tree is from the stiff tough timber being used to make whalebone ribs for women's corsets. The name Handlewood comes from its use for axe and tool handles.

MYOPORACEAE

Myoporum acuminatum

Mangrove Boobialla   **STRf, Sal**
A small leafy tree with pale corky bark, occasionally found in rainforest.
—See COASTAL AND ESTUARINE SPECIES.

MYRSINACEAE

Rapanea howittiana Mez

Turnipwood, Brush Muttonwood   **STRf, Temp Rf**
A small tree 3-10m high, common in subtropical rainforest in the Royal National Park and Illawarra. Similar to *R. variabilis* except the majority of leaves on each plant are toothless.

Range: NSW coast and ranges, and Vic. **Leaves:** glossy, fairly thickish, tough, dull below, hairless. There are always some adult leaves with a few teeth. Leaves on young plants are toothed and cannot be distinguished from *R. variabilis*. **Flowers:** small, in clusters on old wood. The perianth is divided more or less to its base, while that of *R. variabilis* is only divided to about half its length. **Flowering time:** spring. **Fruit:** a yellowish globular drupe. **Name:** *howittiana* = after Alfred William Howitt (1830-1908), the explorer-naturalist who found King, the survivor of the Burke and Wills expedition. He was the nephew of Dr. Godfrey Howitt, whose name is given to *Howittia trilocularis* (Malvaceae).

MYRTACEAE

• *Acmena* De Candolle

A genus with 8 species endemic to eastern Australia, with many more in South-east Asia.

Name: *Acmena* = one of the nymphs of Venus. The myrtle was sacred to Venus.

Acmena smithii (Poiret) Merrill & Perry

Lillypilly, Tdgerail   **Temp Rf, STRf**
A shrub or small tree with dense dark glossy foliage, up to 20m high in rainforest gullies but reduced to a dwarf shrub on exposed coastal headlands. Common in gullies, cliff lines and rainforest.

The fruit (in autumn and winter) is edible with a sour, refreshing flavour, (although exposed coastal specimens are too small and tough). They were eaten by Aborigines.

Range: coastal districts from Vic to northern Qld. **Leaves:** opposite, dark green, thick, tough, glossy, with visible oil dots. **Flowers:** CREAM/WHITE. **Flowering time:** summer. **Fruit:** a fairly succulent white or pink berry containing a single seed, edible, slightly acid. **Name:** *smithii* = honours James Smith (1759-1828), celebrated English botanist. *Tdgerail* is an Aboriginal name from the Illawarra. Lillypilly is of uncertain origin, it may be Aboriginal or a European children's name.

• *Backhousia* J. D. Hooker & Harvey

An endemic genus of 7 species distributed in eastern NSW and Qld.

Name: by J.D. Hooker in honour of James Backhouse, an itinerant Quaker preacher with a botanical bent. He collected

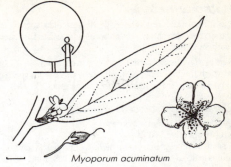

Myoporum acuminatum

anthers

Rapanea howittiana

the type specimen of *B. myrtifolia*. During 1832-38 he travelled by foot throughout New South Wales and Tas, lecturing against the twin evils of alcohol and papism. His *Narrative of a Visit to the Australian Colonies* is the best single portrait of pre-goldrush Australia.

Backhousia myrtifolia J. D. Hooker & Harvey

Grey Myrtle, Lancewood   **Temp Rf, STRf**
A spreading shrub usually 3-4m high, found in dense colonies beside streams in sheltered gullies. Easily recognised by its streamside habitat and dull dark green foliage. The young branches are covered in fine grey hairs.

Range: NSW south coast and ranges, and Qld. **Leaves:** opposite, finely grey-hairy below when young, with distinct oil dots. **Flowers:** with CREAM petals and a persistent GREENISH calyx. **Flowering time:** November-December. **Fruit:** a dry capsule concealed by the greenish sepals. **Name:** *myrtifolia* = Myrtle-leaved. The Myrtle is the European representative of the family.

• *Rhodamnia* Jack

A genus of rainforest trees with 10 Australian species and many others stretching through South-east Asia to Burma and southern China.

Name: *rhodamnia* = Gk. *rhodon*, a rose, *amnion*, a bowl in which the blood of sacrificial lambs was caught (perhaps in reference to the reddish calyx of some species).

Rhodamnia rubescens (Bentham) Miquel

(previously *Rhodamnia trinervia*)
Scrub Turpentine   **STRf**
A small rainforest tree 4-8m high. Occasional in rainforest gullies in Royal National Park, Ku-ring-gai Chase National Park, and the Illawarra. A really beautiful species with scented flowers in spring, bunches of bright red berries in summer, and fine somewhat drooping foliage.

Range: from Durras mountain on the south coast of NSW to southern Qld. **Leaves:** opposite, softly hairy underneath, with 3 main veins. **Flowers:** WHITE, sweetly fragrant, in axillary cymes. **Flowering time:** spring. **Name:** *rubescens* = Lat. flushed.

Syncarpia glomulifera

Turpentine   **Ss, Temp Rf, STRf**
A tall stout leafy tree with coarse fibrous bark, common in or near rainforest.
—See MAJOR FAMILIES: Myrtaceae.

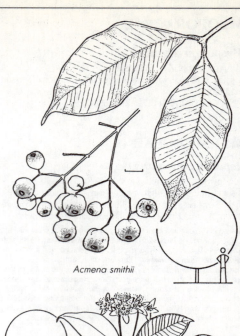

Acmena smithii

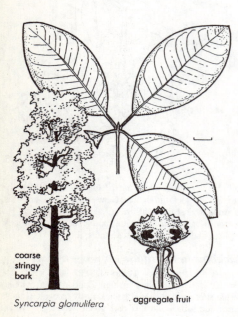

coarse
stringy
bark

Syncarpia glomulifera   aggregate fruit

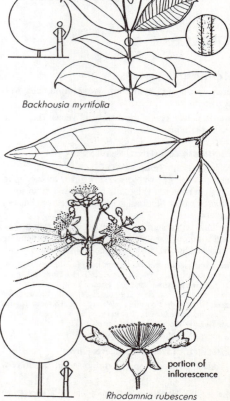

Backhousia myrtifolia

portion of
inflorescence

Rhodamnia rubescens

• *Syzygium* R. Brown ex Gaertner (siz-IDG-ee-um)

A genus with 66 Australian species, mainly tropical, and many other species in Asia.

Name: *Syzygium* = joined, from the paired leaves and branchlets in the original Jamaican species.

Syzygium australe (Wendland ex Link) B. Hyland

(previously included in *S. paniculatum*)
Brush Cherry **STRf**
A small tree, mostly 3-8m high, with dark dense foliage. Fairly common in subtropical rainforest in the Royal National Park and Illawarra. The fruit is edible.

Range: NSW coasts and Qld. **Leaves:** opposite, broad, dark green, glossy, with a drawn-out tip (accuminate), fairly thick and tough, with visible oil dots. **Flowers:** WHITE, with unequal sepals persisting in the fruits. **Flowering time:** summer. **Fruit:** pink to red, succulent, longer than wide. **Name:** *australe* = Lat. southern.

Syzygium paniculatum Gaertner

Magenta Lillypilly
Temp Rf   Endangered 3ECi
A small to medium tree, mostly 3-8m high, with dark dense foliage. Found in rainforest. It was once common around Botany Bay, but now rare, probably entirely restricted to Towra Point in the Sydney area. The fruit (in May) is a large crisp and succulent magenta-red berry which although somewhat sour is quite edible and refreshing. It was probably the first fruit sampled by Cook's party in 1770. Banks' journal records: 'They (Cook and Solander) also found several trees of the Jambosa kind, much in colour and shape resembling cherries; of these they eat plentifully and brought home also abundance, which we eat with much pleasure tho they had little to recommend them but a light acid'.

Range: from Jervis Bay to Bulahdelah, in coastal rainforests. Common in old gardens. **Leaves:** similar to *S. australe*. **Flowers:** WHITE, in small dense axillary cymes, with unequal sepals persisting in the fruits. **Flowering time:** summer. **Fruit:** pink to red, succulent, globular (cherry-like). **Name:** *paniculatum* = having panicles.

Syzygium oleosum (F. Mueller) B.P.M. Hyland

Blue Lillypilly **STRf, Temp Rf**
A small tree, mostly 3-8m high, with dark dense foliage. Found in rainforest gullies. The most common *Syzygium* in the area: fairly common in subtropical rainforest in the Royal National Park and also recorded in the past from Barrenjoey, Kurnell, Manly and Otford. Very similar to *S. paniculatum* but distinguished by the fruit (pink-purple, changing to blue when ripe) and the larger and much more numerous oil-dots in the leaves (best seen with a hand lens). The fruit is edible.

Range: from Illawarra to southern Qld. **Leaves:** like *S. paniculatum* except with numerous visible oil dots and a strong odour when crushed. **Flowers:** WHITE, in axillary cymes, with more or less equal sepals persisting in the fruits. **Flowering time:** summer. **Fruit:** pink-purple, becoming blue when ripe, succulent, globular, similar in shape to *S. paniculata*. **Name:** *oleosum* = Lat. oily, referring to the leaves.

Tristaniopsis laurina

(Smith) P.G. Wilson and J.T. Waterhouse

Water Gum, Kanooka, Wallaya **Temp Rf**
A small spreading tree usually 4-10m high with handsome foliage and distinctive pale bare sheeny bark. A common tree throughout eastern Australia. It shadows the waters of rocky creeks and rivers in mountain valleys and in sandstone gullies in the coastal plateaus, where it occurs with Lillypilly

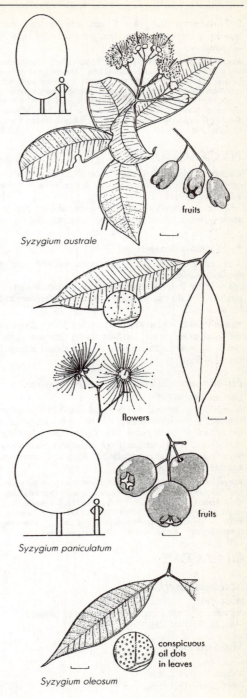

Syzygium australe

fruits

flowers

Syzygium paniculatum

fruits

Syzygium oleosum

conspicuous oil dots in leaves

and Coachwood. The yellow flowers, forming dense leafy bundles at the ends of branches, are a beautiful sight at Christmas.

Range: from Gippsland, Vic to southern Qld. Also a very common street tree in Sydney. **Bark:** smooth, pale, sheeny. **Leaves:** to 14cm long, hairless, satin. **Flowers:** GOLDEN YELLOW, 3 per leaf joint, with prominent stamens. **Flowering time:** December-January. **Fruit:** a 3-valved non-woody capsule. **Name:** *laurina* = Laurel-like, referring to the leaves. *Wallaya* is a local Aboriginal name from Brisbane water. *Kanooka* is a name from Gippsland, but according to Maiden, not an Aboriginal one.

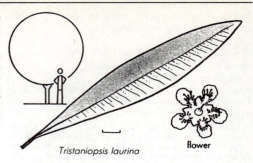

Tristaniopsis laurina

flower

NYCTAGINACEAE

A family with about 300 species in about 30 genera worldwide, especially in the tropical Americas. Australia has 6 native species in 2 genera.

The family includes *Bougainvillea spectabilis*, a popular garden climber, whose flowers have large colourful bracts.

• *Pisonia* Linnaeus (pis-O-nee-a)

A tropical genus with about 50 species worldwide, and 3 species in Australia.

The sticky fruits of *P. grandis*, found on coral cays in northern Australia and elsewhere, are reputed to ensnare and kill small birds.

Name: *Pisonia* = after Willem Piso (died 1648), doctor to the Dutch governor and the West Indian Company in the Dutch South American colonies. He co-authored a natural history of Brasil.

Pisonia umbellifera (J. R. & G. Forster) Seeman
Birdlime Tree   **STRf**

An erect shrub or small tree 3-6m tall found in subtropical rainforest in the Royal National Park where it is uncommon to rare, and in the Illawarra. The flowers have a faint but beautiful and heavy fragrance. The fruits are remarkably sticky when mature, becoming attached to birds and animals as a means of distribution.

Range: uncommon in NSW, in coastal rainforests from Jervis Bay to Qld, also South-east Asia and the Pacific. **Leaves:** large (20-40cm long), firm, glossy, hairless, rather thick, smooth, with rounded tips. **Flowers:** about 6mm long, funnel shaped, with PALE GREENISH CREAM calyx segments and a dull green tube, in a terminal panicle of umbels. **Flowering time:** November. **Name:** *umbellifera* = Lat. carrying umbels.

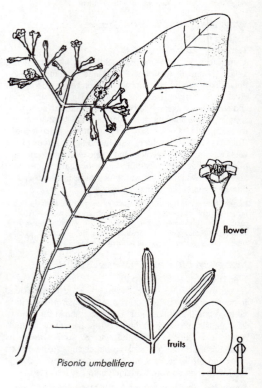

flower

fruits

Pisonia umbellifera

OLEACEAE

Notelaea longifolia
Mock Olive
A shrub 1.5-3m tall, common on the edges of rainforest.
—See LESSER FAMILIES.

Notelaea ovata
Mock Olive
A shrub 1.5-3m tall. Rare.
—See LESSER FAMILIES.

Notelaea venosa R. Brown (no-tel-EE-a)
Temp Rf

A shrub or small tree 2.5-8m tall, found in or near rainforest. Uncommon in the area. Recorded from Wondabyne, Royal National Park (Upper Causeway), and Georges River (The Woolwash). Common in the Illawarra.

Range: coast and ranges of the eastern mainland. **Leaves:** opposite, fairly tough, reticulate but relatively smooth, hairless or furry, drawn out to a fine point. **Flowers and fruit:** bitter blackish olive-like drupes, 10-15mm wide. **Name:** *venosa* = Lat. veiny. **Similar species:** distinguish from *N. longifolia* by the shorter, broader leaves, with lateral veins becoming thinner near the margin (in *N. longifolia* they stay the same thickness).

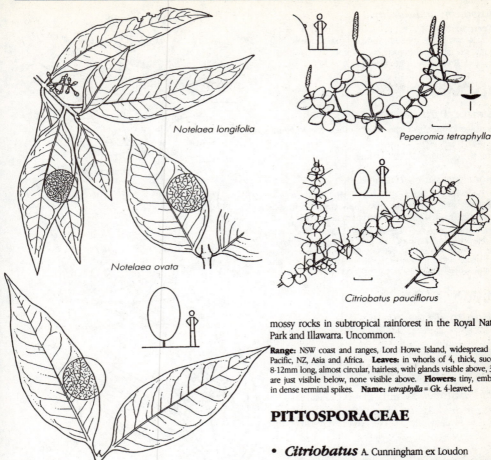

Notelaea longifolia

Notelaea ovata

Notelaea venosa

Peperomia tetraphylla

Citriobatus pauciflorus

PEPEROMIACEAE

A family of small succulent herbs with over 1000 species in 4 genera, widespread in the tropics. There are 7 species in a single genus in Australia.

The family is closely related to Piperaceae.

• *Peperomia* Ruiz and Pavon

A genus with about 1000 species worldwide, including 7 species in Australian rainforests.

Name: *Peperomia* = Gk. pepper-like, from its closeness to *Piper*, the true peppers.

Peperomia tetraphylla

(J.R. Forster) W. J. Hooker & Arnott **STRf**

A weak succulent herb usually about 10cm high, found in mossy rocks in subtropical rainforest in the Royal National Park and Illawarra. Uncommon.

Range: NSW coast and ranges, Lord Howe Island, widespread in the Pacific, NZ, Asia and Africa. **Leaves:** in whorls of 4, thick, succulent, 8-12mm long, almost circular, hairless, with glands visible above, 3 veins are just visible below, none visible above. **Flowers:** tiny, embedded in dense terminal spikes. **Name:** *tetraphylla* = Gk. 4-leaved.

PITTOSPORACEAE

• *Citriobatus* A. Cunningham ex Loudon

A genus of small shrubs with 4 species in Australia and 1 in South-east Asia.

Name: *Citriobatus* = Gk. orange-thorn.

Citriobatus pauciflorus

A. Cunningham ex Ettingshausen

Orange Thorn **STRf**

A stiff wiry shrub 1-1.5m tall, with numerous fine thorns. Very common in subtropical rainforest in the Royal National Park and Illawarra.

Range: NSW coast and ranges, and Qld. **Leaves:** satin both sides, flat, stiff, hairless, more or less circular to rhomboidal, toothed in the upper part. **Flowers:** small, WHITE, solitary, axillary. **Flowering time:** spring-early summer. **Fruit:** a bright orange berry to about 10mm wide. **Name:** *pauciflorus* = Lat. few-flowered.

Pittosporum revolutum

Temp Rf

A shrub 0.5-2.5m tall, common in sheltered places. A pioneer rainforest species.

—See LESSER FAMILIES: Pittosporaceae.

Pittosporum undulatum

Ss, Temp Rf, STRf

Usually a small tree, opportunistic in coastal areas. Large specimens occur in subtropical rainforest.
—See LESSER FAMILIES: Pittosporaceae.

PROTEACEAE

• *Stenocarpus* R. Brown

A genus with 4 Australian species and others extending into NG and New Caledonia.

Name: *Stenocarpus* = Gk. narrow-fruit.

Stenocarpus salignus R. Brown

Scrub Beefwood **STRf, Ss**

A shrub or small tree to 6m high, fairly common in local rainforest gullies and edges of subtropical rainforest.

Range: from Milton to Qld. **Leaves:** glossy, fairly tough, with veins more or less parallel. **Flowers:** WHITE, with a single nectar gland in the base. **Flowering time:** October-November. **Fruit:** a green follicle, rather bean-like. **Name:** *salignus* = Lat. willowy. Scrub is a colonial name for rainforest, beefwood is from the red colour of the timber.

RHAMNACEAE

• *Alphitonia* (Fenzl) Endlicher

A genus of tropical trees with about 20 species, including 5-6 species in Australia.

Name: *Alphitonia* = Gk. *alphiton*, pearl barley, barley meal, referring to the dry, mealy quality of the fruit pulp.

Alphitonia excelsa (Fenzl) Reisseck ex Bentham

Red Ash, Leather Jacket, Murr-rung **STRf**

A small to medium (or tall) rainforest tree usually 6-10m

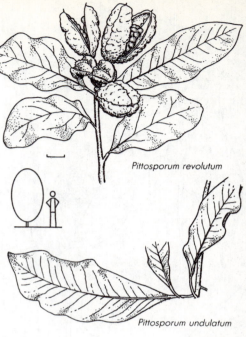

Pittosporum revolutum

Pittosporum undulatum

Stenocarpus salignus

high, with smooth grey bark. Common in subtropical rainforest in the Royal National Park and Illawarra. Rarely in sandstone gullies.

Aboriginal communities in Arnhem Land use the leaves as a skin disinfectant. They are rich in saponin and when rubbed with water produce a good lather. In other places Aborigines used an infusion of bark, root and wood on the body as a liniment, as a gargle for toothache, or as a tonic drink. The young leaf tips were chewed in case of upset stomach.

Range: coastal rainforests north from Mt Dromedary, also Qld, NT, and WA. **Leaves:** 10-14cm long; dark green, glossy, hairless, flat above; whitish with flat white felt and brownish veins below. **Flowers:** tiny (3-6mm wide), pale green, numerous in axillary panicles shorter than the leaves. **Flowering time:** December-March. **Fruit:** black, glossy, shaped like an inverted cup. **Name:** *excelsa* = Lat. excelling, superior. Murr-rung is an Aboriginal name from the Illawarra. **Similar species:** *Alphitonia* is distinguished from similar *Pomaderris* species by having leaves always held parallel to the ground.

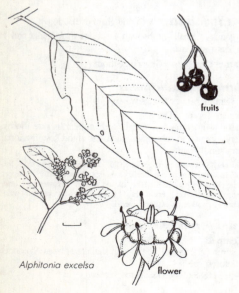

fruits

Alphitonia excelsa

flower

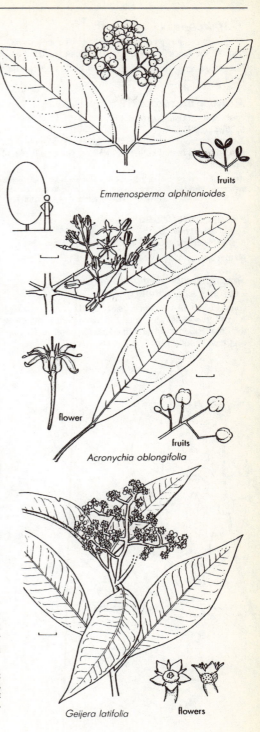

• *Emmenosperma* F. Mueller

A genus of rainforest trees with 3 species, 2 in tropical Australia and 1 in New Caledonia.

Name: *Emmenosperma* = Gk. *emmeno*, to be faithful, *sperma*, seed, referring to the seeds remaining attached to the base of the fruit.

Emmenosperma alphitonioides F. Mueller

Yellow Ash, Bonewood **STRf**
A medium-sized tree, found in subtropical rainforest in the Royal National Park and Illawarra. Uncommon.

Range: coastal rainforests north from Nowra into Qld.   **Leaves:** opposite, 6-9cm long, thin, glossy, hairless, lacking any obvious diagnostic features. **Flowers:** numerous, small, YELLOW-WHITE, in dense terminal cymes shorter than the leaves.   **Flowering time:** September-October.   **Fruit:** orange-yellow, 5-8mm wide, splitting in 2, to reveal 2 seeds.   **Name:** *alphitonioides* = *Alphitonia*-like (in fact it has little resemblance to *Alphitonia*).

fruits

Emmenosperma alphitonioides

RUTACEAE

• *Acronychia* F. R. & G. Forster (ac-ro-NICK-ee-a)

A genus of small rainforest trees with about 25 species widely distributed in Asia and the Pacific. There are 16 Australian species in Qld, NSW and Vic.

Name: *Acronychia* = Gk. claw-tip, from the appearance of the petals.

Acronychia oblongifolia
(A. Cunningham ex W. J. Hooker) Endlicher ex Heynhold

STRf, Temp Rf
A large shrub or small tree 2-8m high, found in rainforest gullies in the Royal National Park. The white crisp succulent fruits are edible, with an oily fragrance.

Range: NSW coastal areas, Qld and Vic.   **Leaves:** 1-foliate, opposite, glossy both sides, thin, flat, with a small notch at the tip, oil dots visible when held up to the light, with a sweet lemon smell when crushed. **Flowers:** WHITE, in dense axillary cymes, with 4 spreading petals and 8 stamens.   **Flowering time:** February-March.   **Name:** *oblongifolia* = Lat. oblong-leaved.

flower

fruits

Acronychia oblongifolia

• *Geijera* Schott (GUY-jer-a)

A genus with 7 species worldwide, including 5 Australia species, distributed in NSW, Qld, NG and the Pacific.

Name: *Geijera* = after J. D. Geijer, an early Swedish botanist.

Geijera latifolia Lindley
STRf (Cumb)
A small tree usually found in subtropical rainforest. Very rare in the area, only recorded locally from a small rainforest remnant, the 'Native Vineyard', near Cobbitty. Relatively common in the Illawarra. Not recorded in the Royal National Park.

Range: north from the Illawarra into Qld.   **Leaves:** glossy, hairless, soft but rather tough, with visible oil dots, aromatic, not sharply pointed, to 10cm long, often with undulate margins.   **Flowers:** in a short pyramidal terminal panicle, YELLOWISH-WHITE.   **Name:** *salicifolia* = Lat. Willow-leaved.

Geijera latifolia   *flowers*

• *Melicope* J.R. and G. Forster

An endemic genus with 10 or more species, found in NSW, Qld, NZ, the Pacific, and widespread in tropical Asia.

Name: *Melicope* = Gk. honey-division, since the nectary glands are 8-lobed.

Melicope micrococca (F. Mueller) T. Hartley

(previously *Euodia micrococca*)
STRf, Temp Rf

A shrub or tree 1-6m high found in light-breaks in subtropical rainforest and humid gullies in the Royal National Park and Illawarra.

Range: Illawarra to Maryborough in Qld. **Leaves:** large, 3-foliate, flat, apparently hairless. **Flowers:** numerous in dense axillary clusters, WHITISH. **Flowers:** summer. **Name:** *micrococca* = Gk. small-seed.

• *Sarcomelicope* Engler

(previously *Bauerella*)

A genus with one species, closely related to *Acronychia*.

Name: *Sarcomelicope* = Gk. fleshy *Melicope*.

Sarcomelicope simplicifolia (Endlicher) T.G. Hartley **ssp.** *simplicifolia*

(previously *Bauerella simplicifolia*) **STRf**

A small tree to 8m high, found in subtropical rainforest in the Royal National Park and Illawarra. Also rarely in Ku-ring-gai Chase National Park.

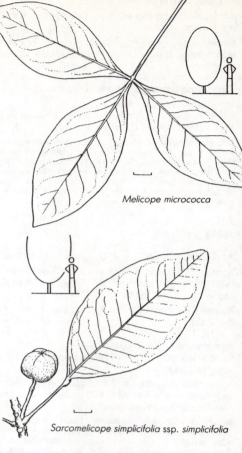

Melicope micrococca

Sarcomelicope simplicifolia ssp. *simplicifolia*

Alectryon subcinereus

fruits

juvenile leaflet

Range: NSW coastal areas, Qld, Lord Howe Island and Pacific Islands. **Leaves:** 1-foliate, opposite, moderately thick and tough, glossy both sides, with a tiny notch at the tip, oil glands present but microscopic, no special odour when crushed. **Flowers:** unisexual (plants dioecious), with 4 fringed petals and 8 stamens. **Fruit:** hard, not succulent, greenish brown. **Name:** *simplicifolia* = Lat. simple-leaved, i.e. not pinnate, as is usual in this family.

SAPINDACEAE

• *Alectryon* Gaertner (a-LEC-tre-on)

A genus of rainforest trees with about 30 species in Indonesia, NG and the Pacific, including 9 endemic species in Australia.

Name: *Alectryon* = Gk. a cock or rooster, from the cockscomb-like aril on the seeds.

Alectryon subcinereus (A. Gray) Radlkofer

Native Quince **STRf**

A small rainforest tree to 8m high, rare in the Sydney area. Recorded from Mitchell Park, Sackville area. Fairly common in the Illawarra. The seeds are edible, although no one seems

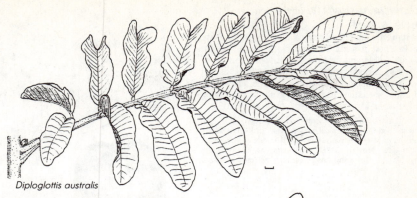

Diploglottis australis

to have recorded this before: they are soft and nutty within the black glossy shell and red aril.

Range: NSW coast, Vic and Qld. **Leaves:** pinnate, with 4-6 leaflets; glossy, thin textured, stiff, hairless, irregularly toothed in the upper part, with prominent reticulation. The juvenile leaves are larger and more strongly toothed. **Flowers:** small, PINK, in open axillary panicles. **Flowering time:** summer. **Fruit:** a capsule with 2 round lobes, each containing a single seed half-enclosed in a fleshy red aril. **Name:** *subcinereus* = Lat. almost ashy, referring to the colour of the leaves.

• *Diploglottis* J. D. Hooker

A genus of trees with 10 species, distributed in South-east Asia and the Pacific, including 8 endemic species in Austalia.

Name: *Diploglottis* = Gk. *diploos*, double, *glottis*, throat, probably referring to small tongue-like glands at the base of each petal.

Diploglottis australis (G. Don) Radlkofer

Native Tamarind **STRf**

A tree to 20m, found in subtropical rainforest in the Royal National Park and Illawarra. Easily recognised by its very large stiff pinnate leaves. The juicy orange fruits are sour, but pleasant to eat, resembling Tamarind.

Range: from the Illawarra to southern Qld. **Leaves:** very large (40-60cm long), pinnate; with leaflets 12-24cm long, rather thick, and often so stiff they rattle in the wind. Stems, rhachis and main veins are densely covered in rusty-golden felt. The juvenile leaves are large (sometimes very large) and papery with 1 or a few leaflets. **Flowers:** about 5mm long, in large stiff axillary panicles projecting above the forest canopy. **Name:** *australis* = Lat. southern.

• *Guioa* Cavanilles (ghee-O-a)

A genus of rainforest trees with about 78 species in South-east Asia and the Pacific, including 5 species in Australia.

Name: *Guioa* = after José Guio, a Spanish botanical artist.

Guioa semiglauca (F. Mueller) Radlkofer

Guioa **STRf, Temp Rf**

A small rainforest tree 8-15m tall, common in subtropical rainforest and littoral rainforest in the Royal National Park and Illawarra.

Range: from Batemans Bay to southern Qld. **Leaves:** pinnate, leaflets usually 4 (2-6), tough, hairless, dull olive green above. The undersurface

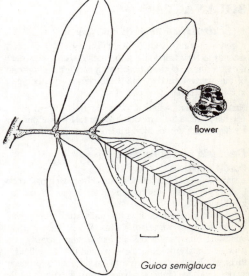

flower

Guioa semiglauca

is very distinctive: grey-green, with a dull waxy lustre, and veins barely visible. **Flowers:** small, about 3mm wide, numerous in dense axillary panicles. **Flowering time:** spring (October-November). **Fruit:** a 3-winged capsule, 6-12mm long. **Name:** *semiglauca* = half-glaucous (grey-green), referring to the leaf undersides.

SAPOTACEAE

A family of tropical trees with about 800 species in an uncertain number of genera. There are 31 species in 6 genera in Australia.

The family is closely related to Ebenaceae.

• *Planchonella* Pierre

A genus with about 20 species worldwide, including about 20 species in Australia.

Name: *Planchonella* = after L. Planchon (1858-1915), a French professor of pharmacy who wrote on exotic plants, including Sapotaceae.

Planchonella australis (R. Brown) Pierre

Black Apple   **STRf**
A tree 8-20m tall found in subtropical rainforest in the Royal
National Park and Illawarra. The large black-purple fruits (in
January) are edible and fleshy with a flavour like Custard
Apple. 'Among the other trees of the colony may be named
the black apple, a tree beautiful in form, outline, and foliage.
It bears a fruit something like a plum in shape, but having
an insipid flavour' wrote the traveller E. C. Booth in 1873.[6]

Range: NSW coastal rainforests north from Gerringong into Qld.
Leaves: shiny both sides, conspicuously reticulate, dark green above,
mid-green and more or less concave below, blunt or slightly pointed,
with a milky juice.   **Flowers:** GREEN, about 9mm long, honey-fragrant;
in axillary clusters.   **Flowering time:** December.   **Name:** *australis* =
Lat. southern.

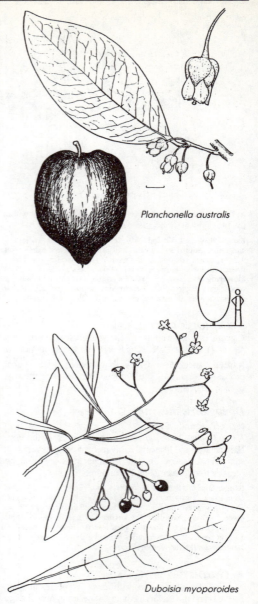

Planchonella australis

SOLANACEAE

• *Duboisia* R. Brown (doo-BOY-zee-a)

A genus of shrubs with 3-4 Australian species, 1 of which
extends to New Caledonia. It includes *Duboisia hopwoodii*,
the Pituri, the best known, but certainly not the most important
of the 'native tobaccos', which are chewed by Aborigines
in inland Australia.

Name: *Duboisia* = after Charles Du Bois (1656-1740), a
London merchant and treasurer of the East India Company.
He kept a private botanical garden and a large herbarium.

Duboisia myoporoides R. Brown

Duboisia, Corkwood   **Temp Rf**
A shrub 3-6m tall (sometimes a small tree) with pale corky
bark, found in rainforest margins in the Royal National Park
and Illawarra.

Its narcotic properties first came to European notice when
a correspondent wrote to William Woolls (about 1860)
informing him that 'It has an intoxicating property. The
aborigines make holes in the trunk and put some fluid in
them, which, when drunk on the following morning, produces
stupor. Branches of this shrub are thrown into pools for the
purpose of intoxicating the eels and bringing them to the
surface.'[7] Further investigation showed that it contained 2
valuable alkaloids, hyoscine and hyoscyamine, which are now
used as sedatives and to widen the pupil in eye surgery.
A hybrid, *D. myoporoides* x *leichhardtii*, is presently grown
in plantations in Qld and the dry leaf is exported, mainly
to pharmaceutical companies in Europe.[8]

Range: north from Clyde Mountain into Qld.   **Leaves:** soft, flat, dull,
thick, light green, hairless, 8-14cm long.   **Flowers:** WHITE, 7-8mm wide;
in a loose terminal panicle.**Flowering time:** October-November.   **Fruit:**
a small shiny black berry, 5-8mm wide.   **Name:** *myoporoides* =
Myoporum-like. It resembles *Myoporum acuminatum* in both the leaves
and the light corky bark.

• *Physalis* Linnaeus (FIZ-al-is)

A genus with about 100 species, mainly in the Americas,
including possibly only 1 native to Australia, and several
introduced species.

Name: *Physalis* = Gk. a bladder.

Duboisia myoporoides

Physalis peruviana [*] Linnaeus

Cape Gooseberry   **Rf margins**
A low bushy shrub with large furry leaves, fairly common
on the edges of subtropical rainforest. The fruit, inside the
inflated calyx, is edible. A native of South America, reaching
Australia via South Africa.

Range: NSW coast, Qld, Vic, SA, Lord Howe Island and South America.
Leaves: dull green, rather triangular, irregularly toothed, covered in fine
furry hairs.   **Flowers:** YELLOW, with 5 purplish spots near the throat.

Fruit: a yellow berry, inside the bladdery green-purple calx.   **Name:** *peruviana* = Peruvian.

• *Solanum aviculare*
—See MINOR FAMILIES.

Solanum pseudocapsicum * Linnaeus
Jerusalem Cherry, Madeira Winter Cherry
Temp Rf, STRf
A small erect shrub, usually 1-1.5m tall, common in or near rainforest on better soils. Introduced from South America.

Range: NSW coast, northern tablelands, inland areas, and South America.
Leaves: shiny, thin-textured, hairless, with prominent veins, 5-10cm long.
Flowers: WHITE, about 10mm wide, 1-3 together, on short lateral stalks.
Flowering time: spring-autumn.   **Fruit:** a red globular berry, about 15mm wide.   **Name:** *pseudocapsicum* = false-*Capsicum*.

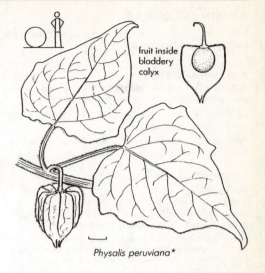

fruit inside
bladdery
calyx

Physalis peruviana *

Solanum pseudocapsicum *

STERCULIACEAE

Brachychiton acerifolius
(A. Cunningham ex G. Don) F. Mueller

Flame Tree   **STRf**
A medium to tall rainforest tree, to 35m high, deciduous in winter, found in subtropical rainforest in the Royal National Park and Illawarra. Also a popular street tree. It is famous for its extraordinary show of flowers about Christmas time, 'a burning accusation against the protest that there is no colour in the Australian bush.'[9] The ground and roasted seeds can be used as a coffee substitute.

Range: coastal districts from Wollongong to Gympie in Qld.   **Juvenile leaves:** 7-lobed, to 30cm long, with stems to 70cm long.   **Adult leaves:** entire or 3-lobed, shiny green both sides, paler on one side, tough, hairless, over 10cm long.   **Flowers:** BRIGHT RED, 1-2cm wide, in large axillary panicles, petals absent.   **Fruit:** a boat-shaped woody follicle about 12cm long.   **Name:** *acerifolium* = *Acer*-leaved. *Acer saccharum* is the European Maple.

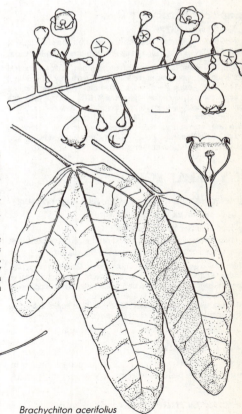

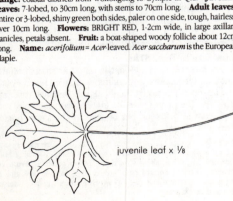

juvenile leaf x ⅛

Brachychiton acerifolius

SYMPLOCACEAE

A family with a single genus, related to Ebenaceae (*Diospyros*) and Sapotaceae (*Planchonella*).

• *Symplocos* Jacquin

A genus with about 350 species distributed in tropical Asia and America. There are 6 species in eastern Australia.

Name: *Symplocos* = Gk. twisted together, referring to the stamens united at the base.

Note: one author considers the 2 local trees to be varieties of the Asian species *S. cochinchinensis*.

Symplocos stawellii F. Mueller

Buff Hazelwood   **SRTf**

A small tree, 4-8m tall. Locally rare, in subtropical rainforest in the Royal National Park and at Little Cattai River. Distinguish from *S. thwaitesii* by the much smaller flowers.

Range: NSW coast, and Qld.   **Leaves:** similar to *S. thwaitesii*.   **Flowers:** similar to *S. thwaitesii*, except smaller (5-8mm wide), and with hairless stalks and calyces.   **Flowering time:** spring.   **Name:** *stawellii* = after Sir William Stawell, Chief Justice of Vic, one of Mueller's patrons.

Symplocos thwaitesii F. Mueller

Buff Hazelwood   **STRf**

A small tree, 4-8m tall, uncommon in subtropical rainforest in the Royal National Park, but more common in the Illawarra.

Range: NSW coast, and Qld.   **Leaves:** alternate, shallowly toothed (mainly on the upper part of the leaf, or the teeth may be obscure), hairless, thick, usually glossy, tough (often quite rigid), with obvious net veins; dull and paler below.   **Flowers:** WHITE, 15-20mm wide, with numerous stamens, in short axillary racemes (the flowers superficially resemble Myrtaceae flowers). The stalks and calyces are finely hairy.   **Flowering time:** spring.   **Name:** *thwaitesii* = after G. H. K. Thwaites, director of the Peradeniya Botanic Gardens near Kandy, Ceylon, who described many species in this genus.

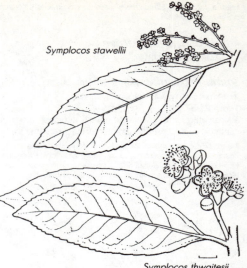

Symplocos stawellii

Symplocos thwaitesii

THYMELAEACEAE

Pimelea ligustrina Labillardière **ssp. *hypericina***

(A. Cunningham ex W. J. Hooker) Threlfall

Tall Rice Flower   **STRf margins**

An erect shrub to 2.5m high, found on the edges of rainforest in the Otford area (also widespread in the Illawarra).

Range: NSW coast and ranges north from Berry.   **Leaves:** opposite, flat, soft, thin, hairless, mostly 4-5cm long.   **Flowers:** WHITE, with orange anthers, numerous in dense terminal heads, protected in bud by 2-3 rows of broad green bracts (visible beneath the expanded head).   **Flowering time:** spring.   **Name:** *ligustrina* = like Privett, *hypericina* = like *Hypericum*, from a similarity of the leaves.

URTICACEAE

A family with about 1900 species in 52 genera, mainly in the tropics. There are 21 species in 9 genera in Australia.

• *Dendrocnide* Miquel (den-drok-NY-de)

A genus of rainforest trees with 37 species in south-east Asia and the Pacific, including 5 species in Australia. The leaves

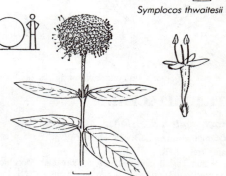

Pimelea ligustrina ssp. *hypericina*

are covered with stinging hairs, which are actually tiny hypodermics filled with an irritant fluid. The Qld town of Gympie is named after the Gympie-gympie (*D. moroides*), the most potent of the stinging trees, whose stings have caused people to require hospitalisation.

Name: *Dendrocnide* = Gk. tree-nettle.

Dendrocnide excelsa (Weddell) Chew

Giant Stinging Tree   **STRf**

A very impressive tree 20-40m tall, with stout smooth whitish trunk, often buttressed, and enormous rounded leaves. Found in subtropical rainforest in the Royal National Park and Illawarra. The purple jelly-like fruiting mass is edible, with a pleasant acid flavour, but be sure to check for stinging hairs.

Range: NSW coastal rainforests from Bega into Qld.   **Leaves:** very large (20-40cm wide), soft, heart-shaped, densely covered in stinging hairs.   **Flowers:** tiny, numerous in short dense axillary panicles.   **Fruit:** (in May-June) a tiny nut seated on a bloated purplish mass, consisting of the swollen perianth and stalk.   **Flowering time:** summer.   **Name:** *excelsa* = Lat. excelling.

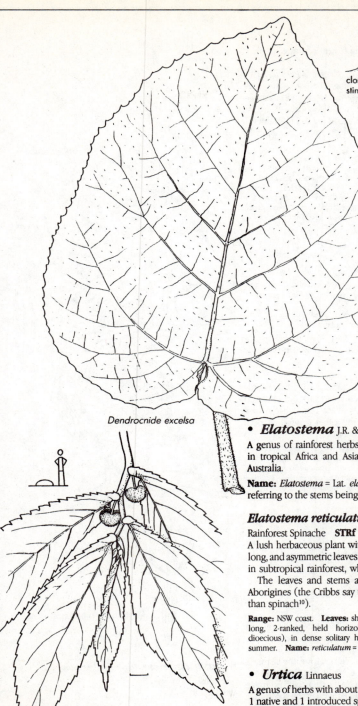

close-up of
stinging hair

Dendrocnide excelsa

Elatostema reticulatum

• *Elatostema* J.R. & G. Forster

A genus of rainforest herbs with about 250 species, mainly in tropical Africa and Asia, including 2 species native to Australia.

Name: *Elatostema* = Lat. *elato*, elevated, Gk. *stemmon*, stem, referring to the stems being held above the ground.

Elatostema reticulatum Weddell

Rainforest Spinache **STRf**

A lush herbaceous plant with thick succulent stems to 50cm long, and asymmetric leaves. Found along fast-moving streams in subtropical rainforest, where it sprawls above the waters.

The leaves and stems are edible and were cooked by Aborigines (the Cribbs say that the young leaves taste better than spinach[10]).

Range: NSW coast. **Leaves:** shiny, soft, thin, smooth, mostly 10-15cm long, 2-ranked, held horizontally. **Flowers:** unisexual (plants dioecious), in dense solitary heads in the axils. **Flowering time:** summer. **Name:** *reticulatum* = Lat. net-veined.

• *Urtica* Linnaeus

A genus of herbs with about 100 species worldwide, including 1 native and 1 introduced species in Australia.

Name: *Urtica* = the Latin name for nettle.

Urtica incisa Poiret

Scrub Nettle   **STRf, Temp Rf**

A weak, erect herb with stinging leaves, common in moist gullies.

The juice of dock (*Rumex*), or plantain (*Plantago*), are reputed to be remedies for the sting. The leaves lose their sting when boiled or steamed; they make a pleasant vegetable. Nettle beer was once a popular non-alcoholic beverage in northern England and Scotland; according to J.H. Maiden it had a 'bite' and was consumed in enormous quantities by the lower classes.

Range: NSW coast, ranges and inland areas, Qld, Vic, Tas, SA, NZ and New Caledonia.   **Leaves:** soft, 2-10cm long, covered in stinging hairs.   **Flowers:** tiny, unisexual (plants dioecious).   **Name:** *incisa* = Lat. cut, referring to the coarsely toothed leaves.   **Similar species:** *U. urens*, an annual cosmopolitan herb, occasionally occurs in waste places. It is monoecious, with male and female flowers mixed in each inflorescence. The leaves are smaller (2-5cm long) and more round (ovate-elliptical) than *U. incisa*.

VIOLACEAE

• *Hymenanthera* R. Brown

A genus of small trees and shrubs with 10 species worldwide, including a single species in Australia.

Name: *Hymenanthera* = Gk. *hymen*, membrane, *anthere*, anther, referring to the thin anther walls.

Hymenanthera dentata R. Brown ex De Candolle

Tree Violet, Scrub Box

Temp Rf, STRf margins

A spreading, much-branched shrub, to 3m tall. It occurs mainly on the edges of rainforest or beside streams, but rarely on sandstone. It is easy to confuse with the common *Bursaria spinosa* (Pittosporaceae), except the leaves are toothed. Both species have branches ending in thorns.

Range: NSW coast, ranges and inland areas, Vic, SA and Tas.   **Leaves:** glossy, thin-textured, toothed.   **Flowers:** waxy, PALE YELLOW, pendant, about 3mm long, like miniature *Pittosporum undulatum* flowers; axillary, mostly solitary.   **Flowering time:** spring-early summer.   **Fruit:** a purplish berry, about 6mm wide.   **Name:** *dentata* = Lat. toothed.

VISCACEAE

Mistletoes

Korthalsella rubra ssp. *rubra*

Jointed Mistletoe
—See MISTLETOES.

WINTERACEAE

A family with about 60 species in 5-7 genera, distributed in rainforests in South-east Asia, South America and Australia, where there are 8 species in 2 genera.

All parts of the plant have oil cells, giving the leaves a hot peppery taste (oil-dots in the leaves are visible with a lens). Lack of water-carrying vessels in the stems, and primitive floral features, make this an ancient family. Botanists consider that it comes nearer than any other modern family to the ancestral prototype of angiosperms.

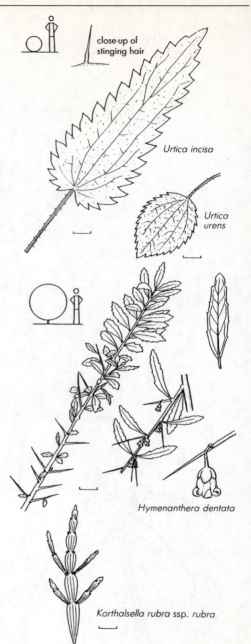

close-up of stinging hair

Urtica incisa

Urtica urens

Hymenanthera dentata

Korthalsella rubra ssp. *rubra*

• *Tasmannia* R. Brown (taz-MAN-ee-a)

(previously Drimys)

An endemic genus with 5 species.

Name: *Tasmannia* = in honour of Abel Tasman (1603-59), Dutch discoverer of Van Diemen's Land (Tas).

Tasmannia insipida R. Brown ex De Candolle

Brush Pepper-bush **STRf**

An erect shrub usually 1-3m tall, found in subtropical rainforest in the Royal National Park and Illawarra.

Range: NSW coast and ranges and Qld. **Leaves:** glossy, firm, with a peppery odour and taste when crushed, widened at the base. **Flowers:** WHITISH GREEN, in terminal umbels, unisexual (plants monoecious), or sometimes bisexual. The male flowers have a dense cluster of stamens and 2 narrow petals. **Flowering time:** September-December. **Fruit:** a purplish berry. **Name:** *insipida* = tasteless, because the leaves are not as peppery as those of other species.

• MONOCOTYLEDONS

ARACEAE

A mainly tropical family with about 2000 species worldwide in about 115 genera. Most species have a dense spike of flowers enclosed in an enormous ear-like spathe, e.g. Arum Lily, Cunjevoi (*Alocasia*), Taro, Monstera.

• *Gymnostachys* R. Brown

An endemic genus with 1 species.

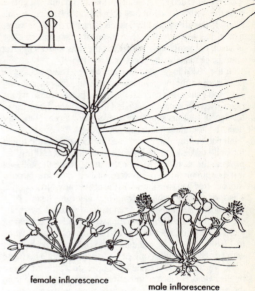

female inflorescence

male inflorescence

Tasmannia insipida

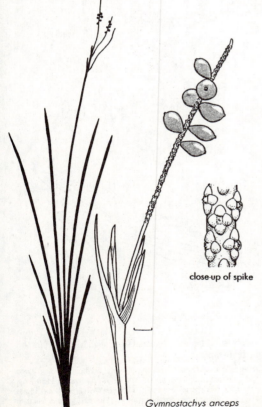

close-up of spike

Gymnostachys anceps

Name: *Gymnostachys* = Gk. *gymno*, naked, *stachys*, a spike of grain, since the spike lacks the usual enclosing spathe.

Gymnostachys anceps R. Brown

Settlers Flax **STRf**

A graceful tufted herb to 2m tall, found in subtropical rainforest in the Royal National Park and Illawarra. The fibrous leaves were used by farmers as cord or string.

Range: NSW coast and ranges, and Qld. **Leaves:** 1-2m long, tough, ribbed, concave, shiny. **Flowers:** inconspicuous, numerous, sessile on the surface of dense slender spikes (to 15cm long) which arise at the tip of a stiff flowering stem to 2m high. **Flowering time:** spring-summer. **Fruit:** large BLUE shiny drupes. **Name:** Lat. *anceps* = compressed, referring to the flattened flowering stem.

ARECACEAE (Palmae)

The Palm family has about 2800 species in 210 genera, mainly tropical. In Australia there are about 52 species in about 21 genera.

• *Livistona* R. Brown

A genus of palms with about 30 species worldwide, including 16 in Australia.

Name: *Livistona* = in honour of Baron Livingstone, founder of the Edinburgh Botanic Garden, Scotland.

Livistona australis (R. Brown) Martius

Cabbage-tree Palm **Temp Rf, STRf**

A tall mop-headed palm, locally common in rainforest gullies near the sea. Colonial history abounds in references to this plant. It was first noted by Joseph Banks in 1770, he wrote that it 'has leaves plaited like a fan; the cabbage of these is small, but exquisitely sweet, and the nuts it bears in great abundance make a very good food for hogs.'[11]

In the 1820s Judge Barron Field wrote: 'These trees once characterised the neighbourhood of Port Jackson; but they have long since been exhausted, the spongy trunks having been used for splitting into hut-logs, and the large leaves for thatch; for thus simply were even the officers of the first fleet, the Romuluses of the colony, lodged.'[12]

All parts of the palm were used by the settlers; the trunks for building, fencing and pig troughs, the pith and fruit for pigfeed, the mature leaves for thatching, while those leaves just beginning to expand were plaited into the popular cabbage-tree hats well known in the last century. Most popular was the 'cabbage', the growing bud at in the heart of the leafy head. 'Several of my companions suffered by eating too much of the Cabbage Palm' wrote Ludwig Leichhardt on his Overland Expedition to Port Essington. Surgeon White in 1788 recorded that while on an excursion to Broken Bay with Governor Phillip '..one of our company shot a very fine duck, which we had dressed for supper, on a little eminence by the side of a cabbage tree swamp, about half a mile from the run of the tide. Here the whole party got as much cabbage, to eat with their salt provisions, as they chose.'[13]

Interestingly, James Backhouse in 1836 was told by Aborigines in Kangaroo Valley that 'they were not aware that the hearts of these Palms were wholesome, till White people came among them; they now form a considerable item of their food.'[14]

It is resistant to all but very severe fires.

Range: the most southerly of palms, the Cabbage-tree Palm grows from Fraser Island, Qld, to Orbost, Vic. **Leaves:** tough, shiny, palmate (i.e. with blades radiating from a central point) on a long stiff stalk lined with large sharp teeth. **Flowers:** small, YELLOWISH CREAM, numerous in massive drooping axillary panicles. **Flowering time:** late August-September. **Name:** *australis* = Lat. southern. **Note:** It is virtually indistinguishable from the exotic species *Washingtonia robusta*, common in old gardens. The best distinguishing feature is the presence of slender strings of fibre which curl off the edges of the leaf segments of that species.

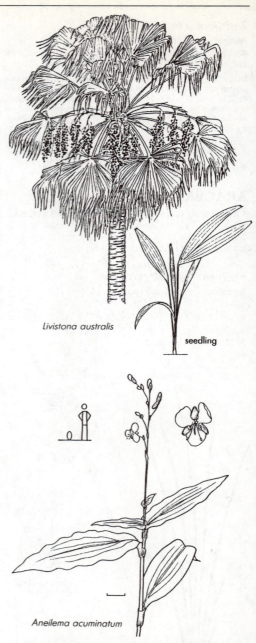

Livistona australis

seedling

Aneilema acuminatum

COMMELINACEAE

• *Aneilema* R. Brown

A genus of weak herbs with about 100 species, including 5 species in Australia.

Name: *Aneilema* = Gk. not rolled up, since the flowers are not folded in a spathe.

Aneilema acuminatum R. Brown

STRf

A weak herb with erect stems to 40cm high, arising from a creeping base. Found on the dark floors of subtropical rainforest. A rare species locally, recorded from subtropical rainforest in the Royal National Park; slightly more common in the Illawarra.

Range: NSW coast north from the Illawarra, northern tablelands, into Qld. **Leaves:** dark green above, pale below, hairless, to 15cm long, on purplish finely pubescent stems. **Flowers:** WHITE, petals about 5mm long; in a slender open terminal panicle. **Flowering time:** summer. **Name:** *acuminatum* = Lat. drawn out at the tip, referring to the leaves.

Commelina cyanea

Ss, Cumb, Temp Rf, STRf margins

A creeping leafy herb with fragile blue flowers. It forms dense tangled groundcover in gullies and edges of rainforest. Very common.

—See MONOCOTS: Commelinaceae.

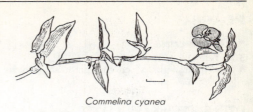
Commelina cyanea

• *Pollia* Thunberg

A genus of herbs widespread in the tropics of Africa and Asia. There are 2 species in Australia.

Name: *Pollia* = after J. van der Poll, the wealthy patron of the Dutch botanist Thunberg.

Pollia crispata (R. Brown) Bentham

STRf

An erect herb to 80cm tall with succulent stems, creeping and rooting at the base. Found in subtropical rainforest in the Royal National Park.

Range: NSW coast north from Sydney, Blue Mountains and Qld. **Leaves:** soft, glossy, slightly thick textured, very wavy at the base before becoming a closed sheath around the stem. **Flowers:** WHITE to BLUE, 8-12mm wide, in a tight terminal panicle, with sheathing leafy bracts. **Flowering time:** summer. **Name:** *crispata* = Lat. wavy.

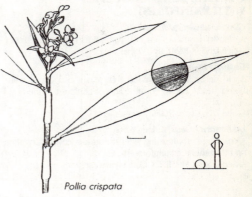
Pollia crispata

Tradescantia albiflora*

Ss, Cumb, Temp Rf

A creeping leafy herb with fragile white flowers. It forms dense tangled groundcover in gullies and edges of rainforest. Very common.

—See MONOCOTS: Commelinaceae.

CYPERACEAE

Sedge species occurring in rainforest are *Carex appressa,* *Cyperus tetraphyllus,* and *Cyperus imbecillis.*
—See SEDGES AND RUSHES.

Tradescantia albiflora

IRIDACEAE

• *Libertia* Sprengel

A genus with 10 species worldwide, including 2 species in Australia.

Name: *Libertia* = after Marie A. Libert (1782-1863), a Belgian botanist who studied Liverworts.

Libertia paniculata (R. Brown) Sprengel

Branching Grass-flag **STRf**

A tufted herb with leaves to 60cm high, found in the dark understorey of rainforest. Rare in the area, in subtropical rainforest in the Royal National Park and Illawarra.

Range: NSW coast, Blue Mountains and northern tablelands, Qld and Vic. **Leaves:** to 10mm wide. **Flowers:** WHITE, in a spreading panicle about as high as the leaves. **Flowering time:** spring. **Name:** *paniculata* = Lat. having panicles.

Libertia paniculata

POACEAE

• *Oplismenus*
STRf, Temp Rf, Ss
A genus of small grasses, very abundant in shady forests.
—See GRASSES.

OTHER SPECIES ASSOCIATED WITH RAINFOREST

Clerodendrum tomentosum
A slender shrub 0.5-3m tall, common in sheltered places.
—See LESSER FAMILIES: Verbenaceae.

Cassinia trinerva
A tall dense shrub with soft thin leaves and dense white flower heads. Found on the edges of rainforest in the Royal National Park.
—See LESSER FAMILIES: Asteraceae.

Dichondra repens, Kidney Weed
A creeping herb, forming extensive groundcovers. Common on moist sheltered rainforest floors.
—See LESSER FAMILIES: Convolvulaceae.

Sigesbeckia orientalis
An erect open herb with strongly toothed leaves, to 1m tall. Common in gullies and rainforest margins.
—See LESSER FAMILIES: Asteraceae.

Trema aspera, Native Peach
A light shrub 2-3m high, common on margins of rainforest and stream banks.
—See LESSER FAMILIES: Ulmaceae.

Viola hederacea, Native Violet
A creeping herb, forming extensive groundcovers, common in moist sheltered rainforest floors.
—See LESSER FAMILIES: Violaceae.

Zieria smithii, Sandfly Zieria.
An aromatic leafy shrub, usually 1-1.5m high. Common in gullies and rainforest margins.
—See MAJOR FAMILIES: Rutaceae.

COASTAL AND ESTUARINE SPECIES

This section includes plants growing in salty coastal environments, that is:
• Estuaries with tidal, brackish waters (salt-marsh and mangrove communities).
• Sand-dunes beside the sea.
• Sea-side cliffs.

Salt is normally injurious to plant tissue. Coastal plants have special adaptations to cope with high salt levels. Many have succulence which dilutes the salt content of the leaves. Others have thick tough leaves with dense cuticle (waxy layer) to protect them from both air-borne salt and high evaporation. Others have special salt-secreting glands (e.g. *Avicennia marina*).

Since European settlement about 75% of Sydney's salt-marsh/mangrove communities have been destroyed, mainly by land reclamation. The largest remaining area is at Towra Point. Limited salt-marsh also survives on the Parramatta River, Georges River and Cooks River.

Sea-side growth forms
A great many non-salt adapted plants have some tolerance for salt. Identification difficulties can arise because of the unusual growth forms adopted by these plants in response to salty conditions. The most common changes are: reduction of leaf size, thickening of leaves, crowding of leaves, increasing thickness of protective coatings such as hairs, waxy cuticle, scales or meal, and reduction of habit to low compact forms.

Key to seacoast and estuarine species

Succulent herbs .... **Group 1**
Non-succulent herbs .... **Group 2**
Shrubs .... **Group 3**
Trees (over 4m tall, with single trunk).......... **Group 4**

Rainforest ferns, climbers, grasses and sedges are treated in separate sections.

> **How to use the key**
> Work your way through by making successive choices: either A or *A, then B or *B etc..
> Where numbers occur (eg. H1, H2, H3) check each one.

Group 1 Succulent herbs

A. Stems jointed, succulent, apparently leafless.
    B. Herb. CHENOPODIACEAE: *Sarcocornia* 396
    *B. Shrub. CHENOPODIACEAE: *Haloscaria* 395
*A. Stems not joined.
    C. Leaves pungent. CHENOPODIACEAE: *Salsola* 396
    *C. Leaves not pungent.
        D. At least some leaves pinnately lobed.
            E. Flowers yellow. ASTERACEAE.
            *E. Flowers pink. BRASSICACEAE: *Cakile* 393
        *D. Leaves not lobed.
            F. Leaves more or less cylindrical.
                G. Leaves finely hairy. CHENOPODIACEAE: *Enchylaena* 395
                *G. Leaves not visibly hairy.
                    H. Leaves channelled on upper surface. CHENOPODIACEAE:*Suaeda* 397
                    *H. Leaves not channelled on upper surface (microscopically hairy).
                        CARYOPHYLLACEAE:*Spergularia* 393
        *F. Leaves not cylindrical.
            I. Leaves triangular in cross-section, opposite. AIZOACEAE:*Carpobrotus* 389
            *I. Leaves flattened.
                J. Flowers tiny, fleshy, a few mm wide. CHENOPODIACEAE 394
                *J. Flowers prominent, white.
                    L. Flowers regular. CONVOLVULUS: *Wilsonia* 397
                    *L. Flowers irregular, hand-like. GOODENIACEAE: *Selliera* 399

Group 2 Non-succulent herbs (may sometimes be succulent in exposed or very salty situations).

A. All leaves along stems.
    B. Leaves compound
        C. Leaves 3-foliate. OXALIDACEAE 401
        *C. Leaves pinnate. APIACEAE: *Apium* 390
    *B. Leaves simple.
        D. Leaves circular with stalk attached to underside. APIACEAE:*Hydrocotyle bonariensis* 390
        *D. Leaves otherwise.
            E. Leaves bluish. Flowers tiny, fleshy, a few mm wide. CHENOPODIACEAE 394
            *E. Leaves green. Flowers prominent.
                F. Leaves opposite.
                    G. Leaves slender. AMARANTHACEAE: *Alternanthera* 124
                    *G. Leaves broad. Creeping herbs.
                        H. Leaves <12mm long. SCROPHULARIACEAE:*Bacopa, Mimulus* 404
                      *H. Leaves >40mm long. ASTERACEAE:*Melanthera* 391
                *F. Leaves alternate.
                  I. Robust sprawling herb with crisp watery leaves 5-10cm long and yellow flowers.
                  AIZOACEAE: *Tetragonia* 389
                  *I. Otherwise.
                    J1. Flowers blue. GOODENIACEAE: *Scaevola* 399
                    J2. Flowers pink-mauve. LOBELIACEAE: *Lobelia* 400
                    J3. Flowers yellow. ASTERACEAE 390
                    J4. Flowers white.
                      K. Several erect stems arising from a rootstock.
                        STACKHOUSIACEAE:*Stackhousia* 404
                    *K. Stems solitary, creeping or erect. PRIMULACEAE:*Samolus* 402

*A. Basal leaves present.
    L. Leaves slender or strap-like, all veins parallel.
        M1. Grasses. POACEAE 407
        M2. Sedges, rushes and similar plants. CYPERACEAE 405 JUNACEAE, JUNCAGINACEAE 406
        M3. Others.
            M. Leaves thick-textured, 1-2m long. LILIACEAE: *Crinum* 406
          *M. Leaves thin-textured, tough.
               O. Leaves toothed at the tip.
                    XANTHORRHOEACEAE: *Lomandra longfolia* (see MONOCOTS) 277
              *O. Leaves not toothed at the tip. LILIACEAE: *Dianella* 407
   *L. Leaves with lateral veins, not strap-like.
        P. Leaves rounded on long stalks. GERANIACEAE: *Pelargonium* 399
       *P. Leaves more or less stalkless, in a basal rosette. PLANTAGINACEAE: *Plantago* 402

Group 3 Shrubs

A. Leaves pinnate. SAPINDACEAE: *Cupaniopsis* 401
*A. Leaves simple.
    B. Leaves whorled. LAMIACEAE: *Westringia* 399
   *B. Leaves not whorled.
        C. Leaves opposite.
            D1. Leaves covered in cotton wool when new. ASTERACEAE: *Chrysanthemoides* 391
            D2. Leaves covered in creamy felt below. RUTACEAE: *Correa* 403
            D3. Leaves green below. Very glossy above. RUBIACEAE: *Coprosma* 403
      *C. Leaves alternate
          E. Leaves <25mm long.
              F. Leaves with several parallel veins. EPACRIDACEAE: *Leucopogon* 398
             *F. Leaves with one main vein. MYRTACEAE: *Leptospermum* 401
         *E. Leaves >25mm long.
              G. Leaves with 2 main veins. MIMOSACEAE: *Acacia* 400
             *G. Leaves with one main vein.
                 H. Leaves slender, with fine shiny scales below. RUTACEAE: *Phebalium* 403
               *H. Leaves broad, green on both surfaces. MYOPORACEAE 400

Group 4 Trees (over 4m tall, with a single trunk).

A. Apparently leafless (leaves reduced to tiny scales). CASUARINACEAE 393
*A. Leaves well developed.
    B. Leaves pinnate. SAPINDACEAE: *Cupaniopsis* 404
   *B. Leaves simple.
        C. Leaves opposite. MYRSINACEAE: *Aegiceras* 401
      *C. Leaves alternate.
          D. Leaves <25mm long. MYRTACEAE: *Leptospermum, Melaleuca* 401
        *D. Leaves >50mm long.
            E1. Leaves green beneath. Bark corky. MYOPORACEAE: *Myoporum* 400
            E2. Leaves grey beneath. AVICENNIACEAE: *Avicennia* 392
            E3. Leaves white beneath. PROTEACEAE: *Banksia integrifolia* 402

• DICOTYLEDONS

AIZOACEAE Mesembryanthemaceae

A family of herbs and shrubs with about 2300 species in about 140 genera worldwide. There are about 60 species in 18-19 genera in Australia.

All the genera have succulent leaves and salt-adapted metabolism. Many are found in arid parts of the world, especially South Africa.

• *Carpobrotus* N. E. Brown

A genus of succulent salt-tolerant herbs with 23 species worldwide, distributed on the west coast of the Americas, South Africa and Australia. There are 4 species native to Australia and 2 naturalised species: *C. aequilateralis* and *C. edulis*, both of which occur rarely in this area.

Name: *Carpobrotus* = Gk. *karpos*, fruit, *brotos*, edible.

Carpobrotus glaucescens (Haworth) Schwantes

Pig Face

A robust creeping herb with succulent leaves, found on exposed places by the sea, especially sand-dunes. Common in the area.

The salty leaves are edible, but only if you're starving. NSW Aborigines used the leaves as an emergency food, steaming them on a fire before eating. Aborigines in Tasmania steamed them as a purgative medicine. The fruits, however, are good to eat. They are purple when ripe and the fleshy pulp can be squeezed out and eaten.

Range: NSW coast, Lord Howe Island and coasts of Qld and Vic. **Leaves:** opposite, succulent, triangular in cross-section, becoming reddish with age. **Flowers:** with numerous BRIGHT PINK staminodes and pale yellow anthers; terminal and solitary. **Flowering time:** much of the year. **Name:** *glaucescens* = Lat. becoming blue-green.

• *Tetragonia* Linnaeus

A genus with about 50 species, mostly native to South Africa. There are 8 species in Australia (3 of which were introduced from South Africa).

Name: *Tetragonia* = Gk. 4-cornered, referring to the fruit.

Tetragonia tetragonioides (Pallas) Kuntze

New Zealand Spinach, Warrigal Cabbage

A robust leafy sprawling herb, with crisp stems to a metre long. Common in moist places near the sea. The whole plant is covered in tiny watery vesicles.

The leaves are edible, although rather bitter unless cooked. Captain Cook served them boiled daily to his crew and Joseph Banks thought they 'eat as well, or very nearly as well, as Spinach.'[1] Nowadays they are mainly enjoyed by native rats and other herbivores.

Range: coasts of NSW, Tas, Vic and Qld, NZ, Polynesia, Japan and South America; also depressions and dry river beds in inland NSW. **Leaves:** triangular, thick, crisp and fleshy, covered with water-filled vesicles. **Flowers:** small, YELLOW, stalkless, solitary or a few together in the leaf axils. **Flowering time:** spring-summer. **Name:** *tetragonioides* = *Tetragonia*-like—this plant was originally placed in the now obsolete genus *Demidovia*.

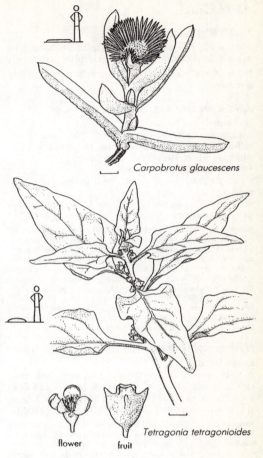

Carpobrotus glaucescens

Tetragonia tetragonioides

flower   fruit

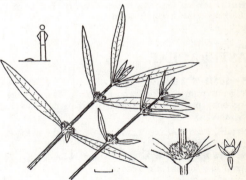

Alternanthera denticulata

AMARANTHACEAE

Alternanthèra denticulata

—See LESSER FAMILIES.

APIACEAE

• *Apium* Linnaeus

A genus of herbs with about 40 species, including 3 in Australia, distributed in all states, with one species introduced.

Name: *Apium* = Lat. the classical name for celery (*Apium graveolens*).

Apium prostratum Labillardière ex Ventenat
Sea Celery

A scrambling herb with stems to 50cm long, found on sea cliffs and beside sandy estuaries. There are two local varieties which are readily distinguished by the leaves:
• **var. *prostratum*:** leaves narrow.
• **var. *filiforme*:** leaves broad; this is the more common variety.
Sea Celery is a superior substitute for parsley, with a crisp and slightly salty taste. It was eaten by Cook's crew in 1770.

Range: coasts of all states except NT; also NZ. **Leaves:** pinnate, hairless, becoming thick in more salty conditions. **Flowers:** WHITE, in small umbels. **Flowering time:** spring-late summer. **Name:** *prostratum* = Lat. prostrate. It was named by the French botanist Labillardière who collected it in Tas in 1793. 'I discovered at a little distance . . . a new species of parsely, which I named *apium prostratum*, on account of the position of its stem which always creeps along the ground. We carried a large quantity of it on board with us, which was acceptable to mariners who felt the necessity of obviating, by a vegetable diet, the bad effects of the salt provisions on which we had lived during the whole of our passage from the Cape of Good Hope to that of Van Diemen.'[2]

*Hydrocotyle bonariensis** Lamarck
Kurnell Curse

A robust creeping herb, rooting along the stems, with erect circular leaves. Introduced from South America and now abundant on seaside sand dunes and cliffs. 'Fairies' Tables' is a fitting old name for a closely related species in England.

Range: coast of NSW, also Lord Howe Island, SA and South America. **Leaves:** shiny, fairly tough, hairless, erect, circular, peltate (i.e. the stalk attached to the middle of the leaf). **Flowers:** tiny, WHITE, in dense compound umbels, on peduncles about the same height as the leaves. **Name:** *bonariensis* = inhabiting Bonaria, a small island off the coast of Venezuela, where it was first collected.

ASTERACEAE

• *Actites* N. Lander

A genus with 1 species, endemic to Australian coasts. Previously placed in the related weedy genus *Sonchus* (Sowthistles).

Name: *Actites* = Gk. a coast dweller, from *akte*, the seashore.

Actites megalocarpa (J. D. Hooker) N. Lander
(previously *Sonchus megalocarpus*)
Coastal Sowthistle

A robust tufted herb found on sand-dunes (e.g. Kurnell, Royal National Park). Often to 1m tall when flowering. Uncommon in the area.

Range: coastal NSW, Qld, Vic, SA, WA and NT. **Leaves:** stiff, fleshy, toothed, dull-green, hairless, tightly clustered in a basal rosette. **Flower-heads:** few, ray flowers YELLOW, disc flowers absent, dense pappus of fine hairs. **Flowering time:** spring-summer. **Name:** *megalocarpa* = large-fruit.

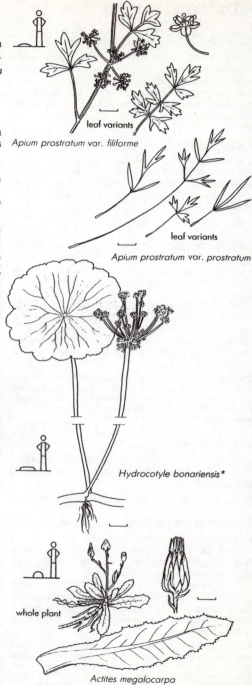

leaf variants

Apium prostratum var. filiforme

leaf variants

Apium prostratum var. prostratum

*Hydrocotyle bonariensis**

whole plant

Actites megalocarpa

*Chrysanthemoides monilifera** (Linnaeus)
T. Norlindh **ssp. *rotundata***

Bitou Bush, Bone Seed

A robust shrub with sprawling stems and ascending branches mostly 1-2m high. A serious weed on coastal sand-dunes. It was originally a native of South Africa, mainly in the south-west Cape district around Cape Town. The first recording in Australia was in 1852, in Sydney. In 1858 it was introduced to Melbourne as a garden plant and in 1892 it reached Adelaide. It is now a serious pest in coastal areas, displacing native sand-dune species.

Range: coastal NSW, Lord Howe Island, Qld and SA. **Leaves:** round, often slightly toothed, rather fleshy, covered in cotton wool when young. **Flower-heads:** a few in a terminal panicle, ray flowers 12, GOLDEN YELLOW, disc flowers GOLDEN YELLOW, pappus absent. The seeds are about half as broad as long, and obscurely ribbed **Flowering time:** mainly spring. **Name:** *monilifera* = Lat. necklace-bearing, referring to the seeds, *rotundata* = Lat. rounded, referring to the leaves.

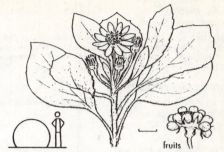

fruits

*Chrysanthemoides monilifera** ssp. *rotundata*

• *Cotula* Linnaeus
Water Buttons

A genus of marsh herbs with about 50 species, mainly in the southern hemisphere, including 7 in Australia.

Name: *cotula* = Gk. little cup, refering to the flowers.

*Cotula coronopifolia** Linnaeus
Waterbuttons, Marsh Daisy

A mat-forming herb with thick succulent leaves. Common in slightly saline conditions on the margins of saltmarshes. The seeds emit a sticky mucus when immersed. This aids dispersal by sticking to birds. A native of South Africa.

Range: coastal Australia and many inland districts, extensively outside Australia. **Leaves:** thick and fleshy, toothed. **Flower-heads:** disc flowers BRIGHT YELLOW, with a single outer row of female flowers. Pappus absent. **Flowering time:** most of the year. **Name:** *coronopifolia* = *Coronopus*-leaved (a genus in Brassicaceae).

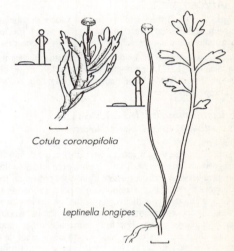

Cotula coronopifolia

Leptinella longipes

• *Leptinella* Cassini
A genus with 33 species, including 4 in eastern Australia.

Name: *Leptinella* = Gk. *lepto*, slender.

Leptinella longipes J.D. Hooker
(previously *Cotula longipes, Cotula reptans*)

A creeping herb with fleshy divided leaves, found in slightly brackish marshes in coastal areas.

Range: coasts of eastern Australia. **Flower-heads:** on long stems, disc flowers YELLOW, 3-4 outer rows female. **Flowering time:** much of the year. **Name:** *longipes* = Lat. long-stemmed.

Melanthera biflora

• *Melanthera* Rohr.
A genus of herbs with about 50 species, including a single species in Australia.

Name: *Melanthera* = Gk. with black anthers.

Melanthera biflora (Linnaeus) Willdenow
A robust scrambling herb with stems usually 1-2 metres long, found on sea-coasts south from Manly.

Range: NSW coast, Qld, NT and Pacific Islands. **Leaves:** opposite, 8-10cm long, slightly toothed. **Flowers:** disc and ray flowers both GOLDEN YELLOW. Pappus absent or consisting of 1-3 awns that fall off early. Each disc flower is protected by a short stiff green bract. The ray flowers are female. **Flowering time:** mainly summer. **Name:** *biflora* = 2-flowered, since the flower-heads occur in pairs on the stems.

Senecio lautus G. Forster ex Willdenow
ssp. *maritimus* Ali

A small erect herb to 30cm high, with fleshy divided leaves, found in wet places on rocks or dunes near the sea, within the range of salt spray.

Range: coasts of all states except NT. **Leaves:** more or less fleshy, deeply divided (except the basal leaves), hairless, margins not recurved. **Flower-heads:** disc and ray flowers both BRIGHT YELLOW. **Flowering time:** most of the year. **Name:** *maritimus* = Lat. pertaining to the sea.

*Sonchus oleraceus**

A weedy annual to 1m high with yellow flower heads, often occurring on or near sand dunes.
—See LESSER FAMILIES: Asteraceae.

AVICENNIACEAE

• *Avicennia* Linnaeus

A genus of small trees with 14 species widely distributed in warm and tropical parts of the world. There are 5 species in Australia. Some authors include it in the family Verbenaceae.

Name: *Avicennia* = in honour of the Persian philosopher Ibn Sina (980-1037). He was called Avicenna in Europe; his Canon of Medicine included many herbal drugs not known in Europe at the time.

Avicennia marina (Forskal) Vierhapper
var. *australasica* (Walpers) Moldenke

Grey Mangrove

A small stout tree, usually about 4-6m high, it is the dominant mangrove in coastal NSW. It forms dense pure groves in the intertidal zone of estuaries where it provides protection for numerous water birds and supports an important ecosystem.

Grey Mangrove is a pioneer coloniser of shallow tidal waters. Its roots breathe by means of fibrous woody *pneumatophores* which arise from horizontal cable roots around the tree. This dense root system helps settle silt, protects banks from erosion and provides a living environment for a host of small marine animals. The animals and algae which form around the roots are a crucial part of the food supply for many species of young fish.

The fruits, no doubt roasted, formed an important part of the diet of Aborigines in northern Australia. The River Mangrove, *Aegiceras corniculatum*, often grows on the landward side of mangrove stands.

Range: coasts of all states, NG, South-east Asia and Pacific Islands. **Leaves:** opposite, 9-12cm long, thick, tough, hairless, shiny above. **Flowers:** GOLD, finely hairy outside, in small dense axillary clusters, producing a rich honey nectar. **Flowering time:** February-June. **Fruit:** a compressed capsule about 3cm wide. The seeds germinate and sprout on the tree, falling in December when the cotyledons are swelling. They float and are distributed by the tide. Swollen green fruit, in various stages of sprouting, are a common sight in coastal waters. **Name:** *marina* = Lat. of the sea. The common name refers to the grey undersides of the leaves, or to the grey colour of the timber.

BRASSICACEAE Cruciferae

Mustards

A family, mainly of annual herbs, with about 3200 species worldwide, in about 375 genera, mainly in the temperate northern hemisphere. There are 160 species in 52 genera in Australia, including a great many introduced weeds and fodder plants.

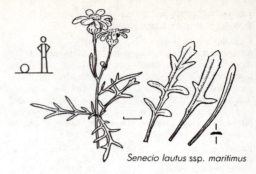

Senecio lautus ssp. *maritimus*

flower   seedling

Avicennia marina var. *australasica*

The flowers have 4 sepals and petals in a cross shape (hence the name Cruciferae).

The family includes many useful plants: Cabbages, Radishes, Broccoli, Cardamine, Cress and Mustard. It is related to Capparaceae (the Caper family) and Papaveraceae (Poppies).

• *Cakile* Linnaeus (kak-ill-y)

A cosmopolitan genus of seaside herbs with 7 species. Two species are naturalised on Australian coasts; it is possible they arrived before European settlement.

Name: *Cakile* = from the Arabic name for the plant, *qaqulla*.

Cakile edentula (Bigel.) W. J. Hooker **var. *edentula***

Sea Rocket

A spreading annual herb, often dense and bushy, to 30cm tall. It grows on open sand-dunes on the coast. It is annual, dying away in summer. Generally uncommon in the area, but populations fluctuate and it can sometimes be abundant. A native of North America.

Range: coasts of all states. **Leaves:** very variable, depending on conditions of salt and moisture, often deeply lobed, fleshy, semi-succulent, pale or bluish green. **Flowers:** MAUVE-PINK, about 8mm wide, in terminal racemes. The fruit is pointed, swollen and fleshy, with 2 chambers, one above the other, the seed often lacking in the lower one. **Flowering time:** much of the year. **Name:** *endentula* = Lat. toothless, referring to the absence of horns on the fruit. **Similar species:** *C. maritima* ssp. *maritima*. This has been recorded at Towra Point and may occasionally occur in the area. It is similar except the fruits have prominent horn-like teeth on the lower segment.

• *Rorippa*
—See AQUATICS.

CARYOPHYLLACEAE

• *Spergularia* Linnaeus

A cosmopolitan genus with about 40 species, including 2 native and 3-4 naturalised species in Australia.

Name: *Spergula*, a genus in the same family, *-aria*, for differentiation.

*Spergularia marina** (Linnaeus) Grisebach

Sand Spurry

A small prostrate plant with many stems 10-30cm long. Uncommon in the area. Early in the century it was well developed at Homebush Bay, growing in salt-marsh with *Sarcocornia*. Elsewhere it occurs in the upper margins of salt marshes, with *Cotula coronopifolia*, or on sea cliffs. Introduced from Europe.

Range: coasts throughout eastern Australia, Tas and Europe. **Leaves:** opposite, succulent, slender, 1-2cm long, with conspicuous transparent stipules (joined half-way along their length). **Flowers:** PINK or WHITE, with 4 stamens, solitary and axillary or in terminal cymes. **Name:** *marina* = Lat. marine. **Note:** *Spergularia rubra*, is a very similar weed in non-saline places. It has 8 (6-10) stamens and stipules which are long and free to the base.

CASUARINACEAE

Allocasuarina verticillata (Lamark) L.A.S. Johnson

(previously *Casuarina stricta*)

Drooping She-oak **Ss**

A small tree 4-10m high with drooping foliage, often grey-green, found on rocky cliffs above the sea (although it has no special preference for salty places, growing on rocky ground throughout southern NSW). Uncommon to rare in the area. Recorded on Narrabeen shales at Scarborough, Coalcliff, Royal National Park, Mona Vale and Newport.

Range: south from near Cobar on rocky hill sites, and on coastal shale patches from Sydney southwards. **Branchlets:** about 1.2mm diameter, pendulous, with 9-12 leaf-teeth. **Cones:** large, spiky, 2-3cm diameter, egg-shaped. **Name:** *verticillata* = Lat. in whorls, referring to the leaf-teeth.

Cakile edentula var. edentula*

Cakile maritima ssp. maritima

Spergularia marina*

Casuarina glauca Sieber ex Sprengel

Swamp She-Oak, Grey She-Oak **Ss, Cumb**

A tree to 20m high, preferring brackish marshes and estuaries, and appearing as a dwarf on exposed coastal headlands. It lines muddy creeks on the Cumberland Plain where its presence is due to saline groundwaters. Neat and pyramidal when young, but maturing into a tall tree with contorted, misshapen branches, often decorated with lichens. It spreads by sucker roots, often forming dense groves in belts just inland

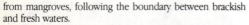

Casuarina glauca

Allocasuarina verticillata

male plant with
inflorescence

female plant with flowers
and fruiting calyces

Atriplex cinerea

from mangroves, following the boundary between brackish and fresh waters.

It was probably the bark of this species which Surgeon Worgan in 1788 saw Port Jackson Aborigines removing in whole cylinders to make canoe hulls.

Range: from Eden to southern Qld (also a common street tree). **Branchlets:** thick, about 1-2mm diameter, 30-50cm long, with 12-16 leaf-teeth. **Cones:** a cylinder, about 14-20mm diameter, with a sunken apex. **Name:** *glauca* = blue-grey, from the grey foliage.

CHENOPODIACEAE

• *Atriplex* Linnaeus (AT-rip-lex)

Saltbush

A genus of salt-tolerant herbs with over 250 species worldwide. There are about 61 species in Australia, mostly in arid areas. They are often a crucial source of feed for cattle.

The leaves are opposite, hairless, thick and fleshy, often with a mealy surface. The flowers are unisexual, tiny, in dense terminal spikes. The fruits are tiny nuts, hidden between 2 swollen fleshy triangular bracteoles.

Name: *Atriplex* = from *atriplexum*, the Latin name for these plants.

Atriplex australasica Moquin-Tandon

An ascending or sprawling annual herb with stems to 1m long, found in salty places on the margins of estuaries but uncommon in the area. Recorded from the Hawkesbury River. It is very similar in appearance to *Atriplex hastata*, but easily distinguished by the leaf shape. The fruits are spread by birds and sea currents, floating for up to 6 months.

Range: Sydney area, south coast, Qld, Vic and SA. **Leaves:** alternate, fleshy, blue-green, not mealy. **Flowers:** in short axillary spikes. **Flowering time:** summer. **Name:** *australasica* = Australian.

Atriplex cinerea Poiret

Grey Saltbush

An erect shrub 1-1.5m high, found in sand dunes by the sea. Now rare near Sydney, it was once plentiful along the shores of Botany Bay. The first fleeters cooked it as a vegetable, likening it to European sage. Surgeon White called it 'a kind of plant resembling balm, which we found to be a good and pleasant vegetable'.[3]

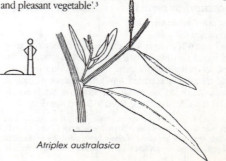

Atriplex australasica

Range: coasts south from Sydney, Vic, Tas, SA and WA.   **Leaves:** alternate, thick, soft, fleshy, pale blue-green, mealy.   **Flowers:** unisexual (plants dioecious), the male in dense brownish spikes, arranged spirally; the female with prominent ruby-red styles, held between 2 silvery bracteoles, in small axillary clusters.   **Flowering time:** summer.   **Name:** *cinerea* = Lat. ash-grey.

*Atriplex hastata** Linnaeus
Orache

An ascending or sprawling blue-green herb with branches to 50cm long. Common in salty places on the edges of estuaries and salt-marshes. A native of Europe and Asia.

Range: Sydney area, Vic, Tas and Europe.   **Leaves:** opposite, triangular, fleshy, blue-green, densely mealy.   **Flowers:** tiny, reddish, in dense terminal spikes.   **Flowering time:** summer.   **Name:** *hastata* = Lat. triangular with spreading basal lobes. Orache is a European name for this and other *Atriplex* species, corrupted from the Latin *atriplexum*, through the French *arrache*.

Atriplex semibaccata

This small prostrate species occasionally occurs in or near salt-marshes e.g. Homebush Bay, Lane Cove River.
—See LESSER FAMILIES: CHENOPODIACEAE.

• *Enchylaena* R. Brown (eng-ky-LEEN-a)

An endemic genus of small succulent herbs with 2 species. The fruits are nuts enclosed in small succulent red globules, formed from the enlarged perianth.

Name: *Enchylaena* = Gk. succulent-cloak, referring to the swollen perianth which encloses the fruit at maturity.

Enchylaena tomentosa R. Brown
Ruby Saltbush

A low spreading shrub with crowded sausage-shaped leaves on stems 20-100cm long. Uncommon in the area, in salty places near the sea.

Range: NSW coast and arid inland areas, Vic, SA, NT and WA.   **Leaves:** alternate, succulent, crowded, erect, finely hairy, cylindrical, light green, to 15mm long.   **Flowers:** tiny, bisexual, solitary, axillary.   **Flowering time:** mainly spring-early summer.   **Name:** *tomentosa* = Lat. felty, referring to the dense layer of fine hairs.

• *Halosarcia* P.G. Wilson

A genus with 23 species worldwide, and 23 species in Australia (all but 1 endemic), found mainly in saline inland areas of all states. The single non-endemic species extends to coasts of Malaysia and Indian Ocean countries.

Distinguished from the similar *Sarcocornia* by 3 (instead of 5-9) flowers per joint, and a shrub-like habit (instead of arising from a creeping stem).

Name: *Halosarcia* = Gk. salt-skinned.

Halosarcia pergranulata (J. Black) P.G. Wilson
ssp. *pergranulata*
Sal

A low rounded shrub to 1m high with swollen succulent jointed stems. Found in salt-marsh. Rare in the area; only known from the Homebush Bay area, on Navy land near Haslams Creek.

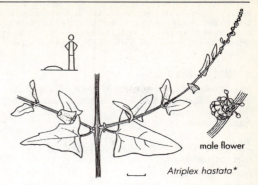

male flower

*Atriplex hastata**

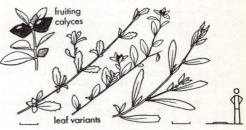

fruiting calyces

leaf variants

Atriplex semibaccata

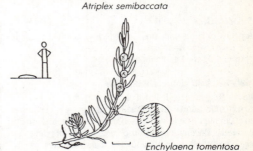

Enchylaena tomentosa

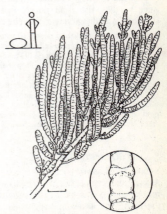

Halosarcia pergranulata
ssp. *pergranulata*

close-up of inflorescence

Range: widespread on saline areas in inland Australia, all mainland states. **Leaves:** reduced to narrow membranous margins on the jointed succulent stems. **Flowers:** 3 per joint, with a single stamen per flower. **Name:** *pergranulata* = Lat. covered with grains, referring to the seed surface.

• *Rhagodia* R. Brown

An endemic genus of shrubs with 11 species. The fruits are nuts enclosed in small succulent red globules, formed from the enlarged perianth.
Name: *Rhagodia* = Gk. berry-like.

Rhagodia candolleana Moquin-Tandon ssp. *candolleana*

(previously *R. baccata*)
Seaberry Saltbush, Coastal Saltbush
A small, dense, weakly ascending or spreading shrub to about 1m tall, occurring on sea coasts, in sand-dune scrub or on rocks. Uncommon in the Sydney area. (e.g. Royal National Park), but quite common in the Illawarra. Easily recognised by its small thick glossy leaves and low habit.

Range: coasts of NSW, Vic, Tas and SA. **Leaves:** alternate (but sometimes opposite), thick, under 3cm long, glossy green above, dull mealy-white below. Stems striate. **Flowers:** tiny, GREEN; in branching terminal racemes. **Flowering time:** summer. **Fruits:** red, succulent, flattened, 4-7mm wide. **Name:** *candolleana* = after Augustin Pyramus de Candolle, (1823-73), influential Swiss botanist.

• *Salsola* Linnaeus

A genus of herbs with over 100 species, including a single species native to Australia.
Name: *Salsola* = Lat. diminutive of salty.

Salsola kali Linnaeus **var. *kali***

Prickly Saltwort, Prickly Roly Poly
A stiff spiky annual herb, usually forming rounded bushes to 50cm high. The leaves are succulent and extremely sharp-pointed. Uncommon in the area, but popping up opportunistically on both sandy and rocky seashores.

In central Australia it abounds in the most arid saline areas. After its dies, the dead prickly ball-like mass becomes detached from the ground and can be blown for kilometres.

Range: coasts and arid inland areas of all states, also Europe. **Leaves:** alternate, stiff, succulent, pale or bluish-green, covered in tiny watery glands, pungent-pointed. **Flowers:** RED; solitary in the axils of short leaves towards the ends of branches. **Flowering time:** summer. **Fruit:** succulent but the perianth continues growing, soon covering it and developing 5 broad red wings. Eventually the whole unit reaches up to 7mm diameter. The wings aid in wind distribution. **Name:** *kali* = from the Arabic name for the plant *al-qili*, hence alkali, a term for a product once obtained from the ashes of its leaves. They are soda-rich, and, like Glasswort, were used in glass making.

• *Sarcocornia* A. J. Scott

Samphires, Glassworts
An endemic genus of salt-marsh herbs with 3 species. Closely related to the cosmopolitan genus *Salicornia*, which includes the European Glasswort, *S. europaea*. The common name Glasswort comes from the use of the ashes as a source of sodium for glass making.

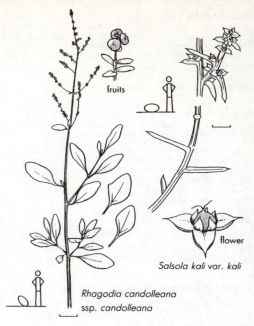

fruits

flower

Salsola kali var. *kali*

Rhagodia candolleana
ssp. *candolleana*

Name: *Sarcocornia* = Gk. flesh-horn, referring to the branches.

Sarcocornia quinqueflora

(Bunge ex Ungen-Sternberg) A. J. Scott

(previously *Salicornia quinqueflora*)
Samphire, Glasswort
A small erect leafless herb with succulent jointed stems to about 30cm high. It occurs in dense colonies in salt-marshes, 'its monotonous stretch of dull-green, stunted herbage, framing the mangroves with a sombre border.'[4]

Reproduction is both vegetative, by sending up shoots from spreading stems, and sexual. It uses the tide for seed distribution; the whole fruiting spike falls off at maturity and floats away.

The stems are edible raw, although rather salty, and good for pickling.

Range: coasts of all states. **Leaves:** reduced to narrow membranous margins on the jointed succulent stems. **Flowers:** tiny, in circlets in the stem joints. The 2-lobed perianth is partly hidden; what you mainly see are the protruding anthers (2 per flower) and styles (2 per flower). **Flowering time:** summer. **Name:** *quinqueflora* = Lat. 5-flowered; in fact they are usually in 7s.

• *Suaeda* Forsskal ex Scolopi

Seablites
A genus of herbs with about 110 species, including 2 native species in Australia.

Name: *suaeda* = from the Arabic name *suwaida*, meaning blackish, given to the Mediterranean species *S. vera*. The name 'blite' comes from the Greek *bliton*, meaning tasteless.

Suaeda australis (R. Brown) Moquin-Tandon

Austral Seablite

A low dense spreading herb to about 40cm high, with slender fleshy erect leaves. Common on the margins of salt-marshes and brackish estuaries, usually alongside Samphire, its 'occasional rival but more frequent ally'.[5]

The young leaves and stems are edible, either raw, when they are tasty and crisp, or steamed.

Range: all coasts in temperate Australia (its relative, *S. arbusculoides*, is widespread on tropical coasts). **Leaves:** alternate, soft, succulent, hairless, often reddish. **Flowers:** GREEN, insignificant, in tiny clusters in the leaf axils. **Flowering time:** spring-early summer. **Name:** *australis* = Lat. southern.

CONVOLVULACEAE

Calystegia soldanella (Linnaeus) R. Brown

A long-creeping herb with stems to a few metres long, found in moist sunny places next to the sea, often on sand-dunes. Not common in the area.

Range: coasts of NSW, Lord Howe Island, Tas and WA; also widespread in temperate parts of the world. **Leaves:** rounded, thick, fleshy, hairless, on long stalks. **Flowers:** PINK-MAUVE, 3-5cm long. **Flowering time:** summer. **Name:** *soldanella* = after the similar-flowered genus *Soldanella* (in Primulaceae). The name is vernacular Italian for little sultan.

Ipomoea brasiliensis (Linnaeus) Sweet

(formerly *I. pes-caprae*)

Coastal Morning Glory, Goatsfoot Convolvulus

A robust runner on beach sand-dunes with stems to a few metres long. Only recorded locally from Jibbon Beach near Bundeena. The roots are edible but very fibrous.

Range: tropical shores of Australia, north from Sydney, also widespread in tropical parts of the world. **Leaves:** round, notched at the tip, tough, hairless, mostly 4-8cm long. **Flowers:** PURPLE, about 4cm long. **Name:** *brasiliensis* = Lat. from Brasil, where it was first collected.

Ipomoea cairica * (Linnaeus) Sweet

Mile-a-minute

A common climber on fences and vegetation near the sea.

Range: coasts of NSW and Qld, tropical Africa and Asia. **Leaves:** palmate, i.e. with 5-7 separate lobes arising from the base of the leaf. **Flowers:** PINK-BLUE. **Flowering time:** spring-summer. **Name:** *cairica* = from Cairo?

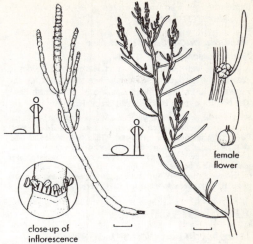

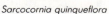

close-up of inflorescence

female flower

Sarcocornia quinqueflora   *Suaeda australis*

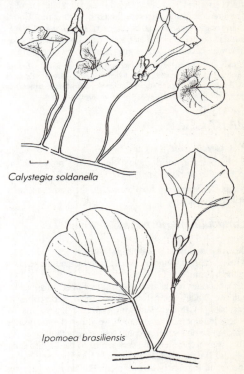

Calystegia soldanella

Ipomoea brasiliensis

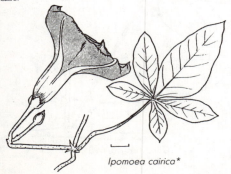

Ipomoea cairica *

• *Wilsonia* R. Brown

A genus of coastal mat-forming herbs with 4-5 species, including 3 in Australia.

Name: *Wilsonia* = after John Wilson, d.1751, an amateur

English botanist who wrote *Synopsis of British Plants in Mr Ray's Method* (1744).

Wilsonia backhousei J. D. Hooker

Narrow-leaved Wilsonia
A prostrate herb, with fleshy erect leaves, forming dense carpets on the edges of salt-marsh. Rare in the area; on the Parramatta River (e.g. Ermington, Concord, Homebush Bay). The best local stand is on Salt Pan Creek, Padstow.

Range: Sydney area (the northern limit is Wamberal Lagoon), Jervis Bay (common), and widespread on the southern coasts of Australia. **Leaves:** thick, fleshy, 6-15mm long. **Flowers:** WHITE, with a slender tube, solitary, axillary, erect. **Flowering time:** spring-early summer. **Name:** *backhousei* = after James Backhouse (1794-1869), an itinerant Quaker preacher with a botanical bent. In the years 1832-38 he walked over the entire settled parts of NSW, holding prayer meetings and collecting plants. He sent the type specimen to J. D. Hooker at Kew Gardens.

Wilsonia backhousei

EPACRIDACEAE

Leucopogon parviflorus (Andrews) Lindley

A bushy shrub usually about 1.5m high, common on open seacoasts and in hind-dune scrubs. The small, white, succulent fruit are edible and were consumed by Aborigines. During D'Entrecasteaux's voyage in search of La Pérouse, 1791-93, the naturalist Riche was lost for 3 days on the south coast of WA, and claimed to have supported himself on the fruits.

Range: all states except NT, also NZ and Lord Howe Island. **Leaves:** flexible, generally concave below, 1-2cm long, soft pointed. **Flowers:** in dense spikes, shorter than the leaves. **Flowering time:** July-September. **Name:** *parviflorus* = Lat. small-flowered.

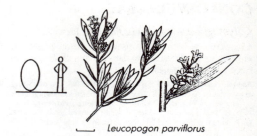

Leucopogon parviflorus

FABACEAE

• *Canavalia* De Candolle

A pantropical genus of trailing vines with 5 representatives in Australia, distributed in WA, NT, Qld and NSW.

Name: *Canavalia* = from *kanavali*, the native name in Malabar, India.

Canavalia maritima (Aublet) Thouars

(previously *C. rosea*)
Beach Bean, Coastal Jack Bean, Sword Bean
A robust creeper, found on exposed coastal sand-dunes north of the harbour.

This species has its own special place in colonial history; Surgeon White's journal on 23 August 1788 describes an excursion to Broken Bay with Governor Phillip. 'As we proceeded along the sandy beach, we gathered some beanes, which grew on a small creeping substance not unlike a vine. They were well tasted, and very similar to the English long-pod bean. At the place where we halted, we had them boiled, and we all eat very heartily of them. Half an hour later, the governor and I were seized with a violent vomiting . . . '6

When properly cooked however they are good eating. Aborigines ate them roasted.

Range: NSW coast from Long Reef into Qld, NT, WA; also in Asia and Africa. **Leaflets:** 3, fairly soft and thin. **Flowers:** PINK to VIOLET PURPLE, in axillary racemes on long stalks. **Flowering time:** summer.

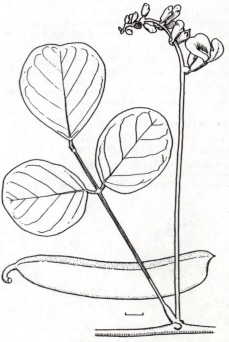

Canavalia maritima

Name: *maritima* = Lat. pertaining to the sea. **Similar species:** distinguish from *Kennedia rubicunda* by the long leaf stalk.

GERANIACEAE

Pelargonium australe Willdenow

Coastal Geranium

An erect herb to about 40cm tall, with leaves along the stem and tufted at the base. Rare in the area, in sand-dune scrubs near the sea (common in the Illawarra).

Range: NSW coast, ranges and western slopes, and all other states. **Leaves:** blades from 2-5cm long, slightly aromatic, covered in downy hairs. The basal leaves are often large and densely tufted. **Flowers:** PINK, to about 10mm wide; in terminal umbels. Fertile stamens 6-8, calyx hairs short and scattered. **Flowering time:** summer. **Name:** *australe* = Lat. southern.

GOODENIACEAE

Scaevola calendulacea (Andrews) Druce

Scented Fan Flower

A robust prostrate herb with ascending flowering stems. It forms large dense mats on sand dunes near the sea. A fairly common species. The purplish berries are edible, 'pleasantly juicy and mildly sweet-salty'.[7]

Range: coasts of NSW, Qld and Vic. **Leaves:** fleshy, usually toothless (sometimes a few teeth towards the tip), covered in fine sparse hairs. They resemble *Chrysanthemoides monilifera* (Bitou Bush), another dune species. **Flowers:** SKY BLUE, in short dense terminal spikes. **Flowering time:** much of the year. **Name:** *calendulacea* = like *Calendula*, a small yellow-flowered genus in the family Asteraceae, known as Cape or Pot Marigolds.

• *Selliera* Cavanilles

An endemic genus with 2 species, found in all states except Qld and NT. *S. radicans* extends to NZ and Chile.

Name: *Selliera* = in honour of Francois Sellier (1737-1800), a French botanical engraver.

Selliera radicans Cavanilles

A creeping herb forming dense carpets in salt-marshes, it also occurs on coastal cliffs. Fairly common in the area. It is less tolerant of salt than other salt-marsh species and so prefers brackish places removed from full tidal flow or located some distance upstream. The fruit capsules float for up to a week, enabling distribution by water.

Range: Sydney area and south coast, Vic, Tas, SA, NZ and Chile. **Leaves:** erect, fleshy, thick, hairless. **Flowers:** solitary, axillary, WHITE with purple-brown markings. The petals lack the wings found in other members of the family. **Flowering time:** summer. **Name:** *radicans* = Lat. rooting, referring to its creeping habit.

LAMIACEAE

Westringia fruticosa (Willdenow) Druce

Coast Westringia

A dense spreading shrub usually 1-1.5m high, common on coastal cliffs and headlands. Often planted in hedges. The flowers have long narrow throats and are white, suggesting pollination by moths.

Range: NSW coast north from Sydney, and Lord Howe Island. **Leaves:** crowded, grey-green, in whorls of 4, narrow, with recurved or revolute margins, and with appressed white felt below. **Flowers:** corolla WHITE, hairy, often with some tiny orange spots; sessile, in short terminal racemes. **Flowering time:** much of the year. **Name:** *fruticosa* = Lat. shrub-like.

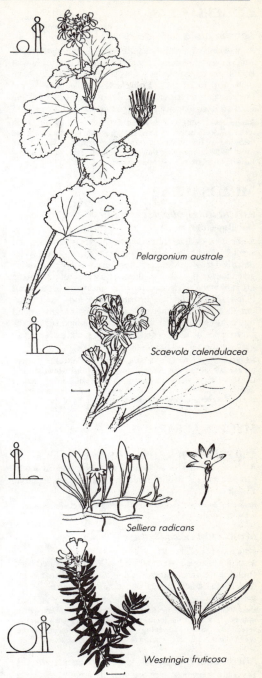

Pelargonium australe

Scaevola calendulacea

Selliera radicans

Westringia fruticosa

LOBELIACEAE

Lobelia alata Labillardière

A small herb with sharply angular stems, common on coastal headlands and beside estuaries. Its habit varies greatly with conditions: on exposed sea cliffs it is compact, under 10cm high, with tufted thick fleshy leaves; while on sheltered brackish stream banks it is a slender, ascending or sprawling plant, to 50cm long, with scattered thin-textured leaves.

Range: coastal parts of all Australian states except NT, also NZ, South Africa and South America. **Leaves:** hairless, soft, becoming thick and fleshy in more salty conditions. **Flowers:** tiny, solitary, axillary, WHITE to SKY BLUE. **Flowering time:** much of the year. **Name:** *alata* = Lat. winged, referring to the angular stems.

MIMOSACEAE

Acacia longifolia var. *sophorae*

(Labillardière) F. Mueller

A robust sprawling shrub with main stems prostrate and smaller branches erect, usually to 1m high. A colonial writer described it as ' . . . lumpish round masses of rich yellowish green foliage, their dark shadows vividly contrasting with the glaringly white sandy shore, and the silvery surf of the broad blue sea. But on climbing the bank of deep loose sand, filling our shoes or boots therewith in the scramble, the round bushes assume the character of crooked stemmed, fantastically twisted trees, bent and driven in all cramped and extraordinary forms by the force of the wind . . . '[8]

Range: coasts of NSW, Qld, Vic, SA and Tas. **Phyllodes:** tough, erect, blunt, much broader and thicker than var. *longifolia* **Flower-heads:** GOLDEN-YELLOW, cylindrical. **Flowering time:** July-October. **Name:** *sophorae* = from its similarity to the handsome yellow-flowered Pacific pea bush *Sophorae tomentosa*, known as Kowhai in NZ.

MYOPORACEAE

• *Myoporum* Solander ex. G. Forster

A genus of shrubs or small trees with 28 species in south-east Asia and the Pacific, including 17 in Australia, found in all states.

Name: *Myoporum* = Gk. closed-pore, referring to the closed appearance of the leaf glands.

Myoporum acuminatum R. Brown

Mangrove Boobialla **Rf**

A small tree usually 4-6m tall with pale corky fissured bark. Found just behind mangroves in *Casuarina glauca* forest, or in rainforest near the sea. Uncommon in the area.

Range: NSW coastal districts, Qld, NT and WA. **Leaves:** thick, fleshy, about 10cm long, hairless, more or less flat, spreading. **Flowers:** WHITE, with purple spots in the throat, about 15mm wide, slightly irregular, several per axil. **Flowering time:** August-October. **Name:** *accuminatum* = Lat. drawn out to a point, referring to the leaves.

Myoporum boninense Koidz. **ssp. *australe***

Boobialla (previously included in *M. insulare*)

A scrambling shrub 50-150cm high, found on rocky sea shores. Fairly common in the area. Fruits said to be edible.

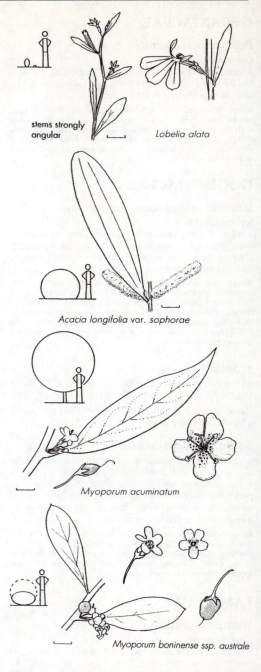

stems strongly angular

Lobelia alata

Acacia longifolia var. *sophorae*

Myoporum acuminatum

Myoporum boninense ssp. australe

Range: coasts of southern Australia. **Leaves:** fairly thick and fleshy, about 5cm long, hairless. **Flowers:** WHITE, sometimes with purple spots, about 8mm wide. **Flowering time:** October-March. **Name:** *boninense* = an inhabitant of Bonin (now Ogaswara-gunto), a small island off Japan.

MYRSINACEAE

• *Aegiceras* Gaertner

A genus of mangrove trees with 2 species, one in Australia, the other in tropical Asia.

Name: *Aegiceras* = Gk. goat-horn, from the shape of the fruits.

Aegiceras corniculatum (Linnaeus) Blanco

River Mangrove

A small mangrove tree, usually 3-4m high, less common than Grey Mangrove and located in less saline water, i.e. upstream and inland from the Grey Mangrove. It breathes through lenticels (air pores) at the trunk base.

Range: south coast of NSW, through Qld to northern Australia; also tropical Asia. **Leaves:** alternate, blunt, thick and leathery, yellowish green, hairless. **Flowers:** WHITE, in dense umbels, terminal or in the upper axils. **Flowering time:** September-October. **Name:** *corniculatum* = having horn-like fruit.

MYRTACEAE

Leptospermum laevigatum

(Solander ex Gaertner) F. Mueller

Coastal Tea-tree

A tall shrub to 8m high forming dense scrubs beside the sea, immediately behind the sand-dunes. This species is very important in coastal ecology. Together with *Banksia integrifolia* it forms a protective barrier against salty winds behind which forests of Bangalay (*Eucalyptus botryoides*) or coastal rainforest communities develop.

Range: NSW coast, WA, Tas, SA and Vic. **Bark:** flaky. **Leaves:** grey-green, 15-30mm long, flat, broad, usually with 3 veins visible. **Flowers:** WHITE, 15-20mm wide. **Flowering time:** August-October. **Capsules:** smooth, 7-8mm wide, green when new, non-woody, with 10 chambers (all other Tea-trees have 5 chambers). **Name:** *laevigatum* = Lat. smooth and polished, referring to the sheeny capsule.

Melaleuca armillaris

A dense fine-leaved shrub with hard corky bark, to 5m high. It occurs in dense heath scrubs near the sea.
—See MAJOR FAMILIES: Myrtaceae.

Melaleuca ericifolia

A fine-leafed paperbark shrub, or small tree, usually 3-6m tall. It has some salt tolerance and often occurs on the fresh side of salt-marshes, near *Casuarina glauca*.
—See MAJOR FAMILIES: Myrtaceae.

OXALIDACEAE

Oxalis rubens Haworth

A small herb with weak stems 5-35cm long arising from branched fibrous roots. Found on beaches and coastal sand dunes, but probably rare in the area.

Range: coasts of NSW, Qld, Vic, SA and NZ. **Leaves:** 3-foliate; leaflets very variable in size, purplish green, somewhat greyish, hairless. The tiny stem hairs are bent upwards. **Flowers:** 1-2 per inflorescence; petals YELLOW, 7-8mm long. **Fruits:** erect, cylindrical, densely furry with fine hairs, 15-18mm long, 3-4mm wide. **Name:** *rubens* = Lat. reddish.

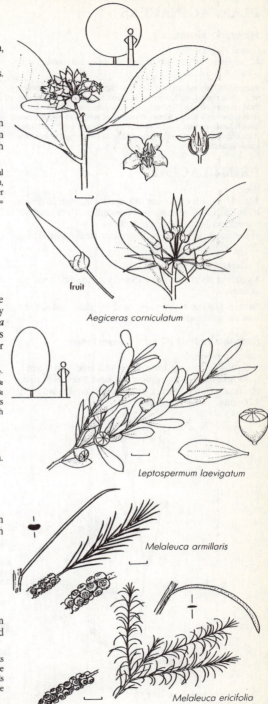

fruit

Aegiceras corniculatum

Leptospermum laevigatum

Melaleuca armillaris

Melaleuca ericifolia

PLANTAGINACEAE

Plantago hispida R. Brown
Coastal Plaintain

A low dense tufted herb, found on rocky sea-coasts. Fairly common in the area.

Range: NSW coast and ranges, and all states except Queensland. **Leaves:** with a few shallow teeth, covered in sparse furry hairs. **Flowers:** in short dense spikes to 10cm tall. The scapes are stout and covered in short soft whitish hairs. **Name:** *hispida* = Lat. rough (an inappropriate name). **Note:** another species found by the sea-side (and elsewhere) is *Plantago coronopus**, easily recognised by its slender, sparsely toothed leaves in dense rosettes.

PRIMULACEAE

Primroses

A family of herbs with about 1000 species in about 20 genera mainly in the temperate northern hemisphere. There are about 6 species in 2 genera native to Australia.

The family is related to the woody family Myrsinaceae.

• *Samolus* Linnaeus
A genus of herbs with about 15 species, including 4 species in Australia.

Name: *Samolus* = the name used by Pliny, possibly for *Samolus valerandii.*

Samolus repens (G. & J. R. Forster) Persoon
Creeping Brookweed

A herb with creeping lower stems and erect upper stems, to 30cm tall, with pretty white star-flowers. It occurs in saline conditions on the edge of estuaries and on wet sea cliffs. A common species in the area.

Samolus repens

growth variants

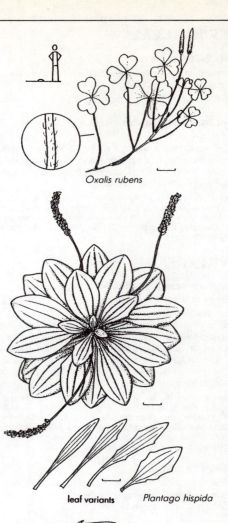

Oxalis rubens

leaf variants   Plantago hispida

Plantago coronopus ssp. coronopus*

Range: coasts throughout southern Australia. **Leaves:** smooth or covered in tiny warty vesicles, green, erect, firm-textured. **Flowers:** WHITE (rarely pink-tinged); solitary, terminal. There are 5 stamens and 5 slender staminodes. **Flowering time:** spring-summer. **Name:** *repens* = Lat. creeping.

PROTEACEAE

Banksia integrifolia Carl von Linné
Coastal Banksia

A shrub or tree 6-16m high, common in coastal scrubs and forests; often abundant in dune successions, on headlands and beside estuaries. Easily recognised at a distance by white leaf undersurfaces that ripple silvery in the wind. Coastal Banksia was once an important timber for biplane construction. Timber getters called it 'Beefwood' because the cut timber looks like a slice of fresh beef with a fatty rind.

Range: from Melbourne to southern Qld. Often planted near the sea. **Bark:** rough, hard, light grey. **Leaves:** entire, stiff, leathery, erect (toothed in juvenile stage), dark green, hairless above, white below due to a layer of fine white felty hairs. **Spike:** PALE YELLOW, to 12cm high. **Flowering time:** mainly winter (January-June). **Name:** *integrifolia* = whole-leaved.

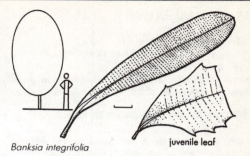

Banksia integrifolia   juvenile leaf

RUBIACEAE

• *Coprosma* G & J. R. Forster

A genus with about 90 species worldwide, half in New Zealand, with 6 species endemic to eastern Australia.

Name: *Coprosma* = Gk. dung-smell, referring to the fetid smell of the leaves of most species.

Coprosma repens * A. Richard

Mirror Bush

A bushy shrub 2-4m tall, very shiny leaves. Introduced from NZ and naturalised in many places along the coast. The succulent fruits are edible, with a sweet flavour.

Range: coasts around Sydney, NSW south coast and NZ. **Leaves:** round, glossy, mid-green, hairless. **Flowers:** unisexual (dioecious). **Fruits:** orange, succulent drupes, edible. **Name:** *repens* = Lat. creeping, since the main stems are often prostrate.

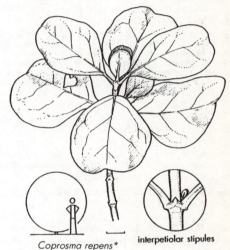

Coprosma repens *   interpetiolar stipules

RUTACEAE

Correa alba Andrews **var.** *alba*

White Correa

A rounded shrub to 1.5m high, always found near the sea, often in exposed, windy, salty and generally hostile conditions, for instance on sand-dunes or rocks subject to spray.

Joseph Banks introduced it to England in 1793 where it became a popular greenhouse plant. The leaves have a refreshing fragrance and make a pleasant tea.

Range: NSW coastal areas, also Vic and Tas. **Leaves:** opposite, round, with a small notch at the tip, and a cream coloured layer of felty star-hairs underneath (and on stems). **Flowers:** WHITE, in small terminal clusters of 1-4. **Flowering time:** June-early spring. **Name:** *alba* = Lat. white.

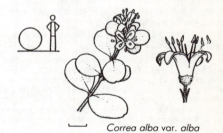

Correa alba var. *alba*

Phebalium squamulosum **ssp.** *argentum*

P.G. Wilson

A dense spreading shrub 1.5-2m tall with somewhat greyish leaves. Abundant in seaside heath and scrub in the Royal National Park.

Range: NSW coastal areas and Vic. **Leaves:** oblong, underside with silver scales and hairs, dull on upper surface, usually just notched at the tip. **Flowers:** petals CREAMISH to WHITE inside. **Flowering time:** spring (from September). **Name:** *argentum* = Lat. silver, referring to the silvery scales.

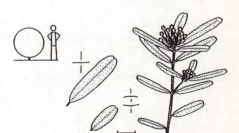

Phebalium squamulosum ssp. *argentum*

SAPINDACEAE

• *Cupaniopsis* Radlkofer

A genus of trees and shrubs with about 60 species, including 5 species endemic to Australia.

Name: *cupaniopsis* = Lat. like *Cupania*, a closely allied genus named in honour of Francesco Cupani (died 1710).

Cupaniopsis anacardioides (A. Richard) Radlkofer

Tuckeroo, Yowarro

A small to medium tree, 3-10m tall in this area, found in humid places near the sea, on windswept headlands or with littoral rainforest. There is a lovely stand behind Jibbon Beach at Bundeena in the Royal National Park.

Range: in near-coastal areas from the Royal National Park to Qld and NT. **Leaves:** pinnate, usually with 6-8 leaflets; leaflets more or less glossy, tough, hairless, strongly veined on both surfaces, with a rounded, often notched, tip. **Flowers:** small, GREENISH WHITE, in axillary panicles. **Fruits:** fleshy 3-chambered capsules, 12-20mm wide, yellow to orange when ripe. **Name:** *anacardioides* = like an *Anacardium* (Anacardiaceae), a tree with similar foliage. *Yowarro* is an Aboriginal name from the Illawarra.

SCROPHULARIACEAE

• *Bacopa* Aublet

A genus of creeping herbs with about 100 species, including 2 in Australia, distributed mainly in tropical areas.

Name: *Bacopa* = origin not known; first described in Guiana, possibly from a native name.

Bacopa monniera (Torner) Wettstein

A small creeping herb with somewhat succulent stems 10-40cm long. Found on the margins of coastal lagoons and marshy places near the sea, and on wet sea cliffs (e.g. Coogee, Maroubra). Uncommon in the area.

In India it is used as a diuretic and laxative, and also as a nerve and heart tonic.

Range: NSW coasts, north from Shellharbour to Qld, also cosmopolitan. **Leaves:** soft, thin, rounded, 4-12mm long. **Flowers:** WHITE, on erect stalks; 2 of the sepals are expanded to enfold the bud and capsule and there are also 2 small bracteoles. **Flowering time:** December-February. **Name:** *monniera* = after Le Monnier, physician to Louis XV. He accompanied the Italian botanist Cassini through the southern provinces of France in the summer of 1739, writing an account of their natural history.

• *Mimulus* Linnaeus

A genus of small aquatic herbs with about 100 species worldwide. There are 4 species endemic to Australia and 2 naturalised.

Name: *Mimulus* = Lat. *mimulous*, little mask, referring to the flowers.

Mimulus repens R. Brown

Creeping Monkey-flower

A small creeping marsh herb with somewhat succulent stems to 10cm long. Uncommon in the area, on the margins of coastal lagoons.

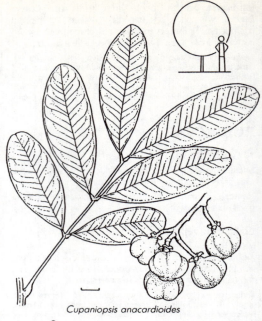

Cupaniopsis anacardioides

Bacopa monniera

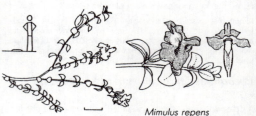

Mimulus repens

Range: NSW coast, Vic, Tas and SA. **Leaves:** 2-6mm long, hairless. **Flowers:** BLUE to PURPLE, with a yellowish tube. **Flowering time:** February-March. **Name:** *repens* = Lat. creeping.

STACKHOUSIACEAE

Stackhousia spathulata Sieber ex Sprengel

A slender erect herb to 45cm high forming dense tufts on sand dunes near the sea. Uncommon to rare in the area.

Range: coasts of eastern Australia. **Leaves:** 15-30mm long, spoon-shaped, thick, soft, usually blunt. **Flowers:** WHITE, 6-8mm long, usually in dense spikes. **Fruit:** consists of 3 nutlets, each with 3 wings. **Name:** *spathulata* = Lat. spoon-shaped.

• MONOCOTYLEDONS

CYPERACEAE Sedges

Baumea juncea

A slender sedge to 1m tall with grey-green stems arising at intervals from spreading rhizomes. Common in freshwater seepages on the edges of salt-marsh.
—See SEDGES & RUSHES.

Carex pumila Thunberg

Strand Sedge

A small grass-like herb to 15cm tall, found on sand-dunes near the sea, usually with *Spinifex hirsutus*. The stems arise from a creeping rhizome.

Range: coasts of eastern Australia, Tas, NZ, Asia and South America. **Leaves:** few, to 6mm wide, 15-30cm long. **Spikelets:** unisexual, in separate spikes, usually with a single upper male spike and several lower spikes. **Name:** *pumila* = Lat. low, small.

Bolboschoenus caldwellii

Often occurs on the edges of salt-marsh.
—See SEDGES & RUSHES.

Cyperus laevigatus Linnaeus

An erect sedge 40-60cm tall, with stiff stems, found in saline estuaries and coastal lagoons.

Range: coast of NSW, Qld, Vic, SA and WA, also widespread in tropical parts of the world. **Leaves:** reduced to sheaths at the base of the stems. **Spikelets:** pale brown, in a dense cluster. **Name:** *laevigatus* = Lat. shining, referring to the stems.

Isolepis cernua (Vahl) Roemer & Schultes

(previously *Scirpus cernuus*)
A minute sedge, forming dense tufts 5-15cm high, on wet sea cliffs and the edges of estuaries and lagoons. Uncommon in the area. Recorded from the Royal National Park.

Range: NSW coast, Blue Mountains, northern tablelands, all states, cosmopolitan. **Leaves:** reduced to sheaths. **Spikelets:** solitary, about 2mm long. The stems are very fine. **Name:** *cernua* = Lat. nodding.

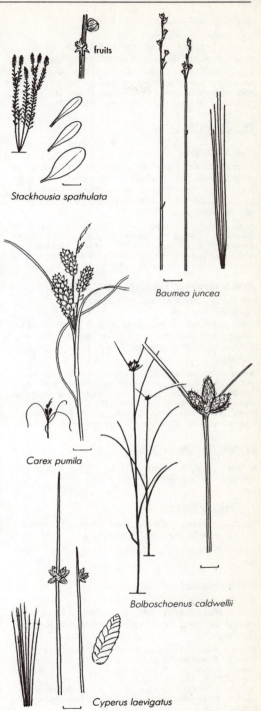

fruits

Stackhousia spathulata

Baumea juncea

Carex pumila

Bolboschoenus caldwellii

Cyperus laevigatus

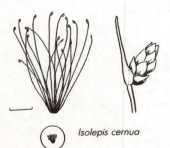

Isolepis cernua

Isolepis nodosus (Rottboell) R. Brown

(previously *Scirpus nodosus*)

An erect sedge forming clumps to 70cm tall, common in moist soil near the sea. Easily recognised by its globular heads.

Range: coasts of southern states, widespread in the temperate southern hemisphere. **Leaves:** reduced to sheaths at the bases of the stems. **Spikelets:** reddish-brown, in dense globular clusters. The stems are cylindrical, about 2mm wide. **Name:** *nodosus* = Lat. nobby.

JUNCACEAE Rushes

Juncus acutus[*] Linnaeus

An erect rush forming radiating clumps, or sometimes dense entanglements, 50-150cm high. Common in salt-marsh in the Sydney area, competing with and displacing *J. kraussii.* It also occurs as a weed in non-salty places. A native of Europe, Asia and North Africa.

Range: NSW coast and ranges except the Blue Mountains, scattered in inland areas, Vic, SA and WA. **Leaves:** rigid, sharply pointed, dull grey-green (slightly bluish), 2-3mm wide, (5mm at base). **Panicles:** dense, rusty coloured, with relatively large capsules 4-6mm long. Stems similar to leaves. **Name:** *acutus* = Lat. pointed.

Juncus kraussii Hochstetter

(previously *J. maritimus* var. *australiensis*)
Sea Rush

A tall, coarse rush, 1-2m high, growing in dense clumps on the edges of brackish estuaries, together with salt-marsh herbs. Usually inundated at high tide. It often occurs in extensive pure stands.

Range: widespread on Australian coasts, except the far north; also NZ and South Africa. **Leaves:** dark-green, 2-3mm wide, to 1.5m tall, sharp-pointed. **Panicles:** dense, each flower subtended by straw-coloured bracts. The capsules are shiny dark brown. The stems are similar to the leaves. **Name:** *kraussii* = after Christian Ferdinand Krauss (1812-90), a German naturalist, who collected the type specimen in South Africa.

JUNCAGINACEAE

A family of aquatic herbs with 14 species in 3 genera worldwide, in both hemispheres.

• *Triglochin* Linnaeus

A genus of aquatic herbs with about 12 species worldwide, 10-11 in Australia, distributed in all states.

Name: *Triglochin* = Gk. 3-barbed, referring to the pointed carpels.

Triglochin striata Ruiz & Pavon

Streaked Arrow-grass

A small erect grass-like herb, found in narrow bands along brackish estuaries, usually where the tidal flow is strong. Common.

Range: NSW coast, all states, Lord Howe Island, South Africa and the Americas. **Leaves:** slender, cylindrical or slightly flattened, to 30cm tall. **Flowers:** small (about 2mm long), with a similar structure to *T. procera* (see AQUATICS) except not all stamens develop; in a slender erect spike-like raceme. There are 3 fertile and 3 sterile carpels. **Flowering time:** summer. **Name:** *striata* = Lat. streaked, referring to the streaked rounded backs of the carpels.

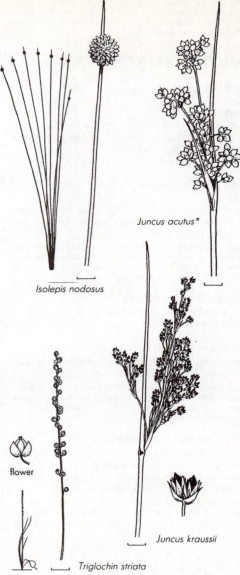

Juncus acutus[*]

Isolepis nodosus

flower

Juncus kraussii

Triglochin striata

LILIACEAE

• *Crinum* Linnaeus

A genus with about 100 species widespread in warm, mainly coastal, parts of the world. There are 5 Australian species, distributed in all mainland states. It is often placed in the family Amaryllidaceae.

Name: *Crinum* = Gk. *krinon*, lily.

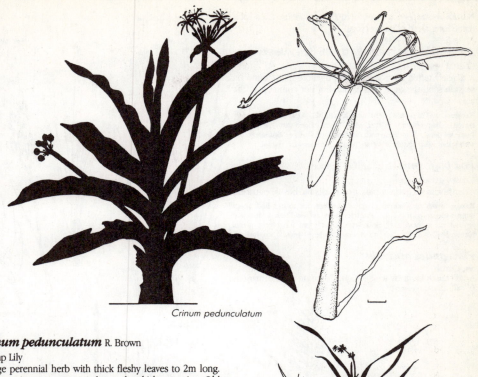

Crinum pedunculatum

Crinum pedunculatum R. Brown

Swamp Lily
A large perennial herb with thick fleshy leaves to 2m long.
Common in swampy ground near brackish estuaries. Qld
Aborigines rubbed crushed leaves on the body as an antidote
to marine stings.

Range: NSW coast, Lord Howe Island, Qld and SA. **Leaves:** thick, tough,
channelled above, to 20cm wide. **Flowers:** WHITE, large, clustered on
a thick fleshy peduncle. **Flowering time:** December-January. **Name:**
pedunculatum = Lat. having a peduncle.

Dianella congesta R. Henderson

Coastal Flax Lily
A tufted herb to 80cm tall, found on exposed seacoasts. So
far not recorded in the area, but abundant north of the
Hawkesbury and in the Illawarra. It resembles *D. caerula*,
except the flowers are fewer and in tight bunches. The
inflorescence stalk is thick and succulent when new,
becoming stiff, winged and deflexed (like a walking stick)
when old.

Range: NSW coast. **Leaves:** hard, stiff, glossy, to about 20mm wide,
30-50cm long, with smooth or finely saw-toothed edges. **Flowers:** RICH
BLUE with yellow anthers. **Flowering time:** spring. **Name:** *congesta*
= Lat. congested, referring to the clustered flowers.

Dianella congesta

Ammophila arenaria° (Linnaeus) Link

Marram Grass, European Beachgrass
An erect grass 60-100cm high, forming dense compact tufts.
Widely planted on the NSW coast to stabilise sand-dunes,
but not common in the area, e.g. Brighton.

Range: NSW coast, north from Sydney area, all states, Europe, North
Africa, North America and NZ. **Leaves:** stiff, grey-green, tough, in-curved,
to 60cm long. **Panicle:** pale, dense, cylindrical, 12-20cm long.
Spikelets: 10-16mm long, stalked, closely overlapping. **Name:** *arenaria*
= Lat. pertaining to sand.

POACEAE Grasses

• *Ammophila* Host

A genus of 2 species of coastal grasses, native to the northern
hemisphere.

Name: *Ammophila* = Gk. sand-loving.

• *Austrofestuca* E.B. Alexeev

Southern Fescues
A genus with 3 species, 2 in Australia and 1 in NZ. Previously
placed in *Festuca*. Closely related to *Festuca* and *Poa*.

Name: *Austrofestuca* = southern-*Festuca*. *Festuca* is a Latin name for a weed of barely crops.

Austrofestuca littoralis (Labillardière) Alexeev

Coastal Fescue

A densely tufted erect grass to 1m or more high, found on seaside sand dunes, e.g. Cronulla, but not common in the area.

Range: coasts of south-eastern Australia and NZ.   **Leaves:** revolute (in-curled), sharp-pointed, 1-2mm wide, often longer than the panicle. **Panicle:** dense, cylindrical, with overlapping spikelets.   **Spikelets:** 12-14mm long, with several flowers.   **Name:** *littoralis* = Lat. coastal.

Poa poiformis (Labillardière) Druce

Coast Tussock Grass

A dense tussock grass, common on coasts and beside estuaries.

Range: coasts of southern Australia.   **Leaves:** flat to in-rolled, about 4mm wide, smooth below.   **Panicle:** more or less linear with few if any spreading branches.   **Spikelets:** about 6mm long, pale green. **Name:** *poiformis* = *Poa*-like (it was originally named *Arundo poaeformis*).

Phragmites australis

Ss, Cumb

A tall reed-like grass to 2m high. Common on the margins of salt-marsh. —See AQUATICS.

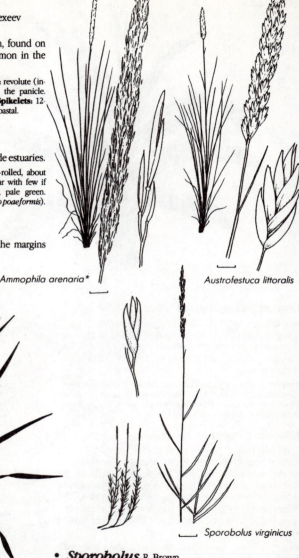

Ammophila arenaria*

Austrofestuca littoralis

Sporobolus virginicus

• Sporobolus R. Brown

A genus of about 150 species, mainly in the tropics and subtropics. There are 13 native and 4 introduced species in Australia.

Name: *Sporobolus* = Gk. seed-throwing, referring to the seed being shed from inside the floral parts.

Sporobolus virginicus (Linnaeus) Kunth

Sand Couch, Salt-grass

A creeping perennial grass forming dense low masses in salt-

Poa poiformis   *Phragmites australis*

marshes and on sand-dunes, usually with *Juncus kraussii* and other saline species. Common in the area.

Range: all states except Tas; cosmopolitan. **Leaves:** short, greyish. Stems about 1mm wide. **Panicle:** short, narrow, spike-like. **Spikelets:** with 2 unequal glumes, about 2mm long, thin-textured, translucent, not fully enclosing the floret. **Flowering time:** spring-summer. **Name:** *virginicus* = from Virginia. **Similar species:** *Zoysia macrantha.*

• *Spinifex* Linnaeus

A genus with 4 species on the coasts of Asia and Australia. Two species occur in Australia. These do not include the desert 'Spinifex', which belongs to a different genus, *Triodia.*
Name: *Spinifex* = Lat. thorn-maker, from an Asian species with sharp leaves.

Spinifex sericeus R. Brown

A coarse robust grass, forming extensive mats on coastal sand dunes. It spreads by means of long creeping stems. The large spidery seed heads are superbly mobile, falling on maturity and rolling for long distances in the wind. It is a most important grass for stabilising coastal dunes.

Range: coasts of all states, NZ and Pacific Islands. **Leaves:** flat, densely silky-hairy. **Panicle:** the plants are dioecious; the male inflorescence is a cluster of racemes or spikes subtended by silky-hairy bracts; the female is a large globular head to 20cm wide. **Spikelets:** each is surrounded by large silky-hairy bracts and attached to an axis which extends as a stout bristle 5-10cm long. **Name:** *sericeus* = Lat. silky

• *Zoysia* Willdenow

A genus with about 10 species, distributed along coasts of the Indian and Western Pacific Oceans.
Name: *Zoysia* = after K. Zoys (1756-1800), a German plant collector.

Zoysia macrantha Desvaux

Coast Couch
A creeping perennial grass with habit similar to *Sporobolus virginicus.* Ranges inland from salt-marsh and dune environments, but often invades *Sporobolus* in patches near seepages. Fairly common in the area. Hard to distinguish from *Sporobolus* when not in flower.

Range: coasts of eastern Australia and South-east Asia. **Leaves:** rigid, flat or in-curled, 2-15cm long, up to 4mm wide. **Panicle:** dark, narrow, spike-like, with spikelets pressed against the flattened, zig-zag axis. **Spikelets:** with a solitary glume, 4mm long, tough-textured, with overlapping edges enclosing the spikelet. **Name:** *macrantha* = Gk. large-flower.

FERNS

The following harsh salt-resistant ferns occur on the Sydney seacoast.

Asplenium difforme
—See FERNS: ASPLENIACEAE.

Cyrtomium falcatum *
—See FERNS: DYROPTERIDACEAE.

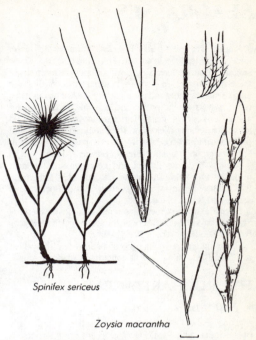

Spinifex sericeus

Zoysia macrantha

OTHER SPECIES FOUND IN SALTY SITUATIONS

Baeckea imbricata
A dense shrub about 1m high, with tiny overlapping leaves, common in heath on the edges of sea cliffs.
—See MAJOR FAMILIES: Myrtaceae.

Centella asiatica
A creeping herb with ascending leaves, common near the sea e.g. damp sea-cliffs.
—See LESSER FAMILIES: Apiaceae.

Crassula sieberana
A tiny herb with succulent crowded leaves, common on sea cliffs.
—See LESSER FAMILIES: Crassulaceae.

Einadia nutans
A small creeping herb, found on sea-coasts in the Illawarra.
—See LESSER FAMILIES: Chenopodiaceae.

Lomandra longifolia
A tufted herb with tough strap-like leaves, common anywhere near the sea.
—See MONOCOTYLEDONS: Xanthorrhoeaceae.

Olearia tomentosa
A shrub about 1m high, on sea-cliffs in the Royal National Park.
—See LESSER FAMILIES: Asteraceae.

SEAGRASSES

Seagrasses are submerged flowering plants which form underwater meadows in sheltered estuaries and bays. These seagrass meadows have a number of important functions in the coastal marine ecosystem. Their matted roots bind the sand or mud together and the friction of the leaf blades helps calm wave action and protect the shoreline. In their shelter a rich ecology of crabs, shrimps, molluscs, algae and microscopic fauna flourishes. The combination of physical protection and rich food supply make seagrass beds important breeding grounds and nurseries for prawns and fish.

Seagrass beds are limited and economically important resources which have suffered much since white settlement. It is estimated that, for instance, only 20% of Botany Bay's seagrass beds remain today.

Extensive seagrass meadows remain in the Hawkesbury River, the bays of Sydney Harbour, the southern parts of Botany Bay, the Georges River and Port Hacking.

Flowering and pollination occur underwater. The pollen is thread-like, drifting until it contacts an exserted stigma.

HYDROCHARITACEAE

• *Halophila* DuPetit-Thouars

A genus of about 10 species, mainly on the tropical coasts of the Indian and Pacific Oceans. There are 4 species in Australia.

Name: *Halophila* = Gk. sea-loving.

Halophila decipiens Ostenfeld

Leafygrass, Sea-wrack
A submerged marine plant with creeping rhizomes, found in sheltered coastal areas at a range of depths to about 20m.

Range: Sydney area, Qld (including Great Barrier Reef), South-east and east Asia **Leaves:** 10-25mm long, 3-6mm wide, often with scattered hairs. **Flowers:** unisexual, (plants dioecious), protected by spathes, to about 5mm long. **Flowering time:** summer. **Name:** *decipens* = Lat. deceptive, perhaps from its similarity to *H. ovalis.*

Halophila ovalis (R. Brown) J. D. Hooker

Leafygrass, Sea-wrack
A submerged marine plant with creeping rhizomes, similar to *H. decipiens* but larger. Found in sheltered coastal waters at various depths to about 10m.

Range: NSW coast, Lord Howe Island, all states: also Africa, Asia and the Pacific. **Leaves:** paired, flaccid, more or less translucent, to 4cm long, often with wavy margins. **Flowers:** as for *H. decipiens.* **Flowering time:** summer. **Name:** *ovalis* = Lat. oval.

POSIDONIACEAE

A marine aquatic family with 1 genus. Related to Zosteraceae.

• *Posidonia* Koenig

A genus of 3 species, 1 in the Mediterranean and 2 in southern Australia. The fruits have a fleshy air-filled outer coat and are often washed up on the shore in summer.

Name: *Posidonia* = after Poseidon, the Greek god of the sea.

Posidonia australis W. J. Hooker

Broad-bladed Strap grass, Marine-fibre Plant, Fibre-ball Weed
A submerged marine plant with grass-like leaves, spreading by rhizomes. Found in sheltered coastal waters on sandy bottoms from 2-10m depth. The grass is highly fibrous and is harvested to make sacks and packing material. Mysterious balls of fibre which sometimes appear on sheltered beaches are created by the action of gently lapping waves on decaying leaves.

Range: Sydney area, south coast, Vic, Tas, SA and WA. **Leaves:** 6-10mm wide, usually about 50cm long, arising from a mass of old fibrous leaf bases. **Flowers:** bisexual or male, in a terminal cluster of slender spikes on a leafless stem, lacking perianths. **Name:** *australis* = Lat. southern.

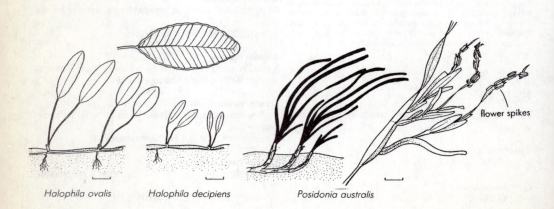

Halophila ovalis   *Halophila decipiens*   *Posidonia australis*   flower spikes

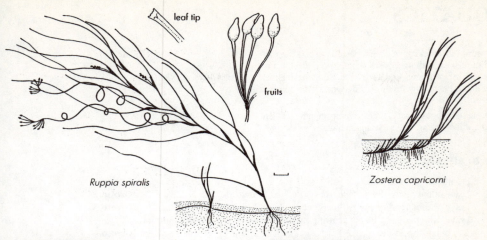

leaf tip

fruits

Ruppia spiralis

Zostera capricorni

RUPPIACEAE

Sea Tassels
A family of submerged herbs of salt, brackish or fresh water. There is a single genus, occuring throughout coastal regions of the world. Related to Potamogetonaceae.

• *Ruppia* Linnaeus

A cosmpolitan genus with about 7 species, including 2 species in Australia.

Name: *Ruppia* = after Heinrich Bernard Ruppius (died 1719), German botanist, author of a flora of Jena.

Ruppia spiralis Dumort

A herb with creeping-floating stems and fine leaves toothed at the tips. Found in brackish coastal lagoons at Dee Why and Manly, usually forming dense masses.

Range: NSW, Tas, SA, WA and widespread in temperate and subtropical parts of the world. **Leaves:** very fine, under 1mm wide, with a broad sheathing base, more or less toothed at the tip. **Flowers:** lacking perianth, with 2 stalkless stamens, and 4 free superior carpels, in a small dense raceme initially enclosed in the basal sheaths of 2 terminal leaves. **Fruits:** the fruiting carpels are beaked; as they mature their stalks elongate. The inflorescence stalk also elongates and often forms a spiral. **Name:** *spiralis* = Lat. spiral. **Note:** this species incorporates *R. megacarpa* and *R. polycarpa*.

ZOSTERACEAE

A family of submerged marine herbs with 18 species in 3 genera.

• *Zostera* Linnaeus

Eel grasses
A genus with about 10 species worldwide. There are 3 species in Australia.

Name: *Zostera* = Gk. a girdle, referring to the ribbony leaves.

Zostera capricorni Martins ex Ascherson

Eel grass
A submerged marine grass-like herb, spreading by creeping rhizomes. Forms dense beds in sheltered coastal waters, especially estuaries, from exposure at low tide to 4-5m depths. In the early days of the colony it was much used for stuffing beds.

Range: NSW coastal waters, Qld, Vic, NZ, NT, NG and Lord Howe Island. **Leaves:** dark green, flaccid, to 5mm wide. **Flowers:** unisexual (plants monoecious), small, protected by short leaf-like spathes. **Flowering time:** summer, although flowers are not common. **Name:** *capricornii* = presumably the tropic of capricorn, where it occurs. The common name refers to its sinuous leaves.

AQUATICS

This section includes native plants adapted to spending part or all of the year with their bases submerged in fresh water or growing in permanently sodden ground. It does not include plants found in marshy heath or sedgeland on the coastal plateaus.

Note: in this book 'marsh' means permanently sodden ground, while 'swamp' refers to standing water.

Key to aquatics

Free floating plants. ....**Group 1**
Leaves floating on the surface, roots attached to mud......................**Group 2**
Leaves submerged or partly emergent...**Group 3**
Leaves all emergent. Plants growing in water or on mud or marshy ground.
    Leaves opposite. ....**Group 4**
    Leaves alternate. ....**Group 5**
    Leaves mostly basal. ....**Group 6**

Note: Sedges and rushes are listed in a separate section.

Group 1 Free floating plants. Roots absent or hanging freely in water.

A. Robust plant to 1m high.
PONTEDERIACEAE: *Eichhornia* 429
*A. Small plants.
  B. Leaves simple <10mm wide.
    C. Leaves hairless.
      D. Plants consisting of one or a few overlapping leaves 0.5-5mm long.
      LEMNACEAE 427
      *D. Leaves 5-10mm long, connected by slender stems.
      CALLITRICHACEAE: *Callitriche* 416
    *C. Leaves hairy:
    SALVINIACEAE: *Salvinia* 434
  *B. Leaves pinnate. Entire plants <30mm long.
AZOLLACEAE: *Azolla* 432

Group 2 Leaves floating on the surface, roots attached to mud.

A. Leaves divided.
  B. Leaves with 4 segments.
  MARSILEACEAE: *Marsilea* 433
  *B. Leaves deeply incised, with numerous slender lobes.
  RANUNCULACEAE: *Ranunculus inundatus* 423
*A. Leaves simple.
  C. Leaves broad, almost circular.
  MENYANTHACEAE: *Nymphoides* 419

*C. Leaves longer than wide.
  D. Flowers with inconspicuous petals.
  POTAMOGETONACEAE 429-30
  *D. Flowers with large white petals.
  HYDROCHARITACEAE: *Vallisneria* 426.

Group 3 Leaves submerged or partly emergent.

A. Leaves >10cm long, ribbon-like, basal.
JUNCAGINACEAE: *Triglochin* 426
*A. Leaves otherwise.
  B. Leaves linear, <1mm wide.
    C. Leaves finely toothed, with stipule-like lobes at the base. NAJADACEAE: *Najas* 428
    *C. Leaves not toothed.
      D. Leaves <10mm long.
        E. Flowers white.
        CRASSULACEAE: *Crassula* 416
        *E. Flowers red or greenish.
        HALORAGACEAE: *Myriophyllum* 417
      *D. Leaves >20mm long.
      POTAMOGETONACEAE:. *Potamogeton pectinatus* 430
  *B. Leaves >1mm wide.
    F. Leaves toothed or lobed.
      G. Submerged leaves with long slender lobes.
      HALORAGACEAE: *Myriophyllum* 417
      *G. Submerged leaves toothed.

H. Leaves 1-3mm wide, whorled.
HYDROCHARITACEAE:
Hydrilla 425
*H. Leaves 5-15mm wide, opposite.
ASTERACEAE: *Enydra* 417
*F. Leaves untoothed, entire.
I. Several main parallel veins present.
POTAMOGETONACEAE 429-30
*I. One main vein present.
ONAGRACEAE: *Ludwigia peploides* 420

Group 4 Leaves all emergent, opposite.

A. Leaves not toothed.
B. Leaves <8mm long.
C. Flowers 2-3mm wide, with 3 sepals and petals. ELATINACEAE: *Elatine* 416
*C. Flowers 2-4mm wide, with 4 sepals and petals.
D. Flowers on stalks >10mm.
LOGANIACEAE: *Mitrasacme* 418
*D. Flowers on stalks <5mm long.
CRASSULACEAE: *Crassula* 416
*B. Leaves >3cm long.
ASTERACEAE: *Eclipta* 414
*A. Leaves toothed.
E. Clusters of scale-like perianth segments in the leaf axils (leaf teeth sometimes absent).
AMARANTHACERAE: *Alternanthera* 124
*E. Otherwise.
F. Flowers conspicuously stalked.
ONAGRACEAE: *Epilobium* 419
*F. Flowers more or less stalkless.
G. Stems very square.
LAMIACEAE: *Lycopus* 417
*G. Stems round or slightly angular.
H. Stems creeping:
ASTERACEAE: *Enydra* 415
*H. Stems erect:
SCROPHULARIACEAE:
Gratiola 423-24

Group 5 Leaves all emergent, alternate.

A. Leaves slender, cylindrical, chambered.
APIACEAE: *Lilaeopsis* 414
*A. Leaves otherwise.
B. Stems prostrate, creeping.
C. Flower in button-like heads, green or reddish. ASTERACEAE: *Centipeda* 414
Epaltes 136 (see also *Cotula* in SEASIDE AND ESTUARINE SPECIES 391).

*C. Flowers not in heads.
D. Flowers white to mauve or bluish, irregular. LOBELIACEAE: *Hypsela* 418
*D. Flowers yellow, regular.
RANUNCULACEAE:
Ranunculus 200-201, 423
*B. Stems erect, often weakly so, but not prostrate.
E. Tall leafy reed-like grass 1-2m or more high.
POACEAE: *Phragmites* 428
*E. Not a grass.
F. Plants 50-200cm tall.
G. Flowers small, pink or white, in slender spikes.
POLYGONACEAE: *Persicaria* 421-22
*G. Flowers yellow, >4cm wide.
ONAGRACEAE:
Ludwigia peruviana* 426
*F. Otherwise. Plants <50cm high.
H1. Flowers yellow.
I. Flowers regular.
J. Flowers with 5 petals.
RANUNCULACEAE:
Ranunculus 200-201, 423
*J. Flowers with 4 petals.
BRASSICACEAE: *Rorripa* 415
*I. Flowers irregular:
GOODENIACEAE:
Goodenia paniculata 175
H2. Flowers white to pale blue.
K. Flowers regular.
L. Flowers with 4 petals.
BRASSICACEAE: *Rorripa* 415
*L. Flowers with 5 petals.
PRIMULACEAE: *Samolus* 422
*K. Flowers irregular:
LOBELIACEAE: *Isotoma* 418
H3. Flowers pink.
ONAGRACEAE: *Epilobium* 419

Group 6 Leaves emergent, mostly basal.

A. Leaves strap-like.
B. Flowers conspicuous, with yellow petals. Leaves hollow. PHILYDRACEAE: *Philydrum* 428
*B. Flowers tiny, in dense heads.
C. Heads globular.
SPARGANIACEAE: *Sparganium* 431
*C. Heads cylindrical.
TYPHACEAE: *Typha* 431-32
*A. Leaves with broad blades.
D. Flowers white. ALISMATACEAE 424-25
*D. Flowers yellow.
MENYANTHACEAE: *Villarsia* 419

• DICOTYLEDONS

AMARANTHACEAE

Alternanthera denticulata
—See LESSER FAMILIES.

APIACEAE

• *Lilaeopsis* Greene
A genus of herbs with about 20 species in Australia, NZ, Central and South America. There are 2 or 3 species endemic in Australia, distributed in all states except WA and NT.

Name: *Lilaeopsis* = Gk. *Lilaea*-like. *Lilaea* is a genus of similar-leaved herbs, known as American quillworts.

Lilaeopsis polyantha (Gandoger) Eichler
Cumb

A small creeping herb, rooting along the stems. Found on the edges of lagoons and streams. Rare in the area.

Range: Sydney area, NSW north coast, ranges and tablelands, south-western slopes, Vic and SA. **Leaves:** reduced to phyllodes 3-10cm, occasionally to 30cm, long, cylindrical, hollow and divided into chambers. **Flowers:** 2-4 per umbel on slender stalks. **Name:** *polyantha* = Gk. many-flowered.

ASTERACEAE

• *Centipeda* Loureiro
A genus of small herbs, with 5 species in NZ, Australia, Asia and South America. There are 3 species endemic to Australia.

Name: *Centipeda* = Lat. hundred-foot, i.e. the centipede, from the creeping growth of the stems.

Centipeda cunninghamii
(De Candolle) A. Brown & Ascherson

Sneezeweed, Old Man's Beard
Cumb

A creeping herb with small toothed leaves. Uncommon in marshy places on the Cumberland Plain (Windsor, Glenfield, Pennant Hills). Not found near the coast or on sandstone. Aborigines in inland areas used the plant medicinally by placing it around their heads, as it was believed to relieve colds. Sneezeweed is surely the first native species to be turned into a range of skin and hair care products, marketed under the name *Koori* and launched in 1990.

Range: a very widespread species, recorded over most of the continent, including Central Australia and WA. **Leaves:** small, with several teeth and a strong unpleasant odour. **Flower heads:** small green buttons, 4-9mm diameter. The flowers are all tubular, green and lack a pappus. **Flowering time:** summer. **Name:** *cunninghamii* = in honour of Allan Cunningham, pioneer botanist of inland NSW, who collected the type specimen.

Centipeda minima (Linnaeus) A. Brown & Ascherson
Spreading Sneezeweed
Ss, Castl

A shy creeping herb with tiny soft leaves. Fairly common in marshy places on the Cumberland Plain. Not found near

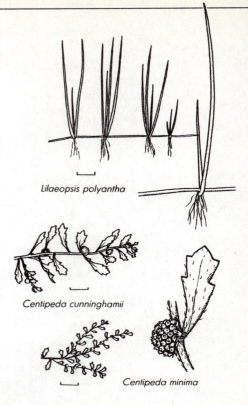

Lilaeopsis polyantha

Centipeda cunninghamii

Centipeda minima

the coast or on sandstone. This and the former species are called sneezeweeds because the leaves make you sneeze. Ferdinand Mueller exhibited a snuff made from powdered leaves and seeds at the Intercolonial Exhibition in Melbourne. In colonial times the plant was brewed as a treatment for inflamed eyes and sold in tins as 'Magic Ophthalmic Cure', a use to which its relatives had long been put in Asia.[1]

Range: NSW coast, ranges and inland areas, all other states except SA, WA, including Central Australia. **Leaves:** small, mostly 3-toothed. **Flower heads:** small green buttons, 3-4mm diameter. The flowers are all tubular, green and lack a pappus. **Flowering time:** summer. **Name:** *minima* = Lat. smallest.

• *Eclipta* Linnaeus
A genus of 3-4 species of herbs found in South America and Australia, where there are 2 native species and 1 introduced.

Name: *Eclipta* = Gk. deficient, since the pappus is often absent.

Eclipta platyglossa F. Mueller
Yellow Twin-heads **Ss, Cumb**

A scrambling herb with weak ascending stems up to 50cm long, often tangled amongst other marsh plants. Found in freshwater marshes near the coast (Narrabeen Lake, Manly, Burning Palms) and Cumberland Plain (Casula, Doonside, Richmond).

Range: all eastern mainland states. **Leaves:** opposite, thin, glossy, covered in tiny stiff (scabrous) appressed hairs. **Flowers heads:** in pairs in the leaf-axils, on long peduncles, disc and ray flowers both YELLOW, pappus absent. **Flowering time:** summer. **Name:** *platyglossa* = Gk. broad-tongue, referring to the broad curved involucral bracts.

• *Enydra* Loureiro
A genus of water plants with 10 species, including 1 in Australia.

Name: *Enydra* = Gk. *enydros,* living in or by the water.

Enydra fluctuans Loureiro
A creeping or floating herb found in coastal freshwater swamps, e.g. Kurnell, Port Hacking, Marly Beach, though these records are old and the species may be locally extinct.

Range: NSW north coast and Sydney area, Africa and Asia. **Leaves:** shiny green above, somewhat succulent, with margins entire or toothed. **Flower-heads:** stalkless, axillary. Disc flowers GREENISH, ray flowers reddish-green, in several rows with very short rays, all enclosed in 4 green bracts. **Flowering time:** summer. **Name:** *fluctuans* = Lat. to flow in waves, referring to its flaccid appearance.

Epaltes australis
Ss, Cumb, Castl
—See MINOR FAMILIES: Asteraceae.

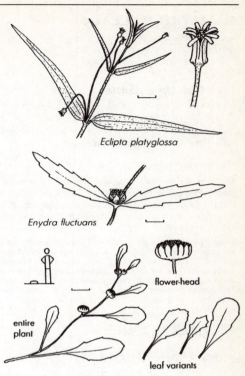

Eclipta platyglossa

Enydra fluctuans

flower-head

entire
plant

leaf variants

Epaltes australis

BRASSICACEAE

• *Rorippa* Scolopi
Marsh-cresses
A genus with about 70 species worldwide, including 4 endemic and 3 introduced to Australia.

Name: *Rorippa* = latinised from a German name.

Rorippa laciniata (F. Mueller) L. A. S. Johnson
Ss, Cumb
An erect herb 10-20cm when flowering, occasionally to 40cm. Found on creek banks and moist disturbed places. Locally recorded from Cheltenham, Hornsby, Cowan, Casula and Sackville areas.

Range: widespread throughout NSW, except in the Blue Mountains, Qld, Vic and SA. **Leaves:** tufted at the base, with deep lobes (pinnatisect), thin-textured, soft, hairless. **Flowers:** WHITE, in an erect expanding raceme. **Name:** *laciniata* = Lat. cut into narrow slender lobes.

Rorippa palustris (Linnaeus) Besser
(previously *R. islandica*) **Cumb**
An erect herb 40-60cm tall, found on the edges of creeks and lakes. Widespread on the Cumberland Plain.

Range: NSW coasts, Blue Mountains, southern tablelands, inland areas, and in all other states. **Leaves:** deeply lobed, thin-textured, soft, hairless. **Flowers:** YELLOW. **Name:** *palustris* = Lat. found in swamps.

Rorippa palustris

Rorippa laciniata

CALLITRICHACEAE

A family of aquatic herbs with a single genus mainly distributed in temperate parts of the world.

The family is related to Lamiaceae.

• *Callitriche* Linnaeus (ca-LIT-rick-ee)

A genus with about 75 species, including 9 species native to Australia.

Name: *Callitriche* = Gk. *kalos*, beauty, *trichos*, hair, referring to the filament of the male flowers.

Callitriche stagnalis Scopoli

A floating aquatic herb in ponds, channels or in mud. It resembles a Duckweed, except the leaves are joined by delicate stems. Common in drainage channels throughout the area. An almost cosmopolitan species, it may have been introduced into Australia.

Range: NSW coast and ranges south from the Sydney area, western plains, also all other states, southern Europe, Asia and North America. **Leaves:** blunt, soft, hairless, thin-textured, lower leaves spoon-shaped. **Flowers:** inconspicuous, unisexual (plants monoecious), usually solitary in the leaf axils, lacking a perianth; the male flowers have a single stamen, the female flower consists of an ovary with 2 hair-like styles. **Name:** *stagnalis* = Lat. not flowing.

CRASSULACEAE

Crassula helmsii (Kirk) Cockayne

Swamp Crassula
A slender floating plant with flaccid stems, found on the margins of streams and channels, often forming mats. Uncommon in the area. A good competitor with undesirable exotics.

Range: Sydney region, NSW ranges, some inland areas, widespread in southern Australia and NZ. **Leaves:** opposite, fleshy, 2-6mm long. **Flowers:** solitary, CREAMY-WHITE, about 2mm wide, with 4 thick petals. **Flowering time:** summer **Name:** *helmsii* = after J.R. Helms, who collected the type specimen near Greymouth, NZ.

ELATINACEAE

A family with 45 species in 2 genera worldwide, including 6 species in 2 genera in Australia.

• *Elatine* Linnaeus

Waterworts
A genus of small aquatic herbs with about 20 species, including 1 species native to Australia.

Name: *Elatine* = according to Mueller, from a supposed resemblance in miniature to the foliage of the Silverfir, called *elate* in Greek.

Elatine gratioloides A. Cunningham

Waterwort **Cumb**
A tiny prostrate herb, creeping in ponds and ditches, submerged or on muddy banks. Fairly common in the area, in ditches on the Cumberland Plain.

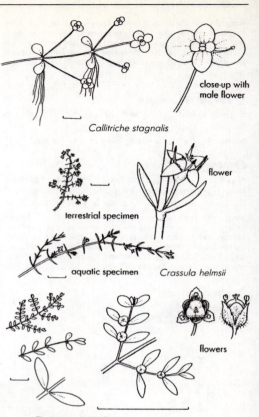

Callitriche stagnalis

terrestrial specimen

flower

aquatic specimen

Crassula helmsii

flowers

Elatine gratioloides

close-up with male flower

Range: widespread in eastern Australia. **Leaves:** opposite, thin-textured, almost membranous, 2-20mm long. **Flowers:** PINKISH, solitary, axillary, under 2mm wide, with 3 toothed sepals, 3 petals, 3 stamens and a 3-chambered ovary. **Fruits:** up to 6mm wide, flattened, with 3 segments. **Name:** *gratioloides* = *Gratiola*-like. *Gratiola* is a semi-aquatic genus in Scrophulariaceae.

GOODENIACEAE

Goodenia paniculata

Ss, Cumb, Castl
—See MINOR FAMILIES: Goodeniaceae.

Goodenia paniculata

HALORAGACEAE

• *Myriophyllum* Linnaeus

Water Milfoil

A worldwide genus of aquatic plants with 36 Australian species. Note the sharp difference between submerged and emergent leaves (which correspond to the floral bracts of other Haloragaceae species). The flowers are tiny and unisexual with 4 hood-like petals, usually male above female on the emergent stem, forming a dense spike.

Name: *Myriophyllum* = Gk. *myrios*, very numerous, *phyllon*, leaves. The common name Milfoil is from Latin *mille*, 1000, *folium*, leaf.

Myriophyllum aquaticum (Vellozo) Verdc.

Brazilian Water Milfoil, Thread-of-Life
Ss, Cumb

A submerged aquatic plant with feathery emergent leaves and stout stems. Common in rivers and ponds. Native to the lowlands of central South America (especially Brazil) but now widely introduced in warm parts of the world.

Range: widespread in southern Australia. **Emergent leaves:** glaucous, in whorls of (4) 5-6, feathery, deeply pinnatisect, mostly 20-35mm long. **Submerged leaves:** similar except with finer segments. **Name:** *aquaticum* = Lat. aquatic.

Myriophyllum gracile Bentham
var. *linear* Orchard

Slender Water Milfoil **Ss**

A small submerged plant with slender stems 10-20cm long. Uncommon or rare in the area, in swamps or boggy marshes in near-coastal heathland.

Range: mainly restricted to the Sydney area. **Emergent leaves:** 6-8mm long, entire or some with a few teeth. **Submerged leaves:** often absent, as the plants seem to be mainly emergent, apparently similar to emergent leaves. **Name:** *gracile* = Lat. slight, *linear* = Lat. straight, referring to the unbranched leaves.

Myriophyllum latifolium F. Mueller
Cumb

A small submerged herb with stout stems up to 1m long. Only recorded locally in Long Neck Lagoon, Pitt Town.

Range: NSW coast and south-eastern Qld. **Emergent leaves:** flat, toothed, in whorls of 2-3. **Submerged leaves:** feathery, with fine segments, in whorls of 2-3. **Name:** *latifolium* = Lat. broad-leaved.

Myriophyllum variifolium J. Hooker

(previously included in *M. propinquum*)
Cumb

A small submerged herb with stout fleshy stems 30-50cm long. Found on the Cumberland Plain. Probably the most common of the local native species.

Range: NSW coast and ranges, south-east Qld, Vic, Tas and SA. **Emergent Leaves:** entire or with a few small teeth, to 2cm long, mostly in whorls of 4-5. **Submerged leaves:** finely branched, in whorls of 4. **Name:** *variifolia* = Lat. variable-leaved.

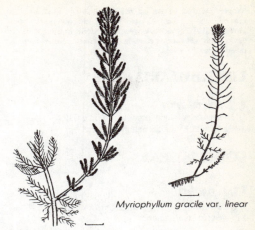

Myriophyllum gracile var. *linear*

Myriophyllum aquaticum

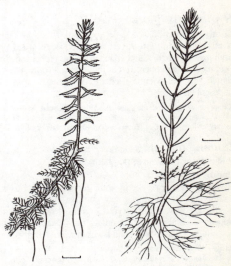

Myriophyllum latifolium   *Myriophyllum variifolium*

LAMIACEAE

• *Lycopus* Linnaeus

Gypsy-wort, Water Horehound
A genus with about 15 species worldwide, including a single Australian species.

Name: *Lycopus* = Gk. wolf-foot.

Lycopus australis R. Brown
Cumb

An erect leafy herb to 1m high, rather weedy in appearance, usually forming dense clumps in swampy ground. Uncommon to rare in the area, but widely scattered.

Range: NSW coast, ranges and inland districts, Qld, Vic, Tas and SA.
Leaves: opposite, 4-ranked, soft, serrated, thin, on square stems.
Flowers: WHITE to very pale green, tiny, sessile, in dense clusters in
the leaf axils. **Flowering time:** January-February. **Name:** *australis* =
Lat. southern.

LENTIBULARIACEAE

• *Utricularia*

All species occasionally occur in standing water.
—See MINOR FAMILIES: Lentibulariaceae.

LOBELIACEAE

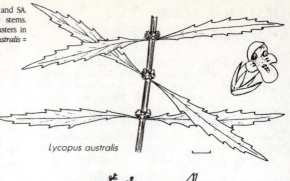

Lycopus australis

• *Hypsela* C. Presl

A genus with 5 species, 3 in eastern Australia, 1 in NZ and
1 in western South America.

Name: Gk. *hypsos*, high, perhaps referring to the habitat of
the type species, in the Andes.

Hypsela sessiliflora E. Wimmer
Cumb Extinct 2X
A small creeping herb. A very rare species, recorded only
from marshes on the Cumberland Plain and probably extinct.
Ferdinand Bauer collected it in the Sydney area in 1803 and
sent it to the Vienna Herbarium where it remained
undescribed until 1957.

Range: only known from the Cumberland Plain. **Leaves:** small (2-4mm
long), blunt, slightly undulate. **Flowers:** WHITE to PALE PURPLE,
solitary, axillary, stalkless. **Name:** *sessiliflora* = Lat. stalkless flowers.

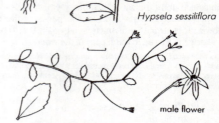

Hypsela sessiliflora

male flower

Isotoma fluviatilis (R. Brown)
F. Mueller ex Bentham **ssp. *fluviatilis***
Cumb
A slender prostrate herb with rooting stems, usually
scrambling but forming a low compact mat in exposed
positions. Found in marshy places on the flood plain of the
Nepean and also once recorded from Narrabeen Lake.
Sometimes found as a weed in lawns in western Sydney.

Range: NSW north coast and Cumberland Plain. **Leaves:** margins
toothed (serrate) or entire, apparently hairless. **Flowers:** SKY-BLUE to
almost WHITE, solitary, axillary, unisexual (dioecious), male and female
similar in shape. **Flowering time:** late September-April. **Name:**
fluviatilis = Lat. pertaining to rivers.

Isotoma fluviatilis ssp. *fluviatilis*

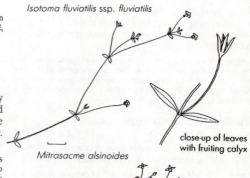

*close-up of leaves
with fruiting calyx*

Mitrasacme alsinoides

LOGANIACEAE

Mitrasacme alsinoides R. Brown
Cumb
A weak annual herb in marshland, usually lost amongst sedges
and swamp flora. Rare in the area, collected from near
Richmond and Elderslie. (It may be the same as *M. paludosa*.)

Range: NSW coast from Buladelah to Camden, also northern tablelands
and Qld. **Leaves:** opposite, 3-8mm long, flat, thin-textured, hairless.
The stems have microscopic hairs. **Flowers:** WHITE. **Name:** *alsinoides*
= like *Alsine*, a genus of small herbs in Caryophyllaceae.

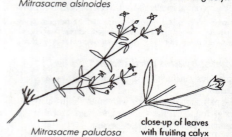

Mitrasacme paludosa

*close-up of leaves
with fruiting calyx*

Mitrasacme paludosa R. Brown
Ss
A weak herb with stems 10-20cm long, found in marshy
ground on the edges of coastal swamps, both brackish and
fresh. Rare in the area. Recorded from the Royal National
Park (Marley lagoon, The Basin near Maianbar) and Narrabeen.

Range: coasts north from Sydney, into Qld, also scattered on northern ranges and inland parts of the state. **Leaves:** opposite, 3-8mm long, flat, thin-textured, hairless. The stems have microscopic hairs. **Flowers:** WHITE. **Name:** *paludosa* = Lat. pertaining to swamps.

MENYANTHACEAE
Marshworts
A family of aquatic and marsh herbs with about 48 species in 5 genera, including 27 species in 3 genera in Australia. It is related to Gentianaceae.

° *Nymphoides* Hill
A genus of aquatic herbs with about 20 species, including 14 species in Australia (11 endemic).

Name: *Nymphoides* = *Nymphaea*-like, from the resemblance to water-lilies.

Nymphoides geminata (R. Brown) Kuntze
Yellow Marshwort **Cumb**
An aquatic plant with floating leaves and yellow fringed flowers. Uncommon in the area: in ponds on the Cumberland Plain.

Range: NSW coast north from the Nepean River and Qld. **Leaves:** more or less circular, 2-8cm wide, on long stalks, often purple below. **Flowers:** YELLOW, to 25mm wide; arising in pairs on a long floating raceme. The petals are densely fringed. There are 4 conspicuously flanged, fringed styles attached to a stout column. **Flowering time:** Spring-Autumn. **Name:** *geminata* = Lat. in pairs.

• *Villarsia* Ventenat
A genus of marsh herbs with about 13 species worldwide, 12 of which are found in Australia (8 restricted to south-western WA).

Name: *Villarsia* = after Dominique Villars (1745-1814), a doctor and professor at Grenoble, southern France, who studied the plants of that area.

Villarsia exaltata (Solander ex Sims) G. Don
Yellow Marsh Flower, Native Buck-Bean
An erect herb with a clump of broad fleshy leaves and a branching inflorescence to 1m high. Found in freshwater marshes, usually in dense colonies. Uncommon in the area, mainly in coastal districts. The leaves are an item of food for herbivores like Swamp Wallabies.

Range: NSW coasts, Blue Mountains, southern tablelands, Qld, Vic and Tas. **Leaves:** erect, soft, fleshy, hairless, light green, to 15cm long, on thick stalks to 40cm long. **Flowers:** YELLOW, with petals winged and densely hairy at the base; arranged in a tall panicle. **Flowering time:** December. **Name:** *exaltata* = Lat. uplifted, referring to the erect habit. Native Buck-Bean is an old name from Tas.

MYRTACEAE
All the paperbark (*Melaleuca*) species, and *Callistemon saligna*, occur in marshy situations.
—See MAJOR FAMILIES: Myrtaceae.

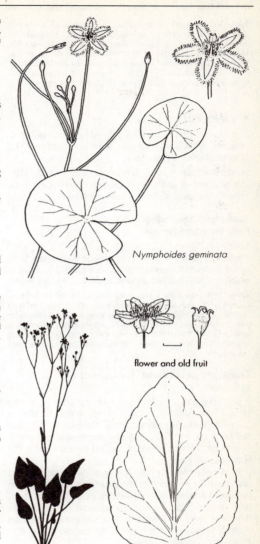

Nymphoides geminata

flower and old fruit

Villarsia exaltata

ONAGRACEAE

Epilobium billardieranum
Séringe in De Candolle **ssp. *billardieranum***
Ss
An erect herb usually 20-40cm tall, found in creeks and edges of freshwater swamps near the coast. Locally restricted to La Perouse, Kurnell and the Royal National Park.

Range: coasts in south-eastern Australia. The Sydney area is its northern limit. **Leaves:** opposite, 2-4cm long, broad (elliptic), finely toothed, thin-textured, soft, shiny, hairless. The stems are typically bright red. **Flowers:** PINK (rarely mauve or white), solitary in the upper axils. **Flowering time:** summer. **Name:** *billardieranum* = after Jacques Julien Houton de La Billardière (1755-1838), botanist on D'Entrecastaux's 1791-93 expedition in search of La Pérouse. He collected the type specimen in Tas.

• *Ludwigia* Linnaeus

A genus of herbs and shrubs with 82 species worldwide, including 45 in South America. There are 4 native and 3 introduced species in Australia.

Name: *Ludwigia* = after Christian Gottlieb Ludwig (1709-73), professor of medicine at Leipzig. He collected plants in North Africa and wrote on botanical subjects.

Ludwigia peploides (Kunth) Raven
ssp. *montevidensis*

Cumb

A yellow-flowering herb with creeping or floating vegetative stems, and erect flowering stems to 50cm tall. Fairly common in the area, in ponds and streams on the Cumberland Plain.

Range: NSW coast, some inland areas, Qld, Vic, SA and the Americas. **Leaves:** 3-6cm long, glossy both sides, hairy, soft, thin-textured, with 2 stipule-like vesicles at the base. Floating leaves are rounder and softer than emergent leaves. **Flowers:** YELLOW, solitary, axillary. **Flowering time:** summer. **Name:** *peploides* = resembling a *Peplis* (now *Lythrum*), *montevidensis* = from Montevideo, the capital of Uruguay, where it was first collected.

Ludwigia peruviana• (Linnaeus) Hara

Ss

A spreading shrub to 2m high, submerged or on marshy ground near streams or ponds, rather similar in habit to *Lantana*. It was first recorded from Eastlakes in 1970 and has since spread widely in freshwater streams and ponds in the inner suburbs, especially around Eastlakes and in the Woronora River system.

It is vigorously opportunistic and clogs marshes and waterways like an aquatic equivalent of *Lantana*. It produces prodigous numbers of seeds—each capsule has as many as 3200 seeds. It also reproduces vegetatively from broken branches. Originally a native of South America, it was only recently introduced into Australia and has the potential to cause great ecological damage.

Range: restricted to the Sydney area, also South America, Florida, South-east Asia and Sri Lanka. **Leaves:** alternate, lanceolate, soft, wavy, finely hairy both surfaces. **Flowers:** large, YELLOW, solitary, axillary. **Flowering time:** late summer. **Fruit:** herbaceous capsules containing many small seeds. **Name:** *peruviana* = from Peru, where it is locally known as *lengua del perro* (tongue of the dog), an appropriate name for the hairy leaves.

POLYGONACEAE

A family mainly of herbs, with about 750 species in 30 genera worldwide, mainly in temperate parts of the northern hemisphere. There are 47 species in 6 genera in Australia.

The family includes buckwheat (*Fagopyrum esculentum*), and rhubarb (*Rheum rhaponticum*), as well as many

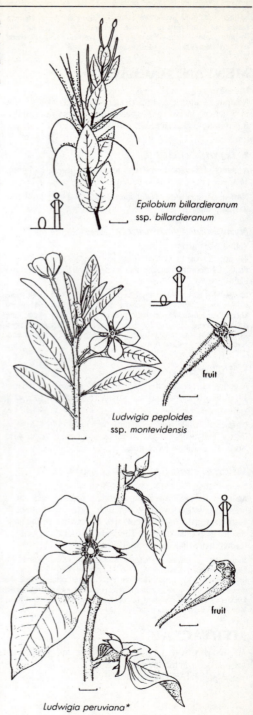

Epilobium billardieranum ssp. *billardieranum*

Ludwigia peploides ssp. *montevidensis*

fruit

Ludwigia peruviana*

fruit

aggressive weed species, such as Sorrel and Dock (*Rumex* species).

It is closely related to Plumbaginaceae.

• *Persicaria* (Tournefort) Miller

Water Peppers, Knotweeds
A genus of semi-aquatic herbs with about 150 species worldwide, including 14 native and 2 naturalised in Australia.

The leaves of most species contain an irritant oil with a strong peppery flavour, as the early Sydney botanist William Woolls observed. 'In order to satisfy myself as to its pungency, I bit one of the leaves and found it so exceedingly peppery that my mouth felt uneasy for an hour afterwards . . . '[2]. Aborigines utilised this quality by throwing the leaves into waterholes as a fish poison. In South Australia the nuts of *P. plebeium* were ground into a paste, cooked and eaten.

A useful identification feature for this genus is the membranous sheath which envelops the stem at the base of each leaf.

Persicaria is selectively parasitised by Dodder (*Cuscata campestris**, see CLIMBERS: Cuscutaceae), a leafless parasitic twiner resembling *Cassytha*.

Name: *Persicaria* = from the similarity of the leaves to those of the Peach tree, *Amygdalus* (now *Prunus) persica*, once known as Persian apple.

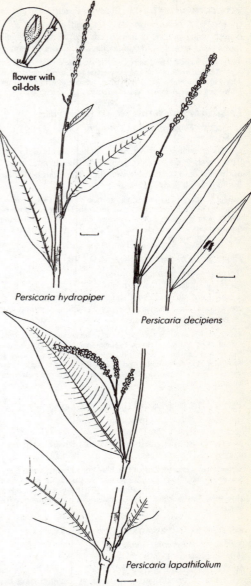

flower with
oil-dots

Persicaria hydropiper

Persicaria decipiens

Persicaria lapathifolium

Persicaria decipiens (R. Brown) K.L. Wilson

(previously *Polygonum decipiens*)
Spotted Knotweed **Ss, Cumb**
An erect or ascending herb usually 0.5-1m tall, found in fresh marshes and beside creeks. Fairly common in the area.

Range: NSW coast and ranges, all other states, Norfolk Island and NZ. **Leaves:** mostly under 10cm long, more narrow than other species, dark green above with veins obscure, usually with a brown marking in the middle of the blade. **Flowers:** PINK, in a dense spike. **Flowering time:** summer. **Name:** *decipiens* = Lat. deceptive, because it is easily confused with the exotic annual European species, *P. minor*, which, fortunately, does not occur near Sydney.

Persicaria hydropiper (Linnaeus) Spach

(previously *Polygonum hydropiper*)
Water Pepper **Ss, Cumb**
An erect or ascending herb to 1m tall. Found in marshes and beside streams. Widely scattered but rare in the area, more common in the Illawarra. It resembles a small-leaved *P. lapathifolium* except the flowers are greenish and covered in tiny oil dots which are just visible to a keen eye.

In Europe it is collected as a medicinal herb. It checks bleeding and relieves menstrual pains. The astringent effect is produced by tannins. In ancient times the ripe seed vessels were used as a substitute for black pepper.

Range: NSW coast, ranges and inland areas, Qld and Vic, also widespread in Europe and Asia, north Africa and the Americas. **Leaves:** to 10cm long. **Flowers:** GREENISH WHITE (or slightly green pinkish), in dense spikes. **Flowering time:** late summer. **Name:** *hydropiper* = Lat. water-pepper.

Persicaria lapathifolium (Linnaeus) S.F. Gray

(previously *Polygonum lapathifolium*)
Knotweed **Ss, Cumb**
An erect or slightly drooping herb, 1-2m tall, found in permanently wet ground beside streams and creeks. The most common of the local species.

Range: all parts of Australia, also widespread in Europe, Asia and the Americas. **Leaves:** 10-20cm long, thin-textured, soft, often drooping. **Flowers:** PINK, in dense, gracefully curving, spikes. **Flowering time:** summer. **Name:** *lapathifolium* = Sorrel-leaved.

Persicaria orientalis * (Linnaeus) Spach

(previously *Polygonum orientale*)   **Cumb**
A stout annual aquatic or marsh herb with stems to 2m tall, found along creeks on the Cumberland Plain. Uncommon.

Ranges: NSW coast, inland areas, Qld, NT, and widespread in India and Asia.   **Leaves:** to 20cm long, soft, covered on both sides with fine furry felt.   **Flowers:** PINK, in large, dense branching terminal spikes. **Flowering time:** summer.   **Name:** *orientalis* = Lat. eastern.

Persicaria praetermissa (J.D. Hooker) Hara

(previously *Polygonum praetermissum*)
Cumb
A weak sprawling herb found in ditches, ponds and creek banks, with stems to about 50cm long. Locally rare, mainly in the Richmond area (also Sackville). The elongated spike distinguishes it from *P. strigosa.*

Range: NSW coast and ranges, Vic, Tas and India.   **Leaves:** narrow-triangular, with stiff recurved hairs on the stalks and stem.   **Flowers:** WHITE, widely separated on a branching inflorescence.   **Flowering time:** summer.   **Name:** *praetermissa* = Lat. overlooked, since it was long included in *P. strigosa.*

Persicaria prostrata (R. Brown) Sojak

(previously *Polygonum prostratum*)
Creeping Knotweed   **Ss, Cumb**
A small prostrate herb with stems to 30cm long, found on creek banks and in marshy ground. Widely scattered but uncommon or rare in the area.

Range: Sydney area, south coast, NSW ranges and scattered inland areas, also all states, and NZ.   **Leaves:** 15-60mm long, covered in fine hairs. The stem sheath has a distinctive ragged curled margin.   **Flowers:** WHITE, in short dense axillary spikes, each flower with a conspicuous sheathing bract.   **Flowering time:** summer.   **Name:** *prostrata* = Lat. lying flat.

Persicaria strigosum (R. Brown) Gross

(previously *Polygonum strigosum*)
Spotted Knotweed   **Ss, Cumb**
An erect or ascending herb to about 1m high, found in fresh marshes and beside creeks. Common in the area.

Range: coastal areas south from Qld, Blue Mountains, India and China. **Leaves:** to about 10cm long, with distinctive shapes. The stems have scattered stiff reflexed hairs.   **Flowers:** WHITE, in terminal spikes. **Flowering time:** summer.   **Name:** *strigosum* = having *strigae*, hair-like bristles.

Persicaria subsessilis (R. Brown) K.L. Wilson

(previously *Polygonum subsessile*)
Hairy Knotweed   **Cumb**
An erect or ascending herb to 2m tall, found along ponds and on creek banks. Rare in the area, in scattered spots on the Cumberland Plain.

Range: coastal districts of all states except NT; also New Caledonia. **Leaves:** similar to *P. lapathifolium*, except with very short stalks and covered with stiff hairs, short above and long below. The hairs are also present on the stems.   **Flowers:** WHITE, in terminal spikes.   **Flowering time:** spring-summer.   **Name:** *subsessilis* = Lat. almost stalkless.

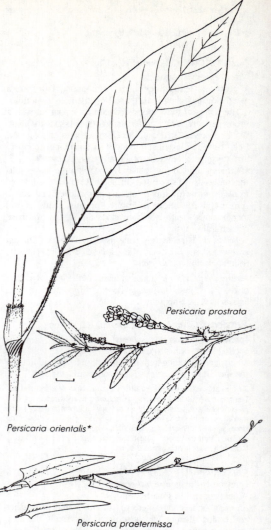

Persicaria prostrata

Persicaria orientalis *

Persicaria praetermissa

PRIMULACEAE

• *Samolus*

Samolus valerandii Linnaeus

Common Brookweed   **Cumb, Aqu**
An erect herb 15-40cm tall, found in marshes and wet creek banks on the Cumberland Plain. Uncommon. William Woolls wrote 'In England the *Samolus valerandi* is commonly called brook weed, or water pimpernel, and its leaves are said to heal wounds and chaps in the skin. It is sometimes also made into a purging syrup. Pliny says that the plant was considered among the Gauls as a specific in all maladies of swine, and was connected with mystic ceremonies.'[3]

Persicaria subsessilis

Persicaria strigosum

RANUNCULACEAE

• *Ranunculus*

All local *Ranunculus* species may occasionally occur in inundated conditions.
—See LESSER FAMILIES.

Ranunculus inundatus R. Brown

River Buttercup **Cumb**
A small weak herb, floating or on marshy ground, common in periodically inundated areas on the Cumberland Plain.

Range: NSW coast, ranges and inland areas, Qld, Vic and Tas. **Leaves:** deeply divided into several narrow segments, which are again divided into narrow lobes. **Flowers:** YELLOW, 12-20mm wide, 2-3 in an erect raceme. **Fruit:** smooth. **Flowering time:** summer. **Name:** *inundatus* = Lat. submerged.

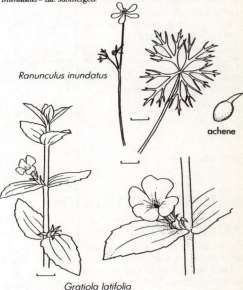

Ranunculus inundatus

achene

Gratiola latifolia

SCROPHULARIACEAE

• *Gratiola* Linnaeus (gray-ti-O-la)

Brooklimes
A genus of small aquatic herbs with about 20 species, including 5 species in Australia, distributed in all states except NT.

Name: *Gratiola* = from *gratia Dei*, Grace of God, a name given in the middle ages for *G. officinalis*, a European medicinal herb. *Brooklime* is an Anglo-Saxon name (lime is from *lemoc*, meaning a small plant).

Gratiola latifolia R. Brown

Austral Brooklime **Ss, Cumb**
A small herb with ascending stems to 30cm high. Scattered in the area on the margins of permanent swamps and rivers, but more common in the Blue Mountains.

Samolus valerandii

Range: NSW coast and ranges, Qld, Vic and Europe. **Leaves:** in a basal rosette and along the stem, thin-textured, hairless, with obscure venation, to 60mm long in the rosette, 15-40mm long on the stem. **Flowers:** petals small, WHITE; on slender stalks, in an erect terminal raceme. Tiny slender staminodes are present. **Name:** *valerandii* = after Valerand Dourez, a sixteenth century herbal botanist in Provence.

Range: NSW coast and ranges, Qld, Vic, Tas and SA. **Leaves:** over 10mm wide, thin, soft, toothed, ovate, hairless. **Flowers:** WHITE, or PALE PINK, on very short stalks (less than 5mm long). **Flowering time:** December-March. **Name:** *latifolia* = Lat. broad-leaved.

Gratiola pedunculata R. Brown
Stalked Brooklime   **Ss, Castl, Cumb**
A small herb with ascending stems to 30cm high, found on the margins of permanent swamps and rivers. Scattered in the area, mainly on clay soils.

Range: NSW coast, ranges and some inland areas, Qld, Vic and WA. **Leaves:** to 10mm wide, thin, soft, toothed, hairless. **Flowers:** WHITE, or PALE PINK, on peduncles at least 10mm long. **Flowering time:** December-February. **Name:** *pedunculata* = Lat. having a peduncle (floral stalk).

Gratiola pubescens R. Brown
(previously *G. peruviana* var. *pumila*)   **Ss**
A small herb with ascending stems to 20cm high, found in swamps in coastal heaths.

Range: parts of the NSW coast and some inland areas, Vic, Tas and WA. **Leaves:** to 6mm wide, thin, soft, toothed, lanceolate. **Flowers:** WHITE, or PALE PINK, on very short stalks (less than 5mm long). **Flowering time:** November-February. **Name:** *pubescens* = Lat. having short soft hairs (a variable feature in this species).

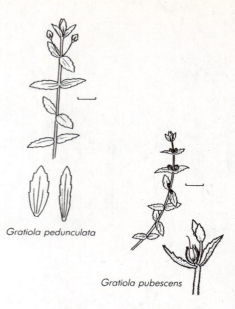

Gratiola pedunculata

Gratiola pubescens

• MONOCOTYLEDONS

ALISMATACEAE

A cosmopolitan family of aquatic herbs with about 100 species in 11 genera. In Australia there are 9 species in 4 genera.

The flowers resemble those of Ranunculaceae, a primitive dicot family. Some botanists regard this family as a missing link, near to the ancester to both monocotyledons and dicotyledons.

• *Alisma* Linnaeus
A genus with about 10 species, including 2 in Australia.
Name: *Alisma* = Gk. *halisma*, the Greek classical name for the plant, meaning salt-loving.

Alisma plantago-aquatica Linnaeus
Water Plantain   **Cumb**
An erect emergent herb to 1m tall, found in ditches, creeks and ponds. Fairly common on the Cumberland Plain. The tubers are edible.

Range: NSW coast and ranges, south-eastern Australia, also widespread in temperate parts of the northern hemisphere. **Leaves:** erect, with blades 10-25cm long, usually with 7 parallel veins. **Flowers:** WHITE or pinkish, about 6mm wide, numerous in a broad branched inflorescence. **Flowering time:** summer. **Name:** *plantago-aquatica* = Lat. Water Plantain, the European name for this plant.

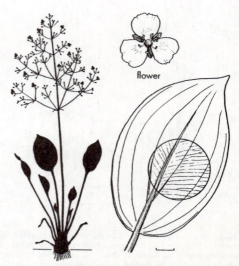

flower

Alisma plantago-aquatica

• *Damasonium* Jussieu

A genus with about 5 species worldwide, widespread in the northern hemisphere

Name: *Damasonium* = Gk. *damazo*, to subdue, because one species was said to overcome poison.

Damasonium minus (R. Brown) Buchenau

Starfruit   **Cumb**

An erect herb to 1m high, with floating or emergent leaves. Moderately common in ditches, creeks and ponds on the Cumberland Plain.

Range: NSW coast and some inland areas; also all states.   **Leaves:** with 3-5 parallel veins, very variable, ranging from erect emergent leaves with blades about 5cm long to flaccid floating leaves with blades about 2cm long.   **Flowers:** about 6mm wide, petals WHITE or PALE PINK, with 6 stamens and about 9 pointed carpels; on tall branched inflorescences. **Flowering time:** November-December. **Name:** *minus* = lesser.

• *Sagittaria* Linnaeus

A cosmopolitan genus with 4 species in Australia.

Name: *Sagittaria* = Lat. shaped like an arrow-head, referring to the leaves.

Sagittaria graminea Michaux
ssp. *platyphylla** Engelm

Arrowhead   **Ss**

An erect emergent aquatic herb 40-60cm high, found along creeks in the Georges River and nearby areas. Introduced from North America.

Range: Sydney area and southern tablelands, Qld and Vic and North America.   **Leaves:** emergent leaves usually have 7 major parallel veins. There are also submerged leaves, to 50cm long, lacking blades.   **Flowers:** fragile, WHITE, unisexual, in an open inflorescence shorter than the leaves, the male flowers above the female flowers. **Flowering time:** late summer.   **Name:** *graminea* = Lat. grassy.

CYPERACEAE

Sedges
All sedges are associated with wet or inundated ground. For convenience they have been grouped in a separate section. —SEDGES AND RUSHES.

HYDROCHARITACEAE

A family of marine and freshwater aquatics with about 160 species in 15 genera. There are 22 species in 12 genera in Australia. The family is primitive, related to Alismataceae.

• *Hydrilla* Richard

A genus with a single species.

Name: *Hydrilla* = Gk. diminutive of *hydra*, water serpent.

Hydrilla verticillata (Carl von Linné) Royle
Cumb

A submerged herb with small whorled leaves on long flaccid stems, forming dense masses in rivers and dams. Found along the Nepean and occasionally in dams. It thrives on nutrient enriched waters.

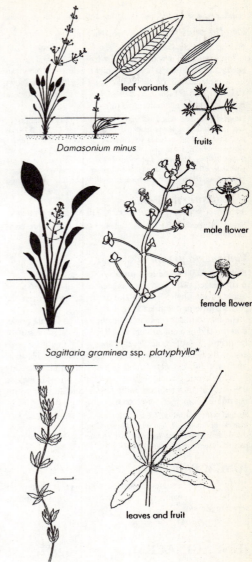

leaf variants

fruits

Damasonium minus

male flower

female flower

Sagittaria graminea ssp. *platyphylla**

leaves and fruit

plant with female flowers   *Hydrilla verticillata*

Range: Sydney area, north coast, some inland districts, all states except NT, also widespread in tropical Asia, Africa and Europe.   **Leaves:** whorled, to 20mm long, finely toothed.   **Flowers:** unisexual (plants monoecious). The tiny male flowers break off and float to the surface before opening. The female flowers float to the surface on a long thread. **Flowering time:** summer.   **Name:** *verticillata* = Lat. whorled.

• *Ottelia* Persoon

A genus with about 40 species, including 2 species in Australia, distributed in all states.

Name: *Ottelia* = from *ottel-ambel*, the name in Malabar, south-west India.

Ottelia ovalifolia (R. Brown) Richard

Swamp Lily **Ss, Castl, Cumb**

A submerged plant with beautiful white flowers and floating leaves, found in dams and slow-moving streams. Now rare in the area, mainly on the Cumberland Plain. Robert Brown collected it in the Sydney area in July 1802 and Ferdinand Bauer painted a magnificent picture of it.

Range: NSW coast, Blue Mountains, inland areas; also all states except Tas. **Leaves:** floating leaves mostly to 10cm long, with 5-7 parallel veins; juvenile leaves submerged, 4-8mm wide, strap-like, lacking blades. **Flowers:** WHITE, 3-4cm wide, solitary, stalkless in an ovoid spathe. Some flowers remain submerged and enclosed within the spathe and are self-pollinating. There are 6-12 anthers and an inferior ovary with 6 styles. **Flowering time:** summer. **Name:** *ovalifolia* = Lat. oval-leaved.

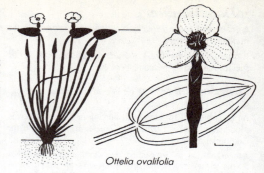

Ottelia ovalifolia

• *Vallisneria* Linnaeus

An aquatic genus with 6-10 species, 3 in Australia, all states.

Name: *Vallisneria* = after Antonio Vallisnieri (1661-1730), Italian doctor and naturalist.

Vallisneria gigantea Graebner

Ribbonweed, Eelweed **Ss, Cumb**

A submerged plant with strap-like leaves, found in rivers and drainage channels. Rare in the area. Recorded from the Nepean River and Port Hacking.

The method of pollination is ingenious. The female flower is at the end of a coiled stem which lets it float at the surface no matter how the water level changes. The tiny male flowers are located in an underwater pod. On maturity this splits open, the flowers detach and rise to the surface like tiny bubbles. Once on the surface they burst open to expose their pollen. After fertilisation the stem recoils and the maturing fruit is submerged for protection.

Range: coast and inland areas of all states and widespread in Asia. **Leaves:** ribbon-like, 1-2cm wide. **Flowers:** unisexual; the female on coiled stems. **Flowering time:** summer. **Name:** *gigantea* = giant (compared to other members of the genus).

JUNCACEAE Rushes

All Juncus species are associated with wet or inundated ground. For convenience they have been grouped into a separate section.

— See SEDGES AND RUSHES.

JUNCAGINACEAE

Triglochin microtuberosum H.I. Aston

Water Ribbons **Ss, Cumb** (previously part of *T. procerum*)

A tufted acquatic herb with erect emergent strap-like leaves. Common in still or gently flowing fresh water in swamps, dams and swampy creeks.

The white tuberous roots were baked and eaten by Aborigines. The small green fruits are also edible.

Range: coastal districts from Myall Lakes in NSW to Sale in eastern Vic. **Leaves:** 30-137cm long, very thickened and spongy towards the base. **Fruits:** of 6 carpels, each with a flat outer surface. **Flowering time:** mainly summer. **Name:** *microtuberosum* = Lat. tiny-tubers, from the small tubers distributed around the rhizome (distinctive of the species).

male flower

female flower

Vallisneria gigantea

flower

Triglochin microtuberosum

Triglochin rheophilum H.I. Aston (not illustrated)

Water Ribbons **Ss, Cumb** (previously part of *T. procerum*)

Similar to the preceding, but all leaves are submerged and flaccid, undulating in a current. Common in gently to swiftly flowing clear streams. The roots and fruits are edible.

Range: costal districts of NSW and eastern Vic. **Leaves:** 41-252cm long, submerged, thin-textured, not thickened or spongy towards the base. **Fruits:** of 6 carpels, each with a strongly ridged outer surface. **Flowering time:** spring-summer. **Name:** *rheophilum* = Lat. current-loving.

LEMNACEAE

Duck Weeds

A family of minute aquatic herbs, floating in still or slowly moving fresh water. There are about 43 species worldwide in 6 genera. In Australia there are 7 species in 3 genera.

The body of each plant is a modified leaf called a cladode. Reproduction is usually vegetative; new cladodes form as branches on existing cladodes, break off and form new plants. Monoecious flowers appear in summer but are rarely seen. Duckweeds are important food for waterfowl and fish.

Key to Lemnaceae

A. Roots present.
  B. One root per plant. = *Lemna minor*
  *B. Roots 2-11 per plant.
    C. Cladode to 3mm long,
      roots usually 2-3.
      = *Spirodella pusilla*
    *C. Cladode up to 5mm long,
      roots 2-11.
      = *Spirodella oligorrhiza*
*A. Roots absent. = *Wolffia*

• *Lemna* Linnaeus

A genus with about 15 species worldwide and 2 in Australia.

Name: *Lemna* = the Greek name for a water weed.

Lemna minor Linnaeus

Rare in the area, in still water.

Range: Sydney area, inland NSW, Vic and Tas. **Cladode:** 1-4mm long, thick. **Roots:** one or none per cladode. **Flowering time:** summer. **Name:** *minor* = lesser.

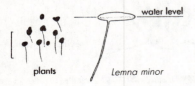

Lemna minor

• *Spirodela* Schleiden (spy-ro-DEEL-a)

A genus with 6 species, including 2 in Australia. Some authors place it in *Lemna.*

Name: *Spirodela* = Gk. spiral, since microscopic spiral vessels are visible in the plant.

Spirodela oligorrhiza (Kurz) Hegelmaier

Cladodes up to 5mm long.

• var. *oligorrhiza*

Roots always 2-5.

Range: NSW coast, Blue Mountains. **Name:** *oligorrhiza* = Gk. few roots.

• var. *pleiorrhiza*

Roots 6-9.

Range: Sydney area, north coast, Blue Mountains. **Name:** *pleiorrhiza* = Gk. more roots.

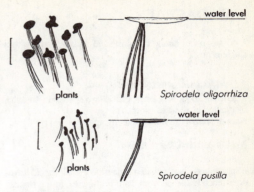

Spirodela oligorrhiza

Spirodela pusilla

Spirodela pusilla (Hegelmaier) Hegelmaier

Duck Weed

In still and slowly running water, in ponds, dams and creeks.

Range: NSW coast, Blue Mountains, northern tablelands, some inland areas, also Vic. **Cladodes:** up to 3mm long. Roots 1-5, often 2-3. **Flowering time:** summer. **Name:** *pusilla* = Lat. weak.

• *Wolffia* (Linnaeus) Wimmer

A genus of tiny floating aquatics with 10 species, including 2 in Australia, distributed in all states.

Name: *Wolffia* = after N. M. von Wolff, an eighteenth century German physician and botanist.

Wolffia australiana

(Bentham) Hartog & Plas

Tiny Duckweed

The world's smallest flowering plant. A tiny, almost microscopic, floating aquatic with a bright green oval body about 1mm long and no roots. Found in dense floating masses on the surface of rivers and dams (in the same habitat as *Lemna* and *Azolla* species), on the Cumberland Plain.

Range: Sydney area, south coast, Blue Mountains, southern tablelands, Vic, SA and NZ. **Cladode:** upper surface convex and rounded at the edge, uniformly green. **Flowers:** with a single anther and ovary arising from an eye-shaped opening on top of the body. **Name:** *australiana* = Australian.

Wolffia globosa (Roxburgh) Hartog & Plas

Similar to *W. australiana* except the upper surface is flat and sharp at the edge, and paler in the centre.

Range: Sydney area, Qld, Vic, SA, WA and Africa. **Name:** *globosa* = Lat. globose.

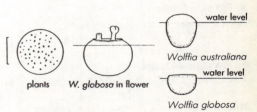

Wolffia australiana

Wolffia globosa

NAJADACEAE

Water Nymphs
A cosmopolitan family of submerged aquatic herbs with a single genus.

- ## *Najas* Linnaeus (NY-ass)

A genus of about 50 species, including 5 species in Australia, distributed in all states except Tas.
Name: *Najas* = Lat. *naias*, water nymph.

Najas tenuifolia R. Brown

Thin-leaved Naiad
A submerged plant with dense masses of small flaccid leaves on a much branched stem. Rare in the area, in the Nepean and Hawkesbury Rivers. Both flowering and fertilisation occur underwater.

Range: Sydney area, north coast, Blue Mountains, inland areas, Qld, Vic, SA, WA, NT and Malaysia. **Leaves:** thin, linear, with almost microscopic teeth, dilated and lobed at the base. **Flowers:** inconspicuous, unisexual (dioecious), solitary, axillary. **Name:** *tenuifolia* = Lat. thin-leaved.

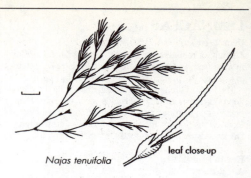

Najas tenuifolia   leaf close-up

PHILYDRACEAE

A family with 6 species in 3 genera. Five species occur in Australia. The flowers are highly evolved and quite different to the usual monocot structure.

- ## *Philydrum* Banks & Solander ex Gaertner

(fill-I-drum)
A genus with one species.
Name: *Phylidrum* = Gk. water-loving.

Philydrum lanuginosum

Banks & Solander ex Gaertner

Woolly Frogmouth   **Ss, Cumb**
A tufted succulent herb to 1.5m high, with numerous yellow flowers on a tall scape. Fairly common in swamps and edges of ponds.

Range: south-eastern Australia, South-east and east Asia and southern Japan. **Leaves:** sheathing, soft, filled with large hollow chambers, tapering from a wide base. **Flowers:** YELLOW, with 2 large petals and 2 much smaller petals enclosing the sexual parts: a single stamen and carpel. Each flower is protected by a green cotton-woolly bract. **Flowering time:** summer. **Name:** *lanuginosum* = Lat. woolly.

POACEAE

- ## *Hemarthria*

Forms bright green swathes on marshy ground.
—See GRASSES.

- ## *Phragmites* Adanson

A genus with 3 species worldwide, 2 of which occur in Australia.

Name: *Phragmites* = Gk. *phragma*, a fence or palisade.

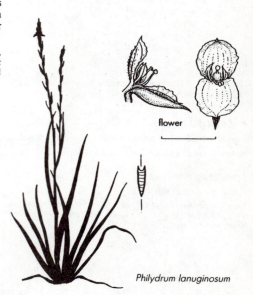

flower

Philydrum lanuginosum

Phragmites australis (Cavanilles) Trinius ex Steudel

(previously *Phragmites communis*)
Native Reed, Thatch-reed
An aquatic grass, cane-like, tall and beautiful, with broad leaves set at right angles to stems about 2m high. Very common in the area. It forms dense stands in marshy ground in fresh or slightly brackish water, spreading by means of creeping rhizomes. The tall willowy floral plumes are a lovely sight in summer, blowing like banners in the wind. The new shoots are succulent and edible, with a pleasant nutty flavour, and were eaten by Aborigines.

Range: most parts of Australia, common in both hemispheres. **Leaves:** 1-3cm wide. **Panicle:** dense, spreading; the spikelets are papery, with several florets. **Name:** *australis* = Lat. southern

PONTEDERIACEAE

A family with 36 species in 9 genera, mainly in the Americas. There are 2 introduced genera (1 species each) and 1 native genus (with 2 species) in Australia.

- ## *Eichhornia* Kunth

A small tropical genus of free-floating herbs, with 1 species introduced into Australia.

Name: after J. A. F. Eichhorn, the Prussian official who collected the type species.

*Eichhornia crassipes** (Martius) Solms

Water Hyacinth **Ss, Cumb**

A free-floating perennial to 1m high. It forms dense masses in slow-moving creeks and ponds and can quickly stretch from bank to bank in an impenetrable mass. Rapid growth is related to nutrient enrichment of the water. Reproduction is by profuse seed-fall, and also by development of daughter plants which appear at the base of the stem, break off and drift away. A native of Central and South America.

Range: Sydney area, north coast, Qld, Vic, SA, WA and widespread in tropical and warm parts of the world. **Leaves:** fleshy, shiny, more or less round, with spongy inflated stalks to 75cm long, becoming less inflated as the leaves mature, the blades are 8-20cm wide. At the base of the plant is a bulbous mass of air-filled floatation cells. **Flowers:** fragile, 5-7cm wide, PALE VIOLET, the upper petal has dark blue-purple suffusions and a yellow marking in the centre. The flowers are short lived (1-2 days). **Fruit:** a capsule. The seeds can be dormant for up to 15 years in dry mud. **Flowering time:** summer. **Name:** *crassipes* = Lat. thick, fat.

POTAMOGETONACEAE

A family of submerged herbs with about 100 species in 2 genera, closely related to the marine families Posidoniaceae and Zosteraceae.

- ## *Potamogeton* Linnaeus

(Pot-a-mo-JEE-tun)
Pondweeds

A genus of small submerged herbs with about 100 species worldwide, including 8 species in Australia, distributed in all states.

All prefer nutrient enriched fresh or brackish water. The plants are sensitive to pollution and are useful indicators of the health of streams. They are an important source of food for water birds.

Pondweeds are perennials with long flexible submerged stems. Floating leaves (if present) are short and broad, while submerged leaves are long and slender. The plants usually die back in autumn and new growth occurs rapidly in spring and summer.

Name: *Potamogeton* = Gk. *potamos*, river, *geiton*, neighbour, referring to its aquatic habitat.

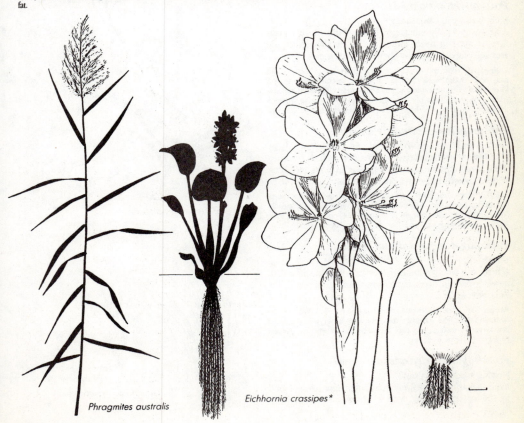

Phragmites australis

*Eichhornia crassipes**

Potamogeton crispus Linnaeus

Curly Pondweed   **Ss, Cumb**

A herb with wholly submerged leaves, scattered through the area, in dams and rivers. Uncommon. It reproduces vegetatively by producing hard burr-like buds at the ends of branches in late summer and autumn. These fall and spend winter in the mud to commence growing the following season.

Range: Sydney area, north coast, Blue Mountains, southern tablelands, some inland areas, all mainland states, widespread in the northern hemisphere.   **Submerged leaves:** with wavy, finely toothed margins, with 3-5 veins.   **Flowers:** few, separated on the spike.   **Name:** *crispus* = Lat. wavy.

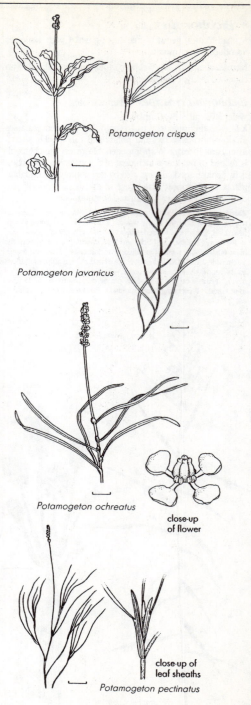

Potamogeton crispus

Potamogeton javanicus Hasskard

Cumb

A herb with both floating and submerged leaves. Found in slow to fast moving water in rivers and dams. Recorded from the Nepean River, uncommon.

Range: Sydney area, north coast, Qld, WA, Asia, Africa.   **Floating leaves:** narrow-elliptic, with 5-7 longitudinal veins.   **Submerged leaves:** slender, up to 2.5mm wide, translucent.   **Flowers:** in a small dense spike on a tall slender peduncle.   **Name:** *javanicus* = of Java, the first place where the species was described.

Potamogeton javanicus

Potamogeton ochreatus Raoul

Blunt Pondweed   **Ss, Cumb**

A herb with wholly submerged leaves, found in still to fast-flowing water in rivers and dams. Widely scattered in the area and probably the most common local species.

Range: NSW coast and ranges, some inland areas, all states, NZ and east Asia.   **Submerged leaves:** strap-like, translucent, with 3-5 longitudinal veins, flat entire margins, 2-5mm wide.   **Flowers:** in dense spikes.   **Name:** *ochreatus* = Lat. a greave, a piece of armour worn on the lower leg, from the shape of the sheath at the base of the leaf.

Potamogeton pectinatus Linnaeus

Fennel Pondweed, Sago Pondweed   **Ss, Cumb**

A herb with wholly submerged leaves on a much branched stem, found in still to fast flowing water in rivers and dams. Widely scattered in the area but uncommon.

Range: Sydney area, north coast, some inland areas, all states except NT and cosmopolitan.   **Submerged leaves:** numerous, very slender (0.5-2mm wide).   **Flowers:** in a small dense spike on a thread-like stalk.   **Name:** *pectinatus* = Lat. comb-like, perhaps in reference to its habit.

Potamogeton ochreatus

close-up
of flower

Potamogeton perfoliatus Linnaeus

Cumb

A herb with wholly submerged leaves, found in still to fast-moving water in rivers and streams. Fairly common in the Nepean River.

Range: NSW coast, ranges and some inland areas, Qld, Vic, Tas and northern hemisphere.   **Leaves:** triangular, with a wavy margin, and a broad rounded stem-clasping base.   **Flowers:** in a dense spike.   **Name:** *perfoliatus* = Lat. stem-clasping.

Potamogeton tricarinatus A. Bennett

Floating Pondweed   **Cumb**

A robust herb with both floating and submerged leaves, found in still or slow-moving water in rivers and dams. Fairly

close-up of
leaf sheaths

Potamogeton pectinatus

abundant along the Nepean River and elsewhere on the Cumberland Plain.

Range: NSW coast, ranges and some inland areas, all states and Asia. **Floating leaves:** large, ovate, with about 11 longitudinal veins. **Submerged leaves:** large, lanceolate, thin, translucent. **Flowers:** relatively large, in a dense emergent spike. **Name:** *tricarinatus* = Lat. 3-keeled.

SPARGANIACEAE

A family with a single aquatic genus.

• *Sparganium* Linnaeus

A genus with 12-19 species native throughout tropical and cool temperate parts of the northern hemisphere, Sumatra, NG, and south-east Australia. There are 2 species in Australia (one introduced).

Name: *Sparganium* = Gk. *Sparganion*, the name used by Dioscorides for this plant, from *sparganon*, a swaddling ribbon, referring to the leaves.

Sparganium subglobosum Morong

(previously *S. antipodum*)
Floating Burr-reed **Cumb, Ss**
An erect grass-like herb usually 50-80cm tall, found on the margins of freshwater ponds and streams. Widely scattered in the area. The fruits form spiky clusters 1-2cm diameter and are a source of food for water birds.

Range: coastal districts from south-eastern Qld to near Melbourne. **Leaves:** erect, grass-like, 3-6mm wide. **Flowers:** unisexual, the male flowers above the female in the inflorescence; clustered in dense globular heads. **Flowering time:** October-March. **Name:** *subglobosum* = Lat. almost globular, referring to the flowers and fruit.

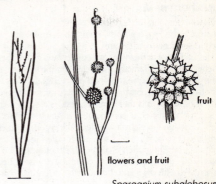

fruit

flowers and fruit

Sparganium subglobosum

TYPHACEAE

A family of tall emergent aquatic herbs with a single genus. It is related to Sparganiaceae.

• *Typha* Linnaeus

Cumbungi, Bullrush
A genus of about 15 species widespread in temperate and tropical regions of the world. There are 2 species native to Australia, and 1 introduced. The plants are distinguished by their dense brown cylindrical flower spikes. These are held on erect scapes, usually shorter than the leaves. Each contains hundreds of thousands of tiny flowers. The upper part of the spike is male and the lower female, the two separated by a short bare space. The male spike disintegrates as soon as flowering finishes, but the female spike remains for most of the year. A single spike can produce up to 200 000 seeds. Both pollen and seeds are wind-dispersed.

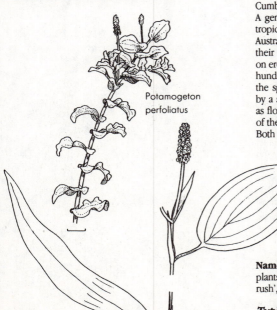

Potamogeton perfoliatus

Potamogeton tricarinatus

Name: *Typha* = Gk. *typhe*, the ancient Greek name for these plants. The European name Bulrush originates from 'pole-rush', meaning pool-rush.

Typha domingensis Presl

Ss, Cumb
An erect herb 1-2m tall. Similar in appearance and habitat to *Typha orientalis*. Widely scattered but uncommon in the area. Distinguish by its narrower leaves and spike.

Range: widespread in NSW, especially in inland districts, also in all states except WA and widespread in tropical and temperate parts of the world. **Leaves:** 5-8mm wide. **Flowers:** female spikes 11-14mm wide. **Name:** *domingensis* = from Santo Domingo in the Caribbean, where the type specimen was collected.

Typha orientalis Presl

Bull-rush, Cumbungi **Ss, Cumb**
An erect herb, 2-3m high. Very common in freshwater ponds and creeks throughout the area.

The fleshy white rhizomes are edible. 'At a certain period, I believe between January and February, the women enter the swamps, take up the roots of these reeds, and carry them back to camp. The roots thus collected are twelve to eighteen inches in length, and they contain, besides a small quantity of saccharine matter, a considerable quantity of fibre. The roots are roasted in a shallow hole in the ground, and either consumed hot or taken as a sort of provision upon hunting expeditions.'[4] The pollen is also edible, being very high in sugar and protein. It other countries it is collected, compressed with water and cooked in the ground as a damper.

Range: throughout NSW, also Vic, SA, WA, NZ, and widespread in temperate Asia. **Leaves:** about 8mm wide (average), stiff, erect, convex. **Flowers:** female spikes mostly about 20mm wide. **Flowering time:** mainly spring-summer. **Name:** *orientalis* = Lat. eastern.

AQUATIC FERNS

This section includes a number of small plants not immediately identifiable as ferns.

Two large fern species with typical fern fronds, *Blechnum indicum* and *Cyclosorus interruptus*, also occur in local marshes. They are listed under FERNS.

AZOLLACEAE

A family with 6 species in a single genus.

• *Azolla* Lamark

A genus with about 2 species in Australia. These are tiny floating plants which often form mats in ponds and dams. Each frond consists of 2 rows of 2-lobed segments, under 2mm long, covered in microscopic water repellant hairs on the upper surface. The upper lobe is thick and photosynthetic with a central cavity containing a colony of the nitrogen-fixing blue-green alga *Anabaena azollae*. The lower lobe is thin and submerged and, when fertile, bears 2-4 sporocarps.

Name: *Azolla* = said to be from Gk. *azein*, to dry, *ollynai*, to kill.

Azolla filiculoides Lamark
var. *rubra* (R. Brown) Strasburger

Pacific Azolla **Aqu**
A small floating fern to 20mm long, fan-shaped, circular or irregular in outline, with many small green or reddish segments. Forms mats on still or slowly moving fresh water.

Range: NSW north coast, central coast, Blue Mountains and southern tablelands, widespread in inland districts, Qld, Vic, Tas, SA, NZ and widespread in the Americas and Europe. **Rhizome:** branched irregularly; with hairless roots. **Fronds:** see description above. **Name:**

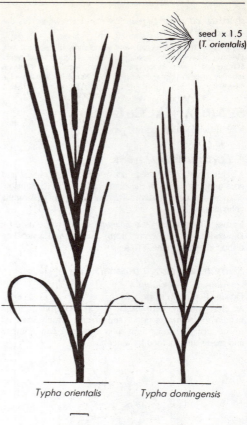

seed x 1.5
(T. orientalis)

Typha orientalis   *Typha domingensis*

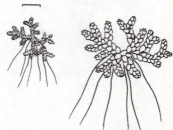

Azolla filiculoides var. rubra

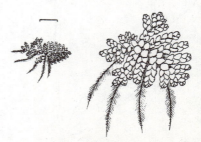

Azolla pinnata

filiculoides = like-*Filicula*, now *Cystopteris*, a genus in Athyriaceae, *rubra* = Lat. reddish.

Azolla pinnata R. Brown
Ferny Azolla   **Aqu**

Similar to the preceding, except the rhizome branches pinnately and regularly and the plant is roughly triangular in outline, usually to 30mm long. The roots are lined with numerous small hairs.

Range: scattered locations throughout NSW, Qld, Vic, NT, SA and tropical Asia.   **Name:** *pinnata* = Lat. pinnate.

MARSILEACEAE

A family of aquatic or semi-aquatic ferns with about 70 species in 3 genera worldwide.

• *Marsilea* Linnaeus
Nardoo

A genus with about 60 species worldwide. There are 7 species in Australia, distributed in all states. The sporangia are borne in a thick-walled, nut-like sporocarp about the size of a pea. The spores are rich in starch and hence the plant was an important source of food for Aborigines in inland Australia.

Nardoo was made famous by the ill-fated Burke and Wills Expedition in 1861. One member of the party, King, survived with the help of Aborigines who showed him how to prepare and consume a species of Nardoo. The Aborigines ground the sporocarps between stones to remove the husks, formed the power into cakes and roasted them in the ground. Wills, who did not survive, was unimpressed by Nardoo: he wrote in his journal 'I cannot understand this Nardoo at all, it certainly will not agree with me in any form ... [but] starvation by Nardoo is by no means very unpleasant'.[5]

Name: *Marsilea* = after Luigi Ferdinando Marsigli, an Italian naturalist.

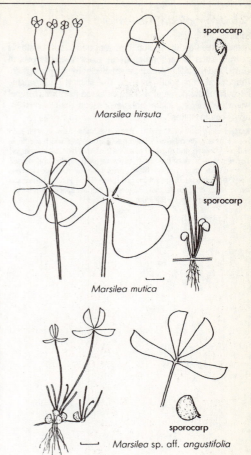

Marsilea hirsuta

Marsilea mutica

Marsilea sp. aff. angustifolia

sporocarp

Marsilea hirsuta R. Brown
A plant with floating or emergent clover-like leaves (fronds). It forms colonies in freshwater marshes. Found in scattered locations on the Cumberland Plain.

Range: extensive in inland parts of Australia, only occasionally found near the coast.   **Rhizome:** creeping, covered with pale brown hairs at the tip.   **Fronds:** with 4 leaflets 5-20mm long, sparsely to densely hairy. **Sporocarps:** solitary on a short stalk, covered in hairs.   **Name:** *hirsuta* = Lat. hairy.

Marsilea mutica Mettenius
Large-leaved Nardoo   **Aqu**

A plant with floating or emergent clover-like leaves (fronds). It forms colonies in permanent freshwater swamps on the Nepean floodplain. Common.

Range: NSW coast and ranges except the northern tablelands, also the north-western plains, all other states, and New Caledonia.   **Rhizome:** long-creeping, much branched, more or less hairless.   **Fronds:** more or less hairless, with 4 leaflets 5-50mm long (narrower in floating plants). **Sporocarps:** up to 4 on a short stalk, hairless.   **Name:** *muticus* = Lat. unarmed, refering to the lack of hairs.

Marsilea sp. aff. *angustifolia*
A plant with floating or emergent clover-like leaves (fronds). It forms colonies in freshwater marshes. Rare in the area: a few recordings from the Cumberland Plain. This species is awaiting formal renaming. True *M. angustifolia* does not occur in the Sydney area.

Range: extensive in inland parts of Australia, only occasionally found near the coast.   **Rhizome:** creeping, covered with pale brown hairs at the tip.   **Fronds:** with 4 leaflets, 4-10mm long, paired.   **Sporocarps:** solitary on very short stalks.   **Name:** *angustifolia* = Lat. narrow-leaved.

SALVINIACEAE

A family with 10 species in a single genus.

• *Salvinia* Adanson
A genus with 1 species naturalised in Australia.

Name: *Salvinia* = after A.M. Salvini (1653-1729), an Italian scholar.

*Salvinia molesta** D.S. Mitchell
Salvinia

A small free-floating aquatic fern, common in still or slowly moving water, often forming dense mats. A serious pest in dams and ponds. Spreads vegetatively by fragmentation. Introduced from South America. The plant is undrownable because of the dense cloak of specialised hairs which repel water by clasping a tiny bubble of air in their basket-like tips (see illustration).

Range: most parts of Australia.   **Rhizome:** short-creeping, with hairs but no roots.   **Fronds:** each frond has 3 leaves, 2 of which are broad and partly folded, and the third much divided, root-like and submerged. The upper surfaces of the broad leaves are partly folded and densely covered with water repellant hairs.   **Sori:** borne in necklace-like rows along the segments of the submerged leaves. There is no evidence that fertile plants occur in Australia, suggesting that the species is a hybrid. **Name:** *molesta* = Lat. troublesome.

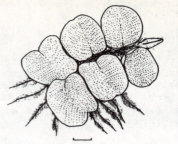

close-up of
frond hair

*Salvinia molesta**

REFERENCES

Using the Field Guide

1 Hamilton, A.G., *Bush Rambles*, Sydney, Angus & Robertson, 1937, p30.
2 Maiden, J.H., *Forest Flora of New South Wales*, Sydney, Government Printer, vol 5, p140.
3 Briggs, J.D. & Leigh, J.H., *Rare or Threatened Australian Plants*, 1988 revised Edition, Canberra, CSIRO Division of Plant Industry.
4 Cronquist, A., *An Integrated System of Classification of Flowering Plants*, New York, Columbia University Press, 1981.
5 Bureau of Flora and Fauna, *Flora of Australia*, Canberra, AGPS, vol 1; 5.
6 Maiden, J.H., George Caley, Botanical Collector in NSW 1800-1810, *Agricultural Gazette of NSW*, Oct. 1903; 988.

Dicolyledons

Myrtaceae

1 Dawson, R., *The Present State of Australia*, London, 1830.
2 McAuley, James, Terra Australis in *Penguin Book of Australian Verse*, Sydney; 1972; 291.
3 Mack, Amy E., *Bush Days*, Sydney, Angus & Robertson, 1911.
4 Maiden, J.H., Sketch of the Botany of the County of Cumberland, in *Handbook for NSW*, British Association for the Advancement of Science, 1914.
5 Mueller, F. von, *Fragmenta*, vol 4.
6 Bunce, Daniel, *Travels with Dr Leichhardt*, London, 1859.
7 Woolls, William, A Glance at the Flora of the Parramatta District, *Sydney Morning Herald*, 24 December 1857.
8 Brooker, M.I.H., and Kleinig, D.A., *A Field Guide to Eucalypts*, Vol 1, Melbourne, Inkala Press, 1983.
9 Pryor, L.D., & Johnson, L.A.S., *A Classification of the Eucalypts*, ANU, 1975.
10 Woolls, William, The Genus *Eucalyptus*, in *Sydney Morning Herald*, 26 August 1867.
11 Cunningham, Peter, *Two Years in New South Wales*, London, 1827.
12 Woolls, William, Myrtaceae II, *Sydney Morning Herald*, 29 May 1857.
13 Smith, James, in White, John, *Journal of a Voyage to New South Wales*, London, 1790; 226.
14 Field, Barron, *Geographical Memoirs of New South Wales*, London, 1825; 320.
15 Maiden, J.H., *Forest Flora of New South Wales*; 1; number 12.
16 Historical Records of NSW; 1 (2); letter dated 18 Nov 1788.
17 Maiden, J.H., *Critical Revision of the Genus Eucalyptus*; number CCXXVIII.
18 Booth, Edward Carlton, *Australia in the 1870s*, London, 1973.
19 Clacy, Ellen, *A Lady's Visit to the Gold Diggings of Australia*, London, 1853.
20 Maiden, J.H., *Forest Flora of New South Wales*; 4; number 144.
21 Meredith, Louisa Anne, *Some of My Bush Friends in Tasmania*, London, 1960; 69.
22 Cribb, A.B. and J.W., *Useful Wild Plants in Australia*, Sydney, Fontana, 1981.
23 Smith, James, Botanical Characters of Some Plants of the Natural Order Myrti, *Linnaen Society of London, Journal of Transactions*; 1796; 3.
24 Cribb, A.B. and J.W., *Wild Foods in Australia*, Sydney, Fontana, 1975; 205.
25 Woolls, ibid.
26 Smith, ibid.
27 Maiden, J.H., *The Forest Flora of New South Wales*; 1; 16.

Mimosaceae

1 Bunce, Daniel, *Travels with Dr Leichhardt*, London, 1859.
2 Woolls, W., Medicinal Plants, *Sydney Morning Herald*, 24 Dec 1856.
3 Ibid.
4. Hamilton, A.G., On the Effects which Settlement in Australia has Produced upon Indigenous Vegetation, *Proc. Linn. Soc.*, NSW; 1892; xxvi; 178.

5. Loudon, Mrs J., *Ladies' Companion to the Flower Garden*, London, William Smith, 1844, p2-3.
6 Worgan, George B., *Journal of a Surgeon of a First Fleet* (1788), Sydney, Library Council of NSW, 1978.
7 Maiden, J.H., *The Forest Flora of NSW*; 4; number 141.
8 Mueller, F. von, *Botanic Teachings*.
9 Booth, E.C., *Australia in the 1870s*, London, 1873.
10 Smith, J.E., *A Specimen of the Botany of New Holland*, London, 1793.
11 Maiden, ibid., number 157.
12 Ibid.

Fabaceae

1 Woolls, W., Papillionaceae II, *Sydney Morning Herald*; 13 Jan 1857.
2 Maiden, J.H., *Illustrations of NSW Plants*, Sydney, Govt Printer, 1907.
3 Woolls, W., A Glance at the Flora of the Parramatta District, *Sydney Morning Herald*; 24 Dec 1857.

Proteaceae

1 Quoted in Woolls, W., Proteaceae, *Sydney Morning Herald*; 8 April 1957.
2 Woolls, W., A Glance at the Flora of the Parramatta District, *Sydney Morning Herald*, 24 Dec 1857.
3 Smith, *Dictionary of Useful Plants*, quoted in Maiden, J.H., *Useful Plants of Australia*, 1889.
4 Mack, Amy E., *A Bush Calendar*, Angus & Robertson, Sydney, 1909.
5 Hamilton, A.G., The Flora of the South Coast, *Handbook for New South Wales*, British Association for the Advancement of Science, 1914.
6 Quoted in Woolls, W., Proteaceae, *Sydney Morning Herald*: 8 April 1957.
7 Woolls, ibid.
8 Maiden, J.H., *Records of Australian Botanists*, Royal Society of NSW, 1908, vol 42.
9 Cunningham, Peter, *Two Years in New South Wales*, Vol 1, London, 1827, p221.
10 Bennet, G., *Wanderings in New South Wales*, Vol 1, London, 1834.
11 Krauss, S., & Johnson, L, *Persoonia mollis*, *Telopea*; 1991; 4(2); 49.
12 Peck, C.W., *Australian Legends*, Sydney, Stafford & Co., 1925.

Epacridaceae

1 Maiden, J.H., *Useful Native Plants of Australia*, London: Trunber & Co., 1889.
2 Atkinson, Louisa, her 1860s articles republished in: *A Voice from the Country*, Canberra: Mulini Press, 1978.
3 Ibid.
4 Field, Barron, *Geographical Memoirs of New South Wales*, London, 1825.
5 Atkinson, ibid.
6 Mack, Amy E., *A Bush Calendar*, Sydney: Angus & Robertson, 1909.
7 Cribb, A.B. and J.W., *Wild Foods in Australia*, Sydney: Fontana, 1975; 36.
8 Ibid; 216.
9 Brewster, A.A., & le Plastrier, Constance M., *Botany for Australian Students*, Dymocks, Sydney (no date).
10 Smith. J.E., *A Specimen of the Botany of New Holland*, London, 1793.

Rutaceae

1 Maiden, J.H., *Flowering Plants and Ferns of New South Wales*, Government Printer, 1895 and on; number 22: 61.
2 Meredith, Louisa Anne, *Some of My Bush Friends in Tasmania*, London; 1866: 98.

Lesser families

1 Woolls, W., Umbelliferae, *Sydney Morning Herald*, 2 Sept 1857.
2 Woolls, W., Asteraceae I, *Sydney Morning Herald*, 3 Nov 1857.

3 Bennet, G., *Wanderings in New South Wales*, London: 1860.
4 Bennet, ibid.
5 Maiden, J.H., *Useful Native Plants of Australia*, Sydney: Govt Printer, 1889.
6 Woolls, ibid.
7 Ibid.
8 Mack, Amy E., *Bush Days*, Sydney: Angus & Robertson, 1911.
9 Baines, J.A., *Australian Plant Genera*, Sydney: Soc. for Growing Aust. Plants, 1981: 342.
10 Woolls, ibid.
11 Sweet, R., *Flora Australasica*, London, 1827-28.
12 Meredith, L.A., *Notes and Sketches of New South Wales*, London: Murray, 1844.
13 Ibid.
14 Henning, Rachel, *The Letters of Rachael Henning*, Sydney, Bulletin Newspaper Co., 1952; letter dated 14 May 1856.
15 Bennet, ibid.
16 Meredith, ibid.
17 Meredith, *Some of My Bush Friends in Tasmania*, London: 1860.
18 Bennet, ibid.
19 Hamilton, A.G., *Bush Rambles*, Sydney: Angus & Robertson, 1937.
20 Hamilton, A.G., Flora of the South Coast, in *Handbook for New South Wales*, British Assoc. for the Advancement of Science, 1914.
21 Maiden, J.H., *Illustrations of New South Wales Plants*, Sydney: Govt Printer, 1907.
22 Mack, Amy E., *A Bush Calendar*, Sydney, 1909; 97.
23 Lucas, A.H.S., notation on specimen sheet held in National Herbarium, Royal Botanic Gardens, Sydney.
24 Meredith, ibid; 58.
25 Field, Barron, *Geographical Memoirs of New South Wales*, London: 1825.
26 Maiden, J.H., *Forest Flora of New South Wales*, vol 3; number 92. Lassack, E.V., & McCarthy, Tara, *Australian Medicinal Plants*, Sydney, Methuen Australia, 1983.
27 Cribb, ibid; 42.
28 Foster, David, *Dog Rock*, Sydney: Penguin Books, 1985.
29 Maiden, J.H., *Useful Native Plants of Australia*, Sydney: Govt Printer, 1889.
30 Meredith, ibid.
31 Caley, G., *An Account of the Journey to Mt Banks in Nov 1804*, Else Mitchell papers ML MSS 960 held in Mitchell Library.
32 Loudon, Mrs J., *The Ladies' Flower Garden*, London: William Smith, 1848.
33 Maiden, J.H., *Descriptions of Three New Species of Australian Plants*, Proc. Linn. Soc. NSW, 1897.
34 Maiden, J.H., & Betche, E., Notes on New South Wales Plants, *Proc. Linn. Soc*, NSW; 1897; 148.
35 Woolls, W., On the Genus *Dodonaea*, Proc. Linn. Soc. NSW, 1890: 764.
36 Cribb, ibid; 94.
37 Bunce, Daniel, *Travels with Dr Leichhardt*, London, 1859.
38 Meredith, L.A., *Some of My Bush Friends in Tasmania*, Second Series, London, MacMillan, 1891.
39 Smith, J., *A Specimen of the Botany of New Holland*, London: 1973.
40 Cribb, ibid; 33.
41 Hamilton, A.G., *On the Methods of Fertilisation of Some Australian Plants*, Assoc. for the Advancement of Science, 7th Report, 1898.

Monocotyledons

1 Backhouse, James, *A Narrative of a Visit to the Australan Colonies*, London, 1843.
2 Cribb, A.B., and J.W., *Wild Food in Australia*, Sydney, Fontana, 1985; 171.
3 Backhouse, ibid.
4 Meredith, L.A., *Notes and Sketches of New South Wales*, London, Murray, 1844.
5 Dahlgren R.M., A Revised System of Classification of the Angiosperms, *Botanical Journal of the Linnean Society*; 1980; 80; 91-124.
6 Mack, Amy E., *Bush Days*, Sydney, Angus & Robertson, 1911.

7 Field, Barron, *Geographical Memoirs of New South Wales*, London, 1825.
8 Hamilton, A.G., *Bush Rambles*, Sydney, Angus & Robertson, 1937.
9 Fitzgerald, R.D., *Australian Orchids*, Sydney, Govt Printer, Vol I, part 1, 1875.
10 Ibid, part 7, 1882.
11 Fitzgerald, ibid, Vol I, part 6, 1880.
12 Meredith, L.A., *Some of My Bush Friends in Tasmania*, London, 1860; 74.
13 Jones, D.L., *Native Orchids of Australia*, Sydney, Reed Books, 1988; 35.
14 Notation on specimen sheet in National Herbarium, Royal Botanic Gardens, Sydney.
15 Fitzgerald, ibid, Vol I, part 7, 1882.
16 Fitzgerald, ibid, Vol I, part 1, 1875.
17 Bunce, D., *Travels with Dr Leichhardt*, London, 1859.
18 Jones, D.L., & Clements, M.A., Reinterpretation of the Genus *Genoplesium* R.Br., *Lindleyana*, vol 1, no 3, Sept, 1989.
19 Fitzgerald, ibid, Vol I, part 5, 1879.
20 Woolls, W., A Glance at the Flora of the Parramatta District, *Sydney Morning Herald*, 24 Dec 1857.
21 Fitzgerald, ibid, part 4, 1878.
22 Ibid, Vol I, part 3, 1877.
23 Ibid, Vol I, part 1, 1875.
24 Ibid.
25 Ibid, Vol II, part 1, 1894.
26 Hamilton, ibid; 121-2.
27 Fitzgerald, ibid, Vol I, part 1; 3.
28 Wheeler, D.J.B., Jacobs, S.W.L., Norton, B.E., *Grasses of New South Wales*, Armidale, University of New England, 1982.
29 Maiden, J.H., Sketch of the Botany of the County of Cumberland, *Handbook for New South Wales*, British Assoc. for the Advancement of Science, 1914.
30 Maiden, J.H., *A Manual of the Grasses of New South Wales*, Government Printer, Sydney, 1898.
31 Cribb, ibid; 180.
32 Cribb, ibid; 187

Primitive plants

1 Loudon, C.J., *Encyclopaedia of Plants*, London, 1836.
2 Hamilton, A.G., *Bush Rambles*, Sydney, Angus & Robertson, 1937.
3 Woolls, W., Australian Ferns, *Horticultural Magazine and Gardeners' and Amateurs' Calendar*, Sydney, May 1867; 114.
4 Hamilton, A.G., The Flora of the South Coast, *Handbook for New South Wales*, British Assoc. for the Advancement of Science, 1914.
5 Hooker, W.J., *Filices Exoticae*, London, 1859.
6 Woolls, ibid: Sept 1867; 214.
7 Bradley, William, *A Voyage to New South Wales, 1786-92*, facsimile edn, Trustees of the Public Library of NSW & Ure Smith, Sydney, 1969.
8 Backhouse, J., *A Narrative of a Visit to the Australian Colonies*, London, 1843; xxxix.
9 Backhouse, ibid.
10 Backhouse, ibid; 55.
11 Woolls, ibid: March 1868; 70.
12 Hooker, ibid.
13 Ibid.
14 Hamilton, A.G., *Bush Rambles*, Sydney, Angus & Robertson, 1937.
15 Woolls, ibid: Feb 1868; 47.
16 Ibid.

Separate groups

Climbers

1 Hunter, Captain J., *Historical Journal of the Transactions at Port Jackson and Norfolk Is.*, London, J. Stockdale, 1793.
2 Baines, J.A., *Australian Plant Genera*, SGAP, 1981.
3 Hamilton, A.G., The Flora of the South Coast, *Handbook for New South Wales*, British Assoc. for the Advancement of Science, 1914.

4 Meredith, Louisa A., *Notes and Sketches of New South Wales*, London, Murray, 1844.
5 Atkinson, Louisa, her 1860s articles reprinted in *A Voice from the Country*, Canberra, Mulini Press, 1978.
6 Woolls, W., Papillionaceae II, *Sydney Morning Herald*, 13 Jan 1857.
7 Cribb, A.B. & J.W., *Wild Food in Australia*, Sydney, Fontana, 1987; 161.
8 Hamilton, A.G., *Bush Rambles*, Sydney, Angus & Robertson, 1937.
9 Hamilton, A.G., Flora of the South Coast, *Handbook for New South Wales*, British Assoc for the Advancement of Science, 1914.
10 Cribb, A.B. & J.W., *Wild Medicine in Australia*, Sydney, Collins, 1981.
11 Meredith, Louisa A., *Some of My Bush Friends in Tasmania*, London, 1860.
12 Cribb, A.B. & J.W., *Wild Food in Australia*, Sydney, Fontana, 1987; 265.
13 Cribb, ibid: 76.
14 Hamilton, A.G., *Bush Rambles*, Sydney, Angus & Robertson, 1937.
15 Lee, Ida, *Early Explorers in Australia*, London, Methuen & Co., 1925; 404.
16 Tench, W., *A Complete Account of the Settlement at Port Jackson*, London, 1793.
17 Woolls, W., A Few Remarks on Medicinal Plants, *Sydney Morning Herald*, 2 Dec 1856.

Mistletoes

1 Lee, Ida, *Early Explorers in Australia*, London, Methuen & Co., 1925; 246.

Rainforest species

1 Cribb, A.B. and J.W., *Wild Food in Australia*, Sydney, Fontana, 1975; 203.
2 Hamilton, A.C., On the Fertilisation of *Eupomatia laurina*, Linnean Society of NSW, *Proceedings*, 1897; 48.
3 For a comprehensive history see *Red Cedar*, John Vader, Reed Books, 1987.
4 Backhouse, James, *A Narrative of a Visit to the Australian Colonies*, London, 1843; 221.
5 Hamilton, A.C., *Bush Rambles*, Sydney, Angus and Robertson, 1937; 114.

6 Booth, Edward Carlton, *Australia in the 1870s*, London, 1973.
7 In Maiden, J.H., *Useful Native Plants of Australia*, London, 1889.
8 Cribb, A.B. and J.W., *Wild Medicine in Australia*, Sydney, Collins, 1981.
9 Mack, Amy E., *Bush Days*, Sydney, Angus and Robertson, 1911.
10 Cribb, *Wild Food in Australia*. Sydney: Fontana, 1975; 135.
11 Banks, Sir Joseph, *Journal ... During Cook's First Voyage in HMS Endeavour in 1768-71*, London, Macmillan, 1896; 299.
12 Field, Barron, *Geographical Memoirs of New South Wales*, London, 1825; 461.
13 White, John, *Journal of a Voyage to New South Wales*, London, 1790; 198.
14 Backhouse; ibid; 436.

Coastal and estuarine species

1 Banks, Joseph, *Journal ... During Cook's First Voyage in HMS Endeavour*, London, Macmillan, 1896.
2 Labillardière, *Voyage in Search of La Pérouse 1791-94*, English edition, London, 1800.
3 White, John, *Journal of a Voyage to New South Wales*, London, 1790.
4 Hamilton, A.A., An Ecological Study of the Saltmarsh Vegetation in the Port Jackson District, *Proc. Linn. Soc. NSW*, 1919; 473.
5 Ibid.
6 White, ibid; 200.
7 Cribb, A.B. & J.W., *Wild Food in Australia*, Sydney, Fontata, 1987; 58.
8 Meredith, Louisa A., *Notes and Sketches of New South Wales*, London, Macmillan, 1844.

Aquatics

1 Cribb, A.B. & J.W., *Wild Food in Australia*, Sydney: Fontana, 1984.
2 Woolls, W., A Few Remarks on Poisonous and Medicinal Plants, *Sydney Morning Herald*, 26 Nov 1856.
3 Woolls, W., ibid, 2 Dec 1856.
4 Krefft, Gerard, Manners and Customs of the Aborigines of the Lower Murray and Darling, Philosophical Society of NSW, *Transactions*, 1862-65; 357-74.
5 Quoted in Cribb, A.B. & J.W., *Wild Food in Australia*, Sydney, Fontana; 83.

GLOSSARY

1-foliate: a reduced pinnate leaf consisting of a single leaflet; recognised by the extra joint between the blade and the leaf stalk.

3-foliate: a compound leaf with 3 leaflets.

Adventitious roots: roots arising in abnormal positions; usually on the stems, as anchoring devices.

aff.: with affinities to.

Achene: a dry single-seeded non-opening fruit, from a single-carpel ovary.

Alternate: arranged at different heights on the stem (i.e. not opposite or whorled). In this book all species have alternate leaves unless otherwise stated.

Anther: the male sexual organ of a flowering plant. The anther produces pollen and consists of 2 cells which usually open by splitting from top to bottom.

Annual: a plant whose life-span lasts only a single season.

Apomictic: plants which produce seeds without fertilisation.

Areole: in Cactaceae, the cluster of hairs and/or spines borne at the nodes of the leafless stems.

Aril: an organ on certain seeds (especially in *Acacia*); often fleshy or oily. Its usual function is to attract animals, especially ants, to help distribute the seeds.

Awn: a bristle-like appendage.

Axil: the upper angle between the leaf and the stem.

Axillary: located in the axils.

Bifid: split in two.

Bipinnate: compound leaves where each pinnate division is itself pinnate.

Bracteoles: a scale or leaf-like appendage attached to the calyx.

Bracts: a scale or leaf-like appendage below a flower, protecting the flower in bud.

Bulb: a short underground stem surrounded by swollen fleshy leaf bases, used as a storage organ (e.g. an onion).

Calli: small projecting structures on the labellum of many orchid species.

Calyx (plural: calyces): the sepals collectively, often partly or wholly joined into a tube.

Carpel: the stigma, style and ovary collectively (i.e. the complete female sexual organ of a flowering plant).

Ciliate: lined with hairs, like an eye-lash.

Cladode: modified stems which perform the same function as leaves.

Cleistogamous: flowers that remain closed and are self-pollinating, producing fertile seed.

Column (gynostemium): a structure formed from the union of the stamens, style and stigmas, as in Orchidaceae, Asclepidaceae and Stylidiaceae.

Corm: a short swollen upright underground stem, formed annually to store food reserves, surrounded by dried protective leaf bases.

Cormil: a corm or cormlike bud in the axil of a leaf or bract.

Corolla: the petals collectively, often partly or wholly joined into a tube.

Corymb: an inflorescence type, where the flowers, although arising at different levels on the stem, are ultimately borne to about the same height in the inflorescence.

Cotyledon: a seed-leaf which swells and opens after germination of a seed. Cotyledons are shaped differently to normal leaves. See monocotyledon and dicotyledon.

Crenate: with the edge cut into rounded teeth or lobes.

Cyme: an inflorescence where the main axis ends in a single flower, further flowers being produced by branchings below that flower which themselves end in a single flower, and so on, often forming highly geometric structures.

Cypsella: the fruit of an Asteraceae: a dry single-seeded non-opening fruit, from a single-carpel inferior ovary, usually tipped by a pappus of hairs, scales or barbs.

Deciduous: falling seasonally, or a plant which loses its leaves for part of the year.

Dicotyledons: the group of flowering plants whose embryos have 2 cotyledons. They include both herbs and woody plants, usually with leaves arranged along the stems, and floral parts in 5s.

Digitate: with 2 or more leaves arising from the same point, like the fingers of a hand.

Dioecious: a plant with unisexual flowers, where the different sexes are on two different plants: see monoecious.

Domatia: small, usually hairy, cavities in the axils of veins on the underside of leaves. Their function is controversial but it seems likely that they were evolved by certan species as homes for microscopic mites which help protect the plant by consuming sap-sucking mites and fungi—a symbiotic relationship.

Drupe: a single-seeded berry with a stone surrounding the fruit, e.g. a peach.

Endemic: restricted to a particular geographical area.

Epicalyx: a whorl of bracts below a flower, resembling a second calyx.

Epicormal: buds, shoots or flowers borne on the old wood of trees.

Epiphyte: plant growing on trees or rocks, but not parasitic.

Felt: a matt of densely interwoven hairs, often star-hairs (the botanical term is tomentum).

Filament: the stalk of a stamen.

Filiform: thread-like.

Floret: the reduced flower of a grass, together with the palea or lemma.

Follicle: a dry fruit derived from a single carpel and opening by a split along one side.

Fronds: the leaves of a fern. They may be sterile or fertile. The fertile fronds carry sporangia on the lower surface.

Gametophyte: see Prothallus.

Glandular hairs: hairs with swollen tips, usually microscopic, often exuding a scent or sticky liquid.

Glaucous: blue-grey; often being covered with a fine protective dust or 'bloom' of that colour.

Globular: more or less spherical.

Glumes: the protective floral bracts of a grass, sedge or rush.

Gynophore: the stalk of a superior ovary.

Gynostemium: see column.

Hastate: (of a leaf) with a pointed tip, and two lobes at the base.

Haustorium (plural: haustoria): the organ through which certain parasitic plants absorb substances from the host plant.

Hemi-parasitic: parasitic in part of its life cycle.

Hispid: bristly.

Incurved: with the margins curled upwards.

Indusia: thin outgrowths of the frond of a fern which protect the sori.

Inferior ovary: when the calyx and corolla are attached above the ovary.

Inflorescence: the flower-bearing system of a plant. Types of inflorescence are:

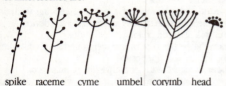

spike raceme cyme umbel corymb head

Inrolled: with margins curled strongly upwards.

Involucre: the whorl of bracts surrounding a flower head, especially of a daisy (Asteraceae).

Irritable: refering to the sensitive parts of some plants which move mechanically when touched, especially the labellum of various orchids.

Keel: a ridge, like the keel of a boat.

Lanceolate: shaped like a lance-blade.

Lateral: positioned on the side, i.e. not terminal.

Laterites: soils produced by the weathering of surfaces which are themselves the product of earlier episodes of weathering. As a soil forms, iron compounds are concentrated in the deeper soil horizons. In time these consolidate into beds of ironstone nodules which are eventually exposed by the erosion of the upper soil horizons. The extensive laterites around Sydney originate from the erosion of Wianamatta Shale which overlaid the Hawkesbury Sandstone.

Lemma: the lower (outer) of 2 bracts immediately enclosing the flower of a grass.

Lignotuber: a woody swelling, wholly or partly underground, at the base of a plant, especially in many Eucalypts.

Ligule: the membranous and/or hairy outgrowth at the junction of the sheath and blade of a grass leaf.

Longitudinal: running along the length of an object, i.e. usually from top to bottom.

Mericarp: a single segment of a fruit which breaks at maturity into a number of segments derived from the individual carpels, e.g. in many Rutaceae genera.

Monocotyledons: the group of flowering plants whose embryos have only 1 cotyledon. They are mostly herbs with floral parts in 3s and leaves with parallel venation.

Monoecious: a species with unisexual flowers, where flowers of both sexes are on the same plant; see dioecious.

Mucilaginous: with a slimy consistency.

Mycorrhizal: a symbiotic relationship between the roots of a plant and a fungus.

Nectary: a gland or disc producing nectar.

Nut: a simple dry non-opening fruit with a single seed and a woody pericarp.

Obovate: ovate, but broadest above the middle.

Operculum: the cap-like covering or lid of some flowers, which falls away at maturity.

Opposite: arranged at the same level on the stem, but on opposite sides (i.e. not alternate). In this book all species have alternate leaves unless otherwise stated.

Ovary: the part of a carpel containing the ovules. It consists of 1 or more chambers. After fertilisation it develops into a fruit.

Ovate: with length 1-3 times the breadth, and broadest below the middle.

Ovule: the seed-germ contained in an ovary; after fertilisation it develops into a seed.

Palea: the upper (inner) of 2 bracts immediately enclosing the flower of a grass.

Panicle: a compound inflorescence consisting of successive branches, where each branch ends in a flower.

Pappus: the cluster of hairs, scales or barbs surmounting the cypsella of an Asteraceae, possibly a modified calyx.

Pedicel: the stalk of a single flower in an inflorescence.

Peduncle: the main stalk of an inflorescence or of a solitary flower.

Perennial: a plant whose life-span extends over more than one growing season.

Perianth: the calyx and corolla collectively, especially when they are similar, e.g. in many monocotyledons. Also used when only 1 floral whorl is present.

Pericarp: the wall of a fruit, developing from the ovary wall.

Petiole: the stalk of a leaf.

Phyllodes: modified leaf-stalks which perform the same function as leaves, e.g. the phyllodes of many species of *Acacia*.

Pinna (plural: pinnae): the leaflet of a pinnate leaf, or the primary branching of the axis of a bipinnate leaf.

Pinnate: compound leaves consisting of leaflets attached to a central stem or rhachis.

Pinnatisect: deeply cut into lobes.

Pinnule: the leaflet of a bipinnate leaf.

Pistil: a carpel, or group of fused carpels.

Pollinium (plural: pollinia): an aggregated pollen mass, especially in Orchids.

Prothallus (gametophyte): the first phase of the life cycle of a fern, a delicate tissue one cell thick and less than 10mm wide which grows from a spore without fertilisation. It contains the fern's sexual organs. The male organs produce mobile sperm which swim to fertilise the ovum of the female organ. The fertilised ovum then grows into the mature (sporophyte) phase.

Pseudo-bulb: the swollen bulb-like stems of many epiphytic orchids, which act as food-storage organs.

Pungent: needle-sharp.

Raceme: an unbranched inflorescence bearing stalked flowers.

Receptacle: the base of the flower, which supports the perianth and sexual parts.

Recurved: with the edges bent downward or backwards.

Reticulation: the pattern of net veins.

Revolute: with the edges rolled underneath (usually of leaves).

Rhachis: the central axis of a compound leaf or inflorescence.

Rhizome: a root-like horizontal underground stem.

Rostellum: in orchids, an area of tissue between the stigma and anther. It secrets drops of sticky liquid which attach to the bodies of passing insects. If the insects then rub against the anther, the pollinia become detached and (hopefully) adhere to the stickiness. Sometimes the name is used simply for the supporting tissue and the secreting gland itself is called the viscidium. Sometimes the name is used for the sticky parts of the stigma.

Saprophyte: a leafless plant deriving nourishment from decaying wood or plant matter, usually through association with a fungus.

Scabrous: stiffly hairy, raspy.

Scape: a flowering stalk arising from near the ground, and usually leafless.

Septate: divided into chambers.

Sessile: stalkless.

Sori: groups of sporangia.

Spathe: large bract(s) surrounding an inflorescence.

Spathulate: spoon shaped.

Spikelet: the unit of inflorescence of a grass, sedge or rush; consisting of one or more florets enclosed in protective glumes.

Sporangia: the spore-bearing organs of a fern.

Spores: microscopic reproductive units, consisting of 1 or a few cells.

Sporocarp: a fruiting body containing sporangia.

Sporophyte: the spore-producing phase of the 2-part life-cycle of a fern. The sporophyte is the mature fern plant.

Stamen: the anther and filament collectively.

Staminode: a sterile stamen, always modified in shape.

Stigma: the receptive part of the style.

Stipules: tiny scales or leaf-like appendages on either side of the base of a leaf stalk, usually triangular in shape. They help protect the leaf in bud. When deciduous their presence can be recognised by tiny scars. Stipules are useful diagnostic features for some families, e.g. Euphorbiaceae.

Striate: lined with longitudinal ridges or grooves.

Style: the tissue joining the stigma to the ovary.

Succession: the process of revegetation on cleared ground or sand-dunes, by succeeding waves of vegetation, each altering the environment to permit the next wave.

Superior ovary: where the calyx and corolla are attached below the ovary.

Synangium (plural: synangia): a composite sporangium, with several cavities.

Tap-root: the main root of a plant, descending vertically into the soil; often swollen as a food storage device.

Terminal: at the tip or apex.

Tuber: the swollen base of an underground stem, containing food reserves (e.g. a potato).

Tubercle: a small warty or pimple-like prominence.

Type specimen: the specimen upon which the original description of the species is based.

Umbel: an inflorescence type, where several flowers arise from the same point on the stem, in a cluster, and are usually borne to about the same height.

Utricle: a small bladder; or a membranous bladder-like sac enclosing an ovary or fruit.

Vascular plants: plants having vessels or veins to conduct fluid. Usually only very primitive plants, such as mosses, are non-vascular.

Vesicle: a small bladder-like cavity in plant tissue, filled with air or water.

Villous: covered with long shaggy hairs.

Viscidium: see Rostellum.

Whorl: a group of 3 or more leaves (or other parts) arising from the same height on the stem or axis.

INDEX